# Genealogica & Heraldica

# *Genealogica & Heraldica*

| Proceedings of the 22nd International Congress of Genealogical and Heraldic Sciences in Ottawa August 18-23, 1996 | Actes du 22$^e$ congrès international des sciences généalogique et héraldique à Ottawa 18-23 août 1996 |

*Edited by/Sous la direction de*
Auguste Vachon   Claire Boudreau   Daniel Cogné

*Reading Committee/Comité de lecture*
Auguste Vachon   Claire Boudreau   Daniel Cogné
Linda Lauzon   Robert D. Watt

*and/et*
Paula Gornescu-Vachon
Augustinus P. Dierick

ACTEXPRESS

UNIVERSITY OF OTTAWA PRESS
LES PRESSES DE L'UNIVERSITÉ D'OTTAWA

The official emblem of the 22nd International Congress of Genealogical and Heraldic Sciences was drawn by Mrs. Cathy Bursey-Sabourin, who is Fraser Herald in the Canadian Heraldic Authority, Office of the Secretary to the Governor General.

The concept was developed by the heralds of the Authority. It uses the maple leaf emblem of Canada in a distinctive arrangement. The central leaf symbolizes Ottawa, the national capital and congress site, with the smaller leaves representing the two sciences: genealogy and heraldry.

Le dessin de l'emblème officiel du 22ᵉ congrès international des sciences généalogique et héraldique est l'œuvre de Mᵐᵉ Cathy Bursey-Sabourin, héraut Fraser à l'Autorité héraldique du Canada, bureau du secrétaire du Gouverneur général.

L'emblème a été conçu par les hérauts d'armes de l'Autorité héraldique du Canada. Au centre, la feuille d'érable du Canada fait allusion à Ottawa, capitale du pays et lieu du congrès. Les deux petites feuilles représentent les sciences généalogique et héraldique.

UNIVERSITY OF OTTAWA
UNIVERSITÉ D'OTTAWA

"Books in the ACTEXPRESS series are published without the University of Ottawa Press's usual editorial intervention. The editorial process for and copy editing of *Genealogica & Heraldica. Ottawa 1996* have been ensured by the publication's Editorial Committee and contributors."

«Les ouvrages de la collection ACTEXPRESS sont publiés sans l'intervention éditoriale habituelle des Presses de l'Université d'Ottawa. Le comité éditorial de la publication et ses collaborateurs ont assumé la responsabilité de la préparation éditoriale ainsi que la révision linguistique de *Genealogica & Heraldica. Ottawa 1996.*»

ISBN 0-7766-0472-4

© University of Ottawa Press, 1998
Les Presses de l'Université d'Ottawa, 1998

*Printed in Canada/Imprimé au Canada*

# Contents / Table des matières

*Genealogical Lectures / Communications généalogiques*

Welcome to the Congress!
Bienvenue au congrès !

Mr. Roger Harmignies, President of the Bureau permanent des congrès during the opening ceremonies of the Congress at the University of Ottawa.
M. Roger Harmignies, président du Bureau permanent des congrès prononce son allocution pendant les cérémonies d'ouverture du congrès à l'Université d'Ottawa.

# The 22nd Congress / Le 22ᵉ congrès

**Under the distinguished patronage of Their Excellencies**
**Sous le haut patronage de Leurs Excellences**

*The Right Honourable Roméo LeBlanc,*
*P.C., C.C., C.M.M., C.D.,*
*Governor General of Canada and Head of the*
*Canadian Heraldic Authority*
*and Mrs. Diana Fowler LeBlanc, C.C.*

*Le très honorable Roméo LeBlanc,*
*C.P. C.C., C.M.M., C.D.,*
*Gouverneur général et chef de l'Autorité*
*héraldique du Canada*
*et M ᵐᵉ Diana Fowler LeBlanc, C.C.*

**President / Présidente**
Mrs. Jean M. Matheson / Mᵐᵉ Jean M. Matheson

**Secretary General / Secrétaire général**
Mr. Robert D. Watt / M. Robert D. Watt

**Organizer / Organisateur**
The Canadian Heraldic Authority / L'Autorité héraldique du Canada

**Co-organizers / Co-organisateurs**
The Heraldry Society of Canada / La Société héraldique du Canada
The Ontario Genealogical Society
La Société de généalogie de l'Outaouais

**Planning Committee / Comité de planification**
Daniel Cogné, Auguste Vachon, Charles Maier, Linda Lauzon
Althea Douglas, Michel Béland, Lionel G. Dixon, James Taylor
Richard Berthelsen, Omar Lindsley-Dixon

**Editorial Committee / Comité éditorial**
Auguste Vachon
Claire Boudreau
Daniel Cogné
Linda Lauzon
Robert D. Watt
*Assisted by* Mrs. Paula Gornescu-Vachon *and* Mr. Augustinus P. Dierick
*Avec la collaboration de* Mᵐᵉ Paula Gornescu-Vachon *et* M. Augustinus P. Dierick

**Sponsors, Donors and Acknowledgements / Commanditaires, donateurs et remerciements**
**Leading Sponsor / Commanditaire principal**
Corel Corporation / Société Corel

**Special Sponsor / Commanditaire particulier**
Burnett-Weston Fund, Toronto

**Major Donors / Principaux bienfaiteurs**
The David and Dorothy Lam Foundation
Dr. Joseph Segal, C.M., O.B.C., and Rosalie Segal
Dr. Helen K. Mussallem, C.C.
The Henry N.R. Jackman Foundation
Bell Canada

**Publication Sponsors / Commanditaires des publications**
The Department of Canadian Heritage / Ministère du patrimoine canadien
The Heraldry Society of Canada / La Société héraldique du Canada

**Canadian Evening Sponsor / Commanditaire de la soirée canadienne**
The McCain Family Foundation

**Congress Events Sponsors / Commanditaires des activités du congrès**
Bruce M. Hicks Education Foundation
Hicks Media
The Honourable Alan A. Macnaughton, P.C., O.C., Q.C.
Brian Hutchison
Théodore J. Arcand
Château des Charmes
Hainle Estate Winery
Sumac Ridge Estate Wineries

**The assistance of the following individuals and organisations is gratefully acknowledged /
Nous remercions vivement les personnes et organismes suivants de leur assistance**
The Honourable Gilbert Parent, M.P., Speaker of the House of Commons of Canada /
L'honorable Gilbert Parent, député, président de la Chambre des communes du Canada
His Excellency the Ambassador of the French Republic / Son Excellence l'ambassadeur de France
His Excellency the British High Commissioner / Son Excellence le haut-commissaire de Grande-Bretagne
Her Worship the Mayor of Ottawa / Son Honneur la mairesse d'Ottawa
Mr. David Smith, C.M. / M. David Smith, C.M.
The staff of Government House, Ottawa / Le personnel de la résidence du Gouverneur général, Ottawa
The Chancellery / La Chancellerie
Cathy Bursey-Sabourin, Charles Maier, Francine Mellor
Lara M^cPherson, Richard Carruthers-Żurowski
Alison Watt, Catherine Watt and Michael Watt
The Canada Post Corporation / La Société canadienne des postes
The Canadian Museum of Civilization / Le Musée canadien des civilisations
The University of Ottawa / L'Université d'Ottawa
The National Archives of Canada / Les Archives nationales du Canada
The National Gallery of Canada / Le Musée des beaux-arts du Canada
The National Capital Commission / La Commission de la capitale nationale
The Canadian Forces / Les Forces canadiennes
The Royal Canadian Mounted Police / La Gendarmerie royale du Canada
Public Works and Government Services Canada / Travaux publics et services gouvernementaux Canada
Sergeant Christian Coulombe / Sergent Christian Coulombe[*]
Master Corporal Monique Fortin / Caporal-chef Monique Fortin[*]

[*] All photographs in the introduction section, except those credited otherwise, were taken by Sergeant Coulombe and Master Corporal Fortin.
[*] Sauf indication du contraire, toutes les photos de la section introductive ont été prises par le sergent Coulombe et le caporal-chef Fortin.

***Opening Ceremony*** Dr. Jean-Claude Loutsch, President of the 21st Congress held at Luxembourg, presents Mr. Robert Watt, Secretary General of the 22nd Congress with the Congress baton. The baton, made by Mr. Tuomas Hyrsky, was designed and given by Messrs. Henrik Degerman and Tom Bergroth at the 16th Congress held in Helsinki in 1984.

***Cérémonie d'ouverture*** Le Dʳ Jean-Claude Loutsch, président du 21ᵉ congrès à Luxembourg, remet le bâton du congrès à M. Robert Watt, secrétaire général du 22ᵉ congrès. Le bâton, œuvre de l'artiste Tuomas Hyrsky, a été dessiné et offert par Henrik Degerman et Tom Bergroth à l'occasion du 16ᵉ congrès tenu à Helsinki en 1984.

Her Excellency Mrs. Diana Fowler LeBlanc, Honorary Patron of the 22nd Congress, in conversation with
Dr. Marcel Hamelin, Rector of the University of Ottawa and Mr. Robert Watt.
Son Excellence Mᵐᵉ Diana Fowler LeBlanc, présidente d'honneur du 22ᵉ congrès, converse avec
M. Marcel Hamelin, Ph.D., recteur de l'Université d'Ottawa, et M. Robert Watt.

*Her Excellency saying farewell after opening ceremonies at the University of Ottawa* (l. to r.) Her Excellency;
Mr. Robert Watt; Mr. Richard Berthelsen, coordinator of special events at the Congress;
Dr. Jean-Claude Loutsch; Mr. Roger Harmignies.
*Son Excellence disant aurevoir après les cérémonies d'ouverture à l'Université d'Ottawa* (de g. à dr.) Son Excellence ;
M. Robert Watt ; M. Richard Berthelsen, organisateur des événements spéciaux du congrès ;
le D' Jean-Claude Loutsch ; M. Roger Harmignies.

*Opening reception at Rideau Hall, official residence of the Governor General of Canada*
Her Excellency with Mrs. Esther de Soaje Pinto and Mr. Teodoro Amerlinck.
*Réception lors de l'ouverture du congrès à Rideau Hall, résidence officielle du Gouverneur général du Canada*
Son Excellence en compagnie de M^me Esther de Soaje Pinto et de M. Teodoro Amerlinck.

# Bureau permanent des congrès internationaux des sciences généalogique et héraldique

M. Roger Harmignies, *Belgique (XI) président*
M. Cecil R. Humphery-Smith, *Royaume-Uni (XIII) secrétaire*

Don Vicente de Cadenas y Vicent, *Espagne (III)*
Chevalier Xavier de Ghellinck Vaernewyck, *Belgique (IV et XI)*
Prof. Dr. Hanns Jäger-Sunstenau, *Autriche (X)*
Prince Alexandre de Merode, *Belgique (XI)*
D$^r$ Ottokar Israel, *Allemagne (XII)*
Vicomte Monckton of Brenchley, *Royaume-Uni (XIII)*
D$^r$ Vagn Dybdahl, *Danemark (XIV)*
M. Nils G. Bartholdy, *Danemark (XIV)*
D$^r$ Jean-Claude Loutsch, *Luxembourg (AIH et XXI)*
Baron Pinoteau, *France (AIH)*
S.A.R. Don Carlos de Bourbon duc de Calabre, *Espagne (XV et IIGH)*
Don Faustino Menéndez Pidal de Navascués, *Espagne (XV et IIGH)*
D$^r$ Kauko Pirinen, *Finlande (XVI)*
M. Tom Bergroth, *Finlande (XVI)*
D$^r$ Eugenio de Andrêa da Cunha e Freitas, *Portugal (XVII)*
D$^r$ Artur Norton baron de São Roque, *Portugal (XVII)*
D$^r$ Franz-Heinz von Hye, *Autriche (XVIII)*
D$^r$ László Czoma, *Hongrie (XIX)*
Prof. D$^r$ Iván Bertényi, *Hongrie (XIX)*
Prof. D$^r$ Stig Strömholm, *Suède (XX)*
D$^r$ Clara Nevéus, *Suède (XX)*
M. Jean-Claude Muller, *Luxembourg (XXI)*
M$^{me}$ Jean M. Matheson, *Canada (XXII)*
M. Robert D. Watt, *Canada (XXII)*

Depuis la clôture du congrès d'Ottawa en 1996 :

— *le secrétariat du Bureau est assuré* par M. Robert D. Watt, *Canada (XXII)*
— *font partie du Bureau au titre du congrès de Turin 1998 :*
    M. l'ambassadeur Ugo Barzini, *Italie (XXIII)*
    M$^{me}$ la dott.ssa Giovana Arcangeli, *Italie (XXIII)*

Her Excellency commenting on Dr. Naomi Griffiths' presentation.
Son Excellence commente la communication de Naomi Griffiths, Ph.D.

*Congress Reception and Registration Hall* In the background a partial view
of the display of grants by the Canadian Heraldic Authority.
*Salle d'inscription et de réception des congressistes* À l'arrière-plan, un aperçu
d'une exposition d'armoiries concédées par l'Autorité héraldique du Canada.

# Programme of the Congress /
# Programme du congrès

# Monday, August 19 / Le lundi 19 août

## HERALDRY / HÉRALDIQUE

| | |
|---|---|
| 9:30<br>9h30 | **CEREMONIAL OPENING**<br>**CÉRÉMONIE D'OUVERTURE** |
| 10:30<br>10h30 | **BREAK /**<br>**PAUSE** |
| 11:00<br>11h | **Halpin, M.** (Canada) - Crest, Image and Story on a Double Totem Pole from the Northwest Coast *(Multimedia Presentation)* |
| 12:00<br>12h | **LUNCH /**<br>**PAUSE DU MIDI** |
| 1:30<br>13h30 | **Swan, C.** (England) - The Aboriginal in Heraldry with Some Examples Drawn from the Heraldic Garden at Boxford House, Suffolk. *(Video Presentation, text not available)* |
| | **Cernovodeanu, D.** (Roumanie) - Les influences de l'art héraldique français sur l'art héraldique roumain |
| 2:30<br>14h30 | **Smith, W.** (USA) - The Relationship between Heraldry and Vexillology: An American Perspective |
| | **Humphery-Smith, C. R.** by **Baker, R.** (England) - Falling Leaves: Heraldic Foliage |
| | **Dogaru, M.** (Roumanie) - L'héraldique et les relations internationales : Le cas des Pays roumains *(conférence annulée, texte non disponible)* |

## GENEALOGY / GÉNÉALOGIE

| | |
|---|---|
| 9:30<br>9h30 | **CEREMONIAL OPENING**<br>**CÉRÉMONIE D'OUVERTURE** |
| 10:30<br>10h30 | **BREAK /**<br>**PAUSE** |
| 11:00<br>11h | **Bouchard, G.-Scriver, C.** (Canada) - Genealogy and Genetics: Two Parts to the Same Story *(text not available)* / Généalogie et génétique deux volets d'une même histoire *(texte non disponible)* |
| 12:00<br>12h | **LUNCH /**<br>**PAUSE DU MIDI** |
| 1:30<br>13h30 | **Roderick, T. H.** (USA) - Umbilical Lines: The Use of Mitochondrial DNA Analysis in Genealogical Research |
| | **Le Clercq, P.** (France) - Les ressortissants de Basse-Bourgogne établis au Canada avant 1730 et leurs racines familiales en France |
| 2:30<br>14:h30 | **Griffiths, N. E. S.** (Canada) - Genealogy as an Historian's Tool: Kin and Community in Acadia |

| | |
|---|---|
| 4:30 | Reception hosted by Her Excellency Mrs. Diana Fowler LeBlanc at Rideau Hall (Bus transportation provided from University Centre at 3:45) |
| 16h30 | Son Excellence, M^me Diana Fowler LeBlanc offrira une réception à Rideau Hall (Le transport par autobus sera disponible au centre universitaire à 15h45) |

\* 6:00 pm meeting and 8:30 pm dinner of the Bureau permanent (by invitation only)
\* 18h réunion et 20h30 dîner du Bureau permanent (sur invitation seulement)

# Tuesday, August 20 / Le mardi 20 août

## HERALDRY / HÉRALDIQUE

9:30 / 9h30   **Kennedy, J. J. F.** (Canada) - When Did Gaelic Irish Chiefs Adopt Heraldry?

**Medvedev, M.** (Russia) - The Towel of King Wenceslas of Luxembourg as a Great Personage of the Late Middle Ages

10:30 / 10h30   **BREAK / PAUSE**

11:00 / 11h   **Duerloo, L.** (Belgium) - Transcending the Frontiers of Reality: The Significance of Heraldic Myths

**Pichette, R.** (Canada) - L'héraldique haïtienne sous le règne du roi Henry I$^{er}$

12:00 / 12h   **LUNCH / PAUSE DU MIDI**

1:30 / 13h30   **Patterson, B.** (Canada) - Trends in University Heraldry: The British Empire and Beyond

**Pinoteau, H.** (France) - Fleurs de lis de France et d'ailleurs

2:30 / 14h30   **BREAK / PAUSE**

3:00 / 15h   **Kennedy, P. L.** (Canada) - Impressions of State Authority

**Loutsch, J. C.** (Luxembourg) - Les pierres tombales des comtes de Lannoy à Clervaux

## GENEALOGY / GÉNÉALOGIE

9:00 / 9h30   **White, S. A.** (Canada) - Problems in Acadian Genealogical Research

**Dubé, J.-C.** (Canada ) - Vraies et fausses généalogies : étude de quelques cas reliés à la Nouvelle-France

10:30 / 10h30   **BREAK / PAUSE**

11:00 / 11h   **Toohey, A. K.** (USA) - Border Relations: Interrelated Families in the United States and Canada

**Mérey, P. D. B.** (Canada) - Charts and Text: A Proposed Method for Recording Family History and Genealogy

12:00 / 12h   **LUNCH / PAUSE DU MIDI**

1:30 / 13h30   **Pinto, E. de Soaje** (Argentina) - Uniones y parentescos entre virreyes de los siglos XVI, XVII y principios del XVIII

**Cory, K. B.** (Scotland) - Immigration from Scotland to Canada

2:30 / 14h30   **BREAK / PAUSE**

3:00 / 15h   **Mildner, S.** (Germany) - Die Aktion Forscherkontakte: Grenzüberschreitende Familienforschung

**Saunders, G.** (Bahamas) - Origins and Impacts: Loyalist Immigration to the Bahamas

---

6:00 pm / 18h   Canadian Evening Barbecue at the Central Experimental Farm
Soirée canadienne barbecue à la ferme expérimentale centrale

# Thursday, August 22 / Le jeudi 22 août

## HERALDRY / HÉRALDIQUE

9:30 **Allpress, P. L.** (Andorra) - The Development of
9h30 Naval and Military Symbols in British Heraldry since the Crusades

**Salter, R.** (Canada) - Medical Heraldry with Four Recent Examples

10:30 **BREAK /**
10h30 **PAUSE**

11:00 **Burnett, C. J.** (Scotland) - The Export of Scot
11h tish Heraldic Symbolism

**Mattern, G.** by **Squire, R.** (Switzerland) - Finding Heraldic Roots in Switzerland

12:00 **LUNCH /**
12h **PAUSE DU MIDI**

1:30 **Roads, E. A.** (Scotland) - The Export of Scottish
13h30 Heraldry

**Alexy, Z.** (Slovakia) - The Links Between Slovakia's Arms and Flags

2:30 **BREAK /**
14h30 **PAUSE**

3:00 **Nevéus, C.** (Sweden) - Heraldic Interaction be-
15h tween Norway and Sweden

**Vachon, A.** (Canada) - La céramique armoriée d'importation (1886-1921) : reflet du nationalisme canadien

## GENEALOGY / GÉNÉALOGIE

9:30 **Miles, M.** (England) - The Kerry Pedigrees:
9h30 A Window on the History and Heraldry of Wales

**Thiébaud, J.-M.** (France) - Les perspectives de constitution de banques nationales et internationales de données généalogiques et héraldiques : l'exemple de la France

10:30 **BREAK /**
10h30 **PAUSE**

11:00 **Yorke, L.** (Canada) - Archival Methodology
11h and Genealogical Research in the Information Age: Two Solitudes or Converging Disciplines?

**Bierbrier, M.** (England) - The Ancestry of the Gardner Family: West Meets East

12:00 **LUNCH /**
12h **PAUSE DU MIDI**

1:30 **Popoff, M.** (France) - L'émigrant italien en
13h30 France : préservation du patrimoine héraldique

**Al-Mousawi, H.** (Oman) - The Genealogy of the Prophet Muhammed and the Royal Houses of the Middle East with Emphasis on the Hashemite Kingdoms

2:30 **BREAK /**
14h30 **PAUSE**

3:00 **Kitzmiller, J.** (USA) - Records Linkage as a Ge-
15h nealogical Tool

**Douglas, P.** (The Netherlands) - Scottish Families and Their Symbols in the Netherlands

---

\*  7:00 pm   Meeting and dinner of the *Conféderation internationale* (by invitation only)
\*  19h       Réunion et dîner de la Conféderation internationale (sur invitation seulement)

# Friday, August 23 / Le vendredi 23 août

## HERALDRY / HÉRALDIQUE

9:30
9h30
**Brownell, F. G.** (South Africa) - The Evolution of a Distinctive South African Heraldic Idiom, 1963-1996

**McColgan, R.** (Canada) - The Armorial Bearings of the King of Scots and Selected Scots Heraldry in Canada

10:30
10h30
**BREAK /**
**PAUSE**

11:00
11h
**ARTISTS SESSIONS/**
**ATELIER DES ARTISTES**

12:00
12h
**LUNCH /**
**PAUSE DU MIDI**

1:30
13h30
**PLENARY WINDUP/ CRITIQUE**
**ASSEMBLÉE PLÉNIÈRE/ DISCUSSION**

## GENEALOGY / GÉNÉALOGIE

9:30
9h30
**Merriman, B. D.** (Canada) - Canada's Loyalist "Mark of Honour": Hereditary Heritage in 18th-Century British North America

**Carruthers-Żurowski, R.** (Canada) - Between Imperial Hinterlands: Reconstituting Families in Bukovina and Saskatchewan, 1775-1940

10:30
10h30
**BREAK /**
**PAUSE**

11:00
11h
**JUDITH REID PANEL**
**PRÉSENTATION JUDITH REID**

12:00
12h
**LUNCH /**
**PAUSE DU MIDI**

1:30
1h30
**PLENARY WIND UP / CRITIQUE**
**ASSEMBLÉE PLÉNIÈRE / DISCUSSION**

---

10:45
10h45
**SPECIAL PRESENTATION (FRENCH-ENGLISH)**
**SÉANCE SPÉCIALE (ANGLAIS-FRANÇAIS)**

**Sakharov, I.** (Russia) - The family of the Beauharnais during the last two centuries, subjects of the kings of France, dukes of Bavaria, members of the Imperial House of Russia, citizens of Germany, France, the United States and Canada. / Sujets des rois de France → ducs de Bavière → membres de la maison impériale de Russie → citoyens d'Allemagne, de France, des États-Unis, du Canada : la famille de Beauharnais, pendant ces deux derniers siècles.

**Sakharova, N.** (Russia) - The Russian, French, Polish, Georgian and Tartar roots of the philosopher Nicolas Berdiaev (1874-1948), and the impact this had on the development of his "self-awareness" and perception of the world. / Les racines russes, françaises, polonaises, géorgiennes et tatares du philosophe Nicolas Berdiaev (1874-1948) : influence sur sa « connaissance de soi » et sa perception du monde.

**Krasko, A.** (Russia) - The Prussian, Russian, German, Romanian and Canadian descendants of L.A.P. Sayn-Wittgenstein (1768-1843), Most Serene Prince, and field marshal of the Russian Army. / Les descendants de L.A.P. Sayn-Wittgenstein (1768-1843), Prince sérénissime, maréchal de l'armée russe : Prusse – Russie – Allemagne – Roumanie – Canada.

\*    6:30 pm for 8pm Closing Gala dinner at the National Gallery of Canada
\*    18h30 pour 20h gala de clôture au Musée des beaux-arts du Canada

*Opening reception at Rideau Hall* (l. to r.) Mrs. Kerry O'Brien; Mr. James Terzian; Mr. Henry Paston-Bedingfeld, York Herald (England); Mrs. Ljerka Alajbeg, Minister Counsellor at the Embassy of Croatia in Canada.
*Réception d'ouverture à Rideau Hall* (de g. à dr.) M^me Kerry O'Brien ; M. James Terzian ; M. Henry Paston-Bedingfeld, héraut York (Angleterre) ; M^me Ljerka Alajbeg, conseillère culturelle à l'ambassade de Croatie au Canada.

A glimpse of the *opening reception* in the gardens of Rideau Hall.
Vue générale de la *réception d'ouverture* dans les jardins de Rideau Hall.

***Opening reception*** Her Excellency and Mrs. Elizabeth Roads, Carrick Pursuivant (Scotland).
***Réception d'ouverture*** Son Excellence et M^me Elizabeth Roads, poursuivant Carrick (Écosse).

***Opening reception in the Tent Room*** Her Excellency greets Mr. Radu Mateescu, Chargé d'affaires
of the Embassy of Romania in Canada, Dr. Thomas Roderick and Mrs. Hilda Roderick.
***Réception d'ouverture dans la Salle de la Tente*** Son Excellence en compagnie de M. Radu Mateescu, chargé d'affaires
de l'ambassade de Roumanie au Canada, M. Thomas Roderick, Ph.D., et M^me Hilda Roderick.

## Message from His Excellency the Right Honourable Roméo LeBlanc, Governor General of Canada, Patron of the 22nd Congress

As honorary patron of the 22nd International Congress of Genealogical and Heraldic Sciences and as Head of the Canadian Heraldic Authority, I am pleased to welcome all delegates to Canada's capital, particularly those who have travelled from afar to attend this Congress, the first to be held outside of Europe.

It seems especially fitting that, as you meet for the first time beyond the birthplace of modern scientific studies in genealogy and heraldry, your theme should be "Families and Symbols Transcending Frontiers." In a world where the globalization of regional and national economies increases the need for greater understanding between countries and peoples, the sciences which you have gathered to explore across various kinds of boundaries offer special insights. After all, genealogy and heraldry are concerned with impulses that have been characteristic of humans for much of their history: the search for origins and lineage and the use of symbols to identify persons and institutions. The way that such origins are recorded and preserved and the types of symbols created have, of course, varied dramatically through time and place.

During your meetings, you will be exploring some of those variations, identifying how one country's experience can influence another's and how technology is creating new opportunities and challenges in both sciences. Ultimately, despite all apparent differences which scholarly analysis reveals, we will recognize our common humanity, the pivotal importance of the family as it unfolds across the years and the creative impulse in such beautiful and enduring inventions as heraldry.

We are proud that Canada has been chosen as the site of this important forum. We are eager to share with you some of the unique symbolic culture of our First Peoples as well as our own experiences of genealogical studies and heraldic practice.

I hope you will enjoy your stay in Ottawa and the tours that some of you will be taking to other communities in Ontario and Quebec. Above all, I extend every good wishes for successful and stimulating discussions during the Congress.

## Message de Son Excellence le très honorable Roméo LeBlanc, Gouverneur général du Canada, président d'honneur du 22e congrès

En tant que président d'honneur du 22e congrès international des sciences généalogique et héraldique, et en tant que chef de l'Autorité héraldique du Canada, je suis très heureux d'accueillir dans la capitale du Canada tous les délégués, notamment ceux qui sont venus de loin pour assister à ce congrès, le premier organisé hors d'Europe.

Comme c'est la première fois que vous vous réunissez à l'extérieur du berceau des études scientifiques modernes en généalogie et en héraldique, votre thème, « Familles et emblèmes par-delà les frontières », me semble particulièrement approprié. Dans un univers où la mondialisation des économies régionales et nationales accroît la nécessité d'une meilleure compréhension entre les pays et entre les peuples, les sciences que vous avez réunies pour explorer diverses limites nous offrent un précieux éclairage. Après tout, la généalogie et l'héraldique sont liées à des motivations présentes chez l'être humain pendant la plus grande partie de son histoire : la recherche de ses origines et de sa lignée, et l'utilisation de symboles pour identifier des personnes et des institutions. Bien entendu, la façon de relever et de préserver ses origines ainsi que les types de symboles créés ont beaucoup varié dans le temps et dans l'espace.

Pendant cette rencontre, vous allez explorer certaines de ces variations, voir comment l'expérience d'un pays peut modifier celle d'un autre et identifier les occasions et les défis nouveaux que la technologie présente aujourd'hui à ces deux sciences. En fin de compte, et malgré toutes les différences apparentes que les analyses des chercheurs peuvent révéler, nous reconnaîtrons notre humanité à tous, l'importance primordiale de la famille au fil des ans et l'impulsion créatrice derrière des inventions aussi belles et durables que l'héraldique.

Nous sommes fiers que le Canada ait été choisi pour accueillir cet important forum. Nous avons hâte de partager avec vous une partie de la culture symbolique unique de nos Premières Nations et notre propre expérience des études généalogiques et de l'héraldique.

J'espère que vous apprécierez votre séjour à Ottawa, de même que les visites que certains d'entre vous ferez dans d'autres communautés de l'Ontario et du Québec. Et plus que tout, je vous souhaite des discussions stimulantes et fructueuses pendant ce congrès.

21

## Message from Mrs. Jean M. Matheson, President of the 22nd Congress

It gives me a great pleasure, on behalf of the members of the Heraldry Society of Canada, to welcome delegates to this the 22nd International Congress of Genealogical and Heraldic Sciences being held in Canada.

Although Canadian heraldry may still be in its youth, the Heraldry Society was formed in Canada in 1966 to proudly carry on the ancient traditions of heraldry and chivalry brought to this country originally by the British and French immigrants. In 1988, significantly as a result of the advocacy of the Heraldry Society of Canada, the Queen granted Letters Patent to the Governor General for the establishment of a Canadian Heraldic Authority. Prior to that time, grants had to be requested and registered outside Canada.

I trust you will enjoy your time in Canada and make many new friends with common interests.

The Heraldry Society of Canada wishes to express its gratitude to the Canadian Heraldic Authority, which has dedicated its time and talents to the planning of this event.

I personally look forward to attending some of the lectures and taking the opportunity to, not only make new heraldic friends, but also to becoming more knowledgeable about heraldry in other countries.

## Message from Mr. Robert D. Watt, Chief Herald of Canada, Secretary General of the 22nd Congress

My colleagues and I on the Planning Committee are honoured to have been entrusted with the first Congress to be held outside Europe. We believe the Congress theme is an apt choice as the Congress meets on another continent at a distance from the birthplace of modern scientific genealogical and heraldic researches.

I want to especially thank Their Excellencies for their patronage, my colleagues in the office of the Secretary to the Governor General, my fellow heralds and the staff of the Heraldic Authority, all our sponsors, donors and volunteers for their special efforts in the preparation of the 22nd Congress.

Canadian genealogists and heraldists look forward eagerly to learning of the newest work of their colleagues overseas and to sharing our researches with them during the Congress and in the Proceedings.

Welcome and thank you.

## Message de M^me Jean M. Matheson, présidente du 22^e congrès

Au nom des membres de la Société héraldique du Canada, je suis très heureuse d'accueillir les délégués de ce 22^e congrès international des sciences généalogique et héraldique tenu au Canada.

C'est d'ailleurs sur la recommandation de la Société héraldique du Canada que la Reine a accordé des lettres patentes au Gouverneur général pour la création d'une Autorité héraldique du Canada en 1988. Avant cette date, les demandes d'armoiries devaient être présentées et enregistrées à l'extérieur du Canada.

Je suis convaincue que vous apprécierez votre séjour au Canada et que vous vous ferez beaucoup de nouveaux amis partageant vos intérêts.

La Société héraldique du Canada tient à remercier l'Autorité héraldique du Canada pour le temps et le savoir-faire qu'elle a consacrés à la planification de cet événement.

Pour ma part, j'ai hâte d'assister à quelques-uns des exposés et d'avoir l'occasion de me faire de nouveaux amis dans le monde de l'héraldique tout en améliorant ma connaissance de l'héraldique dans le monde.

## Message de M. Robert D. Watt, Héraut d'armes du Canada, secrétaire général du 22^e Congrès

Mes collègues du comité de planification se joignent à moi pour vous dire qu'ils sont honorés d'avoir participé à l'organisation du premier congrès à se tenir hors d'Europe. Nous pensons que le thème est approprié pour un congrès qui se tient loin de l'endroit où les méthodes scientifiques de recherche en héraldique et en généalogie ont été élaborées.

Je tiens à remercier plus particulièrement Leurs Excellences de leur parrainage, aussi mes collègues du bureau du secrétaire du Gouverneur général, mes confrères hérauts et le personnel de l'Autorité héraldique, tous les commanditaires, donateurs et bénévoles pour leur dévouement dans la préparation de cet événement.

Les généalogistes et héraldistes canadiens sont enthousiastes à l'idée de prendre connaissance des plus récents travaux de leurs collègues d'outremer et de leur faire connaître les leurs, pendant le congrès et dans la publication qui en résultera.

Je vous remercie et vous souhaite la bienvenue.

## Message from Mr. Marcel Hamelin, Rector and Vice-Chancellor of the University of Ottawa
## Message de M. Marcel Hamelin, recteur et vice-chancelier de l'Université d'Ottawa

Bienvenue à l'Université d'Ottawa.

Au nom de l'Université d'Ottawa, je vous souhaite la plus cordiale bienvenue au 22ᵉ Congrès international des sciences généalogique et héraldique. L'Université est ravie de vous accueillir à cette occasion.

Au cœur de la capitale nationale, à la jonction même du Canada anglais et du Canada français, l'Université d'Ottawa occupe une place unique dans le système universitaire canadien. Depuis sa fondation en 1848, elle constitue un lieu de rencontre de deux des grandes traditions intellectuelles et scientifiques du monde occidental. C'est en fait la plus ancienne et la plus grande des universités bilingues en Amérique du Nord.

As Rector of the University of Ottawa, I welcome you to our campus and hope you will take the opportunity to get to know our university better. I wish each of you a profitable and enjoyable conference.

## Opening Remarks by Her Excellency Mrs. Diana Fowler LeBlanc, August 19, 1996
## Allocution de Son Excellence Mᵐᵉ Diana Fowler LeBlanc à l'occasion de l'inauguration du 22ᵉ congrès, 19 août 1996

Excellencies, Distinguished Guests, Delegates, Mesdames et Messieurs,

Bienvenue au Canada à tous les participants et participantes à ce congrès international.

As co-patron of the 22nd Congress and on behalf of the Governor General as Head of the Canadian Heraldic Authority, I am pleased to welcome delegates to this historic meeting, the first held outside Europe. I hope that you will find the discussions and special events stimulating and that you will have an opportunity to visit some of the historic sites in Canada's capital, between sessions. In particular, I am looking forward to welcoming you to Rideau Hall later today.

C'est maintenant mon plaisir de déclarer ouvert ce 22ᵉ congrès international des sciences généalogique et héraldique.

It is now my pleasure to declare the 22nd International Congress of Genealogical and Heraldic Sciences officially open.

## Allocution de M. Roger Harmignies, président du Bureau permanent des congrès, à la cérémonie d'ouverture le 19 août 1996

Excellence, Messieurs les représentants diplomatiques, Madame la présidente, Monsieur le recteur, Mesdames, Messieurs,

Le congrès international qui s'ouvre aujourd'hui constitue une première à plusieurs égards.

Depuis le début de l'existence des congrès internationaux des sciences généalogique et héraldique, c'est la première fois que l'un de ceux-ci est planifié et mis sur pied directement par une haute autorité nationale. Je tiens donc, avant tout, à exprimer ici nos remerciements à Son Excellence, Monsieur le Gouverneur général, chef de l'Autorité héraldique du Canada, pour avoir bien voulu autoriser celle-ci à se charger de l'organisation de ce 22ᵉ congrès. L'existence même de cette Autorité depuis 1988 témoigne de l'intérêt que le gouvernement canadien porte de nos jours à nos sciences. Son intervention dans ce congrès répond à son désir de participer à leur développement international en pleine expansion, et cela en collaboration avec des associations comme la Société héraldique du Canada, la Ontario Genealogical Society et la Société de généalogie de l'Outaouais, dont la réputation n'est plus à faire.

Tous nos congrès s'étaient jusqu'ici réunis dans un même berceau européen. Il existe certes déjà, depuis des décennies, des rencontres, des congrès plurinationaux, voire inter-continentaux, organisés sous différentes latitudes par certaines associations généalogiques dont les centres d'intérêt dépassent le territoire national. Mais c'est bien la première fois depuis plus de 44 ans qu'héraldistes et généalogistes de 27 nations différentes se rencontrent, non plus en Europe, mais au Nouveau Monde, au-delà cet Océan Atlantique que constituait naguère, aux yeux de beaucoup, une formidable frontière géographique et culturelle, mais aussi psychologique.

Cependant toute frontière, si formidable soit-elle, est forcément un lieu de passage, donc de rencontre. Aussi n'est-ce sans doute pas une coïncidence si nous nous réunissons précisément, ici et maintenant, pour discuter *familles et emblèmes par-delà les frontières.*

Le thème général de ce congrès peut paraître vaste. Ce n'est qu'une apparence, puisqu'il tend simplement à mettre en lumière un fait unique : nos sciences, tout comme leurs objets eux-mêmes, n'ont en réalité jamais connu ni frontières hermétiques, ni barrières infranchissables, ni cloisonnements artificiels d'aucune sorte. Les familles se dispersent, s'unissent, se déplacent ou... sont déplacées, émigrent de plus en plus loin. L'étude des familles, leur histoire sociologique, les généalogies ont toujours eu pour objectif d'en retrouver les racines en amont et d'en suivre les traces en aval, sur toute la surface de la Terre. Comme tous les systèmes signifiants, nos armoiries et nos autres emblèmes sont nés ici et là dans un contexte culturel précis, mais au fur et à mesure de leur développement dans le temps et dans l'espace, ils ont subi des influences extérieures. Toute étude héraldique, insigniologique ou vexillologique scientifique implique par conséquent de disposer et de tenir compte d'un vaste panorama de ces influences.

Nos sciences connaîtront sans doute moins que jamais de frontières, de barrières, de cloisonnements, puisque nous en sommes à la mondialisation des informations et de la Culture. Les progrès constants intervenus dans les procédés de reproduction et de diffusion des documents, comme dans le domaine des communications en général, ont rendu les études et les recherches généalogiques de plus en plus aisées ou – pour être plus près de la vérité – un peu moins laborieuses. Ce qui devient difficile, c'est surtout de rester « branché » et, en particulier, de rester branché sur ce vaste réseau d'information électronique, le « cyberspace ». Il nous faut, comme l'a si bien dit le président de la Confédération internationale de généalogie et d'héraldique dans un récent éditorial, « apprendre à dialoguer et à naviguer comme de parfaits "internautes" à la recherche de liens transcendant les frontières et les accidents de l'Histoire ».

À ce propos, il me paraît assez surprenant qu'au cours du congrès, deux communications seulement évoqueront les banques de données généalogiques et la méthodologie généalogique face à l'informatique, et qu'aucun exposé ne semble annoncé pour traiter spécifiquement de l'informatisation des données héraldiques et de leur traitement. Le sujet pourra sans doute être abordé au cours des discussions en séance pour amorcer une étude plus approfondie en vue des prochains congrès.

Pour le reste, nous pouvons constater que l'ensemble du programme comporte une bonne quarantaine de communications également réparties entre la généalogie et l'héraldique, ce qui implique qu'une sélection sévère a bien été pratiquée par le comité scientifique parmi les très nombreuses propositions qui lui étaient parvenues.

Environ la moitié de ces communications émanent d'orateurs résidant de ce côté de l'Atlantique. Ce qui constitue aussi une première, tout comme le pourcentage particulièrement élevé, plus de 62 pour cent, de participants canadiens et « étatsuniens ». Cette inversion des taux de fréquentation de nos congrès nous montre qu'un océan, si aisément franchissable qu'il soit devenu de nos jours, apparaît peut-être encore comme un obstacle trop difficile à enjamber pour certains.

Par ailleurs, constitue une autre première la mise sur pied d'un atelier d'art héraldique contemporain, greffé sur le congrès. C'est là une très heureuse initiative, à laquelle on ne peut qu'applaudir, car mettre ainsi les congressistes en contact direct avec l'activité d'armoristes renommés ou émergents, ne peut que contribuer à mieux faire connaître les différentes facettes de ce que l'on a appelé le noble Art.

Je ne saurais terminer sans remercier encore Son Honneur M^me la Mairesse d'Ottawa qui a accordé sans réserve l'appui de sa ville aux organisateurs, ainsi que Monsieur le Recteur de l'Université d'Ottawa qui a aimablement mis des locaux du campus universitaire à leur disposition, dès qu'il fut question de réunir le congrès ici, il y a trois ans, presque jour pour jour.

En effet, la première proposition, déjà assez détaillée, de tenir ce 22e congrès à Ottawa était parvenue au Bureau permanent au cours de sa séance du 30 août 1993 à Canterbury. C'est vous dire, Mesdames et Messieurs, amis congressistes, combien les officiers responsables de l'Autorité héraldique et tout spécialement le Héraut d'armes du Canada, Monsieur Robert Watt, et ses proches collaborateurs, ainsi que les membres des trois sociétés co-organisatrices qui leur ont apporté une aide efficace, combien ces personnes dévouées ont dû consacrer de temps, quelle énergie elles ont dû mobiliser pour mener à bien leur projet et être à même de nous accueillir ici aujourd'hui.

Je suis certain d'être votre interprète à tous en les remerciant chaleureusement et en souhaitant que le déroulement et les fruits du 22e congrès, *leur* congrès, les récompensent de leurs généreux efforts.

## Opening Speech by Mr. Robert D. Watt, Secretary General of the 22nd Congress
## Allocution inaugurale de M. Robert D. Watt, secrétaire général du 22e Congrès

Your Excellency, Excellencies, distinguished guests, mesdames et messieurs, ladies and gentlemen.

Over the years since I first represented the Heraldic Authority at the Innsbruck Congress, I have always been struck by the warmth with which our European colleagues welcomed me and the other Canadians who attended. It is a great pleasure and an honour to have been given this opportunity to reciprocate the hospitality. My colleagues and I hope you will feel that the Congress theme "Families and Emblems Transcending Frontiers" will bring forth some fresh interpretations of various themes and topics and stimulate further research to appear at future congresses.

Au cours de la préparation du congrès, l'Autorité héraldique du Canada a bénéficié de l'aide de la Société héraldique du Canada, de la Ontario Genealogical Society et de la Société de généalogie de l'Outaouais. Je voudrais exprimer à leurs représentants et à leur conseil d'administration tous mes remerciements pour leur dévouement, leur appui et leur participation à la planification et à la réalisation de cet événement.

From the outset, corporations, government ministries and agencies and individuals have responded with generous donations and assistance of many kinds to enable us to offer delegates a comprehensive series of lectures and special events. All of these gifts are acknowledged in the delegate guide. However, you will appreciate that one element of the programme deserves special mention. Thanks to our leading sponsor, the Corel Corporation, and major donor, the Burnett-Weston Fund of Toronto, we have been able to organize the world's first heraldic artists workshop, a unique gathering of 11 of the world's masters of the art form. I know you will enjoy meeting with them and seeing their work at the special exhibition at the Museum of Civilization on Wednesday.

Un congrès de cette envergure doit se dérouler dans un endroit approprié. Monsieur le recteur, nous devons une dette de reconnaissance importante à l'Université d'Ottawa qui, grâce à vos bons offices, a pu être le lieu de cette rencontre. C'est l'endroit idéal pour réunir les meilleurs chercheurs en généalogie et en héraldique, disciplines qui s'affirment de plus en plus comme sciences auxiliaires de l'histoire.

L'émission d'un timbre en l'honneur de l'héraldique a grandement contribué à rehausser le prestige national et international de ce congrès. Aussi sommes-nous heureux d'accueillir parmi nous, monsieur Phillippe Lemay, premier vice-président de la Société canadienne des postes.

Earlier I spoke of the warmth of the European welcome. A special component of this has been the advice and assistance received from three leading figures in the world of genealogy and heraldry: M. Roger Harmignies, President of the Bureau permanent des congrès internationaux, Dr. Jean-Claude Loutsch, President of the Académie internationale d'héraldique and Dr. Jean-Marie Thiébaud, President of the Confédération internationale de généalogie et d'héraldique. Gentlemen, thank you very much for your advice and support. I hope you will feel that we have developed a Congress worthy of becoming part of our European predecessors.

As we approach the moment of official opening it remains only to extend the warmest welcome to all delegates.

Puisse ce congrès se révéler une expérience enrichissante pour tous les participants.

I would like to extend a particular welcome to delegates from Germany, Spain and Portugal. While there are not many sessions in your own language, I hope you will find the lectures of great interest and that your visit to Ottawa and Canada is memorable.

Enjoy the Congress, je vous remercie.

### Allocution de M. Roger Harmignies, président du Bureau permanent des congrès, au dîner de gala clôturant le 22ᵉ congrès, le 23 août 1996

Ma brève allocution comprendra deux parties, l'une officielle, l'autre... plus sentimentale.

Tout d'abord, il m'appartient, à la clôture d'un congrès, d'annoncer officiellement le suivant, même si nombre de congressistes sont sans doute déjà au courant.

Le Bureau permanent des congrès a accepté la proposition présentée par la Direction des Archives du ministère italien des Biens culturels de confier l'organisation du 23ᵉ congrès aux Archives d'État de Turin. Outre le patronage du ministère, ce projet est assuré des appuis administratifs et financiers indispensables à sa réalisation. La date exacte reste à fixer et les thèmes doivent encore être précisés au cours d'une réunion prévue à Rome le 23 septembre prochain.

D'autre part, chose rare, nous sommes déjà en possession d'une offre ferme émanant de la Fédération française de généalogie pour organiser le congrès de l'an 2000 à Besançon. L'expérience acquise par cette Fédération dans l'organisation des congrès nationaux de généalogie français est une garantie pour la mise sur pied du 24ᵉ congrès.

Prenant la parole en dernier, je relève une fois de plus que le 22ᵉ congrès constitut une première encore. En ce sens que c'est la première fois que les *cinq* continents y sont representés, puisqu'il compte des participants non seulement d'Europe et des deux Amériques, mais aussi d'Afrique, d'Asie et d'Océanie. Nos congrès s'affirment donc dans le monde entier et il ne fait aucun doute qu'après celui-ci, leur renommée sera plus grande encore.

Après ce qu'ils ont vécu ici, tous les congressistes présents ne pourront que dire le plus grand bien de ce genre de manifestation. Sur le plan scientifique et documentaire, on y entend d'excellents exposés, on y découvre d'intéressantes choses, on s'y fait de nouvelles relations. Sur le plan pratique, l'accueil est chaleureux, les problèmes sont résolus avec célérité et efficacité et, enfin, les réceptions sont aussi grandioses que sympatiques.

Mais le ciel, ce matin, était couvert, le soleil était voilé, la nature plus triste. Nous arrivons au terme de ce congrès en nous lamentant : « Et c'est mon dernier jour ! » Déjà ! C'est, je pense, l'avis de tous les congressistes. Mais de leur côté, Robert Watt, son épouse, ses collaboratrices et collaborateurs, ainsi que l'efficace ordonnateur, M. Berthelsen, vont enfin pouvoir débrayer et pousser un grand « ouf » après cette exténuante semaine.

Nous allons les quitter avec regret. Nous les remercions de tout cœur pour tout ce qu'ils ont fait pour nous, pour leur infini dévouement. Le 22ᵉ congrès qui se termine ici leur doit beaucoup, je dirais même qu'il leur doit TOUT !

Mr. Dan Cernovodeanu greeting Her Excellency.
M. Dan Cernovodeanu présente ses hommages à Son Excellence.

Her Excellency with (l. to r.) Mr. G. Zdenko Alexy; His Excellency Mr. Anton
Hykisch, Ambassador of the Slovak Republic; Dr. Ladislav Vrteĺ.
Son Excellence avec (de g. à dr.) M. G. Zdenko Alexy ; Son Excellence M. Anton Hykisch,
ambassadeur de la République slovaque ; M. Ladislav Vrteĺ, Ph.D.

*Opening reception*  Her Excellency with Mrs. Althea Douglas and Mr. Stephen White.
*Réception d'ouverture*  Son Excellence en compagnie de M^me Althea Douglas et de M. Stephen White.

Her Excellency presenting the Corel Prize for Excellence (Heraldic Art) to Mr. A. Jamieson.
Son Excellence remet le prix d'excellence de la société Corel (art héraldique) à M. A. Jamieson.

# Organizations represented at the Congress / Organisations représentées au congrès

*Académie Heraldique of the Netherlands*, O. Schutte

*Académie Internationale d'héraldique*, A.I.H. : Z. G. Alexy, R. Harmignies, C. Humphery-Smith, J.-C. Loutsch, H. baron Pinoteau, M. Popoff, A. Scufflaire; a.i.h. : J. A. de Boo, L. Duerloo, Bengt. O. Kälde, J. J. F. Kennedy, L. Müller-Westphal, C. Nevéus, R. D. Watt

*Archives générales du Royaume (Belgique)*, A. Scufflaire

*Archives of The Bahamas, Ministry of Education*, G. Saunders

*National Archives of Canada*, P. Kennedy

*National Archives of Sweden, Stockholm*, C. Nevéus

*Public Archives of Nova Scotia, Manuscripts Division*, L. K. Yorke

*Association of Professional Genealogists*, B. D. Merriman

*Canadian Flag Association*, K. Harrington

*L'Association des Familles Roy d'Amérique*, J.-G. Roy

*United Empire Loyalists Association*, J. E. Ruch

*Autorité héraldique du Canada*, C. Bursey-Sabourin, C. R. Maier, R. Pichette, A. Vachon, R. D. Watt

*Bibliothèque nationale de France*, M. Popoff

*South African Bureau of Heraldry*, F. G. Brownell, G. W. Schlemmer

*Center for Human Genetics (USA)*, T. H. Roderick

*Centre d'Entraide Généalogique de Franche-Comté*, D. Foltête

*Centro de Estudios Genea. de Córdoba-Arg*, E. de Soaje Pinto

*Flag Research Center (USA)*, W. Smith

*Ministry of Interior, Heraldry Commission, Slovakia*, L. Vrtel

*Confédération internationale de généalogie et d'héraldique*, H. T. Bruck, D. Cernovodeanu, A. Comnène, A. Cornaro, K. H. Degerman, R. Harmignies, M. F. Harmo, Bengt. O. Kälde, D. Lawson, L. Müller-Westphal, R. Num, L. J. P. Nouel, H. baron Pinoteau, A. Snethlage, J.-M. Thiébaud, A. K. Toohey, L. K. Yorke

*Conseil français d'héraldique*, J.-M. Thiébaud

*Conseil d'héraldique et de vexillologie de la communauté française de Belgique*, A. Scufflaire

*Conseil héraldique Ran & van Adel de Belgique*, A. Scufflaire

*Consulentschap Voor De Heraldeek*, Ir A. Daae

*Court of the Lord Lyon (Scotland)*, C. J. Burnett, E. A. Roads

*Douglas Consultants*, A. Douglas

*Federación Argentina de Genealogia y Heráldica*, E. de Soaje Pinto

*Fédération française de Généalogie*, J.-M. Thiébaud

*Armorial Heritage Foundation*, J. J. F. Kennedy, P. D. B. Mérey

*Gen-Find Research Associates Canada*, B. W. Hutchison

*Gesellschaft für Familienforschung in Franken, Berlin*, E. Friderici

*N.G.V. Branche Heraldiek (Netherlands)*, Ir A. Daae

*Heraldicá komisia, Ministerstvo vnútra (Slovakia)*, L. Vrtel

*Hoge Raad Van de Adel*, O. Schutte

*Ins. Argen. de Ciencias Geneal.*, E. de Soaje Pinto

*Institut d'Études généalogiques (Russia)*, A. Krasko, I. V. Sakharov, D. Sizonenko

*Institut interuniversitaire de recherches sur les populations (IREP) (Cda)*, G. Bouchard

*Institute of Civic Heraldry (U.S.A.)*, J. Croft

*Institute of Heraldic and Genealogical Studies, England*, R. C. F. Baker

*North American Institute of Heraldic & Flag Studies (USA)*, D. F. Phillips

*Institutio Rossica Christiana*, N. Sakharova

*Instituto Araldico Genealogico Italiano*, P. F. D. Uberti

*Instituto Dominicano de genealoja Inc.*, L. J. P. Nouel

*Instituto Historico de Petropolis (Brazil)*, F. J. de Vasconcellos

*Italian Genealogy*, L. Ranieri

*Ancestral File & Authority Systems, Family History Department, Latter Day Saints Church (Salt Lake City, Utah, USA)*, J. M. Kitzmiller II

*The Army Cadet League of Canada*, R. A. McColgan

*Library of Congress (Washington, USA), Local History and Genealogy*, J. P. Reid, A. K. Toohey

*Kungl. biblioteket, Stockholm (Royal) Library*, M. Sandels

*National Library of Canada (Ottawa)*, M. Bend

*National Library of Russia*, A. Krasko, I. V. Sakharov, N. Sakharova, D. Sizonenko

*Maison de la Généalogie (France)*, P. Le Clercq, J.-M. Thiébaud

*Maison de noblesse (Finland)*, K. H. Degerman

*British Museum (Great Britain)*, M. L. Bierbrier

*National Museums of Scotland, Edinburgh*, C. J. Burnett

*Department of National Defence (Canada)*, V. Bezeau

*Recherches et études généalogiques de l'Ain (REGAIN)*, R. Beaubernard

*Riksarkivet, Sweden*, V. A. Sagerlund

*The Royal Orders, The Royal Palace (Stockholm)*, Bengt. O. Kälde

*Societas Heraldica Scandivica*, L. C. Stolt

*Société française de vexillologie*, H. baron Pinoteau

*Société française d'héraldique et de sigillographie*, H. baron Pinoteau, M. Popoff

*Société généalogique de l'Yonne*, P. Le Clercq

*Société généalogique russe*, A. Krasko, I. V. Sakharov

*Société suisse d'héraldique*, G. Mattern

*Bahamas Historical Society*, G. Saunders

*Caledonian Society, Netherlands*, P. Douglas

*Heraldry Australia (Genealogical Society of Victoria)*, R. Num

*Heraldry Society of Canada*, R. Addington, P. L. Allpress, J. Benoit, D. Bowyer, A. Comnène, D. L. C. M. Galles, J. Good, G. Hale, O. Jaakkola, J. J. F. Kennedy, D. Lawson, M. M. Lawson, J. Lofft, C. R. Maier, J. M. Matheson, J. R. Matheson, M. T. McCullough, P. D. B. Mérey, B. Patterson, R. Pichette, L. Ranieri, J. E. Ruch, D. D. Ruddy, D. H. Scholes, D. Scholes, E. N. Taylor, A. Vachon, R. D. Watt, J. Wilkes

*Heraldry Society of Great-Britain*, M. Davies

*Heraldry Society of Scotland*, E. N. Taylor

*Middlesex Heraldry Society*, K. W. Holmes

*New York Genealogical et Biographical Society*, J. Terzian

*Norwegian Heraldic Society*, T. S. Vadholm

*Ontario Genealogical Society*, P. D. B. Mérey, B. D. Merriman

*Society for Creative Anachonism, Inc.*, D .B. Appleton

*Swedish Bookplate Society*, L. C. Stolt

*The Swedish House of Nobility (Riddarhuset)*, L. Wikström

*The Committee on Heraldry (1864) of the New England Historic Genealogical Society*, H. L. P. Beckwith

*The Heraldry Society (England)*, K. W. Holmes, J. Lofft, M. Miles, L. Pierson, E. N. Taylor

*Slovenská genealogická a heraldická spoločnosť (Slovakia)*, Z. G. Alexy

*Swedish National Committee for Genealogy and Heraldry*, Bengt. O. Kälde, M. Sandels, L. Wikström

*Union généalogique de Bourgogne*, P. Le Clercq

*Centre d'études acadiennes, Université de Moncton*, S. A. White

*Département d'histoire, Université d'Ottawa*, J.-C. Dubé

*McGill University - Montreal Children's Hospital, Research Institute*, C. R. Scriver

*The Department of History and the Medieval Institute, University of Notre-Dame*, D. J. D. Boulton

*Université de Moncton*, J. G. P. Delaney

*University of British Columbia*, M. Halpin, J. Ladner

*University of Bucarest, Faculty of History and Heraldic*, D. Cernovodeanu

*University of Toronto*, R. B. Salter

*Vlaamse Heraldische Raad*, L. Duerloo

*World Heraldry Organizations Project*, J. R. Terzian

---

This list was drawn from the registration forms completed by Congress participants. We hope that it is complete and present our apologies should there be involuntary omissions. / La liste suivante a été uniquement élaborée à partir des formulaires d'inscription fournis par les congressistes. Nous ne pouvons garantir son exhaustivité et nous nous excusons des éventuelles omissions.

# List of participants / Liste des participants

**Robert ADDINGTON**
706-565 Talbot Street
London, ON  N6A 2T1
CANADA

**G. Zdenko ALEXY**
Havličkova 3
SK-811 04 Bratislava
SLOVAKIA

**Peter L. ALLPRESS**
& Lucille Allpress
Edifici Puiet 1C
Ordino,
ANDORRA via France

**Anneli AMEE**
Vuorikuja 2 AS 16
FIN-24100 Salo
FINLAND

**T. AMERLINCK Y ZIRIÓN**
Tres Picos 17
MEX-11560 D.F.
MEXICO

**Graham L. ANDERSON**
Suite 204, Cowichan Bay Arms
Cowichan Bay, BC  V0R 1N0
CANADA

**David B. APPLETON**
& Jo Ann Appleton
1610 Vinecrest Circle
Garland, TX  75042-5358
USA

**Robert BEAUBERNARD**
& Michèle M. Teillon-Michallet
Lebourg,
Messimy-sur-Saône
01480 Jassans-Riottier
FRANCE

**Henry L.P. BECKWITH**
& Alice H.R.H. Beckwith
35 Boston Neck Road
N. Kingstown, RI 02852-5704
USA

**Jocelyne BENOIT**
905, Tour du Lac
Val-David, QC  J0T 2N0
CANADA

**Vincent BEZEAU**
Department of National Defence
MGen George R. Pearkes Building
Ottawa, ON  K1A 0K2
CANADA

**M. L. BIERBRIER**
59 Weymouth Street, Flat 24
London W1N 3LG
ENGLAND

**Dietr BIRK**
48 Merkley Square
Scarborough, ON  M1G 2Y6
CANADA

**Hans BIRK**
48 Merkley Square
Scarborough, ON  M1G 2Y6
CANADA

**Mary BOND**
The National Library of Canada
RM 229, Ref. & Info. Services
395 Wellington Street
Ottawa, ON  K1A 0N4
CANADA

**Gérard BOUCHARD**
IREP
555, boulevard de l'Université
Chicoutimi, QC G7H 2B1
CANADA

**D'Arcy J.D. BOULTON**
& Maureen Boulton
625 West Colfax Avenue
South Bend, IN 46601-1401
USA

**David BOWYER**
389 Cooper Street
Cambridge, ON  N3C 3X9
CANADA

**Iain BOYD**
P.O. Box 11-404
Wellington 6034
NEW ZEALAND

**Frederick G. BROWNELL**
Bureau of Heraldry
Private Bag X236
Pretoria  0001
SOUTH AFRICA

**Helene T. BRUCK**
1445 McRobie Avenue
Ottawa, ON  K1H 7E2
CANADA

**Charles J. BURNETT**
Court of the Lord Lyon
H.M. New Register House
Edinburgh EH1 3YT,
SCOTLAND

**James CROFT**
& Claire Johnson-Croft
P.O. Box 365
Northampton, MA 01061,
USA

**Jean-Claude DUBÉ**
Département d'histoire
Université d'Ottawa
Ottawa, ON K1N 6N5
CANADA

**Cathy BURSEY-SABOURIN**
The Canadian Heraldic Authority
1 Sussex Drive
Ottawa, ON K1A 0A1
CANADA

**Marjorie DAVIES**
10 Lawrence Gardens, Mill Hill
London NW7 4JT
ENGLAND

**Luc DUERLOO**
& Tonia Dhaese
Theophiel Reynlaan 46
2640 Mortsel
BELGIQUE

**Richard CARRUTHERS-ŻUROWSKI**
34 A Acacia Avenue
Ottawa, ON K1M OP4
CANADA

**Ir. Anders DAAE**
Jan Steenweg 8
9761 HJ Eelde
THE NETHERLANDS

**Daniel FOLTÊTE**
& Margret Foltête
6, rue du Vivarais
25000 Besançon
FRANCE

**Dan CERNOVODEANU**
30, rue Legendre
75017 Paris
FRANCE

**J. A. DE BOO**
Westersingel 90
9901 GK Appingedam
THE NETHERLANDS

**Elisabeth FRIDERICI**
Fürther Straße 80A
90429 Nürnberg
GERMANY

**Angela COMNÈNE**
& Alexis Comnène
106-505 boulevard St. Laurent
Ottawa, ON K1K 3X4
CANADA

**K. H. DEGERMAN**
Comité National Finlandais
pour la Généalogie
Irjala Gård
03400 Vichtis
FINLANDE

**Duane L. C. M. GALLES**
2546 Cedar Avenue
Minneapolis, MN 55404-4032
USA

**Andreas CORNARO**
Liechtensteinstraße 39
A-1090 Wien
AUSTRIA

**J. G. Paul DELANEY**
Box K336
RR 10 Ammon Road
Moncton, NB E1C 9J9
CANADA

**James C. GERVAIS**
1 Sussex Drive
Ottawa, ON K1A 0A1
CANADA

**Jean-Marc CORREA DE BRITO**
& Elisabeth Correa de Brito-Boudron
Borgoumont 67
4987 La Gleize
BELGIQUE

**Althea DOUGLAS**
3-525 Hilson Avenue
Ottawa, ON K1Z 6C9
CANADA

**Ivan de LEESTHAL GOGALA**
& Mojca de Leesthal Gogala
Collegium Heraldicum
ul. Franje Račkog 82
51 000 Rijeka , CROATIA

**Kathleen B. CORY**
4 Brunstane Road
Edinburgh, EH15 2EY
SCOTLAND

**Percy DOUGLAS**
Leyweg 116A
2545 CT The Hague
THE NETHERLANDS

**Jonathan GOOD**
RR 4
Port Hope, ON L1A 3V8
CANADA

**J. M. GREENSHIELDS**
P.O. Box 749
Stirling, ON K0K 3E0
CANADA

**Naomi E. S.GRIFFITHS**
38 Glencairn Avenue
Ottawa, ON K1S 1M6
CANADA

**Sandra GUILLAUME**
411-51 Grosvenor Street
Toronto, ON M5S 1B5
CANADA

**Grete HALE**
40 Fuller Street
Ottawa, ON K1Y 3R8
CANADA

**Marjorie M. HALPIN**
The Museum of Anthropology,
University of British Columbia
Vancouver, BC V6T 1W5
CANADA

**Roger E. A. HARMIGNIES**
57, rue Martin Lindekens
1150 Bruxelles
BELGIQUE

**M. F. HARMO**
Runeberginkatu 67 A 12
00260 Helsinki
FINLAND

**Kevin HARRINGTON**
50 Heathfield Drive
Scarborough, ON M1M 3B1
CANADA

**Grace HATTAM**
5 Northey Drive
Willowdale, ON M2L 2S8
CANADA

**Kay W. HOLMES**
22 St. Margaret's Road
Ruislip, Middlesex HA4 7N0
ENGLAND

**Cecil R. HUMPHERY-SMITH**
79-82 Northgate
Canterbury, CT1 1BA
ENGLAND

**Brian W. HUTCHISON**
908 34th Street SE
Calgary, AB T2A 0Z6
CANADA

**Tuomas HYRSKY**
Mankkaanpuro 7 B
02180 Espoo
FINLAND

**Oliver JAAKKOLA**
12 Nesbitt Drive
Toronto, ON M4W 2G3
CANADA

**Andrew Stewart JAMIESON**
Home Farm Cottage, 13 High Street
Templecombe, Somerset BA8 0J0
ENGLAND

**Yvonne A. JANSEN-LINSE**
Park Arenberg 14
3731 ES De Bilt
THE NETHERLANDS

**Diethilde Babette JOERRIS**
Glindholzstraße 185
D-47800 Krefeld
GERMANY

**Ilona JURKIEWICZ**
24-3275 McCarthy Road
Ottawa, ON K1V 9M7
CANADA

**Bengt Olof KÄLDE**
Norrtäljegatan 9 A
S-753 27 Uppsala
SWEDEN

**Darrel E. KENNEDY**
352 Imperial Road South
Guelph, ON N1K 1L8
CANADA

**John J. F. KENNEDY**
613-100 Roehampton Avenue
Toronto, ON M4P 1R3
CANADA

**Patricia KENNEDY**
The National Archives of Canada
395 Wellington Street
Ottawa, ON K1A 0N4,
CANADA

**Samy KHALID**
76, rue Langstrom
Ottawa, ON K1G 5J6
CANADA

**John M. KITZMILLER II**
Family History Department
15 East South Temple Street
Salt Lake City, UT 84150
USA

**Alla KRASKO**
The National Library of Russia
18 Sadovaya Street
St. Petersburg, RUSSIA

**Janet LADNER**
4610 Connaught Drive
Vancouver, BC V6J 4E2
CANADA

**Judith A. LAROCQUE**
1, Sussex Drive
Ottawa, ON K1A 0A1
CANADA

**Donald LAWSON**
& Máire Magee Lawson
17 Broadway Street, Box 996
Ridgetown, ON  N0P 2C0
CANADA

**Fred MCGARRY**
RR 4
Cambridge, ON  N1R 5S5
CANADA

**Mikhail Y. MEDVEDEV**
Galernaya ul. 41-14
190000  St. Petersburg
RUSSIA

**Pierre LE CLERCQ**
130, rue Henri-Barbusse
93300 Aubervilliers
FRANCE

**Charles R. MAIER**
Canadian Heraldic Authority
1 Sussex Drive
Ottawa, ON  K1A 0A1
CANADA

**Peter D. Béla MÉREY**
128 Gilmour Avenue
Toronto, ON M6P 3B3
CANADA

**Jonathan LOFFT**
517-31 Alexander Street
Toronto, ON  M4Y 1B2
CANADA

**Donald R. MANDICH**
& Georgia W. Mandich
173 Kirkwood Court
Bloomfield Hills, MI 48304-2927
USA

**Brenda D. MERRIMAN**
201-110 The Esplanade
Toronto, ON  M5E 1X9
CANADA

**Jean-Claude LOUTSCH**
& Douce Loutsch-Weydert
35, rue de Luxembourg
8140 Bridel
LUXEMBOURG

**Baz MANNING**
28B Norwich Road
Bournemouth, Dorset  BH2 5QZ
ENGLAND

**Siegfried MILDNER**
& Gertraude Mildner
Straße der Freundschaft 29
99706 Sondershausen
GERMANY

**Debra MACGARVIE**
636 Glenhurst Crescent
Gloucester, ON K1J 7B7
CANADA

**Terrence C. MANUEL**
626 Clancy Street
Gloucester, ON  K1J 7T9
CANADA

**Marian MILES**
Magpie Cottage, Pondwood Lane
Shottesbrooke, Nr Maidenhead
Berkshire  SL6 3SS
ENGLAND

**D. Ross MCLELLAN**
606-10 The Driveway
Ottawa, ON  K2P 1C7
CANADA

**Jean M. MATHESON**
& Hugh Matheson
1605 Dorion Avenue
Ottawa , ON  K1G 0J7
CANADA

**Hussain AL-MOUSAWI**
10 Ague Drive
Nepean, ON K2E 6S1
CANADA

**Robert A. MCCOLGAN**
& Doris McColgan
442 Guy Avenue
Ottawa, ON  K1K 1C2
CANADA

**John R. MATHESON**
Box 43
Rideau Ferry, ON  K0G 1W0
CANADA

**Lothar MÜLLER-WESTPHAL**
Binsfelder Str. 45
52351 Dueren
Germany

**M. Teresa MCCULLOUGH**
& Francis McCullough
41-4900 Cartier Street
Vancouver, BC  V6M 4H2
CANADA

**Günter MATTERN**
Sichternstr. 35
CH-4410 Liestal
SWITZERLAND

**Clara NEVÉUS**
& Torgny Nevéus
The National Archives
P.O. Box 12541
10229 Stockholm
SWEDEN

**Luis José Prieto NOUEL**
Calle Mercedes No. 204
Apartado Postal 3350
Santo Domingo
REPUBLICA DOMINICANA

**David F. PHILLIPS**
2331 47th Avenue
San Francisco, CA 94116
USA

**Ulrike RÄTZEL**
Querstraße 7
30579 Hannover
GERMANY

**Richard NUM**
P.O. Box 36
Burnside, SA 5066
AUSTRALIA

**Robert PICHETTE**
1015-101, rue Archibald
Moncton, NB E1A 9J7
CANADA

**Judith P. REID**
& J. Norman Reid
Local History & Genealogy
The Library of Congress
Washington, DC 20540-5554
USA

**Jan-Eric OLSSON**
Stocksnäsvägen 9D
S-575 33 Eksjö
SWEDEN

**Leslie G. PIERSON**
& Mary Pierson
27 Longfield Drive
Amersham
Buckinghamshire HP6 5HE
ENGLAND

**Elizabeth A. ROADS**
Court of the Lord Lyon
H.M New Register House
Edinburgh EH1 3YT
SCOTLAND

**Peter ORENSKI**
101-117, Parklane Road
New Milford, CT 06776
USA

**Hervé baron PINOTEAU**
& la baronne Pinoteau
4bis boulevard de Glatigny
78000 Versailles
FRANCE

**Thomas H. RODERICK**
& Hilda K. Roderick
The Center for Human Genetics
4 Seely Road
Bar Harbor, ME 04609, USA

**María-Mercedes COSTA PARETAS**
& María de Gracia Costa Paretas
Consejo de Ciento 181-3º 5ª
08015 Barcelona,
SPAIN

**Esther R. O. R. de Soaje PINTO**
Arenales 843, Piso 5to. 19
1061 Buenos Aires
ARGENTINA

**Jean-Guy ROY**
258, rue Sirois
C.P. 87
Ste-Épiphane, QC G0L 2X0
CANADA

**Henry E. PASTON-BEDINGFELD**
The College of Arms
Queen Victoria Street
London EC4V 4BT
ENGLAND

**Michel POPOFF**
25 Villa Picardie
Chennevieres S/Marne
94430
FRANCE

**John E. RUCH**
1805-71 Somerset Street W.
Ottawa, ON K2P 2G2
CANADA

**Bruce PATTERSON**
55 Colonsay Road
Thornhill, ON L3T 3E9
CANADA

**Luciano RANIERI**
& Eva RANIERI
13189 Dillon Drive
Tecumseh, ON N8N 3P2
CANADA

**D. D. RUDDY**
7A-1390 Pine Avenue West
Montreal, QC H3G 1A8
CANADA

**Julio Genaro Campillo PÉREZ**
Calle Mercedes No. 204
Apartado Postal 407-2
Santo Domingo
REPUBLICA DOMINICANA

**Peter RÄTZEL**
& Regina Rätzel
An Der Buschmühle
Güldendorf
D-15236 Frankfurt (Oder)
GERMANY

**Vladimir A. SAGERLUND**
& Sylvia Kantzy Sagerlund
Nybodavägen 5
S-13547 Tyresö
SWEDEN

**Sunil SAIGAL**
c/o UNDP
One United Nations Plaza
CD-1 Building, 19th Floor
New York, NY 10017, USA

**Leslie SCHWEITZER**
76455 S.W. Bonita Rd
Tigard, OR 97224
USA

**Okill STUART**
700, rue Casgrain
St-Lambert, QC J4R 1G7
CANADA

**Igor V. SAKHAROV**
& Nathalie SAKHAROVA
The National Library of Russia
Institute of Genealogical Research
18 Sadovaya Street
191069 St. Petersburg
RUSSIA

**Charles R. SCRIVER**
Montreal Children's Hospital
Dept. of Biochemical Genetics
709-2300 Tupper Street
Montreal, QC H3H 1P3
CANADA

**Markku SUOMINEN**
Freesenk 4 A 22
00100, Helsinki
FINLAND

**Robert B. SALTER**
The Hospital for Sick Children
555 University Avenue
Toronto, ON M5G 1X8
CANADA

**Andrée E. C. SCUFFLAIRE**
165d/61, av. Winston Churchill
1180 Uccle (Bruxelles)
BELGIQUE

**Conrad SWAN**
Boxford House
Suffolk C010 5JT
ENGLAND

**Marianne SANDELS**
Kyrkogårdsgatan 5A
753 10 Uppsala
SWEDEN

**Whitney SMITH**
Box 580
Winchester, MA 01890-0880
USA

**Lars TANGERAAS**
Royal Ministry of Foreign Affairs
Box 8114 Dep.
0032 Oslo
NORWAY

**Gail SAUNDERS**
Department of Archives
P.O. Box ss-6341
Nassau
THE BAHAMAS

**Dimitri SIZONENKO**
The National Library of Russia
Institute of Genealogical Research
18 Sadovaya Street
191069 St. Petersburg
RUSSIA

**E. N. "Pete" TAYLOR**
& Nan G. Taylor
62 Norman Crescent
Pinner, Middlesex HA5 3QL
ENGLAND

**Gavin W. SCHLEMMER**
c/o F. Brownell
Bureau of Heraldry
Private Bag X236
Pretoria, 0001
SOUTH AFRICA

**Albert SNETHLAGE**
Vyverlaan 3g
3062HH, Rotterdam
THE NETHERLANDS

**James R. TERZIAN**
P.O. Box 4520
Foster City, CA 94404
USA

**David SCHOLES**
& Doris Scholes
14 Barrie Avenue
Ottawa, ON K1Y 1W1
CANADA

**Romilly SQUIRE**
Studio 4
30 Elbe Street
Leith, Edinburgh EH6 7HW
SCOTLAND

**Jean-Marie THIÉBAUD**
& Mme Thiébaud
49, rue des Granges
25000 BESANÇON
FRANCE

**Otto SCHUTTE**
Van Speykstraat 78
2518 GE The Hague
THE NETHERLANDS

**Lars C. STOLT**
& Aino Stolt Thornquist
Birger Jarlsgatan
113 A 4 tr.
1356 Stockholm
SWEDEN

**Margarita TINTÓ**
& Luisa Puig
C/Rec, 34 Granollers
08400 Barcelona
SPAIN

**Anne K. T. TOOHEY**
10901 Knightsbridge Court
Reston, VA 22090
USA

**Pier Felice Degli UBERTI**
Istituto Araldico
Genealogico Italiano
Ordini cavallereschi
Via Belflore, 1
40123 Bologna
ITALIA

**Auguste VACHON**
& Paula Gornescu-Vachon
Canadian Heraldic Authority
1 Sussex Drive
Ottawa, ON K1A 0A1
CANADA

**Tom S. VADHOLM**
Holgerslystveien 23 A
0280 Oslo
NORWAY

**Francisco DE VASCONCELLOS**
& Dionée Cunha Vasconcellos
P.O. Box 90.335
25.621-970 Petrópolis RJ
BRAZIL

**Ladislav VRTEĹ**
Heraldry Commission
Ministry of the Interior
Studenohorská
841 03 Bratislava
SLOVAKIA

**Christopher WALLIS**
RR1
Dashwood, ON N0M 1N0
CANADA

**Robert D. WATT**
& Alison J. Watt
Canadian Heraldic Authority
1 Sussex Drive
Ottawa, ON K1A 0A1
CANADA

**Stephen A. WHITE**
50 Somerset Drive
Moncton, NB E1A 3T7
CANADA

**Lars WIKSTRÖM**
Riddarhuset
Box 2022
10311 Stockholm
SWEDEN

**John WILKES**
57 Larabee Crescent
Don Mills, ON M3A 3E6
CANADA

**Anthony WOOD**
The Society of Heraldic Arts
Quillion House
Over Stratton, South Petherton
Somerset TA13 5LG
ENGLAND

**Lois K. YORKE**
Manuscripts Division
Public Archives of Nova Scotia
6016 University Avenue
Halifax, NS B3H 1W4
CANADA

**Stephen C. YOUNG**
Family History Department
15 East South Temple Street
Salt Lake City, UT 84150
USA

**Closing banquet** *General view.*

**Banquet de clôture** Vue d'ensemble.

**Closing banquet** Music provided by the Canadian Forces String Ensemble.

**Banquet de clôture** Concert de l'ensemble à cordes des Forces canadiennes.

*Closing banquet* (l. to r.) Mr. James Taylor, Mrs. Lucille Allpress and Mr. Peter Allpress.
*Banquet de clôture* (de g. à dr.) M. James Taylor, M$^{me}$ Lucille Allpress et M. Peter Allpress.

*Closing banquet* (l. to r.) Mr. Kay Holmes; Mrs. Nan Taylor; Mr. Pete Taylor; Mr. Anders Daae; Mrs. Marian Miles; Mr. Leslie G. Pierson and Mrs. Mary Pierson.
*Banquet de clôture* (de g. à dr.) M. Kay Holmes ; M$^{me}$ Nan Taylor ; M. Pete Taylor ; M. Anders Daae ; M$^{me}$ Marian Miles ; M. Leslie G. Pierson ; M$^{me}$ Mary Pierson.

***Closing ceremony*** Mr. Roger Lindsay, representative of the Burnett-Weston Foundation, presents
the Burnett-Weston Prize for Excellence (Heraldic Art) to Mr. Baz Manning.
***Cérémonie de clôture*** M. Roger Linsday, représentant de la Fondation Burnett-Weston, remet
le prix d'excellence Burnett-Weston (art héraldique) à M. Baz Manning.

***Closing ceremony*** Mr. Roger Lindsay presents the Burnett-Weston Prize for Excellence (Heraldic Art)
to Mrs. Cathy Bursey-Sabourin, Fraser Herald.
***Cérémonie de clôture*** M. Roger Lindsay remet le prix d'excellence Burnett-Weston (art héraldique)
à M^me Cathy Bursey-Sabourin, héraut Fraser.

**Closing ceremony** Mrs. Mary de Belle-feuille-Percy, master of ceremonies, and member of the Vice-Regal Household, introduces the closing events.

**Cérémonie de clôture** M^me Mary de Bellefeuille-Percy, maître de cérémonies et membre de la maison vice-royale, annonce les événements de clôture.

**Closing ceremony** Dr. Helen Mussallem presents the Mussallem Prize for Exellence (Heraldic Art) to Ms. Debra Mac-Garvie.

**Cérémonie de clôture** M^me Helen Mussallem, Ph.D., remet le prix d'excellence Mussallem (art héraldique) à M^me Debra MacGarvie.

*Closing ceremony* Mr. Patrick Reid, representative of the Corel Corporation, presents the Corel Prize for Excellence (Heraldic Art) to Mr. Romilly Squire.

*Cérémonie de clôture* M. Patrick Reid, représentant de la société Corel, remet le prix d'excellence Corel (art héraldique) à M. Romilly Squire.

*Closing ceremony* Final words by Mr. Roger Harmignies, President of the Bureau permanent des congrès.

*Cérémonie de clôture* Allocution de clôture de M. Roger Harmignies, président du Bureau permanent des congrès.

***Closing ceremony*** Mr. René Bouchard, Vice-President of Bell Canada, presents the Bell Prize for Excellence (Heraldic Art) to Mr. Christopher Wallis.

***Cérémonie de clôture*** M. René Bouchard, vice-président de Bell Canada, remet le prix d'excellence Bell (art héraldique) à M. Christopher Wallis.

***Closing ceremony*** Final words by Dr. Jean-Claude Loutsch, President of the Académie internationale d'héraldique.

***Cérémonie de clôture*** Le Dʳ Jean-Claude Loutsch, président de l'Académie internationale d'héraldique, prononce l'allocution de clôture.

*Closing banquet, National Gallery of Canada, Ottawa* Mr. Henrik Degerman presents the Gustaf von Numers Prize to the Canadian Heraldic Authority recognizing its contribution to a renewed and lively heraldic art within the parameters of traditional heraldry. (l. to r.) Mr. Henrik Degerman; Mr. Robert Watt, Chief Herald of Canada; Mr. Charles Maier, Athabaska Herald; Mr. F. Harmo, member of the Board of Directors of the Foundation Gustaf von Numers; Mrs. Cathy Bursey-Sabourin, Fraser Herald; Mr. Auguste Vachon, Saint-Laurent Herald; Mr. Robert Pichette, Dauphin Herald Extraordinary.
*Banquet de clôture, Musée des beaux-arts du Canada, Ottawa* Remise du prix Gustaf von Numers par M. Henrik Degerman à l'Autorité héraldique du Canada en reconnaissance de sa création d'un art héraldique nouveau et vivant fidèle aux principes traditionnels de l'héraldique. (de g. à dr.) M. Henrik Degerman ; M. Robert Watt, héraut d'armes du Canada ; M. Charles Maier, héraut Athabaska ; M. F. Harmo, membre du conseil d'administration de la Fondation Gustaf von Numers ; M^me Cathy Bursey-Sabourin, héraut Fraser ; M. Auguste Vachon, héraut Saint-Laurent ; M. Robert Pichette, héraut Dauphin extraordinaire.

*Closing banquet* (l. to r.) Mmes Linda Lauzon, Francine Mellor and Lara M^cPherson, staff of the Canadian Heraldic Authority.
*Banquet de clôture* (de g. à dr.) M^mes Linda Lauzon, Francine Mellor et Lara M^cPherson, du personnel de l'Autorité héraldique du Canada.

43

*Closing banquet*  Mr. Robert Watt, his wife, Alison, and their children Michael and Catherine.
*Banquet de clôture*  M. Robert Watt, son épouse, Alison, et leurs enfants Michael et Catherine.

# Special Events / Événements spéciaux

*Civic Reception in the presence of Deputy Mayor Mrs. Joan Wong representing*
*Her Worship the Mayor of Ottawa Mrs. Jacquelin Holzman /*
*Réception municipale en présence du maire adjoint M$^{me}$ Joan Wong représentant*
*Son Honneur le maire d'Ottawa M$^{me}$ Jacquelin Holzman*
City Hall of Ottawa, August 18, 1996, 5:30 p.m. / Hôtel de ville d'Ottawa, 18 août 1996, 17 h 30

*Opening Ceremonies of the 22nd International Congress of Genealogical and Heraldic Sciences in*
*the presence of Her Excellency Mrs. Diana Fowler LeBlanc /*
*Cérémonies d'ouverture du 22$^e$ congrès international des sciences généalogique et héraldique en*
*présence de Son Excellence M$^{me}$ Diana Fowler LeBlanc*
Tabaret Hall, the University of Ottawa, August 19, 1996, 9:30 am /
Pavillon Tabaret de l'Université d'Ottawa, 19 août 1996, 9 h 30

*Canadian Evening Barbecue and Rideau Canal Cruise /*
*Soirée canadienne barbecue et croisière sur le canal Rideau*
The Saunders Building, the Central Experimental Farm, Ottawa /
L'édifice Saunders, ferme expérimentale centrale, Ottawa
August 20, 1996, 6:30 p.m. / 20 août 1996, 18 h 30

*Heraldic and Genealogical Tour*
*The Canadian Museum of Civilization, the Parliament of Canada, the National Archives of Canada*
*Visite à caractère généalogique et héraldique*
*Le Musée canadien des civilisations, le Parlement du Canada, les Archives nationales du Canada*
August 21, 1996, 9:15 am to 4:30 pm / 21 août 1996, 9 h 15 à 16 h 30

*Closing Gala Dinner / Gala de clôture*
The National Gallery of Canada / La Galerie nationale du Canada
August 23, 1996, 6:30 pm / 23 août 1996, 18 h 30

# Exhibitions / Expositions

**A Capital Display of Heraldry / Une célébration capitale de l'héraldique internationale**
City Hall of Ottawa / Hôtel de ville d'Ottawa
August 18, 1996 / 18 août 1996

**Lasting Symbols of a Nation / Symboles durables d'une nation**
National Archives of Canada / Archives nationales du Canada
August 18-23, 1996 / 18 - 23 août 1996

**Eleven Masters of Heraldic Art / Onze maîtres de l'art héraldique**
The Canadian Museum of Civilization / Le Musée canadien des civilisations
August 21- September 2, 1996 / 21 août - 2 septembre 1996

**Letters Patents of the Canadian Heraldic Authority /**
**Lettres d'armoiries de l'Autorité héraldique du Canada**
University of Ottawa / Université d'Ottawa
August 18-23, 1996 / 18 - 23 août 1996

# LASTING SYMBOLS OF A NATION / SYMBOLES DURABLES D'UNE NATION
Exhibition / Exposition
By / par Auguste Vachon

## Foreword

Symbols are the pillars of tradition. The origins of the documents in this display go back to the Middle Ages and beyond, long before the discovery of the New World. Yet it is the same European heraldic, sigilistic and medallic heritage that flourishes here and is preserved in archival collections.

Even when nations disappear, their symbols often live on. Hercules, a hero of ancient Greece, has survived in films, cartoons and people's names. Known as the shorthand of history, heraldic symbols express in concise form the achievements, values and identity of nations. Their representation in stone and durable metals, often precious stones and metals, increase their chance of survival as valuable objects or archeological remains. Their colours are often preserved as baked enamel or registered in the lines and dots (hatchings) that mark a number of coats of arms in this display. Because of their permanence, these objects become in some cases unique witnesses of the past.

Except for a few items identified as "loaned by Government House," the items in this display are from the collections of the National Archives of Canada.

## Avant-propos

Les symboles sont les piliers de la tradition. L'origine des documents figurant dans cette exposition remonte au Moyen Âge et même avant. Pourtant les mêmes traditions héraldiques, sigillographiques et numismatiques de l'Europe, qui précèdent de loin la découverte de l'Amérique, sont demeurées bien vivantes ici et font partie de notre patrimoine archivistique.

Les symboles survivent souvent aux nations qui les ont créés. Hercule, héros de la Grèce antique, est toujours vivant dans des films, des bandes dessinées, des prénoms et surnoms. Les symboles héraldiques expriment, en condensé, l'histoire, les réalisations, les valeurs et l'identité des nations. Souvent représentés en pierre ou en métaux durables, voire en pierres précieuses et métaux précieux, leurs chances de survie comme joyaux ou vestiges sont bonnes. On retrouve leurs couleurs sauvegardées par émaillage au feu ou consignées par des points et lignes (hachures) que l'on peut apercevoir sur bon nombre d'armoiries figurant dans cette exposition. Grâce à leur permanence, ces pièces deviennent parfois des témoins uniques du passé.

Les pièces exposées proviennent de la collection des Archives nationales du Canada sauf celles portant la mention « prêt de la Résidence du gouverneur général ».

5

## The Great Seals of Canada

The Great Seal of Canada was created following Confederation, when a new political entity came into being. Since 1867, there have been seven great seals. One was issued at the time of Confederation as a temporary seal; the others came into being with each successive monarch, except Edward VIII who abdicated before his seal could be completed. Queen Victoria and King George VI are the only monarchs to date for whom two great seals were engraved. Victoria's first seal was a temporary great seal while the second seal of George VI, which came into use in 1949, was a precise copy of the first except that the abbreviation IND. IMP. ("Emperor of India") was deleted from the royal titles in recognition of the Indian Independence Bill. Also, the abbreviation F.D. was expanded to FIDEI DEF. ("Defender of the Faith") to fill the extra space.

The Great Seal of Canada displays the sovereign in majesty with marks of dignity and authority signifying that the executive power of our government flows from the Crown. At a special ceremony with each new ministry, the great seal is entrusted to the registrar general by the governor general of Canada. The great seal is affixed to formal documents of the Government of Canada issued in the name of the reigning sovereign such as the appointments of the governor general, federal cabinet ministers, lieutenant governors, provincial administrators, ambassadors, federal judges, senators, deputy ministers, the commissioner and officers of the Royal Canadian Mounted Police and a variety of other appointments. It is also affixed to other types of documents such as proclamations, Crown land grants, ferry licences

## Les grands sceaux du canada

Ce n'est qu'après la Confédération, alors que le Canada devenait une nouvelle entité politique, que fut créé le grand sceau du Canada. Depuis, sept grands sceaux ont représenté le pays, dont un sceau temporaire gravé au moment de la Confédération. Les autres ont été créés au nom de chaque monarque, à l'exception d'Édouard VIII, qui a abdiqué avant la fabrication de son sceau. La reine Victoria et le roi George VI sont les seuls monarques pour lesquels on a dû fabriquer un second sceau. Le premier sceau de la reine Victoria était le sceau temporaire, tandis que sur le second sceau de George VI, en usage à partir de 1949, l'abréviation IND. IMP. (« Empereur de l'Inde ») a disparu en reconnaissance de l'Indépendance de l'Inde et l'abréviation F.D. (« Défenseur de la Foi ») est devenue FIDEI DEF. pour remplir l'espace libéré.

Le souverain en majesté, avec des insignes de dignité et d'autorité, figure sur le grand sceau du Canada pour signifier que le pouvoir exécutif de notre gouvernement découle de la Couronne. Lors d'une cérémonie spéciale à chaque changement de ministère, le gouverneur général confie le grand sceau au registraire général. Le grand sceau du Canada est apposé sur tous les documents officiels émanant du gouvernement canadien, au nom du souverain régnant, telles les nominations du gouverneur général, des membres du Conseil des ministres fédéral, des lieutenants-gouverneurs, des administrateurs provinciaux, des ambassadeurs, des juges fédéraux, des sénateurs, des sous-ministres, du commissaire et des agents de la Gendarmerie royale du Canada, et sur divers autres types de nominations. On le retrouve aussi sur plusieurs

47

and election writs. Well-known examples of documents bearing the great seal are Canada's flag proclamation of 1965 and the proclamation "repatriating" Canada's Constitution in 1982.

catégories de documents comme les proclamations, les dons des terres de la Couronne, les permis de transbordeurs et les brefs d'élection. Deux proclamations bien connues sont celles du drapeau canadien de 1965 et du rapatriement de la Constitution de 1982.

1. **Temporary Great Seal of Canada, in use 1867-1869.**
Maker unknown.

1. **Grand sceau temporaire du Canada, utilisé de 1867 à 1869.**
Fabricant inconnu.

2. **Queen Victoria's Great Seal, in use 1869-1904.**
Makers: Joseph Shepard Wyon and Alfred Benjamin Wyon, engravers, and Robert Garrard, silversmith.

2. **Grand sceau de la reine Victoria, utilisé de 1869 à 1904.**
Fabricants : Joseph Shepard Wyon et Alfred Benjamin Wyon, graveurs, et Robert Garrard, orfèvre.

3. **King Edward VII's Great Seal, in use 1904-1912.**
Makers: engraver George William De Saulles and the Royal Mint.

3. **Grand sceau du roi Édouard VII, utilisé de 1904 à 1912.**
Fabricants : le graveur George William De Saulles et la *Royal Mint.*

4. **King George V's Great Seal, in use 1912-1940.**
Makers: a Mr. Metcalfe and the Royal Mint.

4. **Grand sceau du roi George V, utilisé de 1912 à 1940.**
Fabricants : un certain M. Metcalfe et la *Royal Mint.*

5. **King George VI's first Great Seal, in use 1940-1950.**
Makers: the artist George Edward Kruger-Gray and the Royal Mint.

5. **Premier grand sceau du roi George VI, utilisé de 1940 à 1950.**
Fabricants : l'artiste George Edward Kruger-Gray et la *Royal Mint.*

6. **King George VI's second Great Seal, in use 1950-1955.**
Maker: the Royal Canadian Mint.

6. **Deuxième grand sceau du roi George VI, utilisé de 1950 à 1955.**
Fabricant : la Monnaie royale canadienne.

7. **Queen Elizabeth II's Great Seal, in use since 1955.**
Makers: the artist Eric Aldwinckle, the engraver Thomas Shingles and the Royal Canadian Mint.

7. **Grand sceau de la reine Élisabeth II, utilisé depuis 1955.**
Fabricants : l'artiste Eric Aldwinckle, le graveur Thomas Shingles et la Monnaie royale canadienne.

13

## The Coat of Arms of Canada

After Confederation, Canada used as its distinctive mark the arms of the provinces and territories united on one shield. This conglomerate of colours was criticized as becoming fuzzy at a distance. In February 1919, a committee was appointed by order-in-council to provide Canada with a suitable coat of arms. The world having known many upheavals during and following the First World War, the members of the committee were especially concerned that the new arms should convey the notion of continuity of which they saw the British Empire as the model. In this vein, they opted for a version of royal arms for Canada in the same fashion that royal arms exist for Scotland. Another strong current within the committee wanted the new arms to express Canada's equal status with other members of the Empire, including England. This approach foreshadowed future developments when members of the Commonwealth would become equal partners and the Crown would be viewed as a shared tradition among sovereign nations, the present sovereign becoming "Queen of Canada."

While creating a version of the royal arms, the committee wanted as well to represent the founding nations by including the individual arms of England, France, Scotland and Ireland. The committee had hoped to convey a stronger Canadian message by placing the sprig of maple leaves at the top of the shield, but when King George V saw the design, he suggested that it was more appropriate for the maple leaves to go below the arms of the older democracies. The red maple leaf that the lion holds above the helmet expresses Canada's

## Les armoiries du Canada

Après la Confédération, le Canada arborait comme marque distinctive les armoiries des provinces et des territoires réunies sur un seul écu. Cet amalgame de couleurs fut l'objet de nombreuses critiques selon lesquelles il devenait flou avec la distance. En février 1919, un ordre en conseil établissait un comité chargé de doter le Canada d'armoiries appropriées. Pendant la Première Guerre mondiale et après, le monde avait connu de nombreuses tribulations. Dans ce contexte inquiétant, le premier souci du comité était de créer un emblème reflétant la continuité que représentait l'Empire britannique. C'est pourquoi il s'efforça de créer une version des armoiries royales pour le Canada, dans le même sens qu'il en existe une pour l'Écosse. Cependant, un autre courant d'opinion au sein du comité voulait que les armoiries expriment le statut égal du Canada vis-à-vis des autres membres du Commonwealth, y inclus l'Angleterre. Dans ce sens, les nouvelles armoiries présageaient les temps à venir où tous les membres du Commonwealth seraient égaux et, la Couronne étant considérée comme une tradition commune à plusieurs nations autonomes, la souveraine actuelle porterait le titre de « reine du Canada ».

Tout en créant une version des armoiries royales pour le Canada, le comité se souciait de représenter les pays fondateurs en incluant les armes de l'Angleterre, la France, l'Écosse et l'Irlande. Il avait espéré mettre le Canada davantage en relief en plaçant la branchette d'érable dans le haut de l'écu. Toutefois, en voyant le dessin proposé, le roi George V avait exprimé le souhait que les feuilles d'érable figurent plutôt sous les armes des plus anciennes démocraties. La feuille d'érable rouge que tient le lion au-dessus du casque symbolise le courage et les sacrifices des

courage and sacrifice during the First World War. The motto is derived from Psalm 72: 8 "*Et dominatur a mari usque ad mare* . . . ", "He shall have dominion also from sea to sea . . . " which is a reflection of Canada's geography and sovereign status.

8. **The conglomerate of provincial and territorial arms used as the emblem of Canada prior to 1921.**
Postcard published by Nerlich & Co., Toronto, ca. 1907.
Loaned by Government House.

9. **Coat of arms proposed for Canada to King George V in the fall of 1920.**
Printed in June 1920 from a drawing by a Mr. Champagne.

10. **Arms granted to Canada by royal proclamation of King George V, dated November 21, 1921.**
Drawing prepared by Alexander Scott Carter and signed by members of the arms committee, April 1921.

11. **1923 version of Canada's coat of arms prepared under the supervision of Ambrose Lee, Norroy King of Arms.**

12. **1957 version of Canada's coat of arms drawn by Alan B. Beddoe. The St. Edward's Crown has replaced the Tudor Crown as requested by Queen Elizabeth II.**

13. **1994 version of Canada's coat of arms drawn by Cathy Bursey-Sabourin, Fraser Herald at the Canadian Heraldic Authority. An annulus added around the shield bears the motto of the Order of Canada.**
Loaned by Government House.

Canadiens pendant la Première Guerre mondiale. La devise provient du psaume 72 : 28 « *Et dominatur a mari usque ad mare...* », « Il régnera depuis une mer jusqu'à l'autre... », sentence qui reflète la situation géographique du Canada et son statut souverain.

8. **L'amalgame des armes des provinces et des territoires utilisé comme emblème du Canada avant 1921.**
Carte postale publiée par Nerlich & Co., Toronto, v. 1907.
Prêt de la Résidence du gouverneur général.

9. **Armoiries du Canada proposées au roi George V à l'automne de 1920.**
Imprimé en juin 1920 d'après le dessin d'un certain M. Champagne.

10. **Armoiries concédées au Canada par proclamation royale du roi George V datée du 21 novembre 1921.**
Dessin réalisé par Alexander Scott Carter et signé par les membres du comité des armoiries, avril 1921.

11. **Version de 1923 des armoiries du Canada, préparée selon les directives d'Ambrose Lee, roi d'armes Norroy.**

12. **Version de 1957 des armoiries du Canada, dessinée par Alan B. Beddoe. Selon le désir de la reine Élisabeth II, la couronne d'Édouard le Confesseur a remplacé la couronne des Tudor.**

13. **Version de 1994 des armoiries du Canada dessinée par Cathy Bursey-Sabourin, héraut Fraser. Un anneau ajouté autour de l'écu porte la devise de l'Ordre du Canada.**
Prêt de la Résidence du gouverneur général.

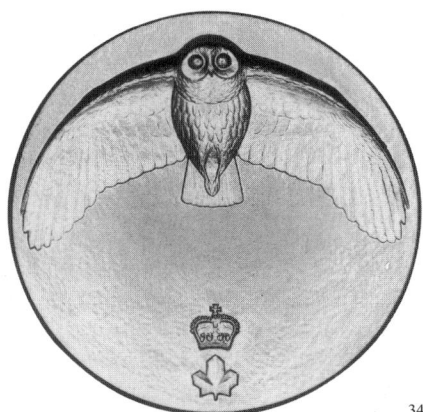

34

## Seals of the Governors General of Canada, 1867-1995

Upon assuming office, governors general of Canada who do not possess a hereditary coat of arms petition for lawfully granted arms to use as a distinctive personal mark on their privy seal. The only exception to this rule has been the Right Honourable Jules Léger, who called upon Alexander Colville, his friend and a well-known Canadian artist, to design his emblem. With minor modifications, the Colville design was granted by the Canadian Heraldic Authority to Léger's descendants in 1990. The governor general's privy seal is affixed to documents that do not require sealing with the Great Seal of Canada such as proclamations concerning the appointment of a governor general, and the death of the sovereign, commissions to the deputy governor general and to officers of the Canadian Forces, pardons and certificates of authentication.

## Sceaux des gouverneurs généraux du Canada, 1867-1995

Après leur nomination, les gouverneurs généraux du Canada qui ne possèdent pas d'armoiries ancestrales demandent à s'en faire concéder officiellement pour meubler leur sceau privé d'une marque personnelle et distinctive. Le très honorable Jules Léger a été le seul à déroger à cet usage, ayant eu recours à son ami Alexander Colville, artiste canadien de renommée, pour lui concevoir un emblème. En 1990, l'Autorité héraldique du Canada a concédé, avec quelques retouches, l'emblème de Colville aux descendants de Jules Léger. Le sceau privé du gouverneur général est apposé sur des documents ne requérant pas l'apposition du grand sceau tels que la proclamation de la nomination d'un gouverneur général, la proclamation de la mort du souverain, la commission du gouverneur général suppléant et celles des officiers des Forces canadiennes, les pardons et les certificats d'homologation.

14. **The Viscount Monck (1867-1868).**

15. **Lord Lisgar (1868-1872).**

16. **The Earl of Dufferin (1872-1878).**

17. **The Marquess of Lorne (1878-1883).**

18. **The Marquess of Lansdowne (1883-1888).**

19. **Lord Stanley of Preston (1888-1893).**

20. **The Earl of Aberdeen (1893-1898).**

14. **Le vicomte Monck (1867-1868).**

15. **Lord Lisgar (1868-1872).**

16. **Le comte de Dufferin (1872-1878).**

17. **Le marquis de Lorne (1878-1883).**

18. **Le marquis de Lansdowne (1883-1888).**

19. **Lord Stanley de Preston (1888-1893).**

20. **Le comte d'Aberdeen (1893-1898).**

| | |
|---|---|
| 21. The Earl of Minto (1898-1904). | 21. Le comte de Minto (1898-1904). |
| 22. Earl Grey (1904-1911). | 22. Le comte Grey (1904-1911). |
| 23. H.R.H. The Duke of Connaught (1911-1916). | 23. S.A.R. le duc de Connaught (1911-1916). |
| 24. The Duke of Devonshire (1916-1921). | 24. Le duc de Devonshire (1916-1921). |
| 25. General Lord Byng of Vimy (1921-1926). | 25. Le général Lord Byng de Vimy (1921-1926). |
| 26. The Viscount Willingdon of Ratton (1926-1931). | 26. Le vicomte Willingdon de Ratton (1926-1931). |
| 27. The Earl of Bessborough (1931-1935). | 27. Le comte de Bessborough (1931-1935). |
| 28. Lord Tweedsmuir of Elsfield (1935-1940). | 28. Lord Tweedsmuir d'Elsfield (1935-1940). |
| 29. Major General The Earl of Athlone (1940-1946). | 29. Le major-général comte d'Athlone (1940-1946). |
| 30. Field-Marshal The Viscount Alexander of Tunis (1946-1952). | 30. Le feld-maréchal vicomte Alexander de Tunis (1946-1952). |
| 31. The Right Honourable Vincent Massey (1952-1959). | 31. Le très honorable Vincent Massey (1952-1959). |
| 32. The Right Honorable General Georges-Philias Vanier (1959-1967). | 32. Le très honorable général Georges-Philias Vanier (1959-1967). |
| 33. The Right Honourable Roland Michener (1967-1974). | 33. Le très honorable Roland Michener (1967-1974). |
| 34. The Right Honourable Jules Léger (1974-1979). | 34. Le très honorable Jules Léger (1974-1979). |
| 35. The Right Honourable Edward Richard Schreyer (1979-1984). | 35. Le très honorable Edward Richard Schreyer (1979-1984). |
| 36. The Right Honourable Jeanne Sauvé (1984-1990). | 36. La très honorable Jeanne Sauvé (1984-1990). |
| 37. The Right Honourable Ramon John Hnatyshyn (1990-1995). | 37. Le très honorable Ramon John Hnatyshyn (1990-1995). |
| 38. Governor General's Academic Medal, the Right Honourable Roméo Adrien LeBlanc (1995- ). Loaned by Government House. Seal is in use. | 38. Médaille académique du gouverneur général, le très honorable Roméo Adrien LeBlanc (1995- ). Prêt de la Résidence du gouverneur général. Le sceau est utilisé. |

45

## Armorial medals

Medals reflect in concise form the achievements and diversity of a country. Not only do they record historical events, institutions and prominent figures, but regional events, institutions and individuals also find their place within the medallic memorial. Medals are an important source of information regarding heraldry as they include both official coats of arms and the more popular types of heraldic devices adopted freely by individuals and corporate bodies. Like ancient coins, medals will survive in the earth if ever our civilization ceases to exist.

## Médailles armoriées

Les médailles reflètent de façon concise les réalisations et la diversité d'un pays. Si elles consignent les événements historiques et rendent hommage aux grandes institutions et personnages, elles commémorent aussi des événements, des organismes et des particuliers à l'échelle locale. Les médailles sont des documents héraldiques importants pour l'étude, non seulement des armoiries officielles, mais aussi des emblèmes de type populaire adoptés librement par des particuliers et des organismes. Comme les anciennes monnaies, elles pourront se conserver dans la terre si jamais notre civilisation cesse d'exister.

39. **Canadian Prize: Great Exhibition, 1851, London, England.**
Arms of Earl of Elgin and Kincardine, governor general of Canada, 1847-1854.
Maker: B. Wyon, engraver, England.

39. **Prix canadien : Grande Exposition, 1851, Londres (Angleterre).**
Armoiries du comte d'Elgin et de Kincardine, gouverneur général du Canada, 1847-1854.
Fabricant : B. Wyon, graveur, Angleterre.

40. **Dominion of Canada medal awarded to Dr. William Saunders for his collection of stuffed birds.**
Dominion of Canada emblem, 1876-1902.
Maker: B. Tasset, sculptor, France.

40. **Médaille du Dominion du Canada décernée à William Saunders pour sa collection d'oiseaux empaillés.**
Emblème du Dominion du Canada, 1876-1902. Fabricant : B. Tasset, sculpteur, France.

41. **Medal of the Army & Navy Veterans in Canada, 1917.**
Particular device of the Army & Navy Veterans.
Maker: Dingwall, Winnipeg.

41. **Médaille des anciens combattants de l'armée et de la marine au Canada, 1917.**
Emblème adopté par les anciens combattants de l'armée et de la marine.
Fabricant : Dingwall, Winnipeg.

42. **Medal of the National War Finance Committee of Canada presented to members of the committee, ca. 1945.**
Arms of Canada, symbols of the nine Victory Loan campaigns on border.
Makers: Thomas Shingles, engraver, and the Royal Canadian Mint.

42. **Médaille du Comité national des finances de guerre du Canada remise aux membres du comité, v. 1945.**
Armoiries du Canada entourées des symboles des neuf campagnes de souscription aux emprunts de la victoire.
Fabricants : Thomas Shingles, graveur, et la Monnaie royale canadienne.

43. **Medal commemorating the 23rd Conference of the Interparliamentary Union held in Ottawa, 1925.**
Arms of Canada in centre, devices on either side appear to be fanciful.
Maker: Birks, Canada.

43 **Médaille commémorant la 23$^e$ conférence de l'Union interparlementaire tenue à Ottawa, 1925.**
Armoiries du Canada entre deux emblèmes apparemment fantaisistes.
Fabricant : Birks, Canada.

44. **Medal commemorating the first visit of a Canadian governor general to Brazil, Viscount Alexander of Tunis, in 1951.**
Arms of Canada, on either side on border, the emblem of Brazil and maple leaves.

44. **Médaille commémorant la première visite d'un gouverneur général canadien au Brésil, le vicomte Alexander de Tunis, en 1951.**
Les armoiries du Canada, de chaque côté sur la bordure, l'emblème du Brésil et des feuilles d'érable.

45. **Medal commemorating the 100th anniversary of Sir George-Étienne Cartier's birth, 1914.**
Cartier's arms as granted by the Heralds of England in 1868.
Maker: Caron Frères, Montreal.

45. **Médaille commémorant le 100$^e$ anniversaire de la naissance de sir George-Étienne Cartier, 1914.**
Les armoiries de Cartier concédées par les hérauts d'Angleterre en 1868.
Fabricant : Caron Frères, Montréal.

46. **Medal presented to His Excellency Jules Léger, Canadian ambassador to France, by the City of Calais, September 27, 1964.**
Arms of the City of Calais.

46. **Médaille offerte à Son Excellence Jules Léger, ambassadeur du Canada en France, par la ville de Calais, 27 septembre 1964.**
Armoiries de la ville de Calais.

47. **Medal commemorating the centennial of George Simpson's arrival at Fort St. James, British Columbia, in 1828.**
Arms of the Hudson's Bay Company assumed in 1680 and granted by the Heralds of England in 1921.
Maker: Elkington & Co., England.

47 **Médaille commémorant le centenaire de l'arrivée de George Simpson au fort St. James (Colombie-Britannique), en 1828.**
Armoiries de la Compagnie de la baie d'Hudson adoptées en 1680 et concédées par les hérauts d'Angleterre en 1921.
Fabricant : Elkington & Co., Angleterre.

48. **Medal struck in 1974 for the 25th anniversary of Newfoundland's entry into Confederation.**
Arms of Newfoundland, granted by King Charles I in 1637.

49. **Medal of the Honourable Onésime Gagnon, lieutenant governor of the Province of Quebec (1958-1961).**
Arms granted by the Heralds of England.
Makers: Marius Plamondon, sculptor, and C. Lamond & Fils, Montreal.

50. **Jewel of Beaver Club instituted in Montreal 1785, awarded 1802.**
The beaver gnawing at a tree is a recurrent symbol in Canadian heraldry.

51. **Medal of the Industrial Exhibition Association of Toronto, ca. 1887.**
Arms assumed by the City of Toronto ca. 1834, granted with modifications by the Kings of Arms of England in 1961.

52. **Medal of the University of Windsor, Ontario.**
Arms of the university granted by the Heralds of England in 1964.

53. **Medal commemorating the Canadian Numismatic Association's Annual Convention held in Ottawa, Ontario, September 1958.**
Arms granted to the City of Ottawa by the Heralds of England in 1954.

54. **Medal of the Manitoba Provincial Rifle Association, instituted in 1871.**
Arms assumed by the Province of Manitoba, ca. 1872; official arms were granted to the province by King Edward VII in 1905.

48. **Médaille frappée en 1974 pour marquer le 25ᵉ anniversaire de l'adhésion de Terre-Neuve à la Confédération.**
Armoiries de Terre-Neuve, concédées par le roi Charles I en 1637.

49. **Médaille de l'honorable Onésime Gagnon, lieutenant-gouverneur de la province de Québec (1958-1961).**
Armoiries concédées par les hérauts d'Angleterre.
Fabricants : Marius Plamondon, sculpteur, et C. Lamond & Fils, Montréal.

50. **Pendentif de la Coterie du castor, instituée à Montréal en 1785, décerné en 1802.**
Le castor rongeant un arbre est un symbole fréquent dans l'héraldique canadienne.

51. **Médaille de l'Association des expositions industrielles de Toronto, v. 1887.**
Armoiries adoptées librement par la ville de Toronto v. 1834, concédées avec modifications par les hérauts d'Angleterre en 1961.

52. **Médaille de l'Université de Windsor (Ontario).**
Les armoiries concédées à l'université par les hérauts d'Angleterre en 1964.

53. **Médaille commémorant le congrès annuel de l'Association canadienne de numismatique tenu à Ottawa (Ontario) en septembre 1958.**
Armoiries concédées à la ville d'Ottawa par les hérauts d'Angleterre en 1954.

54. **Médaille de l'Association provinciale de tir du Manitoba, fondée en 1871.**
Armoiries adoptées librement par la province v. 1872 ; en 1905, le roi Édouard VII lui concédait des armoiries officielles.

55. **Medal commemorating Saskatchewan's creation and entry into Confederation in 1905.**
Arms granted to the province by King Edward VII in 1906.

55. **Médaille commémorant la création de la Saskatchewan en 1905 et son adhésion à la Confédération la même année.**
Armoiries concédées à la province par le roi Édouard VII en 1906.

56. **Academic medal presented by the Anglican bishop of Rupert's Land.**
Arms of Robert Machray, bishop of Rupert's Land, 1865-1893.
Maker: A. Wyon, engraver, England.

56. **Médaille du mérite scolaire décernée par l'évêque anglican de la Terre de Rupert.**
Armoiries de Robert Machray, évêque de la Terre de Rupert, de 1865 à 1893.
Fabricant : A. Wyon, graveur, Angleterre.

### Acknowledgements of the curator

I am indebted to Françoise Houle, Director General of the Client Services and Communications Branch of the National Archives of Canada, for authorizing this display. Thanks are also due to members of the National Archives staff for their unfailing support. Terresa McIntosh of the Art Acquisition and Research Section, Elizabeth Krug of the Custody of Holdings Division, Robert Lamoureux and Brian Schorlemer of the Public Programs Section have all provided assistance in their particular capacity. Their cooperation has facilitated my task and I am grateful.

I would also like to acknowledge the cooperation of Françoise Bouvier, Director of the Communication and Public Programs Division, and of André Martineau, Chief of the Public Programs Section, for organizing the visit at the National Archives of Canada.

Special thanks are also due to Paula, my wife, for her assistance with this display and other aspects of the Congress.

### Remerciements de l'auteur

Mes premiers remerciements s'adressent à Françoise Houle, directrice générale, direction des services aux clients et des communications des Archives nationales du Canada pour avoir autorisé cette exposition. Par la suite, plusieurs autres membres du personnel des Archives nationales me sont venus en aide : Terresa McIntosh de la section d'acquisition et de la recherche en art, Elizabeth Krug de la division de la garde des fonds, Robert Lamoureux et Brian Schorlemer de la section des programmes publics. Leur collaboration dans la préparation de cette exposition me fut précieuse et je leur en suis reconnaissant.

Je désire aussi exprimer ma gratitude envers les organisateurs de la visite aux Archives nationales, plus particulièrement Françoise Bouvier, directrice des communications et des programmes publics et André Martineau, chef de la section des programmes publics.

Paula, mon épouse, m'a secondé dans la préparation de cette exposition et dans les préparatifs du congrès. Je lui en suis particulièrement reconnaissant.

# HERALDRY / HÉRALDIQUE
## ARTIST WORKSHOP / ATELIER DES ARTISTES

A unique feature of the 22nd Congress was the Artists' workshop, the first meeting of its type held anywhere. It was held in Room 215C of the Jock Turcot University Centre at the University of Ottawa from August 12 to 23.

Eleven artists from seven countries, whose brief biographies are given below, worked on one of two themes during the period: symbols for the new millennium and symbols for the new Canadian territory in the high Arctic, Nunavut. Concepts for these themes plus finished work were shown at a special exhibition at the Museum of Civilization, opening August 21, during the delegate's mid-week tour.

These artists explored the nature of heraldic art and its possible evolution and shared their work and ideas with other delegates at set times during the Congress week. We sometimes forget that for many members of the wider public, interest in heraldry is generated especially through the interpretations of master artists. The workshop represented an excellent opportunity to recognise this reality and to meet some of the best heraldic artists currently at work.

## ELEVEN MASTERS OF HERALDIC ART

Symbols have been an important part of human activity for thousands of years. They have served to identify and distinguish one person from another, to celebrate the history and character of human institutions, to tell an important story in a highly memorable way. Of the many symbol systems people have created in different times and places, heraldry has proved one of the most beautiful and enduring.

First appearing in western Europe over 800 years ago, coats of arms and the flags often associated with them have since spread around the world to places far away in every sense from the castles and battlefields with armoured knights where they first appeared. A splendid expression

Une nouveauté dans l'histoire du congrès et l'un des événements saillants du 22ᵉ Congrès a été l'atelier des artistes héraldiques. Il s'est déroulé du 12 au 23 août dans la salle 215C du Centre universitaire Jock-Turcot de l'Université d'Ottawa.

Onze artistes venus de sept pays (voir les notices biographiques ci-dessous) ont réalisé des symboles appropriés pour : (1) le nouveau millénaire, (2) le nouveau territoire du Grand Nord canadien, Nunavut. Les études et les œuvres finies des artistes ont été en montre au Musée canadien des civilisations à partir du 21 août, jour de la visite au Musée.

Les artistes ont exploré la nature de l'art héraldique et ses possibilités pour l'avenir. Ils ont été heureux de discuter de ces questions avec les autres participants à des moments désignés à cette fin lors du congrès. Il est vrai que l'intérêt du grand public pour l'héraldique se développe souvent au contact des grandes œuvres. L'atelier aura permis dans ce but de faire la connaissance d'artistes contemporains de talent et de les observer au travail.

## ONZE MAÎTRES DE L'ART HÉRALDIQUE

Les symboles représentent un élément important de l'activité humaine depuis des milliers d'années. Ils servent à identifier les personnes et à les distinguer entre elles, à célébrer l'histoire et le caractère des institutions humaines et à raconter des faits importants d'une manière mémorable. Parmi les nombreux langages symboliques que les peuples ont créés à diverses époques et en différents lieux, l'héraldique s'est révélée l'un des plus esthétiques et des plus durables.

Les armoiries et les drapeaux qui leur sont souvent associés sont apparus dans l'ouest de l'Europe il y a plus de 800 ans. Depuis, ils se sont répandus dans le monde entier, et on les retrouve dans des endroits bien éloignés – à tous les points de vue – des châteaux et des champs de bataille

of medieval art and ideas, heraldry proved a versatile and adaptable art form, favoured for a wide variety of architectural settings, types of decoration and media. It has continued to evolve to the present day, especially in countries like our own, where new heraldry continues to be created and fresh challenges appear for artists.

Those whose work was in the exhibition are 11 masters of the form and include some of the best heraldic artists in the world today. They worked in a range of different materials, each with his or her own style. The exhibition celebrated their aesthetic achievements.

The Planning Committee of the 22nd Congress acknowledged the following sponsors of the world's first heraldic artists workshop and contributors to the project and the Canadian Museum of Civilization for having hosted this collection.

**Leading Sponsor**
*The Corel Corporation*

**Major Donors**
*The Burnett-Weston Award*
*Dr. Joseph Segal, C.M., O.B.C.*
  *and Mrs. Rosalie Segal*
*The David and Dorothy Lam Foundation*
*Dr. Helen K. Mussallem, C.C.*

**Contributors and Partners**
*The Heraldry Society of Canada*
*The Ontario Genealogical Society*
*La Société de généalogie de l'Outaouais*
*The Canadian Heraldic Authority, Office of the*
  *Secretary of the Governor General of Canada*

de l'époque des chevaliers en armure. Expression splendide de l'art et des idées du Moyen Âge, l'art héraldique a été adapté à une grande variété de cadres architecturaux, de types de décoration et de supports. Il continue d'évoluer encore aujourd'hui, en particulier dans des pays comme le nôtre où la création héraldique se poursuit, et les artistes relèvent de nouveaux défis.

Les personnes dont les œuvres ont figuré dans l'exposition sont 11 maîtres de cet art et comptent parmi les meilleurs artistes-héraldistes au monde. Ils possèdent tous leur propre technique et un style distinctif. L'exposition de plusieurs de leurs œuvres originales a rendu hommage à leurs réalisations.

Le comité de planification du 22ᵉ congrès tient à souligner la contribution des commanditaires ou participants suivants au premier atelier mondial d'art héraldique et à remercier le Musée canadien des civilisations d'avoir accueilli cette exposition.

**Principal commanditaire**
*La Société Corel*

**Principaux bienfaiteurs**
*Le Prix Burnett-Weston*
*Dʳ Joseph Segal, C.M., O.B.C.*
  *et Mᵐᵉ Rosalie Segal*
*La Fondation David et Dorothy Lam*
*Dʳ Helen K. Mussallem, C.C.*

**Donateurs et partenaires**
*La Société héraldique du Canada*
*La Ontario Genealogical Society*
*La Société de généalogie de l'Outaouais*
*L'Autorité héraldique du Canada, bureau du*
  *secrétaire du Gouverneur général du Canada*

Her Excellency greets Ms. Catherine Watt with Messrs. Robert Watt and Jean-Marie Thiébaud, president of the Confédération internationale de généalogie, looking on.

Son Excellence salue amicalement M$^{lle}$ Catherine Watt, sous les regards de MM. Robert Watt et Jean-Marie Thiébaud, président de la Confédération internationale de généalogie.

***Artists' Workshop at the University of Ottawa***
Mr. Sunil Saigal in discussion with Mr. Mikhail Medvedev.
*Photo: Christopher Wallis*

***Atelier des artistes à l'Université d'Ottawa***
M. Sunil Saigal discute avec M. Mikhail Medvedev.
*Photo : Christopher Wallis*

**Artists' Workshop**  Mr. Baz Manning at work with Mr. Anthony Wood intently looking on. *Photo: Christopher Wallis*

**Atelier des artistes**  M. Baz Manning travaillant sous le regard attentif de M. Anthony Wood. *Photo : Christopher Wallis*

**Artists' Workshop**  Mr. Gavin Schlemmer explains his work to Her Excellency. The artist Christopher Wallis looking on.

**Atelier des artistes**  M. Gavin Schlemmer explique son œuvre à Son Excellence. À l'arrière-plan, l'artiste Christopher Wallis assiste à l'entretien.

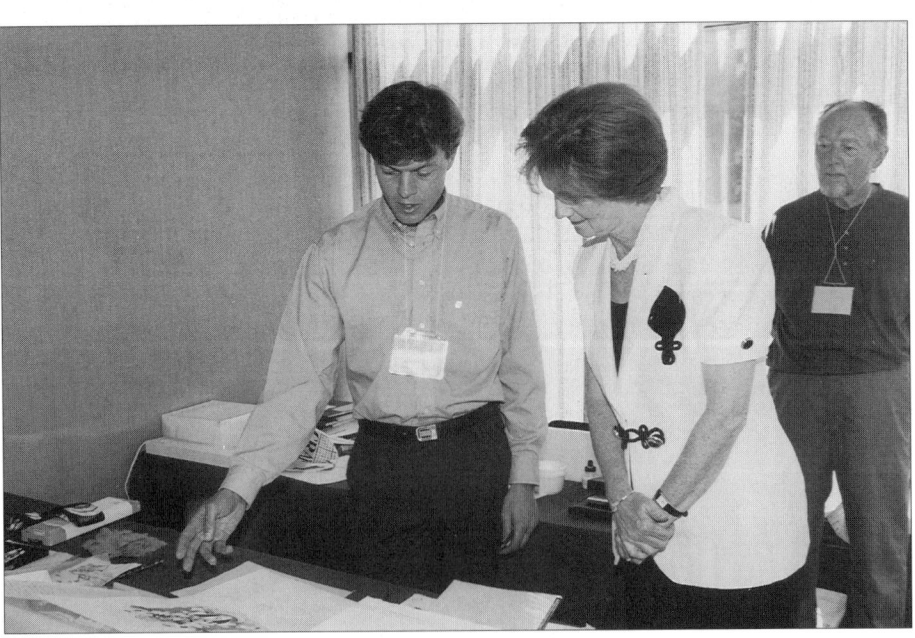

***Artists' Workshop*** In the background a view of Ottawa's University. (From front to back) Mr. Romilly Squire; Mr. Baz Manning; Mr. Andrew Jamieson; Ms. Debra MacGarvie.
***Atelier des artistes*** À l'arrière-plan, vue de l'Université d'Ottawa. (De l'avant vers l'arrière) M. Romilly Squire ; M. Baz Manning ; M. Andrew Jamieson ; M^me Debra MacGarvie.

***Exhibition "Eleven Masters of Heraldic Art"*** Canadian Museum of Civilization, Hull. *Photo: Christopher Wallis*
***Exposition : « Onze maîtres de l'art héraldique »*** Musée canadien des civilisations, Hull. *Photo : Christopher Wallis*

**Zdenko Alexy**, Bratislava, Slovakia (Born 1922)
Mr. Alexy has served his homeland as a commercial engineer, diplomat and civil servant in many capacities from 1945 to 1993. For nearly 40 years, he has been a noted scholar and heraldic artist, creating arms for municipalities and dioceses and more than 300 designs for seals for Slovak parishes and bookplates for clients around the world.

**Cathy Bursey-Sabourin**, Aylmer, Quebec, Canada (Born 1957)
After a career as a commercial and graphic designer in St. John's and Ottawa, Ms. Bursey-Sabourin began her involvement with heraldic art at the Department of National Defence. In 1990, she was appointed as Fraser Herald, the official artist of the Canadian Heraldic Authority, the first woman to hold a state herald appointment in the Commonwealth.

**Tuomas Hyrsky**, Helsinki, Finland (Born 1960)
Mr. Hyrsky pursues jewellery and heraldry design at his own studio, following completion of formal studies in graphic arts and goldsmithing in Helsinki. A particular focus of his heraldic design has been the development of badges and other insignia for the Scout and Guide movements in Finland.

**Andrew Stewart Jamieson**, Templecombe, Somerset, England (Born 1961)
Mr. Jamieson graduated from Reigate School of Art and Design in 1983 where he was a student of Anthony Wood. A native of London, Mr. Jamieson established his own studio in the West Country. There he pursues his love of mediaeval heraldry, especially the art of the 15th century, working in a wide range of materials and on varied compositions.

**Baz Manning**, Bournemouth, Dorset, England (Born 1956)
Attended Hammersmith and West London College and is the heraldic artist for the Honourable Society of Lincoln's Inn and past editor of *Heraldic Craftsmen*. Mr. Manning works mainly with enamels and oil-based pigments on glass and wood and is currently designing and painting renderings of the arms of previous British Prime Ministers.

**Zdenko Alexy**, Bratislava, Slovaquie (1922- )
M. Alexy a servi sa patrie comme ingénieur commercial, comme diplomate et fonctionnaire de 1945 à 1993. Depuis plus de 40 ans, il est bien connu comme érudit et comme maître de l'art héraldique, ayant créé des blasons pour nombre de diocèses et de municipalités, des sceaux pour plus de 300 paroisses slovaques et des ex-libris pour des clients dans le monde entier.

**Cathy Bursey-Sabourin**, Aylmer, Québec, Canada (1957- )
Après avoir fait carrière comme dessinatrice publicitaire et conceptrice graphique à St. John's et à Ottawa, M^me Bursey-Sabourin a commencé à s'intéresser à l'art héraldique au ministère de la Défense nationale. En 1990, elle a été nommée héraut Fraser et artiste officielle de l'Autorité héraldique du Canada, devenant ainsi la première femme à occuper un poste officiel de héraut dans le Commonwealth.

**Tuomas Hyrsky**, Helsinki, Finlande (1960- )
M. Hyrsky a étudié le graphisme et l'orfèvrerie à Helsinki. Il a maintenant son propre studio de bijouterie et d'héraldique. Soulignons qu'il a dessiné des insignes et autres emblèmes pour les Scouts et les Guides de Finlande.

**Andrew Stewart Jamieson,** Templecombe, So-merset, Angleterre (1961- )
Né à Londres, M. Jamieson est diplômé (1983) de la *Reigate School of Art and Design*, où il a étudié avec Anthony Wood. C'est dans son studio, situé dans l'ouest de l'Angleterre, qu'il laisse libre cours à sa passion de l'héraldique médiévale et plus particulièrement de l'art du XV^e siècle, produisant des compositions variées dans une large gamme de matériaux.

**Baz Manning**, Bournemouth, Dorset, Angleterre (1956- )
Ayant fréquenté le *Hammersmith and West London College*, M. Manning est l'ancien éditeur du *Heraldic Craftsmen*. Présentement héraldiste de la *Honorable Society of Lincoln's Inn*, il travaille surtout avec de l'émail et de la peinture à l'huile sur verre et sur bois. M. Manning conçoit et peint actuellement les armoiries des anciens premiers ministres de Grande-Bretagne.

**Mikhail Medvedev**, Saint Petersburg, Russia
(Born 1967)
A graduate of the Saint Petersburg State University and a lecturer in its Department of Mediaeval Studies, Mr. Medvedev has, since 1994, been the principal specialist in the State Heraldry office of the president of the Russian Federation. A scholar and artist, he creates new designs for public bodies and prepares new renderings of historic arms.

**Debra MacGarvie**, Ottawa, Ontario, Canada
(Born 1958)
Ms. MacGarvie graduated with a commercial art degree from Algonquin College. She became involved with heraldic art in 1992 when she began preparing concept renderings and finished paintings under the supervision of Fraser and Athabaska Heralds at the Canadian Heraldic Authority.

**Gavin William Schlemmer**, Pretoria,
South Africa (Born 1961)
A recipient of a National Diploma in Art from Pretoria Technical College, Mr. Schlemmer joined the South African Bureau of Heraldry in 1987 and has become the acting chief heraldic artist there. His work involves preparation of both draft designs and finished paintings on certificates for a very wide range of institutions and individuals.

**Romilly Squire**, Edinburgh, Scotland
(Born 1953)
His formal art education was undertaken at the Glasgow School of Art, where he received a diploma in graphic design. Following a period as an art teacher, he became, in 1983, a freelance heraldic painter and heraldic artist at the Court of the Lord Lyon in Edinburgh. In addition to his work for the Court, he has produced many illustrations of historic Scots arms for a range of popular reference works.

**Christopher Wallis**, Grand Bend, Ontario,
Canada (Born 1930)
A native of London, England, Mr. Wallis was educated at the Hammersmith School of Arts and Crafts followed by an apprenticeship in stained glass in the London studios of Martin Travers and

**Mikhail Medvedev**, Saint-Pétersbourg, Russie
(1967- )
Diplômé de l'université d'État de Saint-Pétersbourg, où il est actuellement chargé de cours au département des Études médiévales, M. Medvedev est, depuis 1994, le principal spécialiste du bureau d'héraldique d'État du président de la Fédération de Russie. Grâce à son érudition et à son talent artistique, il crée des armoiries pour des organismes publics, produisant entre autres des versions modernes d'armoiries anciennes.

**Debra MacGarvie**, Ottawa, Ontario, Canada
(1958- )
M^me MacGarvie, diplômée en art commercial du Collège Algonquin, s'est lancée dans l'art héraldique en 1992, préparant d'abord des esquisses, puis des peintures complètes sous la supervision des hérauts Fraser et Athabaska de l'Autorité héraldique du Canada.

**Gavin William Schlemmer**, Pretoria,
Afrique du Sud (1961- )
Après avoir obtenu le diplôme national d'art du *Pretoria Technical College*, M. Schlemmer est entré au service du bureau d'héraldique de l'Afrique du Sud en 1987 ; il en est maintenant l'artiste héraldique en chef par intérim. Son travail englobe à la fois la préparation des esquisses d'armoiries et l'exécution des versions finales sur parchemin destinées à des particuliers et à institutions de toutes catégories.

**Romilly Squire**, Édimbourg, Écosse
(1953- )
M. Squire détient un diplôme de graphisme de la *Glasgow School of Art*. Après avoir enseigné l'art pendant un certain temps, il est devenu, en 1983, peintre puis artiste de l'art héraldique contractuel à la cour du Lord Lyon, à Édimbourg. Il a aussi produit de nombreuses représentations d'anciennes armoiries écossaises pour plusieurs ouvrages de référence dans le domaine.

**Christopher Wallis**, Grand Bend, Ontario,
Canada (1930- )
Né à Londres, en Angleterre, M. Wallis a étudié à la *Hammersmith School of Arts and Crafts* avant de devenir apprenti en vitrail aux studios de Martin Travers et de Lawrence Lee. Ayant émigré au

Lawrence Lee. He emigrated to Canada in 1956, taught at Fanshawe College and then established his own stained glass studio. His secular and ecclesiastical commissions are now found throughout Canada at major sites including Rideau Hall where three windows, in particular, feature his love of heraldic designs.

**Anthony Wood**, South Petherton, Somerset, England (Born 1925)

Educated in Birmingham and London, Mr. Wood trained as a calligrapher, illuminator and heraldic artist with Daisy Alcock and William Gardner and for many years painted heraldry for various officers at the College of Arms in London. In 1968, he founded a three-year diploma course in calligraphy, heraldry and manuscript illumination at the Reigate School of Art and Design. As a Senior Lecturer there, he had a great influence on the training of many younger heraldic artists even as he continued his own work as a freelance artist.

Canada en 1956, il a enseigné au collège Fanshawe avant de lancer son propre studio de vitrail. On trouve maintenant de ses œuvres profanes et sacrées en de nombreux lieux distingués au Canada, par exemple à Rideau Hall, où trois verrières révèlent sa passion de l'héraldique.

**Anthony Wood**, South Petherton, Somerset, Angleterre (1925- )

Ayant fait ses études à Birmingham et à Londres, M. Wood a fait son apprentissage de la calligraphie, de l'enluminure et de l'héraldique auprès de Daisy Alcock et de William Gardner. Il a ensuite passé plusieurs années à peindre des armoiries pour différents officiers du *College of Arms* de Londres. En 1968, il a créé pour la *Reigate School of Art and Design* un cours de trois ans de calligraphie, d'héraldique et d'enluminure de manuscrits. Comme chargé d'enseignement senior à cet établissement, il a beaucoup influencé la formation de nombreux jeunes artistes de l'art héraldique tout en continuant de travailler pour son propre compte.

**Illustrations (p. 65-66)**

*The New Canadian Territory in the High Arctic, Nunavut /*
*Le nouveau territoire du Grand Nord canadien, Nunavut*
(1) Zdenko Alexy
(2) Cathy Bursey-Sabourin
(3) Tuomas Hyrsky
(4) Andrew Stewart Jamieson
(5) Baz Manning
(6) Mikhail Medvedev
(7) Debra MacGarvie
(8) Gavin William Schlemmer
(10) Christopher Wallis

*The New Millennium / Le nouveau Millénaire*
(9) Romilly Squire
(11) Anthony Wood

1

2

ᓄᓇᕗᑦ
**NUNAVUT**

3

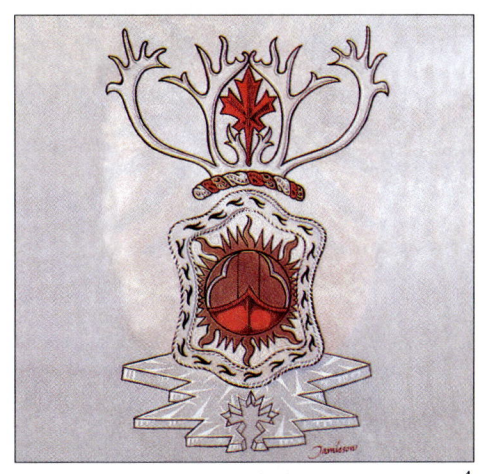

4

5

6

7

8

9

10

11

# HERALDIC COMMEMORATIVE STAMP / TIMBRE HÉRALDIQUE COMMÉMORATIF

Canada Post officially unveiled a new 45¢ commemorative stamp honouring Canadian heraldry in conjunction with the opening ceremonies of the Congress at the University of Ottawa on August 19.

Designed by Derek Sarty of Halifax, Nova Scotia, the stamp highlights the special character of Canadian heraldry, with a particular focus on the diverse nature of our heraldic symbolism. Special first-day covers were available as well as an official Congress postcard featuring a colour photograph of a new heraldic stained-glass window showing the arms of the Canadian Heraldic Authority and its Officers by master glass artist, Christopher Wallis (see p. 69-70).

Lors de la cérémonie d'ouverture du congrès à l'Université d'Ottawa, le 19 août, la Société canadienne des postes a dévoilé un nouveau timbre commémoratif de 45 ¢ dédié à l'héraldique.

Ce timbre conçu par Derek Sarty de Halifax, Nouvelle-Écosse, et dont était disponible une émission du premier jour, met l'accent sur la diversité des manifestations héraldiques au Canada. Une carte postale illustrée du vitrail réalisé par le maître verrier Christopher Wallis en l'honneur de l'Autorité héraldique du Canada était également disponible (voir p. 69-70)

*(p. 67, top)*
**Closing banquet**
National Gallery of Canada.

*(p. 67, en haut)*
**Banquet de clôture**
Musée des beaux-arts du Canada.

*(p. 67, bottom)*
**Closing banquet** Mrs. Judith LaRoque, Secretary to the Governor General and Herald Chancellor of the Canadian Heraldic Authority, presenting Dr. Jean-Claude Loutsch with an Honorary Fellowship in the Heraldry Society of Canada. On the left Mrs. Jean Matheson, President of the Society; on the right, Dr. John Kennedy, Editor of the Society's journal.

*(p. 67, en bas)*
**Banquet de clôture** M^me Judith LaRoque, secrétaire du Gouverneur général et chancelier d'armes de l'Autorité héraldique du Canada, présente au D^r Jean-Claude Loutsch un certificat de Compagnon honorifique de la Société héraldique du Canada. À gauche, M^me Jean Matheson, présidente de la Société ; à droite John Kennedy, Ph.D., rédacteur en chef du bulletin de la Société.

*(Page 69, top)*
Her Excellency with Mr. Patrick Reid of Corel Corporation acompanied by the artists of the workshop, from l. to r.: (back) Messrs. Mikhail Y. Medvedev, Tuomas Hyrsky, Romilly Squire, Baz Manning, Andrew S. Jamieson, G. Zdenko Alexy, Gavin W. Schlemmer, Christopher Wallis, (front) Ms. Debra MacGarvie, Mrs. Cathy Bursey-Sabourin, Her Excellency, Messrs. Patrick Reid and Anthony Wood.

*(page 69, en haut)*
Son Excellence et M. Patrick Reid, représentant de la Société Corel, en compagnie des artistes de l'atelier, de g. à dr. (arrière) MM. Mikhail Y. Medvedev, Tuomas Hyrsky, Romilly Squire, Baz Manning, Andrew S. Jamieson, G. Zdenko Alexy, Gavin W. Schlemmer, Christopher Wallis, (devant) M^mes Debra MacGarvie et Cathy Bursey-Sabourin, Son Excellence, MM. Patrick Reid et Anthony Wood.

*(Page 69, bottom)*
Her Excellency unveiling the commemorative stamp honouring Canadian heraldry with Mr. Phillippe Lemay, Senior Vice-President of Electronic Products and Services, Canada Post Corporation, looking on.

*(Page 69, en bas)*
Son Excellence dévoile le timbre commémoratif honorant l'héraldique canadienne sous le regard de M. Phillippe Lemay, Premier vice-président des produits et services électroniques de la Société canadienne des postes.

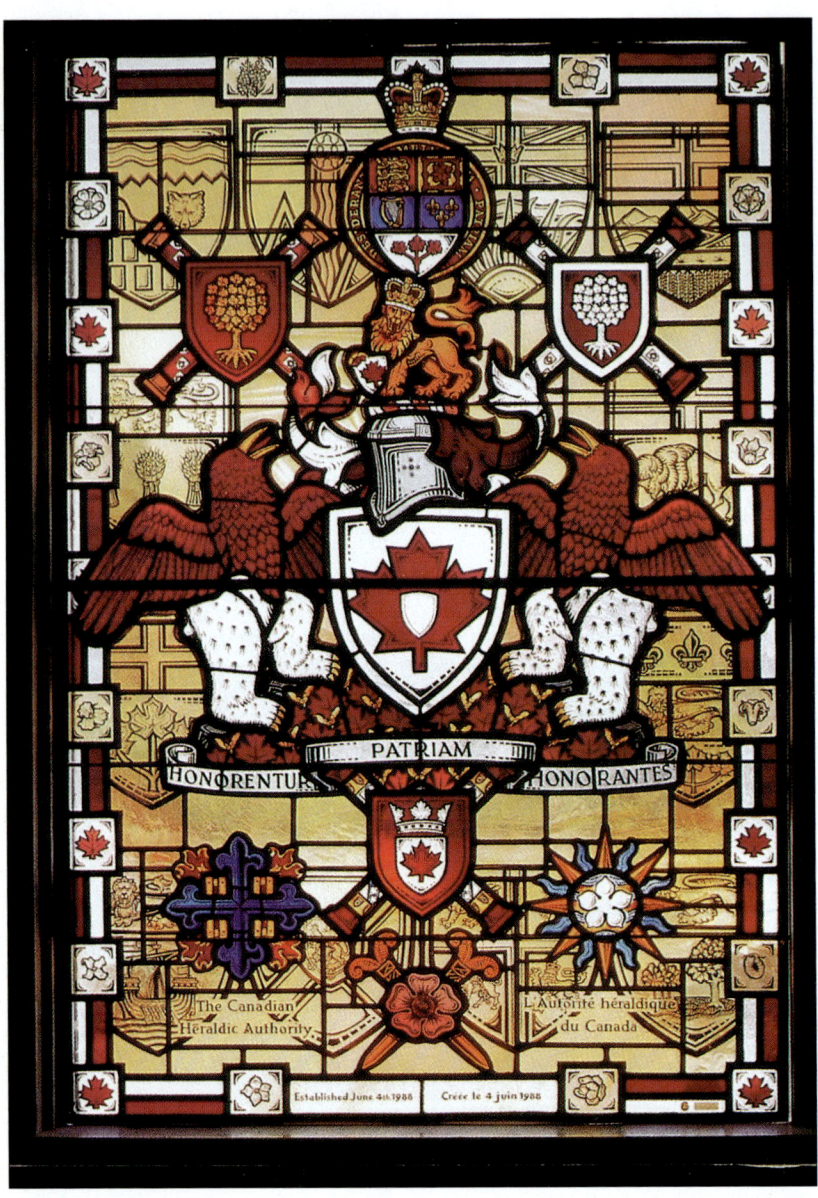

***The arms and insignia of the Canadian Heraldic Authority and its officers*** Stained-glass window designed and produced by Christopher Wallis for the 22nd Congress. This window was donated to the Crown by the artist and was unveiled in its permanent location in Rideau Hall by the Governor General on February 26, 1997.

***Les armoiries et insignes de l'Autorité héraldique du Canada et de ses officiers d'armes*** Vitrail conçu et réalisé par Christopher Wallis à l'occasion du 22e congrès. Il fut offert à la Couronne par l'artiste et installé en permanence à Rideau Hall. Le Gouverneur général l'a officiellement dévoilé le 26 février 1997.

# THE GARDNER FAMILY: WEST MEETS EAST

Morris L. Bierbrier

The theme of this congress is emigration and immigration. Much has been made of the tendency of families to stay put in their native localities, and it used to be implied that emigration and immigration were consequently somewhat exceptional in a family's history until the more fluid modern age. In fact, movement is one of the common features of family history at every point in history, and a genealogical researcher is indeed lucky if a family can be located in one district for any length of time. Most of these movements are gradual from one parish to another because of marriage or economic circumstances, and then perhaps to the nearest town. These changes affect not only the common man but even the gentry or nobility who may move their seat because of inheritance or bankruptcy. When I was attempting to trace the descendants of St. Louis among the British, it was quite noticeable how many lines, especially those of younger sons, simply disappeared.

However, most families usually experience only one major intercontinental migration. Within the British Isles, movements from Scotland to Ireland to England or vice versa may still be classed as local as opposed to the steady migration to America, Australia and India from the 17th century on. Very few of the descendants of permanent migrations returned. The same trends can doubtless be seen with Continental migration to America. We have, however, been rather parochial in the treatment of emigration and indeed genealogy since, of course, similar trends can be observed with regard to non-European races. In the past these have been regarded as of no genealogical consequence as far as Europe and America have been concerned, but this is not strictly true. I do not intend to speak of the early central Asian peoples who either settled in central Europe or pushed the existing inhabitants further west. In more modern times, non-European emigration has always been a feature, however relatively minor, of genealogical life. The mass involuntary emigration of Africans to America is well documented and descendants abound, but much less is known of that to Europe, where the descendants merged with the local population and effectively disappeared except in a few notable cases such as the African Hannibal, slave of Peter the Great of Russia, whose descendants include the present Duchesses of Abercorn and Westminster. As we will see, Eastern genes similarly entered Europe from India. Most of these arrivals had no ancestry of note that can be traced back to their country of origin but this is not always the case.

I wish to outline the history of one family—the Gardners of Coleraine in Ireland—who in the course of 300 years have undertaken at least three intercontinental migrations and whose genes represent a remarkable amalgam of ancestry, which perhaps cannot be equalled in any other British-American family.[1]

The Gardner family first appears in Coleraine in Ireland at the end of the 17th century. The pedigree is headed by one Theophilus Gardner whose son William Gardner is said to have raised a company of men to defend Protestant Londonderry when under siege in 1691 and then to have died young. This at any rate is the version printed concerning the ancestry of William's grandson the first Lord Gardner around 1806 and presumably supplied or vetted by him. A more modern pedigree adds an earlier generation in a Henry Gardner but, if correct, he is still only a name. It may be presumed that the Gardners may have already undertaken a previous immigration from England to Ireland, but if so the Gardners in 1806 had no knowledge of this. It can also be deduced from the designation of the town Coleraine as the ancestral home that the Gardners were not gentry but most probably middle class or burgess although conceivably, but not likely, even lower in the social scale. There is no confirmation of William Gardner's role in Londonderry and the family's fortunes were in fact laid by his son, another William Gardner, who entered the British army and eventually rose to the rank of lieutenant colonel.

Contrary to some modern belief, the officer ranks of the British army in the 18th century were not the total reserve of the noble and gentry class, as, for example, in France where quarters of nobility were required for promotion. The British class system has always been more open and the ranks of officers were available for those who could pay for them—in principle the nobility and the gentry but also the middle class. It was thus possible for those from obscure families, but with financial backing or political patronage, to acquire officer rank. It is not known if William Gardner had a particular patron, perhaps as a reward for his father's services in Londonderry, but probably not. More likely he showed some family aptitude or interest in military affairs, and the family had enough financial resources to purchase a commission for him. The army, as well as being a vehicle for social upward mobility, has also been a vehicle for emigration and, in William Gardner's case, this proved immediately effective. He quitted Ireland never to return. He also demonstrated a new, or perhaps old, family aptitude, that of marrying well. In England he managed to marry a minor heiress from a minor gentry family in Lancashire, although it is true that she was the daughter of a younger son of a younger son who had made his living as a professional man—a doctor, Valentine Farrington. She probably had several royal descents notably from Edward III, although it is unlikely that either she or her husband were actually aware of this fact [TABLE 1]. He would not have been considered suitable unless he was already an officer, but perhaps her money helped in his rise to higher rank since he only became a lieutenant colonel in 1754. He eventually settled in Uttoxeter and in his will is described as esquire showing that he was considered gentry by the end of his career but probably not before.

His sons followed differing careers. The eldest William seems to have reflected the family's origins by becoming a merchant in Liverpool, but the younger sons all entered the forces: Valentine and Henry in the army and Alan in the navy. It is probable that the family's money helped to fund their commissions. Alan Gardner, the youngest, was either more capable or luckier or probably both. The navy in the 18th century was a vehicle for rapid promotion in status as the career of one Horatio Nelson demonstrates. Gardner rose steadily through the officer ranks, no doubt helped by the Gardner facility for marrying well, in this case a Jamaican heiress. After a stint as governor

of Jamaica, he ended up an admiral and the navy's choice for a safe seat to Parliament, where he is recorded as not speaking a word in debate. In due course he became a peer of Ireland and finally a peer of the United Kingdom as the first Lord Gardner. Not at all bad for the grandson of William Gardner of Coleraine and a tribute to Britain's social mobility. More about his descendants later.

His elder brothers were less successful. Both ended up as colonels at the very end of their careers, but Henry died relatively young in Jamaica. Valentine Gardner joined his regiment in America serving as captain in 1765, and later as major in 1776. There he made what he doubtless thought was an equally advantageous match as his younger brother, to Alida Livingston, daughter of Robert Livingston of New York State. Unfortunately for him, the American Revolution intervened and, as a British citizen and soldier, he naturally backed the government side and lost whatever financial gains that he had acquired from his wealthy wife. Indeed, he has been largely expunged from the many Livingston family histories, appearing as Valentine Gardiner of New York with no attempt made to list his descendants. Only the latest Livingston history, while still spelling his name wrongly, actually admits that he was a Loyalist and had a son. The spelling error might be genuine for Valentine Gardiner also appears as such in the army lists. Was he trying to change the spelling of his name to one more up-market or was he the victim of repeated bureaucratic misspellings? It is not likely that he and his heirs were simply ignored because he was a Loyalist as 19th-century American family histories include these lines as well, but the departure of this line from America may have led to their neglect although they were curiously always available to anyone who cared to consult *Burke's Peerage*. Before I deal with the heirs, it would be best to examine the Livingston pedigree.

Robert Livingston, the emigrant to America, was the youngest son of the Rev. John Livingston and a descendant of several generations of pastors. John Livingston in his autobiography claimed that he was a great-grandson of a younger son of the 4th Lord Livingston, who fell at the battle of Pinkie in 1547. There is no contemporary evidence for this death in battle, but there is evidence that Lord Livingston's second son, Master James Livingston, was dead a month after the battle. In view of this evidence, there seems to be no reason to doubt this genealogical link [TABLE 2].[2] No contemporary source mentions a wife or child of James Livingston and it is possible that his son was illegitimate: a fact glossed over by Rev. John and his American descendants, although it would have caused no shame or embarrassment in 16th-century Scotland. The Livingstons were not the most aristocratic of Scottish families. Despite attempts to push the line further back, it can only be traced to the late 13th century and the Livingstons owed their rise to eminence to their military skills and the king's favour. Through the marriage of the 3rd Lord Livingston to Beatrice or Elizabeth Fleming, the later Livingstons could claim two royal descents from Robert II, although it is nowhere stated for certain that she was the mother of the next lord [TABLE 3]. Another royal descent comes in through Barbara Livingston, the grandmother of Robert the emigrant, but this is also not wholly confirmed as Barbara Livingston's parents are deduced, not clearly stated in contemporary sources. It is not even clear that the emigrant Robert was precisely aware of any royal origins, but he certainly would have seen himself as an offspring of Scottish nobility.

In fact, Robert Livingston may have been of good birth but he was virtually penniless. His father had ended up in exile in Holland in opposition to Charles II after previously objecting to Oliver Cromwell. Like many adventurers before him, Robert Livingston went off to America to seek his fortune. This is the first intercontinental emigration in the Gardner ancestry. Livingston had the great advantage of being bilingual in English and Dutch, so naturally he ended up in New Amsterdam, later New York state. I do not propose to go into detail about his rise to wealth and status except that, as usual, it involved an advantageous marriage, to a Dutch heiress Alida Schuyler. By obtaining lucrative land grants, he finished up as lord of the manor of a good part of upper New York state and founded a family defined by a recent author as American aristocracy. His career may be compared to those gentry descendants like Washington, who established themselves in the southern states. His heirs continued his practice of intermarriage with Dutch families so his great-granddaughter, Alida Livingston Gardner, was genetically more Dutch than Scottish and her marriage to the Irish-English Valentine Gardner was a nice genetic mix. The

American Revolution put an end to whatever hopes Gardner had of exploiting his wife's connections and his son, William Linnaeus Gardner, disappeared from the family histories, which the Livingston descendants piously compiled.[3] However, in the recent history,[4] this son, though unnamed, is mentioned as being cared for by his maternal grandfather at the Livingston manor house for several years before it was judged prudent to send him to his father, with whom he ended up back in England—an involuntary intercontinental emigration in reverse. His early upbringing as a grandson of the lord of the manor may well have had some influence in his later career as we shall see. The Livingstons, whose descendants include Eleanor Roosevelt, Mrs. W. B. Astor, and the present Duke of Argyll, were to remain prominent in American society with stately homes along the Hudson River.

William Linnaeus Gardner found himself in a very insecure financial position. The Gardner family had never been wealthy, but had had just enough money to obtain the requisite military positions from which the family members could use their talents to shine or not. His uncle Alan Gardner had been lucky in his career and marriage and had jumped into the aristocracy. Valentine Gardner had been unlucky in the financial side of his marriage. Moreover he had remarried on the death of Alida Livingston so that his own financial resources were now dedicated to his second family. William Linnaeus had to make his own way and, like his father and grandfather before him, had joined the army and ended up in India where the action was in the 1790s. It is to be remembered that Arthur Wellesley had made his initial military career in India as well. I do not propose to follow William Linnaeus Gardner's career in detail as two recent biographies have done so.[5] I would remark that the India of the 1790s was quite a different place from the India of the later British empire. The British were still a minority there in opposition to French interests and even at this stage had no firm intention of actually annexing the country. Most of the country was in the hands of local princes, who had gained power through the disintegration of the Mughal empire in the early 18th century and were fighting for power and influence among themselves. The British and the French were merely two other contending powers to be used by the Indians in their internecine struggles. William Linnaeus soon determined that he would have a freer hand, and perhaps more immediate rewards, in becoming a mercenary leader for Indian factions rather than serving in the regular British or Company forces. He was not alone in this decision as there were many such Western adventurers, English, French or even German, who tried their luck, and sometimes came to sticky ends betrayed by their employers or ending up on the losing side. William Linnaeus was lucky, clever, and successful and ended up rich and respected as the leader of Gardner's Horse.

His inclination to become independent may be reflected in his marriage in the late 1790s to the Begum of Cambay. The relationship between European men and Indian women was not at all unusual at this time. One must forget about the moral and social code that pertained to later Victorian England. In the 18th century in India, European women were few and far between and no one expected the Europeans to remain celibate. Most men had Indian companions and some even married them by native rites or occasionally by Christian ones. The offspring were not noticeably discriminated against and indeed often joined the British forces since, of course, the majority of European men were common soldiers or traders and their Indian companions were in the lower ranks of both societies. The children of those in the upper ranks did not suffer either. Numbers were sent back to Europe for education or even married there with descendants. Money, not birth, counted and whatever social and racial snobbery that existed was then ignored in much the same way that Jewish heiresses were sought in marriage by the Christian nobility and gentry in the 18th century. One may recall that, in Thackery's *Vanity Fair,* the rich mulatto heiress was expensively educated and was expected to make a great match. Such Indian examples are common. The celebrated French mercenary the Comte de Boigne retired to France with his money and Indian children whom he married into the French aristocracy. On a slightly lower level, the merchant Theodore Forbes of Aberdeen sent his children by the local lady Eliza Kewark, possibly an Armenian, back to Scotland where they married into the local merchant class and whose descendants include Diana Princess of Wales and more importantly her sons. In a similar fashion Major-General William Farquhar (1774-1839) resident in Malacca and Singapore had children by a local

woman one of whom married a European official in India and was the ancestor of one Margaret Sinclair Trudeau. The descendants of such unions are no doubt common but have been obliterated from memory by much later Victorian prejudice.

William Linnaeus Gardner's marriage was only unusual in that his bride was a Muslim of good family. The explanation for that was quite simple. She may have been a princess of Cambay, but she was a princess in exile and a pretty nouveau princess at that. Cambay was one of the many minor states formed by the breakup of the Mughal empire in the earlier 18th century, and therefore its ruling house, descended from Persian officials of the previous regime, was not very ancient. This had not prevented infighting in the new royal line, and it is certainly clear that William Gardner met his bride in Surat where her branch of the family had been expelled when it lost the current power struggle. William later asserted that his was a love match although the bride was but thirteen, but he would never have been allowed to see her and indeed marry her if her family did not have high hopes that his mercenary talents might be put to good use in their restoration. It is curious that her father is never mentioned; so it is not absolutely clear where she fits in the Cambay family tree. The Cambay family followed up this match with another one for her sister with another prospective military protector Hyder Young Hearsey. Their hopes in this direction were not satisfied and they were never restored in Cambay although William Gardner did make financial provision for his brothers-in-law on his estates when he made good elsewhere. He ended his career rich and respected and a lord of the manor like, and probably in emulation of, his Livingston grandfather. He obtained extensive land grants in the Khasganj and Chhaoni areas of Uttar Pradesh (formerly United Provinces) 60 miles from Agra and built himself a fine manor house. He kept good relations with the growing British establishment, but was also on excellent terms with the ruling Indian houses, notably that of the Mughal imperial family into which his wife was adopted as a term of respect, and to whose history we now turn.

I have mentioned emigration from the East and the most notable and best remembered of these incursions were the Mongols under the leadership of Genghis Khan, beginning in the early 13th century. Genghis Khan, or more properly Temujin, which was his name and not his title, was not a nobody but a Mongol aristocrat. At the beginning of his career this meant nothing except a genealogy, as he had few material resources, only a name and his character. His ancestry can probably be traced back with certainty to about AD 1000. He and his heirs overran most of Central Asia, China, Iran, Iraq, and Russia. Many Mongols settled in these countries although, apart from the line of the khans, their descendants have by now disappeared without trace in the general populations. By the 14th century, Mongol rule was disintegrating in all directions, but was revived briefly in parts of central Asia, Iran, and Afghanistan by the military career of Timur the Lame known as Tamerlane whose capital was at Samarkand. Timur was not a member of the line of Genghis Khan and was scrupulous in installing a figurehead khan who of course was not allowed any power. His court heralds, for this profession is ancient if not always respected, drew up a detailed genealogy tracing his descent from a distant cousin of Genghis Khan, although his real genealogy probably only went back a few generations. More importantly, Timur allied himself and his sons in marriage to ladies of the khanly line and took the title of Gurgan, which was the prerogative of the khan's sons-in-law. Indeed, his descendants are often known by the last name of Gurgani. The rule of his heirs in central Asia lasted only to the early 16th century, but one member, Babur (1483-1530), sought his fortune in emigration with his followers to India, where he carved out a new empire.

Babur was a highly intelligent and competent leader who was descended in the male line from Timur and the female line from Genghis Khan. Among his legacies are his racy memoirs, which evoked an interest in diary-keeping and patronage of historians among his heirs. Thus we know a great deal about them and their private and genealogical life, which is unusual for Muslim rulers of this period. Babur's grandson, Akbar (1542-1605), began the custom of conciliating his Indian vassals through marriage so that his grandson, the famous Shah Jahan (1592-1666), was only part mongol or Mughal, as it was known in India. His mother and paternal grandmother were princesses from the Rajput Houses of Jaipur and Jodhpur whose lines go back at least to the 11th and 13th centuries respectively. His wife Mumtaz Mahal

(ca. 1593-1631) was a Persian of no great ancestry and later rulers were descended from Indian ladies of untraced ancestry. At the beginning of the 18th century, the Mughal Empire fell apart and the emperor was reduced to the status of a figurehead installed and deposed at the behest of factional leaders. The Emperor Shah Alam II (1728-1806), at the end of the century, stayed in office by playing off various factions, but did it so often that he lost the trust of most and was deposed and blinded in atrocious circumstances. He was eventually restored and ruled as a blind puppet until 1803, when he passed into the hands of the British who used him to legitimize their growing authority. Technically the British, or rather, the East India Company, was appointed vizier of the emperor and his successor Akbar II (1760-1837) in return, of course, for large subsidies.

The chaos in the reign of Shah Alam had tempted some princes to seek refuge in safer havens. His eldest son, Jawan Bakht, who predeceased him, ended up in British Benares, while his fourth son, Sulayman Shikoh (ca. 1762-1838), preferred the protection of the Nawab of Awadh in Lucknow. This arrangement worked well until the British gradually began to renege on their agreements. In order to weaken the fictional but recognized authority of the Mughal emperor, to whom they did not now wish to be beholden to any legal claim to India, the British would only recognize him as king of Delhi and suggested to the Nawab of Awadh that he takes the title of king (shah) as an equal to Delhi. The Mughals regarded this action as a great affront, but worse was to follow as the next king of Awadh demanded the daughter of Sulayman Shikoh as his wife. Like most royal and noble families in India, the Mughals practised cousin marriage and rarely offered princesses outside the family apart from cases of *force majeure* to conquering Persian and Afghan rulers such as Nadir Shah or Ahmad Shah Durrani. The Awadh alliance was obnoxious, as his title was an insult to their family and he was a Shia in religion. The marriage was nonetheless forceably concluded, but the Awadh ruler realized the enmity of his new father-in-law and promptly expelled him from his domains. Sulayman Shikoh sought refuge in Agra but had to leave his harem behind. He needed someone that he could trust to bring his womenfolk to him safely, and that person could only be William Linnaeus Gardner, who responded to his plea for help, little suspecting the future genealogical ramifications.

William Gardner arrived in Agra with his son James Valentine to escort the ladies to safety, but in the course of the journey James Valentine Gardner eloped with the Princess Sultan-ul-zamani Mulka Qamar Chahra Banu Begum, daughter of Sulayman Shikoh. Neither of the two protagonists was exactly inexperienced in the marital arrangements. James already had three children by a local woman whom he later described as his natural children, while the Mughal princess, with three children of her own, was the divorced wife of her cousin Prince Salim, son of the Mughal Emperor Akbar II. Doubtless she believed that her divorce and return to her father's house had put her in limbo and she had seized the opportunity to obtain a new husband. Both in-laws were horrified at the event. William L. Gardner felt that his son had impugned the family honour and took some time to be won over and agree to the formal marriage of the partners. Like himself, his son was married in a Muslim ceremony which today would be considered valid in any law. Other British observers at the time thought the marriage highly romantic.[6] While Gardner forgave, Sulayman Shikoh did not. It is interesting, in the light of future Victorian prejudices, that it was the prince who regarded the union as an insult. From his point of view, James Gardner was not fit to marry his daughter despite his noble maternal line, and he refused to recognize it. In his will he formally declared that the lady was not his true daughter. This led to a later legend in the family that she was only an adopted daughter, but it is obvious that this was invented to cover the family dishonour with the match. Her previous marriage to her cousin proves her imperial birth. However, her brothers were more inclined to accept the *fait accompli* and reap some of the advantages. A few years later, her brother Prince Anjum Shikoh married one of William Gardner's granddaughters, which shows that the Mughals had a more pragmatic approach to the acceptance into the family of daughters-in-law, especially well-dowered ones, as opposed to sons-in-law. This lady's sister made an equally interesting match in marrying her cousin Stewart William Gardner, a grandson of the first Lord Gardner. Being a younger son, Gardner also sought the advantage of an alliance with his wealthy relation, and was not at all bothered by his bride's Indian background.

The history of William and James Gardner and their matrimonial entanglements were regarded as adventurous and romantic by outside contemporary British observers. The Gardners remained well-respected members of both the British and Indian establishment and they did not forget their intercontinental ties. In his will in 1845, James Valentine Gardner specifically mentioned his expectations from the Uttoxeter estate in England and the Livingston estate in America although he obviously had an exaggerated view of his claims. In the 1930s a Gardner descendant named his son Livingstone, keeping the American ancestry alive. His heirs attempted, without success, to live in two worlds: European settlers and Muslim noblemen. Solomon Gardner, otherwise Sulayman Shikoh Gardner, portrayed himself as a European, but lived as an Indian aristocrat with four wives and patronized Urdu literature. The family practised the Indian custom of cousin marriages so that soon all the Gardners were closely related and most of Mughal descent. The first and second generations after James had largely Muslim names such as Sikander Shikoh and Kamran Shikoh and did not register their children or marriages with the British religious authorities. Like the products of mixed marriages in Ireland in the more civilized early 19th century when the different sexes followed different religious persuasions, the boys were brought up as Christians and the girls as Muslims but the high rate of intermarriage of cousins made this separation somewhat theoretical. The problems that the Gardners faced came from two different interrelated sources. Firstly, their imperial connections had led the family to live well above its means and its members were soon in debt and eventually effectively bankrupt, although they did manage to hold onto some land. Secondly, the attitude of the British authorities changed radically in the mid-19th century. Indians no longer were regarded as allies but subjects. The Mughals were considered a nuisance and a threat. Anglo-Indians in general were now viewed as an embarrassment and a social threat to the existence of the white community as racism made a very vigorous appearance. In similar circumstances, Pocahontas and her marriage was romantic in the 17th century, but an alliance with an American Indian squaw in the 19th would have been regarded as beneath contempt for a white man. These new attitudes helped in part fuel the Indian rebellion of 1857, which led to the downfall of the Mughal family, some of whose members later sought refuge with the Gardners. The Gardners of course supported the British as they were also regarded with contempt by the Indian side for their British blood. Afterwards they were lumped with the general and despised Anglo-Indian community, their illustrious ancestry being ignored or forgotten. If the family had preserved its wealth, that might have made some difference but probably not much. It is interesting to find that, at the end of the 19th century, the Gardners abandon, for the most part, their Muslim heritage and reappear in the British religious registers. Now their Christianity demarcated them from local Indian peasants, not their Muslim noble past.

The social snobbery that hampered the Gardners and other Anglo-Indian families is illustrated by the Gardner Barony. The death of the third Lord Gardner without legitimate heirs in 1883 was particularly hard on his three sons. They were born before their father's marriage to their mother, his second wife, as Lord Gardner had had to wait for his first wife to die before legitimizing his long-held union. As bastards in Victorian society, they were of course debarred from claiming the peerage and at a social disadvantage. But, to them, the ultimate insult was that the heir to the title was an Anglo-Indian, a son of the marriage of Stewart William Gardner and the granddaughter of William Linnaeus Gardner. Such a possibility was viewed with horror not only by them but by the British establishment, and no help was offered to Alan Hyde Gardner when he came to claim the title. He was also hampered by the fact that he had no money. Snide implications were made that Muslim or Indian marriages could not be regarded as valid in England. In fact, no such marriages were involved as Alan Gardner's parents' marriage had been a Christian ceremony duly registered as was his own and he and his son had also been duly baptized and registered. Unfortunately these registers were not as easily accessible in the 1880s as they are now from an index in the Indian Office Library. Thus Alan Gardner was unable to prove his claim and the peerage remains dormant. If one of the late Lord Gardner's sons made rather rude remarks about his Indian cousins during a visit to India, another Gardner relation caused consternation by recognizing the relationship. Lady Halifax, wife of the viceroy, of Gardner descent, while travelling, was greeted by a local stationmaster who claimed a relationship as a Gardner and was promptly called cousin by the Vicereine, to the annoyance of her British entourage. It is noteworthy that both she and the stationmaster were aware of the Gardner connection, if only in general terms. Possibly the Indian connections explain the omission of the Gardners from the Livingston genealogy, although sheer ignorance of the facts may also account for this. Apparently, so annoyed were certain quarters by the eventual creation of the Indian peer Lord Sinha, that an objection was made to his heir's succession on the grounds that he was born of an Indian and hence outside a legitimate marriage. Fortunately, this was overruled and a Gardner born of a Muslim marriage would now be able to succeed. The title remains dormant now, not because of problems with the Indian side, but because it cannot be established that Stewart William Gardner's older brother died a bachelor, although he most certainly did. Ironically such proof would have been readily available in the 1880s. Demonstrating that prejudice was not confined to one side, the surviving Mughal family was not very keen on a marriage link with one royal prince since his mother was a Gardner and hence of mixed descent.

The end of British rule in India left the Anglo-Indian community in limbo and many members have emigrated from India since 1947, as part of the major emigration from the sub-continent, which future genealogists must take into account. As I have indicated, not all Indian pedigrees are obscure. Many Gardners have returned to Britain settling in London, Leeds, and Swindon or gone to Australia, while others have moved to Canada or returned to their American roots. There are once more descendants of Alida Livingston resident in the state of New York. One branch has even settled in Germany. Another branch of the family emigrated to Iraq at the end of World War II as one Gardner from India was in the British forces stationed there. His descendants in Basra spread to Kuwait and found themselves in an awkward position during the Gulf war on both sides of the conflict. Some have now managed to return to England, but others remain there. The Gardners in their new countries have all intermarried with local residents so that the blood line of Edward III of England, Robert II of Scotland, Genghis Khan, and Tamerlane is being widely distributed. The Gardners left in India, on the other hand, have intermarried with local

Muslim and Hindu families. We are indeed becoming one world genealogically.

## NOTES

1.   This talk ranges widely over continents and I do not claim to be an expert in all topics mentioned, so there may be inevitably a few suppositions that may bear correction.

2.   E. B. LIVINGSTON, *The Livingstons of Callendar and Their Principal Cadets* (1920).

3.   E. B. LIVINGSTON, *The Livingstons of Livingston Manor* (1910); F. VAN RENSSELAER, *The Livingston Family in America and Its Scottish Origins* (1949); C. BRANDT and A. KELLY, *A Livingston Genealogy* (1982).

4.   C. BRANDT, *An American Aristocracy. The Livingstons* (1986).

5.   N. SAROOP, *A Squire of Hindustan* (1983); L. J. GARD-NER, *The Sabre and the Spur* (1985).

6.   FANNY PARKES, *Pilgrimage in Search of the Picturesque* (1850).

TABLE 1

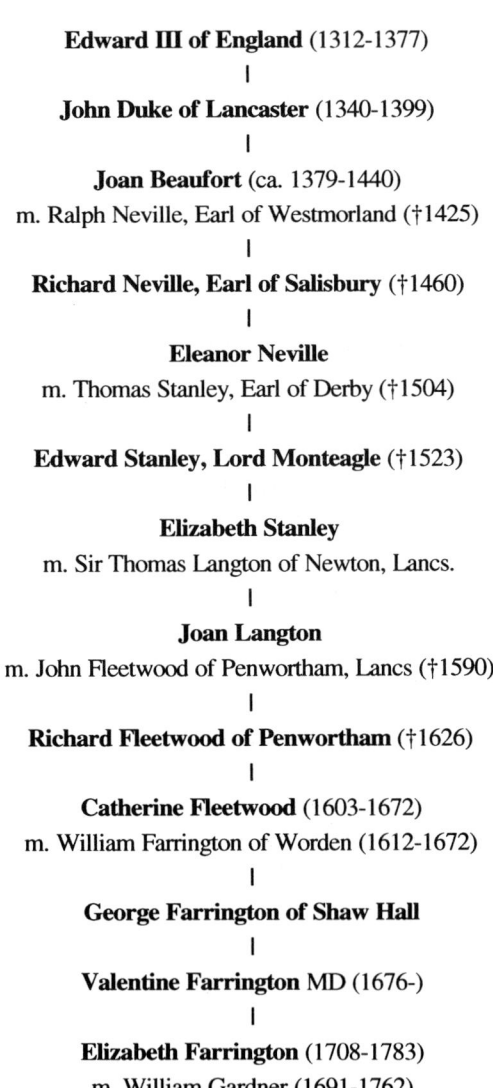

**Edward III of England** (1312-1377)
|

**John Duke of Lancaster** (1340-1399)
|

**Joan Beaufort** (ca. 1379-1440)
m. Ralph Neville, Earl of Westmorland (†1425)
|

**Richard Neville, Earl of Salisbury** (†1460)
|

**Eleanor Neville**
m. Thomas Stanley, Earl of Derby (†1504)
|

**Edward Stanley, Lord Monteagle** (†1523)
|

**Elizabeth Stanley**
m. Sir Thomas Langton of Newton, Lancs.
|

**Joan Langton**
m. John Fleetwood of Penwortham, Lancs (†1590)
|

**Richard Fleetwood of Penwortham** (†1626)
|

**Catherine Fleetwood** (1603-1672)
m. William Farrington of Worden (1612-1672)
|

**George Farrington of Shaw Hall**
|

**Valentine Farrington** MD (1676-)
|

**Elizabeth Farrington** (1708-1783)
m. William Gardner (1691-1762)

TABLE **2**

Andrew de Livingston

|

William de Livingston († ca. 1339)

|

William de Livingston (†1362-4)

|

John de Livingston (†1402)

|

Alexander Livingston (†1451)

|

James 1st Lord Livingston (†1467)

|

Alexander Livingston

|

James 3rd Lord Livingston († ca. 1503)
m. 1472 Elizabeth Fleming

|

William 4th Lord Livingston († ca. 1516-18)

|

James Livingston (†1547)

|

Alexander Livingston († ca. 1598)
m. Barbara Livingston of Kilsyth

|

William Livingston (†1641)

|

John Livingston (1603-1672)

|

Robert Livingston the emigrant

|

Philip Livingston

|

Robert Livingston

|

Alida Livingston (1747-1791)
m. Valentine Gardner

TABLE 3

**King Robert II of Scotland** (1315-1390)

|

**Robert Stewart, Duke of Albany** (1339-1420)

|

**Elizabeth Stewart**

m. Malcolm Fleming (†1440)

|

**Robert 1st Lord Fleming** (†1491)

|

**Elizabeth Fleming**

m. 1472 James 3rd Lord Livingston

# BETWEEN IMPERIAL HINTERLANDS: RECONSTITUTING FAMILIES IN BUKOVINA AND SASKATCHEWAN, 1775-1940

Richard Carruthers-Żurowski[1]

## 1. Bukovina as a focus for research

Many people, North Americans in particular, are daunted by the difficulties of pursuing any investigation into their ancestry in central and eastern Europe. The perceived obstacles, myriad and insurmountable, have become almost legendary in the annals of genealogical research;[2] so much so, that many people throw up their hands in dismay at the prospect and give up the task as being too onerous even before making a start. This is no longer reasonable, and is certainly much to be lamented if carried out by more than a handful.

This paper seeks to demonstrate the application of a radical strategy to a specific research problem. It proposes that, through making common cause in what is, admittedly, one of the more complex areas for genealogical research, the majority of the obstacles to gaining substantial research results can be overcome. It is also believed that such an approach will prove to be of significant benefit to the majority of researchers, amateurs in particular, whose forays into this region have been stymied by difficulties caused through their use of the more traditional method of conducting self-absorbed research into one family at a time. It is hoped that the model discussed, radical at least to most North American and/or non-academic genealogists, will serve as a paradigm for projects of a similar kind in other areas and thereby carry the example of what can be achieved in microcosm to the wider genealogical cosmos. Thus might Bukovina, labelled, in some quarters, like Canada, derisively *tiefste Provinz*,[3] serve to promote a revolution in genealogical methodology among the foot soldiers in the trenches of genealogical endeavour, and thereby gain a lustre that for this vanished land would make her the Atlantis of a New Age Genealogy.

## 2. The historical backdrop

In recent years, with the fall of the Soviet Union and the pulling back of the Iron Curtain, many of the problems associated with attempts to study people from lands formerly under communist sway have been eliminated or, at least, significantly reduced. Consequently, the rewards to the careful, and even the casual, researcher can be exhilarating. Moreover, from the viewpoint of posterity, we have reached a period when the living tradition of our family history needs to be gathered and checked against documentary sources lest the often crucial oral knowledge that provides the necessary linkage between recollection and record pass away forever with its human guardians. Now, then, is an ideal time to start to climb the "Beechwood Tree"[4] and begin an undertaking to benefit current and future generations.

For those concentrating on Bukovina, a former 4,031-square-mile[5] pocket principality, whose very name has fallen into disuse, becoming merely a geographical expression, the situation has improved sharply. Records that once were almost impossible to see are now readily accessible and new links to the former homeland are being forged between members of its North American[6] and European diaspora.[7]

From a genealogical standpoint, this process has been building quietly for years, but the evidence of the liberalisation of genealogical study in the post-communist era was really shown to have gained a noticeable head of steam in 1992 with the publication in *Der Südostdeutsche*[8] of Father Norbert Gaschler's extensive list of Bukovinian parish registers available for investigation—albeit awkwardly in certain cases. The importance of the list was two fold. First, it inventoried a fairly comprehensive mass of records. Second, the very possibility of its compilation augured well for further and more significant developments, which have, indeed, proved to be forthcoming.

The list itself was a roll-call of records of the first order of value to genealogists. Almost all the items had been long held in the close grasp of communist authorities. Through the reverend gentleman's useful, though not exhaustive,[9] accounting sheet, it became clear that new opportunities had opened up for a wider group of the interested to undertake research into Bukovina,[10] a former crownland and duchy of the Austro-Hungarian Empire now, as a unified political entity, at any rate, submerged within the eastern European countries of Ukraine[11] and Romania.[12]

The genealogical importance of this largely unsung[13] enclave is probably already clear to readers with this ancestry. On the wider stage of human history, however, the fact that many North Americans from a broad range of ethno-cultural backgrounds derive their descent from Bukovina is a largely unexplored footnote in the story of global migration. The fact remains, however, that many adult Canadians[14] and Americans, especially those of German, Jewish, Romanian, and Ukrainian ethnicity,[15] are only one to three generations removed from ancestors whose lives began, at least, in Bukovina. In western Europe, especially in Germany and Austria, for the Bukovina German ethno-cultural group, the length of time away from Bukovina is often shorter, dating from late 1940's sudden *freiwilliger Muss*. This latter population movement bears, in literal translation, the title of "Voluntary Compulsion" or resettlement to the Greater German *Reich*. It was, in reality, thrust upon Bukovina's ethnic Germans who had been Romanian subjects since 1919, and is a little-known result of wartime geopolitics. Because the scope of the collections in Father Gaschler's inventory is a direct reflection of the preoccupations of this period, 1940 serves as a watershed, both in Bukovinian history and genealogy.

Hitler's general call of *Heim ins Reich* to the world's *Volksdeutsche* (ethnic Germans)—summoning them "home to Germany" to swell Germany's population and war machine—was made the only viable option in the eyes of most Bukovina Germans by the exigencies of war in Romania, at best a minor power, caught between the Scylla and Charybdis of German and Russian foreign policy. Though strangely allied for the moment, these two great powers had—as was obvious to even the barely politically aware—differing designs on the region. Already, earlier in the year, on June 28, 1940, the Red Army had occupied northern Bukovina on the pretext of reuniting the Ukrainian-speaking majority there to the Ukraine. News of the mass deportations and murders of many members of the classes and ethno-cultural groups deemed undesirable by the Communist authorities did not take long to reach the Germans of southern Bukovina. They quite naturally felt threatened despite the fact that the Germans of the northern part, including those of the provincial capital and largest city, Czernowitz,[16] were allowed to travel to German territory more or less unmolested during the period of the Nazi-Soviet Pact.[17]

Instead of accepting Soviet reassurances that their desires for territorial expansion and ethnic integrity had been satisfied with the annexation of northern Bukovina, most Bukovina Germans in the southern, Romanian-held part of the province took the hint of their northern *Landsleute* (fellow Germans) and left for parts of German-occupied central Europe. Hitler sweetened this necessity by offering compensation for the property that the Bukovina German would have to abandon. Before going, however, Nazi officials working in Romania had to issue those departing with documentation attesting to their racial origins and "purity" for five or six generations.[18] Despite the rigorous vetting of this process, almost all of the nearly ninety thousand ethnic Germans in Bukovina in 1940 chose to endure it and were passed, leaving only a few thousand kinsmen behind to brave the local depredations of the war and its aftermath. Most of those who remained were partners in ethnically mixed marriages who were probably astute enough to realise that they would not fare particularly well in Hitler's German racial "utopia."

Thus, in 1940, eastern Europe experienced yet another wrenching mass population movement. This one effectively marks the end of the 165-year history of the Bukovina Germans as a cohesive ethnic group dwelling in their Carpathian homeland. By direct corollary, 1940 saw the closure for most of the Lutheran parishes and the end of additions to their registers. It also served as the cut-off point for additions to the Roman Catholic registers at least as regards entries pertinent to this ethnic group that are readily available for consultation in western Europe and North America. This makes 1940 a logical end date for the B.R.E.G. project, for the moment at any rate. This said, many of the records both on and off the Gaschler list have yet to be properly assessed as they have themselves only recently become truly open and subject to the examination of scholars and amateurs: so there is plenty of scope for research.[19]

## 3. New developments for research

When the first Bukovinian records were revealed to the world in the Gaschler inventory, they came as an exciting breakthrough, showing that, after years of inaccessibility,[20] there were many sources of information still miraculously in existence and awaiting exploration. The majority of the records in Father Gaschler's list, though created by ecclesiastical authorities, were, for reasons already pointed out above, collected by the *Reichssippenamt*, the German office for the determination of people's Aryan extraction, which was in operation during the years of Hitler's tyranny. As the proverb says, it is an ill wind that blows nobody any good, for it is thanks to the tidy-minded relentlessness of this macabre bureaucracy that we now have access to these records. Virtually purloined from the Romanians by the strong-arm tactics of the Nazis,[21] these records, stashed in damp German tunnels at the end of the war, were retrieved through the diligent searches of a German Mormon, Paul Langheinrich. Through his compliance with the legal niceties, one of the hallmarks of the Mormons, some 360 parish registers and related volumes eventually found their way into the hands of the new authorities, the Soviet army of occupation and thence passed to the East German government. The latter's ideologues established a successor agency to the defunct *Reichssippenamt* for the study of genealogy along Marxist lines, as a means of promoting their version of the brotherhood of man. Thus, from supporting the dubious racial science of the Nazis, the records became part of the socialist agenda at the *Zentralstelle für Genealogie*, which was established, with the transfer of the records from Potsdam to Leipzig in East Germany, on October 1, 1967. Since the reunification of the two Germanies in 1990, this office has been renamed the *Deutsche Zentralstelle für Genealogie* (the German Central Office for Genealogy, hereinafter abbreviated D.Z.f.G.).

Now under the less doctrinaire control of the German federal government, the records have been inventoried in three volumes[22] by the revamped D.Z.f.G. Additionally, the entire collection has been microfilmed[23] for the first time for international use by *The Church of Jesus Christ of Latter Day Saints* (L.D.S., i.e., the Mormons), operating under the subsidiary they have used for their aims in this area since 1894, *The Genealogical Society of Utah* (G.S.U.). The microfilmed records are now available through any of the over 2,500 L.D.S. family history centres around the globe.[24]

In addition to the D.Z.f.G.'s inventory, which generally assigns a volume number composed of four numerals, these newly filmed records have been catalogued by the Eastern European Cataloguing section at the Family History Library in Salt Lake City (hereinafter, F.H.L. and S.L.C.), under the direction of Steven W. Blodgett. There they gained their G.S.U. microfilm numbers, running to seven digits. Some films include several D.Z.f.G. volumes as individual items. The acquisition and accessioning of this material is a long-awaited development. Its excellence has been slightly marred, however, by their previous guardians' erroneous identification of some of the records. This has led to certain items being mislabelled both in the catalogue and on the films themselves. For example, a number of registers are described as Lutheran when they are, in fact, Roman Catholic. Other records have been assigned to the wrong parish,[25] or have been misidentified as to their contents, either in the F.H.L.C. or on item labels within the actual microfilms. This can prove confusing to the researcher and give the impression that the material sought after and ordered on microfilm is, after all, unavailable. Worse still, the researcher may fail to recognise the labelling or cataloguing error and presume that the person sought was not registered, whereas, in fact, they may appear if the correct material is identified and consulted. Additionally, perhaps because of the time the records spent underground, or the haste with which they were gathered in wartime, the logical sequence of parish register volumes is often broken up, so that several microfilms need to be consulted in order to get a continuous and/or complete run of the register type and years available for a given locality and denomination. Some attempt is made to sort out some of these cataloguing and labelling difficulties at the end of this paper.

Even with the material inventoried, catalogued and microfilmed, its availability, however, turned out to be only part of the answer to a genealogist's prayer. There remained the not inconsiderable problem of deciphering and interpreting the records. The microfilms may have become accessible via the Mormons (or by other means in Europe), but few people have the necessary linguistic, paleographic and historiographical skills to gain real access to the data contained on them. In effect, even though the records are on microfilms, most people cannot read them. To meet the challenges of this problem, and to make the records truly accessible to a wide range of researchers, it was recognised that new techniques needed to be employed. Thus the Bukovina Records Extraction Group's project was born.

## 4. The Bukovina Records Extraction Group: serving two agendas

The exigencies of the author's own research led to the discovery of the principle of "whole family" genealogy as a fine method for establishing otherwise elusive lines of descent.[26] It proved useful time and again to contact all people with Bukovinian ancestry—no matter how remote[27]—during the period when direct access to the primary records of greatest interest was almost impossible due to the stultifying weight of the Iron Curtain. Even now, this is a useful adjunct to solitary research into archival material. The next step was, therefore, to expand the definition of the family to its widest regional sense and to adopt the research approach of "whole community" genealogy. This makes the investigation of Bukovina genealogy one that embraces the blood and marriage ties across the entire community, turning what began as a personal project into a kind of genealogical prosopography.[28]

In a practical way, this inclusiveness takes two forms. First, a net is cast widely, choosing, because Bukovina was a remarkably multicultural enclave, to include all its inhabitants, of whatever ethnicity,[29] despite the currently limited coverage afforded some groups in the available material. A natural point of departure is the beginning of modern Bukovina, which can be dated from Austria's official acquisition of the area, previously under Russian occupation (1769-1774), from Ottoman suzerainty, by the Treaty of Constantinople signed May 7, 1775. By a happy coincidence, this year saw, as a logical extension of "Enlightenment" principles by the tidy-minded Austrians, the introduction of the very idea of maintaining civil and ecclesiastical records of the populace. These documents provide the primary resource material needed to undertake a comprehensive and systematic programme of extraction in the first place. Second, as this is a mammoth undertaking, the enlistment of members of the wider Bukovinian "kindred" to help in this endeavour allows one to embrace—with a fitting latitudinarianism—either local[30] people who have direct ties to Bukovina or at least those with links to another area of eastern and central Europe, whether ethnic Germans or not.[31] Such people are often led to join in this project because they recognise that they will benefit from the extraction process and/or its results, in gaining research skills not otherwise easily obtained and/or actual information about their own ancestors, be they direct or collateral.

So, with the problem identified and a core group of helpers found, it remained to gain authorisation and support for the project.

## 5. Practical steps

Work as a non-Mormon volunteer at the local (Ottawa, Ontario, Canada) L.D.S. family history centre put me in touch with one of the largest sources of help available to any genealogist with a project, large or small, and brought awareness of the existence of the L.D.S. extraction programme. This is a L.D.S.-sanctioned process whereby L.D.S. members, and occasionally non-Mormon volunteers, copy necessary identifying information about deceased individuals from the L.D.S. collection of microfilm and microfiche in an effort to determine each person's distinctness from all other people of the same or a similar name so that Mormon proxies can proceed to perform the various L.D.S. ordinances for the dead with a diminished likelihood of duplication. Once put through an L.D.S. temple, the names and their associated events and venues end up on *The International Genealogical Index* (I.G.I.), which makes the information available to researchers after about a three- to five-year timelag.[32]

The local family history library director, Wayne Walker, who was then Stake director for extraction, was sympathetic to this project. He was both willing and able to obtain from Salt Lake City the necessary authorisation of the Church's central extraction bureau to have the desired films, in this case for the Roman Catholic parish of Radautz (1785-1940),[33] assigned to the stake[34] for extraction.

B.R.E.G. undertook to fulfil the L.D.S. requirements for extraction, and was supplied with the forms the Church has designed for this purpose as well as a number of extraction aids to help with the challenges posed by the relevant languages and the vagaries of calendar use in that time and place. In addition to this, a second and somewhat fuller extraction of the information contained in the original records found on microfilm was planned. It involved adapting the L.D.S. forms to B.R.E.G.'s purpose so as to incorporate the extra information found in the originals so that no detail would be ignored and go unextracted.

Eventually, once the original information is extracted, the group established, *The Bukovina Records Extraction Group* (B.R.E.G.; est. February 14, 1994), will use the L.D.S. Universal Data Entry (U.D.E.) software to enter the data found onto computer. The happy upshot of this painstaking process will be that B.R.E.G. will have a complete set of the baptisms (often including birthdates), marriage banns, marriages, and burials (often with the corresponding deathdates) recorded in the subject parishes with which to reconstitute the family ties across the whole community, roughly following the methodology of the *Cambridge School of Local Population Studies.*[35]

With enough time and given the will and hard work on the part of B.R.E.G. working with as many volunteers as possible, this project could be expanded to include all of the records found covering Bukovina[36] and its offshoots.[37]

Such a project has the potential to make genealogical research in Bukovina as systematic and comprehensive a study as that field is in Quebec, and for similar reasons.[38]

## 6. The nature of the records

The records themselves are an extremely rich source of genealogical data. They include baptismal, marriage and burial registers. Kept in Latin, and occasionally in German or Polish,[39] in the case of the Roman Catholic records, a baptismal entry, after 1820, generally includes the baptised's dates of birth and baptism, sex, birth status (legitimate or illegitimate), full names, house number of birth within the community following the Austrian custom of assigning a number to every house in a community for administrative purposes[40] (distinct from the street number), the subject's father with his occupation and place of residence, mother with her former spouse, if previously married, or if not, her parentage including her father's occupation and residence, the midwife and her residence, the priest baptising, the godparents with their occupations and residences. All of this is a far cry from the sparse sort of coverage that most denominations in the British Isles and North America afford for the same event.

The marriage records contain similar data, including, from about 1820, the names and occupations of the parents of both bride and groom as well as the principals' ages, residences and religious affiliations at marriage. The corresponding marriage banns registers often supply the birthplace of the principals and may even reveal where their fathers originated before arriving in Bukovina.[41] Ideally, banns should be used in conjunction with the marriage registers, for one should be aware that not every couple that has banns read ends up at the altar. The banns register often includes the date of marriage, and may even indicate that the marriage took place in another parish, citing the name. Proofs shown to the parish priest at the time that the banns were arranged may provide an indication of baptismal place, military service, schooling, dispensations for reasons of affinity or consanguinity, and as such are much to be valued in spite of the greater difficulty that one generally encounters when trying to decipher the often abbreviated or scrawled format in which they appear.

The burial registers, particularly by the latter part of the 19th century, often furnish the name of the deceased's spouse or parents (dependant on age and marital status).

In addition, there are records of confirmation, and denominational listings of the inhabitants of towns called *Status Animarum*, which are essentially an accounting for souls, or their later, generally Protestant, counterparts, the *Familienbücher* (family registers) or *Gemeindebücher* (community registers). These records generally treat the nuclear family as a distinct unit, recording families in much the same manner as the well-known family group record.[42]

The existence of such a wealth of parish register and allied material makes it relatively easy to reconstitute nuclear families and larger family groups across the whole Bukovina German and allied communities for most of the span of Bukovina's Austrian interlude and the Romanian interwar period. Other material exists to help trace the initial immigration from the various German lands to Bukovina, while the more extensively documented late 19th-century emigration period serves to make it possible to trace Bukovina's Germans and other ethno-cultural communities from Europe to the New World. The existence of emigration, immigration, land grant and naturalisation records, as well as the establishment of new parish registers for the new land, works to allow for a dovetailing of documentation in the Old and New Worlds so that one can undertake a fairly thorough transatlantic migration study of the many thousands of Bukovinians who immigrated to Canada and the U.S. from about 1885 to 1914 and again, in smaller numbers, between the two world wars and then after World War II. Such a project is a logical extension of B.R.E.G.'s extraction and reconstitution work, and serves to bridge the apparent void between remote historical eras and distant localities, demonstrating on a microcosmic level, in a scholarly fashion, how family ties transcend frontiers of time, space, religion, culture, language and technology, which is the theme of the 22nd International Congress of Genealogical and Heraldic Sciences.

## 7. Research inspirations: the birth of B.R.E.G.

Earlier papers on Bukovinian genealogical research detail the precise manner in which direct contact with S.L.C. came about as a result of a successful identification by the current author of a parish register fragment whose identity was then uncertain. The document, which was stumbled upon in a film of mixed items including some Bukovinian material, was listed there and in the Family History Library Catalogue (F.H.L.C.) as possibly pertaining to an unknown town in *Weißrußland*.[43] The F.H.L.C. entry invited anyone with thoughts on the proper designation of the fragment's provenance to contact the S.L.C. cataloguing section. Upon doing so accurately, it took only a few weeks for a grateful cataloguing specialist to telephone the F.H.L.'s agreement with the findings.[44]

In addition, an offer was made to answer any reference queries that might be pressing. Taking full advantage of this link to the informational and research "mecca" of the genealogical world, enquiries were made about recent G.S.U. microfilm projects in central and eastern Europe, in the course of which the parish registers of the Roman Catholic parish of Maria Geburt (The Nativity of Mary) in Radautz[45] were sought.

Radautz was the county town (*Bezirkshauptstadt*) of the Bezirk[46] (i.e., county or district) in which lay the several places housing one of Bukovina's constituent communities, the inhabitants of the "Swabian villages of the plain," whose family registers are listed below. Among them was the village of Deutsch-Satulmare, a German

enclave in a larger village known by the modified name, Satulmare, to the Germans,[47] with a considerably larger, separately administered Romanian section, which, since the departure of most of the German-speaking community in 1940, has now expanded to embrace an entirely Romanianised village called Satu Mare.[48] This village is now located in the present county (in Romanian, *județul*) of Suceava. It was from here that the great-grandparents of the author, Ferdinand Zurowski (1850-1919) and Rosalie/Rosa "Rosi" Bayerle (1852-1926) emigrated in 1898 to take up land at Arrat[49] in the vicinity of the then newly established Bukovina German settlement now known as Edenwold, Saskatchewan, the early hub of much Bukovina German settlement on Canada's prairies, and a current focus of much of the Canadian end of B.R.E.G.'s reconstitution project.

From Christian Armbrüster's 1962 work, *Deutsch-Satulmare: Geschichte eines buchenländischen Pfälzersdorfes*[50] (i.e., *German Satulmare: The History of a Palatine Village in Bukovina*), it was apparent that the village's church operated as a mission chapelry (in German, *eine Filialgemeinde*, literally a daughter community, or filial) of the larger Roman Catholic parish of Radautz.[51] Thus, it was obvious that any parish register entries concerning these ancestors from Satulmare were to be found[52] in the registers of the central parish church at Radautz. Additionally, as earlier forays into "whole family and community genealogy" had revealed that a great many other Bukovina Germans came from village filials whose records were entered in these or the parallel Protestant registers, it was clear that Radautz was a parish that would play a pivotal role in enabling one to research the emigration from Bukovina to Canada. Thus, when the availability of parish registers for the Roman parish at Radautz was made known and the microfilm numbers were furnished, there started in embryonic form in the mind of the author the idea of a project such as B.R.E.G.'s.

When the microfilms were examined on their arrival in Ottawa a few weeks later, their date of microfilming was shown as May 1991. It was realised that, as their numbers had only then been available directly from S.L.C., and not in the catalogues then on microfiche or cd-rom, this was, for all practical purposes, pristine material about to undergo its first thorough examination beyond the S.L.C. cataloguing department by one of the first researchers to have direct access to these records unfettered by East German archivists.[53] It was at that moment that the author conceived of undertaking a full extraction of the material they contained. Extraction of the information imparted in these registers and its reconstitution into an integrated, organic, revivified community of the past became the objective. Nine months later, in February 1994, B.R.E.G.'s work got underway.

As with all projects undertaken in the right spirit, a kind Providence has revealed further details of the expanding horizons of genealogical research in Bukovina and its offshoots. Word percolates through the Bukovinian research grapevine[54] that people have found other, missing material at the Romanian county archives in Suceava, the seat of the district covering the southern section of the former Austrian crownland, duchy and province of Bukovina.

In addition, the second volume[55] of Dr. Patricia Kennedy Grimsted's inventory of archives in the former Soviet Union, covering Ukraine, shows that the State Archives in Chernivtsi, Bukovina's former capital, contain extensive records from the period of Austrian administration, including court records, parish registers, local censuses, and perhaps other revindicated records from the Austrian era, possibly including passport information.

All these invaluable archival fonds may well be microfilmed by the G.S.U. if negotiations proceed smoothly and individual researchers do not forestall any current or future negotiations by contacting these somewhat skittish repositories directly. To do so could possibly endanger any microfilming projects that the G.S.U. may be undertaking. If that excellent umbrella agency is allowed to pursue the necessary steps to ensure the microfilming of this invaluable material for all, then the interested can pool their energies to extract the information they contain in a comprehensive, systematic and scholarly way, working to ensure that all that is available on both sides of the Atlantic is exhaustively examined and mined for all its information.

While Bukovinian research is the topic here, it is obvious the same sort of extraction and reconstitution project could be applied to many other geographical areas or adapted for specific ethnic, linguistic or religious groups. With recent breakthroughs in computer and information exchange technology, as well as hopeful signs in terms of world peace, it is clear that the time is ripe for more family historians and genealogists, amateur and professional, to raise their sights from the simple pursuit of their own families. Instead, as more of us keep our minds open to these new developments, work will expand as a wider group of the genealogical community and those in allied disciplines embraces a broader concept of what is, at the most fundamental and obvious level, a study that shows the kindred nature of this common cause. Tackled together, sense can be made of some of the larger research aims that, once undertaken, could make everybody's research richer, more exact and more successful, truly pushing all our research frontiers across parochial barriers into the wider genealogical universe.

## 8. New records[56] for Bukovinian Protestants and Roman Catholics

An annotated list of the Bukovinian parish registers that B.R.E.G. has on hand or plans to obtain from the Family History Library in Salt Lake City for eventual extraction appears below. These are among the newly accessible records held by the present *Deutsche Zentralstelle für Genealogie* in Leipzig, which were filmed by the *Genealogical Society of Utah* in May 1991. First, the microfilm numbers for Radautz's Roman Catholic parish were obtained directly from the Eastern European Cataloguing librarian, Steven W. Blogdett, in the summer of 1993. Later, the registers of the corresponding Protestant parish of Milleschoutz, later renamed Radautz, and many of its filials' registers, were ordered and examined. In both cases, various cataloguing problems were detected, which the following lists seek to uncover and set to rights.

### 8a. Milleschoutz-Radautz Protestant parish and its chapelries

The F.H.L.C. has a number of problems in connexion with its treatment of this parish. First, it files the records of a parish commonly called Milleschoutz under the rather recondite name Obermilleschoutz [sic]. While this correctly recognizes that the parish, founded at Alt-Fratautz on May 24, 1791, with housing there for the first pastor, Stefan Daniel Wilhelm Hubel, had its offices removed, in October 1792, to the more central village of OberMilleschoutz, commonly called Milleschoutz, or at that period, Millescheuz or Millescheutz, it fails to take note of a later change. In 1862, the parish office was again transferred.

This time it was moved to the larger centre, Radautz, the seat of the local district administration, the better to serve its traditional constituency, the Swabian villages of the central Bukovinian plain. For maximum effectiveness, the records of (Ober-) Milleschoutz must, therefore, be used together with those of Radautz. German researchers have called this entity, really one in tradition and records, Milleschoutz-Radautz. It was the first Protestant parish to be founded in Bukovina. Though Lutherans constituted the bulk of its congregation from the outset until 1862, it officially served both Lutherans and Calvinists.[57] Along with the Protestant parish at Czernowitz, founded in 1795, it alone served Bukovina's Protestants for over 60 years, before having some of its larger filials made into separate parishes. Jakobeny was elevated to parochial status in 1853, with Illischestie, the largest of the German villages, made independent in 1858, and keeping its own registers from that date. Later, other filials, such as Alt-Fratautz, a parish in 1908, were erected into parishes as numbers warranted. In 1923, the united parish of Radautz-Arbora-Badeutz-Milleschoutz-Satulmare was formed with the central church remaining at Radautz. After the departure of the German Lutherans en masse in 1940, the church buildings at Radautz and Badeutz passed into Greek Orthodox hands. Its parish registers date back to 1791, with duplicates lodged at Vienna (1849-1915) and later at Hermannstadt (now Sibiu), Transylvania.

As noted above, Milleschoutz-Radautz and its various filials or mission chapelries had their own Protestant community books, which were registers of the Lutheran families who lived there during the period ca. 1860-1920. They actually refer to people born as early as the 1780s who were still alive when each record was begun, often supplying one with the name of spouses of widowed persons. They appear to have been updated periodically over the next 60 years or so,[58] with the dates of last entries varying from village to village.

| G.S.U. MFM and item (with provenance) | Place | Period | Register Type |
|---|---|---|---|
| 0038958/5 BsA 447 | Milleschoutz | 1796-1829 | Certificate copies[59] |
| 1768050/3 DZfG 3733 | Milleschoutz | 1796-1829 | Certificate copies[60] |
| 0038957/1 BsA 384[61] | Milleschoutz[62] | 1829-1861 | Certificate copies[63] |
| 1768050/4 DZfG 3734 | Milleschoutz | 1829-1861 | Certificate copies[64] |
| 1768387/6 DZfG 3719 | Milleschoutz | 1791-1808 | Baptismal index |
| 1768410/4 DZfG 3723 | Milleschoutz | 1834-1840 | Baptismal index |
| 1768387/6 DZfG 3719 | Milleschoutz | 1791-1808 | Baptismal register[65] |
| 1768410/1 DZfG 3720 | Milleschoutz | 1808-1819 | Baptismal register[66] |
| 1768410/2 DZfG 3721 | Milleschoutz | 1820-1826 | Baptismal register[67] |
| 0038958/1 BsA 311[68] | Milleschoutz | 1826-1834 | Baptismal register[69] |
| 1768410/3 DZfG 3722 | Milleschoutz | 1826-1834 | Baptismal register[70] |
| 1768410/4 DZfG 3723 | Milleschoutz | 1834-1840 | Baptismal register |
| 1768410/5 DZfG 3724 | Milleschoutz | 1840-1845 | Baptismal register |
| 1474917/5 Hexel[71] | Milleschoutz | 1848-1855[72] | Baptismal register[73] |
| 1474918/1 Hexel | Milleschoutz | 1856-1857 | Baptismal register[74] |
| 0038957/2 BsA 340[75] | Milleschoutz-Radautz[76] | 1858-1865 | Baptismal register[77] |
| 1474918/2 Hexel | Milleschoutz-Radautz[78] | 1858-1865 | Baptismal register[79] |
| 1768411/1 DZfG 3725 | Milleschoutz-Radautz | 1858-1865 | Baptismal register |
| 1474918/3 Hexel | Radautz | 1866-1876 | Baptismal register[80] |
| 1474918/4 Hexel | Radautz | 1877-1886 | Baptismal register[81] |
| 1197645/1 AS 2870 | Radautz | 1891-1896[82] | Baptismal register[83] |
| 1474919/1 Hexel | Radautz | 1896-1902 | Baptismal register[84] |
| 1474919/2 Hexel | Radautz | 1903-1915 | Baptismal register[85] |
| 1768050/2 DZfG 3732 | Milleschoutz | 1791-1829[86] | Confirmation register |
| 0038958/4 BsA 411 | Milleschoutz-Radautz | 1859-1890 | Confirmation register[87] |
| 1768249/4 DZfG 3757 | Milleschoutz-Radautz[88] | 1858-1890 | Confirmation register[89] |

| | | | |
|---|---|---|---|
| 0038957/6 BsA 419[90] | Radautz[91] | 1890-1938 | Confirmation register[92] |
| 1768249/5 DZfG 3758 | Radautz | 1890-1939 | Confirmation register[93] |
| 1768412/5 DZfG 3767 | Radautz | 1896-1903 | Banns register |
| 1768413/2 DZfG 3768 | Radautz | 1903-1911 | Banns register |
| 1768413/2 DZfG 3769 | Radautz | 1912-1940 | Banns register |
| 1768049/1 DZfG 3726 | Milleschoutz | 1796-1848 | Mixed marriage index[94] |
| 1768044/4 DZfG 3747/1 | Milleschoutz | 1802-1827[95] | Marriage register |
| 0038957/3 BsA 470[96] | Milleschoutz[97] | 1829-1849[98] | Marriage register[99] |
| 1768049/2 DZfG 3727 | Milleschoutz | 1828-1850 | Marriage register |
| 0038957/4 BsA 467[100] | Milleschoutz[101] | 1851-1857[102] | Marriage register[103] |
| 1768049/3 DZfG 3728 | Milleschoutz | 1851-1857 | Marriage register |
| 1768248/1 DZfG 3753/1 | Milleschoutz | 1857-1858 | Marriage register[104] |
| 1474919/3 Hexel | Milleschoutz-Radautz | 1849-1889 | Marriage register[105] |
| 1474919/4 Hexel | Radautz | 1890-1915 | Marriage register[106] |
| 1768049/4 DZfG 3729 | Milleschoutz | 1791-1824 | Burial index |
| 1768049/4 DZfG 3729 | Milleschoutz | 1791-1824 | Burial register |
| 0038958/3 BsA 310[107] | Milleschoutz | 1825-1844 | Burial register[108] |
| 1768049/5 DZfG 3730 | Milleschoutz | 1825-1844 | Burial register |
| 0038957/5 BsA 322[109] | Milleschoutz[110] | 1844-1857 | Burial register[111] |
| 1768050/1 DZfG 3731 | Milleschoutz | 1844-1857 | Burial register[112] |
| 1474919/5 Hexel | Milleschoutz | 1849-1858 | Burial register[113] |
| 1474920/1 Hexel | Milleschoutz-Radautz | 1859-1888 | Burial register |
| 1474920/2 Hexel | Radautz | 1889-1915 | Burial Register |
| 1768412/1 DZfG 3763 | Radautz | 1869-1898 | Family register[114] |
| 1768412/2 DZfG 3764 | Radautz | 1869-1893 | Family register[115] |
| 0038958/6 BsA 441 | Radautz | 1869-1912 | Conversions book[116] |
| 1768413/3 DZfG 3770 | Radautz | 1869-1912 | Conversions book |
| 1768413/4 DZfG 3771 | Radautz | 1913-1935 | Conversions book |
| 1768246/1 DZfG 3596 | Alt-Fratautz | 1869-1919[117] | Family register |
| 0038934/2 BsA 445 | Alt-Fratautz | 1910-1939 | Family register |
| 1767910/3 DZfG 3608 | Arbora | 1862-1905 | Family register |
| 1768350/2 DZfG 3632 | Illischestie | 1840-1858 | Baptismal register |
| 1768350/3 DZfG 3633 | Illischestie | 1858-1866 | Baptismal register |
| 1474915/3 Hexel | Illischestie | 1858-1874 | Baptismal register[118] |
| 1474915/4 Hexel | Illischestie | 1875-1876 | Baptismal register[119] |
| 1474916/1 Hexel | Illischestie | 1876-1915 | Baptismal register[120] |
| 1768350/4 DZfG 3634 | Illischestie | 1857-1874 | Marriage register[121] |
| 1474917/1 Hexel[122] | Illischestie | 1858-1889[123] | Marriage register[124] |
| 1474917/2 Hexel[125] | Illischestie | 1890-1915[126] | Marriage register[127] |
| 1768351/1 DZfG 3635 | Illischestie | 1858-1873 | Burial register[128] |
| 1474917/3 Hexel | Illischestie | 1858-1894[129] | Burial register[130] |
| 1474917/4 Hexel | Illischestie | 1895-1915[131] | Burial register[132] |
| 0038944/1 BsA 454 | Illischestie | 1860-1936 | Family register/index |
| 1768048/3 DZfG 3639 | Illischestie | 1860-1936 | Family register/index[133] |
| 1768047/2 DZfG 3636 | Illischestie | 1860-1932 | Family register vol. 1 |
| 1768047/3 DZfG 3636 | Illischestie | 1860-1932 | Family register vol. 1 |
| 1768048/1 DZfG 3637 | Illischestie | 1880-1935 | Family register vol. 2 |
| 1768048/2 DZfG 3638 | Illischestie | 1900-1936 | Family register vol. 3 |
| 1768048/4 DZfG 3640 | Illischestie | 1880-1925 | Family register |
| 0038936/1 BsA 442 | Illischestie/Balaczana[134] | 1900-1929 | Family register |
| 1768077/1 DZfG 3641 | Illischestie/Balaczana | 1900-1929 | Family register |
| 1768051/1 DZfG 3735 | Neu-Itzkany | 1904-1937 | Family register |

| | | | |
|---|---|---|---|
| 1768414/1 DZfG 3775 | Satulmare | 1860-1915 | Family register |
| 1768250/3 DZfG 3761 | Tereblestie | 1840-1890 | Combined registers[135] |
| 1768338/5 DZfG 3809 | Tereblestie | 1875-1910 | Family register |

### 8b. Radautz Roman Catholic parish and its chapelries[136]

As with the corresponding Protestant parish, the Roman parish at Radautz was one of the oldest in Bukovina. Czernowitz, Sereth, Suczawa, and Istensegits alone were older, having been founded in the mid to late 1770s. First revitalised as an Austrian garrison town, Radautz became the centre of one of the most important military horse studs in the Empire. As such, there were many visiting soldiers, some of whom stayed long enough to father illegitimate children in Bukovina, and possibly to marry and settle. In the former instance, their names, sheepishly acknowledging paternity, often appear upside-down in the

civilian registers. The presence of others may be recorded in military and field hospital chaplains' registers not listed here. Such records, at any rate, are largely only available from the mid 19th century, and seem not to contain many names of local people, so their relevance to this project is limited. The first registers for the parish filials began, however, with parallel military[137] and civilian[138] baptismal and burial records, which cover only a brief period (1785-1790, 1802). In the case of the latter, they contain some names that later appear among the lists of Catholic and Protestant German colonists.[139] The filials' entries begin again, after a nearly 20-year gap, in 1820.

| G.S.U. MFM and item (with provenance) | Place | Period | Register Type |
|---|---|---|---|
| 1768250/4 DZfG 3762 | Radautz | 1900-1940 | Family register[140] |
| 1768043/2 DZfG 3742 | Radautz[141] | 1785-1817 | Baptismal register[142] |
| 1768250/2 DZfG 3760 | Radautz[143] | 1785-1850[144] | Combined registers[145] |
| 1768043/3 DZfG 3743 | Radautz | 1785-1940 | Baptismal register index[146] |
| 1768043/4 DZfG 3744 | Radautz | 1819-1838 | Baptismal register |
| 1768044/1 DZfG 3745 | Radautz | 1838-1850 | Baptismal register |
| 1768044/2 DZfG 3746 | Radautz | 1850-1860 | Baptismal register |
| 1768250/1 DZfG 3759 | Radautz | 1931-1936 | Confirmation register |
| 1768044/7 DZfG 3750 | Radautz | 1818-1849 | Banns register |
| 1768247/3 DZfG 3752 | Radautz | 1849-1867 | Banns register |
| 1768249/1 DZfG 3754 | Radautz | 1868-1880 | Banns register |
| 1768249/2 DZfG 3755 | Radautz | 1879-1900 | Banns register |
| 1768249/3 DZfG 3756 | Radautz | 1925-1940 | Banns register |
| 1768044/6 DZfG 3749 | Radautz | 1817-1940 | Marriage register index[147] |
| 1768044/3 DZfG 3747 | Radautz | 1786-1817 | Marriage register |
| 1768044/5 DZfG 3748 | Radautz | 1817-1836 | Marriage register |
| 1768247/2 DZfG 3751 | Radautz | 1835-1851 | Marriage register |
| 1768247/4 DZfG 3753 | Radautz | 1852-1883 | Marriage register |
| 1768412/4 DZfG 3766 | Radautz | 1817-1940 | Burial index[148] |
| 1768042/3 DZfG 3765 | Radautz | 1790-1816 | Burial register |
| 1055356/3 KKBA München[149] | Radautz | 1816-1853 | Burial register |

# NOTES

1. **About the author**. Richard Carruthers-Żurowski is a professional genealogist who pursues Bukovinian research as an ongoing project of personal interest. His Bukovinian lines are: *Żurowski* of Czernowitz, Kaczyka and Deutsch-Satulmare; *Bayerle* and *Hoffmann* of Badeutz; *Karst* of Sereth and St. Onufry; *Schröder* and *Zettel* of Karlsberg; *Pöllmann* (alias *Bellmann*) of Fürstenthal; *Engelhardt/Englert* of Mardzina, all of which are Roman Catholic; and *Mang* and *Göttel*, of Badeutz-Milleschoutz, both Lutheran. An honours graduate (1987) in Modern History from Balliol College, Oxford, and former writing and publications officer in the Heritage Cultures and Languages Programme of the federal department of Multiculturalism and Citizenship, he gathered material on the history of the settlement of people from Bukovina in Canada (ca. 1885 to date), for his second chapter, *Between Imperial Hinterlands: Canada's Bukovina German Immigrants 1885-1914*, in the recently published book, *German Emigration from Bukovina to the New World* (Max Kade Center for German-American Studies, University of Kansas at Lawrence, 1996), which was a joint project with the Bukowina-Institut, and the Raimund-Friedrich-Kaindl Gesellschaft, both of Augsburg, Germany. His other chapter, *Climbing the Beechwood Tree: Bukovinian Genealogical Research*, appeared in somewhat different forms, in the journals of the American Family Records Association (*Family Records Today*, October 1994) and the Saskatchewan Genealogical Society (*Bulletin*, June 1995). The author has developed an extensive computer database of individuals with ties to the Bukovina. One can send in queries and contributions in written or diskette form to him at 34a, Acacia Avenue, Rockcliffe Park, Ontario K1M 0P4, CANADA. Tel.: (613) 749-3825. E-mail: cw372@freenet.carleton.ca

2. Visions of burnt out churches and archives and bonfires of parish registers and vital records destroyed by warfare or malicious regimes have filled the heads of more than a generation.

3. W. H. Auden, the English poet.

4. Bukovina means "Land of Beeches," so named because of the extensive forests of beech trees to be found there.

5. 10,422 square kilometres.

6. There is now, thanks to the work of Bukovina genealogist Larry Jensen, and the wonders of "cyberspace," a Bukovina Society of the Americas (B.S.A.) website, under the overarching umbrella organisation the Federation of East European Family History Societies (F.E.E.F.H.S.). It can be accessed two ways, either through the F.E.E.F.H.S. site at: http://feefhs.org or via Larry's address: http://members.aol.com/LJensen/bukovina.html.

This website covers many pages, and, among other items of interest, contains a growing contact list of Bukovina genealogists, with their e-mail and regular postal addresses and interests. This is updated several times a month by the webmaster, to whom one can e-mail or post a submission. One does not even have to be linked to a modem yet to benefit from this research tool, though, of course, this will increase the speed of one's contacts. The website is also "hotlinked" (connected at the stroke of a key) to other websites related to Bukovina, such as that of Chernivtsi State University and the Unofficial City of Chernivtsi homepage. My own project, Bukovina Records Extraction Group, is listed there as is a description of my research interests in brief and detailed form along with a brief sketch of my research collection. Via modem one can exchange entire genealogical databases, though at present, while I am willing to check the over 20,000 Bukovina-related records stored in the L.D.S. Personal Ancestral File (P.A.F.) format for enquirers' surnames, I cannot do this with my file.

On Feb. 28, 1997, a Bukovinian genealogical listserv (e-mail discussion group), with the e-mail address bukovina-gen@gpfn.sk.ca, was opened on the Great Prairie FreeNet in Saskatchewan. The co-owners and chief advisors for the group were Beverly Muntain, G.P.F.N. president, Larry Jensen, and myself. Within a month, the number of subscribers reached 80. The list continues to gain several new subscribers each week, and initial subscription messages should be sent to listproc@gpfn.sk.ca with the simple e-mail message SUBSCRIBE BUKOVINA-GEN followed by one's name. This enables one to post messages to the list, which is one of many interest groups available at the sponsoring service provider.

7. An example of this is the agreement for scholarly cooperation forged between the Bukowina-Institut, Munich, Germany, and the University of Chernivtsi, Ukraine due to be signed in August 1997.

8. This is the organ of the Bukovina German organisation in Germany the *Landsmannschaft der Buchenlanddeutschen*. The article was entitled "*Aufbewahrungsstellen der Kirchenbücher bukowiner Pfarreien*" (i.e., Whereabouts of the Registers of Bukovinian Parishes), and appeared on p. 3-4 of the issue dated April 15, 1992. Apart from the records held by the D.Z.f.G., it lists (i) Roman Catholic registers held by the *Bischöflichen Zentralarchiv* (i.e., Diocesan Central Archive), *St. Peters-Weg* 13, D-93047, *Regensburg*, Germany, (ii) Lutheran and Calvinist registers in the *Archiv des Evang. Oberkirchenrates A. und H.B.* (i.e., Archive of the Evangelical Lutheran and Reformed High Church Council), *Severingasse*, A-1186, Vienna, Austria, (iii) Roman Catholic registers, particularly for parts of northern Bukovina now in Ukraine, held by the *Archivum Archidiencezjalne w Poznaniu (Poznań* Archidiocesan Archives), *ul. Lubranskiego* 1, Pl-61-108 *Poznań*, Poland, (iv) Roman Catholic registers for Andrásfalva, deposited in *Archiv des Rim. kat. ured Žednik-Wojwodina*, in Voivodina, part of the former Yugoslavia, (v) and (vi) registers for individual parishes held parochially in Hungary and Romania, and (vii) in the State Archives of Chernivtsi, Ukraine, the complete set of the original registers of Baptism, Marriage and Burial for the Roman Catholic parish of Czernowitz (1775-1946), partial duplicates and inferior draught copies of which are in the D.Z.f.G., and are what is available on G.S.U. MFMs. Not listed in this inventory are any records housed at the southern part of Bukovina in Suceava. One can now write for inventory information, if not for actual research work, to Professor Gavril Irimescu, *Director, Filiala Arhivelor Statului, Str. Stefan Cel Mare Nr* 33, 5800 *Suceava*, Romania, but a letter sent there by B.R.E.G. did not have any of its questions as to the archives' holdings. Instead, probably due to internal regulations, it was forwarded to the National Archives in Bucharest, from which a brief response was sent to Canada granting access to conduct research in the Suceava County Archives. To ensure delivery, it is advisable to send letters double-registered so that one gets word of the letter's safe arrival. In addition, should one

want a reply, it would be wise to enclose several International Reply Coupons (I.R.C.).

9. The list is made up solely of Roman Catholic and Protestant records, pertaining to two important, but minority, groups in Bukovina. Neither the whereabouts nor the existence of the records of the majority ethno-religious groups, the Greek Orthodox and Catholic Romanians and Ukrainians, as well as other significant Bukovinian minorities, the Jews, Armenian Catholics, Russian Old Believer Philippovans or Lippowaners, etc., is dealt with in this survey.

10. This is the region's correct English-language name which is derived from a Slavic root, meaning land of beech trees, or "Beechwood." Its neighbour, the fabled Transylvania (the German *Siebenbürgen*, "seven citadels"), takes its name from the Latin for "land across the forest," i.e., from the Beechwood. It is an area that was once a political entity, but now exists only in the memories of many people of Bukovina German, and other Bukovinian ancestry, as a vaguely imagined geographical expression that is notoriously difficult for both the neophyte and the well-versed to locate on the map. The Anglo-Saxon world has relegated it to the very edge of any chart of the Balkans, central or eastern Europe, or the former Soviet Union. Even under the best pre-First World War conditions, when it boasted the eastern-most German-language university in the Austro-Hungarian Empire, the Franz-Josef at Czernowitz (founded 1875), and representation in the Imperial diet in Vienna, it was still considered to be '*tiefste Provinz*'—aptly enough a phrase applied by the English poet W.H. Auden to Canada, the land to which many of its sons and daughters immigrated—meaning the deepest province, i.e., the sticks. It was here that those unfortunate enough to be in bad odour with His Imperial and Royal Majesty's government in Vienna were sent on perpetual postings, the usual 19th-century version of exile to Elba under an enlightened Danubian Throne. The best known of these is, of course, Colonel Redl, made famous in the film of the same name.

Bukovina was known under many guises in the lands that adjoined it and fed it with settlers, speaking a plethora of languages, making it what Dr. Sophie Welisch has described as a "microcosm of Europe." It is Bukowina or Buchenland to the Germans, Bukowina to the Poles, Bucovina to the Romanians, and, among others, appears in a Roman-character transliteration of the Cyrillic original as Bukovyna to Ukrainian eyes (a spelling erroneously employed by their intelligentsia even when writing in English in Canada). The correct spelling of the region, though of long coinage, has, perhaps unsurprisingly, been the subject of a lamentable confusion. This is apparent in the multiplicity of odd, bad, and foreign spellings for the area cited, out of contextual circumstances that justify the employment of foreign forms, in a proliferation of family histories and many three-quarter century histories of Saskatchewan localities. Indeed, so profound is ignorance on this point that it is not only amateurs who make errors in this matter, but also, otherwise reputable, professional bodies. Thus, the descriptive placards used on public display in a Ukrainian exhibit at the Canadian Museum of Civilization in Hull honouring the centenary of the arrival of the first Ukrainian settlers in Canada (in 1891) employed a foreign spelling, while some of the photographs used to show the faces of Ukrainian settlers of the Prairie provinces were of known Bukovina Germans, such as Peter Galenzoski, anglicised from the germanised Galenczowsky (1860-1936), a farmer from Deutsch-Satulmare in the county of Radautz in central Bukovina who immigrated via Balgonie to Neu-Tulscha (later Edenwald, now Edenwold, Saskatchewan), two years earlier, in 1889. While the Galenzoskis, originally Gałęcowski, were of Polish descent patrilineally, which is easy enough for the uninitiated to confuse with Ukrainian, the photos also included Carl [*sic*] Mang, clearly an ethnic German.

As we emerge from the Dark Ages, Bukovina was first a region ruled by the Romanian princes of Moldavia and Wallachia, whose principalities were conquered by the Ottoman Turks, remaining, if only nominally, under the suzerainty of the "Sublime Porte" until 1774, when the Austrians demanded it outright from the Russians, who had been occupying it since 1769. The Russian Empire was then at war with what was fast becoming the "sick man of Europe" and had to hand over Bukovina as the price for Austria's continued neutrality. The Habsburg emperors added Bukovina officially to their list of domains and titles on May 7, 1775 under the terms of the Treaty of Constantinople.

From 1775 to 1918, Bukovina was the eastern-most territory of the Austrian and later the Austro-Hungarian Empire. First classified as an Austrian military district (1775-1787), and then as the 19th district (in German *Kreis*, literally circle) of the kingdom of Galicia and Lodomeria (February 1, 1787-March 3, 1849), it was administered from Lemberg (the Polish Lwów, now the Ukrainian city of L'viv, known in German as Lemberg and in Latin as Leopolis, literally "City of the Lion," which the Austrian Habsburgs had gained at the first partition of the Polish-Lithuanian Commonwealth in 1772). It then became separate as a duchy and crownland of the Austrian Empire (March 4, 1849-April 21, 1859). Then, after being reduced in status for another stint as a *Kreis* of Galicia from April 22, 1859 to 1861, it regained its status as a separate crownland of the Austrian Empire pending the signing of a legal act finally dated December 9, 1862. This status did not change when the nomenclature of the Empire itself was revised to reflect the changes made in 1867.

Instead, it saw its final form as an Austrian crownland under the new constitutional arrangements of the Dual Monarchy known to us as the Austro-Hungarian Empire (1867-1918), comprising the Empire of Austria and the restive kingdom of Hungary.

As an entity so-called, Austria dated from 1804, and was elevated to the status of an empire from that of an archduchy to ensure that the Habsburgs remained emperors even after Napoleon began to call for the abdication of the Habsburg Holy Roman Emperor which led, in 1806, to the effective abolition of that 1000-year-old anachronism, the Holy Roman Empire of the German Nation, the first *Reich*, nominally founded by Charlemagne in 800 and later consolidated by Otto II with the agreement of the Pope in the year 962. This was an important question of status to the House of Habsburg because for the previous 400 years tradition had decreed that the throne of the Holy Roman Empire had been occupied by a Habsburg archduke, even though the emperor could in theory be elected by the college of elector princes (such as the Electors of Hanover, who from 1714-1837 were also kings of Great Britain) from any of the many eligible Catholic sovereign rulers of Germany. The political realities of the day, in fact, favoured the Habsburgs against a field of princelings from the various, mostly petty (saving the ambitious Prussia and strategic Bavaria) states known collectively as "the Germanies." This, until Bismarck's masterful declaration of German unification at Versailles in 1871, was the only way one could speak of the ragged patchwork quilt of lay and ecclesiastical fiefdoms that covered an ill-defined area between France and Denmark. Germany, until 1871, was a geographical term only, much as Italy had been until its unification some 20 years prior.

Though the Habsburgs had long before become the royal house of Hungary through marrying the heiress of the House of Arpád, founder of the Magyar's royal dynasty, it was only from 1848 onward that its nobles and burghers gained sufficient force within the Empire to make good on their greater internal autonomy from Vienna as a result of the revolutions which swept Europe, and Hungary under Kossuth, in that year. This emerging clout culminated in a political division of the Empire that led to Bukovina's being designated under the new arrangements of Austria-Hungary as an Austrian imperial crownland, where Austrian German influence predominated over that of Budapest.

After the disastrous 1914-1918 war, Bukovina was briefly at loose ends and free to choose its own course. Austria-Hungary was discredited as an Central power in World War I, and the victorious allies were speedily dismembering her. Bukovina elected to cast its lot with Romania, a minor victorious ally, as the Romanian army was then in occupation and the Russian Empire, under the Bolsheviks, was in turmoil. Thus, it took its last form under a single flag as Bucovina, now an umbrella term rather than a province in the interwar kingdom of Romania (1918-1940), made up of several counties which assumed the administration of the territory.

In 1940, it was partitioned along the Suczawa river, between the then Axis allies, the Soviet Union and a briefly fascist Romania (whose boy-king, Michael, at 16, overthrew in a bloodless palace coup his fascist Iron Guard premier, Antonescu). As such, the partition, though interrupted by three years of German occupation (1941-1944), was, ironically and tragically, one of the few lasting geopolitical legacies of the palmier days of the Nazi-Soviet pact, linchpin of the "phoney war" period of World War II.

This arrangement has been inherited by their successor states, the independent republic of Ukraine, member of the loosely bound Commonwealth of Independent States, and a republic of Romania still ruled by former Communists, who refuse to allow their hero king back into the country from his exile in Switzerland, even to do vital, charitable work or act as a force for stability, reconciliation and the rule of law.

In theory, the Ukraine controls the predominantly Ukrainian-speaking areas north of the Suczawa river, while Romania rules the remaining two-thirds of the former duchy, south of the river, where the indigenous population has always been largely Romanophone.

The minority Jews, Hungarians, Poles and Germans have either left or been assimilated after 50 years of war and Communist tyranny. Some of the despised Gypsies remain, but they pour, instead, into western Europe where they are seen as a threat to public order.

Today, divided Bukovina, a tiny Balkan Switzerland, is a relative backwater, noted for the splendour of its frescoed monasteries, the authenticity of its folk music, and the picturesque quality of its unspoilt scenery. The poverty one encounters there, particularly in the Romanian section, which barely escaped the bulldozing of its villages and the erection of the agro-industrial complexes that the dictator Ceauşescu envisaged in his final megalomania is, by all reports, grinding, and the plight of its inhabitants, truly pathetic. If anything, Bukovina has regressed from the apogee of its modernity, reached in 1914, back to the Middle Ages. The traditional dress of the Romanian peasant and shepherd and the bucolic rusticity of the area are part of everyday life in a region that receives few tourists. All this serves to make it once again what its first Austrian military governor, General V. Spleny, called it in 1775, *"Bukowina: Eine Stille Reserve,"* Bukovina: a quiet backwater, full of undiscovered potential.

11. The part of Bukovina included in the present-day republic of Ukraine is the northern section of the former province, centred on the old imperial crownland's capital, Czernowitz, a city now to be found on maps under the guise of its transliterated Ukrainian Cyrillic name, Chernivtsi, seat of the local county ("oblast") government.

12. Covering the remaining two-thirds of the former duchy, located to the south of the Suczawa river, and centred on the Romanian city of Suceava (formerly Suczawa under the Austrians), the capital of the present-day Romanian county of the same name.

13. Unsung, that is, in the English language, with the notable exception of the scholarly publications of Dr. Sophie Welisch, Professor Emerita of History at the Dominican College at Blauvelt, New York. This is not the case in German, where there are two complementary bibliographies of the region by Erich Beck. There is, however, a useful guide to the region, *Galicia and Bukovina: A Research Handbook about Western Ukraine, Late 19th-20th Centuries*, by Prof. JOHN-PAUL HIMKA, issued in March 1990 as the Historical Sites Service's Occasional Paper no. 20, by the Alberta ministry of Culture and Multiculturalism, but now, unfortunately, out-of-print.

14. Particularly in the district around Regina, notably Edenwold, Southey, Pilot Butte, Cupar, and Markinch, and near Melville, the Catholic settlement at Grayson-Mariahilf, centred on St. Elizabeth's parish, Killaly, childhood parish of the R.C. Archbishop of Vancouver (B.C.), the Most Reverend Adam Exner. In the southwest of the province are the Maxstone district and Spring Valley.

15. Examples of well-known people whose ancestors come from such backgrounds are not hard to find. Canada's recent Governor-General, The Right Hon. Ramon John Hnatyshyn, spoke of his Bukovinian origins on Peter Gzowski's *Morningside* programme shortly before departing the viceregency. I have noted people of his surname in the R.C. registers for Czernowitz, though his family was from nearby Waschkoutz am Czeremosch (in turn-of-the-century Ukrainian in the official gazetteer of Imperial Austria, the *Gemeindelexikon der im Reichsrate Vertretenen Königreiche und Länder*, vol. 13: *Bukovina*, Vienna, 1907, this appears as Waszkiwci nad Czeremoczem) near the southern border of an even larger source of Ukrainian Canadians, Austrian Galicia. The Alberta artist, William Kurelek (1927-1977), produced a book of paintings of Bukovina, celebrating his parents' homeland. Both are of Bukovina Ukrainian origin. Bukovina Germans include the current Roman Catholic archbishop

of Vancouver (B.C.), The Most Rev. Adam Exner, whose parents came from Molodia near Czernowitz, and the actor, John Vernon (formerly Adolf Agopsowicz), star of C.B.C.'s *Wojeck*, now in re-runs, a second cousin of my father.

16. Cernăuți (Romanian), Chernovtsy (Russian, transliterated), Chernivtsi (Ukrainian, transliterated).

17. They were allowed to take many of their smaller movables, but were obliged to leave behind their parish registers. Those parish records that have ended up in western hands were draught copies or imperfect seconds for the most part. Much material remains in the Chernivtsi oblast (county) archives, as yet unmicrofilmed by the Mormons.

18. They were issued with passport documents by the German authorities whom the Romanians were obliged to allow into their country to process the ethnic Germans for resettlement. These papers, called *Ahnenpässe* (literally, ancestry passports), are a valuable, if sometimes inaccurate, source of genealogical data. Many have been collected by the Bukowina-Institut in Augsburg. It should be noted that sometimes a three-generation *Kleiner Ahnenpass* was drawn up for poorer applicants as these documents, which Dr. Welisch reports were not mandatory, had to be paid for by the emigrants.

19. There is the 165-year period for which documentation is on hand via the Mormons. In addition, for those who can present themselves to the authorities in Kiev and Bucharest, there is even limited access to the records housed in the regional archives in Ukraine and Romania. These latter have yet to undergo even a general survey to assess what exists for what years, places and ethno-cultural or religious groups.

20. A minority of the material had been in the Mormon's catalogues since 1949, particularly the Lutheran registers filmed at Berlin-Dahlem in 1949 through the good offices of the German Mormon genealogist and record-searcher, Paul Langheinrich. As late as 1979, Father Gaschler was only able to write of Bukovina's parish registers from the historical perspective, working from occasional fragments to gain an idea of the wider picture. His article *"Die Kirchenbücher der Bukowina,"* which appeared in *Kaindl-Archiv (Mitteilungen der Raimund Friedrich Kaindl Gesellschaft)*, Heft 2, Stuttgart, (1979) surveyed the history of the Lutheran, Reformed, Roman, Greek, and Armenian Catholic, and Greek Orthodox and Russian Orthodox "Old Believer" (Philippovan) parishes and their registers. The inventory of parishes that comes at the end of the article served as the basis for Father Gaschler's later publication.

21. The Romanians transferred the records to the *Reichssippenamt* under contract dated October 24, 1940.

22. *Bestandverzeichnis der Deutschen Zentralstelle für Genealogie Leipzig, Teil I: Die Kirchenbuchunterlagen der österlichen Provinzen Posen, Ost- und Westpreußen, Pommern und Schlesien*, Verlag Degener and Co., Neustadt/Aisch, 1991, and *Teil II: Die archivalischen und Kirchenbuchunterlagen deutscher Siedlungsgebiete im Ausland: Bessarabien, Bukowina, Estland, Lettland und Lituaen, Siebenbürgen, Sudetenland, Slowenien und Südtirol*, Verlag Degener and Co., Neustadt/Aisch, 1992, and a recently published third volume covering the records of pre-World War II Germany.

23. Or re-microfilmed in the case of certain records, mostly Lutheran registers, already filmed once by the Mormons in 1949 at the former records repository in Berlin-Dahlem before worsening relations after the Berlin blockade closed that window of opportunity.

24. The *Genealogical Society of Utah* has not been able to gain access to any of the archives in Romania to begin filming any of the missing parish registers pertaining either to the ethnic German population of Bukovina or to its other ethno-cultural groups. In the case of Ukraine, while the G.S.U. is filming material in a number of archives, the Chernivtsi oblast archives is not among the repositories where microfilming is currently taking place, nor is it currently being planned or negotiated according to my contacts in S.L C. Foremost among these is the personable Steven W Blodgett, of the cataloguing division of F.H.L., whom I have elsewhere credited with giving me an indirect impetus to begin B.R.E.G. He can now be contacted via e-mail at blodgettsw@chqbyu.edu or, for callers in North America, toll-free at 1-800-453-3860 ext. 2312.

25. This has led to some bemusing and tiresome errors. One such is the assertion in the International Genealogical Index (I.G.I.) that there was a united Lutheran-Roman Catholic parish at Czernowitz, which it describes as *Czernowitz evangelisch-katholisch*. An examination of the microfilmed originals reveals that this is likely to have been due to an unqualified person's failing to realise during inventorying that the Lutheran pastor for the congregation at Czernowitz used a pre-printed Roman Catholic baptismal register book to record his Lutheran baptisms. The denominations got on well enough in Bukovina for it to have been mentioned by scholars, but the level of ecumenism that the I.G.I.'s nomenclature implies exceeds even current practice! Reference ought to be made to internal indicators such as the language and terminology used. Most Lutheran records were kept in German, while the majority of Roman Catholic material, apart from the semi-formal banns registers, which could be kept in the vernacular, were kept in Latin.

Recently, I discovered that an item on a microfilm (G.S.U. MFM 0038941, item 3) claiming to contain the burial index (1778-1837) for Czernowitz Roman Catholic parish is, in point of fact, the index for the burial registers, also available (G.S.U. MFM 1766999, item 2, labelled Sterbefälle, 1777-1836. Former D.Z.f.G. vol. 3787), for the Roman Catholic parish of Sereth. All the names that I thought ought to appear in the index (Ganczar, Sanocki, Żurowski) did not appear therein, whereas all sorts of familiar Sereth register names (Karst, Flamann, Henz) did appear in the index, with the correct page numbers from the corresponding burial register.

26. For a good discussion of this, consult EUGENE A. STRATTON'S, *Applied Genealogy* (Ancestry Publishing: 1988).

27. Remoteness is in the mind of the considerer. Most non-genealogists think that anyone beyond a first cousin is remote. In dealing with Bukovina Germans, even when one considers those *"Mischlinge"* (mixtures) such as myself whose Bukovinian blood is not completely German, almost everybody who has any Bukovina German ancestry is related or connected by marriage ties to everybody else of the same ethnicity. Time and again Bukovina Germans who think they are unrelated to one another

turn out to be fourth or fifth cousins, often several different ways, of one another. If there is a qualification to any of this, it appears that there is a bit of a divide between Catholics and Protestants, though even then, in the absence of a direct blood relationship, marriage ties generally exist to connect Bukovina German Catholics to their Protestant compatriots. In the case of B.R.E.G., the three chief officers are all connected by marriage to the Żurowski family. My earlier paper, "Climbing the Beechwood Tree: New Directions in Bukovinian Genealogical Research" describes this phenomenon in greater detail.

28.  Prosopography is group biography, a science very much akin to genealogy. Some other researchers interested in Bukovina have begun similar work. Larry R. Jensen and Sophie Welisch are reconstituting the inhabitants of Bori, alias Boureni, Bukovina. Mr. Jensen's address is 24, Penny Lane, Ithaca, New York 14850-6267, USA. E-mail: LJensen@aol.com, while Dr. Welisch's is 2, Hughes Street, Congers, New York 10920-1816. She is computerised, but not databased with a genealogical software program, and is also not up on the internet via modem.

Johann Christian Dressler's genealogical study of the people of Illischestie has been translated and published by Irmgard Hein Ellingson. She invites submissions from descendants of emigrants for inclusion in a supplement she is preparing. Her address is P.O. Box 97, Ossian, Iowa 52161-0097, U.S.A.

In Germany, the *Arbeitsgemeinschaft ostdeutscher Familienforscher* (AGoFF) (The Work Group for Family Historians of the German East), advises us that the coordination of research into Bukovina, has been handed on to Dipl.-Ing. Kurt Neumann, Platanenstraße 13, D-58644, Iserlohn, Germany, Tel.: (0 23 71) 52 32 37, since the death in August 1994 of the eminent genealogist of Bukovina and Galicia, Ernst Hexel. Since 1995, Herr Neumann has been joined in this work by Manfred Daum, Haferkamp 25, 29525 Ülzen, Germany. Tel.: (05 81) 26 28. Additionally, Dr. Claudius v. Teutul, a native Bukovina German, resident in Germany, has established the *Forschungstelle zur Genealogie im ehemaligen Herzogtum Bukowina* (The Genealogical Research Centre for the former Duchy of Bukovina), for which he launched a website on October 24, 1996 at the following URL, viz.: http://www.pils.de/~cvt/gene with various subsections detailing his interests. The Bukovina-Institut in Germany has launched its own website, temporarily housed on the homepages of member Norbert Rindle, at the URL http://home.t-online.de/home/Norbert-Rindle/buko1.htm where there are several sections dealing with genealogy, language and culture, as well as the holdings of the Institut's library.

29.  Not solely the ethnic Germans so often studied in isolation.

30.  The Ottawa area, where I was fortunate enough to find, via contacts made at the local F.H.C. (then under the 17-year tenure of erstwhile director, Wayne W. Walker, who acted as midwife to B.R.E.G., by gaining the necessary approval for the L.D.S. aspect of the extraction project from S.L.C.), my original group of extractors: Mr. and Mrs. George G. Hopp (both of at least partially German origin, though it is Mrs. Hopp who has ties to Bukovina, her mother having been born in the town of Radautz itself. This lady's sister, Maria Twardochleb married a cousin), Mr. Allan W. Schmidt (whose Roman Catholic Schmidts also hale from my ancestral village of Deutsch-Satulmare, and where, indeed, at least one intermarriage occured when Karl Schmidt wed Ottilie Zurowski), with Bukovinian connexions, and Mrs. Patricia Heaps and Mrs. Fumiko Yamada. All but Mr. Schmidt and the author were Mormons temporarily assigned to work on this project. Of them only Mrs. Hopp, the half-Bukovinian one, has continued to work steadily with B.R.E.G. I, even though she has since been appointed Stake extraction director. Mrs. Yamada, whose knowledge of German language and script was acquired in Japan, an former ally of the *Reich*, has been replaced by a new Mormon extractor, Mrs. Renate Neurauter, a native German speaker, born in Bielefeld, Westphalia. I was hopeful, after a ten-day visit (December 3-14, 1994) to Regina, Saskatchewan, visiting Bukovina German genealogists, that a wider cooperation would result, leading to the establishment of other B.R.E.G. projects. I suggested to the group of people I met that it would be useful to extract the registers of the Protestant (basically Lutheran) parish of Milleschoutz-Radautz (1791-1940), as this would parallel the work of B.R.E.G. in Ottawa, on the registers of the Roman Catholic parish at Radautz (1785-1940). Since then, on July 1, 1996, B.R.E.G. II was established by me at Whitby, Ontario. Two women, one of Bukovina and Galician German origin, Mrs. Elaine Wilma Broughton (née Miller, whose family were originally Müller, of Deutsch-Satulmare and Arbora, Bukovina), and Mrs. Patricia Shumovich (née Osborn), are extracting the duplicate marriage registers (1849-1915) for the Protestant parish of Milleschoutz-Radautz. B.R.E.G. III (Illischestie Protestant, largely Lutheran, marriages, 1858-1915) was begun with one extractor Mr. A. Barry Ginn, and B.R.E.G. IV (Czernowitz Roman Catholic Marriage Banns, 1789-1801 [ed. note not 1803 as prior]) also commenced, on November 3, 1997, with a single extractor, Mr. Steven J. Pusiak, whose e-mail address is puziak@sympatico.ca (of mixed Bukovina German [Sonntag], Polish [Grabowski] and Ukrainian [Pusiak and Makaro] origins from Hliboka, Teprescheny, and Franzthal, all localities north of Radautz in Bukovina).

31.  There are close ties of blood within many ethnically similar populations widely dispersed, but because of the duration of settlement (165 years), excellence of their records and the fact that they lived in distinct communities forming German-language enclaves drawn up along confessional lines, either Lutheran or Roman Catholic, those between the clannish Swabian and Bohemian Germans of Galicia and Bukovina are probably among the easiest to demonstrate.

Nonetheless, here are meant to be included the Romanian and Ukrainian Orthodox and Greek Catholic communities whose registers have not yet appeared in the F.H.L.C. Their existence has been alluded to both by Father Gaschler in an article in German on Bukovinian parish registers, and by the late Johann Christian Dressler in his first work on Illischestie, *Chronik der Bukowiner Landgemeinde Illischestie* (1960).

32.  At present, though the process is to be sped up by new technology and practices.

33.  The registers date from ten years after the acquisition of Bukovina by Austria to the 1940 departure of the ethnic Germans from Bukovina as a fulfilment of one of the clauses of the Nazi-Soviet Pact, and a parallel agreement with the Romanians.

34.  The Mormon term for the local jurisdiction, roughly equivalent to a diocese in Anglican or Roman Catholic parlance.

35. A useful discussion of the parallel German tradition of scholarship in this area is to be found in the F.H.L. publication *Mothers, Fathers, Aunts and Uncles: Learning about German Families and Kinship Ties from Genealogical Sources*, ARTHUR E. IMHOF, Ph.D., World Conference on Records paper series no. 501 (1980).

36. On April 21, 1997, a third B.R.E.G. project was begun on the marriage records (1858-1915) of the Protestant community at Illischestie, thanks to the appearance of another interested individual, Mr. Alan Barry Ginn, whose maternal grandmother was born in Baiaceştie, Bukovina in 1901, of an Illischestie-born mother (Eva Rumpel, Frau Friedrich Uhrich, *1881, Illischestie, †1971; Regina, Saskatchewan), at the Ottawa F.H.C. only the week prior.

37. Under the auspices of the *Saskatchewan Genealogical Society*, B.R.E.G.'s chairman is extracting and indexing for the *Saskatchewan Residents' Index* (S.R.I.) all the names and dates in the published registers of the Lutheran parishes of Edenwold, Saskatchewan, detailed elsewhere in this paper.

38. As in the case of the Roman Catholic Church in Quebec, Bukovina's Roman and Lutheran churches kept excellent records. The French Catholic community in Quebec was served well by such greats as Monsignor Cyprien Tanguay, who started the systematic extraction of entries in parish registers over a century ago, laying the groundwork for a tradition of scholarship that has risen to a level of genealogical demographic research that has no parallel elsewhere in North America. At the apex of their distinguished community of scholar-genealogists is René Jetté, whose work on the origins of the French Canadian nation in Quebec, *Dictionnaire généalogique des familles du Québec* (1983), compiled with the aid of the *Programme de recherche en démographie historique de l'Université de Montréal*, is a masterly synthesis of all the work of the last century along rigorous principles, and whose *Traité de généalogie* (1991) needs to be translated into English and read as a model on genealogical methodology which could serve to help us all avoid some of the most commonly practised errors in researching, compiling and writing in the field of genealogy.

39. The banns registers for Radautz that I have seen date from 1818. In the early years, they contain not just banns for Roman Catholic marriages, but also for ones where both parties were Lutherans. Obviously, then, these volumes should be consulted by those with Lutheran forebears.

The registers were kept almost entirely in German in the case of the Radautz Roman Catholic parish. To complicate matters, this primary usage is combined with an admixture of Latin notes, along with abbreviations that the compilers used alternately in the same entries so that one has to be constantly on guard for a change of scriptorial tradition. Thus, using them properly entails learning to decipher various German and Latin scripts as well as cryptic references.

At Sereth, the banns were kept first in German, then in Polish, and later in both, according to the ethnicity of the priest or the parties concerned. Occasionally, even surnames were translated. Father Gaschler claims to have seen the German name, *Appel*, rendered as the Polish *Jablonski*.

At Radautz, the earliest R.C. records, one set for the military and another for the civilians, were compiled during the incumbency of Father Guido, apparently a military chaplain who served much of central Bukovina using Radautz as his base of operations from 1785-1793. The registers, such as they are, full of cryptic abbreviations, are kept in Latin, in a crabbed hand, and many German surnames take an expert eye to be recognised.

Many of the military personnel presumably moved on when their tour of duty in Bukovina ended, and hence are apparently not terribly important in terms of the reconstitution of the community's ties and origins.

The records of civilians, by contrast, are enormously important, and, at this early period, it should be noted that, perhaps because of the absence of a Lutheran pastor, many events concerning Lutherans appear. One such event is the 1788 marriage of Johann Heinrich Mang, the Younger, of Deutsch-Satulmare to Anna Margarethe Kühl.

Maddeningly, there is a gap in all the registers from March 1793 until May 1802, though apparently Armbrüster saw something at one time in the way of a Roman Catholic register covering this period, for in his work *Deutsch-Satulmare*, p. 67, he refers to the baptism of Heinrich the son of Peter Schmidt *Der Jüngere* of Satulmare, an event that I cannot locate in the registers we now have. Perhaps they were put into the register of another parish, such as Kaczyka, to which I have no access, save via Paul J. Polansky Schneller, who managed to photocopy them (Baptisms, Marriages and Burials, 1792-1890) while they were in the care of their custodian, a Roman Catholic priest in Bukovina, who kept them under his bed, and got beaten by the Romanian secret police for associating with Schneller. (One can write to him at the Czech Research Center, P.O. Box 183, Spillsville, Iowa 52168, U.S.A.).

Alternately, they could be among the records left behind in Romania, now housed in the Suceava county archives, such as, presumably, the baptismal registers for Radautz, 1860-1940, which the Germans did not take with them when they were resettled in 1940, the marriage registers, 1883-1940, and the burial registers after 1853, to which the same applies.

Then, from 1802-1817, the registers maintained during the incumbency of Father Narcissus Lindemann are kept in his increasingly indecipherable handwriting in German script, which is almost like Japanese calligraphy in the minimalism of its execution. Guido was a little latinate in his tendency to translate even German town and district names into Latin. (There is a useful guide to deciphering these, though alas only in Latin and German, called *Latein I für den Sippenforscher* and *Latein II für den Sippenforscher* (Limburg a.d. Lahn: C. A. Starke Verlag, 1965 and 1969 [reprints]). The list of placenames appears in vol. 2, p. 29-73. Fritz Verdenhalven's work, *Familienkundliches Wörterbuch*, 2nd impression, (Neustadt an der Aisch: Verlag Degener and Co., 1969), also contains many of these, though not the Bukovinian ones. Those are not to be found anywhere that I know of, but they are fairly easy to recognise as barely altered derivatives from the German names by which we know them and come up time and again, whereas the German towns and districts may only appear once or twice and may be unfamiliar. It helps if one has a knowledge of German dynastic nomenclature as these are often territorial and help to determine from which part of the Holy Roman Empire or Habsburg possessions (not necessarily one and the same) one's German ancestor came. Lindemann would almost seem to be taking pains to help us lose the thread guiding us back to our ante-Bukovinian *Urheimat*, be it in Bohemia, Galicia, Hungary or the Holy Roman Empire.

If it were not for the fact that he was such a scribbler who clearly did not enjoy writing (perhaps he was in pain, poor man, for his hand becomes more chicken-scratchy as the years pass), never mentioned parents' names at marriage, and at times even neglected to tell us who the parents are in a baptism, we should have an extremely complete record for the period of German settlement.

It is with relief, then, that, in 1818, with the passing of Father Lindemann, that we finally see proper Latin registers instituted. The German script and words in them are reserved for the infrequent signing of a register by a witness or baptismal sponsor, or by those who fathered babes out of wedlock, mostly soldiers, whose traces out of Bukovina to their places of next service or origin will be complicated by the fact that they inscribed themselves in the registers in a thoroughly sloppy manner, perhaps not too surprising in light of their offence, and not infrequently upside-down.

These registers (1818-1853) were kept by the excellent Father Josef Sattfeld, who took amazing care to write in a modified Carolingian script beautiful to behold after the ghastliness of Father Lindemann's work. From 1820, Father Sattfeld strove to give full particulars where Lindemann had been parsimonious.

Whereas the Lutheran registers are barely legible before 1820, that year seems to have been an important one for local Roman Catholic record-keeping practice, with Latin used throughout in a standard vocabulary that one's school Latin can serve to translate with only occasional reference to a dictionary.

It should be noted that, by and large, the regular Latin dictionary will not be of much use for reading parish registers, as such publications tend to be full of Golden and Silver Age words and definitions from the Classical period. The Latin used by the Church, while, of course, containing many of the same words as the ancient tongue, employed a specialised vocabulary that evolved into a bureaucratic language used throughout Europe by both civil and ecclesiastical authorities alike, well into the 19th century.

A number of Latin-English word lists exist, mostly for use with English parish registers of the mediaeval period, which means that they provide a vocabulary rather different from what is required.

With all the deficiencies that one might expect from a work that does not claim to be a Latin-English dictionary for genealogists in the first place, ERNEST THODE'S *German-English Genealogical Dictionary* (Baltimore, Maryland: Genealogical Publishing Company, 1992 edition), is a very useful work. It includes many Latin terms that come up in registers kept for German-speaking populations, and is a boon to the careful sleuth. Any serious researcher, should keep a list, with precise references as to source (G.S.U. MFM no., item no., p. no., and even entry no.) of terms looked up but not found, and send them to Mr. Thode at his address, R.R. 7, Box 306, Kern Road, Marietta, Ohio 45750-9437, U.S.A. Alternatively, he has an e-mail address at the Ottawa National Capital FreeNet: bs113@freenet.carleton.ca

From 1820, apparently following a visit by the vicar-general or some such lofty diocesan authority, the records take on their excellent cast, but even the formal registers of baptism, marriage and burial, do occasionally contain German, in instances similar to those already stated. It seems that banns registers were considered less formal and hence could be kept in the native language of the incumbent or the majority language of the community he served. Certainly, the earliest ones I have investigated, those of Czernowitz Roman Catholic parish, covering the late 18th century, were kept in German and in script.

40. Taxation and the keeping of lists of those eligible for military conscription were two uses.

41. An area largely depopulated under the Turks, Bukovina was resettled under the patronage of the Habsburg emperor, Joseph II, by immigrants from the Holy Roman Empire and various other Habsburg possessions, such as Bohemia (*Böhmen*), Hungary (*Ungarn*) and Galicia (*Galizien*). Indeed, lest one be taken in by the argument, put about by the Ceauşescu regime, that the German-speaking immigrants and others were unwanted interlopers who pushed the Romanians out of their land, it should be noted that even the "native" Romanian population was depleted and needed a large infusion of settlers from Transylvania (the German *Siebenbürgen*) to boost its numbers.

42. If anything, the Lutheran registers of this type, called *Familienbücher,* "family books," or *Gemeindebücher,* "community books," were even more sophisticated than the Roman Catholic records, and, indeed, the Lutherans began even earlier than the Roman Catholics to record the names of the parents of the principals at marriage. Often, these books contain records of a family for two or three generations and even include, in the margin, the date and place of a family's removal to another place (e.g., *Nach Kanada ausgewandert, 1898,* i.e., "emigrated to Canada in 1898").

43. White Russia, Byelorussia/Belorussia or the current Belarus.

44. Thus we have another portion of the confirmation registers (1931-37) (G.S.U. MFM 1055356) of the Roman Catholic parish of Fürstenthal, Bukovina.

45. There is a useful history of this town written by FRANZ WISZNIOWSKI, *Radautz: Die deutscheste Stadt des Buchenlandes* (i.e., Radautz: Bukovina's most German Town) (1966). It contains a *Status Animarum,* which others have estimated was taken ca. 1828/32.

46. Or *Bezirkshauptmannschaft.*

47. To whom it could be rendered *Großdorf,* literally "big village."

48. Not to be confused with the much larger town of Sathmar (in German), which is also called *Satu Mare* in Romanian, but which is located further west in the Transylvanian region of Romania.

49. Or *Arat* as it seems sometimes to have been spelt. The name probably derives from the town of *Arad* in Romania, which the German-speaking population of Bukovina would have pronounced as though the "d" were a "t," hence its North American spelling.

50. Self-published by the author in Karlsruhe/Baden, and now long out of print. It has been translated by Miss Anna Schaffer (originally Schäfer), of Regina, Saskatchewan, and is currently being prepared for publication, with materials supplied, in part, by the Saskatchewan Genealogical Society.

51. Indeed, a similar arrangement obtained in the case of the Lutherans.

52. Insofar as I had not already discovered missing data in the parish registers of the largely Hungarian Catholic settlement of Istensegits, also known as Cibeny, Ţibeni or Zybeny. Because it was a town closer to Satulmare than Radautz, members of the Catholic minority at Satulmare seem to have gone there for the performance of some of the rites of the Church. Here were found some Żurowski events as early as 1807. Local ethnic German Catholics had resort to it until the non-Hungarian communities in the county of Radautz apparently began to be served almost exclusively as daughter communities (with their own chapels-of-ease) of the mother church at Radautz, starting in about 1820.

53. One of the author's family resettled from Bukovina in 1940 is Oswald Zurowski, a second cousin once removed, descended from the emigrant to Canada's (Ferdinand) elder brother Leon (1848-1918), who lives at Ramsen/Pfalz, Germany. He corresponded with the D.Z.f.G. for years, having started long before the reunification of Germany. He has received tidbits of information each time, but only after long intervals of patient waiting on his part. Even then, the D.Z.f.G. staff often failed to locate desired items, and certainly never photocopied them for him to decipher on his own. Instead, they used their own less expert knowledge of both orthography and our particular family history to provide him with poorly translated or transcribed renditions of material that can now be pored over at leisure at L.D.S. F.H.C.'s, outside Europe, until one can construe each entry and decide on its meaning to one's own satisfaction. In going through the registers, the author has found many pertinent entries, including the 1805 baptism at Radautz R.C parish, of the first of the earliest Bukovinian Żurowski's children for which there is a confirmed date of baptism. This item was missed by the D.Z.f.G.

Not surprisingly, then, the author is an advocate of having direct access to records via microfilm over depending on the filtering hand of some archival "expert." Often the people assigned to such a task in an archive cannot for reasons of "resource deployment" be fully qualified archivists, but are instead correspondence clerks. Their expertise is likely to be far less than that of even a keen amateur in search of his own roots.

Though trained as an historian at the undergraduate level, the author is largely self-taught in his knowledge of Bukovinian research; and, even now, cannot read complex passages in German without the aid of a dictionary. The important requirements are time and a drive to learn.

54. There is an English-language group for those interested in the culture, including the genealogical heritage, of this vanished duchy. It is the *The Bukovina Society of the Americas*, founded in 1988, whose address is P.O. Box 81, Ellis, Kansas 67637, U.S.A. It holds an annual Bukovinafest in Ellis and Hays, Kansas, and, though it is largely Bukovina German in its membership, welcomes anyone with a tie to Bukovina. Its publication began as a quarterly newsletter, *The BULLetin* (January 1991-Winter 1993), the name of which alluded to the bull, really a mythical "auroch," which appears so prominently in the coat-of-arms of Bukovina. Currently, their newsletter is called, *The Bukovina Society of the Americas Newsletter* (January 1994-date).

Another such society was the *Bucovinaer Cultural Society*, which was founded in New York in 1967 by a group of Jewish immigrants from Bukovina. It published the *Bukowina Bulletin* in German, but is, apparently, no longer extant. Even older is the *Bucovina Society of Detroit, Michigan*, founded by Romanian-speaking immigrants from Bukovina, which celebrated its 65th anniversary in 1994.

There are also societies elsewhere. In Brazil, there is the *Associaçao Alema-Bucovina de Cultura* (A.B.C., or Association for Bukovina German Culture), headquartered in Rio Negro, where the town council donated a school which has become the Centre for Bukovina Culture and Museum of Bukovinian Culture. Under the direction of Dr. Ayrton Gonçalves Celestino the A.B.C. holds both an annual *Natal Bucovino* (Bukovinian Christmas festival), an annual convention called the *Semana Bucovina* (Bukovina Week) in July, and an annual *Haluschkifest* (Cabbage Roll Festival).

In Germany, there are several organisations, including the *Landsmannschaft der Buchenlanddeutschen (Bukowina) e.V.* (Association of Bukovina Germans), which was founded in 1949 for those resettled from Bukovina and their descendants, now living in Germany and Austria. They publish, *Der Südostdeutsche*, which printed Father Gaschler's seminal article, mentioned at the beginning of this paper. Its editor is Luzian Geier, with offices at *Rankestraße* 12/IV, D-80796 *München* 13, Germany. In Austria, there are two branches of the association, one at Linz, the other at Graz.

In Germany, there are also two research bodies, viz.: the *Bukowina-Institut* (Bukovina Institute), a research and documentation centre for the history and culture of Bukovina and the Bukovina Germans, which was founded in 1988, with Prof. Dr. Johannes Hampel as its director. It is located at *Alter Postweg* 97A, D-86159 *Augsburg*, Germany, and has many records of the Bukovina Germans who were resettled in 1940. According to one of its co-directors, Professor Dr. Kurt Rein, the collection includes many of their genealogical passport documents, known as *Ahnenpässe* (i.e., ancestry passports), showing up to six generations of a person's ancestry on all lines, drawn up to prove people's *Aryan* descent. These contain the names, vital data and sometimes the pre-Bukovinian origins of many who are ancestors to those of Bukovina German background on both sides of the Atlantic.

Dr. Rein is a specialist in Bukovinian German dialects, who speaks and writes English, and has visited Saskatchewan several times. His address is Prof. Dr. Kurt Rein, *Lehrstuhl für Didaktik der Deutschen Sprache und Literatur II, Institut für Deutsche Philologie, Universität München (Ludwig Maximilians Universität), Schellingstraße* 3, D-80799, Germany.

An institutional member of the *Bukowina-Institut* is the *Raimund-Friedrich-Kaindl Gesellschaft* (Raimund Friedrich Kaindl Society) which has offices at *Waldburgstraße* 247, D-70565 *Stuttgart* 80, Germany with Frau Irma Bornemann as president. Named for the foremost historian of Bukovina during the Austro-Hungarian period, who served as professor of history at the Francisco-Josefina in Czernowitz, its purpose is to pursue research on the history and culture of Bukovina and to undertake genealogical studies. It publishes the periodical, *Kaindl-Archiv*, as well as village monographs, genealogies and various brochures.

In Germany, the resettled and/or expelled ethnic German communities of central and eastern Europe are usually sponsored as a group entity by localities that are generally connected to the "returnees" via their forebears. In the case of the Bukovina Germans, the district of Swabia (Schwaben) in southern Germany has, since 1955, been the sponsoring region, chosen, no doubt, because of the large number of Bukovina Germans whose ancestors emigrated from this area to populate the crownland in the 18th century.

55. *Archives and Manuscript Repositories in the USSR*: Ukraine and Moldavia: Book 1, General Bibliography and Institutional Directory. PATRICIA KENNEDY GRIMSTED, 1986. See p. 654-663 incl., which covers the holdings of the State Archive of Chernivtsi Oblast founded in 1940. That institution's address was then 274001 Chernivtsi, vul. Shevchenka, 2.

56. These registers were not included in the edition of the F.H.L.C. consulted in mid-1993, but were in both the latest cd-rom and microfiche editions of the catalogue. B.R.E.G. I is currently extracting records on G.S.U. Microfilms (MFMs) 1768247, 1768248, 1768249 and 1768250. B.R.E.G. now has four segments at work on different parishes, hence B.R.E.G. I-IV.

Also on cd-rom at every fully-equipped F.H.C. is a collection known as *Ancestral File*. This is a collection of pedigrees of three or more generations (in theory) of a contributor's direct or collateral ancestors. Anyone can contribute to it by sending in their genealogical information on a computer diskette using the ASCII protocol for the exchange of genealogical database material between different software packages (such as P.A.F., Brother's Keeper, Roots IV, etc.) known as *GEDCOM*. One's address must appear and contributors are automatically deemed to have agreed to sharing their information with all comers and to answering enquiries as their address must appear appended to the file. Roy Aust Kerth has contributed a great deal of Bukovina-related information to this database, much of which is extremely helpful, particularly in connexion with Illischestie. His information should, however, be used with caution as I have found a number of errors in it, as can be expected with almost any work-in-progress, including my own. One drawback of *Ancestral File* is that its information is entirely unsourced (i.e., lacking in footnotes). One's only recourse is to correspond with the contributor. Unfortunately, as in the case of Mr. Kerth, many files do not show a current address, as people die, lose interest, or simply forget to update their information. In addition, a new edition of *Ancestral File*, which was long overdue, has now appeared, apparently delayed for technical reasons. It still does not contain source information, though it does show a history of any changes to a given record. Corrections and additions to the file are welcome, providing one follows the procedures set out within the software package. Here, one does have to give a source for every alteration, which then appears under the rubric "history of changes."

57. Officially called the *"evangelisch A.B. [Augsburger Bekenntnis] und H.B. [Helvetischer Bekenntnis] Konfession."*

58. One should use the *Deutsch-Satulmare Familienbuch* in tandem with two other publications. The first of these is CHRISTIAN ARMBRÜSTER'S *Deutsch-Satulmare, op. cit.*, which contains the village's *Status Animarum,compiled* 1828-1832, which the author gives with his additions (all of which need to be reviewed carefully because I have found several serious errors), located on p. 200-204. This is followed by a less useful list of extracts from the Lutheran parish of Milleschoutz-Radautz entitled *Kirchenbuchintragungen [sic] 1849-51*, furnished to him by Dr. Karl Deutscher, and found on p. 204-209. The second is *St. John's Evangelical Lutheran Church, 1890-1990: Translations of the earliest church histories, and information on the early families of the congregation, translated from the parish registers of 1890-1927; With records of the work of the early pastors of the St. John's congregation in the wider areas of the Districts of Assiniboia and Saskatchewan (North West Territories) 1890-1905, and later in the Province of Saskatchewan; and family history information from the St. John's parish registers*, a work edited and translated from the German by Dr. RICHARD HORDERN of Luther College at the University of Regina (Saskatchewan), which is unfortunately poorly titled, as nowhere in all the foregoing is the name of the town and district that the church served mentioned as Edenwold (then known as Edenwald to its German inhabitants). It is still in print, and is available from Mrs. Barbara Siebert of P.O. Box 93, Balgonie, Saskatchewan S0G 0E0, Canada, Tel.: (306) 771-2858. It contains a goldmine of genealogical data on the first three generations of Bukovina Germans who settled in that area (as well as other Lutherans, large numbers of whom came between 1890 and 1914 from Satulmare and other villages in the county of Radautz, such as Badeutz and Alt-Fratautz, and elsewhere in Bukovina, such as Unter-Wikow and Illischestie. As with Armbrüster's work, above, HORDERN'S *Edenwold*, needs to be used with caution, not because of any error on his part, but because of the errors of the original pastors who were not always familiar with the correct spelling of Bukovinian surnames and placenames. It is a primary source for events that actually took place in the parish, but should be checked against the actual Bukovinian parish registers when dealing with events that occurred there. In the case of both the *Familienbuch* and *Armbrüster*, one should consider the parish registers of baptism, confirmation, marriage banns, marriage, and burial, as having priority over dates in them. It should be noted that there are *Familienbücher* for other Bukovinian villages including Alt-Fratautz, Arbora, Illischestie and Tereblestie, and Catholic lists for Sereth and its outlying villages, St. Onufry, Terescheny, etc.

One should not fail to consult the excellent 1901 census of the Dominion of Canada or the rather less helpful 1891 Dominion census for that matter. The 1901 census, however, is remarkable in that it provides one with details not encountered before in Canadian censuses. Here the innovation is that in addition to the usual information one encounters, one finds that each person has been asked to give his exact date of birth (again these are subject to error and should be checked against primary sources, namely the baptismal registers), and year of immigration and, if received, naturalisation (if not already a British subject). Taken together these four sources, with the actual parish registers, provide all the material necessary in most instances to carry one's Bukovina German line back from Canada to Austria-Hungary and thence to the ancestral home in Germany or elsewhere.

Another excellent source to help bridge the Atlantic is the collection known as the *Hamburg Passenger Lists*. These exist for the entire period of pre-World War I emigration from Austria-Hungary to Canada, 1889-1914. While not everyone emigrated from Europe via this port, it seems to have been a favoured port of embarkation by Bukovina's Germans. The records of this port are indexed by surname and year, and available on G.S.U. microfilms, making them very simple to search. In addition, Canadian immigration records of ships' passenger lists are preserved on microfilm at the National Archives of Canada. Records of Homestead Entries and Land Grants made under the terms of the *Dominion Lands Act* during the great period of immigration to Canada under the Liberal Interior Minister, Sir Clifford Sifton, are now housed with the provinces concerned as are naturalisation records. For Bukovina German immigrants surviving to the World War II, Canada's 1940 programme of *National Registration*, records much helpful data about all Canadians, but is particularly useful in providing biographical details about birthplace, immigration, naturalisation and name changes of the foreign-born who might be enemy aliens.

Of course, if one wants some other helpful hints as to "old country" origins, and a line on the—fairly—current status of a family in the Edenwold district, one should consult, the Saskatchewan 75th anniversary publication, *Edenwold: Where Aspens Whisper* (1981). It has an excellent brief guide to Bukovina by Hannelore Frombach, the German-born wife, of an Edenwolder of Bukovinian background. It is one of the better Saskatchewan local histories produced in great profusion in time for the 1980 celebration, but, as with all such amateur histories, suffers somewhat from its contributors' lack of primary knowledge, in most cases, of their Bukovinian origins. The spelling of surnames, Christian names and placenames, in particular, should be checked against other records and not treated as Gospel. Many Christian names appear in forms halfway between German and English, such as "Karolina" for the standard German *Karoline* or English "Caroline." Sometime around 1900, the spelling of Christian names in the German language was standardised in what are called their *Rechtschrift* (literally their "right script,", or correct written) forms. It makes sense, if only for indexing purposes, to adopt these spellings, and leave the variants, such as Carl for Karl, for footnoted transcriptions of original records.

59. One of the two sundries books kept by Pastor Andreas Ephraim Schwarz, entitled *Matrikel-Scheine und Zeugnisse*, and containing engrossed copies of birth and baptismal, confirmation, banns, marriage, death and burial certificates he issued from the parish registers as well as other attestations he gave out, including those pertaining to work qualifications, character, etc.

60. Refilming.

61. G.S.U. MFM internal item frontispiece: "Filmed by the Genealogical Society[,] Salt Lake City, Utah at Berlin-Dahlem am Hirschsprung 56-58[,] East-German-Mission[,] Date: 3 May 1949."

62. G.S.U. MFM internal item frontispiece cites "Name of Place:" as "Milleschentzer [*sic*] Pastorat[,] Radautz[,] Bukowina[,] Rumania."

63. G.S.U. MFM internal item frontispiece cites "Title of Record" as "different Document [*sic*] (Marriages, Death, Baptisms)[,] Vol. BSA 384[,] 1829-1861[,] Pages: 1 Title-Page[,] 5-252 (101 following 101a[,] 102 following 102a[,] 103 following 103a)."

64. Refilming.

65. First volume of the original baptismal registers, described as *Geburten* (births), for the Millescheutzer [*sic*] Pastorat, in the F.H.L.C.

66. Second volume of the original baptismal registers for Milleschoutz, described as *Geburten* (births) in the F.H.L.C.

67. Third volume of the original baptismal registers for Milleschoutz, described as *Geburten* (births) in the F.H.L.C.

68. In manuscript, apparently predating the G.S.U. MFM item frontispiece, the reference given is to BsA 111.

69. Extracted by G.S.U. and information on I.G.I.

70. 1991 refilming of the fourth volume of the original baptismal registers of Milleschoutz.

71. Microfilmed by G.S.U. from the collection housed at Ernst Hexel, *Galiziendeutsches Heimatarchiv*, Bad Godesberg, East Germany on January 21, 1987.

72. Gap from the end of 1845 to the beginning of 1848.

73. Duplicate register, tight binding often obscures data, particularly the event date or father's name.

74. Continuation and conclusion of the item begun on the previous film.

75. G.S.U. MFM internal item frontispiece states that this item was "Filmed by the Genealogical Society[,] Salt Lake City[,] Utah[,] at Berlin-Dahlem am Hirschsprung 56-58[,] East-German-Mission[,] Date: 22 April 1949."

76. G.S.U. MFM internal item frontispiece cites "Name of Place:" as "Milleschentzer [*sic*] Pastorat[,] Radautz[,] Bukowina[,] Rumania."

77. G.S.U. MFM internal item frontispiece cites "Title of Record: Birth[,] Vol.: BSA340[,] 1858-1865[,] Pages: 1 Title-Page, 2-284 [recte, 384](1 blank, 83=1 Enclosure, 173=1 Enclosure, 297=1 Enclosure)," while the MFM shows that the original volume's title [from the outside cover of the volume] was "VIII Band[,] Tauf-Matrik des evang. Millescheutzer [the old version of the adjectival form of the place name, Milleschoutz] Pastorat[,] 1858-1865."

78. The Protestant (largely Lutheran) parish established at Milleschoutz (also referred to in the G.S.U.'s Family History Library Catalogue as Obermilleschoutz) in 1791 had its offices transferred to Radautz in 1861. As of the latter date, the parish name was Radautz.

79. Duplicate register.

80. Duplicate register.

81. Duplicate register.

82. Gap in available register series for 1887-1890 inclusive.

83. All left-hand pages filmed first, followed by right-hand pages in reverse order. Wartime filming by the "Reichssippenamt" on March 9, 1942 at Berlin.

84. Duplicate register.

85. Duplicate register. The last available outside of Romania.

86. D.Z.f.G. inventory gives the coverage as 1792-1853.

87. Register microfilmed by G.S.U. in 1949 and birthdate information later extracted so that this material appears in I.G.I.

88. Milleschoutz 1858-1861, then Radautz.

89. This item is miscatalogued as Roman Catholic in the F.H.L.C. where it is stated to be undergoing the extraction process currently (i.e., as of March 8, 1994).

90. G.S.U. MFM internal item frontispiece cites: "Filmed by the Genealogical Society[,] Salt Lake City, Utah[,] at Berlin-Dahlem am Hirschsprung 56-58[,] East-German-Mission[,] Date: 11 May 1949."

91. G.S.U. MFM internal item frontispiece cites: "Name of Place: Milleschentzer [*sic*] Pastorat[,] Radautz/Bukowina[,] Rumania," whereas by this time the name of the pastoral charge was Radautz.

92. G.S.U. MFM internal item frontispiece states: "Title of Record: Confirmations[,] Vol.: BSA 419[,] 1890-1938[,] Pages: 1-192 (38=1 enclosure)."

93. This item is miscatalogued as Roman Catholic in the F.H.L.C., where it is noted to be undergoing the extraction process currently (i.e., as of March 8, 1994).

94. This index was started by government order in 1811 and compiled by Pastor Schwarz of Milleschoutz. He searched out marriages back to 1796 wherein one party was Protestant and the other was of another faith (usually Roman or Greek Catholic, or Greek Orthodox) and recorded later marriages for the period 1811-1848 herein as well. It should be noted that this index covers marriages that took place in other parishes and denominations, thus covering not solely those mixed marriages contracted within his own jurisdiction (i.e., Milleschoutz Protestant parish and its chapelries), but also those involving his own parishioners entering into mixed marriages elsewhere, e.g., Kaczyka Roman Catholic parish. Thus this index furnishes information about marriages recorded in parishes whose registers are not otherwise available for research outside of Romania.

95. The first 20 pages of marriages (1791-1802) are missing. It would appear that they were consulted for the compilation of *Ahnenpäße* in the autumn of 1940, but were lost by 1949 when the material gathered by the *Reichssippenamt* from 1940-1943 was retrieved by Paul Langheinrich from the cellars of Castle Ratsfeld and Rothenburg near Frankenhausen.

96. G.S.U. MFM internal item frontispiece states: "Filmed by the Genealogical Society[,] Salt Lake City, Utah[,] at Berlin-Dahlem am Hirschsprung 56-58[,] East-German-Mission[,] Date: 21 June 1949."

97. G.S.U. MFM internal item frontispiece cites "Name of Place: Millescheutzer Pastorat[,] Jakobeny [one of the filials] u. Andere[,] Bukowina[,] Rumania."

98. Recte 1828-1850, as for the later microfilming of the same original on G.S.U. MFM 1768049/2.

99. G.S.U. MFM internal item frontispiece cites "Title of Record: Marriages[,] Vol.: BSA 470[,] 1829-1849[,] Pages: 2-169 (129 following 129a[,] 130 following 130a[,] 143 following 143a[,] 144 following 144a)." The marriage entries actually start on September 16, 1828 with number 473. Rather than beginning on their proper date, sometime shortly after the last entry in the previous register, there is a gap in the register due to the loss of page 1 of the subject volume which contained the event date and place and the bridegroom's information (page 2, referring to the bride survives), for the intervening entries, numbers 467-472 inclusive, which started from the last noted—number 466, performed November 25, 1827—on p. 138-139 of the prior volume, i.e., the first marriage register volume for the Milleschoutz Protestant Pastoral Charge [Milleschoutzer Pastorat]. Internal evidence, i.e., the notation of the banns dates, makes it possible to supply dates after which the five partially extant marriages could have taken place.

100. G.S.U. MFM internal item frontispiece states: "Filmed by the Genealogical Society[,] Salt Lake City, Utah[,] at Berlin-Dahlem am Hirschsprung 56-58[,] East-German-Mission[,] Date: 20 June 1949."

101. G.S.U. MFM internal item frontispiece cites "Name of Place: Mil\lescheutzer Pastorat[,] Bukowina[,] Rumania."

102. Also includes one inserted baptismal certificate containing the record of a birth and baptism in 1864.

103. G.S.U. MFM internal item frontispiece cites: "Title of Record: Marriages[,] Vol.[,] BSA 467[,] 1851-1857[,] Pages: 1-186 (31-185 blank)." In addition, there is one interleaved baptismal certificate for the 1864 baptism of a Lutheran child born in Kaczyka and baptised there by a Roman Catholic cleric. Strangely, the F.H.L.C. makes no mention of this as a marriage register, citing it instead as *Geburten* (i.e., births), which is wrong, and stating that the contents have been extracted for I.G.I.

104. The F.H.L.C. mislabelled this as a Catholic register, when it is Protestant. As a Catholic register it was assigned to B.R.E.G. for extraction, whereupon the misidentification was discovered.

105. Duplicate register.

106. Duplicate register.

107.　G.S.U. MFM internal item frontispiece states: "Filmed by the Genealogical Society[,] Salt Lake City, Utah[,] at Berlin-Dahlem am Hirschsprung 56-58[,] East-German-Mission[,] Date: 1 April 1949."

108.　G.S.U. MFM internal item frontispiece cites "Title of Record: Death[,] Vol. BSA 310[,] 1825-1844[,] Pages: 3 Title-Pages, 1-223, index 1-13 (134 Enclosure; 110-115 missing; 88—following 88a; 108 following 108a)." On page 226, just before the internal index, it reads: "II[,] Totenbuch[,] Band II[,] 1825-1844."

109.　G.S.U. MFM internal item frontispiece states: "Filmed by the Genealogical Society[,] Salt Lake City, Utah[,] at Berlin-Dahlem am Hirschsprung 56-58[,] East-German-Mission[,] Date: 12 April 1949."

110.　G.S.U. MFM internal item frontispiece cites "Name of Place: Milleschentzer [sic] Pastorat-Bukowina[,] Illischestie, Jakobeny, Dorna Vatra [sic, for Dorna Watra, in German], Eisenau, Freudethal [sic, for Freudenthal], Louisenthal, Bossoritta [sic, for Pozoritta etc.], Mitoka Dragomirna[,] Neujetzkany [archaic, for Neu-Itzkany], Tereblestie[,] usw.."

111.　G.S.U. MFM internal item frontispiece cites: "Title of Record: Death[,] Vol.: BSA322[,] 1844-1857[,] Pages: 1 Title-Page[,] 1-192 (114-191 blank)." The actual volume label on the outside of the original states: "IIItes Todtenbuch des Millescheutzer . . . [the rest is indecipherable due to overexposure of film]." F.H.L.C. says that this material has been extracted by G.S.U., which implies that it should be available in I.G.I.

112.　Labelled *Tote*, i.e., dead.

113.　Duplicate register, vol. 3, stops at 1858, despite being catalogued as running to 1888.

114.　Fragmentary.

115.　Fragmentary.

116.　*Übertretungen*, i.e., conversions. F. H.L.C. describes this as *Austritte* (i.e., resignations), which further states the curious fact that the information was extracted by the G.S.U. and placed on I.G.I. While providing columns for birthdates and places, which were not always completed, this register was principally kept to record the names and dates of people leaving the Lutheran fold. Designed originally to contain only references to defections to Roman Catholicism, many of the entries reflect the conversion of Bukovina German main line church Protestants to the recently arrived Baptist sect. Examples include, on ledger p. 1, Ferdinand Massier, of Alt-Fratautz, on November 14, 1873, described herein as *Confessionslos*, later a well-known Baptist missionary in Galicia, Bukovina and Bessarabia, and, on ledger p. 8, in 1895, the widowed Anna Galenczowski (here rendered Galanschowski), of Satulmare (née Schäfer at Alt-Fratautz), who shortly after, in 1896, emigrated from Austria-Hungary to join her son Peter, who had already settled at Edenwold, Assiniboia district, N.W.T. (now Saskatchewan), Canada in 1889. There she died in 1919, aged 91, receiving a laudatory death notice proclaiming her adherence to the Baptist faith since the death of her husband and baptism at the hand of Brother F. Massier, presumably the aforementioned gentleman.

　　F.H.L.C. also, erroneously states that this item contains *Übertretungen*, i.e., infractions or violations, whereas this material is really *Übertritte*, i.e., moves or transfers, which, in this context, refers to transfers of of denominational allegiance. This item, then, is concerned with conversions, which makes its contents correspond directly to what is indicated by the term employed immediately below it in F.H.L.C., i.e., *Austritte*, meaning resignations, as mentioned above, and, in fact, the contents of the records are exactly the same. The years covered are 1869-1912, and not 1889-1915 as stated in F.H.L.C.

117.　Last entry.

118.　Duplicate register.

119.　Duplicate register.

120.　Duplicate register.

121.　With index.

122.　"*Karton 6*." Filmed at Bad Godesberg, January 21, 1987.

123.　Vol. 1 (1858-1874), vol. 2 (1875-1889).

124.　Duplicate register. Mislabelled "*Taufen*" (baptisms) when it is *Trauungen* or *Heiraten* (marriages).

125.　"*Karton 7*."

126.　Vol. 3 (1890-1891), vol. 4 (1892-1913), and vol. 3 (1914-1915), but 1914 is missing.

127.　Duplicate register.

128.　With index.

129.　Vol. 1 (1858-1872), vol. 2 (1873-1889), and vol. 3 (1890-1894). The last volume is not shown as belonging in this item by the F.H.L.C. Instead, vol. 3 is shown as starting on G.S.U. MFM 1474917/4, whereas that item contains the continuation (1895-1915) of vol. 3 begun here.

130.　Duplicate register.

131.　Vol. 3 (1895-1915), continued from G.S.U. MfM 1474917/3, despite catalogue and internal microfilm frontispiece information that the item starts with vol. 3 (1890-1894), which is, in fact, contained in the previous item.

132.　Duplicate register.

133.　Index to vol. 1-3 inclusively.

134. Balaczana operated as a filial of the independent parish of Illischestie, itself once a dependent filial of Milleschoutz-Radautz Protestant parish.

135. Supplementary register of baptisms, marriages and burials kept by the schoolmaster at Deutsch-Tereblestie, while the village was still served as a filial of Milleschoutz-Radautz parish. Most events should appear in the registers of the mother parish, but there are additional records in this volume. Deutsch-Tereblestie was erected into a separate Lutheran parish in 1905, and obtained its own official parish registers in 1905 or 1906.

136. Parish Church of "Maria Geburt." Parish founded in 1785, with filial chapels in many outlying villages, including Alt-Fratautz, Badeutz, and Deutsch-Satulmare. The mother church was built at an unknown date and was consecrated in 1826. An altar was reserved for the use of a priest ministering to the Greek Catholic community in Radautz, until they obtained a separate church at a later date. In the mid-19th century, the church custodian was the Greek Catholic *Kirchensänger* (cantor), Elias Twardochleb, paternal grandfather of the mother, Anna, of B.R.E.G.'s L.D.S. liaison officer, Mrs. Joyce Hopp, the Ottawa F.H.C. stake director for extraction (through her husband George G. Hopp, of Polish German parentage, a collaborator in the extraction of G.S.U. MFM 1768248/1, she can be reached via his e-mail address: ba943@freenet.carleton.ca).

137. P. 1, heading: *"Vor das Militare [sic] Geborene"* (1785-1786, 1802); p. 2-4, blank; p. 5-6: *"Gestorbene"* (1785-1786).

138. P. 14-17, heading: *"Vor das Civille Geborene"* (1785-1790); p. 18: *"Gestorbene"* (1786-1790, 1816 [military entry], 1817 [date only]); p. 22-23: *"Trauungen"* (1785-1790).

139. Schneeberger, Wolf, Wirth, Matheis, Kurz, Bemer [*sic*, for Böhmer], Rathmacher [later Radmacher], Haas, Mang, Weber, Leib, Hubich, and Nähr.

140. Inhabitants with surnames from A to N only. The remainder of the book appears to have been ripped out at some point. Another fragmentary family register is supposed to appear as D.Z.f.G. vol. 3772, covering the period 1935-1937, but no corresponding G.S.U. microfilm is forthcoming.

141. Labelled *"Bukowina Pojaritta [sic] Radautz und Filialgemeinden X Taufen,"* on the microfilm's internal item frontispiece, when it covers, in fact, the baptismal register for Radautz Roman Catholic parish and its filials. This misidentification seems to have occurred at the point of microfilming, for the D.Z.f.G. contains no such error. *Pojaritta* is a misspelling of a place rendered variously as *Pojorîta* (Romanian), *Pozoritta* (German), *Pożoryta* (Polish), and even *Louisenthal* (popular German) and lay at some distance from Radautz in the former *Bezirk*, i.e., district of, Kimpolung.

142. Gap from March 1793 to May 1802.

143. Parish filials' register.

144. D.Z.f.G. inventory says that the coverage is baptisms (1820-1850), marriages (1820-1835), and burials (1820-1831).

145. Filials' registers for the combined entry of records of baptisms, marriages and burials with gaps 1793-1802 and 1803-1820. More details of the contents are given above in the discussion of the first combined military and civil registers. A typed label in the front of the volume, probably placed there by the D.Z.f.G., states that *"Dieses Kirchenbuch wurde im Jahre 1941 durch Vermittlung des Reichssippenamtes instandgesetzt."* A definite D.Z.f.G. label appears immediately below, viz.: "Radautz[,] Taufen[,] Trauungen[,] Sterbefälle[,] kath.[,] 1785-1850." On the page opposite, a handwritten label reads "Radautz/Bu.[,] KATH.[,] FILIALEN[,] S. INH.[,] *[,] oo[,] +[,] 1785-1850," below which appears the typed label *"Inhaltsverzeichnis. Militär*[,] &[,] 1785-1802[,] Seite 1[;]" [i.e., *Militär*][,] +[,] 1785-1786[,] Seite 5 [;] &[,] 1785-1790[,] Seite 14[;] +[,] 1786-1816[,] *Seite* 18[;] oo[,] 1785-1790[,] *Seite* 22[;] Satulmare[,] & 1820-1830[,] *Seite* 29[;] Altfratautz[,] &[,] 1820-1845[,] *Seite* 41[;] Millescheutz[,] Badeutz, Burla[,] &[,] 1820-1830[,] *Seite* 53[;] Satulmare[,] &[,] 1831-1833[,] *Seite* 57[;] Millescheutz[,] &[,] 1832-1838[,] *Seite* 59[;] Burla[,] &[,] 1832-1835[,] Seite 61[;] Badeutz[,] &[,] 1831-1838[,] *Seite* 63[;] Vadi Vladika[,] &[,] 1833-1840[,] *Seite* 65[;] [blank], &[,] 1833-1838[,] *Seite* 67[;] Altfratautz[,] &[,] 1831-1850[,] *Seite* 73[;] Neufratautz[,] &[,] 1831-1848[,] *Seite* 78[;] Andreasfalva[,] +[,] 1820-1831[,] *Seite* 80[;] Altfratautz[,] +[,] 1820-1831[,] *Seite* 102[;] Andreasfalva[,] oo[,] 1820-1835[,] *Seite* 106[;] Satulmare[,] oo[,] 1824-1830[,] *Seite* 124[;] Millescheutz[,] oo[,] 1821-1829[,] *Seite* 130[;] Altfratautz[,] oo[,] 1820-1830[.] & = Geborene[;] oo = Getraute[;] + = Verstorbene." Immediately below that is the pencilled label, *"Geziffert von Seite 1-135*[;] *Einlagen an Seite 31, 101."* Note non-standard spellings of placenames.

146. Surnames from A to H only.

147. Covers surnames from A to Z.

148. Covers surnames from A to Z.

149. Microfilmed by the G.S.U. at the *Katholisches Kirchenbuchamt des Verbandes der Diözesen Deutschlands, München.*

# FAMILIES AND EMBLEMS TRANSCENDING FRONTIERS

Kathleen B. Cory

I believe that perhaps the earliest people to transcend the "frontiers" of the Atlantic Ocean were the Vikings, who came to North America in about AD 1000 and built a settlement in Newfoundland. This settlement has been designated as one of the World Heritage Sites by the United Nations because it shows the earliest recorded presence of Europeans in the New World.[1] But for the purposes of this paper, I plan to concentrate on later settlers, namely the Scots.

Scotland sent out emigrants of all types—the gentry, some of whom were Lords and Ladies, some of whom were landed gentry with no title but with money and education. Then there were the professional classes—doctors, lawyers, schoolteachers and government officials—and equally necessary were the tradesmen, the farmers, the miners and the labourers. Some of them brought their money and their titles, while others arrived with little in their pockets but with great optimism —hoping and planning to make money in their new world.

What were the most likely things for any emigrant to bring to a new country? Leaving aside the most obvious things such as pieces of furniture, tools of his trade, seeds, perhaps cattle, and very probably a few books and his bible—it surely must have been courage, pride, customs and names.

Scotland's native sons and daughters possess, and always have possessed, a great pride in their nation—this is shown particularly in Canada today by the amount of clan societies that exist, and the number of pipe bands to be found playing at every opportunity. I have taken photographs of kilted Canadians at the Calgary Stampede parade, some piping and others proudly carrying banners bearing the blue and white St. Andrew saltire of Scotland, or, equally proudly, carrying banners bearing the red and white maple leaf of Canada. Surely one very good example of emblems transcending frontiers!

For over 300 years Scots have played a significant part in Canada's history through politics, trade, religion and education, as well as through exploring new ground, building roads, railways and canals; in fact, transcending physical frontiers

within Canada itself. I intend to touch on some of these factors, though there will not be space to expand in detail on any of them.

Even as early as the 1600s, Scotland was creating links with Canada. After the 1603 Union of the Crowns in Britain, King James VI of Scotland (who was the son of Mary, Queen of Scots) became also King James I of England. He created "a new Dignitie between Barons and Knights" with the title of baronet, with the aim of raising money, and in 1624 the Baronetage of Nova Scotia was devised for promoting the plantation of that province. King James announced his intention of creating 100 baronets, each to support six colonists for two years (or pay 2,000 merks instead), and also to pay 1,000 merks to Sir William Alexander, who was afterwards the Earl of Stirling, and to whom the province had been granted in 1621. For this they were to receive a "free barony" of 16,000 acres in Nova Scotia and to become baronets of "his Heines Kingdom of Scotland."

A merk was worth 13s. 4d., which prior to decimilisation was 2/3 of £1. So 3,000 merks would have been approximately £2,000 and 1,000 merks would have been approximately £667, which in those days would have been a very sizeable amount of money.

When King James died in 1625, his son King Charles I carried out the scheme and created the first Scottish baronet on May 28, 1625. In 1629, King Charles granted to all Nova Scotian baronets the right to wear about their necks, suspended by an orange tawny ribbon, a badge bearing an *Azure saltire with a crowned inescutcheon of the arms of Scotland* and the motto FAX MENTIS HONESTAE GLORIA [Peace is the glory of an honest mind].

In 1638, the creation ceased to carry with it the grant of lands in Nova Scotia, and on the union of Scottish and English Parliaments in 1707 —by which time Queen Anne had come to the throne—the Scottish creation ceased. From that date Englishmen and Scotsmen alike received baronetcies of Great Britain.

The 1707 union of the Parliaments together with the union of the Crowns some hundred years earlier, marked another instance of families and emblems crossing frontiers; although even today England and Scotland still retain their own identities, as do the people who inhabit these lands.

The scheme, proposed by King James VI of Scotland, had been a clever idea whereby Nova Scotia got the funds to help support the new settlers, and the Scots got the titles of Baronets of Nova Scotia with the early ones being granted 16,000 acres of land there. In order to save these gentlemen having to spend even more money by journeying to Nova Scotia—which was a hazardous undertaking in the 1600s—the legal ceremony of granting sasine—which is the act of taking possession of land—was allowed to be performed on the ground outside Edinburgh Castle.

A plaque at the entrance of the Castle commemorates this:

> Near this spot in 1615
> Sir William Alexander of Menstrie
> Earl of Stirling received sasine or lawful possession of the Royal Province of Nova Scotia by the ancient and symbolic ceremony of delivery of earth and stone from Castlehill by a representative of the King. Here also (1625-1637) the Scottish Baronets of Nova Scotia received sasine of their distant baronies.

This meant that the new baronets could take possession of their lands with the minimum of inconvenience except to their pockets, or perhaps their sporrans.

These links still exist today in the descendants of the original Baronets of Nova Scotia. The name Nova Scotia alone speaks of its origin.

Looking at the map of Canada it is interesting to note that there is a great preponderance of Scottish place names in the Western Provinces. These are Scottish surnames which have travelled many miles to become Canadian place names, and each one probably has had a book written about it!

Names such as Mackenzie Bay, Fort McPherson, Mt. Campbell, Ogilvie Mt., Mackenzie Mts., Stewart River, Macmillan River, Ross River, Mt. Logan, Mt. Murray are all places named after the intrepid Scots who pushed further the boundaries of settlements and who have left their mark on the map of Canada.

I have marked all the places I could see that had a Scottish or a royal connection. I think nostalgia must have played its part too! Banff in Scotland is a miniature version of Banff in Canada, where Lake Windermere reminded me of the Lake Windermere in England. In Calgary, where my "Canadian" daughter Alison lives with her family, we drive down the Crowchild Trail as well as down the MacLeod Trail—now no longer trails but wonderful highways. In 1882, Calgary was an estate, with what was then described as a modern mansion, in Kildonan Parish, on the Island of Mull in Scotland. My son-in-law Ned tells me that Crowchild was a First Nation Chief, and I am sure someone else will tell me who MacLeod was and why he merited having a trail named after him! MacLeod and Crowchild—these road signs are taken for granted today, but still they are a constant reminder to all travellers in Calgary of the joining together of the Scottish and the Indian cultures within Canada.

This reminder takes us back to the early settlers, more particularly those settlers who were fur traders and worked for either the Hudson's Bay Company of the North West Company. The North West Company, whose men were known as "Nor'westers," was a partnership of traders that emerged under the leadership of Simon McTavish in 1783 and was the first to cross the Rocky Mountains and establish posts on the Pacific slope —a mighty undertaking that needed not only foresight but great courage. The term "nor'wester" seems to have been in use as early as 1761 where I found this entry in the marriage register of Stromness, in Orkney:

> November 7, 1761. Joseph Norris, a norwaster [sic] was contracted with Margaret Robertson, residenter in Stromness. Contracted by Robert Tulloch, Elder.

Having contracted, which is the same as having the banns read, they were married on November 15 of the same year.

By 1787, Alexander MacKenzie (who had been born in Stornoway, on the Island of Lewis, and who had left Scotland when he was 16) had joined the North West Company, and then, when he was aged 24, was appointed to the trading post on Lake Athabasca. This remarkable man led expeditions to the Arctic Ocean in 1789 followed in 1792 by an expedition to the Pacific Ocean, through the Rocky Mountains. By 1793, he had opened the way to transcontinental travel and trade. This he did without the loss of a single man —a remarkable feat when you consider the conditions and hardships they must have endured.

News of this exploit and of Alexander MacKenzie reached Thomas Douglas, the 8th Earl of Selkirk. Lord Selkirk had suffered setbacks in other parts of Canada, owing to disease and an extremely bad harvest, and he went on to attempt to form another settlement in the Red River area of Hudson Bay, which, according to Alexander MacKenzie, was fertile.

To cut a long story short, after a great deal of conflict, the two companies, that is, the North-West Company and the Hudson's Bay Company, were merged in 1821. The first governor to unite the companies was yet another Scot: George Simpson, who was to be knighted and became Sir George Simpson in recognition of his work there and for opening up vast areas of new land.

The preference for Scots as workmen was shown as early as 1682, when Governor John Nixon asked the London committee of the Hudson's Bay Company to send him Scotsmen because they were more stable and better workers. He wrote "they are hardy people both to endure hunger and cold, and are subject to obedience," unlike the men being sent out from London by the London committee.

This was to be the start of men coming to Canada from Orkney—a group of islands off the north of Scotland—to take up service with the Hudson's Bay Company. However, Orkney had been known to them since at least 1670, when their ships called in to Stromness to take on water before their journeys. There is a plaque to commemorate this: "There watered here the Hudson's Bay Company Ships 1670-1891." In fact, I have come across references to Hudson's Bay this in the old parish registers for the parishes of Orkney. These references are sometimes in the birth registers, where the mother of the child states that the father is with the Hudson's Bay Company and promises to marry her on his return!

I have also found some entries which show the intermarriage of fur traders and Indian women. Unfortunately, as we can see from these examples, the wives were not always treated with the respect they deserved. But then, one should never judge past acts by present opinions. They should be judged according to the mores of the times.

It is interesting to note that some of the children born to Indian mothers were brought home to

Scotland by their Scottish fathers to be baptized some years later. In some cases, several years later:

> John, natural [i.e., illegitimate. K. C.] son of John Isbister (of the parish of Harray) late from Hudson's Bay and an Indian Woman was born 8th of January 1811 and baptized the 3rd November 1822 by the Revd. Mr. Marr.

His sister, Ann, had been born in 1817, so John would have been aged 11 and Ann would have been almost 5 when they were baptized.

Only in one case does the Indian name of the mother appear in the old parish register of Stromness, and there she is assumed to have been married as she bears the same surname as the father, and the child is not recorded as a "natural" son. One of the witnesses was John Ballanden, who was an ex-governor. The child was aged 13 at the time of its baptism:

> 1808. Peter Fidlar and an Infidel woman Methwernan Fidlar had a child born in Hudsons Bay in the year 1795; baptized at Stromness October 12th day 1808 by the Revd. Mr. William Clouston named Thomas. Witnesses John Ballanden Esq., and D. Geddes Esq.

In this next entry the session clerk took care to point out that Catherine Spence was an Indian woman. I suspect that she well may have been the daughter of an Indian mother and a British father.

The session clerk recorded the birth as illegitimate by using the word "natural" . . . a natural son. Although this child, William, had been born in York Department of Hudson Bay in 1794, he was not baptized in Stromness until 1813—19 years later.

Compared with the entry in May 1830, where, although James had been born in Moose Factory in 1811, there was no suggestion that either his mother was an Indian or that he was illegitimate, he was the "lawful son" of James Flett. He, too, was aged 19 when he was baptized in Stromness.

In the fur trade, the interdependancy of the emigrant settlers and the indigenous peoples helped to produce a society that reflected both Indian and European customs and technology. These early emigrants arrived as a result of persuasion by agents, or a feeling of adventure or escape. As they seldom brought their womenfolk with them at this point, the resulting intermarriage with the local women led to a greater understanding of both cultures as well as building a greater trust, which proved useful in enhancing trade through the extended families.

Here we have a blending of cultures between Canadian Indians and Scots, which has been well chronicled in Sylvia Van Kirk's book *Many Tender Ties*, published in Canada by Watson and Dwyer. Some Orkney names such as Sinclair, Kirkness and Isbister, still to be found in Calgary, are living evidence of their Scottish origin.

The early traders were content to abide by the customs of their brides' people, and marriage "à la façon du pays," not prostitution, became the usual relationship within the fur trade society. This disregard for the formalities of European marriage rites may have resulted from the lack of clergy to be found in the trading outposts as well as from the strong Scottish influence in the Company. In Scotland at that time, it was possible and not unusual for a legal marriage to be contracted if the couple expressed their consent before witnesses.

One of the stories in Sylvia Van Kirk's book concerns Isobel Gunn, a Scottish girl who disguised herself as a boy and enrolled in the Hudson's Bay Company hoping to join her lover. Her plans went wrong as they were not sent to the same station, but nature took its course and her true sex was discovered when she gave birth to a son . . . the name of the father was not mentioned in this story so I decided to search through the old parish registers of Stromness for Isobel Gunn and found the following entry:

> 1809 Novr. 12th. Isabella Gunn has a child begot in Hudson's Bay by John Scarth born the 29th Decr. 1807 and baptized the 12th day of Novr. 1809 by the Revd. Mr. Wm. Clouston, named James.

So, this was another case where the child was baptized back in Scotland.

Cynthia, a friend of my daughter in Calgary, is the great-great-great-granddaughter of William Sinclair and his Cree wife Nahovway. William Sinclair was a Chief Factor in the Hudson's Bay Company who had been born in Stromness, Orkney, in 1766. Cynthia has married a man of Irish descent and their youngest child rejoices in the names "Aurora Sarah Sinclair O'Flanagan"—a mixture of Scots and Irish, but due to pressure from one of her brothers, the name Sarah was included as this was the name of his favorite dinosaur—perhaps this is a case of crossing boundaries and frontiers by a bridge too far![2]

The number of emigrants to Canada who had British roots was boosted during the eight years of the American War of Independence (1775-1783) by the many thousand American Loyalists who moved northwards. They, too, will have introduced a new element into Canadian life, bringing with them not only ideas and customs from Britain, but ideas and customs from across the American frontier. A colourful kaleidoscope indeed.[3]

From Loyalists we turn to Royalists and yet another link with Britain through Canadian place names. Regina, Alberta, Prince Albert, King William Island, Prince Edward Island, Victoria Island, the Duke of York Archipelago, and so it goes on. Were the first settlers in these places all Royalists at heart? At the risk of sounding flippant, another explanation does spring to mind, however—perhaps they were nostalgically remembering the names of the pubs they had left behind—a remark I am sure that would have been appreciated by many of them!

Then in 1802 came a further boost to the number of Scottish newcomers with the arrival of the Glengarry Fencibles. The Glengarry Fencibles were formed in 1774 from Highlanders who had set out for America, had been shipwrecked and brought back to Scotland. After disbandment in 1802, a thousand men went to Canada and settled there with their families, their chief and their own chaplain. They named their new settlement in Upper Canada, Glengarry County. Another example of not only bringing their old name to their new home, but of bringing their family traditions and their way of worship with them as well. Surely this must have helped them to settle down in their brave new venture.

During the 1860s and 1870s, two Highland units were raised in Canada, both in Nova Scotia, from which time the Scottish influence in the Canadian Army grew. Canada's loyalty to Britain has been amply demonstrated over the years. In 1899, Lord Strathcona raised and equipped a regiment of Canadian horse (known, not surprisingly as Lord Strathcona's Horse!) entirely at his own expense (who ever said the Scots were tight-fisted?!). It is now a tank regiment, something Lord Strathcona could never have envisaged.

In World War I, under the premiership of Robert Laird Borden, another Canadian Scot, Canada entered the struggle wholeheartedly on the British side. The Canadian Expeditionary Force had several battalions with Scottish names such as the Royal Highlanders of Canada, the 48th Highlanders of Canada, and wearing the kilt were Cameron Highlanders of Canada, the Seaforth Highlanders of Canada and the Nova Scotia Highlanders—not to forget all the Canadians who had the good sense to join the navy, but had to eschew the wearing of the kilt for the wearing of bellbottoms! Once again, we see from the chosen names, the strong ties with what many still regarded as "home," or at least as the home of their fathers.

Although between the wars emigration was almost at a halt, the feeling remained, and there was still a strong movement among the militia units towards renaming the Canadian numbered regiments with Scottish titles, as well as adopting the playing of the pipes and the wearing of the kilt.

When World War II was declared on September 3, 1939, Mackenzie King, as prime minister, brought Canada into the fray on the side of Britain; Canadians—army, navy and air force—came in their thousands, for which Britain will be eternally grateful.

On a personal note—I remember dancing with Canadian soldiers in Brighton, on the south coast of England, when I was learning to become a Wren Seaman Torpedoman in the Women's Royal Naval Service.

Frontiers and oceans may have been crossed but strong links still remained.

As the years went by and new techniques were developed, Scottish engineers were involved in the building of canals. The years 1825 and 1829 saw the completion of the Great Erie Canal and the Welland Canal. Is the Welland Canal named after the river Welland in Lincolnshire? Also on the subject of transport, in 1872 two companies were formed to build the Canadian Pacific Railway with a Scot-Canadian at the head of each company, the Hon. David Macpherson of Toronto, and Sir Hugh Allan of Montreal. Then, in 1885, the railway was opened by Donald A. Smith, later Lord Strathcona, who raised the Lord Strathcona's Horse during the Boer War in 1899.

The political scene was dominated over many years by Scots. To name but a few, James Bruce, the 8th Earl of Elgin, who was appointed governor of Canada in 1846; James Douglas who was governor of Vancouver Island, and who in 1856 proclaimed his authority over the mainland, two years before the Colony of British Columbia was established in 1858.

Both George Brown and John A. Macdonald had been born in Scotland and they, with Alexander T. Galt, all helped to achieve a United Canada. John A. Macdonald was later to be knighted for his services and was to become Sir John A. Macdonald. Then there was William Lyon Mackenzie, who in 1828 founded the newspaper *The Colonial Advocate*, and played an active part in the politics of the 1830s. His grandson William Lyon Mackenzie King was prime minister during World War II. And we continue in my own lifetime with John Buchan, Lord Tweedsmuir who combined politics with literature and is known the world over. As a child I lived next door to his sisters in Edinburgh.

Although this paper is Canada orientated, we must not forget that Scots were also helping to shape America, Australia, New Zealand and India, where I spent my early childhood in what is now known as Pakistan. My eldest daughter Elizabeth and I plan to visit Rawalpindi, where the army was stationed and where I lived.

Obviously, to have gained such positions of authority, education must have played an important part in the lives of the settlers. Scots have always held education to be important, and Scottish emigrants took these beliefs with them. Some settlers were able to teach their own children to a high standard and many settlements brought their own teachers with them or they relied on the clergy—both Presbyterian and Roman Catholic.

Through administrators and principals, the Scottish influence is to be seen in the colleges founded in Canada, such as Queen's College, McGill and McMaster Universities and many others. The St. Francis Xavier University of Nova Scotia was founded by the Roman Catholic Highlanders and Gaelic was kept alive there, proving that language, too, can cross borders.

The strict moral principles and great pride in their country that Scottish emigrants have brought with them over the last 300 years are clearly shown today in Scots-Canadians' love for Canada first and Scotland second.

The affection and sympathy of the Scots for Canada is still shown in Scotland; when I was in Oban a couple of years ago, I saw Scottish fishing vessels in the harbour flying the Canadian maple leaf at their mastheads in sympathy with the Canadian fishing fleet war that was going on at that time. The fishermen of Cornwall in England were showing support for Canada in the same manner.

This has been a whistle-stop ride through 300 years of Canada's story, slowing down briefly at points where families and emblems transcended frontiers, and in the case of Scotland, where they first crossed oceans. I have only touched the tip of the iceberg, and at least two-thirds still remains unseen and unsung. I believe that Scots are the third largest ethnic group in Canada, and so somewhere along the line they must be held responsible for introducing golf, curling and whisky drinking as three of their customs and occupations!

But I have tried to focus on what the early Scottish settlers brought with them. They brought their customs, their names, their pride and most importantly, their courage, all of which have transcended oceans and frontiers to make Canada—the Canada of which I am proud to be a small part through my grandchildren Kate, Paul and Liza Kozowyk, whose mother and paternal grandparents have crossed boundaries from Britain and the Ukraine to become Canadians.

## NOTES

1. I am indebted to Maurice Clayton for this information.

2. I am indebted to Douglas A. Sinclair and Cynthia J. O'Flanagan for this information.

3. I hope that after this conference, someone might be persuaded to produce a map with different coloured lines linking Canada with countries from all over the world to show how the many different nationalities have merged together through trade and love to form modern Canada.

# SCOTTISH FAMILIES AND THEIR SYMBOLS IN THE NETHERLANDS OR THE COATS OF ARMS OF DUTCH FAMILIES OF SCOTTISH DESCENT

Percy Douglas[1]

The history of emigration of the Scots to the Low Countries, nowadays the kingdoms of Belgium and The Netherlands, is very old but there are four main ways in which the Scots emigrated to or had contact with the Low Countries.

## The wool staple

From the 13th till the 17th century, Scotland exported wool to the Low Countries, especially to the counties of Flanders and Zeeland, that was used for the textile industry. They had a base in the town of Veere or Campvere on the island of Walcheren in Zeeland. They took tiles as ballast back to Scotland, which can now be seen in many villages around the Firth of Forth. Famous persons exercising this trade were Sir William Davidson, who will follow, and the noble family van Borssele, which was linked by the marriage of one of its members, Wolfaert VI, to Princess Mary Stuart, daughter of King James I and Lady Joan Beauford.

## The Scots Brigade

From 1574 to 1782 the Brigade acted, next to other foreign troops, as the regular standing army of the Federation of the Seven United Dutch-Provinces. In 1574 the Privy Council in Edinburgh decided to raise two regiments to support their Dutch brothers in faith against their Spanish oppressors. They stayed there after 1648, when the Dutch became independent, being hired as mercenaries by some of the provinces like Holland, Friesland, Guelders and Zeeland. The Brigade was disbanded in 1782. Many soldiers had a family there and decided to stay. Among these were the families of Balfour, Balneavis, Colyear, Douglas, Fraser, Gordon, Hamilton, MacAlester Loup, MacGillavry, Mackay, MacLeod, Sandilands, all of which are mentioned below.

## The students of the Universities of Harderwijk and Leiden

When the University of Leiden was founded in 1575, hundreds of Scottish students came to study law and medicine there and upon returning home influenced the development of Scotland in these fields.

## Other trades

Besides wool, the Scots, namely the Dumbars, the Dunlops and the Hopes, worked at many other trades such as shopkeeping, shipping, and banking.

## The coats of arms

In collecting the documentation for this paper, I worked through two huge collections of fiche. First, I worked from April 12, 1978 to June 19, 1981 on the collection of the Nederlandse Genealogische Vereniging at Naarden, North-Holland, which contains about 40,000 fiche. I then researched the collection Muschaert at the Centraal Bureau voor Genealogie, The Hague, with approximately 70,000 fiche, a project that took me half a year. I found approximately 400 descriptions in total.[2]

## 1. Abercromby

Arms of George Carel Abercrombie, January 29, 1771, captain of a company of militia at Paramaribo, Surinam or Dutch Guyana. Married Johanna Hubertine Dieulefit.

Arms: *Argent, on a chevron Gules between three boar's heads couped Azure, an inescutcheon Ermine.*

Wreath and mantling: *Argent and Gules.*

Crest: *A boar's head Azure, armed Argent.*

Motto: MERCY.

Source: Print in sealing-wax in the former notarial Archive of Dutch Guyana, Algemeen Rijksarchief, 1e afdeling, The Hague, reg. 1781 no. 46; BURKE'S *General Armory*, p. 2.

## 2. Armstrong

Arms: *Gules three arms vambraced fesswise in pale Argent.*

Wreath and mantling: *Argent and Gules.*

Crest: *A dexter forearm erect proper holding bendwise sinister a sword Argent hilted Or.*

Sources: *De Nederlandsche Leeuw*, Bulletin of *Koninklijk Nederlandsch Genootschap voor Geslacht- en Wapenkunde* (1958); BLOYS VAN TRESLONG PRINS, *Kerken van Zeeland*; BURKE'S *General Armory*.

### 3. Armstrong

Arms of two persons named Gerard Armstrong who were marksmen of the De Zandburch Guild at Delft from 1748 till 1790.

Arms: *Argent an hour glass Sable.*

Mantling and Crest: *Argent and Gules.*

Crest: *A dexter forearm erect proper holding bendwise sinister a sword Argent hilted Or.*

Source: *Book of the Coats of Arms of the Guild in Delft*, in Museum Meermanno-Westrenianum at The Hague.

### 4. Balfour of Burleigh

Arms of Philip Balfour, buried at Bergen op Zoom, November 27, 1638. Captain at Doesburg, Guelders (1627) and commander of Bergen op Zoom. Direct descendant of David Balfour of Burleigh who has been a colonel of a regiment of the Scots Brigade (1572). Married, Bergen op Zoom, October 30, 1607, to Anna, daughter of Paulus Bax and Elizabeth Joachim.

Arms: *Argent on a chevron Sable an otter's head Argent.*

Wreath and mantling: *Argent and Sable.*

Crest: *Upon a rock a mermaid holding in the dexter hand an otter's head and in the sinister hand a swan's head with neck all proper.*

Supporters: *Dexter an otter and sinister a swan proper.*

Motto: OMNE SOLUM FORTI PATRIA.

Source: Missives of the Council of State, Algemeen Rijksarchief, 1e afdeling, The Hague. *Nederland's Patriciaat*, vol. 11, p. 1020. BURKE'S *General Armory*.

### 5. Balneavis de Carnbadi

Arms of Alexander, son of Henry Balneavis and Caroline or Charlotte Stuart. Ensign 6th Bat. Infantry under Major-General Dundas (1782). Captain Cie. Major Scott. (1792). Captain 2nd regiment Stuart all of the Scots Brigade (1794).

Arms: *Two coats impaled; dexter: per fess Argent and Sable, a chevron between three medlar flowers cinquefoiled all counter charged* (Balneavis); *sinister: Argent a crescent Gules and on a chief three molets* (stars) *Argent* (his wife).

Wreath and mantling: *Argent and Sable.*

Crest: *A dexter hand proper holding in the palm a pallet or cannonball Sable.*

Motto: FORTITUDINE ET VELOCITATE.

Sources: *De Brabantse Leeuw*, vol. 1-2 (1968), p. 19-20. *The chronicle of the family Idema*, vol. 1 (1960); BURKE'S *General Armory*.

### 6. Bell

Arms: *Argent, issuing from the ground in base a tree all Vert, a chief Gules with three hawks-bells Argent.*

Wreath and mantling: *Or and Argent.*

Crest: *A hawks bell Argent.*

Source: DR. J. L. BRABER, *The Genealogy of the family Joppe.*

### 7. Bruce

Arms of M. George Isaac, son of Stewart John Bruce and Christina Schimmelpenninck (Deventer, province Overijssel, October 9, 1803-†Nieuwe Diep, province North-Holland, December 30, 1850). Appointed governor general of the Dutch East-Indies (1850).

Arms: *Or, a saltire and a chief Gules.*

Top of the shield: *A crown of three leaves and two pearls Or gemmed proper.*

Supporters: *Dexter: a lion Or, langued Gules; sinister: a unicorn Argent.*

Motto: FUIMUS.

Source: M. A. VAN RHEDE VAN DER KLOOT, *De Gouverneurs-Generaal en Commissarissen-Generaal van Nederlandsch-Indie, 1610-1888*, (The Hague: 1891), p. 188-189; BURKE'S *General Armory*.

### 8. Colyear

Arms of Count Walter Philip, son of Sir Alexander Robertson of Strowan, Perthshire, who assumed the name of Colyear (1657-†Maastricht, December 8, 1747). Commanding a regiment of the Scots Brigade (1695). Lieutenant-general (1718). Governor of Namur, Austrian Netherlands (1739). Married Alida Riemsburch, of Leiden, Holland (1681).

Arms: *Azure, on a chevron Argent three trees Vert between three boar's heads couped Argent.*

Wreath and mantling: *Argent and Azure.*

Crest: *A unicorn issuant Argent, langued Gules.*

Motto: AVANCE.

Sources: *Genealogie Heemskerck van Beesd*; SIR ROBERT DOUGLAS OF GLENBERVIE, *The Peerage*,

2nd ed. 1813, vol. 1, p. 371. BURKE'S *General Armory*, p. 289.

## 9. Couperus

Arms of the Rev. John Couper (ca. 1555-†1620), minister of Edinburgh. Left the country for safety reasons. Went to Burgwerd, province of Friesland, in The Netherlands, where he became a minister. Married to Theodore, daughter of Theodor Hay.

Arms: *Gules, a dove Argent holding in its beak a twig Or volant towards a sun issuant in dexter canton Or.*

Wreath and mantling: *Or and Gules.*

Crest: *A pair of wings Argent.*

Motto: TUUM EST.

Source: *Nederland's Patriciaat,* vol. 1 (1910).

## 10. Davidson

Arms of Sir William Davidson of Corriehill, Bt. and Kt. (Dundee 1615-†1678). Arrived in Amsterdam as agent and consul for Scotland (1640). Conservator of the Scottish Wool Staple at Veere, co. Zeeland (1661). Married first, Amsterdam, March 14, 1643, to Geertruyt Schuering (1613-†1652); second, Amsterdam, September 24, 1652, to Geertruyt van Dueren (1612-†1658); and third, Amsterdam, March 16, 1660, to Elizabeth Klerck (1630-†1667). His arms are now in the Town Hall at Haarlem, North-Holland.

Arms: *Azure, on a fess Argent between three pheons Or a stag lodged proper, on a canton Argent a sinister human hand Gules. ("The bloody hand of Ulster").*

Wreath and mantling: *Argent and Azure.*

Crest: *A dexter human hand proper holding a pheon surmounted by a molet all Or.*

Source: Bijblad of *Nederlandsche Leeuw*, vol. 1 (The Hague: Koninklijk Nederlandsch Genootschap voor Geslacht- en Wapenkunde, 1951); BURKE'S *General Armory*, p. 266.

## 11. Douglas of Friarshaw (Roxburghshire)

Arms of Robert, son of George Douglas of Friarshaw and Elizabeth Scott (Edinburgh, April 25, 1727-†Zierikzee, Zeeland, December 30, 1809). Ensign regiment Marjorybanks of the Scots Brigade (1745). Lieutenant-general of Infantry, commander of the Marines. Commander of 's Hertogenbosch, States Brabant (1795). Married, Bergen op Zoom, States Brabant, June 24, 1751, to Helena, daughter of Daniel de Brauw and Hester Stavenise (Bergen op Zoom, January 1, 1734-†Zierikzee, January 5, 1802).

Arms: *Argent, a heart Gules ensigned by a royal crown Or lined Gules, on a chief Azure three molets Argent, with a bordure nebuly Azure Celeste.*

Wreath and mantling: *Argent and Gules.*

Crest: *A dexter forearm and hand proper holding a lance sinister bendwise Or the upper half broken dexter bendwise proper the point Argent.*

Motto: DO OR DIE.

Source: *Nederland's Patriciaat,* vol. 71 (The Hague 1987); BURKE'S *General Armory*.

## 12. Dumbar

Arms of Gerhard, son of Jacob Dunbar and Aleida Traes (Deventer, November 14, 1681-†Deventer, April 6, 1744). Secretary of Deventer, province of Overijssel, and chronicler. Married first to Sara Maria van Steenbach (1707) and second to Anna Cuser (1712). Direct descendant of Archibald, son of Garvinus Dumbar, minister at Elgin, and Mary Dundas (Elgin, 1624-†Deventer, Overijssel, September 27, 1685). Shopkeeper at Deventer and member of the "sworn community" (1675-1676). Married, Amsterdam, March 20, 1650, to Jannette, daughter of Claes Jans Jansknegt (Edam, North-Holland, November 16, 1629-†Deventer, May 5, 1660).

Arms: *Argent two lions rampant guardant and respectant Or each holding in their paws a cushion Azure tasselled of the second and between them in base a like cushion with the cords crossed and twisted of the second.*

Wreath and mantling: *Or and Azure.*

Crest: *A pillow Azure tasselled at each corner Or.*

Source: *Procuraties van de Leenkamer in Gelderland 1713.* [Proxies of the Feudal Court of Guelders], Rijksarchief Guelders at Arnhem. *Nederland's Patriciaat,* vol. 8 (1917), p. 145; BURKE'S *General Armory*.

## 13. Dunlop (Fenwick, Ayrshire)

Arms of David Dunlop, born Glasgow, drowned 1778. Poorter (freeman) of Rotterdam (November 27, 1755). Captain of a merchant ship that was lost near Calais (1778). Married, Rotterdam, Scots church, June 13, 1753, to Janet, daughter of Alexander Roberts and Jane Cowie (Rotterdam, November 30, 1734-buried Rotterdam, Grote Kerk, May 17, 1794).

Arms: *Argent a double headed eagle displayed Gules.*

Wreath and mantling: *Argent and Gules.*

Crest: *A dexter forearm proper holding erect a sword Argent hilted Or.*

Motto: MERITO.

Source: *Nederland's Patriciaat*, vol. 38 (The Hague: 1952); BURKE'S *General Armory.*

### 14. Forbes Wels

The family Wels obtained by royal decree no. 39 of April 19, 1885 the right to adopt the name of Forbes.

Arms: *Quarterly: 1 and 4: Or a tree Vert issuing from the ground proper, impalling Azure an increscent moon with a human face Argent* (Wels); *2 and 3: Azure three bear's heads couped Argent muzzled Gules* (Forbes).

Wreath and mantling: *Dexter: Or and Vert; sinister: Argent and Azure.*

Crest: *A tree Vert between two wings the dexter Or and the sinister Argent.*

Source: DR. H. KITS NIEUWENKAMP, *Nederlandse familiewapens*, vol. 2, p. 70; BURKE'S *General Armory.*

### 15. Fraser of Fraserfield or of Balgownie

Arms of Huybrecht or Hugh Fraser (Bergen op Zoom, 1745-†Vlissingen, Zeeland, April 28, 1823). He was an orphan and his origin is unknown. Married, Vlissingen, March 16, 1774, to Adriana Helen, daughter of Bernardus du Moulin and Adriaantje Texse.

Arms: *Quarterly: 1 and 4: Azure, three fraises or cinquefoils Argent* (Fraser); *2: Or a lion rampant Gules debruised by a bend Sable* (Abernethy); *3: Gules a lion rampant Argent* (Ross).

Crest: *An ostrich proper holding in its beak a horseshoe Sable.*

Supporters: *Two angels with wings addorsed proper.*

Mottoes: QUAM SIBI SORTEM and IN GOD IS ALL.

Source: *Nederland's Patriciaat*, vol. 44 (1944); BURKE'S *General Armory*, p. 376.

### 16. Gordon

Arms of Alexander Gordon (Aberdeen, 1729-†Rossum, June 28, 1806). Ensign regiment Marjorybanks (1745). Lieutenant-colonel, infantry of the Scots Brigade (1786). On pension (1795). Mar-

ried, Oosterhout, States Brabant, June 5, 1761, to Maria Petronella Ghyben (1743-1830).

Arms: *Quarterly: 1 and 4: Azure, three boar's heads couped Or (Gordon); 2: Azure three fraises Argent (Fraser); 3: Or three crescents within a double treasure flory-counter-flory Gules (Seton).*

Crest: *a stag's head cabossed affrontee proper antlered Or.*

Supporters: *Two dogs Argent with collars Gules charged with three buckles Or.*

Wreath and mantling: *Or and Azure.*

Source: RIETSTAP'S *Wapenboek; Nederland's Patriciaat*, vol. 19 (1929-1930); BURKE'S *General Armory*, p. 411.

### 17. Graham

Arms of Willem Lodewijk Graham. Councillor of 's Hertogenbosch, States Brabant (1716).

Arms: *Quarterly: 1 and 4: Or on a chief Sable three escallops counterchanged; 2 and 3: Argent three roses Gules barbed Vert all within a bordure quarterly Gules and Sable.*

Wreath and mantling: *Or and Gules.*

Crest: *An escallop Or.*

Source: Collection Musschaert, fiche 22d; BURKE'S *General Armory.*

### 18. Hamilton of Silvertonhill (Lanarkshire)

Arms of Thomas Hamilton of Silvertonhill, 1821. Direct descendant of Sir Robert Hamilton, 2nd baronet of Silvertonhill (†Fort William, 1708). Captain regiment of Earl of Leven of the Scots Brigade (1689). Major regiment of General James Maitland (1700). Married, Goutum, Friesland, March 11, 1683, to Aurelia Catharina, daughter of Taecke van Hettinga and Djeedtje Jans van Runia.

Arms: *Gules a crescent Or between three pierced cinquefoils Ermine and a bordure of the same.*

Wreath and mantling: *Argent and Gules.*

Crest: *An oak tree proper fructed Or and penetrated traversely in the main stem by a frame-saw Or.*

Motto: SOLA NOBILITAT VIRTUS.

Source: *Nederland's Patriciaat*, vol. 56 (1970), p. 47; BURKE'S *General Armory*, p. 446.

### 19. Hope

Arms of extinct family of Dutch nobility (Jonkheer for all).

Arms: *Azure, a chevron Or between three bezants Or.*

Crest: *A broken globe surmounted of a rainbow and clouds and the four gods of the season's*

winds: *Aeolus, Boreas, Favonius and Zephyrus all proper.*
Motto: AT SPES NON FRACTA AT SPES INFRACTA.
Source: *Wapenboeken van Scheltens van Kampferbeke,* vol. C, Municipal archives Rotterdam; BURKE'S *General Armory,* p. 506.

### 20. Van Iterson (orig. Outerson)
Arms: *Argent, three thistle flowers all proper slipped with stem and two leaves.*
Wreath and mantling: *Or and Vert.*
Crest: *A thistle between two wings Or.*
Motto: NOLI ME TANGERE.
Source: *Nederland's Patriciaat,* vol. 35 (1946).

### 21. Kennedy
Arms of Walter Kennedy, councillor of Police and Criminal Justice in Surinam or Dutch Guyana.
Arms: *Quarterly: 1 and 4: Gules three drops Or voided of the field; 2: Gules a lion rampant Or; 3: Argent a helmet affronty barred Or lined Gules ensigned by a crown of the second issuing therefrom a dexter chain-link glove Argent.*
Wreath and mantling: *Or and Gules.*
Crest: *The charge of the 3rd quarter.*
Source: *Gens Nostra,* 1953, p. 102-103.

### 22. Loudon (Forfarshire)
Dutch nobility (Jonkheer for all). Arms of James Loudon (The Hague, June 8, 1824-†The Hague, May 30, 1900), son of Alexander Loudon and Suzanna Gaspardina Valck. Married to Jkvr. Louise Wilhelmina Françoise Félicité de Stuers, Batavia, Dutch East-Indies, August 20, 1855. Direct descendant of Alexander Loudon (Tannadice parish, November 20, 1789-†Rotterdam, October 12, 1839). Naval officer on the fleet of Admiral Sir Robert Stopford at Java, (1811). Resident of Banjuwangi, secretary and temporal resident of Semarang (1811-1816). Sugar and indigo administrator on Java. Naturalised by royal decree of September 17, 1824, no. 107. Married, Semarang, April 10, 1815, to Susanna Gaspardina, daughter of Jan Arend Valck and Johanna Helena Beylon (Kampen, Overijssel, April 10, 1801-†Krawang, November 30, 1828). Minister for the Colonies (1861). King's commissioner for the province of South-Holland (1862-1871). Governor-general of the Dutch East-Indies (1872-1875).
Arms: *Gyronny of eight Ermine and Gules.*

Wreath and mantling: *Argent and Gules.*
Crest: *With a helmet proper barred Or, issuing from a crown of five leaves Or a double headed eagle displayed Gules.*
Supporters: *Two griffins Or langued Gules.*
Source: *Nederland's Patriciaat,* vol. 21 (1933) and vol. 53 (1964); M.A. RHEEDE VAN DER KLOOT, *De Gouverneurs-Generaal etc. van Nederlandsch-Indie, 1610-1888* (The Hague: 1891); BURKE'S *General Armory.*

### 23. MacAlester Loup (originally: of the Loup)
Arms of Robert MacAlester (The Hague-†January 13, 1861), son of Duncan MacAlester and Maria Ouwens. Minister at Zaltbommel. Married, Meeuwen, North-Brabant, November 4, 1830, secondly to Catharina Maria Tierens. Direct descendant of Duncan MacAlester Loup, officer Scots Brigade (1707), married to Johanna, daughter of Arnold Luchtenmaker (1717).
Arms: *Quarterly: 1 Argent a lion rampant Gules; 2 Or a sinister arm vambraced Argent, the hand proper holding a cross-crosslet fitchy palewise Gules; 3 Or a galley Sable with three flags Gules the sails furled; 4, Argent on waves in base Vert a salmon Argent.*
Wreath and mantling: *Or and Gules.*
Crest: *A sinister arm vambraced Argent the hand proper holding a cross-crosslet fitchy palewise Gules.*
Motto: PER MARE PER TERRAS.
Sources: Rijksarchief in Arnhem (Guelders); *Nederlands Patriciaat,* vol. 3 (1912); *Algemeen Nederlandsch Familieblad* (1888); BURKE'S *General Armory.*

### 24. MacDonald de Bowie
Arms of William McDonald. Midshipman at Arnhem (1770) and lieutenant ( 1776).
Arms: *Quarterly: 1 Argent a lion rampant Gules; 2 An arm habited Gules the hand proper holding a cross-crosslet fitchy palewise Sable; 3 Or a galley Sable with three flags Gules, the sails furled; 4 barry wavy Argent and Vert in base a salmon Argent.*
Wreath and mantling: *Argent and Gules.*
Crest: *A dexter forearm erect in pale the hand holding a sword Argent hilt and pommel Or.*
Motto: VINCERE AUT MORI.
Source: Rijksarchief in Arnhem (Guelders); BURKE'S *General Armory,* p. 638.

**25. MacGillavry of Dunmaglas (Argyllshire)**

Arms of Edward John MacGillavry, doctor of law, managing director of the Amsterdam-Rotterdam Bank (Semarang, D.E.I., 1916-†The Hague, August 2, 1997). Direct descendant of William MacGillavry (Elgin, October 22, 1751-buried, Zwolle, Bethlehem church, Overijssel, May 4, 1810). Served regiment Infantry of Major-General Dundas of the Scots Brigade. Teacher English at Zwolle (1794). Married, Zwolle, Michaels church, April 26, 1795, to Elisabeth, daughter of Ernst Landevelt and Geertruyt Jacoba van Kamp (Emmerich, Germany, June 24, 1773-†Zwolle, October 10, 1812).

Arms: *Quarterly: 1 Azure, a galley Or with three flags Gules sails furled; 2 Or three salmons naiant fesswise in pale proper; 3 Or a Malay kris erect Argent hilted proper (Semarang); 4 Azure, an anchor cabled Argent.*

Wreath and mantling: *Or and Azure.*

Crest: *A catamount sejant guardant proper langued Gules holding in the sinister paw palewise a cross-crosslet fitchee Gules, dexter paw resting.*

Motto: VIGILATE (above the crest).

Source: *The Lyon King of Arms' Public Register of All Arms and Bearings in Scotland, in Edinburgh*, vol. 52 (1971), p. 115; BURKE'S *General Armory*, p. 640.

**26. Mackay**

Belongs to both Dutch and Scottish nobility. Arms of Aeneas Baron Mackay van Ophemert en Zonnewijnen (Nijmegen, January 13, 1806-†The Hague, March 8, 1876). Son of Jhr. later Baron Barthold Johan Christiaan Mackay and Anna Magdalena Frederica Henriette van Renesse. 10th Lord Reay (June 2, 1875). Married, The Hague, October 27, 1837, to Jkvr. Maria Catharina Anna Jacoba, daughter of 'Meester' Jacob Baron Fagel and Jacoba Margheretha Maria Boreel (The Hague, September 28, 1817-†The Hague, May 22, 1886). Direct descendant of Donald Mackay (Ribigill, 1721-†Groningen, Province of Groningen, March 25, 1801). Officer of the Scots Brigade (1740). Married, Nijmegen, Guelders, January 15, 1762, to Mayken, daughter of Lambert Mouthaan and Belix van Grevenbroeck (baptised Nijmegen, April 20, 1735-†in a convent in Friesland, after 1801).

Arms: *Azure, on a chevron Or between three boar's heads couped Argent muzzled Gules, a roebuck's head erased between two hands proper issuant from the ends of the chevron each holding a dagger Silver.*

Wreath and mantling: *Argent and Azure.*

Crest: *A dexter cubit arm, holding a dagger in pale all proper, pommel and hilt Or.*

Supporters: *Dexter, a pipeman armed and sinister, a musqueteer all proper.*

Motto: MANU FORTI.

Source: DANIEL BARON MACKAY, *Geschiedenis van het geslacht Mackay* (Koninklijk Nederlandsch Genootschap voor Geslacht- en Wapenkunde/de Walburg Pers Zutphen: 1984).

**27. Maclaine Pont**

Arms of Charles Anthonie Maclaine, minister at Medemblik, Holland.

Arms: *Quarterly: 1 and 4 per fess Argent and Gules an oak branch leaved and fructed proper in chief, in base three tuns of the first resting 1 and 2; 2 Or, two branches raguly in saltire Vert; 3 quarterly (1) Argent a lion rampant Gules; (2) Azure a castle of three towers Argent (Mac-Kinnon); (3) Or a lymphad Sable, sails furled; (4) Argent, two eagle's heads erased respectant Vert in base a salmon naiant Azure.*

Wreath and mantling: *Argent and Gules.*

Crest: *An eagle's head erased Vert.*

Source: KITS NIEUWENKAMP, *Nederlandse familiewapens*; BURKE'S *General Armory*, p. 644.

**28. MacLeod (Invernesshire, Isle of Skye)**

Arms of Norman MacLeod (Invernessshire, 1690). Lieutenant (1719) and captain (1721) regiment of Infantry Douglas of the Scots Brigade. Married, Grave, December 23, 1713, attestation to Beesd, January 14, 1714, to Geertruyt, daughter of 'Meester' Hendrik Schrassert and Johanna Charlotta Schrassert, (baptised Arnhem, Guelders, August 15, 1689-†Elburg, Guelders, January 4, 1764). She married 2nd 'Meester' Andreas Pelgrom Ardesch, November 16, 1632.

Arms: *Azure a castle Argent and Sable, base Vert three towers Argent the middle one higher than the others.*

Wreath and mantling: *Argent and Azure.*

Crest: *An oxhead guardant with neck guardant*

*proper between two flags with staffs Gules.*
Motto: MURUS AHENUM EST.
Source: *Nederland's Patriciaat*, vol. 59 (1970).

### 29. MacLeod

Arms: *Quarterly: 1 Or a rock Sable, inflamed proper; 2 Gules, three legs in armour proper garnished and spurred Or flexed and conjoined in triangle at the upper part of the thigh (Isle of Man); 3 Or a galley Sable sails furled with three flags Gules; 4 Gules a lion rampant Argent.*
Wreath and mantling: *Or and Gules*
Crest: *The sun in splendour Or.*
Mottoes: LUCIO NON URO and
QUO CUNQUE JACERIS STABIT.
Supporters: *Two Savages coming out of a volcano with their head in hand all proper.*
Source: BURKE'S *General Armory*, p. 645.

### 30. Maitland (Earl of Lauderdale)

Arms: *Or a lion rampant dechausee (dismembered or couped at all points) Gules within a double tressure flory-counter-flory Gules.*
Crest: *A lion sejant affrontee Gules, imperially crowned, holding in the dexter paw a sword hilted and pommelled Or, in the sinister a fleur-de-lis Azure.*
Source: *Gens Nostra* (1953), magazine of the Nederlandse Genealogische Vereniging. DR. IR. JOHN MAC LEAN, Bijblad of *De Nederlandse Leeuw*, vol. 6 (*Koninklijk Nederlandsch Genootschap voor Geslacht- en Wapenkunde*); BURKE'S *General Armory*, p. 651.

### 31. Maxwell (Earl of Nithsdale)

Arms found in a collection of sealing-wax prints.
Arms: *Impaled: 1 Argent a double-headed eagle Sable charged on the breast with an escutcheon Argent with a saltire Sable; 2 Azure a chevron between three annulets Argent.*
Wreath and mantling: *dexter, Argent and Sable; sinister, Argent and Azure.*
Crest: *In front of a holly-tree, a stag lodged proper.*
Motto: REVIRESCO.
Source: Collection of sealing-wax prints of "a Museum at Rotterdam"; BURKE'S *General Armory*, p. 671.

### 32. Murray of Falahill (Mid Lothian)

Arms of family.
Arms: *Argent, a hunting horn Sable garnished and stringed Gules on a chief Azure three molets Argent.*
Wreath and mantling: *Argent and Azure.*
Crest: *An arm vambraced, Argent the hand holding per bend sinister a morning star mace Argent all proper.*
Motto: HINC USQUE SUPERNA VENABOR.
Source: BURKE'S *General Armory*, p. 717.

### 33. Sandilands

Arms of Sir William Sandilands, Kt, Laird of Clamannan, Terweer and Melissant (†June 28, 1673). Sergeant major of a regiment of Infantry of the Scots Brigade.
Arms: *Quarterly: 1 and 4 Or a bend wavy Azure (Sandilands); 2 and 3 Argent, a heart Gules imperially crowned Or lined also Gules and gemmed proper on a chief Azure three molets Argent (Douglas).*
Wreath and mantling: *Argent and Azure.*
Crest: *A dexter arm vambraced holding per bend a sword Argent hilted and pommelled Or point to the base.*
Source: His coat of arms on a tomb in the church of St. Servatius at Maastricht, Limburg; BURKE'S *General Armory*, p. 896.

### 34. Stuart

Arms of Edmond Stuart (ca. 1585-†Geertruidenberg, Holland, before February 7, 1622). Bought a house in Geertruidenberg. Married to Anneken Pietersdr Stuards.
Arms: *Or a lion rampant Gules, on a bordure Argent eight demi fleurs-de-lis issuant outward of the second.*
Wreath and mantling: *Or and Gules.*
Crest: *A demi lion rampant Gules.*
Source: *Nederland's Patriciaat*, vol. 50 (1964); BURKE'S *General Armory*, p. 982-983 gives the crest for the Stuarts of Promara, co. Waterford, of Rothesay and of Tillicoultry.

### 35. Tindal

Dutch nobility (Jonkheer for all). Arms of Daniel Tindal. (Dendermonde, 1739- ).
Arms: *Quarterly: 1 Dimidiated, dexter: Or a*

headed eagle halved, unbeaked and no legs, Sable; sinister: Argent three bars couped Azure palewise; 2 Azure a lion rampant Or issuant from the base wavy Argent; 3 Azure a stag trippant on a base all Or; 4 Gules a military tunic and helmet in chief all Argent.
Wreath and mantling: *Or and Gules.*
Crest: *A crown Or with seven pearls proper but shown without a crest.*
Supporters: *Two lions guardant langued Gules.*
Source: *De Navorser* (1889) and (1951).

### 36. Wiselius

Arms of Samuel Wiselius (1769-†1845). Baillie of Muiden, North-Holland. Married to Susanna Le Polle (1772-1813). Direct descendant of Edmund Whisell of Orkney (1304-) who came in 1416 to the Low Countries and established himself at Geertruidenberg, Holland.
Arms: *Azure, three pomegranates ordered 2,1, slipped and leaved Or split to reveal pips Gules.*
Wreath and mantling: *Or and Azure.*
Crest: *Two ostrich feathers and a weasel issuant all Argent, the weasel between the shanks of a compass Or.*
Supporters: *Two griffins guardant, the dexter Sable langued and collared Gules, the sinister per fess Sable and Or.*
Mottoes: DULCIA NON MERUIT QUI NON GUSTAVIT AMARA and OCCULUS IN METAM.

Source: VORSTERMAN VAN OYEN, *Stam- en Wapenboek van aanzienlijke Nederlandsche Familiën*, vol. 3, p. 354; *Nederland's Patriciaat*, vol. 39 (1953).

### NOTES

1.   The theme of this congress was emigration: an excellent topic I would say. Man, from the earliest times, has always migrated to other places. Before I turn to my subject, I want to say that, before our congress took place, it was my privilege to see some parts of the province of Quebec, such as Montreal and Quebec, which I knew only from the history of my family. I state here with pride that at least four Scottish Douglases contributed to the history of Canada, presenting four different trades:

First, David Douglas (1799-1834), a botanist from Scone, in Fife, who discovered the fir tree in British Columbia, which bears his name. Second, Sir James Douglas, 9th Laird of Friarshaw (1704-1787), Captain of HMS Aleide under Sir Charles Saunders, who brought the news of the fall of Quebec in 1759 to the Court of St. James's in London, by which he became a Knight of the Order of the Bath. Third, James Douglas of Lanark (1803-1877), the first Governor of British Columbia from 1858-1863. And fourth, Thomas Douglas, 5th Earl of Selkirk (1771-1820), who colonised parts of Prince Edward Island, Manitoba and Ontario.

2.   It is here that I want to cordially thank three persons who worked closely with me to produce the slides. First, Mr. Andries J. Roelofs (1906- ) at Amsterdam, the Hon. Herald of the Caledonian Society, who worked out the descriptions and published them in our magazine. He enlarged 36 of these 400 coats of arms in colour. Second, my father, Mr. John Douglas (1906-1986), who made the slides out of the enlarged drawings. Third, Mr. Peter Falcon Uff (†1995), who checked the blasoning of the coats of arms.

### Illustrations

1

2

3

4

119

5

6

7

8

9

10

11

12

121

13

14

15

16

17

Sola nobilitat virtus.

18

19

NOLI ME TANGERE

20

21

22

23

24

25

26

27

29

30

31

32

33

34

35

36

# VRAIES ET FAUSSES GÉNÉALOGIES : ÉTUDE DE QUELQUES CAS RELIÉS À LA NOUVELLE-FRANCE

Jean-Claude Dubé

Le 26 avril 1622 s'ouvrait, au siège parisien du grand prieuré de France de l'ordre de Malte, une enquête concernant l'ancienneté de la noblesse de Charles Huault de Montmagny[1].

Son frère Louis présenta une série de documents démontrant que, tant du côté maternel que paternel les ascendants du postulant avaient été, depuis deux siècles au moins, qualifiés d'écuyers ou de chevaliers, qu'ils avaient servi le roi non seulement dans des charges de judicature (ce qui était indéniable), mais aussi dans son armée ; qu'ils possédaient des terres nobles.

Des nombreux détails que contient cet ensemble impressionnant retenons ceux-ci concernant le bisaïeul de Charles Huault — il fallait un minimum de quatre degrés de noblesse pour entrer dans l'ordre : l'arrière-grand-père, donc, Pierre Huault de Montmagny, avait épousé en secondes noces Isabeau Lebret, qui était la fille d'un chevalier ; la mère de ce même Pierre était Alix de Villiers, dont le mari, prénommé Jacques, avait accompagné le roi Charles VIII à Naples en 1495. Or cette dame de Villiers était du même lignage que Philippe de Villiers de l'Isle-Adam, grand maître de l'ordre de Saint-Jean de Jérusalem, qui assura le transfert à Malte en 1530. Il y avait là de quoi impressionner favorablement les officiers du grand prieuré.

Quatre personnages se présentèrent ensuite ; ils avaient connu le père du candidat (mort en 1610) et témoignèrent que celui-ci était :

> gentilhomme de nom et d'armes, d'ancienne et noble maison, qui en son jeune age et même depuis qu'il avoit été pourveu d'office de judicature avoit porté les armes pour le roi, où ils l'avoient vu au siege de Paris et étoit tenu entre la noblesse pour bien gentilhomme.

Ils dirent ensuite un mot des armes des Huault et des Du Drac (la mère de Charles Huault) — retenons celles des Du Drac, bien parlantes

dans son cas : *D'or au dragon de sinople, armé, couronné et lampassé de gueules.*

Les enquêteurs de l'ordre furent aussi dans trois églises parisiennes vérifier les inscriptions figurant sur les tombes, et ils se transportèrent finalement à Montmagny, « lieu de naissance et extraction dudit Charles Huault » ; ils furent impressionnés par le château et le parc, qui démontraient, selon eux, « une grande ancienneté ». Une enquête auprès des notables du lieu confirma la réputation d'ancienneté de la noblesse des Huault.

Trois choses ressortent de ce que nous venons d'exposer : premièrement l'importance du nom — on est « gentilhomme de nom et d'armes » — ce qui signifie qu'on est né noble et que cette noblesse est ancienne, un symbole de cela : les armoiries ; dans le dictionnaire d'Antoine Furetière, de 1690, je note ceci, au mot « Armes » : « ce sont des marques d'honneur qui se mettent sur les Escus et sur les enseignes », et plus loin : « un tel est chef du nom et des armes d'une telle maison »[2]. Deuxièmement le rappel des alliances qui sont révélatrices du statut élevé auquel a accédé une famille, statut que vient parfois rehausser encore la présence d'un personnage célèbre. Troisièmement la profession des armes — l'épée en est le symbole ; on peut bien être dans la robe ; ce qui compte, c'est l'épée[3]. On se trouve en fait, au début du XVIIᵉ siècle, en France, dans une période de transition : la robe — le « service civil », il faudrait dire — se développe rapidement à cause de la centralisation du royaume et du développement des organismes étatiques qui l'accompagne. Pourtant l'épée reste, dans les mentalités, bien supérieure ; elle est perçue comme l'idéal même de la noblesse ; la naissance prime encore sur le mérite personnel, ce qui explique l'intérêt qu'on manifeste pour l'ancienneté des lignages ; les ordres de chevalerie, les couvents de chanoinesses exigent une noblesse immémoriale de leurs membres. D'où le nombre important de fausses généalogies qu'on retrouve dans de nombreux dépôts d'archives.

Le but de notre communication est d'étudier ce phénomène non seulement dans son élaboration — constitution de dossiers de preuves —, mais aussi dans sa transmission par l'imprimé. Nous montrerons ensuite comment, à l'aide de documents dont l'authenticité est incontestable, il est possible de démanteler ces constructions imaginaires et de retrouver la vraie version des choses.

Trois cas seront retenus ; ils ont pour arrière-plan la Nouvelle-France : ceux de Charles Huault de Montmagny, qui y fut gouverneur de 1636 à 1648 ; de Jean-Baptiste Colbert, ministre de la marine et des colonies de 1662 à 1683 ; de Gilles Hocquart, qui fut intendant à Québec de 1731 à 1748.

## Les Huault de Montmagny

Le premier cas, celui des Huault, nous a servi d'introduction. N'insistons pas, sauf à faire remarquer que le tableau généalogique ainsi constitué servit dès 1594 quand il fallut prouver les quatre quartiers de François de Faucon de Ris, dont la mère, Étiennette Huault, était la petite-fille de Pierre, et, en 1613, quand Jean Anjorrant demanda lui aussi son admission dans l'ordre — sa mère se nommait Antoinette Huault. Ce schéma servit encore pour Alexandre Huault de Vayres, un cousin de Charles, qui commença son noviciat à Malte en 1629[4]. On le ressortit en 1714 : les Huault de Bernay, « seuls restants des Huault de Vaires et ce Montmagny » voulurent justifier « leur droit de sépulture sous le maître autel de l'église de Saint-Jean en Grève », à Paris[5].

Ce sont sans doute les Huault de Bernay qui le firent parvenir à l'équipe qui prépara l'édition de 1725 du *Grand dictionnaire historique* que Louis Moreri[6] fit paraître pour la première fois en 1674 ; on le retrouve inchangé dans les éditions subséquentes. Un ouvrage paru en 1978 l'a reprise[7].

Comment a-t-il été possible de démontrer la supercherie ? C'est un acte notarié, en date du 19 mai 1565[8], qui nous a donné les éléments nécessaires. Ce jour-là Louis Huault, le fils de Pierre, fait don à son cousin, marchand orfèvre, bourgeois de Paris, de terrains qu'il possède à Azay-le-Rideau, mais de plus il explique d'où lui venaient ces propriétés : elles avaient appartenu à Mathurin I Huault, le père de Pierre, puis à Mathurin II, son frère, qui avait été « notaire et tabellion » audit lieu. Voilà l'origine des Huault retrouvée.

Pierre commença sa carrière comme clerc d'un secrétaire du roi, Thomas Thioust — fonction qui était donc très proche de celle de son frère Mathurin, le notaire. Quand son patron mourut en 1497[9], il épousa sa veuve, puis réussit à obtenir lui-même une charge de secrétaire du roi. Un secrétaire du roi avait pour fonction de signer et d'expédier les lettres émanant des diverses chancelleries du royaume. Un précieux avantage était attaché à cette charge : elle conférait la noblesse. C'est à ce moment-là, et pas avant, que la famille Huault accéda au second ordre. On connaît la réaction désabusée de Saint-Simon devant cette pratique — il parle en effet à son propos de « savonnette à vilain ». Or un poète satirique du XVIe siècle avait usé brutalement de sa plume pour dénoncer l'accès à la noblesse de personnes qu'il jugeait indignes de cet honneur. Sur Pierre Huault il écrivit ce quatrain assez fielleux :

> Huauld, si de vallet, par impudicité,
> Ta maitresse te fist son seigneur et son maistre,
> Ne te hausse ; le temps, qui desfait et fait estre,
> Te pourra, par retour, réduire à pauvreté[10].

La branche des Huault de Montmagny devint, à la fin du XVIe siècle, passablement riche. Quand elle s'éteignit en 1699, il ne restait plus à Adrien Huault[11] qu'une pension viagère, tout au plus honnête ; rien ne subsistait de leur patrimoine immobilier, au centre ville ou en banlieue de Paris[12].

Voilà un cas intéressant. Pour entrer dans l'ordre de Malte il fallait prouver quatre quartiers de noblesse, c'est-à-dire que les huit bisaïeuls étaient nés nobles. Or pour Charles Huault, quatre seulement sur les huit étaient dans cette situation ; il fallut inventer une généalogie et forger des titres.

## Les Colbert

Nous allons considérer maintenant un autre cas, un peu plus tardif, celui-ci, du milieu du XVIIe siècle, et impliquant un personnage très important, le fameux ministre de Louis XIV, Jean-Baptiste Colbert.

Si l'on va, une fois encore, consulter le dictionnaire de Moreri, voici ce qu'on peut lire : Jean-Baptiste Colbert, né à Paris le 31 août 1619, descendait, suivant un titre du parlement d'Écosse, d'une maison originaire de ce royaume établie en Champagne dans le XIIIᵉ siècle, comme il paraît par le tombeau de Richard Colbert, qui se voit aux Cordeliers de Reims avec cette inscription à l'entour de la pierre, gravée en lettres gothiques :

> ci git li preux chevalier Richard Colbert, dit li Ecossois, kif (ici trois ou quatre mots qu'on ne sauroit lire) 1300 [qui décéda en 1300]. Priez pour l'ame de li ;

et au milieu de la pierre est gravé l'écusson des armes de ce chevalier portant un serpent tortillé mis en pal. Au dessous de cet écusson sont ces vers en lettres gothiques :

> En Ecosse je eus le berceau
> Et Rheims m'a donné le tombeau.

Dans la descendance de Jean-Baptiste je note ceci : son troisième fils, Antoine-Martin, fut bailli et grand-croix de Malte, général des galères de cet ordre, commandeur de Boncourt, colonel du régiment de Champagne, brigadier des armées du roi. Un de ses petit-fils entra aussi dans l'ordre de Malte ; il était connu sous le nom de « Chevalier de Seignelay ».

Donc, si l'on se fie au célèbre dictionnaire, Jean-Baptiste Colbert appartenait à un lignage prestigieux dont la noblesse remontait au moins au XIIIᵉ siècle — une inscription, à laquelle on avait donné des airs d'ancienneté, en faisait foi ; l'entrée dans l'ordre de Malte en apportait une preuve supplémentaire.

Le chevalier de Courcelles, dans un ouvrage de 1820, en rajoute. Il s'agit pour lui d'une famille issue des anciens barons de Castle Hill en Écosse, et connue en France depuis 1285 ; sa postérité fut nombreuse et illustre ; elle s'est alliée à plusieurs maisons souveraines et princières d'Allemagne et d'Italie et aux plus considérables de France [13].

Par contre, si l'on se reporte au *Dictionnaire général du Canada* de Louis Le Jeune, publié en 1931, on trouve une version bien différente de celles qu'on vient de voir : Jean-Baptiste Colbert, selon cet auteur, était « fils d'un marchand de drap » [14]. Cette version n'est pas juste non plus, mais elle se trouve un peu plus près de la vérité.

Arrivé au faîte du pouvoir, Colbert ne pouvait souffrir d'être d'origine obscure, il chargea des généalogistes complaisants de lui trouver des ancêtres honorables. Cela lui permit en plus de bien placer sa progéniture.

Son cas a des points de ressemblance avec celui des Huault. Le 15 mai 1668, Frère Guillaume de Neufville, chevalier de l'ordre de Malte, recevait les preuves de noblesse d'Antoine-Martin Colbert, le troisième fils de Jean-Baptiste. Sont présentés les contrats de mariage des trois générations précédentes : le père, l'aïeul, le bisaïeul y sont qualifiés d'écuyers. La noblesse des ascendants maternels est également clairement exposée ; à noter que, dans l'ascendance de Marie Charron, la mère du postulant, on rencontre la famille Bégon — il s'agit de celle à laquelle appartenait un des intendants de la Nouvelle-France au XVIIIᵉ siècle, Michel Bégon. La référence à la vie militaire s'imposait. L'arrière-grand-père, Jean Colbert, affirme-t-on, a utilement servi le roi Henri IV contre les Ligueurs dans la ville de Reims. Puis, de Jean, c'est la remontée vers l'ancêtre mythique, Édouard Colbert de Castlehill, qui passa d'Écosse en France, en 1285, avec sa femme Damoiselle Marie Lindsay. L'épitaphe de la chapelle des Cordeliers est bien sûr, examinée ; voici comment l'enquêteur la décrit : « sur la tombe paraît un Écossais à l'antique avec une couleuvre [le serpent évoqué plus haut], qui sont les mêmes armes que celle de l'arbre généalogique du présenté » [15]. Suit une imposante série d'actes (ou, plutôt, majoritairement, de pseudo-actes) notariés.

Pour retrouver la vraie version des choses, nous disposons d'un livre écrit par un excellent chercheur, l'historien Jean-Jouis Bourgeon ; il a pour titre *Les Colbert avant Colbert* [16]. Une longue et patiente investigation dans les archives municipales et départementales lui a permis de découvrir ce qu'était le lignage Colbert avant la carrière fulgurante de Jean-Baptiste. À sa suite nous allons, très brièvement, esquisser, mais de façon régressive, l'évolution sociale de la famille, qu'il est maintenant possible de connaître avec assurance jusqu'au XVᵉ siècle.

Une courte description de la carrière de Nicolas Colbert, le père du ministre (plus du tiers du volume de Bourgeon est consacré à cela) mettra en évidence deux choses fort intéressantes : la nette ascension de la famille ; la mise en place d'éléments qui assureront la réussite de Jean-Baptiste.

Dans l'acte de baptême de Nicolas Colbert (en date du 25 mars 1590), son père est dit marchand, bourgeois de Reims ; son parrain, un oncle maternel a le même titre (il sera élu en 1601 échevin de la ville de Reims).

Après avoir fréquenté — peut-être quatre ou cinq ans — le collège des Bons-enfants, Nicolas va faire son apprentissage chez des marchands de Lyon ; il s'agit de marchands merciers, mais engagés dans le commerce de gros, et parfois dans des opérations assez semblables à celles des banquiers. Notons tout de suite que notre homme ne fut jamais marchand de draps[17], comme l'affirmait Le Jeune, mais qu'il œuvrait dans la « marchandise ».

En 1613 il épouse Marie Pussort, qui est fille d'un important marchand de Reims ; ils sont cousins au quatrième degré — l'auteur étudie longuement ce mariage, parce qu'il s'agit d'un bon exemple d'endogamie lignagère et professionnelle. La dot est relativement importante.

Puis c'est l'association avec sa mère, qui a succédé au père à la direction de l'entreprise ; le phénomène est intéressant, parce qu'il montre la cohésion des familles et la participation féminine aux affaires ; elle-même venait, on l'a vu, d'un lignage engagé dans le commerce. Une étude est présentement en cours par un professeur de l'Université d'Ottawa sur les femmes libraires à Paris dans la première moitié du XVIIe siècle[18]. Dans ce milieu-là aussi les réseaux de famille sont très développés et expliquent de nombreux phénomènes.

Puis c'est le départ pour Paris — pratique très courante : se rapprocher du pouvoir ; plusieurs Colbert l'avaient d'ailleurs précédé dans cette démarche ; il acquiert un petit fief, Vandières, au sud de la capitale et, dans les contrats, fait précéder son nom de « noble homme », avant-nom qui n'est absolument pas une preuve de noblesse. Il se lance ensuite dans les finances publiques, mais sans y faire une fortune imposante, comme c'était souvent le cas[19].

Vient finalement la période faste, à partir de 1648. Deux éléments sont à retenir ; premièrement l'obtention de charges honorifiques, mais notons bien qu'aucun des deux offices qu'il finit par détenir ne lui accordait la noblesse, même s'il fait parfois suivre son nom du titre d'écuyer ; deuxièmement la possibilité pour son fils de fréquenter des personnes d'influence.

Parmi les causes de cette réussite, deux éléments sont également à retenir : l'alliance avec les Phélypeaux, famille en rapide ascension, et la réussite du cousin, Jean-Baptiste Colbert de Saint-Pouange, beau-frère de Michel Le Tellier, qui devint en 1643 secrétaire d'État (c'est-à-dire ministre) de la guerre.

Remontons maintenant dans le temps. Jean, le père de Nicolas, est marchand bourgeois, il épouse la fille d'un marchand bourgeois ; mais ce n'est pas un petit commerçant ; il a des relations (grâce, entre autres, à sa famille) avec les villes d'Amiens, Troyes et Lyon. Il acquiert une petite charge de finances, et entre au conseil de la ville de Reims, ce qui ne l'empêche pas de continuer son commerce.

Le père de Jean et son grand-père sont marchands bourgeois de Reims. Dans les deux générations précédentes, on est « masson », mais il s'agit d'artisans d'une certaine envergure, puisque, dans un document de 1433, on voit « Jehan Collebert » à la tête d'une équipe chargée de la démolition d'une tour près de Reims[20]. Parallèlement une autre branche de la famille Colbert réside dans un faubourg de la ville ; ses membres sont laboureurs, donc des paysans disposant non seulement d'une terre (plus ou moins étendue), mais surtout d'un « train de culture », c'est-à-dire de bêtes de trait et d'un outillage, pouvant d'ailleurs servir à autre chose qu'à des travaux agricoles.

Des actes authentiques, échelonnés depuis 1433, ont permis à Jean-Louis Bourgeon de suivre le lignage Colbert jusqu'à Jean-Baptiste et de présenter la véritable généalogie (six tableaux généalogiques accompagnent le volume ; trois autres présentent les alliances). Notons bien qu'à chacune des étapes que nous venons de mentionner des recherches généalogiques se sont imposées pour permettre de bien saisir le phénomène social ; donc partout dans ce livre la généalogie est sous-jacente au travail de l'histoire sociale. Notons encore combien est précieux pour celui qui s'intéresse à l'histoire sociale le fait qu'on ait pu retracer depuis le XVe siècle le destin d'un lignage qui, en l'espace de deux siècles, passa de l'artisanat à la marchandise, puis au sommet de l'appareil étatique.

### Les Hocquart

Un troisième lignage va maintenant retenir notre attention : les Hocquart, dont un représentant passa plusieurs années à Québec au milieu du XVIIIe siècle. Mais notons bien que nous ne nous éloignons pas tout à fait de la famille Colbert, parce que Jean Hocquart, le bisaïeul de l'intendant de la Nouvelle-France avait épousé

Claude Colbert, la fille de Gérard II, lui-même frère du bisaïeul de Jean-Baptiste Colbert, et que cette alliance assura la promotion du lignage.

Or, si j'ouvre un des dossiers des manuscrits de la Bibliothèque nationale de France concernant les Hocquart, je trouve mention d'un acte marqué du sceau de la chancellerie du duc de Bourbonnais et daté du 12 juillet 1453 : Messire Claude Hocquart a déclaré devant témoins que :

> ses ancêtres sont originaires d'Irlande puis qu'ils sont passés en Angleterre, puis en France et que l'un d'entre eux est mort à la Croisade ou il accompagnait Richard dit Cœur de Lion [21].

On sait que pour un noble de l'Ancien Régime, pouvoir compter parmi ses ancêtres un croisé était le suprême honneur. Un événement bien connu dans cet ordre d'idées est l'ouverture en 1839 par le roi Louis-Philippe d'une salle des Croisades au château de Versailles ; les familles nobles qui prouveraient qu'un de leurs ancêtres avait participé à la Croisade, pourraient y voir figurer leurs armoiries — ce qui assura la fortune d'un célèbre faussaire, qui avait nom Vrain Lucas.

Mais revenons aux Hocquart. La généalogie qu'on retrouve dans le fonds précédemment mentionné commence avec Richard O'Cart, chevalier, qui quitta Dublin pour s'établir à Chichester en Angleterre ; il vivait encore en 1170. C'est son fils, prénommé Robert, qui aurait suivi le roi Richard en Terre Sainte ; « il y mourut glorieusement », poursuit le document ; il avait eu d'Elisabeth de Walsingham, sa femme, un fils Donaugh (ou Daniel) qui continua la lignée. Le petit-fils de ce dernier fut écuyer de l'écurie du roi ; mais comme il avait des ennuis avec certains de ses pairs, il décida de quitter l'Angleterre et de passer en France ; il choisit de s'établir à Reims ; son petit-fils quitta cet endroit pour Sainte-Ménehould, petite ville située non loin de là. Un de ses descendants, Jean Hocquart, écuyer, seigneur de Vaux et de la Gravière, aurait épousé Claude Colbert.

Cette famille ne figure pas dans le dictionnaire de Moreri ; mais dans le dictionnaire du chevalier de Courcelles voici ce qu'on peut lire :

> Famille ancienne et distinguée [...] qui d'après les diverses preuves [de noblesse] qu'elle a faites soit au cabinet des ordres

du roi, soit à Malte, soit enfin pour les écoles militaires, remonte à Philippe Hocquart mort vers l'an 1509 [22].

Il se réfère en plus à une sentence des élus du Rethelois (près de Reims) du 4 janvier 1536, qui aurait maintenu la famille dans sa noblesse, laquelle avait été contestée par des collecteurs d'impôts quelque temps auparavant ; ces données sont reprises telles quelles par Le Jeune [23].

Un dossier que j'ai pu consulter récemment aux Archives nationales de France contient une généalogie, réalisée en 1921 par quelqu'un dont la famille était apparentée aux Hocquart, et qui reprend, en les développant, les données du dictionnaire publié un siècle plus tôt [24].

Or la réalité est bien plus sobre. Le premier Hocquart dont l'identité est sûre a pour prénom Jean ; il est marchand à Fismes, petite ville située près de Reims, et dont il fut vraisemblablement maïeur, c'est-à-dire maire [25]. Il épousa Claude Colbert, fille de Gérard, lui aussi marchand.

Leur fils, Jean, est qualifié en 1640 de « bourgeois de Paris » [26] ; il étudia le droit, devint avocat, puis il acquit la charge, anoblissante, de secrétaire du roi, dont nous avons parlé ci-dessus. Une de ses sœurs épousa un médecin, l'autre un bourgeois de Vailly, petite ville située près de Soissons. Ni Jean I, ni Jean II n'accolèrent à leur nom celui d'une seigneurie.

Ce ne fut pas le cas du fils de Jean II, prénommé Jean-Hyacinthe (le père de l'intendant). Au moment de son mariage en 1681, il est dit « écuyer, seigneur d'Essenlis », et on indique comme profession : « secrétaire de M$^{gr}$ Colbert » [27]. Il est sans doute un de ses secrétaires privés ; après la mort du ministre il passa au service de la marine ; il reçut un titre recherché, celui de « conseiller du roi en ses conseils », et, comme son père, il fut secrétaire du roi.

À la toute fin de l'Ancien Régime on retrouve dans sa descendance des titres ronflants : un « écuyer de madame la Dauphine », un « chevalier de Saint-Louis » [28], et probablement trois chevaliers de Malte [29]; on trouve aussi de fort belles alliances : les Cossé-Brissac, le marquis d'Ossun.

Voilà donc une famille qui, au début du XVII$^e$ siècle, appartenait à la bourgeoisie d'une petite ville provinciale, mais qui dans ce milieu restreint jouissait d'une certaine notabilité ; elle eut la chance de s'allier à une famille dont l'ascension sociale commençait — ce qui lui assura une place fort honorable dans la société française de la fin de l'Ancien Régime. Or à cette époque, elle devait mal supporter d'être d'humble origine et, jouant sur une frappante homonymie — O'Cart-Hocquart —, elle se fit fabriquer une généalogie impressionnante.

La liste des cas de fabrication de généalogies pourrait être allongée — en se reportant à l'étude que j'ai faite des intendants de la Nouvelle-France[30]. On pourrait encore parler des Talon, qui prétendirent quelque temps descendre d'un Irlandais, colonel d'infanterie, venu s'établir au début du XVIe siècle en Picardie ; ou également citer Henri de Chazel (qui périt en mer avec le bateau qui l'amenait en 1725 au Canada) — sa généalogie contient aussi des titres inventés tant pour les gens du lignage, que pour les familles alliées.

Il faut donc, quand on consulte certaines séries d'archives — par exemple les fameux Dossiers bleus des manuscrits de la Bibliothèque nationale de France —, ou qu'on ouvre les dictionnaires des XVIIIe et XIXe siècles, être constamment sur ses gardes ; on y rencontre assez souvent des faussetés. Pour retrouver les vraies généalogies, il faut généralement beaucoup de patience ; la recherche peut être longue et même frustrante, car il arrive parfois que les documents pertinents (des registres paroissiaux, ou des minutes notariales, par exemple) soient disparus.

Notons cependant que pour l'historien, cette pratique de forger des filiations à l'aide de documents falsifiés n'est pas sans intérêt : vouloir camoufler une origine obscure derrière un écran de fumée est un phénomène social qu'on ne peut se dispenser d'analyser et d'expliquer.

Quelques réponses ont déjà été esquissées dans notre exposé. On peut tenter, pour conclure, de résumer les motivations qui sous-tendent cette pratique, relativement fréquente, de se forger une ascendance prestigieuse.

Pour certains il s'agit, très banalement, si l'on peut dire, de ne pas payer la taille, impôt sur le revenu, dont la noblesse était exempte. C'est peut-être ce qui arriva aux Hocquart qui habitaient à Sainte-Ménehould. Pour d'autres, le but de l'opération est de conclure une alliance intéressante — beaucoup de nobles n'auraient pas laissé leur fille épouser un roturier. Dans le même ordre d'idées, on s'ingéniait souvent à bien placer sa progéniture — dans l'armée par exemple où les postes d'officiers étaient réservés à la noblesse, ou, comme on vient de le voir, dans un ordre de

chevalerie — or ceci avait beaucoup d'importance dans la société d'Ancien Régime. On ne compte pas moins de 12 chevaliers de Malte dans la famille Colbert entre 1647 et 1795[31]. Pour une biographie, qui devrait bientôt paraître, du gouverneur Charles Huault de Montmagny, j'ai dressé un tableau des relations des Huault et de quelques-uns de leurs alliés (13) avec l'Église du XVe au XVIIIe siècle — j'ai pu recenser, entre 1530 et 1789, 37 chevaliers de Malte.

Et il y a, bien sûr, le sentiment de fierté que pouvait déclencher une ascendance dont les titres étaient prestigieux et remontaient loin dans le temps. On a évoqué la gloire qui rejaillissait d'un ancêtre ayant accompagné le roi dans une campagne militaire, ou, mieux encore, ayant participé à la Croisade. Les armes, les devises rappelaient souvent ce passé mémorable.

Naissance, lignage, maison — souvent synonyme de lignage : ces termes sont liés à l'appartenance au sommet de la société ; ils témoignent d'un fait de mentalité dont doit tenir compte celui qui étudie l'Ancien Régime.

## NOTES

1. Malte, Archives de l'ordre de Malte, Arch. 2926, repris dans Paris, Bibliothèque nationale de France [dorénavant BnF], Carrés d'Hozier ms 345.

2. *Le Dictionnaire universel* (1re éd. 1690), réimpr. Paris, Le Robert, 1978, 3 vols.

3. Voir, entre autres, sur ce sujet : E. SCHALK, *From valor to pedigree. Ideas of nobility in France in the sixteenth and seventeenth centuries*, Princeton, PU Press, 1986 (ce livre a été récemment traduit en français) ; J. MEYER, *La noblesse française à l'époque moderne* (XVIe-XVIIIe siècles), Paris, PUF. (Coll. Que sais-je?), 1991.

4. Malte, Archives de l'ordre de Malte, Arch. 3566.

5. Paris, BnF, Dossiers bleus 362, fol. 2 et suiv.

6. 1643-1680.

7. A. LAPEYRE et R. SCHEURER, *Les notaires et secrétaires du roi sous les règnes de Louis XI, Charles VIII et Louis XII (1461-1515)*, Paris, BnF, 1978, vol. 2, PLANCHE LVI.

8. Paris, Archives Nationales [dorénavant AN], Minutier central, VI, 32 ; repris dans les insinuations du Châtelet de Paris, AN, Y, 106, fol. 59.

9. A. LAPEYRRE et R. SCHEURER, *op. cit.*, vol. 1, p. 306.

10. G. BRUNET *et al.* (éd.), *Mémoires-journaux de Pierre de l'Estoile*, Paris, 1875, t. 1, p. 117.

11. Pontoise, Archives départementales du Val d'Oise, notaire de Montmagny, son inventaire après décès est daté du 16 août ; et son testament, du 23 mai.

12. Ils avaient possédé, au cœur du Marais, un bel hôtel ; il fut vendu à un Parisien qui le revendit au duc de Sully

— l'hôtel que celui-ci y fit construire est encore aujourd'hui un des hauts-lieux de la capitale.

13. J.-B. JULIEN, DIT LE CHEVALIER DE COURCELLES, *Dictionnaire universel de la noblesse de France,* Paris, 1820, 5 vols. Plusieurs des généalogies qu'il propose sont erronées ; il manquait de sens critique ; il publia, souvent sans vérification, ce qui lui était présenté par des gens intéressés à valoriser leur ascendance.

14. LOUIS LE JEUNE, O.M.I., *Dictionnaire général de biographie [...] du Canada,* Ottawa, Université d'Ottawa, 1931, 2 vols.

15. Paris, BnF, Dossiers bleus 204.

16. J.-L. BOURGEON, *Les Colbert avant Colbert,* Paris, PUF, 1973. Les détails qui suivent proviennent de ce livre.

17. Cela aurait signifié un marchand détaillant ; il faut plutôt parler de mercier en gros.

18. Il s'agit de Roméo Arbour, du département des lettres françaises de la Faculté des Arts.

19. Voir sur ce sujet deux très belles études : F. BAYARD, *Le monde des financiers au XVII<sup>e</sup> siècle,* Paris, Flammarion, 1988, et D. DESSERT, *Argent, pouvoir et société au Grand Siècle,* Paris, Fayard, 1984.

20. J.-L. BOURGEON, *op. cit.,* p. 51 et note 30.

21. Paris, BnF, ms Nouveaux d'Hozier 188, fol. 2.

22. J.-B. JULIEN, DIT LE CHEVALIER DE COURCELLES, *op. cit.*

23. LOUIS LE JEUNE, *op.cit.*

24. Paris, AN, AB XIX 4367 et suiv.

25. J.-L. BOURGEON, *op. cit.,* TABLEAU 9 : Les enfants de Gérard II Colbert.

26. J.-C. DUBÉ, *Les intendants de la Nouvelle-France,* Montréal, Fides, 1984, p. 79 et note 41.

27. *Ibid.,* note 49.

28. *Ibid.,* p. 294 et suiv., *Généalogie de la famille Hocquart.*

29. L. DE LA ROQUE, *Catalogue des chevaliers de Malte,* Supplément au *Bulletin Héraldique* (février 1890).

30. J.-C. DUBÉ, *Les intendants de la Nouvelle-France...,* *passim.*

31. L. DE LA ROQUE, *op. cit.*

# GENEALOGY AS AN HISTORIAN'S TOOL: THE LINK BETWEEN KIN AND COMMUNITY IN THE BUILDING OF ACADIAN IDENTITY

Naomi E. S. Griffiths

I am working at present on an examination of how Acadian identity was established and later developed. I have been interested for close to 40 years in the general topic of why people consider a community identity, be it religious, ethnic or national, of crucial personal importance and the history of the Acadians is an almost perfect subject about which to ask this question. In the first place, Acadian identity is a comparatively modern creation. By that I mean that at the opening of the 17th century there were no people who called themselves Acadian and by 1713 there was a small community known by that name. Thus one has a period of about 100 years, no more than three generations, to investigate the ways in which a new community identity was born. Secondly, this community was not only established on the border between competing empires but was ruled now by France and now by England. Imperial influences were thus diverse and their impact, while always of significance, was often less immediately important than other, more local, matters. There is no single tradition, whether European or North American, that can be said to dominate the emerging Acadian identity. Further, those who became Acadian come from very varied backgrounds, although there was strong contingent from the Loudunais region of France. Scottish as well as Basque, Normans and Bretons as well as migrants from the Île-de-France established families in the colony.[1] Finally, in large measure because of the deportation of the majority of the Acadians in 1755, and their subsequent reestablishment within present day Atlantic Canada, one has a vivid example of the way in which history, both as perceived and as experienced, can play a central role in the development of a sense of distinct identity.

In pursuing my historical research, which I both hope and expect to result in the publication of a work entitled *From Migrant to Acadian*, I have come to appreciate how crucial good genealogical data is for my purposes. I have chosen three issues to illustrate the ways in which such material can be exploited to deepen the texture

provided by the more usual historians' tools of official documents and personal memoirs: the first two deal with the provenance of those who migrated to Acadia, their dominant belief systems and their social customs; the third is that of the extraordinary endurance of Acadians in exile, particularly their resistance to assimilation into late 18th-century French society.

The individual ideas and capacities that those who migrate bring to their new society are powerful determinants of how that society evolves. Far too often, as S. F. Wise pointed out in his address as president of the Canadian Historical Association in 1974, historians have written about the founding of new societies in North America at an exalted level of abstraction: "it is not men, women and children who migrate, on crowded decks, or packed in holds and steerages, [but] ideas and symbolic figures . . . "[2] It is only when one gets back to those individuals and discovers what their previous experience had encompassed that one can begin to understand much about the raw material from which these new societies were woven. To talk about European ideas and beliefs —whether French or English—held by the migrants begs the question of what the particular ideas and beliefs of any individual migrants were. It also ignores the complexity of both states. At the opening of the 17th century, France and England were riven by competing visions of Christianity and their politics further exacerbated by competing theories of the foundation of state authority. In both countries, nationalism, a commitment to the ideals of the central government, was something that was of great importance to a comparatively small elite. For the majority in both countries, local and regional identities, encompassing a wide variety of particular and differing customs and conventions, were of much more moment than any all-encompassing a "national" identity.

In analysing what views those who set about establishing a French colony in Acadia held, what political religious beliefs guided their actions, the genealogical details of two of the leading rival families—the La Tours and the d'Aulnays—have been invaluable. The hostility between Charles de la Tour and Charles de Menou d'Aulnay and their competing ambitions for the control and development of the young colony are well chronicled in the official records of the period. Equally well known to present day historians is the bitter and voluminous debate carried on by the supporters of each of these men. For those who favour Charles de la Tour, d'Aulnay is all ambition and no action, all swagger and no accomplishment. For those who support d'Aulnay, Charles de la Tour is nothing more than an adventurous turn-coat, whose unprincipled ambitions overwhelmed any shred of honour.[3] The arguments start over who had what authority from which court, French or Scottish, and whether, indeed, contemporary European international law recognised the right of that particular court over the territory in question. The debates grow more heated over what level of authority at the court in question granted the rights, whether it was the monarch himself, a major advisor, or merely a minor member of the aristocracy. The disputes become most bitter over whether the individual in question carried out the conditions of the grant he obtained.

Genealogical information helps to create some common ground between these opposing judgements. An understanding of family history and of an individual's life experience, looked at against the background of detailed political analysis of time and space, makes the La Tour/d'Aulnay dispute appear much more an issue of personal rivalry between very different men, than an ideological battle of conflicting loyalties. The contrast between the two men is as representative of the France of their day, for each man is equally the valid representative of French experience at the opening of the 17th century. Charles Saint-Étienne de la Tour embodies the element of social mobility and Charles de Menou d'Aulnay that of hereditary status. The former went to Acadia as a teenager and spent his life there. The latter went as a colonial administrator in mid-career and died there. The former acquired considerable establishment respectability by seeking and exploiting commercial and political alliances, the latter exploited his social position to acquire political influence. Both were Catholic, but the former considered the accommodation embodied in the Edict of Nantes both acceptable and wise: the latter

acted as if the toleration accorded Protestants was an unfortunate, temporary necessity. During their life times those who backed La Tour were entrepreneurs in the Atlantic ports and those who supported d'Aulnay held positions of influence at Court.[4]

Charles de la Tour was born in 1593, most probably in Champagne, but perhaps in Paris,[5] the son of Claude de la Tour, who was then in his twenties and had spent his early manhood as a ship's captain, fighting for Henry IV. Claude de la Tour married three times and his first wife was Marie de Salazar, a member of a very well connected family, based in Champagne. Her people were linked by marriage to the Biencourt-Saint-Just family, members of the nobility who had served the monarchs of France well, choosing a careful path in the murderous wars of the 16th century. Claude de La Tour did not so much gain status and prestige by this marriage, as the possibility of advancement.[6] When he was widowed, at some point in the early 1600s, he joined with the Biencourt family and sought his fortune in Acadia in 1610. Charles, then a teenager, accompanied him. Claude de la Tour spent the rest of his life crossing the Atlantic in the pursuit of both status and wealth through the fur trade, ending a baronet of the Scottish Crown, but dying on land governed for France by his son. Charles de la Tour would also marry three times, spend a fair proportion of his life crossing the Atlantic, and receive a title from Charles I. However, unlike his father, his main concern was less personal riches than the funds necessary for the establishment of settlement in Acadia. There was the land that was his heart's home and he brought all that he was to the task.

Whatever his childhood had been, it was in Acadia that Charles de la Tour came to adulthood. In his late twenties, or early thirties, he married a Micmac woman with whom he had three daughters. There is both direct and circumstantial evidence for this. The direct evidence is contained in declarations of one of his daughters who married a Basque fur trader, Martin d'Arpentigny, seigneur de Martignon, who later owned land at the mouth of the Saint-John.[7] The indirect evidence that it was a marriage and not just a private liaison comes from the careers of the other two daughters, both of whom entered convents in France for which legitimate birth was a necessity.[8] One of the daughters is reputed to have had such a magnificent voice that she was brought to sing before members of Louis XIII's court.

It was about the time of this marriage that the territory claimed by France as Acadia was also claimed by Scotland as Nova Scotia.[9] Before the decade was over, attempts would be made to turn a claim into an established settlement. In 1627, Charles de la Tour wrote to France, pleading for help to strengthen the settlement that the French had made. He asked to be given a commission to defend the Acadian coast. He was confident that he had the strength to defend the king's interests, "defendre pour le service de mon roy," with some hundred Micmac families allied to his interests and his small, determined group of Frenchmen, "avec Cent familles de mes alliez . . . et ma petite troupe resolue de francoys."[10] Charles de la Tour consistently used phrases such as "gens du pays," or words such as "peuple" and "alliez" to describe the Micmac rather than the word "sauvages." The 1620s ended with most of Acadia in the hands of the Scots and Charles de la Tour a widower. His second marriage to Françoise-Marie Jacquelin in 1640 was a marriage arranged by one of his agents in France. Her roots were in the bourgeois strata of society, her father very probably a surgeon. She proved to be a woman of great intelligence and courage but died in 1645. There were no children born to this marriage. Charles de la Tour's third marriage was to the widow of his rival in 1653.

This man, Charles de Menou d'Aulnay was about ten years younger than Charles de la Tour and had been born, most probably in 1604, at the castle of Charnisay in Loudun. He was the son of René de Menou, who served the Crown well, both as a soldier and a diplomat. That side of the family was kin to the family of Cardinal Richelieu. His mother was Nicole de Jousserand, wealthy in her own right with a château in Loudun. Little is known about his childhood but, as a young man, Charles de Menou took service in the navy under the command of his cousin, Isaac de Razilly. De Razilly was one of the more important commanders in the French navy, and much trusted by Richelieu, who at that time—the mid 1620s—had established his authority as advisor to Louis XIII.[11] When the Treaty of Saint-Germain-en-Laye was signed in 1632, regulating all outstanding disputes between Charles I and Louis XIII, its third article enjoined the English to:

give up and restore all the places in New France, La Cadie and Canada, occupied by the subjects of his Majesty of Great Britain and to make them withdraw from the said places.[12]

In late March 1632, de Razilly signed an agreement with Richelieu to "receive restitution [of Acadia] at the hands of the English and put New France in possession of it."[13] On the 10th of May 1632, the former received his commission in the name of the king, naming him lieutenant-governor of the king in New France and requesting him to "prendre possession du Port-Royal."[14] When he sailed to take up his position, Charles de Menou sailed with him as his second-in-command. Charles de la Tour had come to Acadia as a migrant in the company of his father, who sought his fortune; d'Aulnay came as a career move, as a government official, in company of powerful friends.

It was a move that would also bring him marriage to a Razilly connection. This was Jeanne Motin, who was the daughter of Louis Motin, an important functionary of the French salt tax bureaucracy as well a member of the nobility and an investor in the Razilly-Cordonnier Company, an enterprise established by the Razilly family to develop Acadia, and one in which Cardinal Richelieu also personally invested.[15] Jeanne Motin and Charles de Menou d'Aulnay married in 1636 and she bore him eight children: four sons, all killed in military action and four daughters, all of whom entered the religious life. D'Aulnay was drowned in a canoeing accident in 1650, and three years later Jeanne Motin married Charles de la Tour, with whom she had five children. Two daughters married into the Mius-d'Entremont family, which had established a settlement at Pobomcoup, in the area of present day Pubnico, and a third married Alexandre Le Borgne, the son of one of the most important merchants of La Rochelle, then trading with Acadia. One of the two sons married into the Melanson family, who had arrived in Acadia sometime in the 1620s and whose origins have recently been traced to marriage between a French Protestant and a Scottish woman.[16]

This specificity of information about the genealogy of particular individuals makes, in my view, for a more reasoned debate about their motives. Together, genealogy and family history build the framework for the interpretation of the social experience of a particular time, allowing one to understand why specific political choices were made by individuals. Prosopography, the collective genealogical data, allows one to trace the ways in which individual choices become community patterns.[17] This, in turn, allows a much more thorough examination of the make-up of communities. One of the more thorny political issues over Acadian identity is that of the nature of its obvious French heritage. The question of the homogeneity of this inheritance, and of the extent to which historical development has brought about a change in the nature of this inheritance, has been a matter of considerable discussion.[18] A number of writers have been unwilling to consider that a sense of nationalism, and the connection between the state and national identity, was a very different matter in the 17th century than it became after 1800. The debate about the links between pre- and post-industrial nationalism is a major issue for Acadian historians.[19] While there is no doubt that a traditional French national culture existed in 1600 there is also no doubt that the France of the early 17th century was a highly fragmented society, one which its rulers from Henry IV to Louis XIV, from Sully to Mazarin were continuously engaged in trying to unify. From the rich plains around Chartres and the cream and butter of the valley of the Loire to the garlic, red wine and olive country of Marseilles, from the dry chalk of Champagne to the slope of the Pyrenees and the Basque people, who were both shepherds and sailors, the country was a complex kaleidoscope of customs, traditions, dialects so different as to be, for practical purposes, distinct languages. All the varying sectors of France had different relations with the power of the Crown and the central governmental structures of the state. From the terms of contract to which Brittany had agreed when finally joining France in 1491, to the immemorial customs of the Île-de-France, the variations of authority recognized within the country were almost numberless. In Champagne the provincial estates met tri-annually, dominated by the landowning class. In the Gironde they met . . . almost never but were dominated by the peasantry when they did. Voltaire remarked that one changed laws in France as often as one changed horses. Thus, the Leblancs coming from Poitou to Acadia would have different traditions about the ways in which authority was exercised than the Roys ar-

riving from St. Malo and having the customs of Brittany as their norm. The Bastarache from the Basque country would have very different ideas about the rights of property holders than the Arsenaults from Rochefort, that marshy city which as late as the 1880s was referred to a place of fevers and barbarity.[20]

The local origins of those who migrated to Acadia are particularly important to disentangle because of the absence of a vision imposed by an external force on the emerging community. Direction from the central governing authorities from France was very haphazard during the crucial decades when Acadian identity was being established, quite apart from 1628 to 1632 and from 1654 to 1668, when the English were the controlling force in the area. There was no major religious vision, such as that which animated the development of Massachusetts or the founding of Montreal, attracting migrants to the community. The Acadians evolved their own particular social and cultural institutions, marriage and family organisation, child rearing and education practices, social customs and religious conventions, speech patterns and leisure activities, not to mention traditional ways of work in the pursuit of their economic livelihood, whether that was farming, fishing, hunting or lumbering. Of course the continued, if not always continuous, connection with France, shaped Acadian culture. But the very variety of this inheritance allowed those who built Acadian identity to select, consciously or unconsciously, what would be most useful for the life in the new circumstances of North America.[21] Detailed meticulous information about the European roots of those who came to Acadia can only illuminate the extraordinary achievement of the early migrants, who brought a common culture from such diversity.

If genealogical information is of crucial importance in the analysis of the early components of Acadian identity, it is also as vital in any attempt at understanding what happened to the community during the period of the Deportation, 1755-1763. This most traumatic period of Acadian history, the era of exile and proscription, is an era dominated by a major world war between France and England. The Acadian survival of the death and destruction that this conflict brought to them is due, above all, to the nature of the Acadian community itself. It was the strength of the Acadians that allowed them to endure the years of

Deportation, to preserve a measure of social coherence and identity in exile and to reroot their community, after a generation of turmoil, in the Maritimes. Leaving aside the questions about why British officials in Halifax decided to send the Acadians into exile, [22] the Deportation meant that the vast majority of the population was shipped away, either in the last six months of 1755 or at some point over the next six years. [23] Those who remained mostly took refuge along the river banks of the St. John and the Miramichi, or survived more or less as prisoners of war within Nova Scotia. In 1764 Acadians were once more permitted to own land in Nova Scotia. Some 165 families are noted as being in the colony at the time, a population of perhaps a thousand. [24] The Acadian population in 1755 in the same territory had been somewhere in the region of 18,000. [25] Whatever one might decide the cause of the Deportation to have been, there can be no disagreement about what the event meant for the Acadians: the exile of somewhere between 75% and 90% of them.

The Acadians deported from Nova Scotia in 1755, who constituted the vast majority of those sent into exile between 1755 and 1763, had as their appointed destination, without exception, one of the British colonies in North America. In the first instance, exile scattered the Acadians into the other British North American colonies from Massachusetts to Georgia. But this was only in the first instance because the years of Acadian exile were years of war. The places of exile were themselves involved, to a greater or lesser extent, in the Anglo-French battle for dominance of North America. What happened to the Acadians immediately on arrival in new lands was often only the beginning of their travails. Nowhere would the Acadians find the conditions of their exile stable and unchanging. The Deportation meant, for many Acadians, far-ranging voyages quite beyond anything imagined by those who supervised their embarkation in Nova Scotia.

For example, a number of those sent to Maryland, South Carolina and Georgia went on to Santo Domingo and some of these then on to either Louisiana or British Honduras. Others first landed in Massachusetts but after 1763 went to the banks of the St. Lawrence. Some had voyages which took them to the Channel islands and then to the islands of Saint-Pierre and Miquelon. Those who were first landed in Virginia were, for the most part, sent on to England and then to France. Many of those who survived this trek sailed from Nantes in 1785 for Louisiana at the expense of Spain, whose territory Louisiana then was.

At the time of the Peace of Paris in 1763, the estimation that there were some 12,000 Acadians alive must be understood in the light of the fact that many of those counted were young children born in exile. For many Acadians, exile was immediately lethal. The *Edward Cornwallis* shipped out of Grand Pré with 417 Acadians on board and arrived in Columbia, South Carolina with "210 dead and 207 in health." While the death toll on board the ships had been no greater than for any other contemporary Atlantic sailing, in some cases it reached 50% and in most cases 30% of those embarked. Once landed, epidemics of smallpox and cholera struck the exiles, who had little experience of, and therefore little immunity to, these diseases. Once more, the death rate was high. For those Acadians who were sent first to Virginia and then on to England, death from smallpox took a third of the group.

For the Acadian population of 1755, the Deportation meant the breaking apart of a community that had endured for more than four generations. How did people survive the trauma of the event itself, the forced abandonment of their homes, the voyage and the arrival into a foreign land? How did they manage not to despair as ravages of disease shook their families? How were they able, not only to survive but also to endure, as more than shattered husks of their former selves? The 20th century has given too many examples of what deportation and exile does to those upon whom it is visited. Losing the familiar, seeing close-knit families founder, has often destroyed an individual's capacity for action. In spite of long sea voyages into unknown circumstances, in spite of epidemic illness, in spite of being subject to alien authority and often poorly lodged, the Acadians survived as a community. Moreover, the coherence of particular groups of exiles was shown by strong leadership, capable of arguing with 18th-century government officials, servants of regimes that were oligarchic at best, aristocratic and autocratic at worst.

It is the records of the officials of these regimes, those of the governments of the American colonies, those of England, France and Spain, whether local or central, that provide a wealth of evidence to show the crucial nature of the Acadian family for the survival of the community.[26] It is not merely that there are census rolls, but that the rolls give details about families and even, in the case of those Acadians who arrived in France after 1763, of Acadian ancestry.[27] Further, there are accounts by contemporaries of the Acadian emphasis on, and knowledge about, the fortunes of their relatives.[28] As well, there is considerable evidence about the struggle that the Acadians fought and won to prevent the breakup of nuclear families in those jurisdictions that helped the poor and destitute by binding out children as servants.[29]

At this point, I think that genealogist and historian work in close cooperation. For the genealogist, I suspect that it is the individual experience that most needs to be disinterred. For the historian it is the collective questions concerning, above all, the experience of families and collections of families, that demand examination. In both cases, meticulous checking of one source against another, the tedious and, at the same time, fascinating work of discovering precisely who was the individual in question, both parentage and issue, are the craft practised. While the genealogist places an emphasis on generational trends, the historian is more often investigating the immediate, selected generation. For both genealogist and historian, however, the Acadian records of the Deportation era illuminate the strength of family and kin connections. And so, to conclude, I want to mention the evidence that, in spite of being separated, not only by the Atlantic ocean, but also by political boundaries, Acadian families nevertheless managed to be informed about what exile had meant for their kin. Officials in Brittany, coping with the Acadians who arrived there after 1763 noted with surprise that they knew where members of the families were. They recorded in their reports that Claude Dion knew that, of his ten brothers and sisters, one brother was in Belle-Isle (France), and another in Saint-Malo. He had also a brother in Halifax (Nova Scotia), a brother and sister in Boston, Massachusetts and another brother in New York, as were two of his sisters. The last sibling, another sister was in Plymouth, England.[30] There are other records of the enduring strength of Acadian family bonds, and the examination of such records by both genealogists and historians reveals the tenacity of human affection and determination in the face of destruction. For both disciplines, the discovery of such knowledge turns the scholar to the foundation of its work—a deeper understanding of what it is to be human.

## NOTES

1. The most important analysis of the origins of the Acadians remains that of GENEVIÈVE MASSIGNON in *Les parlers français d'Acadie : Enquête linguistique*, vol. 1 (Paris: 1955), p. 1-75. The work of STEPHEN WHITE, especially his recent publication "La généalogie des trente-sept familles hôtesses des *retrouvailles 94*", *La Société historique acadienne*, vol. 25, no. 2-3, must also be consulted.

2. S. F. WISE, "Liberal Consensus or Ideological Background: Some Reflections on the Hartz Thesis", Presidential Address, *Historical Papers/ Communications historiques 1974. Canadian Historical Association/ Société Historique du Canada*, p. 1-14.

3. Those interested in this debate should begin with the biographies by: RENÉ BAUDRY, "Charles de Menou d'Aulnay" in GEORGE W. BROWN (ed.), *Dictionary of Canadian Biography*, vol. 1 (Toronto: 1966), p. 502-506; GEORGE MACBEATH, "Charles Saint Étienne de la Tour", *Idem*, p. 592-596.

4. On this aspect of their rivalry, see M. A. MAC-DONALD, *Fortune and La Tour. The Civil War in Acadia* (Toronto: 1983); see also ELIZABETH JONES, *Gentlemen and Jesuits Quests for Glory and Adventure in the Early Days of New France* (Toronto: 1986).

5. Charles' father, Claude de la Tour, was the son of a master mason in Paris and his six brothers and sisters all pursued careers in crafts and trades: M. A. MACDONALD, *op. cit.*, p. 19.

6. On this see ROBERT LEBLANC, *L'ascension sociale d'un aventurier champenois : Claude Turgis* (Paris: BnF, 1974). Paper given, 1970, Congrès national des Sociétés Savantes, section de philologie et d'histoire jusqu'en 1610.

7. October 17, 1672. "Registre des concessions en Acadie" in PIERRE-GEORGES ROY, *Inventaire des concessions en fief et seigneurie, fois et hommages, et aveux et dénombrement, conservés aux Archives de la province de Québec* (1927-1929), p. 11. A full discussion of this is to be found in CLARENCE D'ENTREMONT, *Histoire du cap Sable . . .*, vol. 2, p. 404 *et seq.*

8. A. COUILLARD DESPRÉS, *Charles de Saint-Étienne de la Tour gouverneur, lieutenant général en Acadie et son temps 1593-1666* (Arthabaska: 1930), p. 130-131.

9. The claim made was by letters patent issued to Sir William Alexander by James VI of Scotland and I of England, September 10, 1621: published in JOHN G. BOURINOT, "Builders of Nova Scotia", *Royal Society of Canada, Proceedings and Transactions*, 2nd series, vol. 5 (1899), section 2, p. 104-121.

10. A. COUILLARD DESPRÉS, *op. cit.*

11. PAUL W. BAMFORD, *Fighting Ships and Prisons. The Mediterranean Galleys of France in the Age of Louis XIV* (Minneapolis: 1973), p. 19.

12. Full text in *Coll. Man. N. F.,* vol. 1, p. 86-96. Printed in part in MURDOCH, *History of Nova Scotia,* vol. 1 (Halifax: 1865), p. 88-89.

13. "Convention du 27 mars, 1632", NATIONAL ARCHIVES OF CANADA, MG 1, C$^{11}$ D, I:48.

14. NATIONAL ARCHIVES OF CANADA, C$^{11}$A, I:49; C$^{11}$D, 1:fol. 52; *Coll. des am. N. F.,* vol. 1, p. 110.

15. CLARENCE J. D'ENTREMONT, *Histoire du cap Sable . . .* , vol. 2, p. 519.

16. There has been considerable dispute over the origins of the Melansons. See CLARENCE J. D'ENTREMONT, "Les Melansons d'Acadie sont français de père et anglais de mère", *La Société historique acadienne,* 40$^e$ cahier, vol. 4, no. 10, p. 416-419 and STEPHEN A. WHITE, " La généalogie des trente-six familles . . .", *La Société historique acadienne,* vol. 25, no. 2-3, p. 191.

17. The most innovative work in Canadian history, using such techniques is that of BRUCE S. ELLIOTT, *Irish Migrants in the Canada. A New Approach* (Montreal: 1988).

18. See in particular the work by HAUTECŒUR, *L'Acadie du discours* (Québec: 1975); ROBERT SAUVAGEAU, *Acadie, la guerre de Cent Ans des Français d'Amérique* (Paris: 1987); YVES CAZAUX, *L'Acadie. Histoire des Acadiens du XVII$^e$ à nos jours* (Paris: 1992); JEAN-MARIE NADEAU, *Que le tintamarre commence. Lettre ouverte au peuple acadien* (Moncton: 1992).

19. My own views are a reflection of the work of ERNEST GELLNER, *Culture, Identity, and Politics* (Cambridge: 1987); E. J. HOBSBAWN, *Nations and Nationalism since 1780* (Cambridge: 1990); and JOHN HUTCHINSON, *Modern Nationalism* (London: 1994).

20. EUGENE WEBER, *Peasants into Frenchmen the Modernization of Rural France 1870-1914* (Stanford: 1976), p. 4. For an authoritative account of the diversity of France the work of FERNAND BRAUDEL is without peer in either French or English. The work *L'identité de la France / The Identity of France* was published in Paris and London, 1986, 1988 respectively.

21. One of the most useful analyses of cultural transference can be found in "Forum Albion's Seed: Four British Folkways in America—A Symposium", *The William and Mary Quarterly,* 3rd series, vol. 48, no. 2 (April 1991); see also PETER BENES (ed.), "New England / New France 1600-1850", *The Dublin Seminar for New England Folk Life. Annual Proceedings 1989.*

22. My own views can be found in *The Contexts of Acadian History 1680-1784* (Montreal: 1992).

23. The last attempt at completing the Deportation came in 1763: MURDOCH, *op. cit.,* vol. 2, p. 426.

24. A report of 1767 estimates the Acadian population of Nova Scotia as 1,265: PUBLIC ARCHIVES OF CANADA, *Reports,* vol. 2, App. L, p. 255-256.

25. In their work for *The Historical Atlas of Canada,* JEAN DAIGLE and ROBERT LEBLANC present a lower figure, that of 13,000.

26. An introduction to these resources is provided by the *Inventaire général des sources documentaires sur les Acadiens,* t. 1, (Moncton: 1975).

27. These are in the Archives départementales in Rennes but have been transcribed and published by MILTON P. REIDER JR and NORMA GAUDET RIEDER, *The Acadians in France 1762-1776* (Metarie, Louisiana: 1967).

28. The Archives départementales, Ille-et-Vilaine at Rennes have a rich collection of documents, partly brought together by a doctor who was interested in the exiles. See particularly, series 17F: 2151 *et seq.*

29. On this see N. E. S. GRIFFITHS, "Petitions of Acadian Exiles, 1755-1785. A Neglected Source", *Histoire sociale / Social History,* vol. 11, no. 21 (May 1978), p. 215-223.

30. RENNES, Archives Départementales, Ille-et-Vilaine, 1F: 2158.

# RECORD LINKAGE AS A GENEALOGICAL TOOL

John M. Kitzmiller II

Record linkage, a technique for matching similar records developed by Statistics Canada for the medical field, is now used extensively as a genealogical tool [FIGURE 1]. Employing a technology whereby computer programs use mathematical probabilities to search, match, link, and/or merge records has the potential to revolutionize historical and genealogical research. Types of record linkage that will be discussed are: event linkage, individual linkage, family linkage, and pedigree linkage.

The Genealogical Society of Utah (founded in 1894) by the Church of Jesus Christ of Latter Day Saints (the Mormons) has developed a software application called *FamilySearch*® that utilizes this technology in several of its products. One of these products is *Ancestral File*®, a lineage-linked computer database of approximately 30 million records. This database, like many of the *Family Search*® applications, is available for searching free of charge on CD-ROM at any of the more than 2,000 LDS Family History Centres around the world. Record linkage and its components, such as the Names Recognition System, Locality Resource System, etc., are used in this database to check for proper linkages, names, dates, and places. This helps reduce operational expenses and other file problems.

The better known *International Genealogical Index*® (IGI) contains more than 200 million records that have either been extracted from original sources by the Genealogical Society of Utah or submitted to the file by interested parties [FIGURE 2]. Record linkage is used to help the submitter determine if their submission has duplicate entries already resident within the IGI, and to show them the probable duplicates.

## What is record linkage?

Record linkage is based upon the theory that an algorithm or equation could be written that would simulate the decision-making process that a person makes when comparing one record to another. This is usually done by studying two records, fact by fact, that potentially represent the same person. These facts or individual identifiers are known as fields, and consist of such things as a given name, surname, birth date, etc. Those fields that should be similar if the two records represented the same person are noted, as are the fields that disagree or where information is missing. If one were to add up those fields that agreed and there were enough of them, then there is a high probability that the records are indeed the same or represent the same individual. The same would be true if the fields disagreed, and therefore the outcome would be that the records do not represent the same individual.

## Types of record linkage

Several types of record linkage are possible: event linkage, individual linkage, family linkage, and pedigree linkage. This article mostly discusses the first two types, with event linkage being the basic building block. Event linkage is really at the field level, whereby one wishes to determine if the data in two comparison records represent the same event. Individual linkage is where the sum total of the event comparisons indicate that two records represent the same individual.

Other possibilities exist as well, and the first of these is family linkage. This would compare two proposed matching families, not necessarily by the events, but rather by family structure. For example, if some of the children's names match —are they in the same birth order? Are there children missing that would preclude these families from being the same family? This specifically applies to medieval families, where relationships are more prevalent than actual facts or events.

The other possibility is pedigree linkage, which is another form of family linkage. In many medieval sources or tribal oral genealogies that have been recorded, the only data that is given is a patrilineal or matrilineal descent. This means father to son, or mother to daughter, and gives very little genealogical information. Siblings are seldom mentioned, and other supporting data may be missing. Comparing two different pedigrees can be difficult, especially if they are in different languages. This could perhaps be done using record linkage and using relationships as the matching elements needed.

## Record linkage algorithms

The algorithm or equations used in this process are based upon standard statistical probabilities, whereby the odds (probability) that a record matches or does not match are calculated by the record linkage system. If one were to take the surname field, and that name were McKenzie, the computer would calculate the odds of the surname matching by chance and how often the surname field in general would agree in known records that truly were linked or matched. A value is derived from these measurements that is the odds above chance that the two surnames matched.

Each algorithm can be designed to be specific for a culture or locality, since these factors influence the record keeping and the content of records that are used for genealogical purposes. There is a process whereby these algorithms are created, which starts with a statistically valid sample of the files that are to be compared [FIGURE 3]. Specialists who combine skills from both information science and genealogy examine these records looking for duplicate records, which are termed "duplicate pairs." They study the commonality of fields in these pairs, and then based upon the purpose of the file, choose those elements necessary to build an algorithm called a "Matching Algorithm Parameter," or MAP.

## MAP elements

MAP elements are grouped into three sets of data: blocking, weighting, and thresholds [FIGURE 4]. These three sets take advantage of how databases find and store data internally. Databases store information in some logical format that allows easy access to the data, like chapters in a book. A book's information is located by using an index, which is very similar to how data is located in a database. The ideal (but costly) way to find your ancestor's name in a database would be to compare every record in the database with your query. Instead, most indexes are designed to retrieve records that most likely match your query. *Blocking* is another word for retrieval, which is similar to casting a net into the sea while fishing.

The net will *only* catch (retrieve) fish in the location that the net was cast and will disregard all other fish in the area. The odds of catching the type of fish that is desired increases by casting the net in the proper area. In the computer world, cost savings are incurred by reducing the number of comparisons necessary to retrieve the records that are desired. Blocking effectiveness is measured in two different (and opposing) methods, which are termed "recall" and "precision" [FIGURE 5].

Using the fish metaphor, recall would be the number of fish that were caught of the type desired out of the total number of fish in the net. Precision, on the other hand, would be the total number of fish that were retrieved in the net that were of the type desired. In FIGURE 5 we see the result set based upon the query using the given name of "John." What was really wanted was all of the John Smiths, but all records with John as the given name were retrieved—this is an example of recall.

Another term now needs to be introduced, and that would be "noise." Noise, whether defined by fish or by records, is the number of retrieved names that were *not* wanted. Referring to FIGURE 5 again, all of those individuals that were retrieved that were *not* John Smith would be termed noise. Therefore, precision measures the amount of noise. In computer systems, one can "tune" or maximize the system for recall or precision,which are on opposite ends of the spectrum. If one wants to see more potential records that may be of interest, then the blocking parameters need to be loosened. On the other hand, if one wants to only retrieve those that most closely match one's query, then the blocking parameters need to be tightened. The goal, of course, is to find the necessary balance between these two concepts [FIGURE 6].

There is one way to enhance recall without greatly reducing precision. Record linkage matching parameters are dependent upon the correct information being listed in the fields. A computer searches names or any text field character by character and so, if a surname has one character misplaced or misspelt, record linkage would indicate that this field does not match. Any data field (such as names, dates, places, titles, etc.) can be used with the original spelling. However, due to phonetic and spelling variations, the results become much more precise when the data in these fields are standardized and have appropriate codes attached see ("Building catalogs" below).

## Weighting parameters

The next step in creating an algorithm or MAP is found in the weighting calculations. Blocking (or the net) has retrieved a certain number of records that can be studied to see if they match the query. Of this smaller set of records to compare, each one will be examined field by field and a logarithmic weight or number will be assigned to each field. This number is dependent upon whether the two fields being compared fit into the following categories: agree, partially agree, or disagree. If they agree, a positive weight is calculated; if they partially agree, a somewhat lesser positive weight is assigned; and if they disagree, a negative weight is calculated (see APPENDIX for formulas). These values or weights are then added up to determine the total value or weight of the record for each of the three categories mentioned above.

Weighting parameters, like blocking parameters, can also be specifically designed by culture or locality. Another factor that influences the weighting values of genealogical records has to do with the size of the name pool. A comparison between the United States and Scotland shows that there are a larger number of surnames in the United States than there are in Scotland. This means that the odds of a surname matching above chance in Scotland are higher because there are fewer of them. This also means that the weight for a surname match in Scotland would be smaller than that for the United States. These types of weight calculations are performed on name, locality, date, and gender fields.

When one looks at the total information available for an individual, a very large number of possible weighting fields could result. The cost to weight all fields in a record is usually prohibitive, since it affects computer performance and response time. Therefore, a way to minimize the number of weighting fields is used. By definition, blocking fields are not weighted, but this still could leave ten or more fields available for weighting. An automated process determines which fields are present in the record and how often data actually is found in these fields. Only those fields with data present about 50% of the time are good candidates for potential weighting fields. An example of this would be a death date and death place being recorded in a christening record. This seldom occurs in British genealogical records, but when it does, it is extremely discriminating, meaning that it almost always matches and provides positive identification of the individual. Since it may only occur in less than 5% of the records, it is not cost effective to keep as a weighting field.

## Threshold determinations

Let us review where we are to this point: a sample database has been selected, and the blocking and weighting parameters have been discovered. How does one determine if the two records are duplicates? That is where the threshold value is used, which takes the sum of the logarithmic weights and compares them to a threshold table. This table is statistically created and provides a range of threshold values that may vary from "100% non-duplicates" to "100% duplicates." Generally the threshold is determined from the weights of those records that were known to be truly matched records [FIGURE 7].

Since this range goes from one extreme to the other, there is a certain area where the non-duplicates and duplicates intermingle or coexist. This area is called the "gray area," where it becomes difficult to separate the non-duplicates from the duplicates.

FIGURE 8 shows the distribution curves for two comparison sets—criminals versus citizens. The x-axis shows the log weights, while the y-axis shows the number of individuals. If one wanted to be sure that no citizens would be considered criminals, then the threshold log weight would be -5. If one wanted to make sure that no criminals were considered as citizens, then the threshold log weight of +15 would be chosen. The zone between these two values (represented by the dashed lines) is the gray area. From an automated perspective, all individuals below -5 are considered criminals and above +15 are considered citizens. Since this represents perhaps 80% to 90% of the record comparisons, this can be done by the computer. Judgement decisions are required for the gray area, and these are normally done by skilled staff. There is some possibility that a computer will be able to do even some of this, and this area of study is called "fuzzy logic."

The gray zone comes replete with several inherent problems. One problem is the possibility of a non-matching record scoring high enough to be mistaken for a match (this is called a false positive). Another problem is that a matching record scoring low enough to be mistaken for a non-match (false negative). One factor that contributes to this problem is data missing from a record. The record with the missing data could match on each of its fields with the comparison record, but does not have enough fields to cause the weight to go over the threshold.

## Building catalogs

Catalogs are basically tables of values for a specific field. These are currently available for names and localities, although any field of interest could have a catalog (such as titles, heraldic terms, etc.). Let us talk about the names catalog and how a catalog is created.

First, why build a names catalog at all? The main reason is how a computer searches for names, as was discussed previously. The search will check a name in an index character by character, and if it does not match exactly there will be no record retrieval. This means that a name that was abbreviated or truncated will not be retrieved. Many times in the same document the same name is spelled differently, and these would also not be retrieved. An example of spelling variations that represent the same name: Siver, Syver, Syvert, Sivert, Sigvart, Sigvaardt, Syrverdt, Sirverdt, Sigurd, Siur, and Siul.

The process to build a names catalog is somewhat complicated as is shown in FIGURE 9. Instead of describing each step in this process, let us concentrate on the basic functions. Names are extracted into a computer file so that automated processes can be used. Many times data other than names are placed in a name field, and this needs to be removed or changed. Another step is to group names into a phonetic group, such as the above Scandinavian names that would be all in the same group. This group is represented by a standard name in the index, but any of the variant names that could be used in the query would retrieve the complete group for comparison.

Although the Genealogical Society of Utah does not do the following at this time, the above techniques could also be applied to a multilingual search engine. This means that not only spelling variants would be in the same group, but language variants would be as well. This would help trace immigrants who come from one country and culture to another country with a different culture. In other words, immigrants from Germany to Canada may change their name to an English equivalent. This would make it difficult to match their Canadian record to their German record unless they used this multilingual search engine.

## Heraldic databases

The Genealogical Society of Utah is not involved in this type of database, but many of those attending this Congress may be interested in this topic. A heraldic database can be setup to use record linkage technology. The following example of a multilingual search engine (mentioned above) fits a heraldic situation. This shows a query that is checking heraldic colours, and the query term that is used is "arany." The concept is that the language group would contain all of the language variants for the word gold, and the group would be searched until the actual term of "arany" was found. This points to the center of the wheel in the figure that gives the English equivalent, "gold." The desired language is in the center position (the standard), which can be changed to fit the needs of the system or individual [FIGURES 10].

A multilingual search engine and a heraldic catalog could also be applied to a blazon, where a description occurs in the original language but needs to be in English. The terms for each part of the description would have multilingual equivalents in the database. For this to actually work, the fields in the database need to be set up to match the pattern of a blazon [FIGURE 11].

The next figure shows two shields, and next to them an abbreviated computer blazon. This abbreviated blazon can be changed into the form of a blazon that is normally used. If one were to match different blazons, record linkage could also be of use. Each of the heraldic terms could be assigned weights, and a threshold set that could provide information on a matched blazon. All of the record linkage calculations mentioned in this article can be applied *if* the database is set up to handle the fields that are needed [FIGURE 12].

**Weighting calculations:**

A-Ratio: A measure of how often a field, such as a surname or given name, will agree in two truly matched records.

B-Ratio: A measure of commonality of a specific field value in the database as a whole.

**Agreement weight:**

$$\frac{\text{A-Ratio}}{\text{B-Ratio}}$$

**Disagreement weight:**

$$\frac{1-(\text{A-Ratio})}{1-\text{Sum (B-Ratios Squared)}}$$

**Record linkage algorithm:**

$$W_t = \log_2 A/B$$

$W_t$ = Binit weight. This is a weight assigned to a specific field such as the surname. Binit weights are additive for all weighted fields within a record.

A = Field (such as surname agreement ratio within genuinely linked pairs).

B = Field agreement ratio for pairs brought together for comparison and rejected as unlinkable. This is estimated by using the sum of all of the B-ratios squared.

**Probabilistic Record Linkage**

A Matching Technology
Presented by
John M. Kitzmiller, II

1

# International Genealogical Index (IGI)

2

## Record Linkage Map Creation Process

```
Define
Sample
Database
    │
    ▼                Database                      Yes
Extract Data ◄──────────┐                ┌──────────────►  Map
    │                    │                │
    ▼                    │           Efficient ◄── Yes
Add Authorities ◄────────────┐            │
    │                        │            │ No        Determine
    ▼                        │            └────────►  Thresholds
Identify Duplicates   Locality    Name       Yes
    │                                     Efficient ◄── Yes
No  ▼                                        │
┌── Enough                                   │ No       Determine
│   Dups?                                     └───────►  Weighting
│    │                                                      ▲
│    ▼ Yes                                                  │ yes
│                                                           │
Evaluate Statistics ──────────►  Determine Blocking ◄── No  Efficient
                                       │
                                       └─────────────────►
```

3

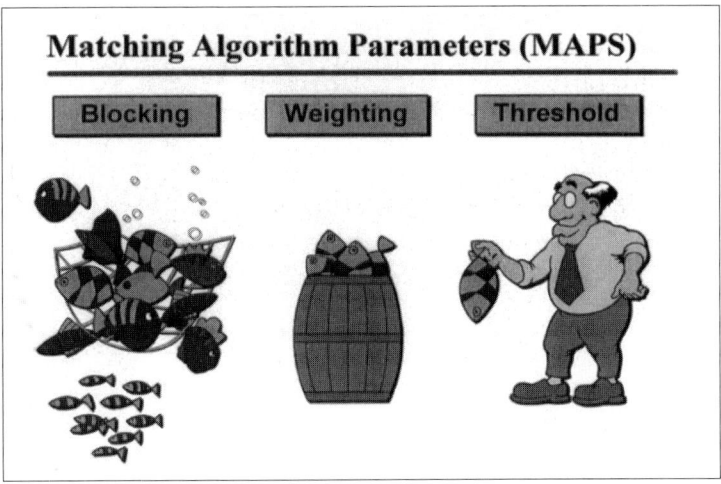

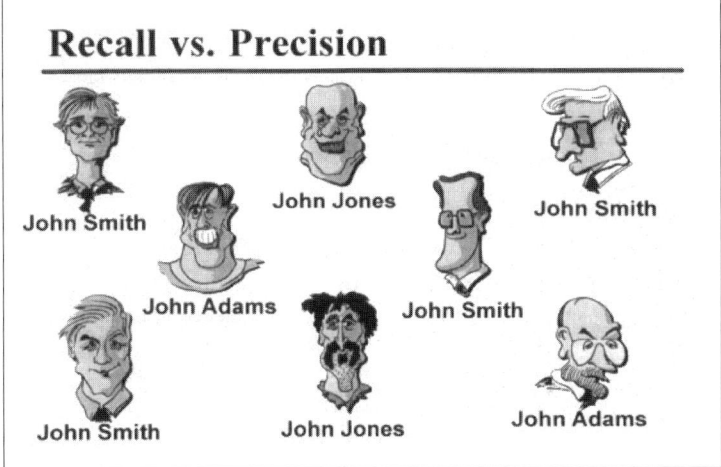

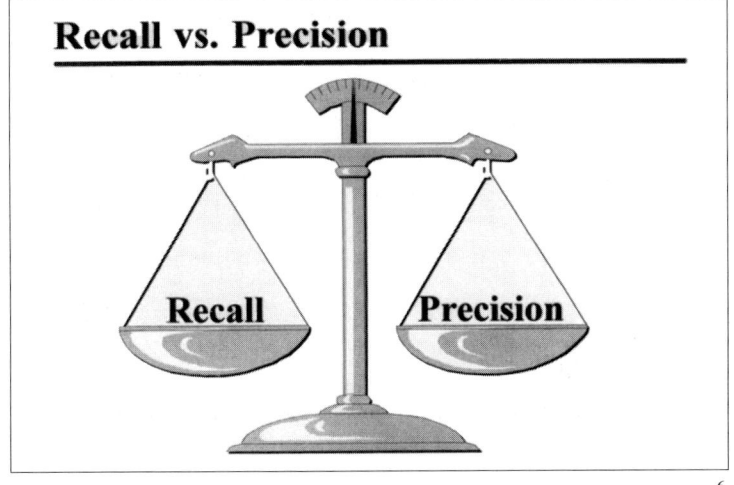

## Threshold Determinations

### Threshold
**The total weight which is used to decide whether a record should be considered a match or nonmatch with the retrievals from the file.**

## Threshold Decision Making

**The threshold decision is based on the purpose of the links**

Threshold

Criminals

Citizens

-50  -40  -30  -20  -10    0   +10   +20  +30  +40  +50

Log Weights

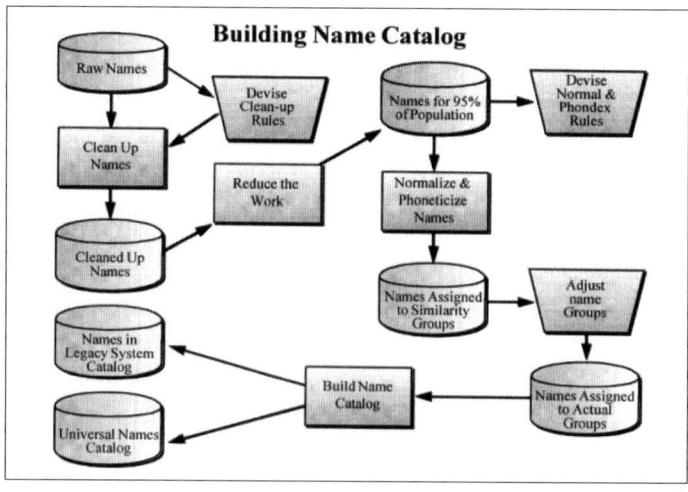

Building Name Catalog

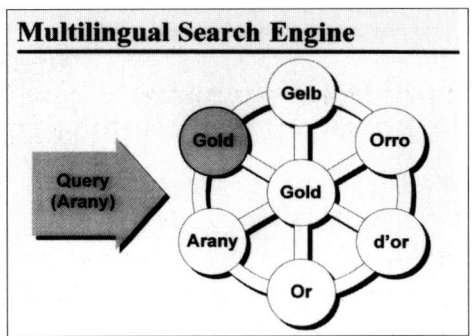

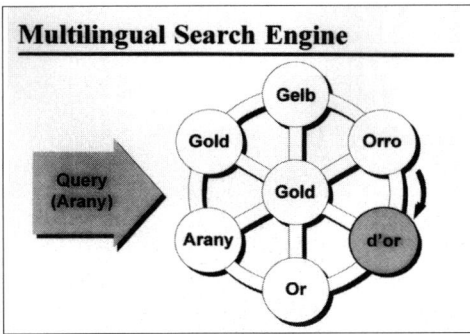

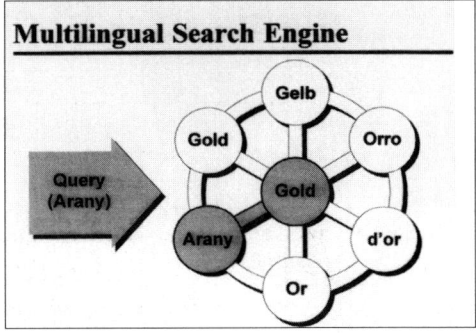

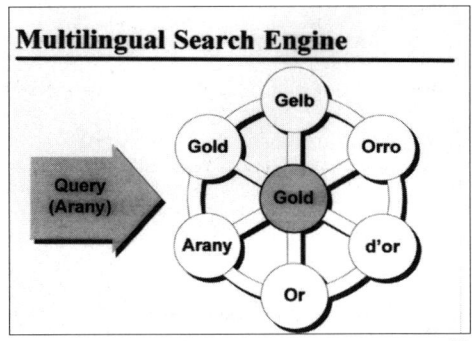

10

**D'Or à la Barre de Sable chargeé de trois Molettes d'Argent**

**Or, on a bend Sable, 3 mullets Argent**

**D'Azur à six Besants d' Argent 3, 2 et 1**

**Azure, 6 plates 3, 2, 1**

**Gules, Fess, Or, Mullet, difference**

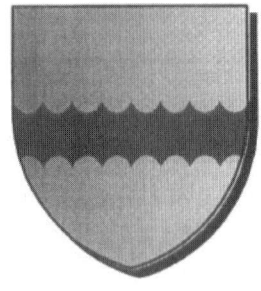

**Argent, fesse, engrailed, Gules**

# THE RUSSIAN, GERMAN, ROMANIAN AND CANADIAN DESCENDANTS OF LUDWIG ADOLF PETER SAYN-WITTGENSTEIN (1768-1843), MOST SERENE PRINCE AND FIELD-MARSHAL OF THE RUSSIAN ARMY

Alla Krasko

For my paper I have chosen a family whose history conforms with the topic of our Congress. Moreover this family has connections with both Russia and Canada, as some family members now live in Ottawa.

The family of the Counts and later the Princes of Sayn-Wittgenstein-Berleburg is of German origin. Its roots go back to the 9th century.

It is well known that many Germans served in the armies of different European countries. In particular, many German noblemen served in Russia, especially since the middle of the 17th century.

In the middle of the 18th century, Count Christian Ludwig Casimir Sayn-Wittgenstein (1725-1797), one of the younger members of the Berleburg branch of the family, was accepted in the Russian military service. The Count took part in the 1756-1763 war against Prussia and in the Russian-Turkish wars, reaching the rank of lieutenant-general. Interestingly, his brother Georg-Ernst was a major-general in the French army of Louis XVI and was executed as a monarchist in 1792 during the French Revolution.

Count Wittgenstein, as he was called in Russia, was first married to a German lady, the Countess Amalie Louisa Finck von Finckenstein. His second marriage was to a Russian lady who belonged to one of the oldest families of the Russian aristocracy: she was born as Princess Dolgorukaya and was the widow of General Count Andrew Bestuzhev-Riumin. The family connections that resulted from this marriage helped the children from his first wife to enhance their careers in Russia. Two of his sons entered Russian military service and became members of the Russian nobility.

Ludwig Adolf Peter (1768/69-1843), called Petr in Russia, the youngest son of Count Christian Ludwig Casimir, knew a brilliant career. It was he, in 1812, who commanded the Russian army, which protected the road to Saint-Petersburg and prevented Napoleon's troops from reaching the capital of Russia, making him a national hero. After the death of Field-Marshal Kutuzov in 1813, he was promoted to the rank of commander-in-chief of the United Army, which fought against Napoleon. His army participated in the liberation of Prussia, at that time a Russian ally. In 1826, Emperor Nicholas I granted him the rank of general field-marshal and, in 1818, Count Wittgenstein became a member of State Council. In 1834, when Europe celebrated the 20th anniversary of the victory over Napoleon, the Prussian King Friedrich-Wilhelm III granted him the title of "Most Serene" Prince. The Russian Emperor confirmed this title and moreover granted it to all his descendants, according to Russian laws.

The Field-Marshal was married to Antonia Snarskaya, who was of Polish origin. They had six sons and one daughter. The daughter was married to Prince Peter Troubetskoy, who later became a senator. His sons were accepted to the Corps of Pages, a privileged military school, and after graduating from this Corps, some of them served in one of the most privileged regiments of guards—the regiment of chevaliers of the Guard, and one son served in the Ministry of Foreign Affairs.

Prince Ludwig Adolf Friedrich (1799-1866), called Lev in Russia, the eldest son of the Field-Marshal, was first married to Princess Stephanie Radziwill, a Polish aristocrat. She was the only daughter of one of the richest landowners of the western provinces of Russia. After his father's death, Prince Lev inherited a large entailed estate in the provinces of Saint-Petersburg and Podolsk and, after the death of his wife, inherited her huge property. This entire estate was destined to the children from his first marriage. His daughter Maria married Prince Chlodwig Hohenlohe-Schillingsfürst, who later became Chancellor of the German Empire. Prince Lev's son, Peter Domenic Ludwig (1831-1887), Petr in Russia, was the Russian military attaché in France for 15 years, from 1861 to

1876, and was promoted to the rank of lieutenant-general and general-aide-de-camp in the Russian army.

Prince Lev's second wife was Princess Leonilla Baryatinskaya, a lady of high Russian aristocracy. After his retirement he lived abroad with his family, from the 1840s to his death. To ensure the property status of his children from the second marriage, he established, in 1846, another entailed estate of Sayn in Germany. These lands had belonged in former times to his German ancestors. Since 1861 he himself and then his descendants (only the eldest in male lines) were called the Most Serene Princes of Sayn-Wittgenstein-Sayn, making the children from his Russian wife Germans again. In fact, they were connected with both Russia and Germany and had double loyalties, double national identities and a double culture.

Prince Peter, the eldest grandson of the Field-Marshal, the owner of an entailed estate in Russia, did not have any children. After his death in 1887, his estate had passed to his half-brother, Prince Theodor Friedrich (1836-1909), Fedor in Russia, who lived in Germany since his birth, but had to settle in Russia. Prince Heinrich (1879-1919), the eldest son of Prince Fedor, became the officer of the His Majesty's Hussar regiment and was the last owner of a Russian entailed estate. He was married to Elisabeth Nabokova, who was the aunt of the famous writer Vladimir Nabokov. Prince Heinrich was killed by the Bolsheviks in 1919 and his family had to flee from Russia to Romania. When the Communists came to power in Romania, Prince Lev (1900/01-1974), the eldest son of Prince Heinrich, with his family again had to move. This time they went to Germany, from where they later emigrated to Canada, where his descendants now live.

Prince Nicholas-Voldemar (1812-1864), the youngest son of the Field-Marshal, was married twice, his first wife was a Catholic of Polish origin, the second was a Russian Orthodox. His daughter from the first marriage married Prince Konstantin Hohenlohe-Schillingsfürst in 1859. Prince Nicholas (1862-1934), his son from the second marriage, a rich landowner in the provinces of Kiev and Podolsk, graduated successfully from the Moscow Agricultural Academy and used his knowledge to cultivate the estate manor. After the revolution of 1917, he and his family escaped to Romania. The history of this family was recorded by his daughter, Countess Ekaterina Razumovskaya in her diary, which was published in German in 1984 and in Russian in 1986.

The table added to this paper illustrates the fact that wives and husbands in this family belonged to different peoples and nations and had different citizenships. In addition to Russians and Germans, there were some of Italian, Romanian, Hungarian and Polish origin. This family also gives us a very interesting example of confessional affiliations. The Field-Marshal belonged to the Reformation Church and his wife was a Catholic. Prince Lev, the eldest son, was baptized a Catholic and then adhered to the Reformers. His first wife and their children were Catholic. His second wife was Orthodox, but then converted to Catholicism. The children from this marriage were also baptized Orthodox, but later, following their father, were brought up in the Reformation spirit. The complicated confessional structure of the family is illustrated by a tomb in Druzhnoselye, the family estate in the Province of Saint-Petersburg, where Catholics, Orthodox, Reformers and Lutherans are buried side by side.

The sense of identity of different members of this family, who were connected with Russia during five generations, was formed in different ways. We can say that the Field-Marshal, though German by origin, felt himself to be a Russian, because he was born in Russia, served in the Russian army for 40 years and became a landowner in Russia. But some of his grandchildren from the branch of the Princes of Sayn-Wittgenstein-Sayn had never been to Russia. Two of them were to be mobilized in the German Army and sent to the eastern front, during the Second World War. Conversely, the diary of Countess Ekaterina Razumovskaya, born as a Most Serene Princess Sayn-Wittgenstein, shows her to have a real Russian consciousness. It is interesting that as an emigrant she was married to Count Andreas Razumovsky, a member of a very famous family in Russian history who, though Russian by his name, belonged to a germanised branch of the family, was a Catholic and did not speak Russian at all. Conversely, his wife, though German by name and origin, inculcated the so to say "Russian spirit" in her children, and one of her daughters, Countess Maria Razumovskaya, living in Vienna, is now a well-known researcher of the works of the Russian poetess Marina Tsvetaeva.

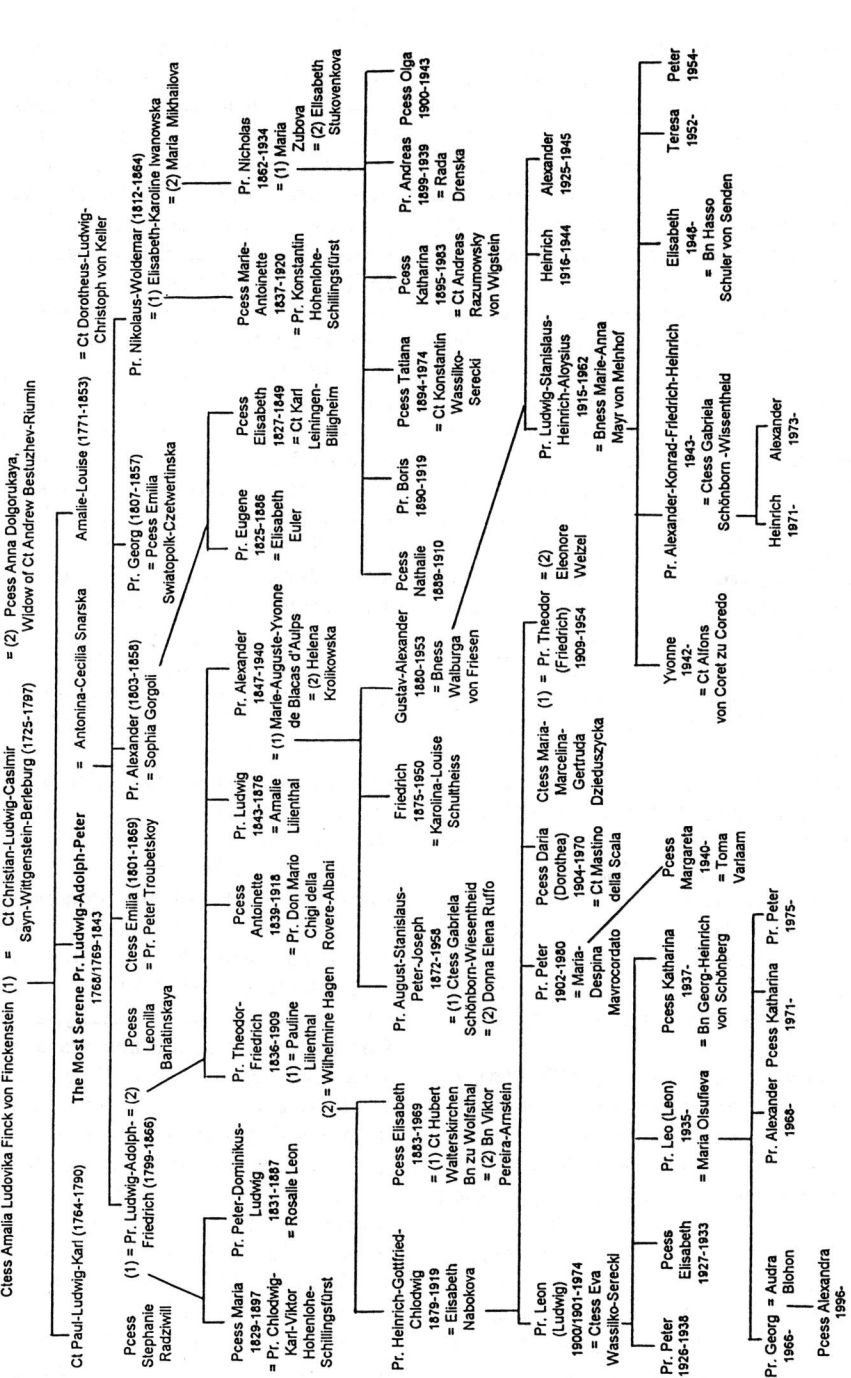

**FIGURE 1:** The descendants of Most Serene Prince L. A. P. Sayn-Wittgenstein, Field-Marshal of the Russian Army

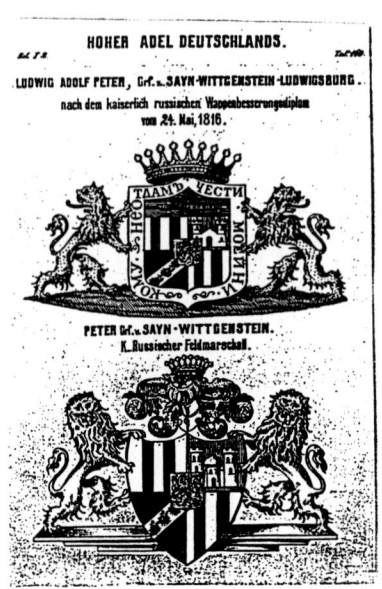

**FIGURE 2:** Russian coats of arms of Count L. A. P. Sayn-Wittgenstein
J. SIEBMACHERS, *Grosses und allgemeines Wappenbuch*, vol. 1, part 3, I, series (Nürnberg: 1878),
table 169.

**FIGURE 3:** Prussian coat of arms of Most Serene Prince L. A. P. Sayn-Wittgenstein
J. SIEBMACHERS, *Grosses und allgemeines Wappenbuch*, vol. 1, part 3, III, series B (Nürnberg: 1888),
table 163.

# LES BAS-BOURGUIGNONS ÉTABLIS AU CANADA AVANT 1730 ET LEURS RACINES FAMILIALES EN FRANCE[1]

Pierre Le Clercq

Depuis quelques années, la Société généalogique de l'Yonne que je représente ici, en tant que vice-président, reçoit des courriers de divers correspondants canadiens, ou bien d'origine canadienne, tous désireux d'en savoir un peu plus sur leur ascendance française dans le nord de la Bourgogne. Certains, très peu nombreux d'ailleurs, ont même fini par adhérer à notre cercle. Or, nous avons constaté que toutes ces demandes, venues de différents horizons, se rejoignent et nous obligent à apporter des réponses identiques à des questions similaires. Aussi, plutôt que de continuer à répéter invariablement les mêmes renseignements au fur et à mesure que lettres et messages nous parviennent d'outre-Atlantique, avons-nous décidé de fournir une réponse globale à tous les cas particuliers qui nous sont exposés.

## Définition des Bas-Bourguignons

On ne saurait débuter une étude sans en préciser le sujet. Par le terme plutôt insolite de « Bas-Bourguignons », appliqué à des gens ayant vécu en France sous l'Ancien Régime, j'entends tous les ressortissants du territoire composite qui, plus tard, en 1790, allait former à jamais le département de l'Yonne, avec la ville d'Auxerre comme chef-lieu. Ce département est divisé actuellement en 36 cantons, que l'on peut regrouper, pour les besoins de cet exposé, en sept contrées traditionnelles. Toutes ces circonscriptions apparaissent sur la carte ci-dessous :

**CARTE 1** : L'Yonne, département français situé dans le nord de la région « Bourgogne »

**Remarque** : Les cantons de Sens et d'Auxerre qui apparaissent sur cette carte sont en fait divisés en plusieurs petits cantons se partageant les deux villes. Par commodité, je n'ai pas tenu compte de ces divisions mineures.

De nos jours, les habitants du département de l'Yonne s'appellent les Icaunais. Ce nom a été créé récemment, à partir du terme « Icauna » dont les Gaulois se servaient pour désigner la rivière de l'Yonne qui, du sud vers le nord, traverse le département. J'ai préféré cependant ne point utiliser ce mot nouveau, employé surtout localement, puisque cette étude est destinée à la communauté internationale des généalogistes. De même, j'ai voulu éviter de parler du département de l'Yonne, dont le nom n'évoque pas grand-chose à l'étranger. Même en France, on rencontre des gens qui pensent que cette circonscription a pour chef-lieu la ville de Lyon ! C'est la raison pour laquelle j'ai choisi des expressions plus accessibles, se référant à une province française connue dans le monde entier. Je parlerai donc ici de Basse-Bourgogne et de Bas-Bourguignons.

## Le corpus des Bas-Bourguignons devenus Canadiens

Deux sources principales existent actuellement pour connaître l'ensemble des familles qui ont fait souche en Nouvelle-France, sous l'Ancien Régime. La première est un ouvrage publié en 1888 par Cyprien Tanguay, intitulé : *Dictionnaire généalogique des familles canadiennes*. La seconde est un livre de René Jetté paru en 1983, portant un titre fort semblable au précédent, à savoir : *Dictionnaire généalogique des familles du Québec*.

C'est ce dernier recueil que j'ai compulsé pour repérer tous les Bas-Bourguignons qui ont émigré au Canada avant 1730. René Jetté, en effet, a accompli avec son équipe de chercheurs un travail considérable, qui permet aux généalogistes de se passer à présent du dictionnaire conçu par Cyprien Tanguay, devenu désuet. Pour réaliser son ouvrage, René Jetté a consulté l'ensemble des actes de baptême, mariage et sépulture qui ont été enre-

gistrés en Nouvelle-France de 1621 à 1730. Il a examiné également tous les contrats de mariage, tous les recensements nominatifs de cette période, et a parcouru la totalité des rôles d'hospitalisation de l'Hôtel-Dieu de Québec. Qui plus est, il a même tenu compte de toutes les publications généalogiques antérieures à son propre livre. On a donc affaire à un dictionnaire qui se veut exhaustif, dans lequel n'ont été oubliés ni les célibataires, ni les gens de passage ayant finalement quitté le Canada.

Dans l'ouvrage de René Jetté, qui présente des milliers de personnages, je n'ai trouvé que 45 Bas-Bourguignons. J'ai déjà publié une liste de 43 d'entre eux [2]. Depuis lors, j'ai découvert deux autres individus originaires de Basse-Bourgogne, ce qui ne change guère l'effectif final. Celui-ci est si faible qu'il ne représente qu'une goutte d'eau parmi les centaines de milliers de personnes qui ont vécu en Basse-Bourgogne à la même époque, de 1621 à 1730. Il apparaît donc clairement que l'émigration des Bas-Bourguignons à destination du Canada fut un phénomène démographique tout à fait marginal, insignifiant.

Les 45 individus en question se répartissent en 17 femmes et 28 hommes. Ils provenaient de 21 paroisses différentes en Basse-Bourgogne, et d'un lieu indéterminé situé dans le diocèse d'Auxerre. Au Canada, ils se sont installés dans 29 localités, le long du fleuve Saint-Laurent. C'est ce que montre le TABLEAU 1, dans lequel figure la liste des 45 Bas-Bourguignons devenus Canadiens avant 1730, classés par ordre alphabétique de leurs noms de famille respectifs et divisés en deux groupes, l'un féminin et l'autre masculin. Par un code numérique, ont été indiquées la provenance en Basse-Bourgogne et l'implantation en Nouvelle-France de chacun de ces 45 émigrants des deux sexes.

**TABLEAU 1** : les 45 Bas-Bourguignons établis au Canada avant 1730

| Les 17 femmes | Yonne | Canada | Les 28 hommes | Yonne | Canada |
|---|---|---|---|---|---|
| BLANVILLAIN Anne | 12 | 25, 27 | ADAM Jean | 04 | 26, 02 |
| CHANCY Marie | 03 | 16 | ANDRÉ Pierre | 20 | 16, 28 |
| COLIN Anne | 19 | 19, 24 | CLAIRAMBAULT | 13 | 16, 13 |
| de BOULLONGNE Barbe | 16 | 16, 13 | François | | |
| de BOULLONGNE Philippe | 16 | 16 | COLLAN Étienne | 19 | 20 |
| de PROVINLIEU Marie | 17 | 16 | COLLERET François | 03 | 21 |
| Marguerite | | | COURTEAU Pierre | 15 | 19, 12 |
| GAUTHIER Marie Jeanne | 06 | 16, 10 | d'AILLEBOUST | 01 | 16, 13 |
| LEPAGE Constance | 14 | 19, 21 | Charles | | |
| LOURY Reine | 14 | 19, 21 | d'AILLEBOUST Louis | 01 | 16, 13 |
| MARTIN Marie | 16 | 13, 04 | de JOINCEAU Jean- | 17 | 08, 13 |
| MICHAUD Françoise | 18 | 05, 16 | Baptiste | | |
| MICHAUD Louise | 18 | 16 | de LACHASSE Pierre | 03 | 15, 16 |
| NORMAND Catherine | 19 | 16 | de LAFOND Jean | 22 | ? |
| NORMAND Madeleine | 19 | 16, 12 | HAY Pierre | 03 | 04, 13 |
| PARIS Françoise | 19 | 16, 20, | HUOT Nicolas | 03 | 16, 07 |
| | | 27 | JANIS François | 02 | 28 |
| SERVIGNIEN Jeanne | 09 | 16, 04 | LEBLANC Auguste | 03 | 22 |
| SOUILLARD Nicole | 08 | 30, 14 | LEGRAIN Louis | 07 | 06 |
| | | | LEMAIRE Claude Louis | 03 | 04, 29 |
| | | | LEPAGE Germain | 14 | 16, 30, 17 |
| **Remarque :** Les codes numériques qui | | | LEPAGE Louis | 14 | 16, 19, 21 |
| apparaissent à la suite du nom de | | | LEPAGE René | 14 | 30, 18, 17 |
| chaque individu, sous les colonnes | | | MARCOUX Pierre | 05 | 16, 03 |
| « Yonne » et « Canada », renvoient aux | | | MAUGRAS Jacques | 11 | 28, 23 |
| lieux cités dans les deux listes de | | | MILLOT Jean | 21 | 13 |
| localités ci-dessous. | | | PÉRILLARD Nicolas | 03 | 13 |
| | | | ROY Antoine | 10 | 16, 01, 09 |
| | | | ROYET Anatole | 03 | 03 |
| | | | THUOT Pierre | 20 | 13, 16, 11 |
| | | | VARAMBOUVILLE | 03 | 16 |
| | | | Antoine | | |

## Yonne (Basse-Bourgogne)

01 Ancy-le-Franc  
02 Argenteuil  
03 Auxerre  
04 Brienon-sur-Armançon  
05 Cry-sur-Armançon  
06 Domats  
07 Domecy  
08 Grange-le-Bocage  
09 Irancy  
10 Joigny  
11 Ligny-le-Châtel  
12 Maligny  
13 Nuits-sur-Armançon  
14 Ouanne  
15 Pontaubert  
16 Ravières  
17 St-Maurice-aux-R. Hommes  
18 Sennevoy  
19 Sens  
20 Tonnerre  
21 Vermenton  
22 Diocèse d'Auxerre

**Canada (Nouvelle-France)**

| | | |
|---|---|---|
| 01 Batiscan | 12 Montmagny | 23 Saint-François-du-Lac |
| 02 Beaumont | 13 Montréal | 24 Saint-Jean (I.O.) |
| 03 Beauport | 14 Ourantage | 25 Saint-Ours |
| 04 Boucherville | 15 Pentagouet | 26 Sillery |
| 05 Cap-de-la-Madeleine | 16 Québec | 27 Sorel |
| 06 Chambly | 17 Rimouski | 28 Trois-Rivières |
| 07 Château-Richer | 18 Sainte-Anne-de-Beaupré | 29 Verchères |
| 08 Lachenaie | 19 Sainte-Famille (I.O.) | 30 Île d'Orléans |
| 09 Lachine | 20 Sainte-Foy | |
| 10 La Férada | 21 Saint-François (I.O.) | |
| 11 Longueuil | 22 Saint-François-de-Sales | |

### L'origine et la destination des Bas-Bourguignons

Les 22 lieux qui sont cités dans la liste des localités de l'Yonne ne couvrent que de façon inégale le territoire du département. On constate en effet que, parmi les sept contrées qui composent la Basse-Bourgogne, certaines ont fourni beaucoup plus de colons à la Nouvelle-France que d'autres. C'est ce que montre le TABLEAU 2 :

TABLEAU **2** : les contrées d'origine

| | FEMMES | HOMMES | TOTAUX |
|---|---|---|---|
| personnes issues du Sénonais | 7 | 2 | 9 |
| personnes issues du Jovinien | 0 | 1 | 1 |
| personnes issues du Florentinois | 1 | 2 | 3 |
| personnes issues de l'Auxerrois | 4 | 13 | 17 |
| personnes issues de la Puisaye | 0 | 0 | 0 |
| personnes issues du Tonnerrois | 5 | 7 | 12 |
| personnes issues de l'Avallonnais | 0 | 2 | 2 |
| lieu indéterminé (diocèse d'Auxerre) | 0 | 1 | 1 |
| **TOTAUX** | **17** | **28** | **45** |

Sur ce tableau, on remarque que les Bas-Bourguignons établis au Canada avant 1730 étaient surtout originaires de l'Auxerrois, du Tonnerrois ou du Sénonais. Ensemble, ces trois contrées regroupent jusqu'à 38 individus, soit 84 % de l'effectif. On note également que, contrairement à l'Auxerrois, qui a envoyé trois fois plus d'hommes que de femmes en Nouvelle-France, le Sénonais se distingue par le fait qu'il a expédié, quant à lui, trois fois plus de femmes que d'hommes. L'origine des Bas-Bourguignons partis au Canada est donc très contrastée : si 41 % des femmes du corpus sont issues du Sénonais, 46 % des hommes viennent en revanche de l'Auxerrois.

À l'intérieur des contrées, le contraste est tout aussi saisissant d'un canton à l'autre. En fait, les Bas-Bourguignons devenus Canadiens n'étaient originaires, en grande majorité, que de quatre cantons à peine, inclus dans les trois contrées mentionnées plus haut. Tout le reste des émigrants,

TABLEAU **3** : les cantons d'origine

|  | FEMMES | HOMMES | TOTAUX |
|---|---|---|---|
| canton de Sens (Sénonais) | 4 | 1 | 5 |
| canton d'Auxerre (Auxerrois) | 1 | 9 | 10 |
| canton de Courson (Auxerrois) | 2 | 3 | 5 |
| canton d'Ancy-le-Franc (Tonnerrois) | 3 | 5 | 8 |
| 12 autres cantons + lieu indéterminé | 7 | 10 | 17 |
| **TOTAUX** | **17** | **28** | **45** |

composé de 17 personnes, venait de 12 autres cantons et d'un lieu indéterminé situé dans l'ancien diocèse d'Auxerre. C'est ce que révèle le TABLEAU 3.

À eux seuls, les cantons de Sens, Auxerre, Courson-les-Carrières et Ancy-le-Franc, qui ne couvrent ensemble qu'un neuvième du territoire de l'Yonne, ont fourni 62 % des Bas-Bourguignons qui se sont rendus au Canada avant 1730. Entre les cantons d'Auxerre et de Sens, on retrouve le même contraste que celui observé entre l'Auxerrois et le Sénonais : dans le premier cas, ce sont surtout les hommes qui ont émigré en Nouvelle-France ; dans le second, ce sont les femmes.

Un dernier point doit être souligné quant aux différents lieu d'origine des 45 individus qui figurent dans le corpus. Ces localités peuvent se répartir en deux groupes : les villes, au nombre de quatre (Sens, Joigny, Auxerre et Tonnerre), et les bourgs et villages de campagne, au nombre de 17. On s'aperçoit alors que si les femmes, à la campagne, ont été presque aussi nombreuses que les hommes à quitter la Basse-Bourgogne pour aller vivre en Nouvelle-France, les citadines, de leur côté, ont beaucoup moins émigré que leurs compagnons citadins. Ce déficit de la gent féminine issue de la ville apparaît nettement dans le TABLEAU 4 :

TABLEAU **4** : les localités d'origine

|  | FEMMES | HOMMES | TOTAUX |
|---|---|---|---|
| personnes originaires de la ville | 5 | 13 | 18 |
| personnes originaires de la campagne | 12 | 15 | 27 |
| **TOTAUX** | **17** | **28** | **45** |

Au Canada, le phénomène s'est déplacé. Les femmes, semble-t-il, après leur arrivée sur le continent nord-américain, ont été plutôt réticentes à s'installer à la campagne : les hommes ont été deux fois plus nombreux qu'elles à s'y établir. On constate en revanche une parité entre les deux sexes dans les villes de Québec et de Montréal. Ces deux agglomérations, avant 1730, n'étaient encore que de

petites bourgades de quelques centaines d'habitants, bien moins peuplées que Sens et Auxerre à la même époque. Elles constituaient cependant des places fortes suffisamment sûres pour inciter les femmes de Basse-Bourgogne à y élire domicile, de préférence à tout autre lieu. Le TABLEAU 5 est tout à fait éloquent à l'égard des choix féminins :

TABLEAU 5 : les lieux d'implantation

|  | FEMMES | HOMMES | TOTAUX |
|---|---|---|---|
| personnes installées en ville | 6 | 6 | 12 |
| personnes installées à la campagne | 5 | 11 | 16 |
| gens en ville puis à la campagne | 5 | 7 | 12 |
| gens à la campagne puis en ville | 1 | 3 | 4 |
| lieux non précisés | 0 | 1 | 1 |
| **TOTAUX** | **17** | **28** | **45** |

En Nouvelle-France, les Bas-Bourguignons se sont établis le long du fleuve Saint-Laurent, autour de quatre pôles d'implantation : les régions plus ou moins peuplées de Rimouski, Québec, Trois-Rivières et Montréal. C'est surtout la région de Québec qui a bénéficié de l'apport humain en provenance de Basse-Bourgogne. Environ 47 % des gens figurant dans le corpus ont choisi comme résidence la ville de Québec ou ses environs.

Cette région était en fait la plaque tournante de la colonisation du Canada. La localité de Rimouski a été fondée en 1696 par des Bas-Bourguignons venus de l'île d'Orléans, près de Québec, et on observe également quelques déplacements de la région de Québec vers celles de Trois-Rivières et de Montréal. Le TABLEAU 6 résume ce que l'on sait des domiciles et changements de régions en question :

TABLEAU 6 : les pôles d'implantation

|  | FEMMES | HOMMES | TOTAUX |
|---|---|---|---|
| région de Québec uniquement | 11 | 10 | 21 |
| région de Trois-Rivières uniquement | 0 | 2 | 2 |
| région de Montréal uniquement | 2 | 6 | 8 |
| régions de Québec et Rimouski | 0 | 2 | 2 |
| régions de Québec et Trois-Rivières | 2 | 2 | 4 |
| régions de Québec et Montréal | 2 | 4 | 6 |
| ailleurs + lieu non précisé | 0 | 2 | 2 |
| **TOTAUX** | **17** | **28** | **45** |

### Caractéristiques des Bas-Bourguignons au Canada

Les gens qui ont quitté la Basse-Bourgogne pour aller vivre en Nouvelle-France, de 1621 à 1730, étaient pour la plupart des hommes et des femmes encore jeunes, libres de partir au loin. Très peu étaient déjà mariés avant leur départ. Dans leur grande majorité, les colons venus des diverses contrées de l'Yonne ont attendu d'arriver sur place, au Canada, pour convoler en justes noces. Ne sont demeurés célibataires que 21 % des hommes (trois laïcs et trois religieux), et 6 % des femmes seulement (une religieuse). Le TABLEAU 7 reprend toutes ces données :

TABLEAU **7** : situations conjugales

|  | FEMMES | HOMMES | TOTAUX |
|---|---|---|---|
| colons du corpus mariés en France | 2 | 3 | 5 |
| colons du corpus mariés au Canada | 14 | 19 | 33 |
| colons du corpus restés célibataires | 1 | 6 | 7 |
| **TOTAUX** | **17** | **28** | **45** |

Les colons originaires de Basse-Bourgogne n'ont point bravé l'océan Atlantique pour mener en Nouvelle-France une vie oisive. Tous ont exercé sur le sol canadien un métier ou une activité quelconque. Les femmes, sauf ladite religieuse, se sont adonnées aux tâches incombant alors aux mères et aux épouses, tandis que les hommes se sont livrés à toutes sortes d'occupations. Parmi les 28 représentants de la gent masculine, on trouve un maçon, deux soldats, trois religieux, un sculpteur, deux taillandiers, un domestique, deux laboureurs, un boulanger, un aubergiste et un tonnelier. On trouve aussi un procureur fiscal, un seigneur de Rimouski, un lieutenant-général civil et criminel de la prévôté de Québec, un subdélégué de l'intendant de Montréal, voire même un gouverneur intérimaire et un gouverneur général de la Nouvelle-France. La grande variété de toutes ces activités montre bien que l'émigration des Bas-Bourguignons vers le Canada n'a pas été un phénomène organisé, de type corporatif comme l'était la migration saisonnière des maçons de la Haute-Marche, des scieurs de long du Forez ou des sabotiers de Laprugne. Tout n'a reposé, en fait, que sur une convergence fortuite de destinées individuelles ou familiales.

Si la corporation professionnelle n'a joué aucun rôle dans le départ des Bas-Bourguignons pour le Canada, il semblerait en revanche que la famille proche, bien souvent, a été un support essentiel à l'émigration. On constate en effet que 53 % des femmes avaient dans leur entourage, en Nouvelle-France, un membre au moins de leur parentèle d'origine. Les hommes, mieux préparés à affronter les dangers et la solitude, n'étaient que 18 % dans le même cas : la plupart ont émigré seuls, sans rejoindre quiconque sur place, comme l'indique le TABLEAU 8 :

TABLEAU **8** : situations familiales

|  | FEMMES | HOMMES | TOTAUX |
|---|---|---|---|
| colons venus au Canada en solitaire | 8 | 23 | 31 |
| colons établis au Canada en famille | 9 | 5 | 14 |
| **TOTAUX** | **17** | **28** | **45** |

Les 14 colons établis au Canada en famille représentent 31 % de l'effectif total des Bas-Bourguignons devenus Canadiens. Il s'agit donc d'une minorité d'une certaine importance, où les femmes prédominent largement. Il convient toutefois de préciser que chaque famille concernée n'est pas venue nécessairement en bloc en Nouvelle-France : on assiste parfois à des arrivées en plusieurs vagues, dans deux cas au moins. Quoi qu'il en soit, regroupées ou venues en une seule fois, les familles de Basse-Bourgogne installées au Canada sont au nombre de quatre, à savoir :

1. **La famille Michaud :** Elle se compose de deux sœurs, Louise et Françoise Michaud, qui se sont mariées toutes les deux en 1670, sur le sol canadien, à l'âge de 25 et 21 ans

respectivement. Les deux jeunes femmes sont probablement venues ensemble en Nouvelle-France.

2. **La famille Normand :** Elle est constituée elle aussi de deux sœurs, Catherine et Madeleine Normand, qui se sont mariées toutes les deux en la ville de Québec, la première en 1665 alors qu'elle était âgée de 21 ans, la seconde en 1670 à l'âge de 23 ans. Les deux jeunes femmes n'ont probablement pas effectué ensemble la traversée de l'océan Atlantique.

3. **La famille Lepage :** Elle est arrivée en deux vagues successives et comprend deux générations de colons issus de Basse-Bourgogne. La première vague a amené en Nouvelle-France deux frères, Louis et Germain, qui ont débarqué à Québec vers l'an 1661. La seconde vague a ensuite déposé sur les rives du Canada trois autres membres de la famille, en 1672 environ : Reine Loury, femme de Germain Lepage ; Constance Lepage, sœur cadette de Louis et Germain ; René Lepage, fils unique de Germain Lepage et Reine Loury.

4. **La famille d'Ailleboust :** Elle est arrivée en trois vagues successives et comporte jusqu'à trois générations de colons originaires de Basse-Bourgogne. La première vague a amené trois personnes en Nouvelle-France : Louis d'Ailleboust et sa femme Barbe de Boullongne, ainsi que la sœur de cette dernière, Philippe de Boullongne, tous trois arrivés sur le sol canadien en 1643. Les deuxième et troisième vagues, quant à elles, ont déposé sur les berges du fleuve Saint-Laurent deux autres colons : d'abord, en 1648, un neveu de Louis d'Ailleboust prénommé Charles, puis, avant 1672, une nièce dudit Charles d'Ailleboust nommée Marie Martin, laquelle s'est mariée à Montréal en novembre 1671.

### Les Bas-Bourguignons dont l'ascendance reste inconnue

Qu'ils aient vécu seuls au Canada ou avec d'autres membres de leur parentèle, les colons originaires de Basse-Bourgogne avaient tous, bien entendu, des racines familiales. Ce sont elles qui intéressent le plus les généalogistes cana-

diens. Malheureusement, il ne m'a pas été possible de trouver l'ascendance de tous les Bas-Bourguignons qui ont émigré en Nouvelle-France de 1621 à 1730. Les raisons à cela sont multiples, que l'on peut classer en quatre catégories :

1. On regrette d'abord, dans deux cas, un manque de sources en France. Les registres paroissiaux et les contrats notariés sont parfois trop tardifs pour permettre de remonter dans le temps.

2. On regrette ensuite, dans un cas seulement, le confinement de certaines sources. Refusant de verser leurs documents anciens aux Archives départementales, certaines mairies en France ont conservé leurs vieux registres paroissiaux, sans aménager des horaires de consultation aussi larges que dans les services départementaux.

3. On regrette aussi, dans quatre cas, que les sources canadiennes soient parfois imprécises. Le nom des parents du colon n'est pas indiqué, ou bien le lieu d'origine est fort vague.

4. On regrette enfin, dans dix cas, que les renseignements fournis par les sources canadiennes soient parfois erronés. On ne trouve pas en France, dans la localité mentionnée au Canada, la famille qui aurait dû y résider normalement.

Toutes ces raisons suffisent à expliquer que, sur les 45 Bas-Bourguignons qui ont émigré de l'autre côté de l'océan avant 1730, il en est 17 dont le berceau familial et géographique en Basse-Bourgogne reste une énigme. Voici la liste alphabétique de ces 17 colons au sujet desquels je n'ai rien pu découvrir de nouveau au cours de mes recherches :

**Adam, Jean :** Né vers 1644, il était originaire de Brienon-sur-Armançon, dans le Florentinois. Il était déjà en Nouvelle-France lors du recensement canadien de 1666. Il avait alors 22 ans. Marié vers l'an 1673 avec Marie Mézeray, à Sillery, il mourut à Beaumont où son corps fut inhumé le 3 septembre 1711. Il avait travaillé comme menuisier puis notaire, et son épouse lui avait donné neuf enfants. Ne connaissant pas ses parents, je n'ai rien pu trouver sur lui en France.

**Colin, Anne :** Née vers 1644 ou 1647, elle était la fille de Nicolas Colin et Isabelle Calende. Originaire de la paroisse Sainte-Croix, à Sens, elle a émigré au Canada où, le 18 octobre 1669, à Sainte-Famille sur l'île d'Orléans, près de Québec, elle épousa Vincent Boissonneau. Lors du recensement canadien de 1681, elle avait 34 ans. Elle mourut le 28 juillet 1719 à Saint-Jean, sur l'île d'Orléans, ceci à l'âge de 75 ans. Elle avait donné 12 enfants à son mari. Je n'ai trouvé aucune trace d'elle et de ses parents dans les registres paroissiaux de la ville de Sens.

**Collan, Étienne :** Originaire de Sens lui aussi, il était fils de François Collan et Françoise Lheureuse. Le 22 octobre 1725, à Sainte-Foy près de Québec, il épousa Thérèse David qui ne lui a donné aucun enfant. Je n'ai rien trouvé sur lui et ses parents dans les registres paroissiaux de Sens. Dans les sources canadiennes, on dit qu'il venait de la paroisse Saint-Étienne de Sens, mais cette ville n'a jamais eu de paroisse de ce nom : il s'agit en fait de la cathédrale.

**Colleret, François :** Originaire d'Auxerre, il était le fils d'Edme Colleret et Anne Gargner. Il se rendit au Canada en tant que soldat, affecté à la compagnie du capitaine Beaubassin. Il y fut surnommé « Bourguignon ». Le 28 février 1718, à Saint-François sur l'île d'Orléans, il convola en justes noces avec Marie Drapeau, dite « Laforge ». Le contrat notarié avait été signé trois jours plus tôt, devant maître Senet. Le couple eut six enfants. Je n'ai rien trouvé sur ledit François Colleret à Auxerre, ni sur ses parents. Il existe toutefois des Colleret dans la région, comme à Bassou où j'ai découvert un mariage entre Pascal Colleret et Perrette Garnier, célébré le 6 juin 1684. Il convient d'ajouter, pour finir, que dans le dictionnaire de René Jetté on précise que François Colleret venait de la paroisse auxerroise de Saint-Germain. En fait, il n'y avait point de paroisse de ce nom à Auxerre : Saint-Germain était une abbaye, située sur le territoire de la paroisse Saint-Loup.

**Courteau, Pierre :** Né vers 1665, il était originaire de Pontaubert près d'Avallon. Ses parents étaient Pierre Courteau et Marthe Marchand.

Le 25 juin 1691, à l'âge de 26 ans, il épousa Marie Saint-Denis en l'église de Sainte-Famille, sur l'île d'Orléans près de Québec. Il rendit l'âme à Montmagny, entre 1712 et 1714. Son épouse lui avait donné dix enfants. Je n'ai rien trouvé sur lui et ses parents à Pontaubert. Il faut dire que dans les registres paroissiaux de cette petite localité les premiers mariages ne commencent qu'en 1668. Les baptêmes débutent en 1649, mais on ne voit aucune mention de celui de Pierre Courteau vers 1665. J'ai cherché aussi à Avallon, où j'ai découvert un couple peut-être apparenté : Pierre Courtot et Marie Bertrand, qui vivaient au XVIIe siècle comme les parents dudit Pierre.

**de Joinceau, Jean-Baptiste :** Originaire de Saint-Maurice-aux-Riches-Hommes, dans le Sénonais, il a émigré au Canada où il vécut à Lachenaie. On le surnommait « Deguise ». Il mourut à l'hôpital de Montréal le 11 février 1700, célibataire. Ne connaissant pas le nom de ses parents, il m'est difficile de trouver son ascendance. Son nom de famille, en tout cas, n'apparaît jamais dans les registres paroissiaux de Saint-Maurice-aux-Riches-Hommes.

**de Lafond, Jean :** Né vers 1647 ou 1652, il était originaire du diocèse d'Auxerre. Il a émigré au Canada où il devint domestique de Nicolas Vérieu. Il avait 20 ans au recensement canadien de 1667, et 29 ans à celui de 1681. C'est tout ce que l'on sait de cet homme. Ne connaissant ni le nom de ses parents, ni le lieu exact où il serait né, il m'est impossible de mener la moindre recherche à son sujet. D'ailleurs, le diocèse d'Auxerre, avant la Révolution française, avait un territoire qui s'étendait jusque dans l'actuel département de la Nièvre, où l'on trouve quelques Delafond dans les anciens registres paroissiaux de Saint-Amand-en-Puisaye.

**de Provinlieu, Marie Marguerite :** Originaire de Saint-Maurice-aux-Riches-Hommes, elle était la fille de Louis de Provinlieu et Madeleine de Trota. Le 11 octobre 1672, en la ville de Québec, elle épousa un Irlandais de Dublin nommé Jean Houssy. Le couple n'eut point d'enfants. Je n'ai rien trouvé sur cette femme, ni sur ses parents dans les registres paroissiaux tenus par les curés de Saint-Maurice-aux-Riches-Hommes sous l'Ancien Régime.

**Gauthier, Marie Jeanne :** Née vers 1639, elle était originaire de Domats, dans le Sénonais. Ses parents étaient Honoré Gauthier et Jacqueline Mabile. Le 17 octobre 1668, en la ville de Québec, elle épousa Gilles Masson à qui elle donna quatre enfants. Elle avait 42 ans lors du recensement canadien de 1681. Elle décéda le 9 octobre 1713, dans une localité appelée La Férada. Comme les registres paroissiaux de Domats ne commencent qu'en 1685, je n'ai pas pu vérifier si cette femme était bien née dans ce village de Basse-Bourgogne, et si ses parents étaient bien ceux indiqués dans les sources canadiennes.

**Janis, François :** Né vers 1676, il était originaire d'Argenteuil, dans le Tonnerrois. Ses père et mère étaient Jean Janis et Marie Paquet. Le 14 novembre 1704, à Trois-Rivières au Canada, il convola en justes noces avec Simone Brosseau qui lui donna 11 enfants. Il avait 40 ans lors du recensement canadien de 1716. Il était alors aubergiste. Je n'ai rien trouvé sur lui, ni sur ses parents, dans les registres paroissiaux d'Argenteuil. Il faut dire que l'on déplore une lacune dans ces registres, de 1676 à 1681.

**Leblanc, Auguste :** Né à Auxerre le 23 novembre 1649, il entra dans les ordres chez les Jésuites en 1666, à Paris, puis se rendit en 1696 au Canada. Là, il fut envoyé comme missionnaire auprès des Indiens Abénaquis, à Saint-François-de-Sales. Il rentra ensuite en France dès l'an 1700, où il mourut le 26 février 1723, à Beaugency, près d'Orléans. Je n'ai pas pu reconstituer son arbre généalogique à Auxerre, car, dans aucun des registres paroissiaux de cette ville, on ne trouve son acte de baptême à la date indiquée dans les sources canadiennes. En revanche, dans l'un des registres de l'église Notre-Dame-la-d'Hors, on peut voir un acte de mariage daté du 11 janvier 1635, unissant un certain Pierre Leblanc à une femme qui s'appelait Germaine Guesnier. Il s'agit peut-être des parents du futur Jésuite en mission temporaire au Canada.

**Legrain, Louis :** Né vers 1649, il était originaire de Domecy-sur-Cure ou Domecy-sur-le-Vault, dans l'Avallonnais. Ses parents étaient Pierre Legrain, ou Challegrain, et Françoise Béguen. Le 14 novembre 1686, à l'âge de 37 ans, il passa un contrat de mariage en Nouvelle-France, devant maître Normandin, notaire à Chambly près de Montréal. Cet acte notarié l'unissait à une certaine Louise Bonnet, qui lui donna un fils. Louis Legrain mourut à Chambly, le 14 février 1711. Je n'ai pas pu remonter son ascendance en France, ceci pour deux raisons : 1) les registres paroissiaux de Domecy-sur-le-Vault commencent en 1648, mais je n'y ai trouvé aucun Legrain ou Challegrain ; 2) ceux de Domecy-sur-Cure débutent en 1612, certes, mais il faut aller les consulter en mairie, loin des Archives départementales de l'Yonne qui ne possèdent pas les microfilms correspondants.

**Lemaire, Claude Louis :** Né vers 1658, il était originaire d'Auxerre. Ses parents étaient Louis Lemaire et Marguerite Bardolat. Il est arrivé au Canada avec les armées du roi de France, comme sergent affecté à la compagnie du capitaine Marin. Le 30 novembre 1686, à Boucherville près de Montréal, il épousa Marie Charlotte Charron qui lui donna deux enfants. Il mourut à Verchères avant 1693. Je n'ai rien trouvé sur lui, ni sur ses parents, dans les registres paroissiaux des 12 églises d'Auxerre[3].

**Paris, Françoise :** Née vers 1646, elle était originaire de la paroisse Saint-Pierre, à Sens. Ses parents étaient Edme Paris et Cyrette Baron. Le 11 septembre 1673, à Québec, elle se maria en premières noces avec Pierre Petitclerc. Puis, le 12 février 1714, à Sainte-Foy près de ladite ville de Québec, elle convola en secondes noces avec Pierre Elie. Elle avait 70 ans environ lors du recensement canadien de 1716. Elle mourut 12 ans plus tard et son corps fut enseveli le 16 mars 1728, à Sorel. De son premier mariage, elle avait eu 11 enfants. Je n'ai rien trouvé sur elle, ni sur ses parents, dans les registres paroissiaux des églises Saint-Pierre-le-Donjon et Saint-Pierre-le-Rond, à Sens. On peut voir cependant, dans un registre de la seconde église, deux actes de baptême se rapportant à des enfants d'un certain Edme Paris et de sa femme Cyrette Carduelle, *alias* Cairduille. Le premier nourrisson, une fille prénommée Étiennette Françoise, fut baptisé le 25 juin 1653. Le second nouveau-né, un garçon prénommé Edme comme son père, fut tenu sur les fonts baptismaux le 19 juillet 1655. Dans l'hypothèse où Cyrette Baron et Cyrette Carduelle seraient une seule et même personne, portant le nom de son père dans un cas et celui de sa mère dans l'autre, il y aurait de fortes chances pour que

Françoise Paris, mariée à Québec en 1673, corresponde en fait à la petite Étiennette Françoise, baptisée à Sens en 1653.

**Périllard, Nicolas :** Né vers 1652 ou 1661, il était originaire d'Auxerre. Ses parents étaient Nicolas Périllard et Nicole Baraton. Le 10 janvier 1695, à Montréal, il épousa Jeanne Sabourin qui lui donna 14 enfants. Il avait 34 ans lors de son mariage, et exerçait l'activité de taillandier et forgeron. On le surnommait « Bourguignon ». Il décéda le 10 novembre 1726 en ladite ville de Montréal, à l'âge de 74 ans. Je n'ai rien trouvé sur lui, ni sur ses parents, dans les registres paroissiaux des 12 églises d'Auxerre.

**Royet, Anatole :** Né vers 1681 à Auxerre, il est arrivé au Canada le 2 juin 1715, comme prêtre. En 1719, il fut nommé curé de Beauport, près de Québec. Il y fit aussitôt bâtir une église, qui fut inaugurée en 1722. Il mourut à Beauport le 5 janvier 1731 et son corps fut inhumé au sein de cette nouvelle église. Je n'ai rien pu trouver sur lui à Auxerre, car je ne connais pas le nom de ses parents.

**Souillard, Nicole :** Née vers 1636 ou 1642, elle était originaire de Grange-le-Bocage, dans le Sénonais. Ses parents étaient Michel Souillard et Jeanne Bourdon. Le 16 novembre 1665, devant maître Duquet, notaire à l'île d'Orléans près de Québec, elle convola en justes noces avec Louis Gaboury. Elle avait 24 ans au recensement canadien de 1666, puis 45 ans à celui de 1681. Après son trépas, elle fut enterrée le 25 mars 1707, à Ourantage. Elle avait donné sept enfants à son mari. Je n'ai pas pu remonter son ascendance car les registres paroissiaux de Grange-le-Bocage ne commencent qu'en 1681.

### Les Bas-Bourguignons dont la parentèle a été retrouvée

Les 17 colons qui figurent dans la liste ci-avant sont ceux au sujet desquels, pour des raisons diverses, on ne peut rien ajouter à ce que nous apprennent déjà les sources canadiennes : aucun acte n'a été découvert en France qui vienne enrichir les données de base. Dans la nouvelle liste qui suit, sont présentés en revanche d'autres Bas-Bourguignons, dont j'ai pu retrouver la trace en France, ou bien celle d'un membre quelconque de leur parentèle proche. On a donc

ainsi la confirmation que ces gens venaient bien de Basse-Bourgogne, qu'ils étaient originaires des localités mentionnées dans les sources canadiennes, sans que l'on connaisse pour autant leur ascendance au-delà de leurs parents. Voici cette nouvelle liste, composée elle aussi de 17 Bas-Bourguignons établis au Canada avant 1730 :

**André, Pierre :** Baptisé le 30 juillet 1663 en l'église Notre-Dame, à Tonnerre, il était le fils de François André et Marie Thierriat. Son père était avocat, chevalier du guet, et receveur de l'abbaye Saint-Michel à Tonnerre. Sa mère mourut le 3 juin 1674, et fut ensevelie le même jour dans ladite abbaye. À l'âge de 20 ans, Pierre André perdit aussi son père, qui décéda à Tonnerre le 22 février 1683. Les obsèques eurent lieu en l'église Notre-Dame, puis le corps fut inhumé en l'abbaye Saint-Michel. Le défunt avait 58 ans lors de son trépas. Le 15 janvier 1694, à l'âge de 30 ans, Pierre André signa un contrat de mariage devant maîtres Valet et Vatry, notaires en la ville de Paris. Il s'unissait de la sorte à Claudine Frédin, qui lui donna six enfants, dont les quatre premiers naquirent à Québec. Peu après la cérémonie nuptiale, en effet, Pierre André se rendit avec son épouse au Canada, où il remplaça son beau-frère Jean Frédin au poste de secrétaire de l'intendant Jean Bochart de Champigny. Il regagna ensuite la France en 1702, et s'installa aussitôt au Havre pour y occuper l'office de prévôt général de la Marine et des Galères. En 1718, il retourna au Canada. Pendant les 26 années qui suivirent, il y assuma la charge de lieutenant général civil et criminel de la prévôté de Québec, remplissant aussi, pour un temps plus court, la fonction de lieutenant général de l'Amirauté. En 1744, à l'âge avancé de 81 ans, il démissionna pour se retirer chez sa fille à Trois-Rivières, où il rendit sont dernier soupir le 7 mars 1748.

Pierre André avait eu quatre frères et une sœur, tous nés à Tonnerre et baptisés comme lui en l'église Notre-Dame, à savoir :

- Françoise, baptisée le 7 janvier 1659. Elle épousa Jean-Baptiste Jamin le 7 janvier 1683, en ladite église Notre-Dame à Tonnerre, ceci le jour même de ses 24 ans.
- Jean, baptisé le 11 mars 1661. Il se maria le 31 octobre 1685 avec Geneviève Ravigneau, devant l'autel de l'église Saint-Pierre à Tonnerre. Il était alors ancien mousquetaire

du roi, mais poursuivait néanmoins une carrière militaire comme lieutenant des dragons. Il portait aussi le titre de « sieur de Leigne », à l'instar de son frère puîné Pierre.

- François, baptisé le 27 février 1665, deux ans environ après la naissance dudit Pierre.
- François, baptisé le 4 janvier 1668.
- Fabio, baptisé le 18 mars 1671.

**Blanvillain, Anne :** Baptisée le 26 mai 1643 à Maligny, dans le Florentinois, elle fut tenue sur les fonts baptismaux par Jacques Olivier et Anne Foutrier, ses parrain et marraine. Ses parents étaient Guillaume Blanvillain, procureur fiscal de Maligny, et Jeanne Logeron. Vers l'âge de 12 ans, Anne Blanvillain fut deux fois marraine dans son village natal, les 30 mars et 31 octobre de l'année 1655. Elle savait déjà écrire son nom à l'époque. Ses deux filleuls furent un garçon nommé Edme Blanvillain, fils de Louis Blanvillain et Anne Guiot, puis une fille qui s'appelait Anne Barbier, issue d'Edme Barbier et Jeanne Rolland. Moins de six ans après ces deux baptêmes, la jeune marraine perdit son père, décédé dans une localité voisine, à Ligny-le-Châtel. Le corps du défunt fut enterré le 1ᵉʳ janvier 1661 à Maligny. Dix ans plus tard, en 1671, Anne Blanvillain fut appelée au Canada comme « fille du roi ». À ce titre, elle était dotée par le roi de France pour aller épouser un colon de l'autre côté de l'océan. Le 1ᵉʳ janvier 1672, elle fut donc unie à Louis Charbonnier devant maître Christophe Richard, notaire à Saint-Ours près de Montréal. Elle avait alors 28 ans. Elle vécut ensuite avec son mari à Sorel, où naquit son fils Pierre, baptisé le 19 octobre 1677. Anne Blanvillain mourut en 1681, juste après le recensement qui eut lieu au Canada cette année-là. Son époux convola aussitôt en secondes noces avec Barbe Celles-Duclos, le 25 novembre 1681. Deux mois plus tard, il trépassa lui aussi et sa dépouille fut ensevelie le 13 janvier 1682, à Montréal.

**Hay, Pierre :** Baptisé le 4 novembre 1660 à Auxerre, en l'église Saint-Pierre-en-Vallée, il fut tenu sur les fonts baptismaux par Jacques Desloges, chanoine d'Auxerre, et Catherine Charlotte de La Magdeleine, fille de Claude de La Magdeleine, comte de Rigny. Les parents du nouveau-né étaient Gabriel Hay, marchand à Auxerre, et Catherine Baudoin. À l'âge de 12 ans, Pierre Hay fut le parrain de sa petite sœur Marie Rose, bap-

tisée comme lui en l'église Saint-Pierre-en-Vallée, le 2 septembre 1673. Son père mourut à Auxerre cinq mois plus tard, le 18 février 1674 à l'âge de 44 ans. Puis vint le tour de sa mère, qui décéda au même lieu le 3 mai 1679, âgée de 43 ans. Tous deux furent enterrés dans le grand cimetière public de l'église Saint-Pierre-en-Vallée, le jour même de leur trépas. Devenu orphelin, Pierre Hay se mit à exercer le métier de tailleur de pierre, maçon et maître sculpteur. Il se rendit au Canada, où, le 21 février 1689, il se maria à Boucherville avec Geneviève Benoît. Il avait alors 28 ans. Après le décès de son épouse, qui ne lui a donné aucun enfant, il convola en secondes noces avec Catherine Campeau, le 10 décembre 1696 à Montréal. C'est dans cette dernière ville qu'il rendit l'âme, à l'âge de 48 ans : son corps y fut enseveli le 3 décembre 1708. De sa seconde femme, Pierre Hay avait eu huit enfants.

En Basse-Bourgogne, ses parents lui avaient donné quatre sœurs et un frère, tous nés à Auxerre après lui, et tous baptisés en l'église Saint-Pierre-en-Vallée. Voici cette fratrie :

- Anne, baptisée le 6 janvier 1663. Elle épousa un maître menuisier qui s'appelait Edme Hay, le 31 mai 1695, en ladite église Saint-Pierre-en-Vallée.
- Gabriel, baptisé le 23 août 1665. Il se maria à Auxerre avec Germaine Bersonnet, le 15 avril 1694, en l'église Notre-Dame-la-d'Hors.
- Catherine, née le 25 janvier 1668 et baptisée le même jour.
- Germaine, baptisée le 31 juillet 1670. Elle prit pour époux Pierre Petit, le 30 avril 1696, en l'église Saint-Pierre-en-Vallée.
- Marie Rose, baptisée le 2 septembre 1673. Elle convola en justes noces avec Félix Billaut, le 8 janvier 1695, en l'église Saint-Pierre-en-Vallée. Son mari était notaire à Saint-Bris.

**Huot, Nicolas :** Baptisé à Auxerre le 3 octobre 1631, en l'église Saint-Loup, il fut tenu sur les fonts baptismaux par Nicolas Savier, marchand à Auxerre, et Edmée Imbault, femme de Germain Coulon. Les parents du nouveau-né n'étaient pas mariés ! Le nourrisson, en effet, était le fils naturel d'un marchand auxerrois nommé Laurent Huot, célibataire, et d'une femme qui s'appelait Edmée Beauvillain, veuve de Nicolas Laurain, maître pâtissier. Dans l'acte de baptême, le curé de l'église Saint-Loup a même précisé que

« ladite Edmée Imbault, et Gillette Martin, femme de Pierre Champeaux, vigneron à Auxerre, m'ont attesté et dit savoir bien que ledit enfant est fils naturel dudit Laurent Huot ». Ce témoignage formel suffisait pour attribuer au nouveau-né le nom de famille de son géniteur, sans demander l'avis de ce dernier. En 1658, à l'âge de 26 ans, le jeune Nicolas Huot s'engagea dans la milice pour servir pendant trois années en Nouvelle-France. Parti de la Rochelle entre la mi-mai et la fin du mois d'août, il débarqua à Québec, où, dès le 7 septembre 1658, il passa un contrat avec Charles Pouliot et Guillaume Couture, devant maître Guillaume Audouart. Pendant trois ans, le jeune milicien travailla au service de Jean Bourdon, procureur du roi à Québec. Il quitta ensuite la ville pour aller s'installer à Château-Richer, dans une maison achetée le 12 novembre 1661 devant maître Claude Aubert. Le 24 juillet 1662, à l'âge de 30 ans, il se maria à Québec avec une femme nommée Marie Fayet, déjà enceinte de cinq mois. Cette union fut suivie dix ans plus tard par la signature d'un contrat de mariage, passé le 1er juin 1672, devant maître Paul Vachon, notaire seigneurial en Nouvelle-France. Nicolas Huot, qui exerçait l'activité de marchand à Château-Richer, ainsi que d'huissier et de procureur fiscal, fut le père de 11 enfants. Étant devenu « sieur de Saint-Laurent », il prit l'habitude d'ajouter ce nom patrimonial à la suite de son nom patronymique, se faisant appeler communément « Huot de Saint-Laurent ». Il mourut à l'Hôtel-Dieu de Québec en 1693, à une date inconnue située entre le 22 janvier et le 23 juillet. Il avait alors 61 ans. Sa femme décéda quant à elle deux décennies plus tard : elle fut inhumée le 16 avril 1713 à Saint-Nicolas. Étant fils naturel, Nicolas Huot n'avait pas eu de frères et sœurs issus de ses deux parents. Par sa mère, toutefois, il avait eu une demi-sœur née six ans avant lui, à savoir :

- Marie Lorain, baptisée le 28 septembre 1625 à Auxerre, en l'église Saint-Eusèbe. Elle était la fille de Jean Lorain, maître pâtissier, et d'Edmée Beauvillain. Les parrain et marraine qui la tinrent sur les fonts baptismaux furent Michel Dubois et Anne Beauvillain, femme d'un marchand vannier nommé Abraham Monnot. On remarque que, dans l'acte de baptême de Marie Lorain, le nom du père de l'enfant est « Jean Lorain », alors que six ans

plus tard, dans l'acte de baptême de Nicolas Huot, ce nom devient « Nicolas Laurain ». Il s'agit bien, cependant, du même personnage.

**Lepage, Constance :** Baptisée le 11 juin 1645, à Ouanne dans l'Auxerrois, elle fut tenue sur les fonts baptismaux par Pierre Gaufillet et Constance Duchamp, ses parrain et marraine. Ses parents étaient Étienne Lepage et Nicole Berthelot. À l'âge de 16 ans environ, elle vit ses frères aînés Louis et Germain quitter Ouanne à jamais, pour aller travailler ensemble au Canada. Elle partit les rejoindre une dizaine d'années plus tard, en 1672, avec sa belle-sœur Reine Loury, femme de Germain, et son neveu René Lepage. À l'âge de 28 ans, Constance Lepage convola en justes noces. Le 5 février 1674, elle épousa un domestique nommé François Garinet, près de Québec, en l'église de Sainte-Famille sur l'île d'Orléans. Le couple vécut en la paroisse de Saint-François, sur la même île. C'est là que mourut Constance Lepage, une quinzaine d'années après son mariage. Elle fut ensevelie en ladite paroisse le 18 août 1688, à l'âge de 43 ans. Elle avait donné à son mari cinq filles et un garçon. Son époux décéda à son tour une trentaine d'années plus tard. Il fut inhumé au même lieu le 29 mars 1715, au lendemain du trépas. Il avait atteint l'âge de 75 ans environ. Constance Lepage, sa femme, avait eu quatre frères et une sœur, à savoir :

- Germain, né avant 1634. Sa biographie est publiée ci-après.
- Jean, baptisé à Ouanne le 29 août 1635. Il est probablement mort en bas âge.
- Loup, baptisé en 1636. Sa biographie est publiée ci-après, sous le prénom de Louis.
- Étiennette, baptisée à Ouanne le 9 janvier 1641, quatre ans avant sa sœur Constance. Elle est vraisemblablement décédée en bas âge.
- Pierre, baptisé trois ans après sa sœur Constance, le 26 octobre 1648 à Ouanne. Lui aussi est sans doute mort en bas âge.

**Lepage, Germain :** Né vers 1627, son acte de baptême ne figure pas dans les anciens registres paroissiaux de Ouanne. Il était le fils, en tout cas, d'Étienne Lepage et Nicole Berthelot. À une date qui demeure inconnue, mais que l'on peut situer avant 1653, il prit pour épouse une femme qui s'appelait Reine Loury. Il est possible que les noces furent célébrées à Ouanne : une lacune dans les registres de mariages de cette localité, de 1632 à 1654, laisse le champ libre à cette hypothèse. En 1661 environ, Germain Lepage partit travailler au Canada avec son frère Louis. Il laissait derrière lui, à Ouanne, sa femme et ses trois enfants. Pendant trois ans, il vécut en la ville de Québec, puis, le 9 juillet 1664, la famille d'Ailleboust lui octroya des terres dans la seigneurie d'Argentenay, sur la pointe nord de l'île d'Orléans. C'est là que le rejoignit son épouse quelques années plus tard, en 1672 ou environ. Elle était accompagnée de son fils René Lepage, seul enfant survivant du couple, ainsi que de Constance Lepage (voir ci-avant). Jusqu'en 1686, Germain Lepage cultiva ses terres. Il finit toutefois par les céder entièrement à son fils René, lors du mariage de celui-ci avec Marie-Madeleine Gagnon, le 10 juin 1686 en l'église de Sainte-Anne-de-Beaupré. Étant âgé de plus de 50 ans, le père passait ainsi le relais à son fils unique, à charge pour ce dernier de subvenir aux besoins de ses parents jusqu'à la fin de leurs jours. Reine Loury, la mère du jeune marié, rendit l'âme quelque temps après les noces, à une date qui reste inconnue. Germain Lepage, quant à lui, était toujours en vie. En 1696, il quitta l'île d'Orléans à jamais, pour suivre son fils René jusqu'au site de Rimouski. C'est dans cette région encore sauvage qu'il vécut désormais, jusqu'à sa mort. Décédé le 26 février 1723, près de cinq ans après le trépas de son propre fils, Germain Lepage avait eu le temps d'assister au lent développement de la localité de Rimouski, au bord du Saint-Laurent. Personne ne sachant vraiment son âge, on a avancé celui de 101 ans! Il est certain, en tout cas, qu'après avoir vécu 25 ans au moins à Ouanne, puis 3 ans à Québec, 32 ans sur l'île d'Orléans et 27 ans environ à Rimouski, le vieil homme avait 87 ans au minimum lors de son décès.

**Lepage, Louis :** Né à Ouanne, dans l'Auxerrois, il y fut baptisé le 7 décembre 1636, sous le même prénom que celui de son parrain, maître Loup Gramain. Sa marraine était Edmée Bernardin. Fils d'Étienne Lepage et Nicole Berthelot, Loup Lepage, devenu Louis, partit travailler au Canada en 1661 environ, avec son frère Germain (voir ci-avant). Il vécut alors pendant trois ans à Québec, où il servit comme domestique jusqu'en janvier 1664 au moins, chez Charles Le Gardeur.

Quelques mois plus tard, ayant achevé sa période de trois années de travail contractuel, il obtint de la famille d'Ailleboust une concession de terres dans la seigneurie d'Argentenay, située sur l'île d'Orléans près de Québec. C'est là qu'il vécut dorénavant, comme en témoignent les recensements canadiens de 1666 et 1667. Contrairement à son frère Germain, il était toujours célibataire. Le 24 août 1667, il finit cependant par signer un contrat de mariage devant maître Pierre Duquet, notaire à Québec : à l'âge de 30 ans, il s'unissait ainsi à une jeune fille nommée Sébastienne Loignon, âgée d'une quinzaine d'années à peine. Celle-ci lui donna 14 enfants, nés de 1669 à 1699 sur l'île d'Orléans : les cinq premiers furent baptisés en l'église de Sainte-Famille, et les neuf suivants en celle de Saint-François. Sébastienne Loignon mourut à Saint-François le 2 décembre 1702. Louis Lepage, son mari, décéda à son tour huit ans plus tard : il fut enterré en ladite paroisse de Saint-François le 27 novembre 1710, à l'âge de 74 ans.

**Lepage, René :** Baptisé le 10 avril 1656, à Ouanne dans l'Auxerrois, il fut tenu sur les fonts baptismaux par Edme Bernardin et Renée Chevallier, ses parrain et marraine. Ses parents étaient Germain Lepage et Reine Loury. Il n'avait que 5 ans environ lorsque son père, en 1661, quitta la France pour aller travailler au Canada. Le jeune garçon resta quant à lui dans son village natal avec sa mère, ainsi qu'avec son frère Guillaume, âgé de 3 ans à l'époque. Ce dernier trépassa une dizaine d'années plus tard, le 12 avril 1670. C'est après cette mort subite que René Lepage quitta la France à son tour, avec Reine Loury sa mère, et Constance Lepage sa tante. Tous trois se rendirent ensemble au Canada, pour y rejoindre Germain Lepage et son frère Louis. Le voyage à travers l'océan eut lieu probablement en 1672. Pendant une quinzaine d'années, René Lepage vécut alors avec ses parents sur l'île d'Orléans, près de Québec. Le 10 juin 1686, à l'âge de 30 ans, il finit pourtant par se marier en l'église de Sainte-Anne-de-Beaupré avec Marie-Madeleine Gagnon, âgée de tout juste 15 ans à l'époque. Le jour de ses noces, le jeune époux reçut de ses parents tous les biens que ceux-ci possédaient sur l'île d'Orléans, à charge pour le bénéficiaire de subvenir aux besoins de ses père et mère jusqu'à la fin de leurs jours. Dix ans plus tard, après la mort de sa mère, René Lepage quitta l'île d'Orléans à jamais, avec sa femme, ses enfants et son père. Le 10 juillet 1694, en effet, il avait échangé tous ses biens contre la seigneurie encore sauvage de Rimouski. C'est là qu'il s'installa avec sa famille, en juillet 1696. Il avait alors 40 ans. En tant que seigneur des lieux, il devait participer au peuplement du Canada en octroyant des terres à des colons, toutes situées à l'intérieur de sa seigneurie. Il fit donc venir à Rimouski ses cousines Constance et Marie-Madeleine Garinet, filles de François Garinet et Constance Lepage, qui arrivèrent en 1701 avec deux compagnons : Pierre Saint-Laurent, mari de Constance, et Pierre Gosselin, fiancé de Marie-Madeleine. Un prêtre itinérant vint aussitôt à Rimouski pour marier les deux fiancés, le 1ᵉʳ septembre 1701. Dès lors, trois familles vécurent dans la seigneurie : celle de René Lepage et celles de ses deux cousines Garinet. En l'absence de tout prêtre résidant sur place, c'est Germain Lepage, le patriarche de la famille, qui était chargé de diriger la prière dominicale de toute la communauté, d'ondoyer les nouveau-nés et d'enseigner le catéchisme aux enfants. Une fois par an, au cours de l'été, le prêtre itinérant venait à Rimouski pour baptiser les nourrissons déjà ondoyés. En 1711, René Lepage fit bâtir une petite chapelle sur le territoire de sa seigneurie. Il put ainsi accueillir un prêtre en permanence à partir de 1714. Le seigneur de Rimouski, qui était aussi sieur de Sainte-Claire, mourut le 4 août 1718, à l'âge de 62 ans. Il fut enterré le même jour, en présence de son père, de son épouse et de toute la communauté. Sa femme décéda à son tour le 31 janvier 1744, âgée de 72 ans. Elle avait donné 16 enfants à son mari, nés de 1687 à 1714. Ce sont les descendants de cette famille nombreuse qui, au nombre de deux mille environ, se sont rassemblés à Rimouski les 12, 13 et 14 juillet 1996, pour fêter tous ensemble le tricentenaire de la fondation de cette localité par René Lepage, leur ancêtre commun.

**Loury, Reine :** Originaire de Ouanne, dans l'Auxerrois, elle était vraisemblablement née dans un tout autre lieu. C'est à Ouanne qu'elle vécut quelque temps, en tout cas, après avoir pris pour époux Germain Lepage (voir ci-avant). Le mariage fut célébré avant 1653. En 1661 environ, Reine Loury vit son conjoint partir pour le Canada, la laissant seule à Ouanne avec ses enfants. Une dizaine d'années plus tard, cependant, elle put le rejoindre en Nouvelle-France, accompagnée de son seul fils survivant et de sa belle-sœur Constance Lepage (voir ci-avant). La traversée de l'océan eut lieu probablement en 1672. Arrivée au Canada, Reine Loury vécut avec son fils et son mari sur l'île d'Orléans, près de Québec, comme en témoigne le recensement canadien de 1681. Elle était encore en vie lors du mariage de son fils René, le 10 juin 1686 à Sainte-Anne-de-Beaupré. Elle mourut toutefois avant 1696, année au cours de laquelle son fils et son mari quittèrent l'île d'Orléans pour aller s'installer ensemble à Rimouski. De son union avec Germain Lepage, elle n'avait eu que trois enfants, tous baptisés en l'église paroissiale de Ouanne, à savoir :

- Marie Lepage, baptisée le 17 septembre 1653. Elle mourut probablement en bas âge.
- René Lepage, baptisé le 10 avril 1656. C'est lui qui fonda Rimouski en 1696 (voir ci-avant).
- Guillaume Lepage, baptisé le 31 janvier 1658. Il mourut à Ouanne le 12 avril 1670.

**Marcoux, Pierre :** Né en 1631 environ, il était le fils de Claude Marcoux et Marie Junot. On ne trouve pas son acte de baptême dans les registres paroissiaux de Cry-sur-Armançon, d'où il était originaire : les premiers actes ne commencent qu'en 1644. Il existe toutefois une table générale des baptêmes de Cry-sur-Armançon, qui débute dès 1630, mais on n'y trouve pas le nom de Pierre Marcoux. Deux conclusions sont alors possibles : soit Pierre Marcoux n'a point été baptisé dans cette localité du Tonnerrois, soit le baptême a eu lieu avant 1630. Il est certain, en tout cas, que cet homme a bien vécu à Cry-sur-Armançon. C'est là que mourut sa mère, en effet, ainsi qu'en témoigne un acte de décès figurant à la page 115 du registre mortuaire. On y apprend que ladite Marie Junot, veuve de Claude Marcoux, trépassa audit lieu le mercredi 11 janvier 1651, et qu'en plein accord avec le curé elle avait « délaissé en aumône à l'église vingt sols à la confrérie du Saint-Rosaire ». Pierre Marcoux était âgé d'une vingtaine d'années lors de ce décès. Orphelin de ses père et mère, il quitta la France en 1652 environ, pour aller travailler pendant trois ans au Canada. Au terme de ces trois années de travail contractuel, il reçut une première concession de terres le 15 octobre 1655. Puis, le 4 novembre 1658, il obtint une seconde concession, située à Beauport près de Québec. Il était toujours célibataire à l'époque. Il finit toutefois par se marier le 8 janvier 1662, à Québec, avec une jeune fille de 15 ans environ, qui s'appelait Marthe de Rainville. Le couple vécut à Beauport, comme l'attestent les recensements canadiens de 1667 et 1681. Pierre Marcoux avait 36 ans lors du premier recensement, et 50 ans lors du second. Il exerçait le métier de maçon. C'est à Beauport qu'il mourut, le 11 juin 1699. Il avait atteint l'âge de 68 ans. De son union avec Marthe de Rainville, il avait eu 11 enfants, tous nés à Beauport mais baptisés à Québec. En 1994, ses descendants canadiens ont fait apposer une plaque commémorative sur une vieille maison de Cry-sur-Armançon. On peut y lire l'inscription suivante : « Pierre Marcoux arrive à Québec en 1652 et meurt le 12 juin 1699 à Beauport »[4].

**Maugras, Jacques :** Baptisé le 19 mars 1636 à Ligny-le-Châtel, dans le Florentinois, il fut tenu sur les fonts baptismaux par Jacques Leblanc et Anne Jossot, ses parrain et marraine. Il était le fils de Claude Maugras et Françoise Flogny. Sa mère rendit l'âme entre 1644 et 1651, et son père la suivit dans la tombe une douzaine d'années plus tard : il fut inhumé à Ligny-le-Châtel le 6 février 1662, à l'âge de 70 ans environ. Orphelin de ses deux parents, Jacques Maugras décida de partir travailler au Canada, à une date qui reste inconnue. C'est là qu'il épousa Marie-Jeanne Moral, en tout cas, ceci par contrat de mariage signé le 5 novembre 1668 devant maître Ameau, notaire à Trois-Rivières.

Le couple eut huit enfants. Jacques Maugras décéda entre 1690 et 1692, à Saint-François-du-Lac. Il avait eu deux frères et trois sœurs, tous les cinq baptisés comme lui à Ligny-le-Châtel. Voici la liste de ces personnages :

- François, baptisé le 16 avril 1625. À l'âge de 26 ans, il épousa Marie Louat, le 11 novembre 1651 à Ligny-le-Châtel.
- Claude, baptisé le 13 décembre 1627. Il mourut sans doute en bas âge.
- Jeanne, baptisée le 22 août 1630, soit six ans environ avant son frère Jacques.
- Anne, baptisée le 27 novembre 1638, deux ans et demi après ledit Jacques, son frère.
- Françoise, baptisée le 24 mars 1644.

**Michaud, Françoise :** Baptisée le 18 août 1649 à Sennevoy, dans le Tonnerrois, elle fut tenue sur les fonts baptismaux par Marceau Sardin et Françoise Comperot, ses parrain et marraine. Ses parents étaient Briside Michaud et Marguerite Matret, domiciliés au hameau de La Loge en ladite paroisse de Sennevoy. Ceux-ci, dans le dictionnaire de René Jetté, apparaissent sous les noms de Brésitte Michel et Marguerite Maistre. Françoise Michaud se rendit au Canada avec sa sœur aînée, Louise, à une date qui reste inconnue. C'est là qu'elle épousa Gilles Dupont, en tout cas, par contrat de mariage signé le 10 août 1670 devant maître Ameau, notaire au Cap-de-la-Madeleine. La jeune conjointe allait avoir 21 ans. De cette union, naquirent sept enfants, ceci de 1671 à 1683. Après le décès de son mari, Françoise Michaud convola en secondes noces avec Paul Hubert, le 8 février 1685 à Québec. Elle n'était âgée que de 35 ans à l'époque, mais ne donna aucun enfant à son nouvel époux. Elle mourut une quinzaine d'années après ses secondes épousailles, vers 1698. Elle avait eu deux sœurs et quatre frères, tous baptisés à Sennevoy avant elle, à savoir :

- Pierrette, baptisée le 23 août 1638.
- Edme, baptisé le 2 septembre 1637.
- Nicolas, baptisé le 8 octobre 1643. Il mourut le 29 octobre suivant.
- Edme, baptisé le 8 octobre 1643. Frère jumeau du précédent, il mourut deux jours avant lui.
- Louise, baptisée le 5 avril 1645. Sa biographie est publiée ci-après.
- Jean, baptisé le 20 octobre 1647.

**Michaud, Louise :** Baptisée le 5 avril 1645 à Sennevoy, dans le Tonnerrois, elle fut tenue sur les fonts baptismaux par Jean Calmeau et Françoise Guinot, cette dernière agissant au nom de sa fille Louise Le Nief, âgée de 7 ans. Les parents de la jeune baptisée étaient Briside Michaud et Marguerite Matret. Ceux-ci, dans le dictionnaire de René Jetté, figurent sous les noms de Brésil Michaud et Marguerite Tessier. Le nom de famille « Tessier » était peut-être celui que portait la mère de ladite Marguerite : les femmes, en effet, transmettaient parfois leur nom à leurs filles comme simple surnom. Quoi qu'il en fût, Louise Michaud se rendit au Canada avec sa sœur cadette Françoise, à une date encore inconnue. Elle s'y maria le 10 septembre 1670, à Québec, avec un homme nommé Jean Daniau, lequel venait d'abjurer le calvinisme quatre jours plus tôt. La jeune conjointe avait 25 ans à l'époque. Elle mourut une quinzaine d'années plus tard : son époux se remaria en juin 1686 avec Françoise Rondeau. Louise Michaud avait eu quatre enfants avec lui.

**Millot, Jean :** Baptisé le 11 novembre 1624 à Vermenton, dans l'Auxerrois, il fut tenu sur les fonts baptismaux par Jean Breschat, demeurant à Lucy-sur-Cure, et Jeanne Bourdillat. Ses parents étaient Philibert Millot et Chrétienne Saunois. Il se rendit au Canada, où il fut vite surnommé « le Bourguignon ». Il y exerça le métier de marchand taillandier. Le 7 janvier 1654, à l'âge de 29 ans, il se maria à Montréal avec Marie Marthe Pinson, qui lui donna six enfants. Puis, le 26 novembre 1663, à l'âge de 39 ans, il convola en secondes noces avec Mathurine Thibault, dans la même ville. Six enfants supplémentaires naquirent de cette seconde union. Jean Millot décéda à Montréal le 3 novembre 1699, alors qu'il était âgé de presque 75 ans. Il avait eu au moins une sœur et deux frères, tous baptisés avant lui à Vermenton. On peut imaginer que d'autres frères et sœurs avaient été mis au monde avant décembre 1614, date à laquelle commence le tout premier registre paroissial de ladite localité. Toutefois, en l'absence d'actes les concernant, la liste des gens composant la fratrie de Jean Millot se réduit aux trois personnes suivantes :

• Jean l'aîné, baptisé le 27 septembre 1616.
• Louis, baptisé le 5 septembre 1618.
• Antoinette, baptisée le 16 décembre 1620.

**Normand, Catherine :** Baptisée le 17 mai 1644 à Sens, en l'église Saint-Hilaire, elle fut tenue sur les fonts baptismaux par Alexandre Égreville et Catherine Mansajer, femme d'Edme Pageot. Ses parents étaient Baptiste Normand et Catherine Pageot. Une vingtaine d'années plus tard, elle se rendit au Canada pour y épouser un homme portant le même nom de famille qu'elle, Pierre Normand, originaire de Normandie. La cérémonie nuptiale eut lieu à Québec, le 7 septembre 1665. Catherine Normand, qui avait 21 ans lors de ses noces, était encore en vie lors des recensements canadiens de 1666 et 1681. Après avoir donné

11 enfants à son époux, elle mourut à Québec le 7 février 1703, à l'âge de 58 ans. Elle n'avait eu qu'une sœur, dont la biographie est publiée ci-après.

**Normand, Madeleine :** Baptisée le 29 août 1646 à Sens, en l'église Saint-Hilaire, elle était la fille de Baptiste Normand et Catherine Pageot. Ses parrain et marraine furent Étienne Périllault et Madeleine Gasteau. En 1665 environ, elle vit sa sœur aînée Catherine partir pour le Canada, afin de s'y marier. Madeleine Normand resta probablement en France : son nom ne figure point sur les rôles du recensement canadien de 1666. Elle finit toutefois par rejoindre sa sœur quelques années plus tard, sans doute en 1669. Le 10 février 1670, en effet, à l'âge de 23 ans, elle se maria à Québec avec un homme nommé Alphonse Morin. Elle était encore en vie lors du recensement canadien de 1681. Après avoir donné 11 enfants à son époux, elle trépassa le 27 avril 1690 à Montmagny, près de Québec. On ne lui connaît qu'une sœur, Catherine Normand (voir ci-avant).

**Roy, Antoine :** Baptisé le 23 mars 1635 à Joigny, en l'église Saint-Jean, il était le fils d'un maître tonnelier nommé Olivier Roy et de Catherine Baudard. Il fut tenu sur les fonts baptismaux par Antoine Baudard et Marie Collard, ses parrain et marraine. Il était déjà adulte lorsqu'il perdit ses parents. Sa mère fut enterrée le 20 décembre 1659, puis son père le 6 décembre 1661, les obsèques de l'un et l'autre ayant eu lieu en l'église Saint-Jean, à Joigny. Quelques années après la mort de ses parents, Antoine Roy partit pour le Canada. Il arriva sur place le 18 juin 1665, comme soldat de la compagnie du capitaine Froment, dans le régiment de Carignan-Salières. Trois ans plus tard, le 11 septembre 1668, il se maria à Québec avec Marie Major. Il était âgé de 33 ans à l'époque. Il vécut avec sa conjointe près de Trois-Rivières, à Batiscan où il exerça le métier de tonnelier. Le couple ne fut pas très heureux : Marie Major ne donna qu'un seul fils à son époux ; ce dernier fut ensuite assassiné le 10 juillet 1684 à Lachine, surpris en flagrant délit d'adultère avec Anne Godeby, femme de Julien Talva. Antoine Roy avait 49 ans lorsqu'il fut occis par le mari trompé.

Grâce à son fils unique, qui a engendré neuf enfants, il eut néanmoins de nombreux descendants, dont le chanteur canadien Roch Voisine.

Le défunt avait eu six sœurs et deux frères, tous baptisés en l'église Saint-Jean à Joigny, à savoir :

- Catherine, baptisée le 11 juillet 1627.
- Marie, baptisée le 13 février 1629.
- Edmée, baptisée le 19 mars 1632.
- Geneviève, baptisée le 8 juillet 1633, soit deux ans avant son frère Antoine.
- Élie, baptisé le 13 juillet 1636, un an après ledit Antoine, son frère.
- Suzanne, baptisée le 31 juillet 1638.
- Jean, baptisé le jeudi 31 août 1640.
- Catherine, baptisée le 19 septembre 1643.

### Les Bas-Bourguignons isolés dont l'ascendance est connue

Sur les 45 colons qui figurent dans le corpus [voir TABLEAU 1], nous venons de voir qu'il en est 17 au sujet desquels je n'ai rien pu découvrir de nouveau par rapport à ce que l'on sait déjà au travers des sources canadiennes, et 17 autres dont j'ai pu retrouver la trace en France. Ne restent donc que 11 cas à traiter : il s'agit tous de Bas-Bourguignons aux racines familiales étoffées, que des recherches plus heureuses ont permis de développer sur plusieurs générations. Dans la liste qui suit, six premiers cas sont présentés, rassemblant des colons qui sont partis seuls au Canada. Les cinq autres cas seront exposés dans le dernier chapitre de cette étude.

**Chancy, Marie :** Baptisée le 11 mars 1657 à Auxerre, en l'église Notre-Dame-la-d'Hors, elle fut tenue sur les fonts baptismaux par Jean Louat, avocat au bailliage et siège présidial d'Auxerre, et Marie Bérault, femme de Claude Martineau, sieur de Monjou. En 1673, alors qu'elle n'avait que 16 ans, elle partit pour le Canada en tant que « fille du roi », dûment dotée par le roi de France pour aller épouser un colon au-delà des mers. Elle se maria donc le 2 octobre 1673, à Québec, avec un homme qui s'appelait Michel Prézeau, dit « Chambly ». Un contrat unissant les deux parties avait été signé le 18 septembre précédent, devant maître Rageot : la mariée apportait des biens estimés à 200 livres. De cette union, naquirent sept enfants, dont deux qui moururent très tôt. Marie Chancy était la fille de Gaspard Chancy et Étiennette Frappé, qui suivent en 2 et 3 :

2. **Gaspard Chancy :** Baptisé le 6 novembre 1632 à Auxerre, en l'église Notre-Dame-la-

d'Hors, il exerçait l'activité de vigneron lorsqu'il convola en justes noces, à l'âge de 21 ans. Il se maria en effet avec Étiennette Frappé le 2 août 1654, en l'église Saint-Eusèbe à Auxerre. Il devint ensuite drapier drapant. Un mois et demi après la mort de son épouse, il se maria en secondes noces avec Bénigne Armant, le 22 septembre 1663 en l'église Notre-Dame-la-d'Hors, à Auxerre. Il avait alors 30 ans. Gaspard Chancy était le fils de Gaspard Chancy et Françoise Michau, qui suivent en 4 et 5.

3. **Étiennette Frappé :** Baptisée le 31 août 1631 à Auxerre, en l'église Saint-Eusèbe, elle allait avoir 23 ans lorsqu'elle épousa Gaspard Chancy, ci-avant. Elle mit au monde au moins trois enfants, trépassant une semaine après ses dernières couches. Son corps fut inhumé le 16 mai 1663 à Auxerre, après des obsèques en l'église Notre-Dame-la-d'Hors. Étiennette Frappé, âgée de 31 ans au moment de sa mort, était la fille d'Edme Frappé et Edmée David, qui suivent en 6 et 7.

4. **Gaspard Chancy :** Né sous le règne du roi Henri IV, il se maria trois fois. Il épousa d'abord Françoise Michau, par contrat de mariage signé le 22 janvier 1617[5]. Puis il convola avec Marie Prévost, le 7 janvier 1657 en l'église Saint-Eusèbe, à Auxerre. Enfin, le 6 septembre 1660, il se maria en l'église auxerroise de Saint-Pèlerin avec Anne Chartier. Il était encore en vie en 1663. Gaspard Chancy, marchand et vigneron à Auxerre, était le fils de Germain Chancy et Perrette Cirebon, qui suivent en 8 et 9.

5. **Françoise Michau :** Née elle aussi sous le règne du roi Henri IV, elle donna à son mari trois filles et huit garçons, tous baptisés de 1620 à 1643 en l'église Notre-Dame-la-d'Hors, en la ville d'Auxerre. Elle décéda dix ans après la dernière naissance. Son corps fut alors enterré le 7 novembre 1653, après des funérailles en ladite église Notre-Dame-la-d'Hors. Françoise Michau était la fille de François Michau et Marthe Leclerc, qui suivent en 10 et 11.

6. **Edme Frappé :** Baptisé le 10 août 1593 à Auxerre, en l'église Notre-Dame-la-d'Hors,

il avait 21 ans lorsqu'il fut uni à Edmée David, par contrat de mariage signé à Auxerre le 1er février 1615[6]. Il exerçait alors l'activité de joueur d'instruments, mais devint aussi, par la suite, maître couvreur en tuiles. Il mourut entre 1650 et 1654. Edme Frappé était le fils d'Edme Frappé et Marie Riot, qui suivent en 12 et 13.

7. **Edmée David :** Née sous le règne du roi Henri IV, elle donna à son mari au moins quatre filles et cinq garçons, dont la plupart furent baptisés de 1618 à 1636 en l'église Saint-Eusèbe, à Auxerre. Elle était encore en vie en 1654. Edmée David était la fille de Jean David et Marie Lasnier, qui suivent en 14 et 15.

8. **Germain Chancy :** Il était déjà décédé lorsque son fils Gaspard épousa Françoise Michau, par contrat de mariage signé à Auxerre le 22 janvier 1617[7].

9. **Perrette Cirebon :** Baptisée le 10 février 1566 à Auxerre, en l'église Notre-Dame-la-d'Hors, elle était toujours en vie en 1622, date à laquelle on la retrouve marraine d'un petit-fils. Perrette Cirebon était la fille de Germain Cirebon et Jeanne Lamy, qui suivent en 18 et 19.

10. **François Michau :** Né pendant les guerres de religion, il épousa Marthe Leclerc le 24 février 1587, ceci par contrat notarié signé devant maître Loup Horry, notaire à Auxerre. Il exerça l'activité de sergent royal au bailliage de ladite ville. Mort sous le règne de Louis XIII, son inventaire après décès fut établi le 20 janvier 1620, par maître Étienne Daulmoy, notaire auxerrois[8]. C'est dans cet inventaire qu'est signalé le contrat de mariage de 1587 : l'acte original, depuis, a disparu.

11. **Marthe Leclerc :** Elle donna à son mari au moins deux filles et un garçon, les seuls qui fussent encore vivants en 1620 pour hériter de leur défunt père (voir ci-dessus). Elle était toujours en vie, elle aussi, à cette époque.

12. **Edmé Frappé :** Il exerçait le métier de joueur d'instruments, et mourut après 1618.

13. **Marie Riot :** Elle donna deux fils à son mari, tous deux baptisés de 1590 à 1593 en l'église Notre-Dame-la-d'Hors à Auxerre. Dans le premier acte de baptême, elle apparaît sous le nom de « Marie Réau », dans le second sous celui de « Marie Régault ». Elle décéda avant 1615.

14. **Jean David :** Je ne sais rien de lui pour le moment.

15. **Marie Lasnier :** Je ne sais rien d'elle non plus.

18. **Germain Cirebon :** Il épousa Jeanne Lamy avant l'an 1554.

19. **Jeanne Lamy :** Elle donna à son mari quatre filles et trois garçons, tous baptisés de 1554 à 1566 en l'église Notre-Dame-la-d'Hors, à Auxerre.

**Clairambault, François :** Baptisé le 26 mars 1659 à Nuits-sur-Armançon, dans le Tonnerrois, il fut tenu sur les fonts baptismaux par son grand-père paternel François Clairambault, contrôleur des écuries du prince de Condé, et par sa grand-mère maternelle Jeanne Louet, veuve d'Hilaire Triboullard, argentier dudit prince de Condé. En 1684, à l'âge de 25 ans, il travailla auprès de l'intendant de Dunkerque comme secrétaire. Puis, le 1er juin 1701, il fut nommé commissaire de la Marine en Nouvelle-France. Arrivé à Québec le 4 septembre de la même année, il occupa cette fonction jusqu'en 1703. Il exerça aussi la charge de subdélégué de l'intendant à Montréal, ceci de 1701 à 1728, et redevint commissaire de la Marine en 1717. Il mourut à Québec le 1er décembre 1728, à l'âge de 69 ans. Il était resté célibataire. François Clairambault, sieur d'Aigremont, était le fils de Claude Clairambault et Françoise Triboullard, qui suivent en 2 et 3 :

2. **Claude Clairambault :** Originaire d'Asnières-en-Montagne, en Côte-d'Or, il épousa Françoise Triboullard le 11 octobre 1655, à Nuits-sur-Armançon dans le Tonnerrois. Après avoir résidé quelque temps à Nuits-sur-Armançon, il retourna vivre avec sa femme à Asnières-en-Montagne. Claude Clairambault, qui exerçait les activités de marchand, juge et notaire royal, était le fils de François Clairam-

bault et Madeleine Le Boyteux, qui suivent en 4 et 5.

3.  **Françoise Triboullard :** Elle donna au moins deux filles et deux garçons à son mari, baptisés de 1659 à 1673. Le premier enfant naquit à Nuits-sur-Armançon en 1659, alors que les trois suivants furent mis au monde à Asnières-en-Montagne, de 1667 à 1673. Françoise Triboullard était la fille d'Hilaire Triboullard et Jeanne Louet, qui suivent en 6 et 7.

4.  **François Clairambault :** Originaire de Séboncourt, dans l'Aisne, il vécut un certain temps à Montreuillon, dans la Nièvre. C'est de cette dernière localité qu'il venait lorsque le 4 juin 1629, à Asnières-en-Montagne, en Côte-d'Or, il épousa Madeleine Le Boyteux. Depuis 1627, la famille Clairambault était installée à Asnières-en-Montagne. François Clairambault y retrouva son oncle Jacques Clairambault, ses cousines Geneviève et Madeleine, et même son frère cadet Pierre Clairambault. D'abord notaire au marquisat de Cruzy-le-Châtel, dans l'Yonne, il devint marchand royal pour la fourniture de la ville de Paris, et contrôleur de l'écurie du prince de Condé. En 1658, il résidait avec son épouse à Fulvy, dans l'Yonne.

5.  **Madeleine Le Boyteux :** Elle donna à son mari au moins deux filles et quatre garçons, mais je n'ai retrouvé dans les registres paroissiaux d'Asnières-en-Montagne que les actes de baptême de quatre de ces six enfants, ceci de 1633 à 1648. En 1658, elle vivait à Fulvy avec son époux. Madeleine Le Boyteux était la fille de Claude Le Boyteux et Madeleine de Sènevoy, qui suivent en 10 et 11.

6.  **Hilaire Triboullard :** Il travaillait au service du prince de Condé, comme argentier. Il était déjà mort en 1655.

7.  **Jeanne Louet :** Elle eut au moins deux enfants, dont un garçon prénommé Edme, baptisé le 8 juillet 1632 à Nuits-sur-Armançon dans le Tonnerrois. Apparemment, sa fille Françoise n'est pas née dans cette localité. Jeanne Louet était encore en vie en 1659, lors

du baptême de son petit-fils François Clairambault.

10.  **Claude Le Boyteux :** Il exerçait l'activité de procureur fiscal en la terre de Rochefort. Il mourut après 1638.

11.  **Madeleine de Sènevoy :** Elle donna au moins deux filles et deux garçons à son mari, le dernier de ces enfants ayant été baptisé le 15 octobre 1614 à Asnières-en-Montagne.

**de Lachasse, Pierre :** Baptisé le 7 mai 1670 à Auxerre, en l'église Saint-Pierre-en-Château, il fut tenu sur les fonts baptismaux par son oncle Pierre Delachasse, curé de l'église auxerroise de Saint-Regnobert, et par Marie Chevallier, femme de l'avocat Henri Vilain. Le 20 octobre 1685, à l'âge de 15 ans, il fut choisi pour servir de parrain à sa sœur Élisabeth, en ladite église Saint-Regnobert. Il entra ensuite dans les ordres chez les Jésuites, le 14 octobre 1687 à Paris. Il avait alors 17 ans. Une douzaine d'années plus tard, en 1699 environ, il fut envoyé au Canada comme missionnaire de la compagnie de Jésus. Pendant près de deux décennies, de 1700 à 1718, il accomplit sa tâche apostolique à Pentagouet, puis il fut nommé supérieur des missions jésuites en Nouvelle-France, le 15 juillet 1719. Il occupa cette fonction jusqu'en 1728. Cette année-là, au mois de février, c'est lui qui prononça l'oraison funèbre de monseigneur de Saint-Vallier, deuxième évêque de Québec. Ayant pris la direction du collège des Jésuites de Québec en 1726, il resta à ce poste jusqu'à sa mort, survenue à Québec le 27 septembre 1749. Il avait atteint l'âge de 79 ans lors de son trépas. Pierre de Lachasse était le fils de Joseph Delachasse et Edmée Roussel, qui suivent en 2 et 3 :

2.  **Joseph Delachasse :** Né en 1641 environ, c'est peut-être lui qui, sous le prénom de « Claude », fut baptisé à Auxerre le 16 juin 1641, en l'église Saint-Pierre-en-Château. En prenant plus tard le prénom de « Joseph », il a voulu sans doute se différencier de son frère aîné Claude, né en 1621. Quoi qu'il en fût, Joseph Delachassse devint conseiller du roi au bailliage et siège présidial d'Auxerre. Il occupait déjà cette fonction lorsque le 5 septembre 1666, en l'église auxerroise de Saint-Regnobert, il convola en justes noces avec

Edmée Roussel. C'est dans cette même église qu'eurent lieu ses obsèques. Mort à Auxerre le 6 février 1721, à l'âge de 80 ans, il fut inhumé le lendemain en présence du curé de ladite église. Joseph Delachasse était le fils de Claude Delachasse et Anne Girard, qui suivent en 4 et 5.

3. **Edmée Roussel :** Née en 1645 environ, elle donna à son mari neuf filles et cinq garçons, tous baptisés à Auxerre de 1667 à 1690. Les deux premiers enfants reçurent le baptême en l'église Saint-Regnobert, les trois suivants en celle de Saint-Pierre-en-Château, puis tous les autres en la même église que les deux premiers. Edmée Roussel mourut à Auxerre le 8 février 1738, à l'âge de 93 ans. Elle fut enterrée le lendemain en présence du curé de Saint-Regnobert. Elle était la fille d'André Roussel et Jeanne Lasné, qui suivent en 6 et 7.

4. **Claude Delachasse :** Baptisé le 11 mai 1597 à Vézelay, en l'église Saint-Étienne, il avait le titre d'avocat en parlement lorsqu'il épousa Anne Girard à Auxerre, le 13 novembre 1617 en l'église Saint-Regnobert. Il devint ensuite conseiller du roi, doyen des conseillers au siège présidial d'Auxerre, puis bailli du marquisat de Saint-Bris, Augy et Chitry. Il mourut en la ville d'Auxerre à l'âge de 81 ans, et son corps fut enseveli le 3 octobre 1678 en présence du curé de Saint-Regnobert. Claude Delachasse était le fils aîné de Gabriel Delachasse et Jeanne Leclerc, qui suivent en 8 et 9.

5. **Anne Girard :** Baptisée le 30 novembre 1601 à Auxerre, en l'église Saint-Regnobert, elle avait presque 16 ans lorsqu'elle épousa Claude Delachasse le 13 novembre 1617. Elle donna quatre filles et sept garçons à son mari, tous nés de 1621 à 1644. Les cinq premiers furent baptisés en l'église Saint-Regnobert, à Auxerre, et les suivants en celle de Saint-Pierre-en-Château. Anne Girard mourut à Auxerre le 17 novembre 1647. Ses funérailles eurent lieu le même jour en l'église auxerroise de Saint-Regnobert. Âgée de 46 ans, ou presque, lors de son trépas, elle était la fille de Pierre Girard et Jeanne Chappotin, qui suivent en 10 et 11.

6. **André Roussel :** Bailli de Cosne, dans la Nièvre, il décéda avant 1667.

7. **Jeanne Lasné :** Elle rendit l'âme après 1667.

8. **Gabriel Delachasse :** Marié à Jeanne Leclerc avant 1597, il fut d'abord avocat au bailliage et siège présidial d'Auxerre, puis grènetier du roi au grenier à sel de Vézelay. Il rendit l'âme à Vézelay, dans l'Avallonnais, entre 1610 et 1617.

9. **Jeanne Leclerc :** Elle donna à son mari sept garçons, tous baptisés en l'église Saint-Étienne de Vézelay de 1597 à 1610. Le 20 mars 1605, elle fut mise à l'honneur en étant l'une des deux marraines de la nouvelle cloche de ladite église. Elle mourut à Vézelay après 1635.

10. **Pierre Girard :** Marié à Jeanne Chappotin avant 1601, il était marchand à Auxerre, et chef du gobelet de la reine Marie de Médicis. Il décéda entre 1609 et 1617.

11. **Jeanne Chappotin :** Elle donna à son époux deux filles et trois garçons, tous baptisés de 1601 à 1609 en l'église Saint-Regnobert, à Auxerre. Dans les deux premiers actes de baptême, elle n'apparaît point sous le nom de « Chappotin », mais sous celui de « Regnauldin » : ce dernier nom de famille était sans doute celui de sa mère. Jeanne Chappotin mourut à Auxerre le 12 juin 1635. Ses obsèques eurent lieu le même jour en l'église auxerroise de Saint-Regnobert.

**Servignien, Jeanne :** Baptisée le 16 février 1646 à Irancy, dans l'Auxerrois, elle fut tenue sur les fonts baptismaux par Jean Regnard et par sa tante Jeanne Servignien. En 1665, elle partit au Canada comme « fille du roi », dûment dotée par le roi de France pour aller épouser un jeune colon dans le Nouveau Monde. Elle se maria donc le 13 octobre 1665, à Québec, avec un homme nommé Jean Ronceray. Elle avait alors 19 ans. Un contrat unissant les deux futurs conjoints avait été signé le 6 octobre précédent, devant maître Duquet. De cette union, naquirent six enfants, dont deux qui moururent en bas âge. Jeanne Servignien décéda le 21 février 1683 à Boucherville, non loin de Montréal. Elle était la fille de Nicolas Servignien et Jeanne Vatard, qui suivent en 2 et 3 :

2. **Nicolas Servignien** : Baptisé le 18 août 1607 à Irancy, dans l'Auxerrois, il allait avoir 19 ans lorsque le 1ᵉʳ août 1626, dans la même paroisse, il convola en justes noces avec Jeanne Vatard. Il était le fils de Germain Servignien et Barbe Villette, qui suivent en 4 et 5.

3. **Jeanne Vatard** : Née à Auxerre, dans la paroisse de Notre-Dame-la-d'Hors, son acte de baptême n'a pas pu être retrouvé, malheureusement, en raison d'une lacune que l'on constate dans les registres de cette paroisse de 1598 à 1616. Elle donna toutefois six filles et trois garçons à son mari, tous baptisés à Irancy de 1629 à 1646. Elle était la fille aînée de Denis Vatard et Marguerite Marie, qui suivent en 6 et 7.

4. **Germain Servignien** : Marié à Barbe Villette avant 1603, il décéda à Irancy le 26 mai 1630.

5. **Barbe Villette** : Baptisée à Irancy le 24 janvier 1579, elle donna à son époux trois filles et trois garçons, qui furent tous tenus sur les fonts baptismaux dudit lieu d'Irancy de 1603 à 1617. Elle était la fille de Michel Villette et Chrétienne Coquard, qui suivent en 10 et 11.

6. **Denis Vatard** : Maître imprimeur domicilié à Auxerre, en la paroisse de Notre-Dame-la-d'Hors, il décéda dans cette même ville entre 1626 et 1634.

7. **Marguerite Marie** : Elle donna au moins cinq filles et deux garçons à son époux, tous baptisés en l'église Notre-Dame-la-d'Hors de 1604 environ jusqu'à 1626 (à cause d'une lacune, je n'ai pu retrouver que les actes de baptême des cinq derniers enfants, de 1618 à 1626).

10. **Michel Villette** : Marié à Chrétienne Coquard avant 1577, il décéda avant 1625.

11. **Chrétienne Coquard** : Elle donna à son mari deux filles et trois garçons, tous baptisés en la paroisse d'Irancy de 1577 à 1586.

Elle mourut audit lieu d'Irancy le 20 février 1625.

**Thuot, Pierre** : Baptisé le 9 août 1681 à Tonnerre, en l'église Saint-Pierre, il fut tenu sur les fonts baptismaux par Pierre Testard et Marguerite Thomas. Il émigra au Canada à une date qui reste inconnue. Naquit alors de ses œuvres, le 23 janvier 1710 à Montréal, une fille naturelle qu'il avait conçue avec une certaine Elisabeth Guilbert. C'est une tout autre femme qu'il épousa cependant, nommée Marie Fournier : la cérémonie nuptiale eut lieu à Montréal le 11 juillet 1712. Pierre Thuot, âgé de presque 31 ans lors de ses noces, exerçait le métier de boulanger. De son union avec Marie Fournier, il eut dix enfants : les quatre premiers naquirent à Montréal, puis les cinq suivants à Québec, et le tout dernier de nouveau en la ville de Montréal. C'est à Longueuil qu'il mourut, près de Montréal : il y rendit l'âme le 29 septembre 1730, à l'âge de 49 ans. Pierre Thuot était le fils d'Edme Thuot et Louise Duval, qui suivent en 2 et 3 :

2. **Edme Thuot** : Né avant 1649, il épousa Louise Duval le 4 juin 1668 à Tonnerre, en l'église de Notre-Dame. Il exerça le métier de maître boulanger en la paroisse Saint-Pierre, à Tonnerre, et mourut entre 1684 et 1690. Edme Thuot était le fils d'Edme Thuot et Huguette Bourgoin, qui suivent en 4 et 5.

3. **Louise Duval** : Elle donna à son mari sept filles et trois garçons, tous baptisés en l'église Saint-Pierre à Tonnerre, ceci de 1671 à 1684. Elle décéda elle aussi entre 1684 et 1690, sans doute à Tonnerre. Louise Duval était la fille de François Duval et Marguerite Pitoiset, qui suivent en 6 et 7.

4. **Edme Thuot** : Marié à Huguette Bourgoin avant 1649, il exerça le métier de maître boulanger à Tonnerre, en la paroisse Notre-Dame, et rendit l'âme après 1668.

5. **Huguette Bourgoin** : Elle donna au moins deux filles et trois garçons à son époux, les quatre derniers enfants ayant été baptisés de 1649 à 1657 à Tonnerre, en l'église Notre-Dame. Elle mourut entre 1657 et 1668.

6. **François Duval** : Il exerçait l'activité d'huissier royal, et décéda après 1668.

7. **Marguerite Pitoiset** : Elle était déjà morte lors du mariage de sa fille Louise Duval en 1668.

**Varambouville, Antoine** : Baptisé le 9 octobre 1699 à Auxerre, en l'église Saint-Loup, il fut tenu sur les fonts baptismaux par un tailleur de pierre prénommé Antoine, et par Anne Goubinat, femme d'un autre tailleur de pierre qui s'appelait Edme Doyen. Il se rendit au Canada à une date qui demeure inconnue. C'est là qu'il convola en justes noces avec Marguerite Joubert, à Québec, le 7 février 1729. Son épouse lui donna cinq enfants. Antoine Varambouville était le fils unique de Jacques de Varambouville et Jeanne Poupin, qui suivent en 2 et 3 :

2. **Jacques de Varambouville** : Né en 1649 environ, sans doute à Rouen, il était âgé d'une dizaine d'années lorsqu'il vint s'établir à Auxerre avec ses parents, avant 1659. Devenu adulte, il se mit à exercer le métier de maçon et tailleur de pierre. Il se maria trois fois à Auxerre. Il épousa d'abord Françoise Bourbon, le 22 juin 1679 en l'église Saint-Mamert ; puis Jeanne Boulanger, le 7 janvier 1681 en l'église Saint-Loup ; et enfin Jeanne Poupin, le 30 août 1694 en l'église Notre-Dame-la-d'Hors. Il n'eut point d'enfant de sa première femme, décédée le 11 août 1680 en la paroisse Saint-Loup. Il eut en revanche quatre filles et deux garçons de sa deuxième épouse, décédée le 9 juillet 1694 en la paroisse Notre-Dame-la-d'Hors. Quant à sa troisième conjointe, elle ne lui donna qu'un fils. Il semblerait que Jacques de Varambouville quitta ensuite la ville d'Auxerre avec sa famille : on ne trouve pas son acte de décès dans cette localité. Il était le fils de Philippe de Varambouville et Jeanne Bruzet, qui suivent en 4 et 5.

3. **Jeanne Poupin** : Baptisée le 23 octobre 1671 à Auxerre, en l'église Saint-Pierre-en-Vallée, elle n'avait que 22 ans lorsqu'elle épousa Jacques de Varambouville en 1694, lequel était âgé de 45 ans environ à l'époque. Elle ne donna qu'un fils à son mari, en 1699, puis elle quitta la ville d'Auxerre où on ne trouve pas son acte de décès. Jeanne Poupin était la fille d'Edme Poupin et Jeanne Gallereux, qui suivent en 6 et 7.

4. **Philippe de Varambouville** : Natif de Rouen, il s'installa à Auxerre avant 1659, avec sa femme et ses enfants. Il exerça sur place le métier de maître charpentier de maison. Il fut inhumé à Auxerre le 27 mars 1662, après des obsèques en l'église Notre-Dame-la-d'Hors.

5. **Jeanne Bruzet** : Née en 1618 environ, elle était âgée d'une quarantaine d'années lorsqu'elle vint s'établir à Auxerre avec son mari, avant 1659. Elle donna à son époux au moins trois filles et deux garçons, les deux derniers enfants de la fratrie ayant été baptisés en 1659 et 1661 à Auxerre, ceci en l'église Notre-Dame-la-d'Hors. Après la mort de son conjoint en 1662, elle resta à Auxerre où elle décéda le 1er mai 1686, chez son fils Jacques de Varambouville en la paroisse Saint-Loup. Elle avait atteint l'âge de 68 ans au moment de son trépas.

6. **Edme Poupin** : Originaire d'Augy, dans l'Auxerrois, c'est à Auxerre qu'il convola en justes noces avec Jeanne Gallereux, le 23 novembre 1665 en l'église Saint-Pierre-en-Vallée. Il était vigneron et ne savait pas signer son nom. Il mourut avant 1694, en dehors d'Auxerre où son acte de décès ne figure point dans les registres. Edme Poupin était le fils de Georges Poupin et Perrette Romeraux, qui suivent en 12 et 13.

7. **Jeanne Gallereux** : Originaire de Coulanges-la-Vineuse, dans l'Auxerrois, elle résidait à Vaux lorsqu'elle épousa Edme Poupin en 1665. Elle donna au moins deux enfants à son mari, baptisés en 1671 et 1677 à Auxerre, en l'église Saint-Pierre-en-Vallée. Elle mourut après 1694. Elle était la fille de Florentin Gallereux et Claudine Foudriat, qui suivent en 14 et 15.

12. **Georges Poupin** : Il mourut à Augy, dans l'Auxerrois, avant le mariage de son fils en 1665.

13. **Perrette Romeraux** : Elle était encore en vie en 1665, lors du mariage de son fils.

14. **Florentin Gallereux :** Il décéda avant le mariage de sa fille en 1665.

15. **Claudine Foudriat :** Elle était toujours vivante en 1665, lors du mariage de sa fille.

### L'ascendance des d'Ailleboust et consorts

Les six Bas-Bourguignons qui viennent d'être présentés, ci-avant, étaient tous des colons partis seuls au Canada, n'ayant retrouvé sur place aucun membre de leur famille. En dehors de ce groupe d'individus dont on connaît les ancêtres, il existe toutefois cinq autres personnes qui méritent, eux aussi, un traitement particulier : il s'agit d'un ensemble composé d'hommes et de femmes qui appartenaient tous, soit directement soit par alliance, à la famille d'Ailleboust.

**d'Ailleboust, Charles :** Baptisé en juin 1621 à Ancy-le-Franc, dans le Tonnerrois, il fut porté sur les fonts baptismaux par Charles Henri de Clermont, comte de Tonnerre et seigneur d'Ancy-le-Franc, capitaine de 100 hommes d'armes. Sa marraine était Anne Le Foul. Dès l'âge de 5 ans, il fut choisi à son tour comme parrain, lors d'un baptême célébré à Ravières le 30 juillet 1626. On lui confia de nouveau cette responsabilité quelques années plus tard, les 27 avril 1633 et 31 mai 1635 en l'église de Ravières. À ces deux occasions, en 1633 et 1635, il apposa sa signature au bas des actes de baptême. Il avait 27 ans lorsqu'il partit au Canada avec son oncle Louis d'Ailleboust. Arrivé à Québec le 19 août 1648, il fut mis à la tête d'un groupe de colons armés pour repousser les Iroquois qui menaçaient la région de Montréal. Le 3 septembre 1652, devant maître Guillaume Audouard, notaire résidant à Québec, il signa ensuite un contrat de mariage qui l'unissait à une femme nommée Catherine Le Gardeur. Les noces furent célébrées à Québec le 16 septembre suivant. De cette union, naquirent 14 enfants. Charles d'Ailleboust, sieur des Musseaux, exerça le métier de marchand de fourrures. Il fut aussi gouverneur intérimaire de Montréal, ainsi que juge civil et criminel. Il mourut à Montréal le 19 novembre 1700, à l'âge de 79 ans. Ses parents, qui s'appelaient Nicolas d'Ailleboust et Dorothée de Menteth, suivent en 2 et 3 :

2. **Nicolas d'Ailleboust :** Originaire d'Ancy-le-Franc, dans le Tonnerrois, c'est à Paris qu'il épousa Dorothée de Menteth, par contrat de mariage signé le 6 mai 1620 devant maîtres Dupuys et Nutrat, notaires parisiens[9]. Il portait alors le titre de sieur de Collonge, à cause des terres qu'il possédait à Collonge-la-Madeleine, près d'Autun. Il vécut avec sa femme à Ancy-le-Franc jusqu'en 1625 environ, puis s'installa avec elle et ses enfants à Ravières, dans le Tonnerrois. Entre 1636 et 1646, il fut nommé commissaire du roi et maître des magasins de munitions en l'artillerie de Thionville. Il rendit l'âme entre 1655 et 1678. Ses parents, qui s'appelaient Antoine d'Ailleboust et Marie Genevois, suivent en 4 et 5.

3. **Dorothée de Menteth :** Originaire d'Argentenay, dans le Tonnerrois, elle entra au service de la duchesse de Mercœur à Paris, comme fille d'honneur. C'est dans la résidence parisienne de cette dame qu'elle signa, en 1620, le contrat de mariage qui la liait à Nicolas d'Ailleboust. Cet hôtel particulier était situé dans le faubourg Saint-Germain-des-Prés, en la paroisse de Saint-Sulpice. Dorothée de Menteth donna six filles et cinq garçons à son époux : les trois premiers enfants furent baptisés à Ancy-le-Franc de 1621 à 1624, les huit suivants à Ravières de 1626 à 1645. La femme de Nicolas d'Ailleboust était la fille de Jean de Menteth et Suzanne Hotman, qui suivent en 6 et 7.

4. **Antoine d'Ailleboust :** Originaire d'Autun ou des environs, en Saône-et-Loire, il épousa Marie Genevois avant l'an 1580. Il était alors avocat au bailliage d'Autun. Le 30 juillet 1580, il fut condamné avec sa femme, par le parlement de Paris, à verser 300 écus à Jean Fichot père et Jean Fichot fils, domiciliés à Châtillon-sur-Seine en Côte-d'Or. Dès le 24 août suivant, il fit établir une procuration aux noms de François Logerot et Jacques Lestorchier, devant maître Jean Fameley, notaire à Cruzy-le-Châtel dans le Tonnerrois : ceux-ci étaient chargés de remettre ladite somme de 300 écus auxdits Fichot. Ces derniers firent établir un reçu dès réception de l'argent, le 8 novembre 1580 devant maîtres Edme Deguettes et Vorle Fricauldot, notaires royaux à Châtillon-sur-Seine[10]. Antoine d'Ailleboust devint ensuite conseiller au bailliage d'Auxois. Pendant la guerre de la Ligue, il se rangea du côté du roi Henri IV. Le 17

décembre 1591, en raison des services qu'il rendit au roi, et en considération de la perte de ses maisons pillées par les partisans de la Ligue, il reçut du souverain des lettres patentes signées lors du siège de Rouen : celles-ci annulaient toute dette en rentes et en argent qu'il avait contractée auprès de Léonard Boullon, Anne Dumey, Quentin Bouchu et François Morin, tous ligueurs et réfugiés en des villes rebelles au pouvoir royal. Ces lettres patentes furent enregistrées le 14 décembre 1595 à Dijon, par le parlement de Bourgogne[11]. Après la mort de Marie Genevois, son épouse, Antoine d'Ailleboust convola en secondes noces avec Suzanne Hotman, veuve de Jean de Menteth. Les noces furent célébrées à une date inconnue, entre 1594 et 1612. En 1602, il dut subir un procès engagé contre lui par son cousin germain Jean d'Ailleboust, qui désirait recevoir une partie de la seigneurie de Collonge, située à Collonge-la-Madeleine près d'Autun. La totalité de cette seigneurie resta néanmoins entre les mains d'Antoine d'Ailleboust. Ce dernier mourut en 1619 ou 1620 : il était encore en vie le 15 novembre 1619, date à laquelle il fut parrain d'un enfant à Ancy-le-Franc ; mais il était déjà mort le 6 mai 1620, lorsque son fils Nicolas d'Ailleboust épousa Dorothée de Menteth à Paris. Il était à cette époque conseiller ordinaire au conseil du prince de Condé. Dans un ouvrage intitulé *La famille d'Ailleboust*, publié en 1917 à Montréal, Aegidius Fauteux prétend que le père d'Antoine d'Ailleboust était le premier médecin du roi Henri IV, Jean d'Ailleboust. Cette thèse, tout à fait erronée, repose sur le dossier de maintenue de noblesse qui fut enregistré en France le 11 juin 1720, à la requête des descendants canadiens dudit Antoine[12]. Or, le premier médecin du roi Henri IV était en fait l'oncle, et non le père, d'Antoine d'Ailleboust : il n'était pas distinct d'un autre Jean d'Ailleboust, oncle d'Antoine et médecin à Sens, mais formait avec lui une seule et même personne. Le vrai père d'Antoine d'Ailleboust était André Ailleboust, moins prestigieux que son frère Jean. Je n'ai pas encore trouvé de preuves directes de cette filiation, mais celle-ci est la seule qui reste possible en procédant par élimination. André Ailleboust, en effet, avait cinq frères, dont quatre qui devinrent chanoines à Autun. Le cinquième

frère, Jean d'Ailleboust, médecin à Sens puis premier médecin du roi Henri IV, n'avait que trois enfants survivants à sa mort, en 1594, tous calvinistes comme lui : Suzanne, Marie et Jean. André Ailleboust, en revanche, était resté catholique et portait le titre de sieur de Collonge, comme Antoine d'Ailleboust et ses descendants canadiens. Bref, sauf preuve du contraire, les parents d'Antoine étaient sans doute André Ailleboust et Odotte Rolet, qui suivent en 8 et 9.

5. **Marie Genevois :** Son nom n'apparaît que dans la quittance du 8 novembre 1580, par laquelle Jean Fichot père et Jean Fichot fils reconnaissent avoir reçu la somme de 300 écus d'Antoine d'Ailleboust et de son épouse Marie Genevois, par l'intermédiaire des procureurs François Logerot et Jacques Lestorchier[13].

6. **Jean de Menteth :** Natif du comté de Sterling, en Écosse, il était issu de la vieille maison des comtes de Menteith puis de celle des barons de Kerse. Par l'une de ses grands-mères, il descendait aussi des comtes écossais de Montrose. Entré au service du roi de France, il finit par acquérir la seigneurie d'Argentenay, dans le Tonnerrois. Le 18 juillet 1594, il signa un contrat de mariage devant maître Hugues Babynet, notaire à Paris, par lequel il prenait pour épouse Suzanne Hotman. Parmi les témoins, figurait son cousin issu de germain Jean de Gordon, gentilhomme de la chambre du roi Henri IV, qui descendait lui aussi des comtes écossais de Montrose. Jean de Menteth mourut avant 1612.

7. **Suzanne Hotman :** Elle se maria en premières noces avec Jean de Menteth, par contrat notarié signé à Paris le 18 juillet 1594, puis, en secondes noces, elle épousa Antoine d'Ailleboust, ceci avant 1612. Elle donna au moins une fille à son premier conjoint, puis une fille et un garçon au second. Elle mourut après 1638. Ses parents, qui s'appelaient François Hotman et Claude Aubelin, suivent en 14 et 15.

8. **André Ailleboust :** Né à Autun, en Saône-et-Loire, il épousa Odotte Rolet en 1547. Le

29 août de cette année-là, en effet, conformément aux clauses de son contrat de mariage, il reçut de sa mère la somme de 807 livres et 10 sols tournois. Il fit aussitôt établir une quittance par maître Lazare Chastel, notaire à Autun[14]. Après avoir exercé l'activité de marchand, ceci dès 1547, il devint économe de l'abbaye Saint-Martin, à l'extérieur des murs d'enceinte de sa ville natale. Le 29 juin 1570, lors du pillage de cette abbaye par les troupes calvinistes de l'amiral de Coligny, on lui déroba tous ses meubles et une grande quantité de blé. Dès que son frère Charles eut été nommé évêque d'Autun, en 1573, il fut engagé par celui-ci comme percepteur des droits de mainmorte et de régale, des rentes et redevances de l'évêché. Une semaine après la mort du prélat, André Ailleboust racheta à son frère Jean, médecin à Sens, sa part de la seigneurie de Collonge-la-Madeleine : l'acte de vente fut signé le 7 mai 1585. Quatre ans plus tard, le 20 mai 1589, les troupes de la Ligue s'emparèrent de la ville d'Autun. Dès lors, la position d'André Ailleboust, partisan du roi Henri III puis de son successeur, fut inconfortable : en août 1589, il fut arrêté et rançonné par les ligueurs de la ville. Après l'abjuration du roi Henri IV en 1593, le camp royaliste se renforça, et les villes ligueuses commencèrent à se soumettre une à une au pouvoir royal. La soumission de Paris, le 22 mars 1594, provoqua l'ire des ligueurs d'Autun : les partisans du roi durent se réfugier à Lucenay-l'Évêque dès le mois d'avril, auprès de l'évêque Pierre Saulnier. Parmi ces rescapés se trouvait André Ailleboust. Celui-ci contribua à l'effort de guerre du roi : répondant à une convocation des nobles vassaux inscrits au ban et arrière-ban du bailliage d'Autun, il versa une contribution de 20 écus, enregistrée le 10 décembre 1594 par le receveur du bailliage[15]. Il ne put rentrer à Autun qu'après la soumission de la ville au roi Henri IV, imposée par les armes le 16 mai 1595. Mort entre 1595 et 1602, André Ailleboust était le fils de Pierre Ailleboust et Perrette de Séez, qui suivent en 16 et 17.

9. **Odotte Rolet :** Mariée en 1547 audit André Ailleboust, elle reçut de son mari des joyaux d'une valeur de 30 écus lors de ses noces[16]. Elle donna la vie à trois enfants au moins : une fille prénommée Antoinette, qui épousa Antoine Pigenat par contrat de mariage signé le 1er janvier 1574 ; un fils prénommé Pierre, qui devint chanoine d'Autun en 1576 ; et sans doute un fils prénommé Antoine, qui se maria en premières noces avec Marie Genevois, avant 1580 (voir ci-avant). Odotte Rolet était la fille d'Hugues Rolet et Guillemette Micheletet, qui suivent en 18 et 19.

14. **François Hotman :** Né à Paris le 23 août 1524, il fit des études de droit civil à l'université d'Orléans. De retour à Paris avec le grade de licencié, il ouvrit dans la capitale, en 1546, un cours privé de droit civil, puisque l'université de Paris n'enseignait encore, à l'époque, que le droit canonique. Converti à la réforme calviniste, il partit se réfugier à Lyon, d'où, le 17 juin 1548, il écrivit à Calvin pour lui demander asile. Il arriva à Genève en octobre de la même année, en même temps que Théodore de Bèze (originaire de Vézelay dans l'Yonne). En mai 1549, Calvin lui confia la charge d'enseigner le latin à l'école protestante de Lausanne, la chaire de grec étant attribuée audit Théodore de Bèze. C'est après son séjour à Lausanne que François Hotman épousa Claude Aubelin : les noces furent célébrées le 15 mai 1553, ceci en l'église réformée de Saint-Pierre à Genève[17]. Un mois après ce mariage, le 22 juin 1553, il fut reçu officiellement comme habitant de Genève. C'est dans cette ville que naquit son premier enfant, Jean Hotman, baptisé en l'église Saint-Pierre le 15 avril 1554, dont le parrain fut Jean Calvin en personne. En 1555, François Hotman finit pourtant par quitter Genève, pour aller vivre à Strasbourg avec sa famille.

Le 24 juin 1556, il y signa un contrat d'engagement pour cinq ans, comme professeur de droit civil au gymnase luthérien de la ville. Lorsque la première guerre de religion éclata en France, le 1er avril 1562, il rejoignit aussitôt le prince de Condé à Orléans, pour entrer au service de celui-ci comme secrétaire particulier. Après la paix d'Amboise, signée le 17 mars 1563, il s'installa à Valence avec sa famille : il y enseigna le droit civil à l'université pendant quatre ans. En avril 1567, il partit s'établir à Bourges, à l'invitation de la duchesse Marguerite de Savoie. Il dut cependant quitter la ville quelques mois plus tard, lorsqu'éclata la deuxième guerre de religion, en septembre 1567. Il se réfugia aussitôt à Orléans, tombée aux mains des calvinistes. En août 1568, il partit s'enfermer derrière les murs de Sancerre, où, pendant cinq semaines, il participa à la défense de la ville assiégée. Deux ans plus tard, après la signature de la paix de Saint-Germain-en-Laye en août 1570, il put retourner à Bourges pour y enseigner le droit féodal. Il échappa de justesse au massacre de la Saint-Barthélemy. Réfugié à Genève, où il arriva le 2 octobre 1572, il y devint professeur de droit romain. C'est dans cette ville que naquit sa dernière fille, prénommée Théodore : baptisée le 27 mars 1574 en l'église Saint-Pierre, elle fut présentée au pasteur par Théodore de Bèze en personne[18]. En août 1578, François Hotman partit vivre à Bâle avec toute sa famille. Il quitta toutefois cette ville quatre ans plus tard, pour fuir une épidémie de peste qui s'était déclarée au cours de l'été, en 1582. Il vécut près d'un an à Montbéliard, où sa femme mourut de la peste le 28 février 1583. Après un court séjour à Bâle, il retourna à Genève en septembre 1584. Il y demeura pendant cinq ans, jusqu'en septembre 1589. Il finit par repartir à Bâle, où il rendit l'âme le 12 février 1590. François Hotman était le fils de Pierre Hotman et Paule de Marle, qui suivent en 28 et 29.

15. **Claude Aubelin :** Née à Orléans de parents devenus calvinistes, elle se réfugia à Genève où elle épousa François Hotman en 1553. Elle donna 11 enfants à son époux, baptisés de 1554 à 1574 dans les diverses villes où le couple a résidé : Genève, Strasbourg, Sancerre et autres. Elle mourut de la peste le 28 février 1583, à Montbéliard. Claude Aubelin était la fille de Guillaume Aubelin et Françoise Brachet, qui suivent en 30 et 31.

16. **Pierre Ailleboust :** Il serait originaire d'Allemagne, si l'on en croit ses descendants de la branche française qui, le 4 juin 1717, firent enregistrer à Paris un dossier de maintenue de noblesse[19]. Cette tradition familiale, reprise par tous les auteurs dont Aegidius Fauteux, est fausse ! Pierre Ailleboust était né en

fait dans le Perche. C'est lui même qui l'a écrit, de sa propre main, lorsqu'il s'inscrivit à l'université de médecine de Montpellier, le 4 octobre 1510. Ce jour-là, il nota en effet dans le registre d'immatriculation qu'il était *francus perticensis*, c'est-à-dire un Français du Perche[20]. Pierre Ailleboust était donc un Percheron, venant d'une province où l'on trouve encore, de nos jours, un hameau appelé « les Aillebouts », situé dans la commune de Bonsmoulins dans le département de l'Orne. À Montpellier, notre étudiant du Perche suivit les cours du professeur Antoine Romier, qui enseigna la médecine de 1508 à 1536 à l'université de la ville. Devenu médecin, avec le grade de docteur, Pierre Ailleboust alla exercer son art à Autun, où il épousa Perrette de Séez. Le 9 mai 1517, il acheta à Jean et Pierre Rolin, écuyers, une rente annuelle et perpétuelle de sept livres tournois, ceci pour le prix de 100 livres tournois. Cet acte fut enregistré ce jour-là par maître Jean Desplaces, notaire à Autun[21]. Pierre Ailleboust fut ensuite engagé comme médecin ordinaire par le roi François Iᵉʳ, à une date qui reste inconnue. Une hypothèse peut être formulée cependant : sachant que le souverain a séjourné deux fois à Autun, du 1ᵉʳ au 28 août 1521, puis du 12 au 14 février 1530, on peut penser que le monarque s'est attaché les services du médecin autunois à l'une de ces deux occasions. Quoi qu'il en fût, Pierre Ailleboust mourut le 5 septembre 1531 au château de Fontainebleau. Son cœur fut enterré dans la chapelle Saint-Côme-et-Saint-Damien de l'église Saint-Jean-de-la-Grotte, à Autun.

17. **Perrette de Séez :** Elle était originaire de la région d'Autun, où l'on trouve un hameau qui porte le nom de « Séez » dans la commune de Saint-Didier-sur-Arroux. Or, dans cette localité, vivait une famille de Séez, *alias* de Sez, comme l'atteste un acte daté du 19 avril 1544 : ce jour-là, Emiland de Sez, fils de Jean, domicilié au village de Marolles situé dans la paroisse de Saint-Didier-sur-Arroux, reconnut être redevable envers les chanoines d'Autun d'une rente de 26 livres et 8 deniers[22]. Devenue la femme de Pierre Ailleboust, entre 1510 et 1517, Perrette de Séez donna à son époux plusieurs enfants, dont

deux filles et six garçons qui parvinrent à l'âge adulte. Après la mort de son mari, elle acheta la seigneurie de Collonge-la-Madeleine, pour la somme de 82 livres tournois : l'acte fut enregistré le 27 janvier 1532 (n.s.), devant maître Jean Desplaces, notaire demeurant à Autun[23]. Perrette de Séez passa ensuite un acte notarié le 27 novembre 1540, par lequel elle reconnut devoir aux chanoines d'Autun une rente annuelle de dix livres tournois, pour la maison qu'elle occupait à Autun. Dans cet acte, elle donne la liste de ses enfants encore vivants, à savoir : Jean l'aîné, chanoine, puis Charles, Anatole, André, Hugues, Jean le jeune, et Françoise[24]. Elle avait eu aussi une fille prénommée Ferrine, déjà décédée en 1540, qui avait été l'épouse de Jean de Montrambault, docteur en droit et avocat au bailliage d'Autun. Le dernier document que j'ai pu retrouver concernant Perrette de Séez fut établi une quinzaine d'années plus tard : le 29 juillet 1555, en effet, son gendre Jean Lalemant, à qui elle avait donné procuration le 5 juillet précédent devant maître Lazare Chastel, notaire à Autun, reçut en son nom la somme de 200 livres que lui devait tous les six mois la municipalité de Lyon, à prendre sur les aides et gabelles de la ville[25]. Perrette de Séez, encore en vie en 1555, mourut avant 1560 : le 24 janvier 1660 (n.s.), ce furent ses fils qui touchèrent la rente semestrielle qui leur était due par la municipalité de Lyon, à savoir les chanoines Charles, Jean et Anatole Ailleboust, le bénéficier Hugues Ailleboust (futur chanoine), ainsi que le médecin Jean Ailleboust et André Ailleboust, tous frères germains[26].

18. **Hugues Rolet :** Marié à Guillemette Micheletet au début du XVIe siècle, il fut greffier au bailliage d'Autun en 1515, notaire en 1517, maître forestier et contrôleur du grenier à sel d'Autun en 1523, échevin d'Autun du 24 juin 1523 au 23 juin 1536, puis maire de ladite ville d'Autun du 24 juin 1540 au 23 juin 1541. Le 7 octobre 1559, il partagea ses biens entre ses quatre fils Nicole, Antoine, Jean et Denis, devant maître Lazare Chastel, notaire domicilié à Autun[27]. Il était alors seigneur d'Aigrevault.

19. **Guillemette Micheletet :** Elle donna au moins une fille et quatre garçons à son conjoint, tous parvenus à l'âge adulte. Elle décéda avant le partage du 7 octobre 1559 (voir ci-avant).

28. **Pierre Hotman :** Sieur de Villiers-Saint-Paul, il épousa Paule de Marle avant 1524. Il exerça l'activité de lieutenant général des eaux et forêts de Compiègne, puis devint conseiller au parlement de Paris le 5 septembre 1544. En 1548, il tenta en vain d'empêcher son fils aîné François de devenir calviniste. Il mourut le 27 mars 1554 à Paris, et fut enterré aux Carmes. Ses parents, qui s'appelaient Lambert Hotman et Catherine de Vic, suivent en 56 et 57.

29. **Paule de Marle :** Mariée à Pierre Hotman avant 1524, elle donna sept garçons à son mari, et décéda après 1554. Elle était la fille de Vaast de Marle et Jacqueline Dupuy, qui suivent en 58 et 59.

30. **Guillaume Aubelin :** Originaire d'Orléans, il devint calviniste et se réfugia à Genève avec sa femme et sa fille avant 1553. Il était sieur de La Rivière.

31. **Françoise Brachet :** Elle donna au moins une fille à son conjoint, mariée à Genève en 1553.

56. **Lambert Hotman :** Originaire de Breslau en Silésie, il vint en France vers l'an 1470, avec les hommes qui accompagnaient Angilbert de Clèves, comte de Nevers. Il épousa en troisièmes noces Catherine de Vic, et mourut à Paris le 24 décembre 1514. Son corps fut enseveli dans l'église des Innocents à Paris. Lambert Hotman était le fils de Gérard Hotman, qui suit en 112.

57. **Catherine de Vic :** Elle donna à son époux deux filles et six garçons.

58. **Vaast de Marle :** Il était seigneur de Vaugien et de Villiers-Saint-Paul, dans le Beauvaisis.

59. **Jacqueline Dupuy :** Elle donna au moins une fille à son époux.

112. **Gérard Hotman :** Il vivait en Allemagne.

**d'Ailleboust, Louis :** Né vers l'an 1612 à Ancy-le-Franc, dans le Tonnerrois, on ne sait quand il fut baptisé car le premier registre paroissial de son village natal ne commence qu'en 1615. À l'âge de 7 ans, il fut choisi comme parrain lors d'un baptême célébré à Ancy-le-Franc, le 13 décembre 1619. Devenu adulte, il partit vivre dans la paroisse Saint-Étienne-du-Mont à Paris, dans un logement de la rue de Bièvre. C'est à Paris qu'il épousa Barbe de Boullongne : le contrat de mariage fut signé le 6 septembre 1638 à l'hôtel des « Deux Anges », sur la place Maubert, devant maître Philippe Périer, notaire parisien. Louis d'Ailleboust avait alors 26 ans. Quelques années plus tard, il se rendit au Canada avec sa conjointe, débarquant à Québec le 15 août 1643. Il fut nommé gouverneur intérimaire de Montréal en octobre 1645, pour organiser la défense de la ville contre les attaques des Iroquois : c'est à lui que l'on doit la construction des fortifications de Montréal, puis du fort de Trois-Rivières. En 1647, il rentra en France, mais, le 2 mars 1648, on le nomma gouverneur général du Canada. Il repartit donc vers le Nouveau Monde, accompagné de son neveu Charles d'Ailleboust (voir ci-avant). Arrivé à Québec le 19 août 1648, il occupa ledit poste de gouverneur général jusqu'en 1651. Il se retira alors sur sa terre de Coulonge, qu'il avait achetée en 1649, près de Québec. En 1655, il retourna en France où il séjourna pendant un an et demi. Il reprit ensuite le bateau en sens inverse, arrivant à Québec le 29 juillet 1657. Dès le mois de septembre suivant, il devint gouverneur intérimaire du Canada : il abandonna son poste le 11 juillet 1658, lorsqu'il fut remplacé par le gouverneur en titre. Il quitta alors la ville de Québec un mois plus tard, le 21 août, pour aller s'établir à Montréal. C'est là qu'il rendit l'âme, le 31 mai 1660. Il n'avait que 48 ans lors de sa mort. Ses parents étaient Antoine d'Ailleboust et Suzanne Hotman : comme ces deux personnages figurent aussi dans l'ascendance de Charles d'Ailleboust, qui précède, il suffit de se reporter aux ancêtres 4 et 7 dudit Charles pour dresser l'arbre généalogique de Louis d'Ailleboust.

**de Boullongne, Barbe**[28] **:** Baptisée le 7 avril 1614 à Ravières, dans le Tonnerrois, elle fut tenue sur les fonts baptismaux par Jean Rigollet et Barbe Jazu. Le 21 juillet 1632, à l'âge de 18 ans, elle fut choisie à son tour comme marraine, lors d'un baptême célébré dans son village natal. On lui confia de nouveau cette responsabilité les 25 juillet 1633, 11 mars 1634 et 10 octobre 1634, en l'église de Ravières. Après son mariage avec Louis d'Ailleboust, en 1638, elle résida avec son époux à Paris, dans un logement de la rue des Morfondus, laquelle était située dans le vieux faubourg Saint-Marcel, en la paroisse de Saint-Étienne-du-Mont. Elle partit ensuite avec son conjoint pour le Canada, en 1643. Sur place, elle s'occupa d'œuvres de charité, apprenant aussi la langue des Indiens pour mieux les convertir au catholicisme. Après le décès de son époux, en 1660, elle se retira d'abord à l'Hôtel-Dieu de Montréal, puis elle partit s'installer à Québec en 1663, auprès des sœurs Hospitalières de la ville. Cette année-là, le 31 juillet 1663, elle fonda la confrérie de Sainte-Famille, toujours en activité de nos jours. Elle mourut à Québec le 7 juin 1685, à l'âge de 71 ans, sans avoir donné le moindre enfant à son époux. Ses parents, qui s'appelaient Florentin Boullongne et Eustache Quéau, ou Cuot, suivent en 2 et 3 :

2. **Florentin Boullongne :** Marié à Eustache Quéau avant 1603, il exerçait le métier de recteur des écoles à Ravières, dans le Tonnerrois. Il décéda entre 1614 et 1632.

3. **Eustache Quéau :** Elle donna à son mari quatre filles et trois garçons, tous baptisés de 1602 à 1614 en l'église de Ravières. En 1638, elle se rendit à Paris pour assister à la signature du contrat de mariage qui devait unir sa fille Barbe de Boullongne à Louis d'Ailleboust : elle logea à l'hôtel des « Deux Anges », où le contrat fut signé le 6 septembre 1638[29].

**de Boullongne, Philippe**[30] **:** Baptisée le 7 février 1605 à Ravières, dans le Tonnerrois, elle fut tenue sur les fonts baptismaux par Jean Moreau et Philippe Cuot. Devenue adulte, elle accepta à son tour d'être la marraine de plusieurs nouveau-nés, dans l'église de sa paroisse : ceux-ci, au nombre de huit, furent reçus au baptême les 29 septembre 1632, 28 octobre 1634, 2 mai 1635, 28 août 1636, 7 mars 1637, 17 mai 1637, 10 août 1637, et 12 mai 1638. Quand Philippe de Boullongne apprit que sa sœur Barbe allait partir au Canada, elle la rejoignit à Paris pour faire partie du voyage. Arrivée à Québec le 15 août

1643, elle finit par entrer comme novice chez les sœurs Ursulines de la ville, le 2 décembre 1648. Elle avait alors 43 ans. Elle vécut dès lors une vie de religieuse pendant une vingtaine d'années. Décédée à Québec le 20 août 1667, elle était âgée de 62 ans lors de son trépas. Ses parents étaient Florentin Boullongne et Eustache Quéau, *alias* Cuot (voir ci-avant).

**Martin, Marie :** Née en 1648 à Ravières, dans le Tonnerrois, elle fut baptisée à une date qui reste inconnue : l'année de son baptême, 1648, apparaît bien dans une table récapitulative, mais on ne trouve pas les actes de cette année-là dans les microfilms reproduisant les registres de Ravières. Devenue adulte, Marie Martin rejoignit son oncle Charles d'Ailleboust au Canada. Elle y épousa Christophe Février le 16 novembre 1671, à Montréal, à l'âge de 23 ans. Après avoir mis au monde sept enfants, elle rendit l'âme le 14 juillet 1680, à Boucherville près de Montréal. Elle n'était âgée que de 32 ans lors de son décès. Ses parents, qui s'appelaient Abraham Martin et Suzanne d'Ailleboust, suivent en 2 et 3 :

2. **Abraham Martin :** Il semblerait qu'il ne fut point né à Ravières. Il vint pourtant y habiter dès l'an 1630 avec ses parents, année au cours de laquelle il devint le parrain d'un enfant de cette localité, baptisé le 19 mai. On retrouve ensuite sa signature au bas de trois autres actes de baptême, datés des 31 juillet 1638, 26 février 1641 et 30 septembre 1643. C'est en 1647 qu'Abraham Martin épousa Suzanne d'Ailleboust, entre les mois d'avril et de décembre. Il exerça l'activité de marchand à Ravières, où il vivait encore en 1654. Il était le fils de Jacques Martin, qui suit en 4. Le nom de sa mère n'est pas encore connu.

3. **Suzanne d'Ailleboust :** Baptisée le 28 juillet 1622 à Ancy-le-Franc, dans le Tonnerrois, elle fut tenue sur les fonts baptismaux par Paul Cosquinot et Suzanne Hotman, la seconde épouse de son grand-père Antoine d'Aille-boust. À l'âge de 13 ans, elle fut choisie comme marraine à son tour, lors d'un baptême célébré le 1ᵉʳ novembre 1635 en l'église de Ravières. Elle savait déjà signer son nom à l'époque. Avant de se marier, elle fut marraine 13 autres fois dans la même église, ceci de 1639 à 1647. Lors du dernier baptême, daté du 29 avril 1647, elle était encore célibataire : elle fut désignée dans l'acte comme « fille de Nicolas d'Ailleboust », et non point comme étant déjà la femme d'Abraham Martin. Elle épousa toutefois cet homme avant la fin de la même année 1647, entre les mois d'avril et décembre. Elle était alors âgée de 25 ans. Trois filles et trois garçons naquirent de cette union : les cinq premiers enfants furent baptisés à Ravières, de 1648 à 1654, et le dernier à Argenteuil, en 1656. Suzanne d'Ailleboust était la fille de Nicolas d'Ailleboust et Dorothée de Menteth. Leur ascendance est détaillée dans la notice consacrée à Charles d'Ailleboust (voir ci-avant, à partir des ancêtres 2 et 3 de ce personnage).

4. **Jacques Martin :** Il exerçait la fonction de lieutenant en la prévôté de Ravières, puis celle de prévôt de cette même localité. Il était encore en vie en 1653, année au cours de laquelle il fut le parrain de son petit-fils Jacques Martin, baptisé à Ravières le 19 juin.

**Conclusion : l'exemple des Bas-Bourguignons**

Si l'objet principal de cette étude était d'apporter une réponse globale à l'ensemble des demandes particulières qui sont adressées à la Société généalogique de l'Yonne, j'ai voulu aussi donner un aperçu de ce que tout cercle, en France, est en mesure de fournir aux généalogistes du Canada, ou originaires de ce pays. Sur les 45 Bas-Bourguignons du corpus, en effet, il en est 28 dont j'ai pu retrouver la trace dans les archives françaises, soit un peu moins des deux tiers de l'effectif. Cette proportion est-elle un indice du résultat final qu'obtiendraient d'autres cercles dans d'autres régions? Une comparaison des travaux menés par différentes associations en France serait riche en enseignements : outre le fait qu'elle permettrait de mieux évaluer la proportion, sur le plan national, des recherches fructueuses, elle apporterait surtout une bien meilleure connaissance du comportement des Français partis pour le Canada avant 1730.

Le comportement des Bas-Bourguignons devenus Canadiens a-t-il valeur d'exemple ? J'ai pu montrer que ceux-ci, très peu nombreux à l'échelle de tous les habitants de Basse-Bourgogne, et célibataires pour la plupart avant le départ, agissaient différemment selon qu'ils appartenaient à la gent féminine ou masculine. C'est en famille, ou bien pour rejoindre sur place de proches parents, que les femmes émigraient au Canada le plus souvent. Les femmes isolées, quant à elles, étaient « filles du roi », munies d'une belle dot royale qui leur donnait l'assurance de trouver au-delà des mers un mari. Il ressort de ces deux constats que le comportement féminin, chez les Bas-Bourguignons, était surtout dicté par une recherche de la sécurité. D'ailleurs, originaires de la campagne en majorité, les femmes se sont surtout fixées, au Canada, dans les deux villes bien protégées qu'étaient Québec et Montréal. Les hommes, au contraire, semblent avoir été plus aventureux. Souvent venus seuls, sans rejoindre quiconque sur le sol canadien, ils ont préféré élire domicile au contact direct de la nature, restant parfois célibataires. Ce qui les avait poussés à s'établir au Canada, ce n'était ni la volonté de maintenir ou de renouer des liens familiaux, ni l'envie d'en créer de nouveaux. Ce n'était pas non plus le désir d'accompagner des amis d'enfance au sein d'une même équipe de travail, comme le faisaient autrefois les scieurs de long du Forez. En fait, en partant au Canada, les hommes de Basse-Bourgogne ont surtout voulu se créer un avenir meilleur, dans un monde nouveau.

**Dépôts d'archives fréquentés pour cette étude :**

| | |
|---|---|
| Auxerre : | Archives municipales (AM, AUXERRE) ; Archives départementales de l'Yonne (AD, YONNE) |
| Paris : | Archives nationales (AN) ; Bibliothèque nationale de France (BnF) |
| Autun : | Bibliothèque municipale (BM, AUTUN) |
| Mâcon : | Archives départementales de Saône-et-Loire (AD, SAÔNE-ET-LOIRE) |
| Dijon : | Archives départementales de Côte-d'Or (AD, CÔTE-D'OR) |
| Lyon : | Archives municipales (AM, LYON) |
| Salt Lake City : | Family History Library (FHL) |

## NOTES

1.  Cette étude est dédiée à la famille Lepage, qui, les 12, 13, et 14 juillet 1996, s'est réunie à Rimouski pour célébrer le tricentenaire de la fondation de cette ville par René Lepage, né en 1656 à Ouanne, dans l'Yonne. Je tiens à remercier, pour l'aide qu'ils m'ont apportée : Ronald LePage, John Roch LePage, Firmin et Lucette LePage,

ainsi que Sylvie Biton et Étienne Meunier.

2.  Dans le *Bulletin de liaison*, no. 11 (1984) de la Société généalogique de l'Yonne.

3.  De nouvelles recherches, menées à Salt Lake City en mai 1997, m'ont permis de découvrir enfin l'origine de Claude Louis Lemaire. En fait, il a été baptisé le 26 août 1658 à Entrains-sur-Nohains, localité qui faisait partie, sous l'Ancien Régime, du diocèse d'Auxerre, et qui se trouve actuellement dans le nord du département de la Nièvre. Baptisé sous le prénom de Claude, il était le fils non pas de Marguerite Bardolat, mais de Jeanne Bardolat. Après le décès de sa mère, inhumée à Entrains le 30 septembre 1664, son père, Louis Lemaire, s'est remarié le 22 juin 1665 avec Claire Parmentier, à Entrains. Claude Louis Lemaire a eu un frère et une sœur de sa mère, et trois demi-frères et quatre demi-sœurs de sa marâtre.

4.  La date du 12 juin est en fait celle de l'inhumation. Le décès avait eu lieu la veille.

5.  AD, YONNE, 3E14/157.

6.  AD, YONNE, 3E14/155.

7.  AD, YONNE, 3E14/157.

8.  AD, YONNE, 3E7/30.

9.  AN, MINUTIER CENTRAL, ET/VIII/604.

10.  AD, CÔTE-D'OR, E2335, fol. 180.

11.  AD, CÔTE-D'OR, B12085, fol. 87.

12.  Paris, BnF, ms n. acq. fr., dossier n° 9279, fol. 46.

13.  AD, CÔTE-D'OR, E2335, fol. 180.

14.  AD, SAÔNE-ET-LOIRE, 3E9661, p. 5-9.

15.  AD, CÔTE-D'OR, C3589.

16.  AD, SAÔNE-ET-LOIRE, 3E9661, p. 5-9.

17.  FHL, microfilm n° 0128360.

18.  FHL, microfilm n° 0128360.

19.  Paris, BnF, ms, pièces originales n° 16, pièce 422, fol. 3-5.

20.  MONTPELLIER, Bibliothèque interuniversitaire, fonds ancien de médecine, registre S 19, fol. 25.

21.  AD, SAÔNE-ET-LOIRE, 3E9631, p. 283.

22.  AD, SAÔNE-ET-LOIRE, 3E9637, fol. 255v.

23.  AD, SAÔNE-ET-LOIRE, 3E9630, p. 47.

24.  AD, SAÔNE-ET-LOIRE, 5G90, fol. 125-126.

25.  AM, LYON, CC1025.

26.  AM, LYON, CC1080.

27.  AD, SAÔNE-ET-LOIRE, 3E9662, fol. 169-172.

28.  Son prénom était Barbe à sa naissance et lors de son mariage. Ce n'est qu'à partir de 1664, au Canada, qu'elle s'est fait appeler Marie-Barbe dans les contrats notariés. Dans les actes de baptême, à Ravières, elle signait « Barbe Deboullougne » (voire « Deboullogne »).

29.  Dans cet acte notarié, elle apparaît sous le nom de Quéau. Dans les actes religieux de Ravières, en revanche, elle figurait sous le nom de Cuot.

30.  Dans les actes de baptême, en France, elle signait « Philippe Deboullougne ».

ANNEXE 1 : la famille Ailleboust

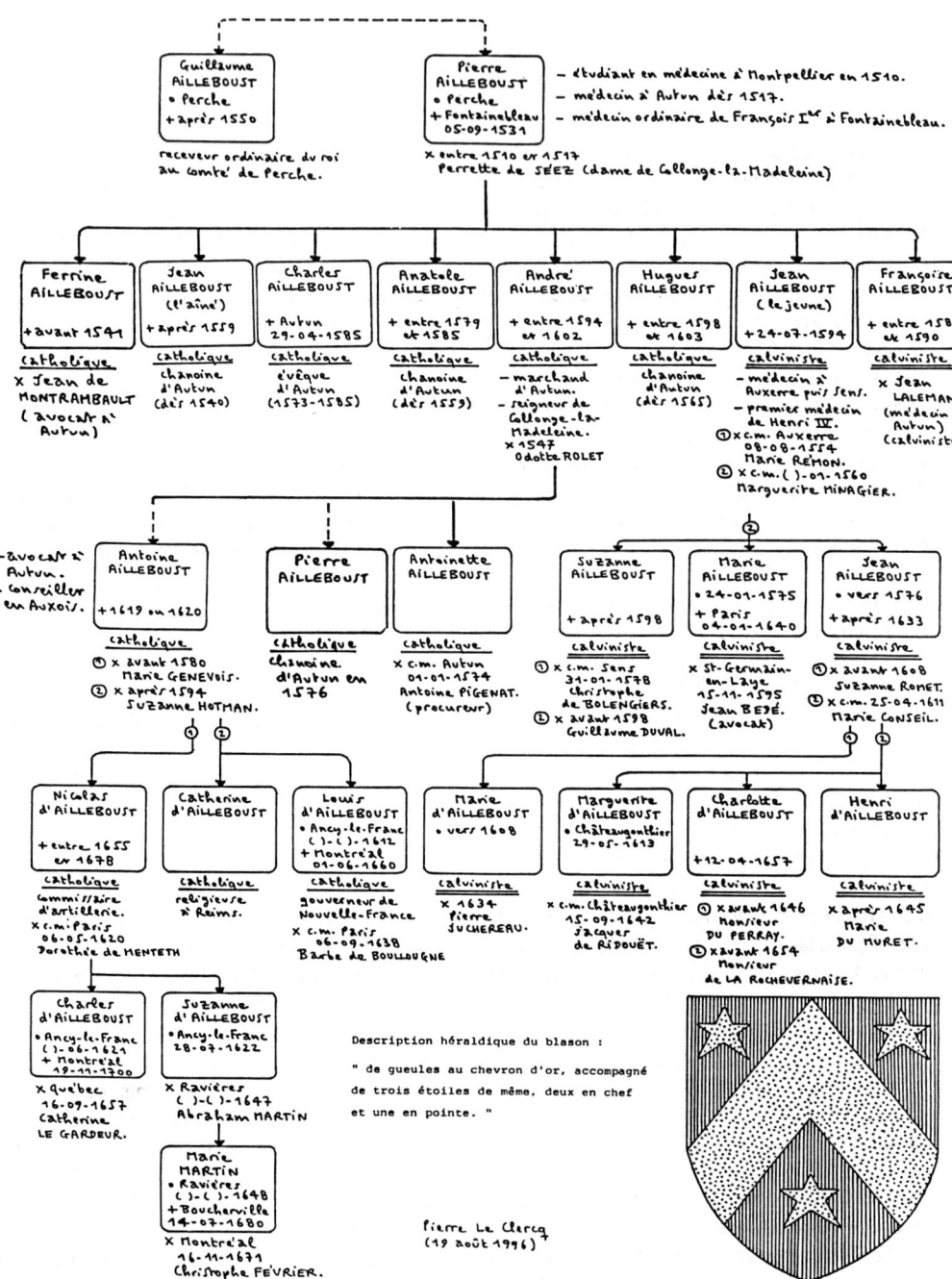

Description héraldique du blason :

" de gueules au chevron d'or, accompagné
de trois étoiles de même, deux en chef
et une en pointe. "

Pierre Le Clercq
(19 août 1996)

# CHARTS AND TEXT COMBINED: A PROPOSED METHOD FOR RECORDING FAMILY HISTORY AND GENEALOGY [1]

Peter D. B. Mérey

How often does one encounter family histories without an index, with little or no regard for sources, or containing family charts that appear to follow some obscure, contorted formula? When it comes to the text, some methods assign a long series of numbers and markings to every family member's name (these are meant to indicate such things as position in the genealogy, the generation number, the child number, the distance from the first ancestor, and so on), but it can become ponderous to read through such a document, constantly having to recall the meaning for each pointer. Then there are family charts with connecting lines and names positioned in a such a convoluted way that one may simply avoid the effort needed to unravel the recorded lineage.

The various guidelines described below aim to avoid the more common shortcomings and introduce an effective standard in chart design and the publishing of family histories.

In compiling a family history and genealogy, one might keep in mind an imaginary reader who, 50 years hence, will be searching the library shelves, selecting dozens of books for research; or it may be a family member browsing through our holdings. Now let us consider the features in our presentation that will prompt that person to select it and then to encourage reading it—for what is the use of painstaking research and all the work put into it, if no one will read it? At the very least, the publication should provide the means for a quick understanding of the recorded information. So an easy-to-follow set of genealogical charts will certainly be of great assistance to our reader.

## Recording history and genealogy

Every family history is made up of stories, experiences, dates and places of events, traditions, recollections and accomplishments.

The challenge is to present this variety of detail in such a way that our imaginary reader can follow it without difficulty. Years of experience in helping others compile their respective histories have resulted in the development of a method that combines the use of text and charts to record family history in an orderly, straightforward manner. The method has been further refined through its presentation and discussion at seminars and speaking engagements.

It provides a means of handling any type of situation, whether it be four marriages, 16 children, cousins intermarrying, widows marrying a second time, or tracing a genealogy from the year AD 1000 to the present. While it is not necessarily a new way of recording information, the method does bring together a set of procedures containing features that are more likely to serve the reader well: clarity, pleasing for the eye to follow, detailed in scope, yet not cumbersome to understand.

## The method

The salient aspect in this method is its combination of the use of family charts (the outline of a genealogy) and historical text (the details), with cross-references throughout acting as guidelines so that the reader is never left to flounder alone.

The goal of family charts should be to record lineages in such a way that their relationship is easy to understand and follow. Charts are the maps pointing the way. Therefore, one should aim for simplicity in their layout, reserving the fuller details for the text. For example, the charts may indicate only the years of birth and death while the accompanying text will also have the day, month and the place names where events occurred. For each generation, the names are positioned on the same line in the charts—never intermixed. To keep the presentation as simple as possible (making it easier to follow), detailed identification numbers are left out from the text.

Shown in the accompanying illustrations are sample outlines of a text and chart [FIGURE 3], and on the following pages are excerpts from a published history [FIGURES 4-5] that illustrate the application of this method. Various features are shown:

**For the charts:**
- date format: day, month (spelled), year, e.g., 29 January 1877 (no intervening commas used);
- the charts have a clear, uncluttered appearance;
- there are no vertical lines drawn between the names of brothers and sisters;
- each generation is placed on one line;
- drawn lines are kept at a minimum, using outside "drop" lines and a triangle to indicate lines of descent;
- the family name is indicated just once rather than repeated with each name;
- use of superscript/subscript numbers to denote several marriages and their offspring;
- cross-references to preceeding and following charts;
- children listed in order of birth;
- "drop" arrows to indicate continuing lines;
- spouses' family names are shown in bold when a new line is introduced.

**For the text:**
- cross-references to the charts (the overview);
- use of the "5-generation I.D.," no other identifying numbers needed;
- from the first ancestor, follow the line of descent for the first child down to the present generation, then continue with the next sister or brother of that first child;
- text format: name, titles, degrees, career, experiences, memberships; date and place of birth, date and place of death, date and place of marriage, name of spouse (if a new line, highlight the family name in upper case or bold), titles, degrees, career, experiences, memberships; name of spouse's father, name of spouse's mother—include mother's family name (e.g., Norma Evans or, in the case of a widow, Mrs. Norma Evans, née Millard), spouse's date and place of birth, date and place of death.

In the text section one may also include additional details on each person such as places of residence, travels, description of accomplishments, using the narrative style to relate family stories, adventures, special events, viewpoints and personality characteristics.

**Family charts—some additional points:**
- assist the reader to be always aware of the location within the genealogy;
- in the case of large genealogies, break up the text into chapters;
- place "guiding posts" atop each page: references to charts and sub-headings;
- the simple I.D. system is entirely flexible; there is no re-numbering required in the case of new members being added;
- concerning the I.D. numbers, only one set of five should be used within each section (there is no need to add one set to another since the connection to the original ancestor is already evident via the charts).

**Other features**

Using this methodology also introduces a particular consistency in style that helps the reader further. Of note is the absence of any convoluted system for identifying each person, or having individual names accompanied by the first names of each ancestor back to the original known progenitor. It seems to serve little purpose to record in the text that a given descendant is the sixth child, or that this person is a member of the seventh generation from the first known ancestor (the charts already indicate such details at a quick glance).

Having to read a genealogical text with identifying numbers or letters attached to each name may lead the reader to either ignore their meaning or find the reading too obtrusive (or boring) to follow. Furthermore, these details add nothing to our knowledge or understanding of a given individual. While it may be that some see these details as useful or interesting (certain genealogical societies even encourage their use), from our reader's point of view the simple and easy-to-follow style may serve one better.

Certainly, some form of identifying reference is needed to assist the reader in following each line of descent. For this purpose the "5-generation I.D." format is suitable. It uses alternating numbers and letters to indicate relationships (Roman numerals I, II, III, IV, upper-case letters A, B, C, D, numbers 1, 2, 3, 4, lower-case letters a, b, c, d, and Roman numerals i, ii, iii, iv), without interrupting the flow of reading. As shown in the accompanying chart and text illustrations, taken from a book published in 1993 [FIGURES 4-5], the more simple system proves to be quite effective.

Overall, the recommended method is fastidious for straightforwardness, for ease of reading, for fast understanding in an age when "time poverty" forces us to overlook or simply bypass what is not well presented. So the user-friendliness of this method will certainly help increase readership.

## Software for genealogy

There is a veritable plethora of genealogical software that will allow one to print out reams of group records, charts or telephone-book style of listings. Each package comes with a variety of features. And, if the intention is to create just such records and listings, then these software packages will certainly be suitable.

But here is a cautionary note. Software is generally created according to a given set of conditions and therein lie its limitations. For example, does it accommodate three marriages? If so, what happens when there is a fourth one? If the program is able to fit 12 children on one page, how does one handle the family of 13? The advantage of computer packages is the automated handling of large volumes of data with great accuracy and speed. But the final printout may not be the one that is intended for publication where layout, styling and data arrangement have to be given particular consideration—ever keeping in mind the needs of our reader.

Each family history can be as unique as the persons making up a family. Therefore it appears unlikely that every possible situation can be included in an automated program. While some may prefer to let the computer set up the charts, for those who wish to have a direct control over the final design, the process of compiling the final text and chart needs to remain entirely open (not automated with constricting options). For this task, our suggestion is to use a desktop publishing software or any similarly structured software that allows full freedom in creativity. Then, every marriage, adoption, lineage, date, first and second (even third) names can all be included as one may wish.

When selecting a software package, therefore, the best guide is provided by your own needs. If you wish to compile a database for quicker access to researched data then a genealogical software package may be appropriate. But, if the intent is to create charts that follow a similar style as shown here, a desktop publishing software is more likely to provide the needed support.

## Conclusion

In outlining the features of the method under review, the intention is to raise awareness of the need to improve the way family histories are being published. A given standard should be followed so that future family histories will be more "reader-friendly" and genealogical charts will avoid layouts that appear more like contorted roadmaps than records of family relationships.

While no one method can be considered to meet every need, the set of guidelines given here has been devised to at least take care of the basic aspects in style, presentation and layout. These have not been arrived at merely on the basis of preferential whim. Through years of research, reviewing many sources, designing family charts and publishing family histories, it seemed that certain features better lent themselves to this purpose: to publish a family genealogy or history containing charts that are easy to follow, a narrative that is informative and a lineage whose description can be readily understood.

## NOTES
1. Portions of this article were previously published in the journal of the Ontario Genealogical Society, *Families*, vol. 35, no. 4 (November 1996), p. 223-230.

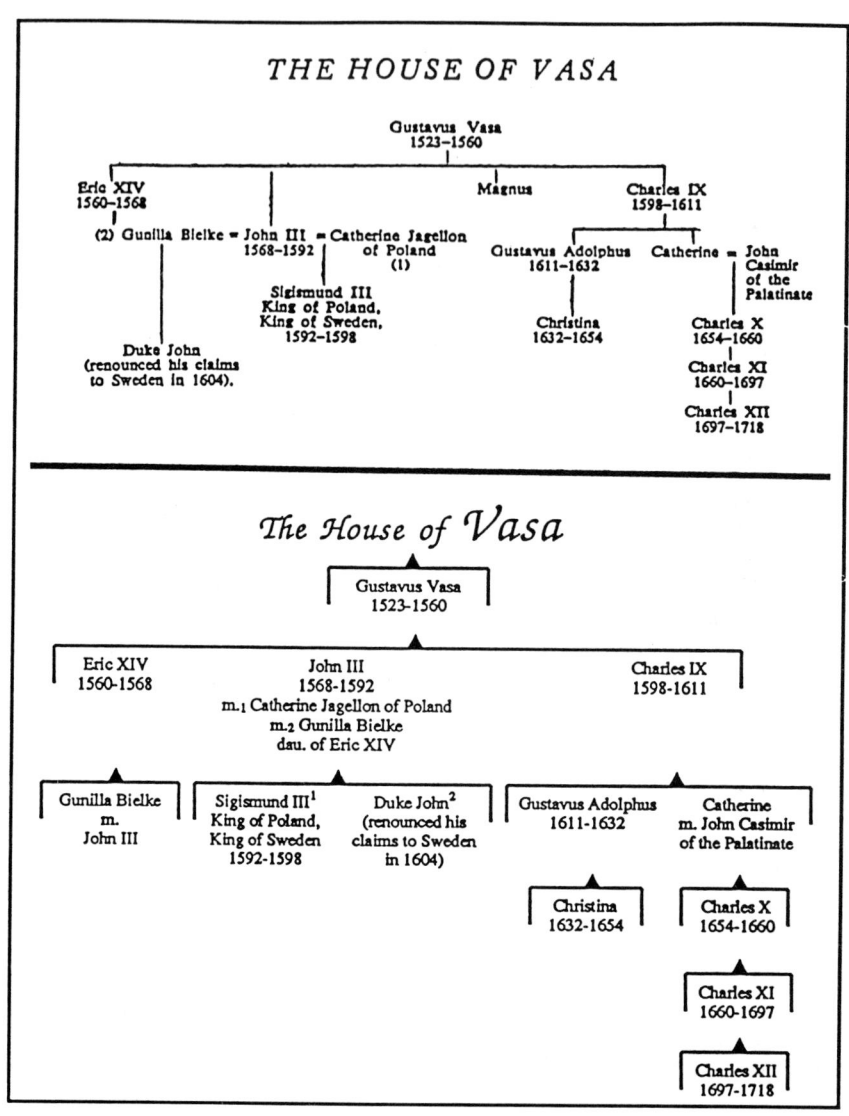

## THE HOUSE OF VASA

Gustavus Vasa
1523–1560

Eric XIV
1560–1568

Magnus

Charles IX
1598–1611

(2) Gunilla Bielke ▪ John III ▪ Catherine Jagellon
1568–1592     of Poland
(1)

Gustavus Adolphus
1611–1632

Catherine ▪ John
Casimir
of the
Palatinate

Sigismund III
King of Poland,
King of Sweden,
1592–1598

Christina
1632–1654

Charles X
1654–1660

Duke John
(renounced his claims
to Sweden in 1604).

Charles XI
1660–1697

Charles XII
1697–1718

## The House of Vasa

Gustavus Vasa
1523-1560

Eric XIV
1560-1568

John III
1568-1592
m.1 Catherine Jagellon of Poland
m.2 Gunilla Bielke
dau. of Eric XIV

Charles IX
1598-1611

Gunilla Bielke
m.
John III

Sigismund III[1]
King of Poland,
King of Sweden
1592-1598

Duke John[2]
(renounced his
claims to Sweden
in 1604)

Gustavus Adolphus
1611-1632

Catherine
m. John Casimir
of the Palatinate

Christina
1632-1654

Charles X
1654-1660

Charles XI
1660-1697

Charles XII
1697-1718

**FIGURE 1**

The two charts titled "The House of Vasa" and "The Leveridge Family" [FIGURE 2] are taken from S. M. TOYNE, *The Scandinavians in History* (London: 1948) and L. TIVY, *Your Loving Anna, Letters from the Ontario Frontier* (Toronto: 1972), respectively. The top half presents the charts as they were published, while the bottom half shows their appearance when using the suggested method. Both are representative of a style commonly found in publications, with various connecting lines and the intermixing of generations; the overall effect is somewhat confusing and the lines of descent not easily followed. By applying the method described in this article, the layout is clearer and relationships can be easily determined. In addition, more space becomes available for adding pertinent details such as full dates or place names, which renders the charts more informative and interesting.

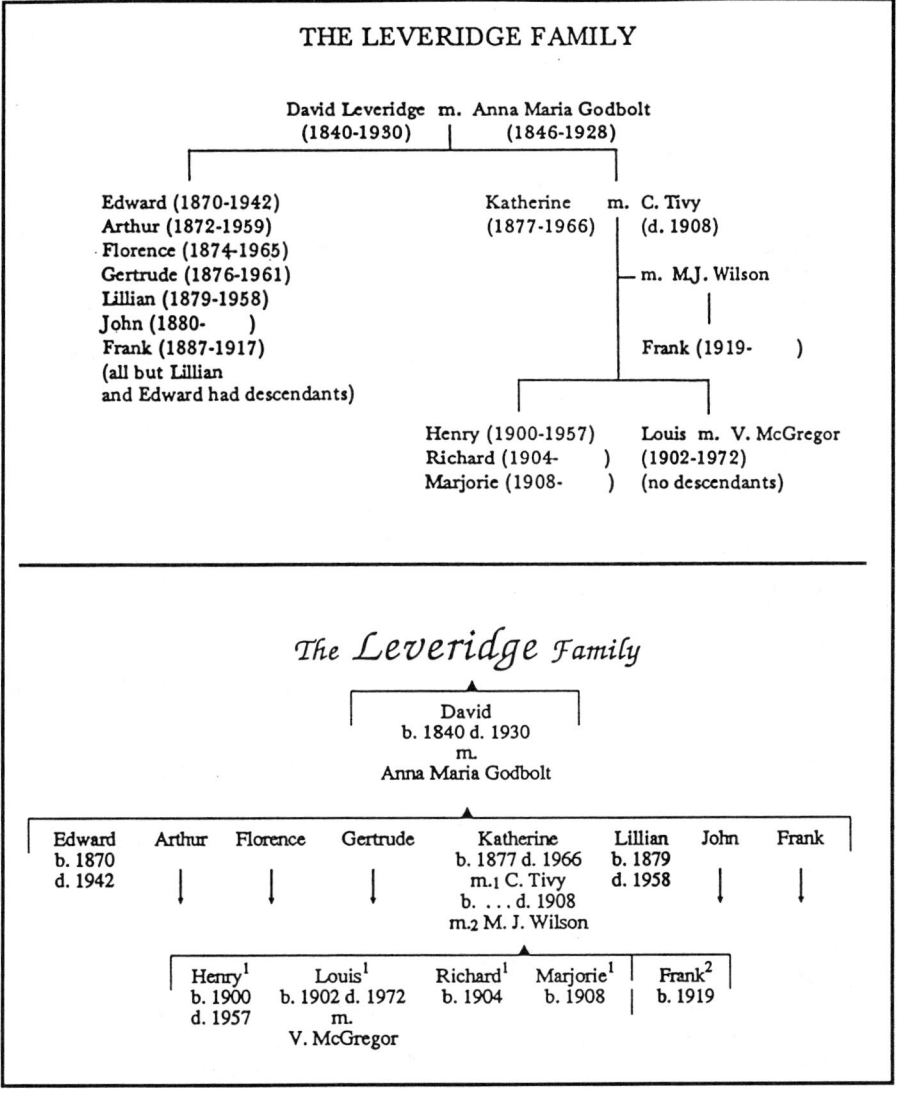

# THE LEVERIDGE FAMILY

David Leveridge  m.  Anna Maria Godbolt
(1840-1930)  |  (1846-1928)

Edward (1870-1942)      Katherine    m.  C. Tivy
Arthur (1872-1959)      (1877-1966)  |  (d. 1908)
Florence (1874-1965)
Gertrude (1876-1961)                 — m. M.J. Wilson
Lillian (1879-1958)                     |
John (1880-    )
Frank (1887-1917)                    Frank (1919-    )
(all but Lillian
and Edward had descendants)

Henry (1900-1957)    Louis  m.  V. McGregor
Richard (1904-    )  (1902-1972)
Marjorie (1908-    )  (no descendants)

## The Leveridge Family

David
b. 1840 d. 1930
m.
Anna Maria Godbolt

| Edward | Arthur | Florence | Gertrude | Katherine | Lillian | John | Frank |
| --- | --- | --- | --- | --- | --- | --- | --- |
| b. 1870 |  |  |  | b. 1877 d. 1966 | b. 1879 |  |  |
| d. 1942 | ↓ | ↓ | ↓ | m.1 C. Tivy | d. 1958 | ↓ | ↓ |
|  |  |  |  | b. ....d. 1908 |  |  |  |
|  |  |  |  | m.2 M. J. Wilson |  |  |  |

| Henry[1] | Louis[1] | Richard[1] | Marjorie[1] | Frank[2] |
| --- | --- | --- | --- | --- |
| b. 1900 | b. 1902 d. 1972 | b. 1904 | b. 1908 | b. 1919 |
| d. 1957 | m. |  |  |  |
|  | V. McGregor |  |  |  |

FIGURE 2

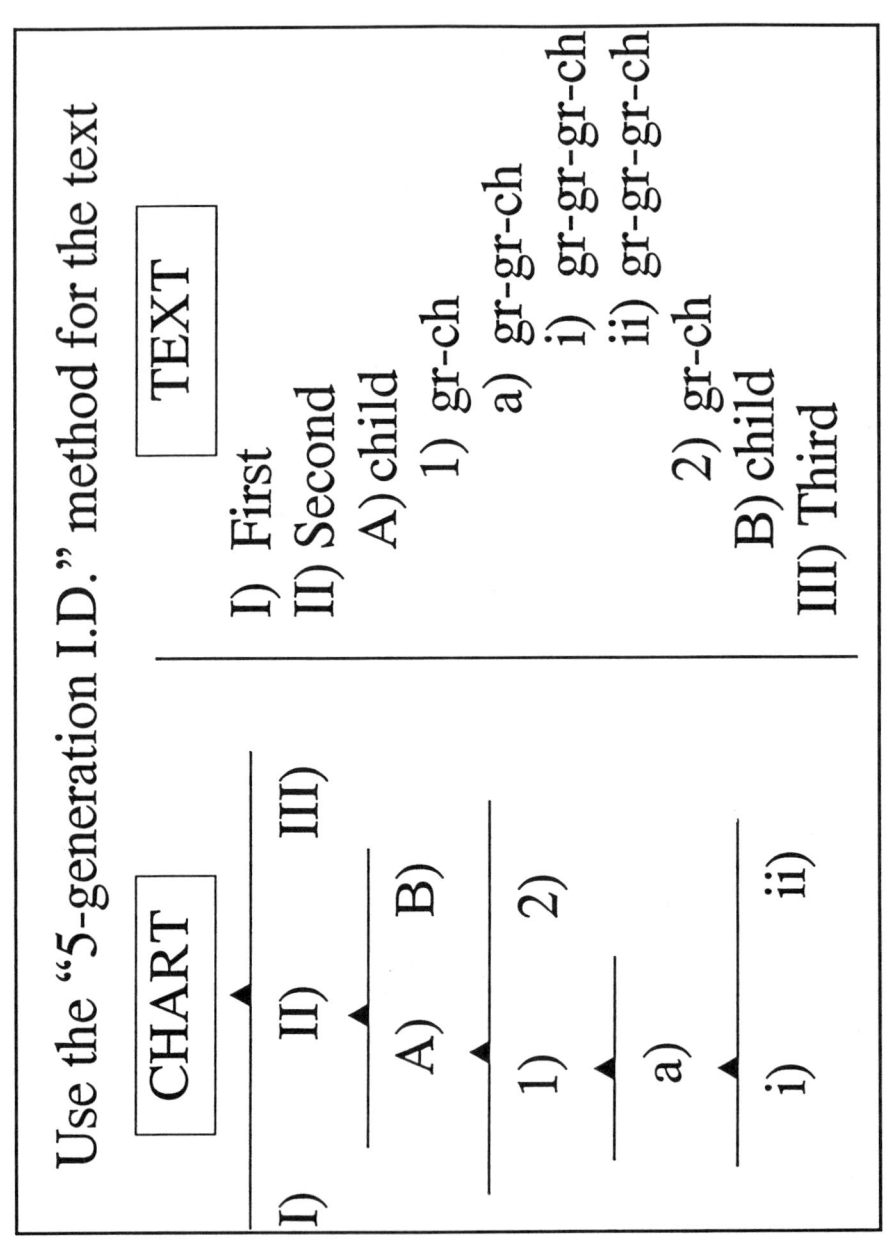

**FIGURE 3**

Outline of the "5-generation I.D." format. Note the cross-references between chart and text. In the chart, members of each generation are recorded on one line only. In the text, different generations are indented and the names carry no other identifying numbers or letters. A published example is given in FIGURES 4-5.

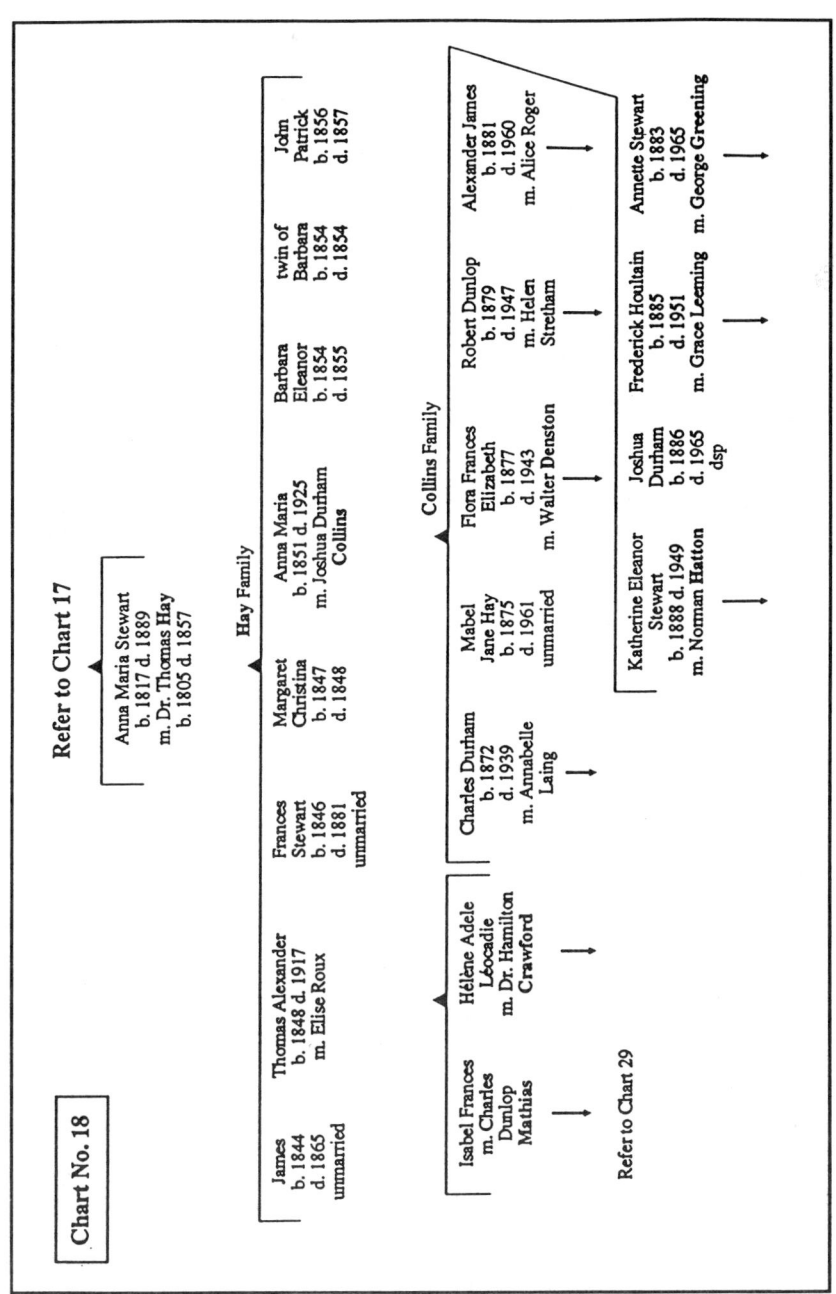

Chart No. 18

Refer to Chart 17

Anna Maria Stewart
b. 1817 d. 1889
m. Dr. Thomas Hay
b. 1805 d. 1857

Hay Family

James
b. 1844
d. 1865
unmarried

Thomas Alexander
b. 1848 d. 1917
m. Elise Roux

Frances
Stewart
b. 1846
d. 1881
unmarried

Margaret
Christina
b. 1847
d. 1848

Anna Maria
b. 1851 d. 1925
m. Joshua Durham
Collins

Barbara
Eleanor
b. 1854
d. 1855

twin of
Barbara
b. 1854
d. 1854

John
Patrick
b. 1856
d. 1857

Isabel Frances
m. Charles
Dunlop
Mathias

Hélène Adele
Léocadie
m. Dr. Hamilton
Crawford

Charles Durham
b. 1872
d. 1939
m. Annabelle
Laing

Collins Family

Mabel
Jane Hay
b. 1875
d. 1961
unmarried

Flora Frances
Elizabeth
b. 1877
d. 1943
m. Walter Denston

Robert Dunlop
b. 1879
d. 1947
m. Helen
Stretham

Alexander James
b. 1881
d. 1960
m. Alice Roger

Refer to Chart 29

Katherine Eleanor
Stewart
b. 1888 d. 1949
m. Norman Hatton

Joshua
Durham
b. 1886
d. 1965
dsp

Frederick Houltain
b. 1885
d. 1951
m. Grace Leeming

Annette Stewart
b. 1883
d. 1965
m. George Greening

FIGURE 4

195

**Chart 18**  *HAY Family* **(continued)**

V) Anna Maria Hay, born 7 October 1851 in Peterborough, died 4 January 1925; married 20 June 1871 at Malone, Ashburnham, Ontario, Joshua Durham COLLINS, son of Dr. Robert Collins of Cookstown, Co. Antrim, Ireland, and Elizabeth, née Dunlop, born in 1839, died in 1927. Their children:

  A) Charles Durham, born 13 June 1872 in Peterborough, died 17 February 1939 in Waterloo; married 2 October 1901 in Dundas, Annabelle Louise Laing, daughter of Reverend John Laing and Elizabeth, née Smith, born in 1876, died in 1962. Their children:

    1) John Laing, born 10 August 1903 in Dundas, died 30 March 1988 in Kitchener; married 3 December 1932 in Ottawa, Helen Irene MacPhail, daughter of Ewen Stewart MacPhail and Julia, née Tuplin. Their children:

      a) John MacPhail, born 17 July 1933 in Kitchener, married 7 April 1956 in Kingston, Mary Myrtle Gollan, daughter of Ian Andrew Gollan and Myrtle, née Leishman. Their children:

        i) Brian Douglas, born 18 February 1957 in Halifax, married 14 September 1979 in Toronto, Leslie Kathleen Thorpe, daughter of John T. Thorpe and Shirley, née Valliant. Their children: Erin Lindsay; Andrea Kathleen; John Alexander Thorpe.

        ii) Elizabeth Marie, born 15 October 1958 in Halifax, married 10 August 1990 in Toronto, Stephen Arthur MATTHEWS, son of Arthur Norman Matthews and Mary Adele, née Chamberlain.

        iii) Patricia Joanne, born 17 August 1965 in Sarnia, married 22 June 1991, David Abel BONFOFS.

      b) Helen Mary, born 25 June 1935 in Kitchener, married 29 September 1956 in Waterloo, David Leonard HAHN.

**FIGURE 5**

The chart [FIGURE 4] and text (above) are taken from E. S. HALL and J. SHEARMAN, *A Sense of Continuity: The Stewarts of Douro* (Toronto: 1993). These illustrate the application of the "5-generation I.D." format, the cross-references between chart and text, and the highlight of family names when a new line of descent begins. Chart 18 indicates its connection to Chart 17 and continuation with Chart 29 (the text also provides the same reference); the drop arrows indicate continuing lines of descent, which are recorded in the text. The information at the top of the text page tells the reader the location of this lineage in the overall genealogy. The identifying numbers/letters for each generation are aligned and indented to show the connection to each descendant. Family names appear in upper case where a new line is being introduced.

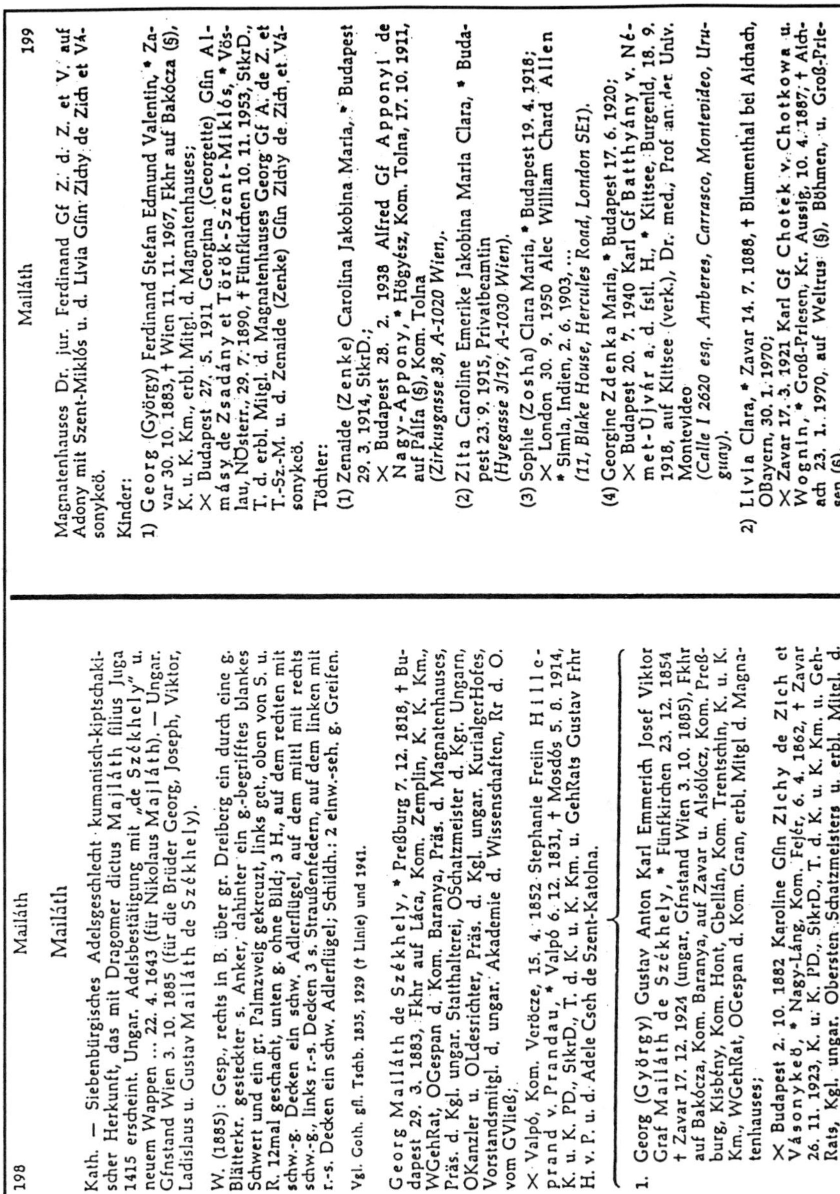

198 Mailáth

## Mailáth

Kath. — Siebenbürgisches Adelsgeschlecht· kumanisch-kiptschaki-scher Herkunft, das mit Dragomer dictus Majláth filius Juga 1415 erscheint. Ungar. Adelsbestätigung mit „de Székhely" u. neuem Wappen ... 22. 4. 1643 (für Nikolaus Majláth). — Ungar. Gfnstand Wien 3. 10. 1885 (für die Brüder Georg, Joseph, Viktor, Ladislaus u. Gustav Mailáth de Székhely).

W. (1885): Gesp., rechts in B. über gr. Dreiberg ein durch eine g-Blätterkr. gesteckter s. Anker, dahinter ein g-begrifftes blankes Schwert und ein gr. Palmzweig gekreuzt, links get., oben von S. u. R. 12mal geschacht, unten g- ohne Bild; 3 H., auf dem rechten mit schw.-g. Decken ein schw. Adlerflügel, auf dem mittl mit rechts schw.-g., links r-s. Decken 3 s. Straußenfedern, auf dem linken mit r.-s. Decken ein schw. Adlerflügel; Schildh.: 2 einw.-seh. g. Greifen.

Vgl. Goth. gfl. Tschb. 1935, 1929 († Linie) und 1941.

**Georg Mailáth de Székhely**, * Preßburg 7. 12. 1818, † Budapest 29. 3. 1883; Fkhr auf Láca, Kom. Zemplin, K. K. Km., WGehRat, OGespan d. Kom. Baranya, Präs. d. Magnatenhauses, Präs. d. Kgl. ungar. Statthalterei, OSchatzmeister d. Kgr. Ungarn, OKanzler u. Oldesrichter, Präs. d. Kgl. ungar. KurialgerHofes, Vorstandsmitgl. d. ungar. Akademie d. Wissenschaften, Rr d. O. vom GVließ;

× Valpó, Kom. Veröcze, 15. 4. 1852. Stephanie Freiin Hille- prand v. Prandau, * Valpó 6. 12. 1831, † Mosdós 5. 6. 1914, K. u. K. PD., StkrD., T. d. K. u. K. Km. u. GehRats Gustav Frhr H. v. P. u. d. Adele Csch de Szent-Katolna.

1. **Georg (György)** Gustav Anton Karl Emmerich Josef Viktor Graf **Mailáth de Székhely**, * Fünfkirchen 23. 12. 1854 † Zavar 17. 12. 1924 (ungar, Gfnstand Wien 3. 10. 1885). Fkhr auf Bakócza, Kom. Baranya, auf Zavar u. Alsólócz, Kom. Preß-burg, Kisbény, Kom. Hont, Gbellán, Kom. Trentschin, K. u. K. Km., WGehRat, OGespan d. Kom. Gran, erbl. Mitgl. d. Magna-tenhauses;

× Budapest 2. 10. 1882 Karoline Gfin Zichy de Zich et Vásonykeß, * Nagy-Láng, Kom. Fejér, 6. 4. 1862, † Zavar 26. 11. 1923, K. u. K. PD, StkrD., T. d. K. u. K. Km. u. Geh-Rats, Kgl. ungar. Oberstem-Schatzmeisters u. erbl. Mitgl. d

199 Mailáth

Magnatenhauses Dr. jur. Ferdinand Gf Z. d. Z. et V. auf Adony mit Szent-Miklós u. d. Livia Gfin Zichy de Zich et Vá-sonykeß.

Kinder:

1) **Georg (György)** Ferdinand Stefan Edmund Valentin, * Za-var 30. 10. 1883, † Wien 11. 11. 1967, Fkhr auf Bakócza (§), K. u. K. Km., erbl. Mitgl. d. Magnatenhauses;

× Budapest 27. 5. 1911 Georgina (Georgette) Gfin Al-másy de Zsadány et Török-Szent-Miklós, * Vös-lau, NÖsterr. 29. 7. 1890, † Fünfkirchen 10. 11. 1953, StkrD., T. d. erbl. Mitgl. d. Magnatenhauses Georg Gf A. de Z. et T.-Sz.-M. u. d. Zenalde (Zenke) Gfin Zichy de Zich et Vá-sonykeß.

Töchter:

(1) **Zenalde (Zenke)** Carolina Jakobina Maria, * Budapest 29. 3. 1914, StkrD.;
× Budapest 28. 2. 1938 Alfred Gf Apponyi de Nagy-Appony, * Högyész, Kom. Tolna, 17. 10. 1911, auf Pálfa (§), Kom. Tolna
(Zirkusgasse 38, A-1020 Wien).

(2) **Zita** Caroline Emerike Jakobina Maria Clara, * Buda-pest 23. 9. 1915, Privatbeamtin
(Hyegasse 3/19, A-1030 Wien).

(3) **Sophie (Zosha)** Clara Maria, * Budapest 19. 4. 1918;
× London 30. 9. 1950 Alec William Chard Allen
* Simla, Indien, 2. 6. 1903, ...;
(11, Blake House, Hercules Road, London SE1).

(4) **Georgine** Zdenka Maria, * Budapest 17. 6. 1920;
× Budapest 20. 7. 1940 Karl Gf Batthyány v. Né- met-Ujvár a. d. fstl. H., * Kittsee, Burgenld, 18. 9. 1918, auf Kittsee (verk.), Dr. med., Prof an. der Univ. Montevideo
(Calle I 2620 esq. Amberes, Carrasco, Montevideo, Uru-guay).

2) **Livia** Clara, * Zavar 14. 7. 1888, † Blumenthal bei Aichach, OBayern, 30. 1. 1970;
× Zavar 17. 3. 1921 Karl Gf Chotek v. Chotkowa u. Wognin, * Groß-Priesen, Kr. Aussig, 10. 4. 1887; † Aich-ach 23. 1. 1970, auf Weltrus (§), Böhmen, u. Groß-Prie-sen (§).

**FIGURE 6**

Sample text from *Genealogisches Handbuch der Gräflichen Häuser*, vol. 9, 1983. The differences between this method and the one under review include the use of "universal" symbols representing events such as birth, death, marriage; the date format consists of numbers only, with intervening periods necessary to separate day and month (but 2. 9. 1949 could still mean either February 9 or September 2); in the identifying format only numbers are used followed by a period, a single bracket or a double bracket (the text indentation further differentiates generations).

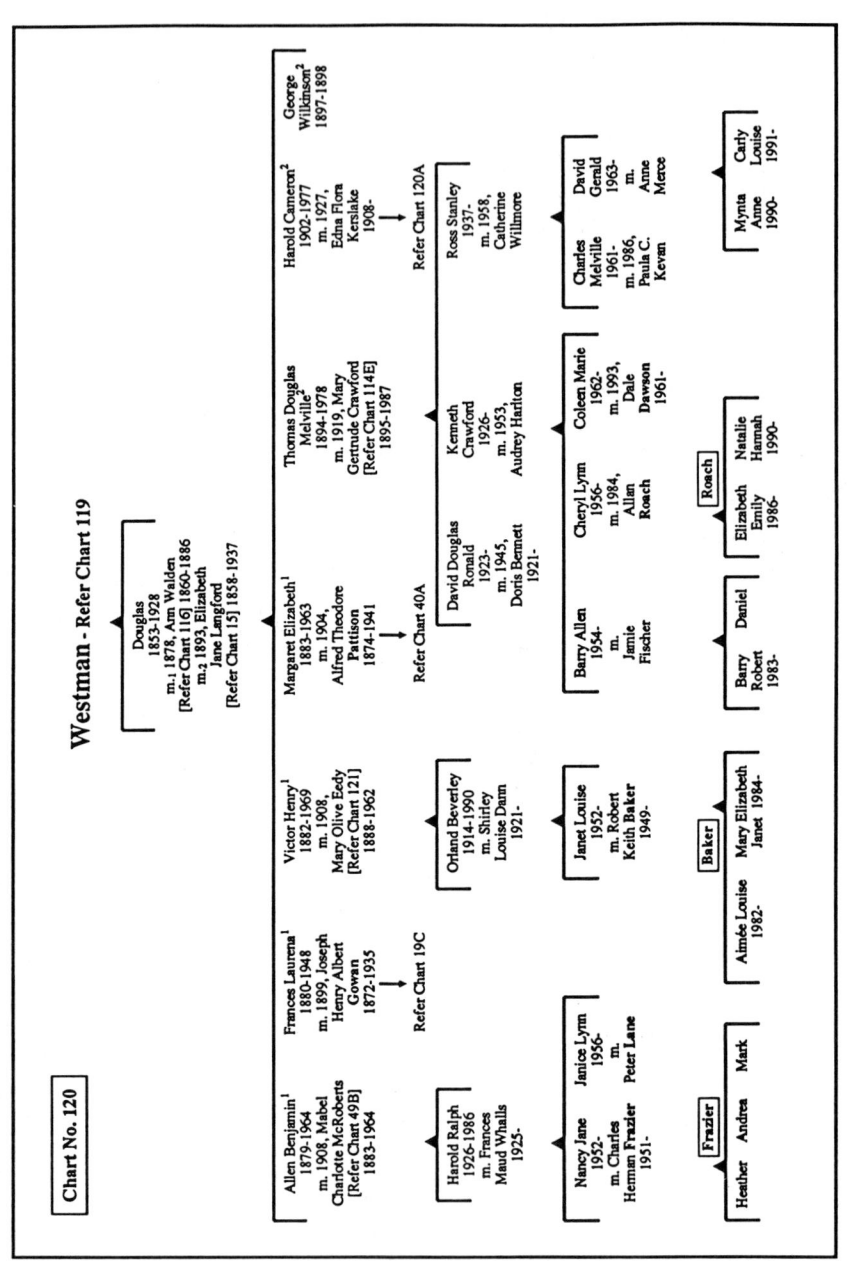

**FIGURE 7**

Sample chart from the upcoming publication, J. E. SCHEIDING, *Langford, Westman and Related Families. Their History and Genealogy* (Toronto: 1997). Part of a genealogy recorded in over 300 charts, it illustrates the number of cross-references given to guide the reader.

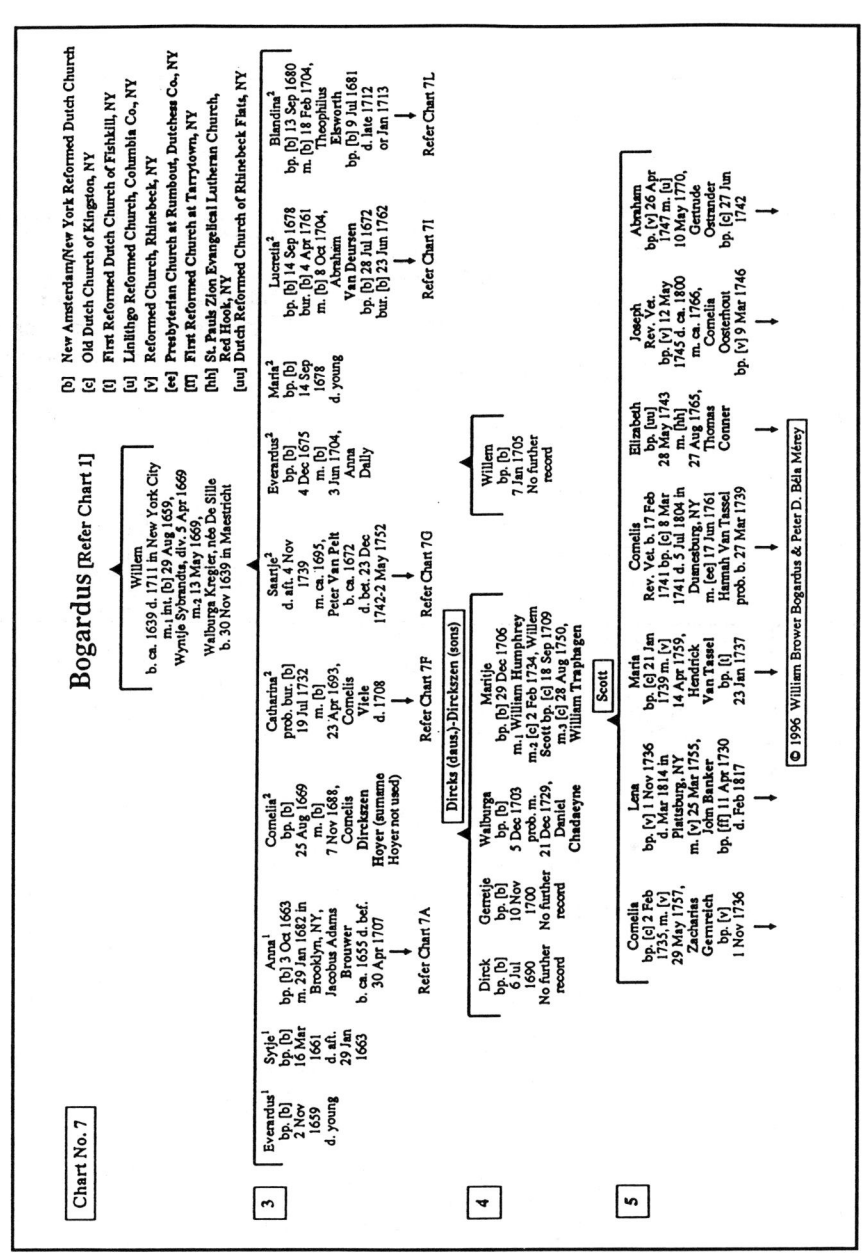

**FIGURE 8**

Sample chart from the recently published work, W. B. BOGARDUS, *Dear "Cousin": A Charted Genealogy of the Descendants of Anneke Jans Bogardus (1605-1663) to the 5th Generation* (Wilmington, OH: 1996). Notwithstanding the considerable amount of data recorded, including references to various church locations, the overall layout still retains balance, a careful order and the ease to understand the relationships.

199

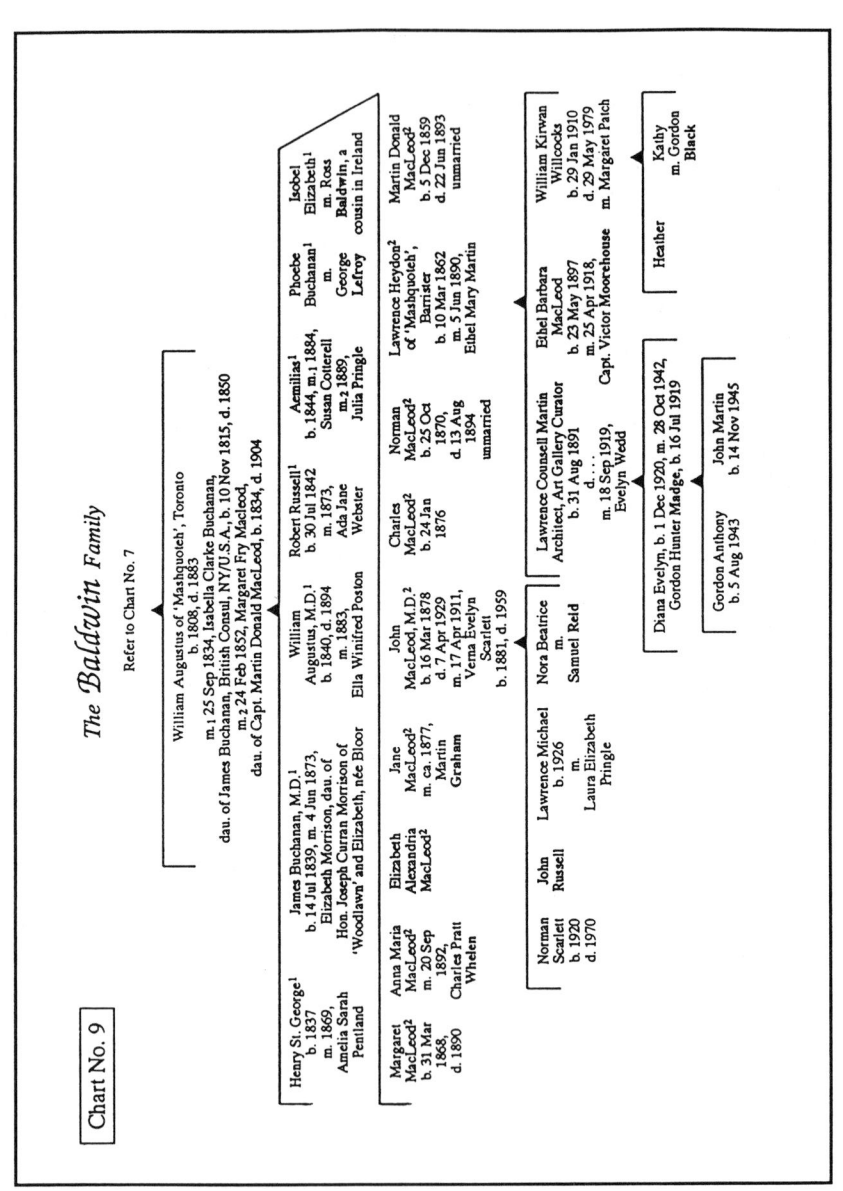

**FIGURE 9**

Sample chart from G. L. SAUNDERS, "Joseph Willcocks—Politician to Traitor," *The York Pioneer*, vol. 85 (1990). Even with the difficulty posed by limited space (5 in. x 8 in.), the chart still contains much detail and handles the challenge of recording 16 children from two marriages.

# CANADA'S LOYALIST "MARK OF HONOUR": HEREDITARY HERITAGE IN 18TH-CENTURY BRITISH NORTH AMERICA

Brenda Dougall Merriman

Canada has a unique hereditary honour that was created 207 years ago. The postnomial designation "UE" means "Unity of Empire" and is borne by thousands of descendants of the United Empire Loyalists who fled the revolting colonies in America in the late 18th century. Unlike other North American hereditary societies based on a mutual ancestral experience (The Mayflower Society, Daughters of the American Revolution, and so on), the UE designation originated with a vice-regal proclamation.

## Who were these Loyalists and how did this happen?

When the American Revolution began to affect the life of every colonist, the majority of Loyalists were overt supporters of the traditions and policies of the monarchy in America. Some men immediately left their families to fight under the British Royal Standard; others bided their time, believing the British would soon quell the disturbance. Some supported the Loyalist cause for more pragmatic or opportunistic interests. "Deeply rooted convictions guided some; momentary circumstances guided others." [1] Even some families were divided. Regardless of motivation, more than 50 Loyalist Corps were raised in the American colonies, as provincial support troops for the British army. American Patriots tried to press the Loyalists into rebel service, imposing fines for noncompliance; they punished those who refused an oath of allegiance to the newly declared republic; they destroyed and seized property. The largest effect of this persecution was to turn even neutral parties into Loyalist sympathizers. Each side viewed the other as traitors.

Fear of roving Patriot gangs made anything resembling a normal life impossible for those who tried to remain in their homes. "Tarring and feathering, and the rail, the intimidation of women and children, the plunder and defacement of property, the maiming of horses and cattle, were worse than war." [2] Eventually they were forced to leave through threats or eviction or military action. Thousands of refugees streamed away from the rebelling colonies, not only after the Treaty of Separation in 1783, but all through the eight years of the war. This paper deals with those who came to the still-British northern colonies of Quebec and Nova Scotia, but recognizes that varying numbers of Loyalists also went to Florida, the West Indies, Prince Edward Island and Newfoundland, and some returned to Britain.

By the end of the war, such British forts and settlements as Halifax, Shelburne, Parrtown on the Saint John River, the Saint Croix River area, Fort William Henry at Sorel, Montreal, and the forts at Carleton Island, Niagara, and Detroit were swarming with homeless refugees, disbanded men from the Loyalist Corps, and the ranks of regular British army soldiers. Every manner of assistance was needed in various quarters—food, shelter, clothing, medical attention, transportation, and essential tools for wilderness farming.

It was the responsibility of "local" Governors John Parr of Nova Scotia, and Frederick Haldimand of Quebec, to oversee the ultimate disposition of these displaced people. This was augmented in 1784 with the creation of a new province, New Brunswick, governed by Thomas Carleton. It is important to note that *this* province, once called Upper Canada and now known as Ontario, was originally an extension westward of the colony or province of Quebec. It received over 10,000 Loyalists in 1783-1784. Lesser numbers were being settled in parts of old Quebec, mainly the Gaspé region and the Eastern Townships (now called l'Estrie). Finally, in 1786, the former commander-in-chief of British Forces, Guy Carleton, was named governor-in-chief of all the British colonies in North America. Foremost among the administrative duties was the allocation of land to the Loyalist newcomers, according to royal instructions first issued in 1783 to all the colonies. The instructions were specific in the amount of acreage to be given, and that the usual administrative fees would be waived.

By 1788 in the "new" western part of Quebec, the amount of land for each Loyalist, his family members, and/or his rank in the service of a Loyalist corps had been satisfactorily defined. Four land boards were established to oversee land allocation; properties were surveyed, assigned, settled, and cultivated, but final title of ownership was to be accorded after the initial commotion and disorder had calmed. It was the *recording* of those privileged land grants, in what became Upper Canada, that helps descendants to identify a Loyalist ancestor. While this appears to be a straightforward matter, the truth is not so simple. It took years for some Loyalists or their children to make the official application for property title. Many died before receiving recognition on a UE list. While alive, their most immediate goal was survival.

During the 1780s the British also set up a commission to hear "Claims for Losses" from the Loyalists, to make some compensation for their lost possessions and property in the American colonies. Hearings were held in London, Halifax, and Montreal. Unfortunately the March 1784 deadline for submitting claims was quite unrealistic for those people in the hinterlands; moreover, news of the Commission sittings did not reach many of these people until far too late. An extension of the mandate until the spring of 1786 made it possible for two commissioners to travel to various settlements in Upper Canada and Nova Scotia to take evidence, thus accommodating many more Loyalists.

In late 1789, His Majesty's representative (Carleton was now Lord Dorchester), in discussion with his Executive Council about the allotment of lands not only to Loyalist heads of families, but also to their sons and daughters, told them:

> ... it was his wish to put a mark of honour upon the families who had adhered to the unity of the Empire and joined the Royal Standard in America before the Treaty of Separation in 1783.[3]

This was to be achieved by each district land board establishing a registry or roll of Loyalists and their children (which would also serve as a basis for potential militia purposes):

> ... to the end that their posterity may be discriminated from future settlers, in the parish registers and rolls of militia of their respective districts and other public remembrancers of the Province, as proper objects, by their persevering in the fidelity and conduct so honourable to their ancestors, for distinguished benefits and privileges.[4]

In his subsequent dispatch to the King in May 1790, Dorchester included his Order in Council along with the form that the district militia roll would take, including:

> N.B. Those Loyalists who have adhered to the Unity of the Empire, and joined the Royal Standard in America before the treaty of separation in 1783, and all their children and descendants by either sex, are to be distinguished by the following Capitals affixed to their names: UE, alluding to their great principle The Unity of Empire.

The initials UE started to be used in land documents relating to the new expansion of Quebec. SUE (son of a Loyalist) and DUE (daughter of a Loyalist) now also became common designations on land petitions, fiats, warrants, and other government paperwork. They did not become routine or frequent notations in early parish registers, as suggested. And as Elizabeth Hancocks, UE, CG, points out, rarely if ever did the Loyalist or his family use the initials with his own signature.[5]

Why then did the UE postnomial designation take special hold in Upper Canada, and not in Lower Canada (Quebec) or the Maritime Provinces? Part of the answer lies in the fact that Dorchester's supreme position as governor-in-chief involved separate commissions for each of the colonies; his authority overruled the lieutenant governors only when he was *present* in one of their colonies. His proclamation of 1789, made in Quebec, may not have seemed as applicable to the far-off Atlantic colonies as to the newly developing portion of Quebec, which would soon be called Upper Canada.

Another part of the answer relates to Col. John Graves Simcoe becoming the first lieutenant governor of Upper Canada in 1791. Simcoe wanted many more new settlers, and his offers of inexpensive large land grants attracted crowds of Americans. He ordered a proclamation in 1795 that required the Loyalists to turn in their previous land certificates or documents for an official deed of title, called a patent. By 1796 the land boards in Upper Canada were kept busy with their district rolls, distinguishing Loyalists from newcomers, who often claimed retroactive loyalty in order to obtain the desirable grants for their children as well. In other words, Simcoe continued to honour the privileges first proclaimed by Lord Dorchester.

In Nova Scotia and New Brunswick, it seems that less attention was paid to distinguishing privileges for Loyalists. Those who settled there did not receive free land for their children. Many discovered that their land "grants" had first been deeded to a few wealthy and favoured men, who were not inclined to issue patents to the Loyalists. A fair number of Loyalist families, who first found themselves in New Brunswick or Nova Scotia, eventually moved on to Upper Canada although they could not claim free land again there.

Sometimes those Loyalists who were in British territory by 1789 are called First Loyalists. Other "categories" of sympathizers have been called:

- **Associated Loyalists:** groups who had served the British cause by assisting refugees, without direct attachment to a regular army regiment;

- **Late Loyalists:** who had not been within the British lines by 1783 for various reasons, but claimed UE benefits when they did arrive;

- **Simcoe Loyalists:** who remained in the United States until Simcoe's 1791 invitation to new settlers; they may have claimed retroactive loyalty, but had not suffered the loss of property, and usually had no evidence of joining the royal standard before 1783;

- **Treasury Loyalists:** who had removed to England during and after the War and were given provisions and assistance there by the Treasury Board; some came later to Upper Canada, where they could not claim additional compensation;

- **Pre-Loyalists:** who left the American colonies before the war began, to reside in Nova Scotia, and therefore did not take part in the fighting;

- **Maritimes Loyalists:** who received a grant in Nova Scotia or New Brunswick, but who later came to Upper Canada, or their children did, where they could not again claim free land.

Women were not considered Loyalists in their own right, although the widows of men killed in action who came to Canada could submit the husband's name to the UE list so their children would acquire free land grants.

This brings us to the definition of a true Loyalist. Several of the above categories were cause for much discussion in the governing circle of Upper Canada. Evidence in contemporary documentation shows that even bureaucratic officials were at times inconsistent in the recognition of Loyalists. As with the Claims Commission, the news of Simcoe's 1795 proclamation to enroll all Loyalists was not comprehensively circulated. The lists created by the district land boards were being changed up until the 1830s with the removal or insertion of names.

We can say that a Loyalist was *not* someone who retained property in the American states after the war, and was *not* a paid soldier in the regular British army. Discharged soldiers who decided to stay in Upper Canada were also given preferential land grants, noted as "military claimants" (MC), but of course their children were not eligible for free grants. In theory, a Quaker and other religious pacifists were not true Loyalists because they could not bear arms. However, many were overt sympathizers, providing practical assistance, and were recognized with free land grants.

In light of contemporary sources, with their sometimes contradictory messages, genealogical authorities agree that a true Loyalist was:

- A person who was in the American colonies before hostilities began on April 19, 1775, who joined the royal standard before the Treaty of Separation in 1783 or "otherwise demonstrated loyalty to the Crown,"[6] who sacrificed homes and/or possessions in the former colonies, and who removed to territory still ruled by Britain, OR

- A Six Nations Indian of the Tyendinaga or Grand River Reserves who served the British

203

cause, and whose migration to this country was under the same circumstances as above.

Associations of descendants of the Loyalists were formed in several provinces after centennial observances in 1883-1884. In 1914, a federal charter was granted to the United Empire Loyalists' (UEL) Association of Canada to represent and unite descendants across our nation, to honour the spirit of loyalty, to preserve, collect, and publish Loyalist heritage. It is the UEL Association that determines who has the right to the initials "UE," a right that has been extended to Loyalists (and their descendants) who came to *any* part of the British territory that became Canada. Regular membership is contingent on (1) providing acceptable evidence of the ancestor's contemporary eligibility for UE status, (2) providing documentation of the applicant's direct-line descent from that ancestor, and (3) the applicant bearing allegiance to the Crown. Affiliate membership can be granted to a descendant who fulfills the regular requirements, but who cannot claim allegiance to the Crown of Canada. This applies, of course, to citizens of other countries, notably the United States, where thousands of Loyalist descendants now live.

Each of the UEL branches across Canada has a Branch Genealogist to whom application is made; the Branch Genealogist forwards the completed application to the Investigating Committee for final review and ultimate acceptance or rejection. The UEL Association, like many other lineage societies, has gone through periods of improving and refining its application procedures to meet today's standards of sound and stringent genealogical presentation. While lineal descent is documented in conventional genealogical fashion from as many sources as possible, it is the identification of the ancestor as a Loyalist that presents the greatest challenge and fascination.

Primary evidence of a Loyalist ancestor may be found in contemporary documents such as successful petitions for land grants, various land and court records, discharge papers from a Loyalist corps or sworn statements from commanding officers, approval for compensation by the Claims Commission, lists of refugees or Loyalist corps muster rolls, lists of Loyalists made at different times and places, or possibly government correspondence. The challenge lies in finding the documents—if they were created, or have survived

—and identifying the "right" ancestor. As already mentioned, names on the district rolls were often removed; several men of the same name compounded the difficulties; fathers and sons and cousins of the same name were sometimes confused on lists; children in one family may have encountered conflicting results with their petitions at different times. The overlap between military and civilian record-keeping presents another obstacle, in locating source material that can be in national or provincial archives, in government papers or private manuscripts, and even in regional or localized repositories. Land granting policy and procedure evolved in complex bureaucratic fashion; over the years, government officials tried to resolve the confusion between military claimants and militia or Loyalist corps service, and separate them from some regular settlers who also tried to claim the desirable UE grants.

Lists are often the first source a family genealogist will consult.[7] If such a list does have an ancestor's name, they are merely starting points in the quest for primary material. If a man's name appears on the District UE Rolls or on the Executive Council UE List (derived from the former after their passage to the central government), this is considered good evidence. So also are names on refugee and invalid lists made at the forts where Loyalists had gathered, and provisioning lists. Muster rolls of the Loyalist corps are another excellent source. The ones that concern us most here are the corps that were affiliated with the Northern (Canadian) Command, and to some extent, the Central Command.

But there are always cautions in "claiming" a name on a list. How can you know, of eight Archibald McDonalds or three John Werts, which one is "yours"? Muster rolls have not survived on a regular sequential basis for every Loyalist unit. Your man may have been transferred, or disabled, before the extant lists were made; he may have joined the company or corps after the list was made. A name on a list is not enough by itself. None of the lists are considered comprehensive for each and every Loyalist.

Claims for losses in personal property and possessions left behind them, or confiscated, were submitted by about 5,000 Loyalists to the British Claims Commissioners in the 1780s. This number is a fraction of the total who fled their former homes, but if a man's claim was approved, it is considered undoubted evidence of his Loyalist status. The minutes of interviews with claimants and supporting witnesses in Montreal and Halifax, with the lists of their losses, including documentary evidence when available, went into British Audit Office records. Researchers can view this material on microfilm at several Canadian sites. Although books have been published containing some of the Audit Office information, the combination that nominally indexes *all* the claims heard by the two commissioners to British North America is Bruce Antliffe's *Loyalist Settlements 1783-1789: New Evidence of Canadian Loyalist Claims* together with the published claims in the *Second Report (1904)* of the Bureau of Archives for Ontario. These two replicate the Audit Office 12 series.

Along this same vein referring to former property and possessions, it is possible to find evidence in records of the American states that a Loyalist ancestor was mistreated, fined, or imprisoned. In this case, it is necessary to know in which state the man lived, and preferably in which community. Some records can be found for the confiscation of goods and property, forfeiture of lands and estates, banishment or proscription notices, and perhaps prisoner lists.

Land records and documents, particularly in Upper Canada, probably constitute the most-used sources for determining a Loyalist ancestor. A crucial finding aid to Crown land grants from the 18th to the 20th century was compiled by the provincial Archives of Ontario, alphabetically indexed by personal names or by township names. This index includes grants made to Loyalists and their children, among many other Crown grants, and tells the researcher that some original sources are available.

If the Loyalist himself did not make a claim for losses, nor appear in court to substitute his original land certificate for a patent deed (and thus be placed on the District UE Roll), he may have formally petitioned the government to substantiate his claim as a Loyalist for a certain piece of property. Accompanying this would be a discharge paper from a Loyalist corps, or perhaps a sworn statement from a former commanding officer, in proof of his service. However, the majority of evidence comes from the petitions of the children (upon reaching the age of 21, or the marriage of a daughter) for their own free 200-acre land grants. These petitioners were required to name their Loyalist father, usually his residence, and quite often, whether he was then deceased. A daughter would also name her husband. Supporting affidavits for identification of the petitioner and/or the eligibility of the father would come from some prominent local official. In one document, the Loyalist and one of the next generation would be identified.

The petitions were annotated to indicate approval or rejection. Government officials seemed mainly concerned with whether the alleged Loyalist's name was on the then Executive Council UE list, and whether the particular petitioner had previously received a grant of land. None of this process went without flaw: occasionally children in the same family found different results, due to the changing UE list. Upper Canada Land Petitions is a microfilmed series of nominally indexed records that are widely available.

Fiats and warrants were documents produced by assorted departments of government administration. Like the petitions, they usually use the initials "UE" and they are contained within their own series of land records. Old land board certificates and location tickets for Loyalists have not been collected in a series of records. They are found, if they exist, in a variety of records series, such as township papers or Heir and Devisee Commission files.

In Lower Canada, some of the same land records can be found—petitions and Crown grants—when previously ungranted land was involved. However, the French seigniorial system of land had been retained after the conquest, which did not please the American Loyalists, who were accustomed to the right of ownership. A few Loyalists moved onto seigniory lands along the banks of the Ottawa River, but the majority went to new territory in the Gaspé and the Eastern Townships. In Nova Scotia and New Brunswick also, petitions for land, maps and descriptions of land grants, and patent deeds are important sources for Loyalist research. And in all places, the extant lists of Loyalist militia corps, refugees, and claims for losses also apply.

Records of the Heir and Devisee Commission in Upper Canada are another worthwhile source for descendants hunting a Loyalist ancestor. The first commission was established in 1797, but it is actually from the date of the second commission in 1805 for which we have surviving individual files. The mandate of the commissions was to clarify land titles in cases where the original

Crown nominee for a piece of property had never received a patent deed. Loyalists (and other settlers) often sold or assigned their claims to a property to another person, perhaps a relative, perhaps not. In some cases, a piece of property changed hands many times before settlement obligations were performed, or before the patent was finally granted. The commission's job was to trace these pre-patent transactions and verify their authenticity up to the person then requesting clear title. In some cases, we can learn of the Loyalist who died without a will or without an assignment to a son and heir; occasionally we learn of the eldest son and heir having left the province.

The inevitable result of the American Revolution was the creation of not one, but two, new countries. On the one hand, we have the American credo of "life, liberty, and the pursuit of happiness," while the Canadian principle of "peace, order, and good government" continues. The American Loyalists came into British territory from every state and settled region that existed at the time, south of our current boundary; they left the generally comfortable homes and businesses it took years to develop; most were forced to pioneer in the wilderness again; some of them were separated for generations from dissenting family members. Now, in this century, descendants on both sides of the Canada—United States border are seeking and appreciating their Loyalist ancestors through the UEL Association. Truly, these are families transcending frontiers.

## NOTES

1.  PATRICIA L. KENNEDY, *How to Trace Your Loyalist Ancestors* (Ottawa: Ontario Genealogical Society, Ottawa Branch, 1971, revised 1982), p. 9.

2.  CHESTER MARTIN, "The Loyalists in New Brunswick," *Papers and Records of the Ontario Historical Society*, vol. 30 (1934), p. 163.

3.  National Archives of Canada, RG 1, L 1, Executive Council Land Book A, 1787-1790; minutes of 3 November 1789; published in *Seventeenth Report of the Department of Public Records and Archives of Ontario, 1928*, p. 68.

4.  *Idem.*

5.  ELIZABETH HANCOCKS, "Resources for Loyalist Research," *in* TRUDY MANN and JAN SPEERS (eds), *Papers of OGS Seminar '84*, Ontario Genealogical Society, 1984.

6.  Article 5.01 A. (I), The By-Laws of the United Empire Loyalists' Association of Canada.

7.  Published lists are readily available, such as WILLIAM D. REID'S *The Loyalists in Ontario: Sons and Daughters of the American Loyalists*, or ESTHER WRIGHT'S *The Loyalists of New Brunswick*.

# DIE AKTION FORSCHERKONTAKTE
Siegfried Mildner

## 1. Darstellung des Problems

Es ist sehr nützlich, wenn man bei der Suche nach seinen Ahnen einen Forscherkollegen findet, mit dem sich gemeinsame Ahnenlinien ergeben (Ahnengemeinschaft), und dieser bereit ist, einen Datenaustausch vorzunehmen. Die Aktion Forscherkontakte (FOKO) ist eine Aktivität der deutschen Arbeitsgemeinschaft genealogischer Verbände (DAGV).

Ein Beispiel um das Problem darzustellen : Der Daniel Weißflog starb 1694 in Zwönitz.

Diesen Weißflog haben in den letzten 100 Jahren, schätzungsweise, etwa 30 Familienforscher, unabhängig voneinander, gesucht, die Daten ermittelt und in ihre Ahnenliste aufgenommen.

Ein organisierter Forscherkontakt soll das in Zukunft vereinfachen.

## 2. Ziel der Forscherkontakte

Ziel ist es, weltweit einen Kontakt zwischen den einzelnen Forschern herzustellen. Es sind oft mit Mühe und erheblichen Kosten viele Daten von einzelnen Forschern ermittelt. Diese Daten sollen nicht nochmals gesucht werden. Die Forscherkontakte sollen nicht dem Zufall überlassen werden. Die Aktion Forscherkontakte organisiert den Prozeß.

Forscher die gemeinsame Ahnen (Ahnengemeinschaft) haben, sollen das erkennen, aktiv den Kontakt mit dem anderen Forscher herstellen und Daten austauschen.

## 3. Methoden der Arbeit

Die Methoden werden erläutert, und über die Ergebnisse wird berichtet.

Die Teilnehmer an der Aktion Forscherkontakte reichen eine Liste, die FOKO-Liste, ein. Diese enthält zu jedem Ahn folgende Angaben :

|  |  | in unserem Beispiel |
|---|---|---|
| 1. | Namen | Weißflog |
| 2. | Religiöses Bekenntnis | ev. (evangelisch) |
| 3. | Staat | D (Deutschland) |
| 4. | Postleitzahl | 08297 |
| 5. | Ort | Zwönitz |
| 6. | Territorium | SN (Sachsen) |
| 7. | Matrikel (Geburt, Heirat, Tod u.a.) | T |
| 8. | Jahreszahl | 1694 |
| 9. | Einreicher mit Anschrift | Dr. Mildner |

Die im Verein von den Mitgliedern eingereichten Daten werden zusammengefaßt, nach Namen und nach Orten sortiert und als Buch oder Diskette veröffentlicht. Dabei beschränkt sich der Verein nur auf die Daten in seinem Arbeitsgebiet. Die anderen Daten kommen im Datenexport zu den zuständigen Vereinen. Andererseits erhält der Verein durch Datenimport die Daten für seinen Bereich.

Eine besondere Rolle spielen dabei der Zentralcomputer und die Mail-Box. Die bisherigen Daten sind in einer CD-ROM erfaßt.

## 4. Ausblick

Die Aktion Forscherkontakte und der Einsatz der Computertechnik sind geeignet, neue Wege in der genealogischen Forschung zu gehen.

Wer einen Ahnen sucht und Ort und Zeit angeben kann, könnte einen Forscherkollegen finden, der schon viele der gesuchten Daten kennt. Durch Forscherkontakt wird eine weltweite genealogische Forschung wirkungsvoller.

Das ist aber ein Prozeß, an dessen Anfang wir erst stehen.

Mein Beitrag soll der allseitigen Verbreitung dieser Methode zum Nutzen der Genealogie, weltweit, dienen.

# THE KERRY PEDIGREES: A WINDOW ON THE HISTORY AND HERALDRY OF WALES

Marian Miles

A Kerry family, whose children I taught some years ago, were in possession of a Kerry pedigree roll, but they knew nothing of its history and had no evidence proving that it related to their own family. I sought, and was granted, permission to research the pedigree and see if I could establish a real connection for them. The information that gradually emerged gave a fascinating insight into several aspects of Welsh history.

The vellum roll measured some 25 cm by 4 m and was in a very distressed condition. The title had all but disappeared but the words "Belihut" and "Belingate" seemed to be there, and at the end the title stated that it was drawn in 1680 by T. Francis. This may have been a "Thomas Francis in Montgomery," who is known to have drawn other pedigrees at that time. The pedigree claimed that the Kerry family traced their line back to the Lords of Kerry in pre-conquest times, but only one date was mentioned, 1598, and this was noted against several people who were not of the family line.

The first few coats of arms (shields 1-4) that head the pedigree relate to the ancestors of Tudor Trevor. He was head of the "Tribe of the March" and was Earl of Hereford, King of Gloster and Baron of Stafford in the 10th century; that is to say, he controlled these lands at that pre-conquest period. The Welsh took the view that if arms are hereditary then arms used by one generation must also be relevant for earlier generations. They can be said to have "attributed" their own later arms to their ancestors. We shall see evidence of this in several cases.

Shield 1 represents the great-great-grandfather of Tudor Trevor. The name-roundel is blank, and, I think, always has been. Tudor Trevor's father is given as the Lord of Gal Bromfield, Maesbrook and Oswestry.

Shield 2 represents the great-grandfather of his mother, whose grandfather was Caradoc Eirich, King of Gloster. These arms are derived retrospectively from Bleddyn ap Maenarch of Breconshire.

Shield 3 represents the father of Tudor Trevor's maternal great-grandmother. The name-roundel shows "King Pel . . ." These arms are given by Papworth for a Morgan family of Monmouthshire.

Shield 4 represents Rhodri Mawr, or Broderick the Great, the last Great King of all Wales, who died in 870. His eldest son inherited N. Wales, and a younger son, Cadell (who died in 909), inherited S. Wales. Cadell was the grandfather of Tudor Trevor's wife Greladus.

Tudor Trevor had three sons and on his death his lands were divided between them. His eldest son, Grenwy (the Welsh "w" is pronounced "oo"), inherited the English titles while the next inherited the Lordship of Bromfield and the third the Lordship of Melverley and Maesbrook. In this way, Welsh Lordships were broken down over generations.

Shield 5 is for Severus, the grandfather of Cyhelyn who married Reingar, daughter of Tudor Trevor's son Grenwy and she is said on the pedigree to have "carried away the Earldom of Hereford." From Severus, Cyhelyn inherited Buellt, Radnor, Kerry and Melinydd, and it is here that the Kerry story really begins. The area to which the pedigree relates is Montgomery (in Wales) and Shropshire (in England).

The arms (shield 6) for the marriage of Cyhelyn and Reingar are a 16th-century style marshalling of arms for a pre-heraldic marriage that brought together the English lands of Hereford and Gloster and the Welsh lands of Buellt, Radnor, Kerry and Melinydd. The son of this marriage was Elystan Glodrudd, born in 933, who is shown on the pedigree as King of Gloster and Earl of Hereford. He married Gwenllia, another descendant of Rhodri Mawr (shield 7). This marriage is represented by another 16th-century style quartering (shield 8). Their son, Cadwgan, is shown as Lord of Radnor, Buellt, Kerry and Melienydd, the titles inherited from his paternal grandfather. There is no sign now of the English titles.

Shield 9, the dexter coat, is that which is recognised as Elystan Glodrudd I and it has been "attributed" back to his paternal ancestor, Severus. The sister of Elystan Glodrudd, Jane, married Lord Cardigan and the present Lord Cardigan still bears these arms.

The sinister coat in shield 9, *Gules, three chevrons Argent*, is for Iestyn, 11th-century King of Galad Morgan or Glamorgan and founder of the Fifth Royal Tribe, whose sister, Eva, was Cadwgan's bride.

The eldest son of Cadwgan was Idnerth and he was probably the last hereditary Lord of Melienydd (temp. William Rufus ca. 1100). His son, Madoc, was Lord of Kerry and he married Jane, a daughter of Crwmbawck, but I cannot find any evidence for the arms (shield 10). He died in 1139 and, once again, the lands were divided between his five sons.

The eldest son, Cadwallan, inherited Kerry; he is said to have founded the Cistercian Abbey of Cwmhir in Melienydd in 1143 and died in 1179. Cadwallan's son, Maelgwn, married his cousin, Sioned, and, as both parties of this marriage descended from Elystan Glodrudd, one might expect this to be reflected in the arms (shield 11)—but in both cases the tinctures are reversed from those associated with Elystan Glodrudd. Other examples of this practice are known to occur. Maelgwn, who was probably the last to be called Lord of Kerry, died in 1197. Over the next century, the control of these lands passed back and forth between the Welsh and the English Mortimer family.

In the pedigree, the reversal of tinctures of the dexter coat of arms continues through the next few generations. The eldest son of Maelgwn was Madoc, who married a daughter of Sir Roger Mortimer, an example of intermarriage between Welsh and English. Madoc was executed in 1212 at Bridgnorth, along with his uncle Howel and others, for killing William de Moid in a border feud. Mredd, the second son, carries this pedigree forward. He was another benefactor of Abbey Cwmhir. The pedigree states he married Ann, daughter of Sir John Skitmore of Kentchurch and shield 12 shows the well-known Skitmore/Scudamore arms, *Gules, three stirrups Or*. There must be some error here as this Sir John Skitmore was alive ca. 1400, over a century later.

So far the pedigree just sets the Kerry line in the context of Welsh history. Now it enters a new phase, where it concentrates on a wide range of people related by marriage and culminating in a set of men all alive in 1598—the only date on the pedigree itself. The descents of each bride's family as well as her forbears are given in some detail.

In the next four generations, all the brides claim descent from Elystan Glodrudd and the normal Elystan Glodrudd I is used for them all, still with the reversed colours to the dexter (shields 13-16).

Madoc married Joyce, who descends from Howel ap Tudor of Mochdre, who was steward of Ceri (Kerry) and Kedewain, probably for the Mortimers (shield 13). Also descended from Howel ap Tudor of Mochdre are the Prys family of Newton, three of whom are shown on the pedigree with the date 1598. One of these descendants, Rees ap David Lloyd, was Esquire to the Body of Edward IV and was slain at the Battle of Banbury in 1469. Madoc's son, David, married Sioned, a cousin of his mother, who also descended from Howel ap Tudor of Mochdre; from Sioned's brother descends another Lloyd family (shield 14).

Their son, a second David, married Llenki whose grandfather was Howel of Kerry (shield 15). From her brother descend the Broughton family of which the last mentioned here was Richard Broughton, who is labelled "one of the Council." Richard Broughton was born in 1524, admitted to Inner Temple in 1568, and served on the Council of the Marches at Ludlow in 1586. He was a founding member of the Society of Antiquaries, and Devereux, Earl of Essex, procured for him the position of deputy judge of Chester. In 1596 the Corporation of Shrewsbury notes "Wine given to Mr. Justice Broughton 6s. 4d.," so one may assume that he was alive in 1598 even though the date is not entered.

The third David, son of David and Llenki, married Elen, granddaughter of Madoc ap Tirbrodir (shield 16). From her brother, Howel ddu, descends Hugh Lloyd of Bettwys, another of the people dated 1598.

The son of the third David was Griff and he married Ales Dwnn, the last of this series of apparently important Welsh brides. Griff was the first to surname himself Kerry and it is with him that we enter the English period.

Griff's wife, Ales, was the sister of David Dwnn, from whom Lewis Dwnn, the Welsh Herald, descends. Lewis Dwnn, born ca. 1550, deserves a little of our attention. He was a Deputy Herald appointed in 1585 by Clarenceux (Cooke) and Somerset (Glover) (acting as Marshal to Norroy Flower) "to record, register and make entrances of all discented, marriages, funerals and Obites of the knights esquires and gentlemen within the principality or the dominions or lordships thereof." One imagines that a Welsh-speaking Deputy Herald was essential! Cooke died in 1592 and Flower in 1588, but Lewis Dwnn continued with his work until at least 1614 and probably until his death in 1616. Lewis Dwnn lived near Kerry, at Garthgellin near Bettws Cedewain, probably at a house called Glanbechan. He prepared many pedigrees, but he was also a poet in the Welsh language. Not unnaturally, the family arms are a matter of record (shield 17).

Griff's son, Jenkin Kerry, is given as "of Worthen," which is a township south-west of Shrewsbury, near the border and on the way to Montgomery. Jenkin Kerry married Ann, a granddaughter of Corbet of Awston. I have found no authority for the arms shown here (shield 18), but I wonder if an error has been made and the arms below should have been in this place. A manuscript in Shrewsbury[1] gives *Or, two ravens in pale proper* for Corbet of Awston.

Jenkin's son, John Kerry, married Marged Lac, a granddaughter of Raff Botvel or Ralph Botfield, ancestor of the Marquesses of Bath. Shield 19, which stands for John Kerry's marriage to Marged Lac, seems to have a Corbet flavour and I cannot trace anything to connect these arms with Lac or Botvel. As I have said, this bride is the granddaughter of Raff Botfield/Botvil/Botville. Several generations later John (Botville), known as John of the Inn (Inns of Court, London), was living 1461-1483 (temp. Edward IV) and his son Ralph was the maternal grandfather of Marged, our bride. This Ralph Botville, or Thynne, as the family became known, was the grandfather of the Sir John Thynne who founded Longleat (the seat of the Marquesses of Bath) and whose son John, knighted in 1603, is given the date 1589 on this Roll.

Another John Kerry, son of John and Marged, married Joyce Semper of Pontesbury (shield 20). Their son Humphery Kerry married Christian Ambler (shield 21). Here the arms appear to be *Barry of four Argent and Sable (or Azure) a canton*(?). A Shrewsbury manuscript[2] gives the canton as *Gules*.

The Kerry family had now entered the period of its greatest prosperity (at least since pre-conquest times). They were living at Binweston, a sizeable property just outside Worthen, where the parish records list many of the family. The house, described as based on a seven-bay hall house, has existed since the 15th century so it is possible that they had been there ever since the move from Wales. It is now a listed building (category II) and was fully refurbished some 12 years ago. The Kerry family lived here for the rest of the period of this pedigree.

George Kerry, son of Humphery, was the first to style himself "of Binweston." This is also the first appearance of the Kerry coat of arms (shield 22) which was confirmed at the visitation of Shropshire in 1569 as *Per saltire Ermine and Azure* with one quartering. This quartering is tricked in the visitation records as Elystan Glodrudd I quartering Elystan Glodrudd II. The arms are very indistinct on the pedigree, but appear to have been intended as the visitation records describe.

In November 1554 George married Ann Oteley, daughter of a distinguished family with their seat at Pitchford in Shropshire. The Oteley arms (shield 22), are well documented and can be seen in several forms at the private chapel at Pitchford today.

Thomas Kerry, the son of George and Ann, was the armiger at the time of the 1623 visitation of Shropshire. He married Mary Hopton, daughter of William Hopton of Churbury, who was Sheriff of Shropshire in 1591 (shield 23). The Kerry arms (dexter) show a complete quarter of Elystan Glodrudd II. Thomas himself was Sheriff of Montgomery in 1618, although it is noted that he had no property in that county.

In these last two shields, as in the painting of all the Kerry arms in the pedigree, there is evidence of muddle and alteration. FIGURE 1 shows how these arms are tricked in the Harleian ms 1396 version of the 1623 visitation and you will see that the arms are given two different interpretations on this one folio. Perhaps there was some misunderstanding of the position of the tinctures of the "per saltire" arms. The accepted form of the one quarter confirmed in the visitations is also shown here. It is interesting to note that in the Montgomery Collection only the Elystan Glodrudd quartered arms are given for Thomas as their Sheriff.

Thomas and Mary's son, George Kerry, married twice and it is his second wife, Elinor Turbridge, who is shown here (shield 24). Their son Edward Kerry married Sara, daughter of Ponsbury Owen of Eaton. The arms for this family, who had the Ponsbury Christian name in several generations, are recorded as quarterly (but not tricked or tinctured), though the first quarter is a lion rampant (shield 25). Burke gives *Or, a lion rampant Gules* for Owen of Albrightly, Co. Salop, so this seems to tie up.

With Edward and Sara the fortunes of the family declined swiftly. In spite of a marriage settlement with Sara's mother, the lands at Binweston were heavily mortgaged and Edward slipped into debt. He obtained a common release on the property, which I believe meant that he broke the entail, and in 1698 the family presented a Private Bill to Parliament in the ninth year of the reign of William III, that is 1697/1698, to secure the portions of the children. By this time I suspect that Edward was very ill because he died in May 1698.

The eldest son, Edward, himself had an eldest son Edward, probably sold Binweston in 1735/1736 for £8,550—soon after the birth of his own son, Edward, in 1734.

So now I had a pedigree of one family with many details of other loosely related families, drawn in the 17th century, but apparently relating to an event in the 16th century, starting in Wales and finishing in England. What was it all about?

At this stage, a much delayed visit to the National Library of Wales produced an amazing stroke of luck. The Library had just received a new purchase—a Kerry pedigree.[3] Examination showed that this was a copy of the same pedigree as I had seen, but this time the title was clear. It *might* be the same as that of the original but this copy, which had been drawn by a Jos. (Joseph) Patrick, was dated 1792. You will remember that the Kerry family had moved from Wales into Shropshire and here, in this later title, we are told why:

> The Pedegree of Edward Kerry Esq. of Binweston In the County of Shropshire, Griffith Kild a man in the Sepp of Kerry, Lost his Lands, and Fled to Binweston.

Griffith Kerry was Son & Heir of David Lloyd of Malgwyn Lord of Kerry Kerry Buellt Melicaydd Between Ich & Wye King of Gloster Baron of Stafford Lord of Radnor Buellt Mitienydd & Gloster & Severus son of Cador Lord of Buellt Radnor Milwydd Kerry & Wigmore Lineally Descended of Belinus Who Builded Belinsgate. Jos Patrick. 1792.

Presumably Griff Kerry needed to remove himself from the sphere of Welsh Law at a time when the disputes between England and Wales were still active. If he had "merely" committed murder, I doubt if he would have been safe at so short a distance from Kerry (15 miles/ 24 km), yet he made no attempt to hide his origin, being the first member of the family to take the surname Kerry.

The reference in the title to Belinus and Billingsgate may have some connection with the Salters' Company with which at least two members of the family, not in the direct line, were associated in the 16th century. Unfortunately the records of the Salters' Company for that period no longer exist.

Comparison of the two versions of the Roll show several significant differences in the heraldry, although the text is probably intended to be identical throughout. The field of the Severus shield (shield 5) has been changed to azure. From shield 6 onwards, retrospective attribution of arms, as practiced in Wales, reaches extremes. The Kerry arms first used in the 16th century have now been carried back to the first mention of Kerry in the pedigree in the early 11th century. In the next quartering (shield 5), it seems that they are loath to part with the *reguardant lion* of Severus and have placed it overall on the Kerry arms. In shields 10 and 17 the azure has become vert. In the last four shields (shields 22-25) quarters 1 and 4 of the dexter arms show a "vert and ermine" version of the Kerry arms.

George Kerry, who married Ann Oteley (shield 22), was probably the first to use the Kerry arms and was certainly the earliest confirmed in the first visitation of 1569. The later visitation of 1623 also confirms one quartering—the quartered coat of Elystan Glodrudd I and Elystan Glodrudd II.

a    b

**FIGURE 1:** The "tricked" arms of Kerry from the visitation
of Shropshire 1623 (ms Harley 1396). (By permission of the British Library).

I think that this caused a lot of trouble for the artist in 1680. Perhaps he got them all wrong the first time and had to redo them and the later paint has partly disappeared. Whatever the reason, the 1680 Roll is difficult to read and the errors have been compounded in 1792. The inclusion of a "vert and ermine" coat in the Kerry quarters may arise from this confusion as I cannot find any other support for it and it is very odd that it should be placed first and fourth quarters anyway.

These muddled quarterings continue to the end of the pedigree. Here an 18th-century style full achievement reverts to the azure and ermine version of the single Kerry coat of arms with three of the early Welsh ancestral arms on the sinister side.

What light does this throw on the reasons for compiling the earlier pedigree and the sole date of 1598? On this I can only theorise at present, but I feel that the story goes something like this.

Griff Kerry kills his man in Kerry and flees to England where he settles at Binweston right from the start. He may have lost all his land in Wales, but he was certainly not destitute and the family makes good over the next few generations and is confirmed as armigerous under the English system in 1569. Here I noted that the pedigree shown at that visitation is sketchy and differs from the later visitation.

At the end of the 16th century, two things happen. Lewis Dwnn is actively researching Welsh pedigrees and Thomas Kerry is going into politics *in Wales*. I mentioned earlier that it is noted in the Montgomery Collection papers that he held no land in that county. So here we have a man who has no land in Montgomery and who is descended from a Welshman who fled the country some generations before. I think it was important for him to establish his Welsh descent to qualify for his position of Sheriff of Montgomery. So Lewis Dwnn sets to work on behalf of his relative. Now the people dated 1598 have a new sort of importance, so I looked more closely at their connection with the Kerrys and each other. Five sets of people were involved, if we include Richard Broughton (who was certainly alive then), and each set relates to a *separate* generation of the Kerry line. It seems to me that these were the *living* sponsors of the Kerry claim to their Welsh descent—each vouching for a different generation based on its link by marriage with their own line.

213

**FIGURE 2:** Comparison of some of the arms that illustrate the two pedigrees.

| Shield Number | 1680 Roll | 1792 Roll[4] |
|---|---|---|
| |  | |

6

8

24

So now I have a pedigree drawn in 1680 built on the work of Lewis Dwnn a century earlier. Why was another copy made a hundred years later in 1792? This later copy has not been extended—it still finishes with Edward son of Edward—the two Edwards involved in the Private Act of Parliament in 1698. I know that there were three further Edwards in the line—the last I have identified was born in 1771. Which of all these Edwards did the scribe of 1792 have in mind when he wrote his title?

From the previous owner of the 1792 pedigree, I obtained a family tree and I was able to use this to establish a line back to the last Edward of the pedigree. From this I was also able to track the siblings of one of the post-pedigree Edwards. He had a younger brother named Dryden who turns out to be the ancestor of my Kerry pupils. But why was the copy made?

The last of the Edward Kerrys was born in 1771 and probably married in 1791/1792. A Joseph Patrick was born in the same year as Edward and, like him, baptized at St. Phillips in Birmingham (now Birmingham Cathedral). They may well have gone to the same school and other evidence suggests that both families were artistic.

Did Joseph Patrick paint this new pedigree as a wedding present for his friend? Did his friend Edward then give the old and tatty 1680 pedigree to his artistic little brother, then aged 8? I am not likely to be able to prove or disprove this, but it rounds the story off nicely!

So what can we learn from this that is relevant for this Congress dealing with the effects of migration? A need for those who migrate to record all the details they can for their families. A need for those dealing with Welsh records to remember the peculiarly Welsh habit of retrospective attribution of arms. A need for all who study armorial records to beware of the changes that can arise due to faulty copying of damaged or misunderstood records, and the need to be aware that any document found may not be the original, however impressive it may be.

**NOTES**

1.  Ms 4360.

2.  Ms 2795.

3.  National Library of Wales, ms 23219G.

4.  By permission of the National Library of Wales, ms 23219G.

**APPENDIX 1:** The main line of the Kerry pedigree

| | | Shield No. |
|---|---|---|
| Cyhelyn ap Ifor ap Severus    m. | Reingar da Grenwy ap Tudor Trevor | 6 |
| Elystan Glodrudd    m. | Gwenllia da Enion ap Owen ap Howel dda ap Rhodri Mawr | 8 |
| Cadwgan Lord of Radnor, Buellt and Kerry    m. | Eva, sister of Iestyn King of Galad Morgan | 9 |
| Idnerth Lord of Radnor, Buellt, Kerry and Melienydd    m. | Gwervyl | |
| Madoc, Lord of Kerry    m. | Jane Crwmbawck | 10 |
| Cadwallan, Lord of Kerry    m. | ? | |
| Maelgwn, Lord of Kerry    m. | Sioned (cousin) | 11 |
| (1. Madoc) 2. Mredd    m. | Ann Skitmore (Scudamore) | 12 |
| Madoc    m. | Joyce | 13 |
| David    m. | Sioned | 14 |
| David    m. | Llenki | 15 |
| David    m. | Elen | 16 |
| Griff Kerry    m. | Ales Dwnn | 17 |
| Jenkin Kerry of Worthen    m. | Ann Corbet | 18 |
| John Kerry    m. | Marged Lac | 19 |
| John Kerry    m. | Joyce Semper | 20 |
| Humphery Kerry    m. | Christian Ambler | 21 |
| George Kerry    m. | Ann Oteley | 22 |
| Thomas Kerry    m. | Mary Hopton | 23 |
| George Kerry    m. | (2) Elinor Turbridge | 24 |
| Edward Kerry    m. | Sarah Owen | 25 |
| Edward Kerry | | |

1. *Per bend sinister Ermine and Sable a lion rampant Or.*
2. *Sable a chevron between three spearheads Argent.*
3. *Argent a wyvern's head erased Vert holding in its mouth a hand couped Gules.*
4. *Gules a lion rampant and a bordure indented Or.*
5. *Gules a lion rampant reguardant Or.*
6. 5 impaling *Quartely, first as 1, second as 2, third as 3, fourth as 1.*
7. *as 4.*
8. *Quartely, first as 5, second as 1, third as 2, fourth as 3.*
9. 5 impaling *Gules three chevrons Argent.*
10. 5 impaling *Azure a wolfe (?) courant Argent.*
11. a) *Or a lion rampant reguardant Gules* impaling.
    b) *Sable three boars heads couped Argent.*
12. *11a* impaling *Gules three stirrups Or.*
13-16. all *11a* impaling *5.*
17. *11a* impaling *Azure a wolfe rampant Argent.*
18. *11a* impaling *Azure (?) on a pile in bend Argent a (bird) Sable.*
19. *11a* impaling *per fess Sable and Argent two (birds) in pale counterchanged.*
20. *11a* impaling *Or on a bend Sable (?) three Gold annulets.*
21. *11a* impaling *Barry of four Argent and Sable (?) and a canton (?).*
22. Kerry Quarterly impaling *Argent on a bend Azure three garbs Or.*
23. Kerry Quarterly impaling *Gules a lion rampant Or.*
24. Kerry Quarterly impaling *Argent in fess a masoned bridge Gules.*
25. Kerry Quarterly impaling *Or a lion rampant Gules.*

# THE GENEALOGY OF THE PROPHET MUHAMMED AND THE ROYAL HOUSES OF THE MIDDLE EAST, WITH EMPHASIS ON THE HASHEMITE (ALAWAITE) KINGDOMS [1]

Hussain al-Mousawi

## Quraish, Hashem and the Prophet

Genealogy played an important part in Arab culture as the basic social structure within which stories from the past and other manifestations of its collective memory intermingled. Every individual wanted to be sure that the tribe to which he belonged was an honourable one being connected with the great names of the past. In about AD 800, Ibn al-Kalbi, established an Arabic genealogical system of which late 19th-century Western scholars questioned the validity, but which modern scholars now accept as being a true reflection of genealogical facts. Using that system the Arabs, with their strong interest in ancestry, linked traditional Arab genealogies with those of the Bible from Adam to Ismai'l (the oldest son of Ibrahim). In its genealogical list the Bible recorded Ismai'l's sons as they became "the heads of twelve tribes." They are "Nebejoth, Kedar, Abdeel, Mibsam, Mishma, Dumah, Massa, Hadad, Tema, Jetur, Naphis, and Kedmah" (Chronicles 1: 28-31). "Those were the ancestors of twelve tribes and their names were given to their villages and camping places" and they "lived in the territory between Havillah and Shur to the east of Egypt on the way to Assyria" (Genesis 25: 16,18).

In this paper, we will discuss the historical background of Prophet Muhammed's descendance from the biblical Prophet Ibrahim and we will present a general idea on the ruling dynasties in the Middle East descended from the Prophet in ancient, recent and present times. We will focus on Morocco, Jordan and the Shia'h Ismai'li Muslims Imam, Aga Khan. Unless quoted, the biblical terms used herein are Arabic: Ibrahim for Abraham, Ismai'l for Ishmael, Ya'koob for Jacob, I's'haq for Isaac, Esa for Jesus, Basmah for Mahaleth and so on. [2]

Ismai'l, eldest son of Ibrahim gave his daughter, Basmah, in marriage to Esau, son of his brother I's'haq. "Esau's sons were Eliphaz, Reuel, Jeush, Jalam, and Korah." "Eliphaz became the ancestor of the following tribes: Teman, Omar, Zephi, Gatam,

Kenaz, Tunna and Amalek." "Reuel became the ancestor of Nahat, Zerah, Shammah and Mizzah" (Chronicles 1: 35-37). The obvious Arabic features in these names would seem to indicate that a good number of Arabic tribes were descended from I's'haq and not just from Ismai'l. Arab scholars have noted that, upon dying, Ismai'l designated his brother I's'haq as his heir.

Arab scholars regarded Adnan (the 19th great-grandfather of the Prophet Muhammed) as being a direct descendant of Ibrahim through his son Ismai'l. The Kura'n says: "As Ibrahim and Ismai'l were raising the house's foundation, [they said]: Our lord accept this [Shrine] from us for you are the knowing and the hearing. Our Lord make us Muslims (surrendering to your will) and of our descent a Muslim nation" (S. 11: 127, 128). The Prophet Muhammed said: "God chose Ismai'l from the sons of Ibrahim and from the sons of Ismai'l the Quraish and from Quraish the Bani Hashem." This saying proves that all prophets genealogically, were cousins and belonged to one family tree from Muhammed upward to Esa, Ya'koob, I's'haq and Ismai'l and are all associated with one founder Ibrahim. This saying could also link all three monotheistic religions, Judaism, Christianity and Islam, along with other Ibrahamite monotheistic religions (the Sabians, for example) somewhat like the rings of a chain.

However, Arab scholars have identified 12 different groups (in numbers and in names) for the ancestry of the Prophet Muhammed from Ma'ad to Ismai'l. Some scholars link the lineage of Ma'ad to Ismai'l's son Qaydar and others to Nabit. The number of names varies from six to 40. Al-Tabari contends that a certain genealogist told him that some Arab scholars had memorized 40 ancestors from Ma'ad to Ismai'l quoting Arabic verses as evidence, and that he collected these names from the People of the Book (Jews and Christians). He states that the genealogist "dictated these names to me and I wrote them down." The above number of names (40), from Ma'ad to Ismai'l, when added to the number of names (20), from the Prophet Muhammed to Ma'ad is 40 + 20 = 60. If Ismai'l can be dated to 1800 BC and the Prophet Muhammed's birth was in AD 571, then the time between the Prophet Muhammed and Ismai'l is, 1800 + 571 = 2,371 years. Measuring this span of time (2,371 years) against the above total number of names (60), makes this figure more acceptable, keeping in mind that time scale and memory could be an important factor.

## Hashem the Lord of Mecca

In Mecca, the tribe of Jurham had exercised control over the Ka'bah. This control passed from Jurham to Khuza'ah, but they were prevented from exercising it by Qussay (grandfather of Hashem and third great-grandfather of the Prophet Muhammed), who brought his supporters (Quraish) to settle in the area round the Ka'bah. He gave land close to the Ka'bah to the more important supporters who came to be known as (Quraish al-Bitah), while less important (Quraish al-ZZawahir) were settled at greater distances. The meaning of Quraish's name seems to have various interpretations. It has been interpreted as supporters or loyalists. It was given also to the ancestor of either Fihr or al-Nadr. Some suggested that Quraish's name means "The Little Collection" while others associated it with the control and the organization of the Ka'bah. However, the meaning of Quraish's name remains mysterious. It is perhaps more ancient and complicated than what has been presented would indicate.

Hashem is the founder of the Hashemites of today, the grandson of Qussay and the great-grandfather of the Prophet Muhammed. The nickname "Hashem" was not used in his father's time. The family was then called Abd al-Munaf his father while Hashem's real name was Amr. The nickname "Hashem" was never given to anyone before him, a mark of his unique and outstanding qualities. The name perhaps relates not just to social but also to religious realities. After his father's death, Hashem succeeded to the office of Mecca and became the chief master of Quraish. He began looking after the Ka'bah by providing food and drink to the pilgrims of the Holy Place. He was extremely generous and kind. Hashem used to break bread (Arabic: Hashem al-Khubz or Kasr al-Khubz) with his own hands to feed the poor and the hungry. As we have said, Hashem's name seems to have been both a social and a religious one. Perhaps it was associated with the practice of "breaking the bread," which was prevalent in early Christianity. Hashem was also a politically and commercially skilful person who had a strategic vision that has had a far-reaching impact on Arab history in its entirety. He established treaties with the Romans, the Persians, and Yemen, guaranteeing immunity for the Quraish that allowed them to travel to those countries for business and helped them to create wealth. It is said that Hashem was the first to regulate the movement of trade by instituting the two annual caravans known in the Kura'n by Rihlatu al-Shita' wal-Ssayf—the commercial land journeys of the winter and the summer (the winter journey was to Yemen and the summer one to Rome and Persia, with Mecca becoming the transit station). Hashem died in Gaza, which was known in Arabic history as Gazzet-Hashem (Gaza of Hashem). After Hashem's death, his son Abd al-Muttalib took over his father's office, and carried on his activities. After the death of Abd al-Muttalib, his son Abu-Talib succeeded to the same office. Hashem passed his name and qualities on to his sons and to his great-grandsons the Prophet Muhammed and Imam A'li, who then endeavored to change not just the Arab world, but the entire world.

## The Prophet Muhammed

The Prophet Muhammed, founder of Islam, is descended directly from the biblical Prophet Ibrahim [TABLE 1]. He was born in AD 571 in Mecca. His father, Abdullah, had died before he was born, and his mother, Aminah (bt. Wahab b. Munaf b. Zhrah, from the lineage of Kilab), died when he was six years old. He was brought up by his nanny, Halymah al-Sa'dyyeh, and was cared for, first by his grandfather Abd al-Muttalib, then by his uncle Abu-Talib, Imam A'li's father. At the age of 25, Muhammed was employed in the commercial activities of Khadija, his future wife. From their marriage was born a son, al-Kasem (who died in childhood), and a daughter, Fatimah, by whom the descent of the Prophet was continued through her two sons al-Hassan and al-Hussain, their father being A'li b. Abu-Talib, direct cousin of the Prophet.

Obviously one cannot escape both historical and religious aspects when discussing the Prophet Muhammed. In this section we will answer a question that was raised by some regarding the religion of the Prophet and his family prior to

Islam. Did the Prophet Muhammed and his family adhere to some kind of monotheistic belief prior to Islam? The answer is yes, but the discipline on which it was based is not very clear. It obviously entailed great respect for Moses and Jesus Christ and was probably close to the Christian Order of the Circumcision, followers of James, Christ's brother. There is historical evidence that Muhammed's ancestors worshipped God much along the lines of traditional biblical beliefs.

Arabia was not isolated from the two religions of Judaism and Christianity. Since Ibrahim, the Bible is full of events that took place in Arabia in very ancient times. As the Arabs are Semitic, the Bible is in fact a reflection, not just of a religion, but also of Semitic social traditions that are deeply rooted in the Arab traditions of today. From Ibrahim and Ismai'l to Sulaiman and the Queen Balqis of Sheba (Yemen today) down to the birth of Esa, the Arabs have made a great contribution to these religions. With the Three Wise Kings and their Arabian gifts (Myrrh and Frankincense), they paid homage to the newborn Christ. The journey of St. Paul to Arabia in the 1st century is another example of the exchange between Arabs and Christians.

At the age of 12, Muhammed accompanied his uncle Abu-Talib on a visit to Syria. On their way, they visited the Christian monk Bahira (also known as the Gorgeous), who warmly welcomed his guests into his monastery and gave them generous hospitality. This warm welcome seems to indicate that the monk had a special relationship with Abu-Talib or his family. It is said to have been this monk who discovered signs of a prophet in the child Muhammed, and told his uncle to look after him. Arab historians noticed that in one of his early business visits to Yemen, the Prophet met with the bishop of Najran, with whom he entered the church and recited the Christian evening prayer (Ssalaat-ul- Ghuroob al-Masihiyeh). It is said that Waraqah b. Nofel, nephew of Hashem, great cousin to the Prophet and a Christian Priest, told Khadija (Muhammed's wife) that Muhammed's experience as a prophet was similar to that of Moses as recorded in the Bible. During his office, Muhammed befriended Arab Christians and signed treaties of coexistence with them. Muhammed himself never doubted that he shared with Jews and Christians the same beliefs and one God. The Kura'n says: "All those who believe in God and  the  day of Judgement [such as] Jews,

Christians and Sabians and those who do righteousness are rewarded by their Lord" (S. 11: 62).

Muhammed received his divine call in AD 610. He began to proclaim Quraish, the oneness of God, the moral responsibility towards God and the Day of Resurrection. Also, Muhammed's aim was to change the social system and make the Arabs a unified nation believing in one God. He delivered to the Muslims the Kura'n, which is the word of God transmitted to the Prophet through the angel Gabriel. It is also known as al-Kitaab (the book), which unites it to other kutub (books) of God that were delivered to prophets before Muhammed. Muhammed also launched a campaign ridiculing the idol-gods, always affirming the oneness of God.

During the pre-Islamic era, Arab pilgrims went to Mecca every year to pay homage and worship God and several other idol-gods, al-Laatu the Sun, al-Uzza  the symbol of might, Manat Goddess of fortune, and al-Hubal al-A'ala, Hubal the highest. Quraishs were angered by the new religion, and decided to kill Muhammed, and torture his followers. He advised some of his followers to seek refuge in Ethiopia, and asked for the Christian Ethiopian king's protection.

In AD 622 Muhammed fled Mecca for Medina. This marks the start of the Muslim calendar, and the beginning of Muhammed's religious and political centre, then the capital of the Muslim world. In 630 Muhammed returned to Mecca after a peaceful agreement with the Meccans. He entered into the Ka'bah and destroyed all the idols, then he dedicated the Ka'bah only to God and declared Mecca the holiest city of Islam. The pillars of Islam are five: Ssalaat (prayer), Zakat (charity), Hajj (pilgrimage to Mecca), Ssaum or Sseyaam (fasting) in Ramadan and Shahadeh (confirmation of the oneness of God, and that Muhammed is the messenger of God—Arabic: Ash-hadu a'n-la-Ilaaha i'lla-llah, Wa a'sh-hadu anna Muhammadan Rasul-ellaah). To believe in Islam is to believe in God, his books, his prophets and the Day after.

From 636 Islam spread to Palestine, Syria, Mesopotamia (Iraq), Egypt (642), Persia (651), North and Northwest Africa, Spain, Sicily (715), India (1030), and it reached up north to Central Asia, Northwest China. Later, Islam spread down south to Indonesia and Malaysia by the ancient routes of commerce and through business travellers and sailors.

The Prophet Muhammed died in AD 632. On the basis of his age and his friendship with the Prophet, Abu-Bakr was selected as first successor Caliph immediately after the Prophet's death. According to Arab Scholars, there appears to be two different opinions about the Prophet's succession. Some believe that he did not leave clear instructions regarding his successor, while others believe that the Prophet actually appointed his cousin A'li as his successor at Ghadir Khumm and clearly highlighted this issue. What does matter, however, are the events that took place after the death of the Prophet and which prove that a serious defect had occurred in his succession. First, the question of succession created serious friction in the body of Islam between those who thought that A'li was the legitimate person to become the Caliph, known as Shia'tu- A'li (A'li's supporters), and those who thought otherwise and who are known as Sunnis (Sunnah: loyal to the conduct of the Prophet). Second, the tragic events that followed totally influenced Islamic history. Only one Caliph enjoyed a natural death, the other three being killed in a most dramatic way.

Abu-Bakr ruled for only a short time, dying two years after his succession. U'mar, who was elected as Caliph in 634, ruled ten years before being assassinated in 644. U'thman was elected the same year and was killed in 656 by revolting soldiers returning from Egypt. That same year A'li was elected Caliph, but had opposition on two fronts: from A'isha, widow of the Prophet who blamed him for killing her brother U'thman, and from Mua'wiyeh (governor of Syria), who was not loyal to A'li. A'isha fought against A'li in a battle called Harb al-Jamel (the war of the Camel) because A'isha was riding a camel. A'li's and Mua' wiyeh's army engaged in the al-Sseffyn battle. To save lives, however, both parties decided to negotiate a truce during which A'li was assassinated in 661. The assassination of A'li caused the further division of Islam into three sects, Sunnis, Shia'hs, and now Kharijis (Arabic: Sunnah, Shia'h and Khawarij). Because it disliked the negotiations undertaken with Mua'wiyeh, the Khawarij party assassinated A'li.

With A'li's assassination, the way was paved for Mua'wiyeh to establish himself as sole Caliph, ruling his Omayyad Empire, that extended from Northwest China to southern France. After A'li's assassination, al-Hassan, his eldest son, became the head of the Hashemite now Alawaite House.

He managed to coexist with Mua'wiyeh, who died on 18 April 680 and was succeeded by his son, Yazyd, the succession question becoming an issue again.

Al-Hassan, however, was mysteriously poisoned and died in AD 670 during the lifetime of Mua'wiyeh. Shia'h's finger points to Mua'wiyeh as being behind this poisoning. Al-Hussain, the second full brother of al-Hassan, succeeded his brother and became the head of the Hashemite. He managed to coexist with Mua'wiyeh, but not with his son, Yazyd. Al-Hussain, supported by all the House of the prophet, decided to reestablish the Caliphate under the Hashemite house in Kufah (Iraq). He sent his cousin Muslim b. A'qil to organize the loyalists, but Muslim was arrested and was executed by Ubayd-ullah b. Ziyad, governor of Kufah. Although he was told about the fate of Muslim, and the failure of the movement in Iraq, Al-Hussain refused to retreat and continued his march with his small group, mainly of his own family. On the way, he was intercepted by Ubayd-ullah's troops near Karbala. He fought with his small number of supporters, but he and his family were outnumbered and slaughtered on 10 October 680. His two sons A'li al-Akbar, A'bdullah (infant), his nephew al-Qasem (son of al-Hassan) and his half brother al-Abbas all were killed. Only one son, A'li zain al-A'abideen, was saved because of his illness. Hussain's head and those of others were severed from their bodies and sent to Damascus, as proof of death for Yazyd. The rest of his family, mainly women, were taken to Damascus as prisoners of war. Thus the House of the Prophet suffered tragedy from their own fellow Muslim Arabs. It was the greatest tragedy ever to shake and tear apart the entire Arab and Muslim world.

The above events have also influenced the distribution of the Prophets descendants throughout the Arab and the Islamic world. From al-Hussain, two main lines of beliefs and dynasties were derived: Shia'h Imami, descendants of his brother al-Hassan (the Idrisi of Morocco, Libya, Tunisia, Spain) and Shia'h followers of his own descent: the Ismai'lis, and Shia'h Ithna'sharis (twelvish) from Ismai'l and his brother Mousa, son's of Ja'afar al-Ssadik, second grandson of al-Hussain. Genealogically, however, we have to note that Hussain married Shahnaz, daughter of the latest Persian King. Therefore, after Hussain, the Prophet's lineage is linked with the Persian royal lineage through Hussain's wife, mother of the fourth Imam Zainal A'abideen.

In 750 the Omayyad dynasty was overthrown by the Abbasid. Although the Abbassids were close cousins to the Prophet, they inflicted worse treatment to the children of the House of the Prophet Al al-Bait than the previous dynasty. They established their centre at Baghdad (Iraq) and the first Abbasid Caliph was Abdullah, known as al-Saffah the butcher. In 756 in al-Andalus (Andalusia, Spain), a fleeing Omayyad prince from Syria established an independent European Arab state. By 935, however, the Abbasid Empire had completely disintegrated and, from 1258, several dynasties ruled in the Middle East until the 15th century. Then the Ottoman Turks took over the entire Arab world until the early 20th century. The Islamic centre of power shifted for the fifth time, now to Constantinople (former Byzantine capital) in Southeast Europe.

In Mecca the Hashemite continued to occupy the attention of the people who kept selecting them for their leadership. They managed to overcome all measures of repression and restrictions imposed on them by different Islamic governments and survived there till the 20th century. Whenever there were grievances or important social or political matters, people normally turned to them for consultation and leadership and to stand up to the established order if necessary. They became the best representatives of the people's interests. Because of their readiness to express public concerns and support public causes, people trusted them. This trust became a dynastic tradition and their responsibilities expanded. They included looking after social, religious, scientific and educational matters, which led to the establishment of great institutions of knowledge and science. They were addressed as Sayyid or Sharif. Although the title Sayyid was mainly given to the descendants of al-Hussain and the title Sharif to the descendants of al-Hassan, both titles could be interchanged between descendants of al-Hussain, or al-Hassan. It is a given title, not an acquired one. Some of them use the title Sayyid followed by al-Mousawi, al-Hashimy, al-A'lawi or al-Hassani and al-Hussaini al-Ja'fari. These titles are found in most eastern parts of Arab countries, Persia, the Persian Gulf and around the east (Mesopotamia) and southern parts of Mediterranean, along its North African Coast from Egypt to Morocco. In some countries, for example, Israel, Palestine, Jordan, Lebanon and Syria, descendants of the Prophet are known by their own nucleus units such as al-Kawakibi, al-Dajani, al-Rababia'h, al-Milkawiyeh, and al-Ssamadiyeh. People by tradition know them and call them Sayyid or Sharif to show respect for the House of the Prophet. It should be noted that the titles Sayyid/Sharif (Lord/Noble descendant from the House of the Prophet) should not be confused with similar common titles such as Sayyid/Sharif which are equivalent to Mister/landlord or notable member of the community. Some ruling houses adopted such titles, which had nothing to do with descent from the Prophet, to boost their own social and political status.[3]

## The dynasties descendant from the Prophet Muhammed

The Prophet has said: "All the sons of one mother trace themselves back to an agnate, except the sons of Fatimah, for I am their nearest relative and their agnate."

### The ancient dynasties

**Lineage of al-Hussain:** (Central Asia) Tabaristan 860-, (Arabia) Persian Gulf Oman and Bahrain and Yemen (from 894 to 944). North Africa the Fatimi Empire (from 909 to 1171).

**Lineage of al-Hassan:** (Morocco), Shia'h Idrisi of Fez, (Spain) Malaga and Algesiras (Hamudis branch of Idris of Fez from 788 to 922).

### The recent dynasties

- Kingdom of Hijaz, the last king, A'li b. al-Hus-sain b. A'li (1925)
- Kingdom of Sybya, the last king, Muhammed b. A'li al-Idrisi (branch of Idrisid of Fez, Morocco) Kingdom of Syria, the first and last king, Faisal I b. al-Hussain b. A'li (1926)
- Kingdom of Tunisia, the last king, Reshad al-Mahdi (1957)
- Kingdom of Iraq, the last king, Faisal II (1958)
- Kingdom of Libya, the last king, al-Hassan al-Ridha (1969)
- Kingdom of Yemen, the last king, Muhammed al-Bader Sayful-Islam (1962)

## The contemporary dynasties

- Kingdom of Morocco under H.M. King Mulay al-Hassan II (A'lawi line from al-Hassan b. A'li + Fatimah).
- Hashemite Kingdom of Jordan under H.M. King Hussain (al-A'un line from al-Hassan b. A'li + Fatimah).
- The dynasties of the imamate of the Shia'h Ismai'li under H.H. Prince Karim al-Hussain (Fatimi from al-Hussain b. A'li + Fatimah). [4]

## Moroccan dynasties

In 640 Morocco joined the Islamic Empire after the arrival of the Islamic leader U'qbah b. Nafe'. In spite of some difficulties, Islam became the official religion of the country. Morocco, prior to Islam, was influenced by Jews and Christians, but they were not regarded as professing Judaism and Christianity. However, they were regarded as having prepared the ground for the adoption of Islam as a monotheistic religion. The Berbers also have contributed to the consolidation of Islam through the great theologian Ibn Tumart of the Atlas. In 788 the Moroccans gained their independence under Idris I (788-792), who was the son of Abd al-Kaamel, son of Hassan II. It is said that he fought in Kerbala beside his uncle al-Hussain (son of al-Hassan, son of A'li + Fatimah, daughter of the Prophet Muhammed). The Idrisi who were Shia'h Imami became kings and leaders of Libya, Tunisia, Sybya (A'syr, South Arabia, on the West Coast), Malaga and Algesiras in Spain. Muhammed al-Nafs al-Zakeyah, Idris I's brother was ancestor of Falili Sharifs, who rules Morocco today. Idris became the first national saint and ruler of Morocco.

In 786 in Arabia, at Fakh, near Mecca, a confrontation took place between the Al al-Bait party and the Abbasid state. The forces being unequal, the Al al-Bait party was defeated and, those still living, butchered. Idris, son of Abd al-Kaamel, escaped to Morocco, where the Aouraba Berbers, knowing his origins, welcomed him. He consolidated his relations by marrying a lady from that tribe. Because of his noble descent and high personal qualities, the tribes of Aouraba, Telmicen, and south Bu-Regreb made him their chief and sovereign. Idris I was assassinated, probably by an emissary of the Abbasid Caliph Haroun al-Rashid. He was succeeded by his only son, Idris II, who established his new capital at Fez in 809.

Fez became one of the most important spiritual centres of Islam. In 1062 the Idrisi were succeeded by several dynasties: the Mohads (1062-1147), the Merinids (1147-1158) and Sa'diyyn in 1517. In 1666 at Fez, the founder of the Alawaite dynasty that is ruling over Morocco today, Mulai Mohammed, ascended to power and liberated and unified the country. Mulay Muhammed died in 1672. He was succeeded by his brother Mulay Ismai'l (1672-1727), the restorer of the Moroccan armed forces and liberator of Moroccan territories. Having formed the finest cavalry in the world, he gave Morocco long years of peace and prosperity. In 1682, at the château de Saint-Germain-en-Laye, Louis XIV and the ambassador extraordinary of Moulay, Ismai'l Hadi Muhammed Tamim, signed the first treaty of friendship between France and Morocco. During this period, Arabs and Jews expelled from Spain settled in Morocco and the country has since flourished. This period was known as a Renaissance in Morocco's history.

By 1700 the Moroccans had regained control of many coastal towns that had previously been in Portuguese hands. Through three centuries, they had to fight for their independence and freedom. Early in 1904, Morocco was divided between France and Spain, with the former receiving the larger area. In 1911 a German gunboat was sent to the Moroccan port of Agadir to provoke the nationalists against the French, but negotiations resulted in an agreement that France could continue her control over Morocco, in return for concessions elsewhere for Germany. In 1920, Moroccans fought for their independence and drove the Spanish forces out of Morocco. In 1926, France and Spain jointly attacked Morocco and regained their influence on the territory. By 1942, during World War II, American forces occupied Morocco and the country was used as a supply base and as a meeting-place for the Allies.

## King Muhammed b. Yousef V

From 1929, King Muhammed acted as guardian of Moroccan national integrity and sovereignty. Contrary to previous rulers who had accepted the French protectorate, his view was that the time had come for a transition period from the Morocco of yesterday to the modern free state of today.

King Muhammed reigned for all Moroccan people regardless of race or religion. In 1940, during World War II, King Muhammed V refused to apply the anti-Semitic laws that targeted Jews although asked to do so by the French (Vichy) government. From time immemorial Morocco had protected Jews, who were under the personal care of the sovereign. In Morocco, the Jewish quarter has always been near the royal palace.

In 1943 the al-Istiqlal (independence) Party was founded and submitted its manifesto to the king. The king believed in the justice of his cause and that he would finally triumph. After long unrest in Morocco, King Muhammed V was forcibly deported from his country on August 20, 1953 by the French and forced to live in exile in Corsica, Madagascar, and then in Tahiti. With him were his two sons Maulay Abdullah and the Crown Prince Maulay Hassan. On November 1, 1955, at the château de Saint-Germain-en-Laye, in the pavilion of Henry IV, the total independence of Morocco was proclaimed. King Muhammed V and his family could now return to their motherland and, under his leadership, a new Morocco was born. It is impossible to understand the history of modern Morocco without reference to King Muhammed. In 1957, Morocco regained control of the rest of the country from Spanish occupation. In the same year, on December 7, the king formed his first government.

In 1960, King Muhammed V visited most of the al-Mashreq al-Arabi (eastern Arab countries), where he also visited the holy city of Mecca, the land of his ancestors. It was as if, when he was biding farewell in the Ka'ba and the Mausoleum of the Prophet, he was biding farewell to the world as well. In the following year, on February 16, 1961, King Muhammed died just one year after his visit to the Holy Land. In the Arab world, his death was regarded as the loss of a great Arab national leader. But he left behind a determined nation and a man who continued his great work, H.M. King Hassan II [TABLE 2].

## H.M. King Hassan II

H.M. King Hassan was born in Rabat on July 9, 1929. As a child H.M. was first educated in the palace. He studied Islam with his teacher, Si Muhammed al-Kesbi, and to him H.M. used to recite—often in the presence of his father—verses of the Kura'n. H.M. spoke French fluently from the age of two, due to Mrs. Deville, his governess, who also became his French tutor. He eventually specialized in law.

H.M. was seven years old, when on the day of E'id al-Adha (the feast of sacrifice), in 1936, he was crossing the court in front of the palace, heading to the throne room. A number of notables ran up to kiss his hand. When he joined his father, he took him aside and whispered to him gently: "My son . . . the loyalty of the people to our family is of a spiritual and moral order. It cannot be expressed by the kissing of hands."

At the age of 14, during World War II (1943), at Afna near Casablanca, H.M. King Hassan II was with his father King Muhammed V at a dinner in his honour with President Roosevelt of the United States. The guest list was: British Prime Minister, Winston Churchill, the American president's personal adviser, Harry Hopkins, Colonel Elliott Roosevelt, the son of the president and Captain John D. McRea, naval attaché at the White House. At that dinner, Roosevelt promised that Morocco could become an independent country according to the principles of the Atlantic Charter and that, after the war, the politico-economic situation of human society there would be recognized. After this interview and as a result of these promises, King Muhammed V was encouraged to lead the Moroccan people on the road to independence. At this early age King Hassan witnessed an important turning point in the history of his country and after World War II in 1949, H.M. served a term as naval officer on the *Jeanne d'Arc*.

In 1961 H.M. King Hassan II succeeded his father and, in 1962, proclaimed: "our constitution guarantees to the citizens the following freedoms and rights: freedom of opinion, of assembly, and of expression in all its forms. Freedom of movement within the kingdom, freedom of political and trade union association. All citizens have an equal right to education and employment. Both sexes possess equal political rights, and members of the House of Representatives enjoy parliamentary immunity." On December 12 he stated: "Both the Jewish and Christian religions are accorded full liberty." These are "the religion of the book" permitted by Islam. They are not only permitted—we are expressly encouraged to listen to their prophets.

On H.M.'s 60th birthday, Maurice Druon said: "some people had first predicted that King Hassan II's reign would be short-lived . . . but we are celebrating his 60th birthday and 28 years of this rule. His achievements are due largely to the perfect marriage, nature and character between him and his country." He "like his people, has a gift for knowledge, bravery, and dreams. This descendant of the Prophet, and hence of an oral civilization and culture, educates himself by listening as well as by reading." Hassan II, he said "inspired in the arts a style which brings together tradition and modernity, and which gives to the Morocco of today the appearance which will keep for many centuries. He has founded an impressive number of institutions, one of the greatest being the Academy of the Kingdom. Education is one of his major preoccupations, an education which is open to the world." When he inaugurates a dam "he will have discussed its location and capacity with hydrologists and engineers." This king, he said, "will remain in the memory of all as a great irrigator."

Today Morocco is one the United Nations' important members and has relations with most countries in the world. It is very active in Arab world issues as well as in African ones.

H.M. Hassan II has two sons: the Royal Crown Prince Sydi Muhammed and Prince Maulay Rashid. He also has three daughters: Princess Lala Maryam, Princess Lala Aasmat and Princess Lala Hasn'a. He also has three grandchildren: Maulay Idriss and Lala Sukayna, son and daughter of Princess Lala Maryam and Maulay Yazid, son of Princess Lala Aasmat.

### Kingdoms of Hijaz, Iraq, and Jordan

Mecca's history is closely linked to Quraish and the Prophet Muhammed. At the beginning of this section, we briefly presented the changes in the religious and the political status of Mecca prior to Islam and after Islam. During the Omayyad period, Mecca came under direct control of the ruling centre in Damascus. By the end of the Abbasid period, the pilgrimage became unsafe; the state became weak and disintegrated.

In 964 Ja'far al-Musawi (from the line of al-Hassan) ascended to power as Emir of Mecca to restore order and control the Hajj. He was the first to establish an independent Principality of Mecca. In 969, when the Fatimi took over Egypt, they acknowledged the al-Musawi Dynasty over Mecca. The new Emirs made their own appointments and showed a tendency for independence and to have their own features, separate from the rest of the Islamic world. Two incidents illustrated this tendency. In 976 Mecca refused to pay homage to the Fatimi Caliph, and in 1011

Abu-'l-Futuh instated himself as Caliph against the Fatimi one. However, the al-Musawis' and the Fatimi's relations never developed into a serious confrontation. The end of the Fatimi period witnessed also the end of the al-Musawi dynasty. Al-Musawi are descendants of Musa bin Abd b. Musa b. Hassan II b. Hassan b. A'li b. Abu-Talib + Fatimah.

In 1171 the Ayubis succeeded the Fatimis and exercised their direct authority over Mecca. In 1200 Sharif Qatadah, from the same lineage of al-Mousawi, seized power and established a new dynasty of Sharifs who continued to hold the Meccan Emirate.

In 1241 descendants of Sharif Qatada began to quarrel over the Emirate. The Rasuli of Yemen (1228-1454) took this opportunity to control Mecca and keep and the Qatada family. In 1500 Mecca came under the control of the Mamelukes of Egypt, but from 1514-1517 Sharif Barakat and his son Numai turned against the Mamelukes and sided with the Turks. In 1517 Sharif Barakat visited Cairo to recognize the Ottoman sovereignty over the Holy City, and the Ottoman Sultan confirmed him and his father as the Emirs of Mecca. In 1631 a new quarrel developed within the Sharif family and divided them into two Houses; the House of Abdallah (known as al-A'un family) and the House of Hussain (the one that ruled Syria, Iraq and Jordan).

In 1745 Mecca came under direct threat from a fanatic religious movement known as Wahabi with support of Sa'udi chieftain from Central Arabia. The movement condemned all Muslim practices that were not strictly in keeping with their understanding of Islam. They opposed visits to graves and tombs including that of the Prophet, which they are said to have destroyed. It is also said that when they attacked Iraq, they destroyed the grave of al-Hussain b. A'li in Kerbala.

In 1806 the Wahabi's captured Mecca and stripped the Ka'bah of its traditional adornments. They returned again that same year and the Emir Sharif Ghalib (from the Zaid House 1787-1813) was forced to come to terms with them.

In 1811-1812 Sharif Ghalib joined Muhammed A'li of Egypt to expel the Wahabis from Mecca and Hijaz. In 1827 Sharif Ghalib was removed and replaced by his nephew Yahaya b. Srur, and soon afterwards by his son Abd al-Mutalib; the latter also being replaced by Sharif Abd al-Mui'n (1827-1851) of al-A'un family. By the 19th century, with the emergence of colonial powers, the Sharifs of Mecca became aware of the modern international influences on events close to them. In 1839 Britain seized Aden in southern Arabia and, in 1882, occupied Egypt and, as a result, diplomatic contacts between the Sharifs of Mecca and the British were initiated. From 1882 to 1905 Mecca was ruled by Sharif Aun al-Rafiq, who worked in harmony with the Ottomans.

During the 19th century, Arab intellectuals started to challenge the Ottoman Turks. They adopted nationalistic ideas rather than religious ones, seeking an Arab identity for their leadership. An Arab scholar, Abd al-Rahman al-Kawakibi (Native Syria), repudiated the Ottoman Turk's claim as Caliphs. He argued that "The Caliph of Islam was supposed to be an Arab of Quraish descent, and that he would be even more acceptable if he was from Al al-Bait. The Turks were neither Arabs nor from Al al-Bait." He pointed out "if there must be a Caliph then it should be an Arab like the Meccan Sharif." This issue became more important when, from 1908, the Ottoman undertook policies that abandoned their pluralistic and pan Islamic methods to adopt instead a secular Turkish nationalism. The formerly cosmopolitan and tolerant Ottoman empire began to discriminate openly against all other non Turk nations. Arabs in particular were faced with political, cultural and linguistic persecution. This prompted the Arab nationalist groups in Syria, Iraq, and Arabia to revolt. They all rallied behind the Sharif and his two sons, Faisal and Abdallah. This gave Sharif Hussain great support for his plans to form an Arabic state independent from the Ottomans.

## Sharif Hussain b. A'il King of Hijaz

Al-Sharif Hussain (1853-1931) was the great-grandfather of H.M. King Hussein of Jordan. He was born in Istanbul (Turkey) and was educated with the Ottoman privileged society. He became the grand Sharif and Emir of Mecca, the hereditary custodian of the Muslim Holy Places and head of the Hashemite family in the Middle East. He believed in the Arab cause and dreamt of a unified Arab state stretching from Syria to Hijaz.

In 1914, during World War I, the Ottomans sided with the central powers and, during this period, arrested many Arab nationalist figures in Damascus and Beirut. Arabs were further threatened by the construction of the Hijaz Railway, which connected Damascus to Mecca, and facilitated the mobility of Turkish troops into the Arab hinterland. Therefore on June 10, 1916, as head of the Arab nationalists, and in alliance with Britain and France, Sharif Hussain declared the Great Arab Revolution against the Turks. That was a turning point in Arab history. His sons, Abdallah and Faisal, led the Arab forces and liberated southern Syria, Jordan, Palestine and most of the Arabian Peninsula. Britain promised to help the Sharif achieve an independent Arab state, should he join the Allies against the Turks during World War I. But the promises were not kept and the Arab world was divided between the major two colonial powers, Britain and France. The interests of the colonial powers took precedence over promises made to the Arabs. While accepting the principles of Arab independence laid down in the Hussain-McMahon correspondence, the Sykes-Pecot Agreement signed by Britain, France and Russia in 1961, divided the area into zones of permanent colonial influence. The agreement fostered French interests in greater Syria and Northern Iraq and acknowledged British influence from the Mediterranean to the Persian Gulf.

King Faisal was elected by the General Syrian Congress in 1920. However, shortly afterwards, the newly founded League of Nations awarded Britain the mandates for Transjordan, Palestine and Iraq. France was given the mandate for Syria and Lebanon. France had to take Damascus by force, removing King Faisal from the throne to which he had been elected. King Faisal claimed the throne of Iraq in 1921. After his death, his son Ghazi, King of Iraq, took over, and then in 1958 his grandson Faisal II, King of Iraq, was killed during a coup led by Colonel Abd al-Karim Kasim. It is interesting to recall that King Faisal II joined a series of Al al-Bait who had been killed in Iraq within the last 14 centuries starting with Imam A'li, Muslim b. A'kil, and Imam al-Hussain b. A'li and so on.

Abdallah, son of Sharif Hussain, King of Transjordan, founder of the Hashemite Kingdom of Jordan, was born in Mecca in 1882. After World War I, he joined his father in Mecca, during political negotiations to liberate Arab lands from Turkish rule. He entered into difficult negotiations with the British to establish a national government in Transjordan. In 1946 the country was proclaimed the independent Hashemite Kingdom of Jordan. Government offices were built and infra-structure development was initiated. King Abdallah wanted peaceful relations between all faithful believers, Muslims, Christians and Jews. On July 20 King Abdallah was assassinated in the al-Aqsa Mosque in Jerusalem, an event that echoes the assassination of A'li b. Abi Talib in the Mosque of al-Kufah in similar circumstances, 14 centuries before.

King Abdallah founded a modern country with an ancient multi-culture and history, since parts of Jordan today are linked with the dominions of ancient Iraq, including the Sumerian, Akkadian, Babylonian, Assyrian and Mesopotamian empires. From the west, Egypt extended its power and culture into Jordan. The Nabatians built their great empire in Jordan. Their impressive monuments are witness to the greatness of their civilisation. Jordan also was incorporated into the classical civilisation of Greece, Rome and Persia. From the mid-17th century the land of Jordan has remained almost continuously in the hands of various Arab and Islamic dynasties: the Omayyads (661-750), the Abbasids (750-969), the Fatimis (969-1174), the Mamelukes (1250-1516) and the Ottomans (1516-1918).

In 1951 Talal, son of Abdallah, was inaugurated, but he abdicated within less than a year for health reasons. He was born in Mecca in 1909 and died in Istanbul in 1972.

### H.M. King Hussain b. Talal [TABLE 3]

He is the first king from the Prophet line to be born in Jordan (1935) since all his ancestors were born in Hijaz (West coast of Arabia). H.M. King Hussain went to school in Alexandria (Egypt), and then at Harrow and Sandhurst (England). He was 17 when he ascended the throne on May 2, 1953. He introduced a series of liberal reforms including freedom of speech and of the press. In 1960 the economy of Jordan started to take off and the kingdom witnessed high rates of economic growth and stability. Jordan was transformed from a tribal and semi-nomadic society to a fully modern state.

H.M. King Hussain has a large family of 12 of his own children and one adopted daughter, Princess A'bir Muhaisen, who lost her parents in a tragic accident. From his first marriage to Princess Dina Abd al-Hamid, he has one daughter, Princess Alia. From his second marriage to a British woman, Antuanate Gardner, who became

Princess Muna al-Hussain, King Hussain has two sons, Prince Abdallah and Prince Faisal and also two daughters, Princess Zein and Princess Aisha. From his third marriage with Queen Alia Tokan, he has one daughter Haya and one son A'li. From his fourth marriage to Lisa Halaby, who became Queen Noor al-Hussain, H.M. has two sons, Hamzah and Hashem, and two daughters, Iman and Raiyah.

H.M. has two brothers and one sister: Crown Prince al-Hassan (the youngest brother of H.M.) and H.R.H. Prince Muhammed (b. 1940.) and H.H. Princess Basma (b. 1951).

### H.M. Queen Noor of Jordan

Their Majesties King Hussain and Queen Noor were married on June 15, 1978. Her Majesty Queen Noor, whose former name was Lisa Najeeb Halaby, was born on August 23, 1951, in the USA to a distinguished Arab-American family. She spent her childhood in the USA and attended schools in Los Angeles, Washington, D.C., New York City and the Concord Academy in Massachusetts. In 1974 H.M. obtained a B.A. in Architecture and Urban Planning from Princeton University.

H.M. Queen Noor devotes a great deal of her time to promoting international understanding between different cultures. In 1980 she convened the first Arab Children Congress to discuss the contemporary challenges and the ancient bonds of culture shared by all Arabs. She also established the Noor al-Hussain Foundation (NHF) to consolidate the administration of her diverse and expanding development initiatives since 1978, namely to set standards of excellence in social-economic development models and in national health care, education, culture and the arts.

### The Crown Prince al-Hassan b. Talal

Crown Prince al-Hassan was born in Amman on March 20, 1947. He is the youngest brother of H.M. King Hussain of Jordan. H.R.H. began his primary education in Jordan. He then joined the Summerfield Preparatory School followed by Harrow, in England. Afterwards he went to Christ Church and onto Oxford, from which he received a B.A. (Hon.) in Oriental Studies in 1965 and an M.A. In April 1967, H.R.H. was officially invested as Crown Prince and heir to the Hashemite throne of Jordan. Since then he has officially served as H.M. King Hussain's Regent in his absence. H.R.H. has initiated and directed a number of Jordanian and international institutes and committees. In Jordan he has chaired the National Development Plan Committee from 1973 to 1990. He has founded a number of cultural, social, educational, and humanitarian institutions and in 1981 addressed the 36th session of the United Nations General Assembly and proposed the establishment of a new national humanitarian order. This led to his founding and co-chairing the Independent Commission on International Humanitarian Issues (I.C.I.H.I., 1983).

H.R.H. initiated a series of contacts that encouraged interfaith dialogue. This involved consultations with the Orthodox Centre of the Ecumenical Patriarchate (Chambesy), the Pontifical Council for Inter-Religious Dialogue (Vatican) and the Independent Commission on Christian Muslim Relations (Deanery and Windsor) in 1987. He has written and published a number of articles and four books on political and regional issues.

### The present Shia'h (Ismai'li) Imam

H.H. Prince Karim al-Hussaini (Aga Khan) is the present imam (spiritual leader) of the Ismai'li Muslims. He is the 49th imam. H.H. does not exercise sovereignty over any country. As imam, he is concerned with the spiritual and material well-being of the Ismai'lis who live in some 25 countries, mainly in Africa, Asia and the Middle East, as well as in Europe and North America. He has adopted a system of administering the Ismai'lis that is responsive to the needs of time and place. Wherever the Ismai'lis live, they have elaborated a well-defined institutional framework to carry out social, economic and cultural activities.

In common with other Shia'h Muslims, the Ismai'lis affirm that, after the death of the Prophet Muhammed, his cousin and son-in-law A'li, became the first imam of the Muslims. They believe that this spiritual leadership, known as the imamate, continues through the hereditary line of A'li and his wife Fatimah, the Prophet's daughter. According to the Shia'h doctrine and tradition, succession to the imamate is by designation. It is the absolute prerogative of the imam to appoint his successor from among his male descendants.

During its long history, Ismai'lism has come to include peoples from many different traditions and cultural diversity. This continues to characterize the Ismai'lis today. During the course of history, the Ismai'lis have, under the guidance of their

imams, made a major contribution to the growth of Islamic civilization. The Academy of Sciences, Dar al-Ilm and the University of al- Azhar (which is one of the oldest universities in the world, and which has a great influence on Islamic thought and culture) in Cairo and indeed the city of Cairo itself, exemplify the Ismai'lis' contributions to the cultural, religious, social and intellectual life of the Muslims.

The ancient history of this family goes back to the Fatimis. Historians conventionally divide Ismai'li history into several broad periods. The achievements of the Fatimi Empire dominate accounts of the early period ranging from the beginnings of Islam through the 11th century. Named after the Prophet's daughter Fatimah, the Fatimi dynasty created a state that stimulated the development of art, science and trade in the Mediterranean and the Middle East over two centuries. Its centre was Cairo, founded by the Fatimis, which was designed by the great Fatimi Sicilian military leader Jauhar al-Sikally. Following the Fatimi period, the Ismai'li's geographical centre shifted from Egypt to Syria and Persia. Their centre in Persia, Alamut, fell to the Mongol conquerors in the 13th century. After this event, the Ismai'lis lived in several centres within dispersed communities mainly in Persia and Central Asia, but also in Syria, India and elsewhere.

H.H. Prince Karim Aga Khan is the fourth of the new dynasty which came to be known as the Aga Khans. This dynasty raises a great deal of interest genealogically and historically because its history has taken place on three continents and at a variety turning points between Arabia, North Africa, Persia, India and Europe. We will try to cover briefly this long history, but our main interest in this subject is the genealogy and the modern period of the Aga Khans.

In Persia, Imam Shah Khalil Allah was highly regarded as a religious leader by the Nizaris of India (known as Khoja). They used to come to Kahak to receive his blessings and guidance. Khalil Allah was killed in a riot in Yezd in 1817. He was succeeded by his son Muhammed Hassan al-Hussaini also known as Hassan A'li Shah (the 46th imam), who became the first Nizari imam to be known as the Aga Khan (an honorary, hereditary title conferred on him by the Shah of Persia).

In 1835 Aga Khan I (Hassan A'li Shah) became the governor of the Kirman region. Following the termination of his governorship in 1837, he moved to Afghanistan and then, in 1841, to India, where he initiated the modern period of Nizari Ismai'li imams. Nizari Khojas found direct access to the imam and they began to send him their community contributions. In 1881 Aga Khan I died, and was succeeded by his eldest son, Aga A'li Shah Aga Khan II, who spent his early childhood with his mother in Iraq and studied Arabic, Persian, Islam and the doctrines of the Nizari Ismai'lis. He died in 1885 in Poona, India, but his body was taken to Najaf, Iraq, where he was buried in the family mausoleum. In the same year, he was succeeded by his son, Sultan Muhammad Shah (Aga Khan III), who became the 48th imam. He was 8 years old when he was installed. He grew up under the close supervision of his capable mother, Shams al-Muluk, known as Lady A'li Shah. Under her supervision, Aga Khan III received a rigorous education, taking lessons in Arabic, Persian literature, Islam and Ismai'li tariqah (persuasion). Until her death in 1938, Lady A'li Shah played an active role in administrating the affairs of the Nizari-Ismai'li through a council and had a lasting influence on her son.

From 1907 onwards Aga Khan III established his chief place of residence in Europe and his involvement in international affairs at Geneva culminated in his election as president of the League of Nations from 1937 to 1939.

In Europe, through the marriages of the Aga Khans, the lineage of the Prophet Muhammed intermingled with genealogies of European descent, namely Italian and English. In 1908 Aga Khan III married Miss Theresa Magiliano, of Turin, Italy who, in 1911, in her native city, bore A'li (father of the Prince Karim). She died in Cairo in 1926. In 1929 Aga Khan III married his third wife, Miss Andrée Carron, who bore his second son, Sadr' al-Din. In 1936 Aga Khan III's son A'li married the former Joan Yarde-Buller, a daughter of Lord Churston. On December 13, 1936, she bore the first of A'li Khan's two sons, Karim (the present imam who was to succeed his grandfather Aga Khan III to the imamate in 1957); the second son, Amyn, was born in 1937. A'li Khan also had one daughter, Yasmin, from his second marriage with Rita Hayworth.

Aga Khan III died on July 11, 1957 in Switzerland. His body was taken to Egypt, the glorious centre of his ancestors, the Fatimis. He was buried in a permanent mausoleum in Aswan. Sultan Muhammed Shah Aga Khan III was imam for 75 years, a critical period in the modern history of the Ismai'lis. His leadership played a crucial role in enabling the Ismai'lis to adapt to historical change, notably through the transformation of their institutions. During this period, centrally administered medical facilities, schools, housing societies and cooperative banks were created mainly in the Indian sub-continent and in East Africa. Many of them still exist today as parts of the Aga Khan Development Network (AKDN) ,which is a group of institutions working to improve living conditions and opportunities in specific regions of the developing world, for the common good of all citizens from all faiths, regardless of their origin or religion. Aga Khan III was succeeded by his grandson H.H. Prince Karim Aga Khan IV.

### H.H. Prince Karim Aga Khan

H.H. Prince Karim Aga Khan IV was born in Geneva, Switzerland on December 13, 1936. He spent his early childhood in Kenya, attended Le Rosey school in Switzerland and completed his studies in 1959 at Harvard University with a B.A. (Hon.) in Islamic History. Aga Khan IV has a brother, Prince Amyn and a half sister, Princess Yasmin. Aga Khan has one daughter, Princess Zahra, born in 1970, and two sons, Prince Rahim born in 1971 and Prince Hussain born in 1974, from their mother Princess Salimah Aga Khan (formerly Sarah Croker-Poole).

In view of the importance that Islam places on maintaining a balance between the spiritual and material well-being of an individual, the imam's guidance deals with both these aspects of the life of his followers. In the Islamic tradition, as Imam, H.H. is not only concerned with the spiritual well-being of his followers, but also with the improvement of the quality of their life and that of people in societies where Ismai'lis live. This is obvious in the activities of the Aga Khan Development Networks (AKDN). The AKDN has three main areas of activities—social development, economic development and culture. It cooperates with various international agencies mainly located in Asia and Africa. It carries out an increasing number of development activities whose benefits are available to all. The AKDN'S mandate covers health, education, architecture, rural development and the promotion of private sector enterprise. Its programmes respond to the challenges of social, economic and cultural changes within Muslim society. The Aga Khan Trust for Culture focuses on problems of buildings and spaces and is directly involved with the Aga Khan programme for Islamic Architecture at Harvard University and the Massachusetts Institute of Technology in the USA.

In 1977, under the patronage of the Aga Khan, the Institute of Ismai'li Studies was established with the object of promoting scholarship and learning of Islam and a better understanding of its relationship with other faiths. The Institute, which is based in London, UK, and has been associated with McGill University in Montreal, Canada, offers a number of scholarships for different programmes.

Aga Khan IV's brother, Prince Amyn, entered the United Nations Secretariat following his graduation from Harvard in 1965. In 1968 he joined the Aga Khan's secretariat and is closely involved with the imamate's development activities and the governance of its principal institutions. Aga Khan IV's uncle, Prince Sadr' al-Din, has been UN High Commissioner for Refugees in addition to serving in various other positions with the UN.

H.H. Prince Karim Aga Khan IV is indeed a modern Muslim leader with an international outlook who believes that the wisdom of Prophet Muhammed in seeking new solutions for problems that could not be solved by traditional methods. He provides an inspiration for Muslims to conceive a truly modern and dynamic society without affecting the fundamental concepts of Islam. Aga Khan IV's significant contributions to Islam and humanity have been recognized by various universities and other institutions, through the conferment of awards and honorary degrees.

## Conclusion

As the end of 20th century approaches, we look at the descendants of the Prophet, not in terms of their noble descent, but in the context of what they are doing in this modern world. Needless to say that they continue to be leaders utilising modern and progressive ideas inspired by their founder, the Prophet Muhammed, who with Islam brought not just a new religion, but a modern way of thought. It is well known that it is the Islamic and Arabic civilizations that produced the foundations for modern science in mathematics, medicine, astronomy, etc., and changed the method of thought even in the non-Islamic world. The present descendants of the Prophet are implementing changes which not only help the development of their own countries and people, but also contribute

to the stability and development of the whole world. They do this with an open mind and heart, without prejudice or fanaticism and reflect the liberal discipline of their ancestor the Prophet Muhammed who said: "Bashiru walaa tunaffiru, yassiru walaa tua'ssiru" [Preach but don't put (people) off and ease but don't complicate (issues)]; "Ta'allamu min-al mahdi ila-allahd" [Keep learning from cradle to grave]; "Al-Muslim Man salama al-nas min lisanahu wa-yadeh" [A Muslim is that person from whom people are safe, from his hand and his tongue]. His cousin and son-in-law Imam A'li has said: "Law kaana-l fakru rajulun lakataltuh" [If poverty was a man I would have to kill him]; "Man tasaawa yawmah fahuwa maghboon" [He whose two days are the same (without progress or change) is underprivileged].

As they lead their people in this final stage of the 20th century and with the 21st century approaching, time will tell whether the present descendants of the Prophet Muhammed and their future descendants will keep on progressing and continue meeting the fundamental and modern requirements of their own people. The challenges they face are many. But, if they keep on following the commandments of their founder, they will continue improving their quality of life and will establish enlightened constitutions that will foster social equality and social justice. With this progressive approach, their people will work with them and under their leadership for future generations to come.

## BIBLIOGRAPHY

ABIDI, HASAN and HAYDER AQIL, *Jordan A Political Study* (New York: 1948) p. 157; ABU-SAUD, M., *Concept of Islam* (USA: 1990); ABU-NOWAR MA'AN, *The History of the Hashemite Kingdom of Jordan*, vol. 1 (Oxford: 1981); GHABBOOSH AHMED A., *Al-Da'wah al-Islaamiyeh (Islamic Propagation)* (Cairo, Beirut: 1978); AHMED KHURSHID (ed.), *Islam, Its Meaning and Message* (Islamic Foundation: 1980); AL-AKKAD, ABBAS., *M Dhu- al- Noorain, Uthmaan Ibna Affaan; Uthman son of Affan of Two Lights* (Beirut: 1969); AL-HASSAN AL-THANI MALIK AL-MAGHRIB (Hassan II King of Morocco), *Inbia'ath Ummah; Resurrection of a Nation* (Royal Palace publications, vol. 36, Morocco, Alribat: 1991); ANTONIUS, GEORGE, *The Arab Awakening* (Lebanon: 1969); ARURI, NASSER, *Jordan: A Study in Political Development* (1921), p. 65; ESPOSITO, JOHN L., *Islam the Straight Path* (New York: 1988); AL-MOUSAWI, HUSSAIN AL-SAYYED HASHEM, *A History of the British Omani Relations* (Unpublished Ph.D., Glasgow: 1990); ARBERY A. J., *The Kura'an Interpreted* (1955); BACHARACH, *A Middle East Studies Hand Book* (Washington: 1976); BAKER, RANDALL, *King Hussain* and the Kingdom of Hejaz (New York: 1979); BOSWARTH, CLIFFORD E., The Islamic Dynasties (Edinburgh: 1967); BRILLS, E. J. (ed.), First Encyclopedia of Islam (vol. 7, New York: 1987); BROCKELMAN, CARL, History of the Islamic People (New York: 1947); BURKES, Genealogy of the World Ruling Royal Families (London); CORBIN, HENRY, Cyclical Time and Ismail'i Gnosis (London: 1983); DAFTARY, FARHAD, The Ismai'lis, Their History and Doctrines (Cambridge: 1990); DAN, URAL, King Hussain and the Challenge of Arab Radicalism (New York: 1989); DEARDEN, ANN, Jordan Birth of a Kingdom (London: 1958); ESMAIL, AZIZ and AZIM NANJI, The Ismai'lis in History in S.H.; NASR (ed.), Ismai'li Contributions to Islamic Culture (Imperial Academy of Philosophy, Tehran: 1977); GILB, HAR and KRAMERS J. H., Shorter Encyclopedia of Islam (New York: 1953); GLUB, J. B., The Life and Time of Mohammed (Hoder & Stangton: 1970); GRAVES, PHILIP (ed.), Memoirs of King Abdullah (London: 1950); H.M. KING HUSSAIN OF JORDAN, Uneasy Lies the Head, (London: 1962); HASSAN II, The Challenge (Memories of H.M. King Hassan II of Marocco), (translated by RHODES, ANTONY, London: 1978); HERWITZ, J. C., The Middle East and North Africa in World Politics (vol. 2, London: 1972); HODGSON,MARSHAL, The Venture of Islam (Chicago: 1961); HOLT, P. M., The Cambridge History of Islam, (vol. 1a, 2b, London: 1956); HORANY, ALBERT, A History of the Arab People (London: 1991); HOTINGER, A., The Arabs (London: 1963); HURGRONJE, C. S., Mecca in the Later Part of the 19th Century (London: 1931); JAFRI, S. H. M., The Origins and Early Development of Shi'a Islam; JARADAT, WALEED MUHAMMED, Hathihi-al-Douhah min Hashem Ila-al- Hussain (These series from Hashem to Hussain, Jordan n.d.); KHAALID MUHAMMED KHAALID and KAMAA TAHADDATHA AL-RASOOL, As The Prophet Has Spoken (part 2, Beirut: 1973); LAPIDUS, IRA. M., A History of Islamic Societies (New York: 1988); LEWIS, BERNARD, The Origin of Ismai'lism (New York: 1940); LENT, J., Glub Pasha: A Biography (London: 1984); LUGAN, BERNARD, Histoire du Maroc (Paris: n.d.); LUNT, JAMES, Hussein of Jordan (London: 1989); MANSOUR, ALI AL-SHAREEA'H AL-ISLAAMIYEH WA KAANOON AL-DUWALY AL-AAM., The Islamic Law and the International Law (Cairo: n.d.); MARTÍNEZ, JOSEFA FERNANDES, Libro de las Generaciones (Valencia: 1963); MCNEIL, W., The World History (New York: 1979); MORIS, JAMES, The Hashemite Kings (London: 1959); NASR, SEYYED HOSSEIN (ed.), Ismai'li Contributions to Islamic Culture (Tehran: 1977); NENO, J. and PAPE, I. (ed.), The Hashemite Monarchy (USA: 1994); NOWFAL, ABD AL-RAZZAQ and AL-KURA'AN WAL IILM AL HADIYTH, The Kura'an and the Modern Science (Beirut); OLSON, ROBERT (ed.), Islamic and Middle Eastern Societies (Brattleboro: 1987); PATIA, RAPHAEL, The Kingdom of Jordan (New Jersey: 1958); PEAK, FREDRICK G., History and Tribes of Jordan (Miami: 1950); PIPES, DAVID, In the Path of God (New York: 1983); RENARD J., In the Footsteps of Mohammed (New York: 1992); LACEY, ROBERT, The Kingdom (London: 1981); DR SA'AB, HASAN. and AL-ISLAAM WA TAHDDIYAAT AL-ASSAR, Islam and the Challenge of Time (Beirut: 1970); SALIBI, KAMAL, The Modern History of Jordan (London: 1993); SCHACT and BOSWORTH (ed.), The Legacy of Islam

(Oxford: 1974); SNOW, PETER, Hussain a Biography (New York: 1972); SPARO, GERALD, Hussain of Jordan (1960); WATT M. and MCDONALD M. V. (transl.), The History of al-Tabari (vol. 6., New York); WILSON, King Abdullah, Britain and the Making of Jordan (New York: 1987); WILLIAM, ALDEN, Islam (New York: 1961); ZEPP, JR. and IRA G., A Muslim Primer (1992).

## DOCUMENTS AND CONFERENCES

Al-Akaadimiyyeh Acaddemia (Morocco: 1988); AL-KITAAB AL-MUQADDES, The Holy Book (Bible); Al-Muhyt al-Arabi (special ed., Dubai: 1992); Al-Ssayyad (special ed., Dubai: n.d.); The Holy Bible; The Holy Kura'an; AL-MOUSAWI, HUSSAIN, AL-SAYYED HASHEM, Understanding Islamic Civilisation (Lecture, Algonquin College, Ottawa, Canada: March 30, 1996); AL-ISLAM WAL-TAHADDIYAAT AL-MUA' ASIRAH, Islam and Modern Challenges (conference, Islamic Culture Center, Malta: 1987); Augustan Society, Omnibus 7:81 (USA: 1986); CORLEIR SOCIETY, History of Egypt (London: 1904); H.M. QUEEN NOOR OF JORDAN (CV); H.R. H. CROWN PRINCE AL-HASSAN BIN TALAL (CV); The New Encyclopedia Britannica (vol. 8, London: 1985); Encyclopedia of Islam (vol. 5, 6, 9, New York: 1987); Encyclopedia Americana (vol. 15, USA: 1980); JORDAN MEDIA GROUP, Keys to the Kingdom (Amman: 1995); HASSAN BIN TALAL (Crown Prince of Jordan), Jordan's Quest for Peace in the Middle East (Lecture, May 19, 1984); H. M. QUEEN NOOR THE HASHEMITE KINGDOM OF JORDAN (CV); Jordan Home Page (Internet: Morocco Home Page); H. M. KING HUSSAIN KING OF THE HASHEMITE KINGDOM (CV); KNOX PRESBYTERIAN CHURCH (Commonwealth Day, Ottawa: March 1996; Le Matin (Newspaper, Morocco Le Point, No. 984, July 27, 1991); MINISTRY OF INFORMATION, Kingdom of Morocco, Morocco Land of Promise the Spirit of a King and a People (1991); AL-RISALEH, The Prophet (film); RICHARD, B. et al., The Pillar of Islam (BBC Books); SALINI J., Islam: A Primer; Middle East Editorial Ass. (Washington, DC: 1983); SECRETARIAT OF AGA KHAN PUBLICATION, His Highness the Aga Khan Biography (Aiglemont, France: 1993); Idem, The Aga Khan Development Network (Aiglemont, France: 1995).

## NOTES

1. This work would have been impossible without the cooperation and kind assistance of: (Abuna) Father Sulaiman al-hajjar, Rector of Saint Peter and Paul Church, (Ottawa); Professor Abdallah Obeid, Professor of Arabic Chair at Ottawa University; Dr. Nabeel Mezher, Professor of Statistics and Demography, Ottawa University; H. E. Muhammed Sa'd A'li, Ambassador of The Yemen Republic in Canada; H.E. Tajedine Baddou, Ambassador of The Kingdom of Morocco in Canada; H. E. Samir Khalifah, Ambassador of The Hashemite Kingdom of Jordan in Canada. Many thanks for their support.

My thanks also to all staff members of Lincoln Fields Resource Center, Nepean, who helped to prepare part of my work, especially Catherine Morin and Rouba Dabboussi. My great thanks to my friend Isam Adi and the Motani family in Ottawa for their assistance and the valuable documents they provided. To my family in Scotland (UK): my wife Khadija Zainal, my son Ahmed, my daughters Tarneem and Vinous (al-Mousawi's) who, from Glasgow, copied and sent to me valuable information necessary to this work, thanks for their support.

2. The Editorial Committee does not take responsibility for this personal choice nor for discrepancies that may have occurred in the spelling of Arab names.

3. There are some rumors that African and European ruling families, and some Anglo-Americans, for example, the King of Ethiopia and President Nixon, are descendants of the Prophet. We will keep this issue, if possible, for a future presentation.

4. Some descendants of the Prophet managed to establish ruling dynasties as far as the southeast of the earth, as Sayyids from Hadramout (Yemen south) are strongly represented in the Malay Archipelago and to them belong the founders of the Sultanate of Siak and Pontianak. This is also a possible subject for a future presentation.

**TABLE 1:** Lineage of the Prophet Muhammed from the Prophet Ibrahim.

(1) The Prophet Ibrahim

(2) Ismai'l — Is-haq

Nabit — (3) Qaydar — Basmah.................m.................Isu

(3) Qaydar
(the first to be king)
also known as
Jutham, and Uram

(4) Sanf'a, it is said , 'was the most generous king on earth'
(5) Marz'a or Marhar
(6) Sammi
(7) Zarih
(8) Muqsir (was the most just king to reign)
(9) Tahmar (known as Daws al-ltq)
(10) Qanadi
(11) A'sir
(12) Dasan
(13) A'qara I
(14) Ra'wani
(15) Yalhani
(16) Bahrani
(17) Bathrani
(18) Bashmani
(19) Hamaada, (to whom the Arabain horses of A'waji breed was ascribed)
(20) Abda'i
(21) Banda'a (known by his generosity and first to establish houses for guests in every Arab Town)
(22) A'qara II
(23) A'qara III
(24) Ma'jala
(25) Mahsha
(26) Jahma
(27) Tahba
(28) Badlana
(29) Bildasa
(30) Hazana
(31) Kusdana
(32) Yamana (lived during the time of King Sulaiman)
(33) Shuhha
(34) Bura
(35) A'ws
(36) Nbit
(37) Salman
(38) Hamayta
(39) Hamaysa
(40) Uddaad
(41) Adnaan
(42) Ma'aad
(43) Nizaar
(44) Mudar
(45) I'lyaas
(46) Mudrikah
(47) Kuzaymah
(48) Kinanah
(49) al-Nadr
(50) Malik
(51) Fahr (by whom it is said that Quraish was known)
(52) Gualib
(53) Lu'ayy
(54) Ka'ab
(55) Murrah
(56) Kilab
(57) Qussay
(58) Abd Munaf
(59) Hashem (the founder of the Hashemite tribe to whom the Prophet and then the Alawaite belong)
(60) Abd al-Muttalib

(61) Abdallah — Abu talib

(62) Prophet Muhammed

(63) Fatimah.................m.................Imam A'li

Hassan *     Zainab     Hussain *          *Ancestors of the modern Hashemite dynasties

234

**TABLE 2:** Lineage of King Hassain of Morocco.

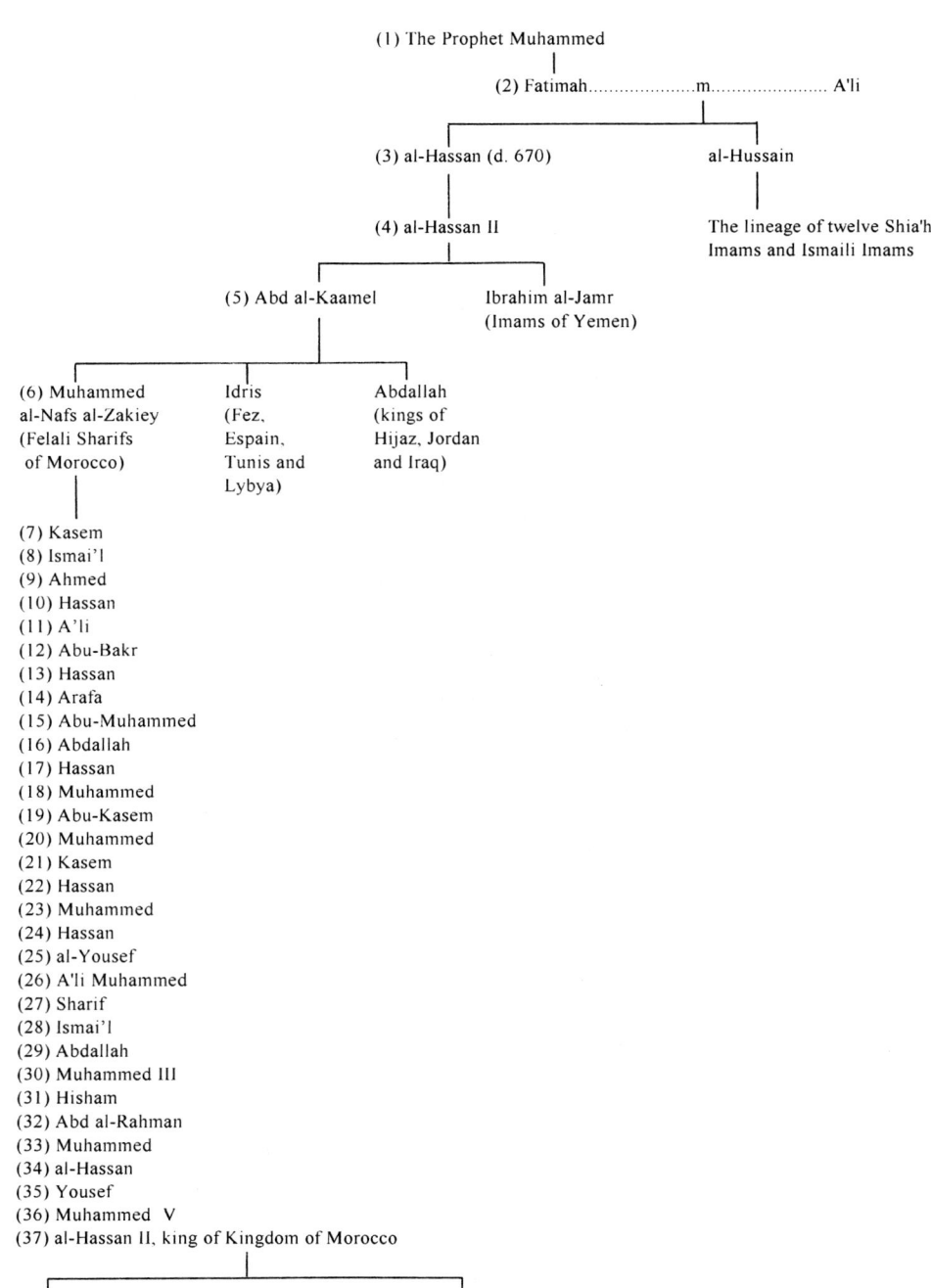

(1) The Prophet Muhammed

(2) Fatimah....................m...................... A'li

(3) al-Hassan (d. 670)          al-Hussain

(4) al-Hassan II          The lineage of twelve Shia'h Imams and Ismaili Imams

(5) Abd al-Kaamel          Ibrahim al-Jamr (Imams of Yemen)

(6) Muhammed al-Nafs al-Zakiey (Felali Sharifs of Morocco)

Idris (Fez, Espain, Tunis and Lybya)

Abdallah (kings of Hijaz, Jordan and Iraq)

(7) Kasem
(8) Ismai'l
(9) Ahmed
(10) Hassan
(11) A'li
(12) Abu-Bakr
(13) Hassan
(14) Arafa
(15) Abu-Muhammed
(16) Abdallah
(17) Hassan
(18) Muhammed
(19) Abu-Kasem
(20) Muhammed
(21) Kasem
(22) Hassan
(23) Muhammed
(24) Hassan
(25) al-Yousef
(26) A'li Muhammed
(27) Sharif
(28) Ismai'l
(29) Abdallah
(30) Muhammed III
(31) Hisham
(32) Abd al-Rahman
(33) Muhammed
(34) al-Hassan
(35) Yousef
(36) Muhammed V
(37) al-Hassan II, king of Kingdom of Morocco

Rashid          (38) Muhammed, Crown Prince

**TABLE 3:** Lineage of King Hussain of Jordan.

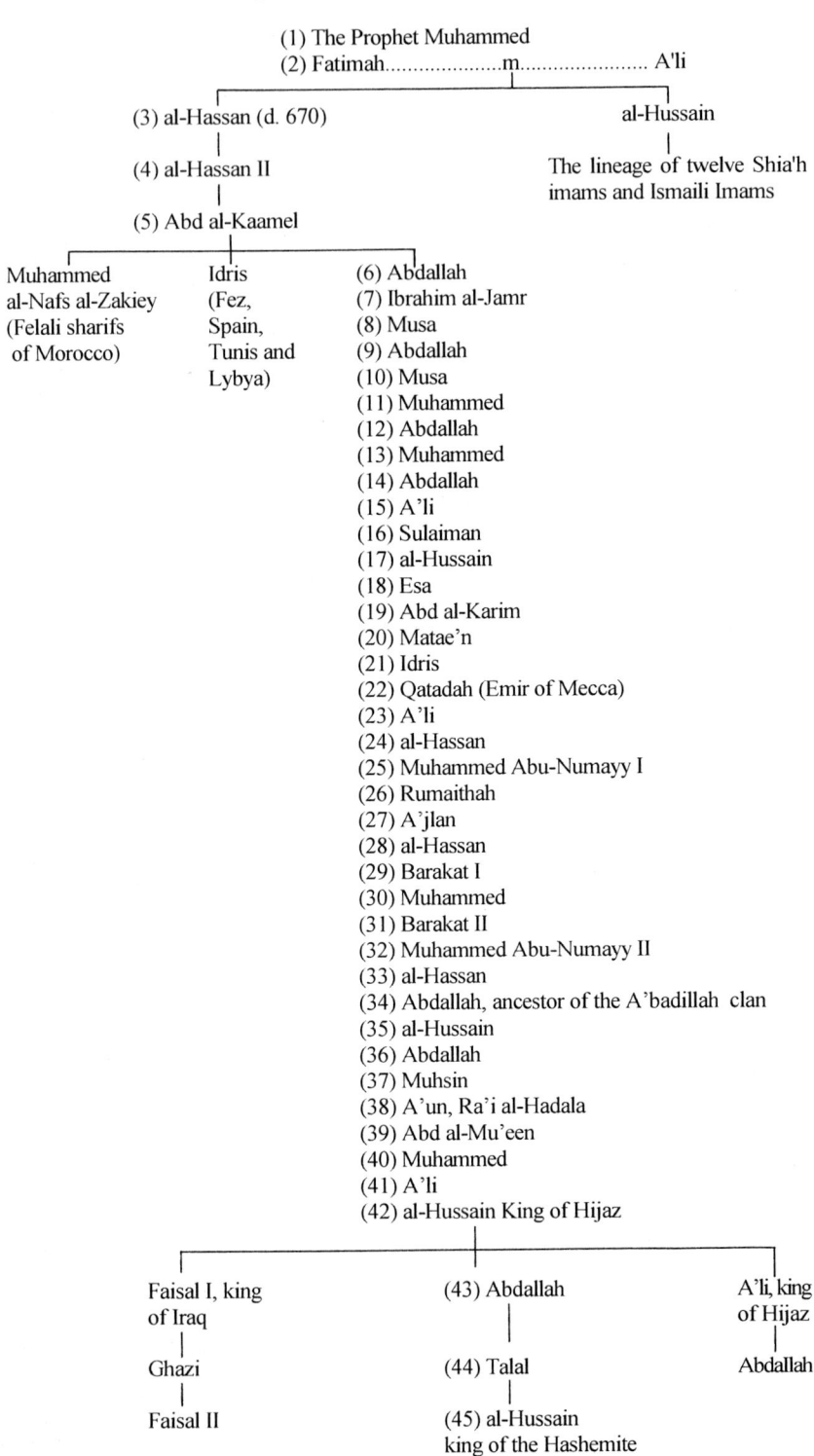

(1) The Prophet Muhammed
(2) Fatimah...................m...................... A'li

(3) al-Hassan (d. 670)

(4) al-Hassan II

(5) Abd al-Kaamel

al-Hussain

The lineage of twelve Shia'h
imams and Ismaili Imams

Muhammed
al-Nafs al-Zakiey
(Felali sharifs
of Morocco)

Idris
(Fez,
Spain,
Tunis and
Lybia)

(6) Abdallah
(7) Ibrahim al-Jamr
(8) Musa
(9) Abdallah
(10) Musa
(11) Muhammed
(12) Abdallah
(13) Muhammed
(14) Abdallah
(15) A'li
(16) Sulaiman
(17) al-Hussain
(18) Esa
(19) Abd al-Karim
(20) Matae'n
(21) Idris
(22) Qatadah (Emir of Mecca)
(23) A'li
(24) al-Hassan
(25) Muhammed Abu-Numayy I
(26) Rumaithah
(27) A'jlan
(28) al-Hassan
(29) Barakat I
(30) Muhammed
(31) Barakat II
(32) Muhammed Abu-Numayy II
(33) al-Hassan
(34) Abdallah, ancestor of the A'badillah clan
(35) al-Hussain
(36) Abdallah
(37) Muhsin
(38) A'un, Ra'i al-Hadala
(39) Abd al-Mu'een
(40) Muhammed
(41) A'li
(42) al-Hussain King of Hijaz

Faisal I, king
of Iraq

Ghazi

Faisal II

(43) Abdallah

(44) Talal

(45) al-Hussain
king of the Hashemite

A'li, king
of Hijaz

Abdallah

**TABLE 4:** The genealogy of Ismaili Imams.

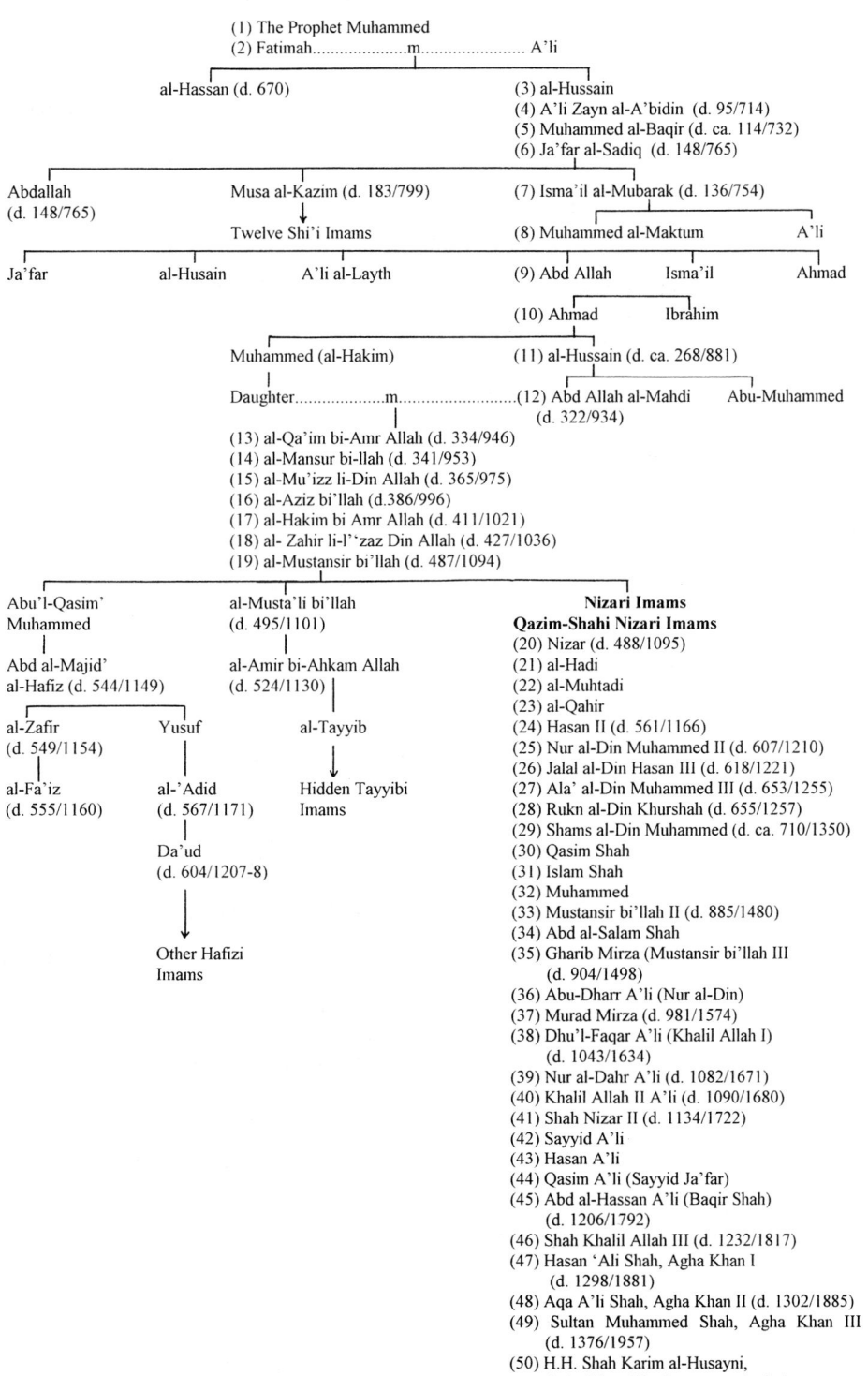

(1) The Prophet Muhammed
(2) Fatimah.............m.............A'li

al-Hassan (d. 670)

(3) al-Hussain
(4) A'li Zayn al-A'bidin (d. 95/714)
(5) Muhammed al-Baqir (d. ca. 114/732)
(6) Ja'far al-Sadiq (d. 148/765)

Abdallah (d. 148/765)

Musa al-Kazim (d. 183/799)
Twelve Shi'i Imams

(7) Isma'il al-Mubarak (d. 136/754)

(8) Muhammed al-Maktum          A'li

Ja'far          al-Husain          A'li al-Layth

(9) Abd Allah          Isma'il          Ahmad

(10) Ahmad          Ibrahim

Muhammed (al-Hakim)

(11) al-Hussain (d. ca. 268/881)

Daughter.............m.............(12) Abd Allah al-Mahdi          Abu-Muhammed
(d. 322/934)

(13) al-Qa'im bi-Amr Allah (d. 334/946)
(14) al-Mansur bi-llah (d. 341/953)
(15) al-Mu'izz li-Din Allah (d. 365/975)
(16) al-Aziz bi'llah (d.386/996)
(17) al-Hakim bi Amr Allah (d. 411/1021)
(18) al- Zahir li-l''zaz Din Allah (d. 427/1036)
(19) al-Mustansir bi'llah (d. 487/1094)

Abu'l-Qasim' Muhammed

al-Musta'li bi'llah (d. 495/1101)

**Nizari Imams**
**Qazim-Shahi Nizari Imams**
(20) Nizar (d. 488/1095)

Abd al-Majid' al-Hafiz (d. 544/1149)

al-Amir bi-Ahkam Allah (d. 524/1130)

(21) al-Hadi
(22) al-Muhtadi
(23) al-Qahir

al-Zafir (d. 549/1154)          Yusuf          al-Tayyib

(24) Hasan II (d. 561/1166)
(25) Nur al-Din Muhammed II (d. 607/1210)

al-Fa'iz (d. 555/1160)          al-'Adid (d. 567/1171)          Hidden Tayyibi Imams

(26) Jalal al-Din Hasan III (d. 618/1221)
(27) Ala' al-Din Muhammed III (d. 653/1255)
(28) Rukn al-Din Khurshah (d. 655/1257)
(29) Shams al-Din Muhammed (d. ca. 710/1350)

Da'ud (d. 604/1207-8)

(30) Qasim Shah
(31) Islam Shah
(32) Muhammed
(33) Mustansir bi'llah II (d. 885/1480)
(34) Abd al-Salam Shah
(35) Gharib Mirza (Mustansir bi'llah III (d. 904/1498)

Other Hafizi Imams

(36) Abu-Dharr A'li (Nur al-Din)
(37) Murad Mirza (d. 981/1574)
(38) Dhu'l-Faqar A'li (Khalil Allah I) (d. 1043/1634)
(39) Nur al-Dahr A'li (d. 1082/1671)
(40) Khalil Allah II A'li (d. 1090/1680)
(41) Shah Nizar II (d. 1134/1722)
(42) Sayyid A'li
(43) Hasan A'li
(44) Qasim A'li (Sayyid Ja'far)
(45) Abd al-Hassan A'li (Baqir Shah) (d. 1206/1792)
(46) Shah Khalil Allah III (d. 1232/1817)
(47) Hasan 'Ali Shah, Agha Khan I (d. 1298/1881)
(48) Aqa A'li Shah, Agha Khan II (d. 1302/1885)
(49) Sultan Muhammed Shah, Agha Khan III (d. 1376/1957)
(50) H.H. Shah Karim al-Husayni, Agha Khan IV, the present *hadir* imam

237

**TABLE 5:** The twelve imams of the Iithna A'shari Shia'h imams and their connections with the present royal dynasties.

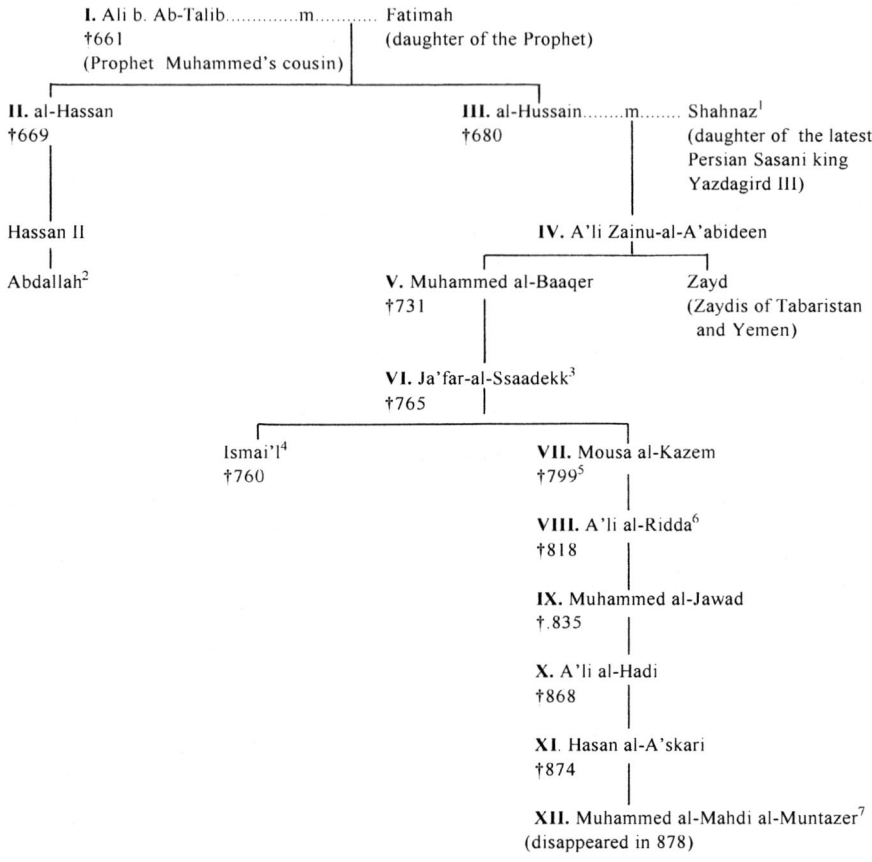

I. Ali b. Ab-Talib..............m............ Fatimah
†661                                         (daughter of the Prophet)
(Prophet Muhammed's cousin)

II. al-Hassan                    III. al-Hussain........m........ Shahnaz[1]
†669                             †680                             (daughter of the latest
                                                                 Persian Sasani king
                                                                 Yazdagird III)

Hassan II                        IV. A'li Zainu-al-A'abideen

Abdallah[2]                      V. Muhammed al-Baaqer          Zayd
                                 †731                          (Zaydis of Tabaristan
                                                               and Yemen)

                                 VI. Ja'far-al-Ssaadekk[3]
                                 †765

Ismai'l[4]                       VII. Mousa al-Kazem
†760                             †799[5]

                                 VIII. A'li al-Ridda[6]
                                 †818

                                 IX. Muhammed al-Jawad
                                 †.835

                                 X. A'li al-Hadi
                                 †868

                                 XI. Hasan al-A'skari
                                 †874

                                 XII. Muhammed al-Mahdi al-Muntazer[7]
                                 (disappeared in 878)

---

1. Shahnaz, mother of A'li Zainu al-A'abideen, witnessed two tragedies in her life: one being the loss of her father's empire and his death, and the second, the killing of her husband Imam Hussain.

2. Ancestor of the dynasties of: Fez, Malaga and Algaseras Libya, Tunisia Mecca (Hijaz) A'syr, Iraq and the present Hashimite Kingdom of Jordan and Kingdom of Morocco.

3. A great scholar and teacher known to have been running a university in Baghdad, Iraq to teach science, art and theology. The university was in his name in Arabic: Madrasat (the School) of al-Imam Ja'far al-Ssadek. Thousands of Arab theologians artists and scientists were graduates from his school, for example, the chemist Jaber ibn Hayyan al-Koofi and the theologian Imam Abu-Hanyfah and other famous scientists.

4. Ismai'li known also as A'lawis in Syria and Mehdis in North Africa and then Fatimi dynasty in Egypt and Nizary Aga Khans. The eastern branch known in Oman Bahrain and the Persian Gulf area as Karamitah Kurmutians who were (ahead of time) republican socialists!

5. From this imam onwards there are some allegations that a number of ruling dynasties had been established in different parts of the world, a subject for possible future research.

6. He became the son-in-law of the Abbasi Chalif al-Ma'moon and became his crown prince, but later al-Ma'moon feared him and killed him.

7. He is also known by al-l haadi al-mahdi and al-Kaaem. He is highly honored and glorified. According to the Shia'h he did not die, but disappeared. They believe that he will come again to rule the world with justice and peace after chaos. They pray for him by standing up and saying: "Allahumma A'jjil farajeh, wa sahhil makhrajeh" [God make his release quick and ease his coming back].

# UNIONES Y PARENTESCOS ENTRE VIRREYES DE LOS SIGLOS XVI, XVII Y PRINCIPIOS DEL XVIII

Esther de Soaje Pinto

La enfermedad de doña Juana, su madre y el testamento de Fernando de Castilla y Aragón, su abuelo, impuso a Carlos I, nacido en Gante, a asumir la Corona de un reino que no conocía pero con el que se identificó hasta llevarlo a su mayor esplendor.

Educado por los más sabios preceptores de su época, supo afrontar los problemas que traía aparejado el descubrimiento de un continente y resolverlos con justicia y equidad.

Durante los primeros 20 años de su reinado seguirían apareciendo tierras. A sus habitantes de culturas desconocidas había que atraerlos, conquistarlos y gobernarlos en la fe, esa fe que lo guió siempre y lo llevó a hacer de su vida una cruzada.

Superada la primera etapa de exigencias y ensayos, se impone establecer una forma de gobierno que consolide la conquista. En el primer tercio del siglo XVI la Corona establece en América un representante de su autoridad, semejante a las delegaciones reales que Aragón, en el siglo anterior, había designado en sus poblaciones ultramarinas de Sicilia y Cerdeña y que los Reyes Católicos habrían de extender a otros territorios de la península como Cataluña, Valencia, Navarra, Aragón y Mayorca.

Este delegado, con el título de virrey que representa la figura misma del monarca, es acompañado por un organismo, la audiencia, creado para asesorarlo y administrar justicia. En perfecto equilibrio de funciones, el virrey y la audiencia formaron en Indias la base de la organización político-administrativa de las provincias españolas. Se establece en Nueva España, México en 1535 y pocos años después, (1544) en el Perú. La extensión de los dominios y las dificultades para comunicarse dificultan el buen gobierno y dos siglos más tarde son creados los otros dos virreinatos: Nueva Granada y Río de la Plata que no entran en el tema de mi trabajo, pues su gobierno ha pasado a ser ejercido por funcionarios probos que no siempre pertenecen a la alta nobleza, aunque al final de su mandato reciban títulos honoríficos.

Esta forma de gobierno consolida la conquista, dirige las nuevas fundaciones y robustece la colonización.

Carlos I el emperador tiene en su entorno los hombres más preclaros del reino: sus parientes o primos, agraciados con la grandeza de España en 1520, y es entre estos señores de ilustración, poder y linaje entre los que designa los primeros virreyes. Su hijo Felipe II y sus sucesores obran en la misma forma y hacia 1722 en Nueva España y 1745 en el Perú, todos los virreyes pertenecen a familias de la más rancia y antigua nobleza castellana y están unidos entre sí, y con el monarca, por lazos de sangre o matrimonio. Excepciones a esta regla son los cortos períodos ocupados por la autoridad eclesiástica, los obispos, que por la muerte del virrey, por su llamado o destitución, ocupan el cargo, uniendo a la autoridad religiosa la civil, hasta que se produce la llegada del nuevo representante de la Corona.

Los linajes de Mendoza, Velasco, Zúñiga, Cerda, Manrique, Enríquez, etc., trajeron e implantaron en América el pensamiento, el señorío, la cultura y los adelantos de la metrópoli, por entonces la más importante de Europa.

Haremos una rápida referencia al origen de cada uno de ellos y la categoría social que ostentan cuando Carlos I, consagrado Emperador, empieza a gestar el gobierno que dará a sus posesiones de América.

**1. Mendoza.** Descendiente de los antiguos señores de Vizcaya toman el nombre de Mendoza, su casa solar. Ocupan los cargos más importantes junto a los reyes, recibiendo en premio a su lealtad grandes heredades, señoríos y títulos que los equiparan a los primeros ricos hombres de Castilla, destacándose además en las letras y en las artes. Dos miembros de esta casa recibieron la grandeza: don Diego Hurtado de Mendoza, III duque del Infantado y don Rodrigo Díaz de Vivar y Mendoza, I marqués del Cenete.

**2. Velasco.** Pertenece al linaje montañés (santanderino) que desde el siglo XV ostentaba el título de condestable de Castilla. Fue creado grande don Iñigo Fernández de Velasco, II duque de Frías, condestable hereditario de Castilla.

**3. Manrique.** Descienden de la noble casa de Lara, derivada a su vez de los condes soberanos de Castilla. Se inició el apellido con uno de los hijos del conde don Pedro, llamado Manrique de Lara cuyas virtudes militares y cristianas, según Salazar y Castro hicieron tan recomendable su nombre, antes poco usado en Castilla que lo tomaron por apellido propio sus descendientes varones. En 1520 dos caballeros de esta casa fueron agraciados con grandeza: Antonio Manrique de Lara, II duque de Nájera y Luis Fernández Manrique, II marqués de Aguilar de Campóo.

**4. Zúñiga.** Linaje riojano con señoríos en Las Cuevas y Cameros unido a la casa de Haro por matrimonio. Dos caballeros de esta familia son agraciados con grandeza en 1520, Alvaro de Zúñiga, III duque de Béjar y Francisco de Zúñiga y Avellaneda, III conde de Miranda del Castañar.

**5. Guzmán.** El primitivo solar de este linaje estuvo en Burgos, desde donde se extendió por toda Castilla y de allí a Andalucía, tomando el nombre de la Casa y Torre de Guzmán, cuyo señorío les pertenecía. El primer título que recibieron fue el condado de Niebla. El III conde recibió el ducado de Medinasidonia, elevado a grandeza con Juan Alonso de Guzmán, IV duque, casado con Ana de Aragón, nieta natural del Rey Católico.

**6. Cerda.** Linaje que comienza con don Fernando el de la Cerda, hijo de Alfonso el Sabio, yerno de San Luis IX, rey de Francia. El título que reciben es el condado de Medinaceli, elevado a ducado en el V conde. Recibe la grandeza el II duque, don Juan de la Cerda.

**7. Álvarez de Toledo.** Desciende esta familia de "valerosos caballeros cristianos de estirpe goda", según Argote de Molina. Estos valerosos caballeros ganaron tierras y títulos hasta convertirse en unos de los primeros rico hombres del reino. Los títulos que ostentaban eran los de conde de Oropesa y de Alba de Tormes. Este último es elevado a ducado y Fadrique Álvarez de Toledo, II duque, recibe la grandeza.

**8. Fernández de Córdoba.** Procede de la villa de Montemayor en el reino de Córdoba de donde tomaron su nombre. Ha dado origen a esclarecidas estirpes y a ella perteneció don Gonzalo de Córdoba, el Gran Capitán, una de las mejores lanzas de Europa. Los títulos que tienen son el ducado de Sessa, el marquesado de Priego y el condado de Cabra. Los tres fueron elevados a grandeza en Catalina Fernández de Córdoba, II marquesa de Priego, Diego Fernández de Córdoba, II conde de Cabra y Luis Fernández de Córdoba, II marqués de Comares.

**9. Enríquez.** Originados en el almirante don Alfonso Enríquez, hijo del maestre de Santiago, don Fadrique y nieto por tanto de don Alfonso XI y doña Leonor de Guzmán. No pertenecen a este linaje los Enríquez de Almansa y Enríquez de Guzmán, varias veces virreyes de México y Perú. Éstos tienen su origen en Sevilla y están entroncados también con los linajes castellanos antes nombrados.

### Virreyes de México y Perú

#### I. Antonio de Mendoza. Virrey de México y Perú (1535-1550)

III conde de Tendilla, bisnieto del marqués de Santillana por su abuelo Iñigo López de Mendoza, II conde de Tendilla y I marqués de Mondejar.

#### II. Luis de Velasco (1551-1564)

Señor de Salinas. Nieto paterno de Pedro de Velasco y Carrillo de Mendoza y nieto materno de Isabel Manrique y Enríquez de Rivera. Casado con Ana de Castilla y Mendoza, hija del señor de Gor y de Beatriz Hurtado de Mendoza, es prima del primer virrey don Antonio de Mendoza, nieta de don Diego Hurtado de Mendoza, II duque del Infantado y de su segunda mujer Isabel Enríquez de Noroña. Es padre de don Luis de Velasco el Joven, dos veces virrey de México y una vez de Perú.

#### III. Gastón de Peralta (1566-1568)

III marqués de Falces. Es hijo de Antonio de Peralta y Velasco y de Ana du Bosquet. Navarro de nacimiento, casa tres veces, (1) con Ana de Velasco, (2) con Leonor de Mur, y (3) con Inés Díez de Aux, tía carnal del XVI virrey don Lope Díez de Aux.

**IV. Martín Enríquez de Almansa (1568-1580/ Perú 1581-1583)**

Señor de Valderrábano. Pertenece al linaje de los Enríquez de Sevilla y enlaza por matrimonio con los Manrique y Velasco al casar con María Manrique de Castilla Pimentel y Velasco. Es tío abuelo del XXI virrey Luis Enríquez de Guzmán y bisabuelo materno de García Sarmiento y Sotomayor, XIX virrey de México.

**V. Lorenzo Suárez de Figueroa (1580-1583)**

IV conde de Coruña. Tercer nieto de don Iñigo López de Mendoza, I marqués de Santillana y de su mujer Catalina Suárez de Figueroa, de quien toma el nombre. Sobrino de don Antonio de Mendoza, I virrey, de don Luis de Velasco, señor de Salinas, II virrey, y primo por tanto de don Luis de Velasco el Joven, VIII virrey. Casa con Catalina de la Cerda y Silva, hija de don Juan de la Cerda, II duque de Medinaceli, II conde del Puerto de Santa María, grande de España, y de doña María de Silva, su segunda mujer. Nuestro virrey es grande de España nato.

**VI. Pedro Moya de Contreras (1584-1585)**

Obispo de México no pertenece a la primera nobleza española.

**VII. Alvaro Manrique de Zúñiga (1585-1590)**

I marqués de Villamanrique. Zúñiga por padre y por madre. Nieto paterno de Alonso Sotomayor y Enríquez, es casado con la hija del III virrey del Perú don Diego López de Zúñiga, doña Blanca Manrique de Aragón o Blanca Enríquez de Velasco, sobrina materna del IV virrey Martín Enríquez de Almansa.

**VIII. Luis de Velasco el Joven (1590-1595/ Perú 1596-1607/ México 1607-1611)**

Recibe el título de I marqués de Salinas del Río Pisuerga en 1609. Hijo del II virrey don Luis de Velasco y de su mujer Ana de Castilla y Mendoza. Es casado con su prima doña María de Mendoza, hija de Martín de Ircio, acaudalado comerciante indiano y de María de Mendoza, hija natural de don Iñigo de Mendoza, II conde de Tendilla, media hermana por tanto de don Antonio de Mendoza el I virrey de México y Perú.

**IX. Gaspar de Zúñiga y Acevedo (1595-1603/ Perú 1603-1606)**

V conde de Monterrey. Nieto materno de don Iñigo Fernández de Velasco y Mendoza, III nieto del marqués de Santillana por su hija doña Mencia casada con el Condestable de Castilla.

**X. Juan de Mendoza y Luna (1607-1615)**

III marqués de Montesclaros, pertenece a la línea de don Diego Hurtado de Mendoza y Luna, III duque del Infantado, grande de España. Por su madre es Manrique de Padilla. Casa dos veces, la primera con Ana Messía de Mendoza y la segunda con Luisa Antonia de Portocarrero Mendoza y Luna, su sobrina, hija de su hermana doña Francisca Mendoza y Luna.

**XIII. José Diego Fernández de Córdoba y Melgarejo (1612-1621/ Perú 1621-1629)**

I marqués de Guadalcázar, I conde de Posadas. Nieto paterno materno de doña Brianda de Mendoza, llamada así por su abuela materna, la condesa de Teba.

**XIV. Diego Carrillo de Mendoza y Pimentel (1621-1624)**

X conde de Priego. Hijo segundo de don Pedro Pimentel, II marqués de Távara y de Leonor Enríquez de Guzmán. Lleva el apellido Carrillo de Mendoza por imposición del título de conde consorte por su mujer, la condesa propietaria doña Juana Carrillo de Mendoza.

**XV. Rodrigo Pacheco y Osorio de Toledo (1624-1635)**

III marqués de Cerralvo. Es Enríquez por su abuela paterna, doña Ana Enríquez de Toledo, mujer de su abuelo Rodrigo Pacheco y Osorio.

**XVI. Lope Díez de Aux de Armendáriz (1635-1640)**

I marqués de Cadreita. Es Enríquez por su matrimonio con Antonia de Sandoval y Rojas, hija de doña Inés Enríquez de Távara y de Pedro Suárez de Castilla y Rivera, Per Afán de Rivera. Sobrino político por la mujer de don Gastón de Peralta, III virrey, suegro del XXII virrey, Francisco Fernández de la Cueva, VIII duque de Albuquerque, grande de

España, por el matrimonio de su hija Juana Francisca.

### XVII. Diego López Pacheco Cabrera y Bobadilla (1640-1642)

VII duque de Escalona, marqués de Villena, grande de España. Por sangre está unido a los importantes linajes que se repite en su primer matrimonio con Bernarda Cabrera de Padilla, su parienta. En su segundo matrimonio con doña Juana de Zúñiga Sotomayor y Mendoza, hija del VI duque de Béjar, grande de España, entronca con los otros linajes que estamos estudiando. (El conquistador del Tucumán, fundador de Córdoba, pertenecía a este linaje.)

### XVIII. Juan de Palafox y Mendoza (1642)

Arzobispo de México, es una excepción entre los virreyes interinos. Figura como hijo de una señora apellidada Mendoza en algunas genealogías, pero que aún no ha sido bien identificada.

### XIX. García Sarmiento de Sotomayor y Enríquez (1642-1648)

II conde de Salvatierra, I marqués del Sobroso. Su abuela materna es Isabel Enríquez de Almansa, hija del IV virrey de México, don Martín Enríquez de Almansa. Su abuela paterna es doña Leonor Sarmiento, hija de don Luis Sarmiento y Mendoza.

### XXI. Luis Enríquez de Guzmán (1650-1653)

IX conde de Alba de Liste, II marqués de Villaflor, grande de España. Nieto paterno de Juan Enríquez de Almansa y Ulloa. II marqués de Alcañices y conde de Almansa, hermano del IV virrey de México y V de Perú, don Martín Enríquez de Almansa.

### XXII. Francisco Fernández de la Cueva (1653-1660)

VIII duque de Albuquerque, VIII marqués de Ledesma, VIII conde de Huelma, VI marqués de Cuellar, grande de España. Hijo del tercer matrimonio de Francisco Fernández de la Cueva con Ana Enríquez de Cabrera y Colonna. Casa con Juana Francisca Díez de Aux, II marquesa de Cadreita, hija del XVI virrey, López Díez de Aux. Es abuelo paterno materno de Francisco Fernández de la Cueva, X duque de Albuquerque, XXXIV virrey de México.

### XXIII. Juan Francisco de Leiva y de la Cerda (1660-1664)

V marqués de Leiva y La Adrada. Perteneciente al linaje de la Cerda, entra por su abuela paterno materna en el de los Mendoza, por ser ésta Catalina de Mendoza y Ximenez de Cisneros. Casa con Isabel de Leiva y Mendoza, su prima.

### XXV. Antonio Sebastián de Toledo Molina y Zalazar (1664-1673)

II marqués de Mancera, grandeza de España personal. Hijo del segundo matrimonio de don Pedro de Toledo y Leiva, XIV virrey del Perú y de doña María o Ana Enríquez de Navarra. Es nieto paterno de don Luis de Toledo y Mendoza y de su sobrina y mujer, doña Isabel de Leiva y Mendoza.

### XXVI. Pedro Nuño Colón de Portugal (1673)

V duque de Veragua, IV duque de la Vega. Casa dos veces, la primera con Isabel de la Cueva Enríquez, entroncada directamente con el XXII virrey, don Francisco Fernández de la Cueva.

### XXVII. Fray Payo Enríquez de Rivera (1673-1680)

Arzobispo de México. Hijo bastardo de don Fernando Afán de Rivera y Enríquez, III duque de Alcalá de los Gazules, grande de España y de doña Leonor Manrique de Lara.

### XXVIII. Tomás Antonio de la Cerda y Aragón (1680-1686)

XII conde de Paredes de Nava, III marqués de la Laguna de Camero Viejo, grandeza de España personal. Hijo de don Antonio Juan Luis de la Cerda, VII duque de Medinaceli, grande de España y de su mujer Ana María Enríquez de Rivera, V duquesa de Alcalá de los Gazules, grande de España.

### XXIX. Melchor Portocarrero y Lasso de la Vega (1686-1688)

III conde de Monclova, recibe la grandeza en 1700. Hijo de don Antonio Portocarrero y Enríquez de la Vega, I conde, y de doña María de Rojas Manrique de Lara.

### XXX. Gaspar Melchor Baltasar de Silva Mendoza Sandoval y Cerda (1688-1696)

VIII conde de Galve. Hijo de don Rodrigo de Silva y Mendoza, IV duque de Pastrana y de doña Catalina de Sandoval y Mendoza, VIII duquesa del Infantado, era cuarto nieto de doña Ana de Mendoza, Princesa de Éboli.

### XXXIV. Francisco Fernández de la Cueva Enríquez (1702-1711)

X duque de Albuquerque. Era nieto paterno materno de don Francisco Fernández de la Cueva, VIII duque de Albuquerque, XXII virrey de México y pariente político del XXVI virrey, don Pedro Nuño Colón de Portugal. Casa con doña Juana de la Cerda y Aragón, hija del VIII duque de Medinaceli.

### XXXVI. Francisco de Zúñiga y Guzmán Sotomayor y Mendoza (1716-1722)

II marqués de Valero, IV duque de Ayamonte, I duque de Arión, grande de España. Hijo de don Juan de Zúñiga y Sotomayor y de doña Teresa de Zúñiga y Guzmán, su mujer. Casa con Guiomar de Mendoza, hija de los duques del Infantado don Iñigo López de Mendoza y doña Isabel de Aragón. Primo del XXX virrey, Gaspar Melchor Baltazar de Silva Mendoza Sandoval y Cerda.

Con este virrey llegamos hasta el año 1722, con una continuidad ininterrumpida de grandes títulos y linajes. Como parentescos aún nos quedaría por ver los virreyes XLI y LII, Francisco Güemes y Horcasitas y su hijo Juan Güemes Pacheco de Padilla, condes I y II de Revillagigedo. A don Matías de Gálvez, sucedido por su hijo Bernardo, I conde de Gálvez, como virreyes XLVIII y XLIX y al marqués de Croix Carlos Francisco y Teodoro su sobrino, XLV virrey de México y XXXVIII de Perú.

En el virreinato del Perú encontramos hasta el año 1745 nueve de estos virreyes favorecidos por su fidelidad a la Corona con el nombramiento en la sede de Lima, territorio más rico, donde tenían más posibilidades de acrecentar sus fortunas.

A éstos que ya nombramos en México se añaden otros de categoría similar, que en nada desdicen en linaje y poder.

A don Antonio de Mendoza que inicia y encarrila el virreinato del Perú, le sucede su pariente:

### II. Don Andrés Hurtado de Mendoza (1556-1560)

III marqués de Cañete. Es hijo de don Diego Hurtado de Mendoza, I marqués, y de su mujer Isabel de Cabrera y Bobadilla, hija de los marqueses de Moya. A esta casa pertenece don Jerónimo Luis de Cabrera, conquistador y fundador de Córdoba del Tucumán, hoy República Argentina. Casa con María Magdalena de Manrique.

### III. Diego López de Zúñiga y Velasco (1560-1564)

IV conde de Nieva. Velasco y Zúñiga por sus padres es nieto de doña María Enríquez de La Carra, mujer de don Sancho de Velasco. Casa con María Enríquez de Almansa, hermana del IV virrey y V de Perú, Martín Enríquez de Almansa.

### IV. Francisco de Toledo (1568-1580)

Hijo de don Francisco Álvarez de Toledo y Pacheco, III conde de Oropesa, señor de varias villas y de doña María Manuel de Figueroa, hija del II conde de Feria, Gómez Suárez de Figueroa y de su mujer doña María de Toledo, hija del I duque de Alba de Tormes, grande de España.

### V. García Hurtado de Mendoza (1590-1596)

IV marqués de Cañete. Hijo del II virrey don Andrés Hurtado de Mendoza. Casa dos veces: primero con Teresa de Castro y de la Cueva y segundo con Ana Florencia de la Cerda. Por este virrey que ordena la fundación de Mendoza, hoy República Argentina, esta provincia ha tomado su nombre (con él vino Alonso de Ercilla y Zúñiga, autor de "La Araucana").

### XIII. Luis Gerónimo Fernández de Cabrera y Bobadilla (1629-1639)

IV conde de Chinchón. Casa primero con doña Ana de Osorio, hija de doña Blanca Manrique y Aragón, y segunda vez con doña Francisca Enríquez de Rivera, hija de Per Afán de Rivera y de doña Inés Enríquez de Távara, tía del XXVII virrey de México, Payo Enríquez de Rivera.

### XIV. Don Pedro de Toledo y Leiva (1639-1648)

I marqués de Mancera. Hijo de Luis de Toledo y Mendoza, IV señor de Mancera, es nieto materno de don Sancho Martínez de Leiva y de su mujer doña Leonor Hurtado de Mendoza y Leiva, y nieto paterno de don Enrique de Toledo y de su mujer doña Isabel de Mendoza y

Castilla. Casa por segunda vez con doña María Luisa de Salazar y Enríquez de Navarra.

## XVII. Diego Romualdo de Benavídez y de la Cueva (1661-1666)

VIII conde de Santisteban del Puerto, I marqués de Solera. Su abuela paterna era doña Leonor de Toledo, hija de don Pedro Dávila, II marqués de las Navas y de doña Gerónima Enríquez de Guzmán. Su tercera mujer es doña Ana de Silva Mendoza y de la Cerda, descendiente de la princesa de Éboli.

## XVIII. Pedro Antonio Fernández de Castro Andrade y Portugal (1667-1672)

X conde de Lemos, VII marqués de Sarría, VIII conde de Castro, duque de Taurisano, conde de Villalba y Andrade. Nieto materno de doña Catalina Francisca Enríquez de Rivera, está emparentado con el XXVII virrey, don Payo Enríquez de Rivera y con doña Francisca Enríquez de Rivera, mujer de don Luis Gerónimo Fernández de Cabrera y Bobadilla, XII virrey de México.

## XIX. Baltasar de la Cueva Enríquez Arias de Saavedra (1674-1678)

Conde de Castellar. Su padre es don Baltasar de la Cueva Enríquez y su madre doña Teresa María Arias de Saavedra Enríquez de Ulloa, prima del IV virrey, Martín Enríquez de Almansa, del XXI virrey, Luis Enríquez de Guzmán y del III del Perú, Diego López de Zúñiga y Velasco por su mujer doña María Enríquez de Almansa y Ulloa.

El último virrey enrolado en esta maraña de parentescos es:

## XXIX. Don Antonio José de Mendoza Caamaño y Sotomayor

III marqués de Villagarcía. Quedan todavía once virreyes en el Perú, pero no tienen ni la importancia ni la categoría social de los primeros.

Esta enumeración de los entronques entre los antiguos linajes, es una prueba del cuidado que había en las uniones matrimoniales como medio de estrechar lazos de sangre dentro de una nobleza a veces aislada en sus propios señoríos.

Durante los siglos XIV y XV la vinculación entre la nobleza y los monarcas de los reinos peninsulares se hizo más frecuente y más estrecha y la procedencia de los reyes de Asturias, León, Navarra, Aragón y por supuesto Portugal, no es extraña a los personajes que tratamos. Más bien y con seguridad podemos afirmar que todos los primeros virreyes tenían por si mismos o por matrimonio entronques reales.

Al transcurrir los siglos XVI y XVII, al original deseo del vínculo de sangre se agregó el de poder, al buscar una relación más directa con la casa reinante. Comienza a desarrollarse una vida cortesana y es la asiduidad y el trato permanente, el que multiplica y acentúa los matrimonios dentro de ese mismo grupo selecto de nobles.

Los virreyes son una muestra del profundo respeto que tuvieron los reyes de España en la formación y el desarrollo de sus provincias de ultramar, equiparadas desde el principio a las peninsulares, pues al enviar a ellas vástagos de sus mejores familias, cumplían con el deseo de la reina Isabel de Castilla de considerar a todos sus súbditos iguales ante la Corona.

# UMBILICAL LINES AND THE USE OF MITOCHONDRIAL DNA ANALYSIS IN GENEALOGICAL RESEARCH

Thomas  H.  Roderick

In genealogical work, we primarily use the written record as our source for information. We occasionally also use an oral record and give it validity if it is made by a person having first-hand knowledge. From these we develop hypotheses about relationships and then test these hypotheses by examining other written primary sources to confirm or deny the hypotheses. Today the genealogist has a larger armamentarium than oral and written sources. With modern molecular genetic technology, genealogists now have new approaches to study and confirm genealogical relationships. One of the foremost is utilizing mitochondrial DNA, which is inherited through umbilical lines. Because DNA is composed of identifiable molecular segments arranged in sequences, just as sentences are written in sequences of letters, this is genealogical history written in a new sense, that is, written in the DNA. And we can read it!

## Genetic inheritance

First, a few details should be given about genetic inheritance. In general, but for minor exceptions, we receive half of our genetic component (DNA) from each parent. Carrying it further, we therefore get one-quarter from each grandparent and one-eighth from each great-grand parent, and so on back. Genetically, each of us then is a composite of our ancestors from each generation, but we carry a smaller fraction of the genes of each ancestor the farther back in generations we go.

## Mitochondrial DNA (mtDNA)

One of the minor exceptions to this general rule of inheritance is the small fraction (about 1/200,000) of our DNA that we inherit only from our mothers and that is called mitochondrial DNA (hereafter mtDNA): it is a 16,589 base pair closed circular molecule present in thousands of copies in each of our cells.[1] Besides its important function in providing energy for our cells, it is long and distinctive enough to be enormously useful in distinguishing families from each other.

Located outside the nucleus of the cell, the cytoplasmic mtDNA has a unique mode of inheritance coming to us from our mothers only. Our mothers in turn inherited that same mtDNA from their mothers, and so on back only through the special maternal line called the umbilical line.

## The umbilical line

An umbilical line is defined as that unique matrilineal ancestral line which passes back *only* through our mother and her mother and her mother and her mother. . . and so on, *only* through females with *no* intervening male. In some circles[2] it has also been referred to as the "uterine line." Thus, except where the *propositus* could be a male as well as a female, this line is comprised of only one sex. Genealogists are well aware that this particular line is usually the most difficult to establish with certainty for two main reasons. (1) Under traditional systems of naming, the surname is inherited from the father, and, of course the surname is one of the major crutches in establishing connections among members of the same family over generations. (2) Women in history have been given short shrift. In historical records important to genealogists, they are not mentioned, even though they might be (in the case of a birth record) the mother! Furthermore, women have not had occupational, professional, decision-making and voting opportunities that men have had, and thus have been comparatively left out of the written record. Admitting that the umbilical ancestral line is the most difficult to extend, we can say, however, that once it is genealogically established, it probably has more validity than any of our ancestral lines, for the true mother is always present at the birth of her children.[3]

## mtDNA inheritance

Through our umbilical lines we, both males and females, inherit this special mtDNA called mitochondrial DNA. In an ancestor table, this type of DNA would therefore be inherited by us through individuals numbered 3, 7, 15, 31, 63,

127, etc. [see FIGURE 1].[4] Thus, for example, in the fourth generation back, I inherit my mtDNA from only individual no. 31, my mother's mother's mother, and she from her mother, and so on back. Males, just as females, inherit this mtDNA through their umbilical lines, but only females pass it on. So for example, I and all my full siblings as well as anyone who has an umbilical line that intersects my umbilical line, will share the same mtDNA. To be sure, as we go much farther and farther back we would encounter mutational changes that took place in the mtDNA. Molecular geneticists and genealogists could probably expect to find changes in the mtDNA over 4,000 years, but probably not often in 400 years. This means that most of the time when two umbilical lines can be genealogically traced to a common ancestor, we will find *no* differences in the mtDNA. Put in another way, if three or four of us have independent umbilical lines back to a common immigrant ancestor, say 12 generations ago, we will probably all exhibit the same mtDNA. If one of us has a slightly different mtDNA, the reason could be a mutation in that line or it could be due to genealogical error in compiling the pedigree. There are ways to help distinguish between these possibilities. For example, if only one change is noted, then the probability is high that a mutation occurred and was fixed in one line. If, on the other hand, many differences are found between two individuals with the same umbilical line ancestress, then the probability is very high that one or the other line (or perhaps both!) is flawed in its genealogical research.

The specific characteristics or sequence of our own mtDNA can be determined from a small sample of blood or certain other body tissues, including bones. And, as stated, the particular type of mtDNA that is found in my blood, for example, will usually be identical to the mtDNA found in all individuals in my umbilical line for many generations. And it will most likely be identical to the mtDNA in those individuals who have umbilical lines that intersect mine. This type of analysis therefore will be particularly useful to the genealogist in verifying umbilical lines and in discovering possible connections among umbilical lines farther back than written records reveal.

## The use of mtDNA and umbilical lines in anthropological and genealogical research

Molecular comparisons of the mtDNA of various populations on earth indicate that all our umbilical lines meet at least back in Africa in one woman about 200,000 years ago.[5] These and other studies further show that there are racial, subracial, and ethnic differences in mtDNA that can be used to track the migrations of ancient peoples and to determine their interrelationships.[6] This approach is being used intensively to understand the origins and relationships of human and other populations, including insects.[7] Another use of mtDNA is to determine ethnic relationships of mummies[8] and other ancient human remains.[9]

An interesting genealogical-genetic question has been resolved using mtDNA comparisons. In 1991, nine skeletal remains were found in a mass grave near Yekaterinburg, Russia, believed to include Tsar Nicholas II, the Tsarina Alexandra and three of their daughters. Prince Philip of England shared the same umbilical line as the Tsarina, the Tsarina having been his mother's mother's sister. A comparison of his mtDNA with that of the skeletal remains proved with little doubt that some of the remains were indeed the Tsarina and her three daughters.[10] Further analysis comparing mtDNA from umbilical line relatives of Tsar Nicholas II (including mtDNA from the bones of the Tsar's brother Georgij Romanov) with the remaining skeletons proved with little doubt that one of the other skeletons in the grave was the Tsar.[11] The remains of two other children of this royal couple have yet to be found. Mitochondrial DNA analysis also rules out the identity of Anastasia with pretender Anna Anderson,[12] although some people close to Anna Anderson cannot yet believe she could have been a Polish peasant.[13]

## mtDNA for the genealogist

So having knowledge of racial and many ethnic types of mtDNA, we could find the ethnic or perhaps a more specific national type origin of our own ancient umbilical ancestress by analyzing our own mtDNA. We would not even need to know our own biological mother's name or ancestry to find this out from mtDNA analysis. Furthermore, if our genealogical research shows that our umbilical line intersects with another genealogists' umbilical line several generations back, a comparison of our mtDNAs will support the validity of our genealogical research if our mtDNAs are the same.

### The mtDNA genealogical study underway

In collaboration with Robert Charles Anderson, F.A.S.G., and Dr. Mary-Claire King, we inaugurated a search for umbilical lines leading back several generations. [14] We have welcomed now the collaboration of Dr. Douglas C. Wallace of Emory University, Atlanta, Georgia, and Dr. Bryan Sykes of the University of Oxford, Oxford, England. This is a genealogical and genetic study that has four goals: (1) for the genealogist, to define and document long umbilical lines and verify many of them through genetic analysis; (2) for the genealogist and population geneticist, to gain further insight into the structure of early colonial populations, and to get further information on the genealogical and genetic background of European immigrants to North America; (3) also for the genealogist and population geneticist, to determine and establish differences in the mitochondrial DNA due to different ethnic or geographical backgrounds, and to use this information to study genealogical origins of families and genetic origins of populations; (4) for the geneticist, to determine more precisely the mutation and evolutionary rates in various portions of the mitochondrial DNA. Umbilical lines extending farther back than colonial times into Europe, Great Britain, or Asia are especially valuable. It is these longer lines that provide the best opportunity for further genealogical and genetic analysis. However, any umbilical line extending into the 1700s into any region of the world could be useful.

At present over 500 lines have been submitted, and several distant connections have been found. Mitochondrial DNA analysis has been done on one connection between two umbilical lines extending into Sudbury, Mass. in the 1600s; this analysis is being prepared for publication. Through mtDNA analysis, ethnic origins of several other lines are being explored. Results will be communicated to participants as quickly as possible. In the meantime, a newsletter called *Umbilical Lines* will be sent to all participants.

Genealogists interested in collaborating in this study should assemble their umbilical lines with full citations to vital records, deeds, probate records, or other primary sources that prove the connection between generations. Good secondary sources fully cited will sometimes suffice if primary sources are not available. It is not necessary to send photocopies of birth certificates and other original records.

When pedigrees have been received and collated, some will be chosen for mtDNA analysis depending on the length of the line and how many other umbilical lines have the same origin. If the material is not sufficiently documented, we will contact the submitter and ask for more detail or work with him or her to provide minimal but good documentation. At that time participants will be notified and asked to provide a small sample of blood or buccal cells. The small blood samples are easily drawn (and usually without charge) at a hospital clinic or by an interested physician, as long as the study is for scientific purposes. The buccal cells are collected with a small sterile brush by scraping gently the inside of the cheeks. Both methods are being used. Emphasis should be made that this study concerns natural variation in mtDNA only and does not concern genetic problems or genetic disorders. Participation is voluntary and a participant's withdrawal from the project is possible at any time, with no further commitment. Umbilical lines can be sent to: mtDNA-Umbilical Line Project, Center for Human Genetics, P.O. Box 770, Bar Harbor ME 04609-0770, U.S.A.

### NOTES

1. D. C. WALLACE, "Mitochondrial DNA variation in human evolution, degenerative disease, and aging," *Am. J. Hum. Genet.*, 57 (1995), p. 201-223.

2. Eminent French-Canadian genealogist René Jetté told me "uterine line" was commonly used in his experience, and this term clearly has the same connotation as "umbilical line." For example, the term "uterine brother" means a brother with a common mother, whether half brother or full brother. Dr. George E. McCracken, F.A.S.G., former editor of *The American Genealogist*, said to me in personal correspondence that the term "umbilical line" was coined by Dr. Bradley Arthaud. The term has now been widely used and in general use in American genealogical periodicals.

3. In the last half of this century, however, this time-honored "truth" no longer holds, because a conceptus brought about by the union of a sperm and egg in vitro (i.e., in an artificial environment) can now be implanted

into the uterus of an unrelated woman, who can bring the fetus to term and deliver it. In this case the true biological mother is not the woman who nurtured the embryo and gave birth. The unrelated birthing mother would be a surrogate mother.

4. This number in the ancestor table can be calculated as $2^n-1$, where n is the number of the generation beginning, with oneself.

5. R. L. CANN, M. STONEKING and A. C. WILSON, "Mitochondrial DNA and human evolution," *Nature*, 325 (1987), p. 32-36. See also M. STONEKING, S. T. SHERRY, A. J. REDD, and L. VIGILANT, "New approaches to dating suggest a recent age for the human mtDNA ancestor," *Phil. Trans. R. Soc.*, 337, Lond. B (1992), p. 167-175. These studies do not imply that we descend from only one woman at that time, but rather that our umbilical lines intersect most recently in one ancestral woman. She has been dubbed in the popular press as "Mitochondrial Eve." Of course, this Eve's mother also is our common umbilical ancestor and so on back.

6. A. TORRONI and D. C. WALLACE, "mtDNA haplo groups in native Americans," *Am. J. Hum. Genet.*, 56 (1995), p. 1234-1236. See also M. RICHARDS, H. CÔRTE-REAL, P. FORSTER, V. MACAULAY, H. WILKINSON-HERBOTS, A DEMAINE, S. PAPIHA, R. HEDGES, H.-J. BANDELT, and B. SYKES, "Paleolithic and neolithic lineages in the European mitochondrial gene pool," *Am. J. Hum. Genet.*, 59 (1996), p. 185-203. Another study of related populations is by F. CALAFELL, P. UNDERHILL, A. TOLUN, D. ANGELICHEVA and L. KALAYDJIEVA, "From Asia to Europe: mitochondrial DNA sequence variability in Bulgarians and Turks," *Ann. Hum. Genet.*, 60 (1996), p. 35-49.

7. G. K. RODERICK. "Geographic structure of insect populations: Gene flow, phylogeography and their uses," *Annu. Rev. Entomol.*, 41 (1996), p. 325-352.

8. M. V. MONSALVE, F. CARDENAS, F. GUHL, A. D. DELANEY, and D. V. DEVINE. "Phylogenetic analysis of mtDNA lineages in South American mummies," *Ann. Hum. Genetic*, 60 (1996), p. 293-303.

9. B. HERRMANN and S. HUMMEL (ed.), *Ancient DNA, Recovery and Analysis of Genetic Material from Paleontological, Archaeological, Museum, Medical, and Forensic Specimens* (New York: Springer-Verlag, 1993).

10. P. GILL et al. "Identification of the remains of the Romanov family by DNA analysis," *Nature Genet.*, 6 (1994), p. 130-135.

11. P. L. IVANOV, M. J. WADHAMS, R. K. ROBY, M. M. HOLLAND, V. W. WEEDN, and T. J. PARSONS, *Mitochondrial DNA sequence heteroplasmy in the Grand Duke of Russia Georgij Romanov establishes the authenticity of the remains of Tsar Nicholas II.*

12. P. GILL et al, *Nature Genet.*, 9 (1995), p. 9-10.

13. R. R. SCHWEITZER, "Anastasia and Anna Anderson," *Nature Genet.*, 9 (1995), p. 345.

14. T. H. RODERICK, M.-C. KING and R. C. ANDERSON, "Mitochondrial DNA: a genetic and genealogical study," *Nexus* IX(5) (1992), p. 145-146. See also T. H. RODERICK, "Umbilical lines and the mtDNA project," *National Geneal. Soc. Quart.*, 82 (1994), p. 144-145.

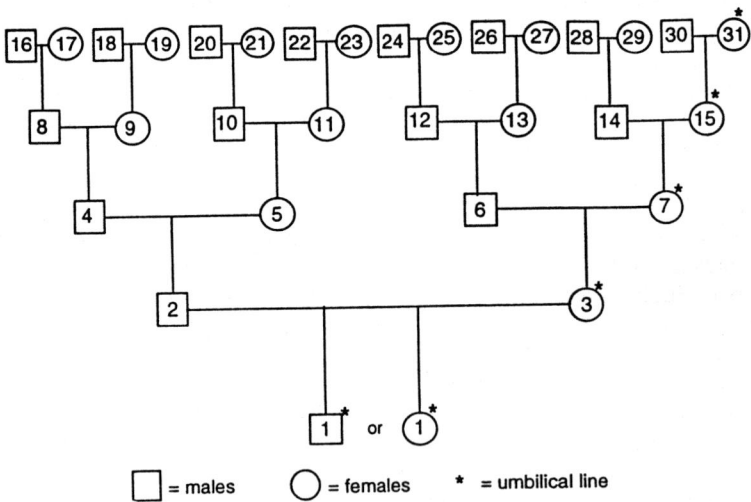

**FIGURE 1:** Ancestor table numbers showing the umbilical line, 1, 3, 7, 15, 31, etc. (asterisks) through which mitochondrial DNA is inherited. No. 1* and all his or her full siblings (or half siblings through the mother) will have the same mtDNA. Numbers are ancestor table numbers.

# SUBJECTS OF THE FRENCH KINGS → BAVARIAN DUKES → MEMBERS OF THE RUSSIAN IMPERIAL HOUSE → CITIZENS OF GERMANY, FRANCE, CANADA, USA: THE BEAUHARNAIS OVER THE LAST 200 YEARS

Igor Sakharov

The Beauharnais are an ancient line of the Orléanais nobility. At the end of the 17th century and in the first half of the 18th century, some of them held important posts in the Royal French Navy and in French overseas territories: for instance, François Beauharnois de la Chaussaye, Baron de Beauville (1665-1746) was intendant of New France and his brother Charles Beauharnois de la Boische, Marquis de Beauharnois (1671-1749) was governor general of New France. So it is not by chance that a town not far from Montreal is named Beauharnois.

The Beauharnais became especially famous at the time of the French Revolution of 1789, when two brothers actively stepped into the political arena and found themselves in opposite camps —the marquis François, the royalist, and the vicomte Alexandre, who supported the Revolution. The latter became one of the commanders of the revolutionary army, then was nominated minister of war, but didn't accept this post and was condemned for treason and guillotined in Paris in 1794. His widow, Josephine, became the wife of the general Napoleon Bonaparte, the future emperor of France, who adopted her children from her earlier marriage, and her son Eugène de Beauharnais (1781-1824) became a distinguished general and statesman.

This study is devoted to the curious and dramatic story of Eugène's direct male descendants up to the present day. We examine how they changed their countries of residence over five or six generations, along with formal changes of nationality or citizenship and religious denominations. We also examine their total change in world outlook, revised loyalties, and dislocation of their ethnic, linguistic and confessional identity.

The principal milestones are as follows:

In 1806, Eugène de Beauharnais married Princess Augusta, daughter of the Bavarian *Kurfürst* and the first king of Bavaria Maximilian I. Having settled in his wife's country, he became the owner of the former principality of Leuchtenberg, which

had been recreated as a mediatised duchy and, having been granted the appropriate Bavarian title of duke of Leuchtenberg and prince of Eichstätt, his family was raised to the highest ranks of Bavarian society.

The son of Duke Eugène, Maximilian (1817-1852), having married the daughter of the Russian Emperor Nicholas I, Grand-Duchess Maria (1819-1876) in 1839, gave up his Bavarian nationality and moved to Russia. The new country became the homeland of his children and grandchildren, who were brought up in the traditions of the Russian Orthodox Church. In 1852, after their father's death, they were granted the title of Princes Romanovsky (while retaining the right, on the basis of *primogeniture*, to the Bavarian title of dukes of Leuchtenberg), and were officially included in the Russian Imperial House with the titles of imperial highnesses.

Some members of this family took an active part in different spheres of Russia's social life. For example, Duke Maximilian, who became honorary member of the St-Petersburg Academy of Science and president of the Russian Academy of Arts, played a prominent role in the development of mining, metallurgy and the construction of railways in Russia. Duke Maximilian was also famous as a benefactor, and today there is an important medical center in St-Petersburg, called the Maximilian clinic, reminding us of his charitable activities. His son Duke Nicholas became famous in the field of mining, geology and mineralogy. Several princes Romanovsky and dukes of Leuchtenberg served in the Imperial Russian army, and one of them, Prince Serge, was killed in 1877, during the war for the liberation of Bulgaria against Turkey.

Two of Duke Maximilian's four sons, Nicholas and Eugène, contracted morganatic marriages (see TABLE 2). Their untitled wives were granted the titles of countesses of Beauharnais by the Russian Emperors; their sons and daughters lost the title of princes and princesses of Romanovsky but received the hereditary *Russian* title (as a kind of echo of the *Bavarian* one) of dukes of Leuchtenberg. Thus their surnames and titles and, respectively, their coats of arms became a strange mixture of French, Bavarian and Russian elements; and we could say that the French and Bavarian elements that had already vanished in France and Bavaria were "restored" on Russian soil.

The title of countess of Beauharnais was also given to Darya, daughter of Eugène, the fifth duke of Leuchtenberg, a case that is of a specific interest to the main theme of our Congress. Countess Darya's father was a grandson of Eugène de Beauharnais, general in Napoleon's army, while her mother was a great-grand-daughter of the Russian field marshal Koutouzov, and so her forefathers confronted each other in battle during the War of 1812.

After the Russian Revolution of 1917, all members of this aristocratic family were forced to flee the country. Only the Countess Darya de Beauharnais, princess Kotchoubey by her first marriage, and baroness Graevenitz by her second, remained in Soviet Russia after the revolution. In 1937, she was arrested and shot in a prison in Leningrad. As *émigrés*, most of the dukes and duchesses of Leuchtenberg settled in the lands of their forebears—some in Germany, some in France, and, after World War II, a few crossed the ocean to Canada and the USA. In time, they and their children became citizens of their respective countries.

The death in Rome of the unmarried Prince Serge (1890-1974), the eighth duke of Leuchtenberg, marked the end of this *Bavarian* dynasty, as well as the end of the line of the Russian princes Romanovsky. The male lines of the so to say "post-Russian," i.e., "French" and "American" (including the "Canadian") branches of the *Russian* dukes of Leuchtenberg have now also died out. For instance, speaking of the "Canadian" line, Duke Konstantin died in Ottawa in 1983, and his daughters, Duchess Ksenia (countess Grabbe by her marriage) and Duchess Olga (Gaydebourova by her marriage) are now living in the USA. The latter's cousin Duchess Elena (who was a lieutenant in the Canadian Army during the World War II) became a nun, with the name Elisabeth, and actually lives in the Russian Orthodox Convent at Bussy-en-Othe, in France. The male line of the dukes of Leuchtenberg continues only in the "German" branch in the person of Duke Nicholas, born in 1933, his sons Nicholas and Konstantin and his younger cousin Duke Serge (born in 1955) now living in the USA. As for the female lines, they are represent-ed in various countries by such names as vom Bruch, Mogilevsky, de Pasquale, Stout, Newburgh, Kraft, Ugrichich-Trebinsky, Karanfilov, Vsevolozhski, the Counts Grabbe, Gaydebourov, Bataille, the Princes Kotchoubey, Laguerre, the Counts Tyszkiewicz etc. None of them lives in Russia.

At the present time, depending on the prevailing ethnic, linguistic and confessional milieu in which they find themselves, the various branches of this international and cosmopolitan family are subject to different kinds of contradictory ethnic and social processes. This takes place mostly at the individual level, and generally, as a result of the nature of their marital links. One can suppose that after two or three more generations, second or even first cousins will lose all that they formerly had in common, socially and culturally. They are not even likely to share a common mother tongue.

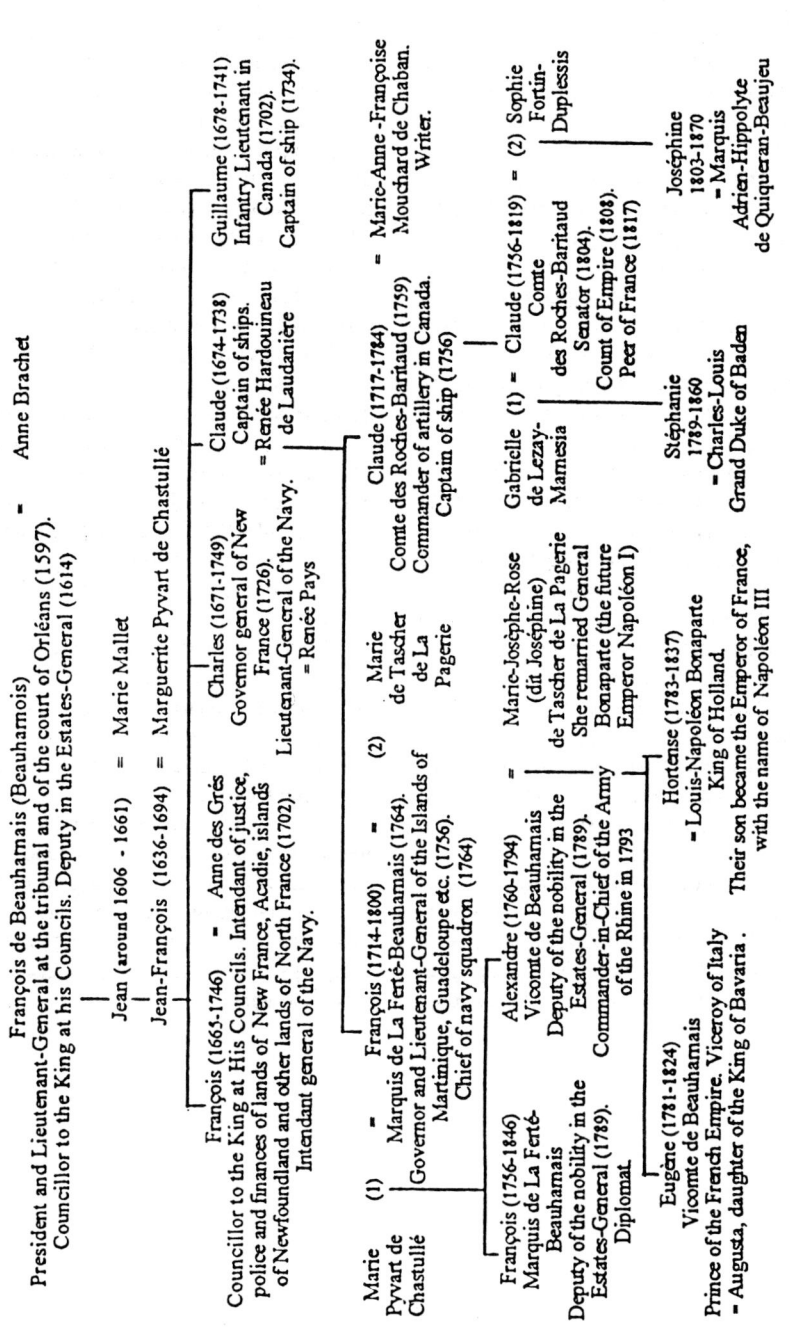

**FIGURE 1:** Simplified genealogy of the Beauharnais (Beauharnois, Beauharnoys)

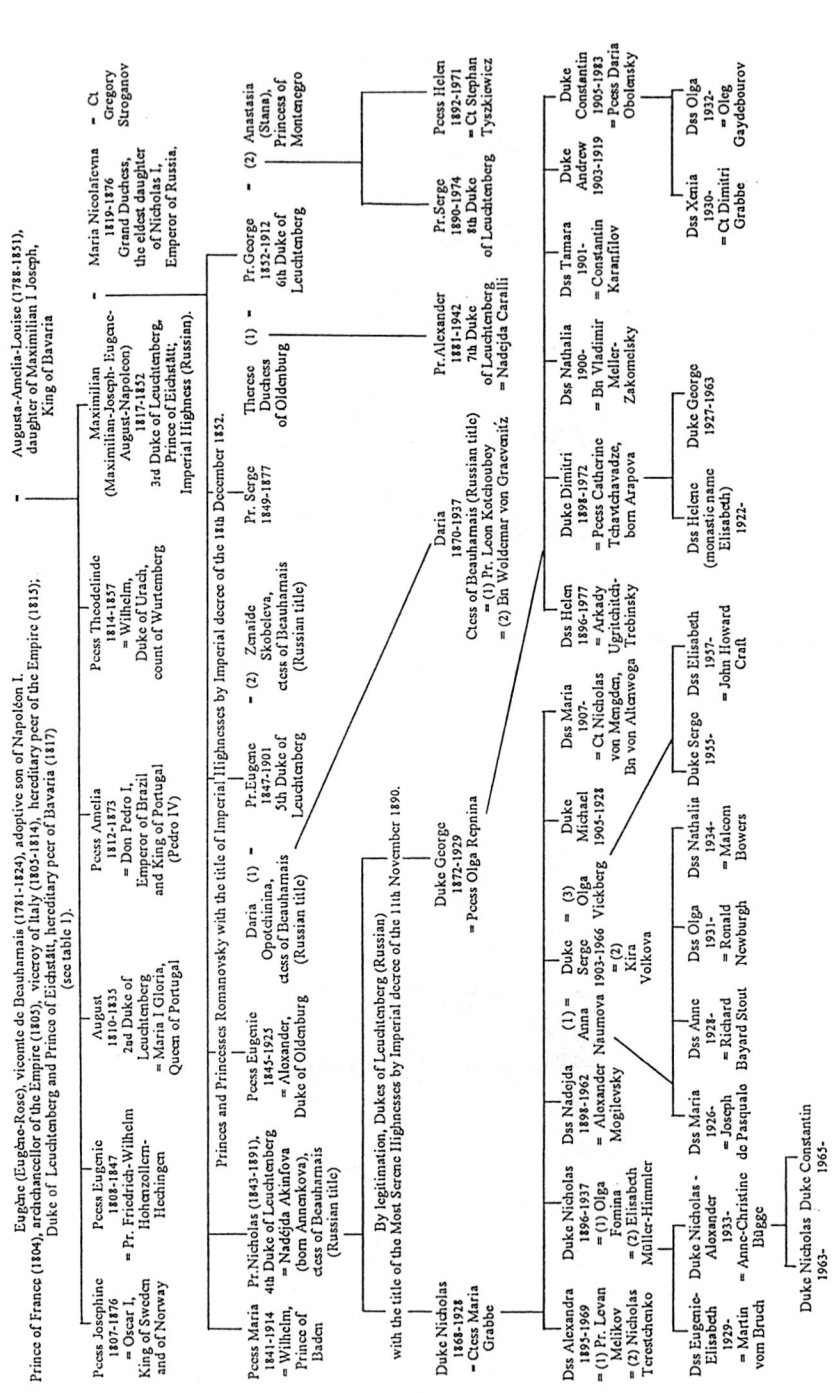

**FIGURE 2:** The dukes of Leuchtenberg, Bavaria and Russia

**FIGURE 3:** Coats of arms of counts de Beauharnais, of marquis de Beauharnais and of landgraves de Leuchtenberg, J. SIEBMACHERS, *Grosses und allgemeines Wappenbuch*, vol.1, part. 3, III, series B (Nürnberg: 1888), table 41.

**FIGURE 4:** Russian Coat of arms of Maximilian, duke of Leuchtenberg
J. SIEBMACHERS, *Grosses und allgemeines Wappenbuch*, vol. 1, part. 3, III, series B (Nürnberg: 1888), table 40.

253

# LES RACINES RUSSES, FRANÇAISES, POLONAISES, GÉORGIENNES ET TATARES DU PHILOSOPHE RUSSE NICOLAS BERDIAEV (1874-1948) ET LEUR INFLUENCE SUR SA « CONNAISSANCE DE SOI » ET SA VISION DU MONDE

Nathalie Sakharova

Cette communication est consacrée à la généalogie de Nicolas Berdiaev (Kiev, 1874-†Clamart, près de Paris, 1948), un des plus grands philosophes russes du XXe siècle, dont les lignées ascendantes sont constituées d'un mélange plutôt inhabituel. Les Berdiaev appartenaient à la noblesse traditionnellement militaire reconnue, depuis le XIVe siècle, dans la région de Smolensk. Du côté de son père, l'élément russe domine (sauf que la famille de sa grand-mère paternelle, née Bakhmetiev, remontait à de lointaines racines tatares, et l'arrière-grand-père de sa mère, née Dounina, était un Polonais qui s'était installé en Russie, au début du XVIIIe siècle). Les ancêtres de sa mère, d'origines ethniques variées, appartenaient à des confessions différentes et représentaient diverses traditions culturelles. La mère de Berdiaev appartenait à la famille des princes Koudachev, d'origine tatare assez récente : au XVIIe siècle, ses ancêtres étaient encore musulmans et seul le grand-père de son grand-père s'était fait baptiser. Le passage à l'orthodoxie contribuait à la russification rapide des mourzas tatares d'hier ;

mais dans le cas des ancêtres de Berdiaev, la russification n'était que relative. En effet, la grand-mère paternelle de la mère du philosophe était née princesse Baratov : les princes Baratov, ou Baratachvili, appartenaient à la très ancienne noblesse géorgienne. La grand-mère maternelle du philosophe, une comtesse Choiseul-Gouffier, était de la haute aristocratie française. Quant à la mère de celle-ci, elle appartenait à une grande famille de l'aristocratie polonaise, les Potocky. Ainsi, au niveau des huit quartiers du philosophe, c'est-à-dire pour ce qui est de la génération de ses bisaïeux et bisaïeules, il y avait cinq Russes (dont deux d'origine tatare et un de récente origine polonaise), une Géorgienne, un Français et une Polonaise (ces deux derniers étant catholiques, à la différence des autres qui étaient orthodoxes). Comme il le disait lui-même, Nicolas Berdiaev avait conscience de son origine « bariolée » et en premier lieu de ses composantes russe et française, qui constituaient les fondements de son « sol mental ». Tout ceci transparaît, à travers quelques traits essentiels de la personnalité et de l'œuvre de ce grand penseur.

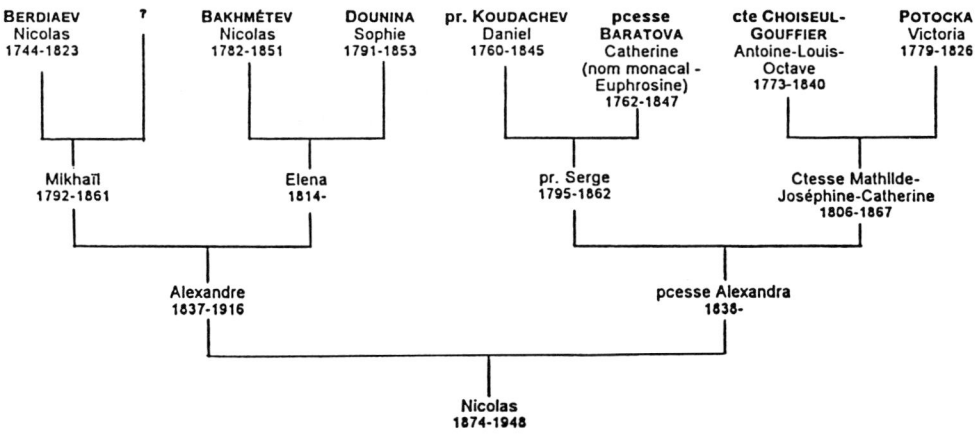

**FIGURE 1 :** Généalogie ascendante de Nicolas Berdiaev

Les Berdiaev

Les Bakhmétev

Les Dounine

Les pr. Koudachev

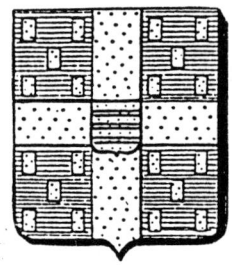

Les comtes
Choiseul-Gouffier

Les Potocki

# ORIGINS AND IMPACTS: LOYALIST IMMIGRATION TO THE BAHAMAS

Gail Saunders

The origins of the division that produced "Loyalism" in the American society is difficult to pinpoint but the Stamp Act crisis of 1765 probably saw its beginning. It was the Declaration of Independence in July 1776, however, that demarcated the Whigs from the Tories or Loyalists. The former were for the establishment of an independent Republic, the latter opposed independence and favoured reconciliation with Great Britain.

Why people chose to remain Loyalists is difficult to explain. Wallace Brown contends that most Loyalists thought that the break with Britain would lose them something "material" or "spiritual."[1] Some feared the loss of their jobs, trade, prestige, and the Anglophiles, the Empire. Many were alienated from whiggish circles; some thought the British were invincible; many opposed independence but some simply followed their leaders.[2]

The persecution of the Tories, which began in earnest after 1774, was terrible. Each State passed legislation requiring inhabitants to take oaths to the new United States or be deemed traitors. Some Loyalists had their property confiscated; others were socially ostracised and their businesses boycotted. All types of atrocities in the name of patriotism were inflicted against the Loyalists, the most infamous and common being that of tarring and feathering.

Loyalists were fined, pressured socially, mobbed and deprived of earning a living and some were banished. Others left voluntarily, initially finding sanctuary within the British lines, especially in East Florida. Formerly a Spanish colony, East Florida was ceded to Britain after the Seven Years' War and was favoured by the southern Loyalists, especially those from Georgia and the Carolinas. Later they left the country altogether.

Estimates calculate that between 80,000 and 100,000 Loyalists fled from the United States.[3] A trickle went to Great Britain while the majority settled in the Maritime Provinces of Canada, especially in Nova Scotia. Some went to the West Indies, including Jamaica, Barbados, Dominica and the Bahamas.

Before the coming of the Loyalists and their slaves, the Bahamas were sparsely populated, the whole population amounting to between 4,000 and 5,000 people, a great proportion being free.[4] Except for New Providence, Eleuthera and Harbour Island, most Bahamian islands were as yet unsettled or sparsely so. Only those three places named were represented in the House of Assembly. The inhabitants were very poor and owned little property, usually comprising a few small vessels and a few slaves. There was no plantation system as such.

Principally occupied in a seafaring life of fishing, wrecking and turtling, the early inhabitants also engaged in woodcutting, mainly dye-woods and other varieties such as Madeira (Bahamian mahogany) and boxwood. There was no staple crop and very little agriculture. The inhabitants took to rambling when the plantation soil failed. Schoepf, a German traveller, described the older inhabitants of Nassau as "amiable," "courteous" and "hospitable" and as liking to drink and dance the time away.[5]

No sheep or cattle were raised and the diet comprised mainly of fish, probably conch, turtle, iguanas, vegetables and fruit. Salt was gathered by the settlers prior to the coming of the Loyalists, but was mainly for local consumption. According to William Wylly, a Loyalist, who became attorney general of the islands, the total exports, which included wrecked goods and probably salt and dye-woods, to Great Britain in 1773-1774 amounted to £5,216 8s.10d. and the imports to £3,581 0s. 0d.[6] No account was kept of imports or exports to and from other countries.

Nassau, the chief town located on the strategically placed New Providence Island, was a shabby little port overgrown with shrubs and trees. It comprised one narrow unpaved street, mostly wooden buildings and a few unimpressive public buildings. Schoepf described the now famous Bay Street, then the only "tolerably regular street"[7] as a narrow and shore-winding one that was lined with houses and shops on one side and an open harbour on the other.

With such little information about the Bahamas, not many Loyalists wished to come to the Bahamas at first. The Treaty of Versailles agreed to on February 10, 1783 had ceded the Bahamas back to Britain, and alarmingly, East and West Florida to Spain. However, not aware of the Treaty, Colonel Andrew Deveaux, of the South Carolina Militia, who was exiled in Florida, had with other Loyalists and a band of volunteers from Eleuthera and Harbour Island daringly taken New Providence by force from the Spanish in April 1783.[8]

Reports by Lewis Johnson, of Georgia, and Lieutenant Wilson, acting engineer, both examined the islands of the Bahamas. Their reports were not very favourable.[9] However, encouraged by grants of land, the Loyalist refugees made their way to the Bahama Islands between 1783 and 1785. The first group of American Loyalists left New York for Abaco in September 1783 and founded the town of Carleton named for Sir Guy Carleton, the British commander-in-chief at New York. Other settlements in Abaco such as Marsh Harbour, Coca Plum Creek, Spencer's Bight, Cherokee Sound and Maxwell Town were formed from the original settlement of Carleton because of disagreements among the settlers. The Loyalists also settled elsewhere in Abaco, such as Hope Town and also in many other Bahamian islands including New Providence, Eleuthera, Exuma, Cat Island, Long Island, Crooked Island, Acklins, Watlings Island (now San Salvador) and Turks and Caicos, which was then a part of the Bahamas.

Population-wise, the Loyalists revolutionized the Bahamas. Between 1783 and 1789, the white population doubled and the black population trebled. Williams Wylly estimated that in 1788 the white inhabitants numbered 3,100, the slaves 5,696 and the "people of colour" 500, giving a total of 9,296. This did not include some ten others who were scattered on the smaller cays.[10]

Included among those blacks accompanying the Loyalists were some free Negroes who had deserted their patriot masters and gone behind British lines and had been declared free. After Britain's defeat, and the cession of East Florida to Spain, many free Negroes came with the Loyalists to the Bahamas to start new lives. Some did. Others unfortunately were recaptured by the American Loyalists and resold into slavery.

According to Governor John Maxwell, who was under some pressure from some of the Loyalists, there were two classes of Loyalists—the farmers who settled on the Out Islands with large families and 10, 20 or 100 slaves, and the second group, who were officers, merchants and professionals, many of whom wished to return to America when conditions settled down. The governor praised the former group, but stated that nothing could satisfy the second group, his main critics, who faulted the way he conducted business in general. He complained of their demanding behaviour and saw them as a threat.[11] The latter group settled mainly in New Providence and the northern Bahamas.

Among the Loyalists who settled and remained in the northern islands was the Curry Family. Joseph Curry's five sons, Joseph, John, Richard, Benjamin and William, moved to the Bahamas from South Carolina after the Revolutionary war and intermarried with the Conchs. It is said that all the Currys in the Bahamas today can trace their ancestry to these brothers.[12]

Those Loyalists who went south and southeast settled islands (which Dr. Peters called the plantation islands)[13] and which for the most part had few, if any, inhabitants. Such islands included Crooked, Acklins and Long Cay, Cat Island (which in 1783 and for most of the 19th century was referred to as San Salvador), Watlings, Rum Cay and the Exumas. The Loyalists, using slave labour and a staple crop pattern that they had known in Georgia and South Carolina, established cotton plantations.

Denys Rolle of East Florida was one of the principal settlers on Exuma, Charles Farquharson and Burton Williams were among those at San Salvador and William Moss, perhaps the largest slave owner settled Crooked Island and Acklins. He owned several plantations including Prospect Hill Estate and the True Blue Estates on Crooked Island. True Blue survives as a settlement on that island today. Duncan and Archibald Taylor settled Ragged Island and the capital of the Island Duncan Town is named for one of the brothers. Among those Loyalists who settled in Cat Island were Joseph and Oswell Eve, the former inventor of a wind-turned cotton gin. However, most of the settlers had little aptitude and training for agriculture in the rocky and thin soil of the Bahama Islands.[14]

New Providence in the strict sense was not a plantation island. Many of the Loyalists who settled there were businessmen, professionals and government officials. Quite a number of the plantation Loyalists who owned estates on the Out

Islands bought business and residential properties in Nassau. Among the 80 Loyalists described by Lydia Parrish in her unpublished manuscript, three were medical doctors, one a surgeon, one a cabinet-maker, two ship captains, one a mariner and one a school teacher—the latter doubling up as an auctioneer. [15]

Prominent among the New Providence Loyalists were Adam Chrystie, secretary of the Bahamas and a member of the Council, Stephen Delancey, chief justice (after whom Delancey Town is named), and William Wylly, a former captain in the Carolina Rangers. Wylly, who owned three plantations on New Providence including one at Clifton, quickly rose to the position of attorney general and perhaps was the most controversial figure in Bahamian politics for a quarter of a century. John Wells, the first newspaper publisher in the Bahamas, also settled in Nassau and helped the Loyalists in their fight to gain political power. [16]

Feuds developed not only between the Loyalists and the old inhabitants or Conchs, whom they considered inferior, and the local colonial government headed by the governor, but friction also raged between refugees from West Florida and the merchant-planters from East Florida. Most of the latter had close ties of either blood or friendship and were clannish. Some families, sought plantations in the same islands, for example, the Bellinger and Kelsall families, who settled at Little Exuma. [17]

Besides expanding the population and laying down racial lines for centuries to come, the Loyalists and their slaves affected the Bahamas economically, socially and politically.

In the economic sphere the Loyalists failed to transform the Bahamas. They attempted to introduce new crops, especially the growing of cotton. However, they brought short-lived prosperity and some development, even if on a modest scale to many hitherto uninhabited or scarcely inhabited islands. Introducing a plantation economy in the south they infused new life into the commercial activity of the islands.

The planter Loyalists who went south and those who settled in the north both had an economic impact on the Bahamas. Loyalist shipbuilders who included John Russell, William Begbie and Daniel Manson introduced a prosperous trade bringing much foreign capital into the Bahamas. With the influx of professionals, such as doctors, lawyers, accountants and merchants, commercial life was given a further boost. Stores "blossomed over Nassau." Some companies that had successfully traded with the Indians in the southern states moved their headquarters to Nassau. One firm was Panton, Leslie and Company. There were others, including Miller, Bonnamy and Company. But it was the planter Loyalists who mainly went south, who tried, albeit unsuccessfully, to revolutionize the Bahamian way of life. [18]

Those Loyalists who went south mainly to Watlings, Exuma, San Salvador (that is Cat Island), Long Island and Crooked and Acklins Island between 1784 and 1785 to set up cotton plantations, had great hopes of prosperity. By November 1785, over 2,000 acres of cotton were under cultivation in the Bahamas. For a few years it looked as though the Loyalists' hopes would be fulfilled. However, cotton as a successful commercial crop was brief.

In 1785 the Bahamas produced 124 tons of cotton from 2,476 acres. Production for the years 1786 and 1787 was 150 tons and 219 tons from 3,050 and 4,050 acres respectively. However, by 1800, most of the cotton planters were facing ruin and the Bahamian government's questionnaire in that year to 25 leading cotton growers, revealed that failure was principally due to the exhausted state of the soil, the inexperience of the planters and consequent injudicious planting, the attack of the chenille and red bug, bad management and climate. The soil was thin and the slash and burn method usually employed to clear the fields eventually led to soil exhaustion. Manure was difficult to obtain; many planters had no cattle. [19]

Because many of the Loyalists had invested all that they had in their plantations, they were tied to them. A good number tried to sell them in the late 18th and early 19th centuries. When cotton failed, the planters were forced to leave or resort to the old subsistence crops such as guinea corn and yams, stock-raising, salt-raking (for example Duncan and Archibald Taylor in Ragged Island) and took to the seafaring life of the older inhabitants. Some cotton was still grown in the 1860s according to Governor Rawson's *Report on the Bahamas' Hurricane of October 1866* and also in the late 19th century. [20]

Socially, the Loyalists greatly influenced Bahamian life. They introduced their own concept of plantation life and that of the relationship of master and slave. The increase in the slave population made for more stringent controls by the ruling class. Because of the increased number of black slaves, the Loyalists passed harsh vagrancy laws and regulations to separate the races on New Providence in the early 1790s. An "Act for Regulating the Police of the Town of Nassau and Suburbs," passed between 1795 and 1798, demanded that all people of colour be off the streets of the town of Nassau after 9:00 p.m. when the Town bell rang. [21]

The two main areas near Nassau that were inhabited by blacks during slavery were Grant's Town, a wooded swampy area surveyed in the 1820s under the administration of Governor Grant, and Delancey Town, named after a slave owner and chief justice of the Bahamas, Stephen Delancey.

While Grant's Town or "Over-the-Hill" was much poorer and had more humble dwellings, Nassau was revitalized by the Loyalists. Besides important architectural changes, streets were cleaned, and repaired, and new ones built. Docks and wharves were improved and new regulations passed, prohibiting thatched roofs in Nassau. Architecturally, the Loyalists had a tremendous impact on the town. Much of the architectural style of the southern states was transported to Nassau. Many Loyalist houses were built after the Georgian style but adapted to meet Bahamian climatic and economic conditions. [22]

Not only did the Loyalists affect private architecture in the town, its suburbs and on the Out Islands, they also greatly influenced public construction. Lord Dunmore, himself, in his mania for building, directed the building of Forts Charlotte and Fincastle and batteries at Winton, Hog Island and Potter's Cay. He also built Dunmore House (formely known as The Priory but now demolished) on West Street. For his private enjoyment, he built two summer residences, the Hermitage on East Bay Street and a house, now demolished, on Harbour Island in Dunmore Town, which he also laid out. [23]

The public buildings completed between 1812 and 1816 were based on Governor Tryon's palace in New Bern, the ancient capital of North Carolina. Similarly, the Nassau Public Library, built between 1798 and 1799, was said to have been inspired by the old Powder Magazine in Williamsburg, Virginia. Government House was also said to have been inspired by the Loyalists,

as well as St. Matthew's Anglican Church and the St. Andrew's Presbyterian Church. [24]

On the Out Islands, the modest Loyalist plantation house—made of stone with separate kitchen, fireplace and chimney, bakery, stable and slave quarters—changed the life on the hitherto uninhabited or scantily inhabited islands. Recent archaeological excavations on plantation sites in New Providence and the Family islands give a "general idea of plantation life in the Bahamas as a whole" and reinforce the written record, which indicate, that "productivity of these plantation was consistently low." Grace Turner argues that while many planters moved away, their slaves were left to manage the estates. They resorted to subsistence farming, and also adapted to the Conchs' (old inhabitant's) way of life. [25]

Culturally, the Loyalists and their slaves made a big impact on Bahamian and especially New Providence life. Record-keeping and education were improved, a lending library started, and drama entertainment begun. The British legal system, which still survives today, was reinforced.

The first Bahamian newspaper, *The Bahamas Gazette*, was published for the first time on August 7, 1784 by John Wells, a Loyalist from Charleston, South Carolina. Besides the Bahamas, Wells' newspaper was circulated in Charleston, Savannah and Bermuda. Wells also opened a book and stationery store, the only one in Nassau, and published various items including the *Bahamas Almanac*.

Two other Loyalist printers functioned for a while. Joseph Eve for a time was a printer to the House of Assembly and Alexander Cameron, a Virginian Loyalist, founded a second, largely unknown Nassau newspaper, *The Lucayan Royal Herald*. [26]

Religious and education life were also strengthened by the Loyalists' advent. By an act of 1795, six new parishes were created on recently settled islands. An enlightened "School Act" was also passed in 1795 providing for the establishment of an additional school at Nassau. Soon after, in 1804, a "High School Act" was passed thereby creating the first High School in the Bahamas. The Loyalists were also responsible for introducing private schools in the Bahamas. [27]

The slaves of the Loyalists also greatly influenced religious and social life. They kept alive many of their African customs diluted by their new environment and tribal dispersal. Additionally, many of the slaves of Loyalists had been born in America or the West Indies. However, they brought their beliefs and practices with them, and much of their folklore was passed on from generation to generation and still affects Bahamian culture today. Especially significant are the use of bush or herb medicine, the practice of Junkanoo, the Baptist religion, story-telling, music and dance, obeah, food and games. [28]

Bush medicine was most certainly used in slavery days and is still practised today. It is possible to trace Junkanoo back to the plantation. In the religious field, it is interesting to note that Joseph Paul, a freed slave, was the first Methodist in the Bahamas and Brother Amos and Samuel Scriven, formerly slaves, were among the first Baptists in the Bahamas. [29]

Politically, the Loyalists created factional feeling and challenged the older Bahamian ruling party. The older inhabitants disliked the newcomers. A feud developed between the Loyalists, the Conchs and the established colonial administration. Gradually gaining prominence, the Loyalists caused the downfall of two successive governors, John Maxwell and John, Earl of Dunmore. Becoming a "party" of opposition to the existing government in the islands, the American Loyalists criticized the administration and challenged the *status quo*.

Representation was extended to include Abaco, Exuma, Long Island, Cat Island and Andros. Previous to that date, only Nassau, Eleuthera and Harbour Island returned representatives. In 1799 additional seats were created for Turks and Caicos, San Salvador, Rum Cay, Crooked Island, Acklins and Long Cay. [30]

The election of 1785 gave the Loyalists some members in the House of Assembly, but the old "party" was still in control. The Loyalists gained ascendancy through by-elections. They owned more property than the older inhabitants and soon held the majority of the high positions in government. The rowdy, troublesome newcomers, especially ring leaders James Hepburn, formerly attorney general of St. Augustine and Robert Johnston, a lawyer, successfully agitated against Governors Maxwell and Dunmore. Gradually the Americans became the stronger party in the Bahamas.

The American Loyalists greatly influenced political life. By their very numbers and their settlement in the Out Islands, they posed a challenge to the old order. They also passed laws that profoundly affected the social lives of the inhabitants of the Bahamas. Included in the legislation were acts to reinforce the fledgling police force and a militia, to establish schools and to regulate fire protection and cemeteries. As discussed above, acts were passed defining more stringently the colourbar. In the political sphere, the Loyalists passed legislation to limit the House of Assembly to a five-year term. Although this was amended from time to time, the Loyalist law was of some significance. The present day Parliament sits for five years. [31]

The coming of the Loyalists to the Bahamas was formerly characterized as the transformation of the islands by a new and more progressive type of white colonists. However, as Michael Craton and this author argued, "it could easily be portrayed as the transformation of such Loyalists in the Bahamas." [32]

Quantitatively, there was a transformation in the Bahamas' population. The Loyalists set up many new settlements especially on the Out (Family) Islands and have left permanent imprints in the Bahamas on place names such as Glenton's Sound, and Buckley's Long Island, named after Henry Glenton, Loyalist from New York, and John Buckley, formerly a resident of East Florida. Moss Town, Great Exuma and Forbes Hill, Little Exuma were named after William Moss and Thomas Forbes. Lyford Cay, western New Providence was named after William Lyford, a Georgia Loyalist.

It was in fact the enormous increase in the black population that perhaps was of greater significance. "It was probably the slave and free black majority of newcomers who most indelibly shaped the social history of the Bahamas." [33] As the plantations declined, many of the white planters returned to the United States, went to England or settled in New Providence. There they developed as a mercantile oligarchy controlling commerce, land and politics. [34]

The white merchants, planters and professionals were forced to pass more stringent laws and regulations to control the large black population. The ruling class made sure that the black population, then in a majority, knew their place. The result was the hardening of racial barriers, which was to affect Bahamian society for over 150 years. Separated by colour and class, the division in the society was reflected in the cultural aspects of Bahamian life.

While the powerful elite transformed the architecture of the white section of Nassau where it lived and worked, it paid little attention to the "over-the-hill" or the black section where the perceived "social inferiors" lived and which ultimately became a slum. Loyalists strived to improve the tone of literary and drama societies. At the same time, the slaves perhaps imperceptibly passed on their customs such as Junkanoo and obeah, with African origins but which were creolized.

In the economic sphere, the experiment in cotton growing was short-lived and largely a failure, although there is evidence that cotton production was revitalized in the 1860s and 1890s on some Bahamian islands. As the plantations failed, the Loyalists, their slaves and their descendants learned to adapt to the lack of resources and the unyielding soil of the Bahamas. They learned to survive as subsistence farmers and reinforced old Bahamian industries and putting farming on a more stable basis. Ship building, commerce, salt-production and, to a minor extent, stock-raising also remained important to the Bahamas, especially in rural areas. The Loyalists adapted to the ways of the old inhabitants and were themselves changed by local conditions.

## NOTES

1. WALLACE BROWN, *The Good Americans. The Loyalists in American Revolution* (New York: 1969), p. 80.

2. *Ibid.*, p. 81.

3. *Ibid.*, p. 192.

4. WILLIAM WYLLY, *A Short Account of the Bahama Islands* (London: 1789), p. 5-7.

5. J. D. SCHOEPF, *Travels in the Confederation 1783-1784* (Philadelphia: 1911), p. 273.

6. WILLIAM WYLLY, *op. cit.,* p. 7.

7. J. D. SCHOEPF, *op. cit.,* p. 262.

8. MICHAEL CRATON and GAIL SAUNDERS, *Islanders in the Stream. A History of the Bahamian People,* vol. 1 (Athens and London: The University of Georgia Press, 1992), p. 169-171.

9. GAIL SAUNDERS, *Bahamian Loyalists and Their Slaves* (London: Macmillan Education Limited, 1983), p. 8.

10. WILLIAM WYLLY, *op. cit.,* p. 8.

11. Maxwell to Sydney, May 17, 1784, PUBLIC RECORD OFFICE, London, CO, 23/25, p. 104-105.

12. GAIL SAUNDERS, *Bahamian Loyalists . . .,* p. 13.

13. THELMA P. PETERS, *The American Loyalists and the Plantation Period in the Bahama Islands* (Ph.D. Thesis, University of Florida: 1960), p. 62-66.

14. GAIL SAUNDERS, "The Loyalists—General Influences," *Journal of the Bahamas Historical Society,* vol. 5, no. 1 (October 1983), p. 5.

15. See LYDIA A. PARRISH, *Records of Some Southern Loyalists,* unpublished manuscript about some 80 families most of whom immigrated to the Bahamas during and after the American Revolution, 1940 to 1953.

16. GAIL SAUNDERS, *Bahamian Loyalists . . .,* p. 14; MICHAEL CRATON and GAIL SAUNDERS, *Islanders . . .,* p. 190, 297-303.

17. MICHAEL CRATON and GAIL SAUNDERS, *Islanders . . .* p. 233-242.

18. GAIL SAUNDERS, *Bahamian Loyalists . . .,* p. 37; MICHAEL CRATON and GAIL SAUNDERS, *Islanders . . .,* p. 191-195.

19. GAIL SAUNDERS, *Slavery in the Bahamas,* The Nassau *Guardian* (Nassau: 1985), p. 23-27; MICHAEL CRATON and GAIL SAUNDERS, *Islanders . . .,* p. 196-197.

20. GAIL SAUNDERS, *Bahamian Loyalists . . .,* p. 41.

21. *Ibid.,* p. 44-45; See also GAIL SAUNDERS, *Slavery in the Bahamas . . .,* p. 32.

22. GAIL SAUNDERS, *Bahamian Loyalists . . .,* p. 48-57; MICHAEL CRATON and GAIL SAUNDERS, *Islanders . . .,* p. 192-195.

23. GAIL SAUNDERS, *Bahamian Loyalists . . .,* p. 49-51. See also GAIL SAUNDERS and DONALD CARTWRIGHT, *Historic Nassau* (London: 1979), p. 29-32.

24. GAIL SAUNDERS and DONALD CARTWRIGHT, *op. cit.,* p. 18-20.

25. GRACE TURNER, "An Archaeological Record of Plantation Life in the Bahamas," *Journal of the Bahamas Historical Society,* vol. 14, no. 1 (October 1992), p. 38. See also LAURIE WILKIE and PAUL FARNSWORTH, "Archaeological Excavations on Crooked Island," *ibid,* vol. 17 (October 1995), p. 34-36; PAUL FARNSWORTH, "Excavations at Promised Land Plantation, New Providence," *ibid,* vol. 16, no. 1 (October 1994), p. 21-27.

26. *The Bahama Gazette* (1784); *The Lucayan Herald* (1789), (PUBLIC RECORD OFFICE, London, CO 23/30, 194-195A).

27. *Bahama Gazette,* April 9-11, 1785 and Manuscript Laws of the Bahamas, 1795-1799, Department of Archives.

28. GAIL SAUNDERS, *Bahamian Loyalists . . .,* p. 59-66.

29. *Ibid.,* p. 63-64.

30. *Ibid.,* p. 66-67; See also Manuscript Laws of the Bahamas, 1795-1799, Dept. Of Archives, 40 Geo. III, c. 7.

31. *Ibid.,* p. 67-70; See also *Journal of The House of Assembly,* 1784-1794, Department of Archives.

32. MICHAEL CRATON and GAIL SAUNDERS, *Island-ers . . .,* p. 179.

33. *Ibid.*

34. Michael Craton, *Bay Street, Black Power and the Conchy Joes: Race and Class in the Colony and Commonwealth of the Bahamas, 1850-2000* (Draft unpublished paper: 1996).

# LA BRANCHE RUSSE DES DANZAS (D'ANZAS), AU COURS DE DEUX SIÈCLES : CHANGEMENT DE PAYS, D'APPARTENANCE CONFESSIONNELLE ET D'IDENTIFICATION ETHNO-PSYCHOLOGIQUE

Dimitri Sizonenko

De tout temps et à la suite de diverses circonstances, des ressortissants des pays de l'Europe occidentale appartenant à toutes les couches de la société (depuis les artisans jusqu'à l'aristocratie titrée) sont venus s'installer en Russie. Pour beaucoup de familles, ce pays devenait une seconde patrie. C'est là que naissaient leurs enfants et leurs petits-enfants et le destin de leur descendance s'accomplissait dans le contexte de certains processus ethno-culturels qui avaient lieu à la suite d'une assimilation ethnique due à l'altérité linguistique, confessionnelle et culturelle du milieu ambiant. Ces processus d'adaptation présentent un intérêt pour la science historique et, pour les étudier à travers plusieurs générations, la généalogie est un instrument irremplaçable.

Les Français ont toujours constitué une part considérable des émigrés s'étant établis en Russie. Ce fait était en premier lieu notable à Saint-Pétersbourg, la capitale de l'Empire de Russie, étant donné leur nombre et le rôle qu'ils jouaient dans différentes sphères de la vie sociale. Une des grandes vagues de l'émigration française s'est dirigée vers la Russie à la suite des événements de la Grande Révolution. Cette vague a entraîné quelques membres de la famille d'Anzas, de la branche gasconne de cette ancienne famille qui avait fait souche en Alsace, au XVIIIᵉ siècle.

En accord avec le thème principal du 22ᵉ congrès, cette communication présente l'histoire des d'Anzas (devenus Danzas ou Dansas, en Russie), à partir du moment où, ayant quitté leur pays pour un autre, ils passèrent par l'adaptation et l'acculturation à un milieu nouveau et vécurent des changements occasionnés par des mariages mixtes et par le passage à une autre confession. Leurs carrières sont caractérisées par des modifications de statut social (certains d'entre eux occupaient des postes très importants dans l'armée ou le service civil).

Le « retour » dramatique des Danzas dans leur patrie d'origine, à la suite de la révolution russe de 1917, présente un intérêt particulier. Cette famille était déjà tout à fait « russifiée » : pour Jacques Danzas, qui avait dû fuir en France, la composante française n'était représentée que par un de ses huit quartiers de noblesse, tandis que, pour son fils Pierre, le dernier représentant masculin de cette famille russe portant un nom si français, elle n'était représentée que par un quartier sur 16. Ainsi, depuis plus de deux siècles, cette famille se définit ethniquement et culturellement en fonction de ses rapports complexes avec ses deux patries.

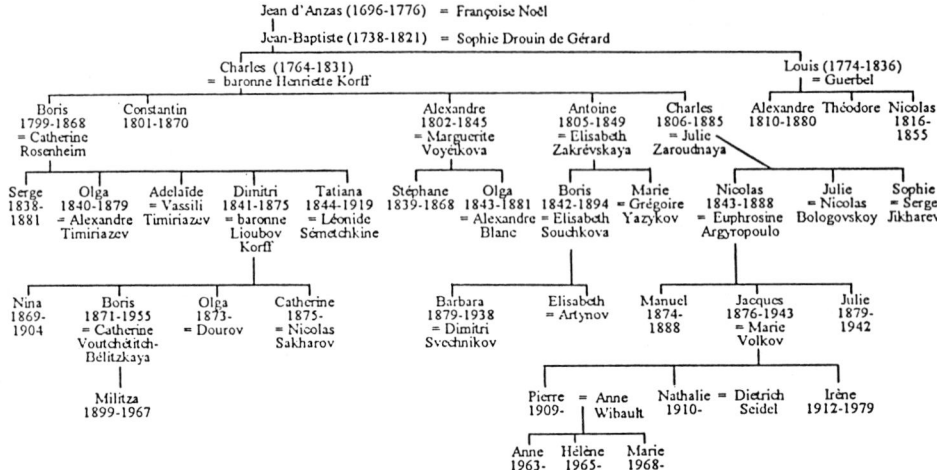

**FIGURE 1 :** Généalogie de la branche russe des Danzas (d'Anzas)

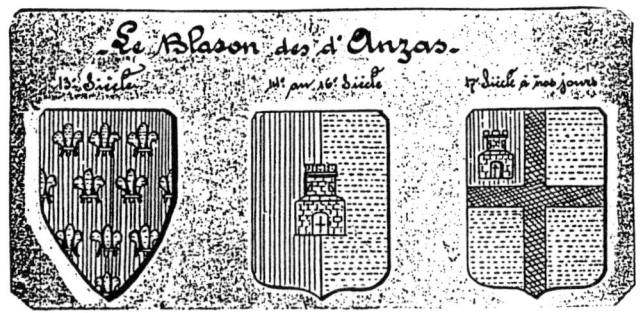

**FIGURE 2 :** Le blazon des d'Anzas
Document des archives familiales de M. Pierre Danzas (Paris)

# LES PERSPECTIVES DE CONSTITUTION DE BANQUES NATIONALES ET INTERNATIONALES DE DONNÉES GÉNÉALOGIQUES ET HÉRALDIQUES : L'EXEMPLE DE LA FRANCE

Jean-Marie Thiébaud

Ayant rapidement dépassé le stade affectif des recherches familiales personnelles visant à établir des filiations ascendantes et descendantes, les généalogistes français se sont lancés — surtout depuis 15 à 20 ans — dans des travaux collectifs qui eussent laissé pantois d'étonnement des générations entières de bénédictins.

Tout a commencé par des entreprises isolées, sans méthodologie ni aucun plan d'ensemble conçus à l'échelle nationale. Comme les lois qui s'adaptent presque toujours aux mœurs *a posteriori*, la méthodologie a suivi d'assez loin l'émergence de cette science nouvelle. En un mot, l'action a précédé la réflexion. Une fois de plus, *Primum vivere, deinde...* et tant pis si dans quelques cas, il conviendra de relire des travaux réalisés voici quelques décennies, à la lumière d'une rigueur scientifique enfin parvenue à maturité. L'essentiel était au départ de créer une formidable impulsion.

En effet, bien avant la naissance des associations généalogiques, des villes avaient ouvert la voie : à Besançon, capitale de la Franche-Comté, des archivistes-bibliothécaires municipaux ont, vers 1950-1960, complètement classé par ordre alphabétique et dactylographié les actes d'état civil de 1540 à 1800, mettant ainsi à la disposition des lecteurs un ensemble de plus de 300 000 documents sous forme de grands registres reliés consultables dans la salle des usuels. La hantise de la destruction toujours envisageable des originaux (surtout après l'exemple malheureux de l'état civil de Paris, disparu dans l'incendie de l'hôtel de ville lors de l'insurrection de la Commune en 1871 et bien avant la campagne de microfilmage systématique des documents) ne fut sans doute pas étrangère à cet étrange besoin de déchiffrer, de recopier et de classer. N'est-ce pas ainsi que le Moyen Âge servit de relais aux chefs-d'œuvre de la littérature grecque et latine?

Pendant huit ans et demi, j'ai personnellement mené une expérience semblable dans la commune voisine de Pontarlier (Doubs), à proximité de la frontière suisse. Les registres très complets couvrent sur trois paroisses une période allant de 1537 à 1792. Si le nombre d'actes étudiés et classés est moins important (environ 48 000), il est d'une toute autre ampleur car, au lieu de se limiter à de simples listes alphabétiques de naissances, mariages et décès avec dates et cotes archivistiques (comme à Besançon), ici, chaque acte a été analysé et retranscrit *in extenso*, selon des grilles bien précises, avec noms des parents, des parrains et marraines, des témoins des mariages et sépultures, sans oublier les titres, les professions, les localités d'origine et les mentions les plus diverses. Un tel fichier permet des études généalogiques portant sur plusieurs siècles sans être contraint de se reporter aux actes originaux. De plus, la consultation en est grandement facilitée par des fiches rappelant toutes les variantes graphiques rencontrées pour chaque patronyme. Et c'est là un des intérêts majeurs de la transcription systématique de tous les actes : elle seule permet — par le biais de reconstitution des familles — de retrouver des graphies parfois très déformées des noms patronymiques. L'ensemble a été complété récemment par un fichier alphabétique des personnes admises au cours des siècles dans le corps de bourgeoisie ce qui fournit une source supplémentaire d'information sur les migrants et les origines géographiques des familles.

Le professeur Dupâquier, démographe, a parallèlement mené une vaste enquête sur la France entière en étudiant, grâce à l'aide de généalogistes amateurs bénévoles, tous les Français, hommes et femmes, dont le nom commence par « Tra ». Ainsi s'est constituée une importante banque de données sociologiques permettant d'étudier les mouvements de population du XVIIIᵉ siècle à 1982 inclus. L'alliance de la généalogie et de ses sciences annexes autorise tous les espoirs pour la connaissance toujours plus affinée de l'histoire des familles. Il est déjà loin le temps où Ernest Renan pouvait ironiser sur les sciences historiques qu'il qualifiait de « petites sciences conjecturales, qui se défont sans cesse après s'être faites »[1]. La rigueur chirurgicale de la généalogie moderne s'apprête à servir d'ossature à des disciplines historique et sociologique entièrement repensées à une échelle dont n'osaient rêver les chercheurs du XIXᵉ siècle, contraints de travailler sur des sondages de trop faible amplitude pour être susceptibles d'entraîner une totale adhésion.

Ces travaux de pionniers (qui ne sont que des exemples parmi d'autres) se poursuivaient tandis que le mouvement associatif en France naissait et se développait, prenant des formes de courbes exponentielles. Après le Centre d'entraide généalogique de France (et il convient de noter au passage le terme d'*entraide* qui a toujours été le mot clé du fonctionnement de la vie généalogique associative dans notre pays), la Fédération française de généalogie est née en 1968. Puis le réseau associatif s'est vite étendu au pays tout entier. À l'heure actuelle, ce sont quelque 44 000 amateurs qui adhèrent à près de 300 associations et 36 000 d'entre eux relèvent de la Fédération nationale.

Ces chercheurs bénévoles ont compris que les richesses archivistiques de la France font de ce pays une mine d'or généalogique. Aussi, après une formation préalable en paléographie, ont-ils commencé à mettre sur fiches et à informatiser la totalité des actes des registres paroissiaux et d'état civil, en privilégiant toutefois les mariages, du début du XVIᵉ à la fin du XIXᵉ siècle. Certes, c'est en 1539 (et donc quelques années avant le concile de Trente) que François Iᵉʳ, roi de France, promulgua au château de Villers-Cotterêts une ordonnance pour la tenue obligatoire de l'état civil, mais, en réalité, nombreuses étaient les paroisses qui avaient déjà commencé à posséder des registres dès les premières années du XVIᵉ siècle, et même avant.

L'ensemble des documents conservés concerne environ 320 millions de Français (en tenant compte du fait qu'on ne peut consulter les registres postérieurs à 1896 car la législation actuelle impose un délai de 100 ans, limite qui sera peut-être révisée à la baisse dans un très proche avenir). Il représente *grosso modo* un milliard d'actes, chaque personne étant au minimum référencée socialement par deux actes (naissance et décès), mais aussi, le plus souvent, par un, voire plusieurs actes de mariage.

Ces travaux, qui présentent de surcroît pour les générations actuelles et futures le formidable avantage de faire sauter les barrages des difficultés paléographiques ou de la traduction latino-française, ont été entrepris dans toutes les régions géographi-

ques, partout où rayonnent des associations généalogiques. Leur sérieux (avec double lecture systématique et une bonne connaissance des noms du terroir que possèdent ces spécialistes de la micro-histoire que sont les généalogistes) les a fait considérer bientôt comme de précieux auxiliaires des archivistes au point que les Archives nationales de France leur ont accordé des subventions pour l'acquisition de micro-ordinateurs. Le seul bémol à concéder pour tempérer ce bel optimisme est que si la saisie des données s'est toujours effectuée sur des fiches de modèle quasi identique, l'informatisation, elle, s'est accomplie par le biais de logiciels différents, commerciaux ou même artisanaux, ce qui pose encore des problèmes de compatibilité pour de possibles et nécessaires interconnexions. Mais les informaticiens deviennent de plus en plus capables de résoudre ce type de problème et M. Xavier Guyot, président du club de généalogie IBM-FRANCE, siège au Conseil d'Administration de la Fédération dont il anime, bien évidemment, la commission informatique.

À côté de ces banques de données relatives à l'état civil, les généalogistes français ont ouvert plusieurs autres chantiers d'importance nationale ou internationale. Parmi ceux-ci, quelques-uns sont très parlants.

L'association « Ancêtres italiens » qui regroupe des Français d'origine italienne, a créé en 1995 une base militaire historique baptisée INVAL, regroupant tous les militaires blessés nés en France ou à l'étranger et reçus à l'Hôtel des Invalides à Paris entre 1673 et 1796. On y trouve quantité d'Allemands, d'Anglais, de Belges, d'Écossais, d'Irlandais, d'Italiens, de Suisses, etc. Il s'agit de données textuelles avec texte libre indexé et lexique. Pour chaque militaire, apparaît après le numéro du volume du Service Historique de l'Armée de Terre (S.H.A.T., château de Vincennes), le numéro et la date de l'acte original, une reproduction intégrale de l'acte (avec respect de l'orthographe) avec : prénoms, nom, nom de guerre, nationalité, lieu de naissance (16 % de ces soldats sont nés à l'étranger), diocèse, grade, compagnie, régiment, description de l'invalidité, batailles, profession dans le civil, lieu de mariage, date et lieu de décès.

Une des originalités de cette base réside dans la multitude des accès possibles pour le lecteur. On peut sortir à volonté les données se rapportant à une commune, à un département actuel, aux noms ayant une même finale (par exemple, se terminant par -audeau), aux invalides nés en Toscane, aux tailleurs de pierre ou à toute autre profession dans le civil, aux originaires d'un même diocèse, aux blessés de telle ou telle bataille (Fleurus, par exemple), aux villes de mariage, aux invalides originaires des Grisons dont les villes de naissance sont actuellement en Italie, aux noms de guerre, aux noms de compagnies, aux motifs de réception à l'Hôtel des Invalides, à la liste des batailles du début du XVIIIe siècle, à la localisation géographique de ces batailles, aux chirurgiens militaires, aux catégories bien précises de militaires en fonction de leur origine géographique (les Écossais, les Suisses, les Comtois) ou de leur spécialité (mousquetaires, sapeurs, canonniers).

À terme, ce seront 111 394 actes contenus dans 39 volumes qui seront analysés et informatisés. L'équipe qui travaille sur cette base en avait déjà classés 9 762 en juin 1995 et 15 596 en mars 1996 (avec 29 486 mots clés) ce qui donne une idée du rythme de progression.

Pour les informaticiens, précisons que l'association a choisi pour support un compatible PC avec pour logiciel de saisie un documentaire CDS/ISIS de l'Unesco et pour logiciel de consultation un convivial Heurisko, ne demandant aucune formation spécifique préalable[2].

Autre exemple bâti sur le même modèle et par la même association : une base de données regroupant tous les actes de naturalité de la généralité de Provence de 1650 à 1705, avec index des patronymes, les villes de naissance et de résidence et surtout le mode de francisation des noms de famille, ce qui ouvre la voie pour de vastes études franco-européennes. Ces actes regroupés aux Archives nationales, dans la série E, sous le titre *Rolle des Sommes de Naturalité*, donne la liste des sommes à payer par des étrangers ou leurs héritiers pour leur droit de résider en France. À titre d'exemple, l'association, en effectuant un dépouillement systématique intégral de 532 actes relatifs aux versements ordonnés le 5 septembre 1702 aux immigrés dans le port méditerranéen de Toulon[3], les a indexés par ordre alphabétique de noms de famille, de villes de naissance et de professions. On y découvre des habitants originaires de tous les pays d'Europe : Allemagne (Brandeburg, Dantzig, Hamburg, Lübeck, Mecklenburg, etc.), Angleterre (Bristol, London, etc.), Belgique (Bruxelles, Liège, etc.), Espagne, Écosse, Pays-Bas, Russie, Crète (port de Candie), mais aussi du Canada (ville de Québec, Terre-Neuve) ou de « Barbarie » (nom donné autrefois aux États barbaresques et corres-

pondant à la zone géographique qui recouvre de nos jours les régions de l'Afrique du Nord à l'ouest de l'Égypte : Maroc, Algérie, Tunisie et Libye). Les plus nombreux et pour d'évidentes raisons de proximité géographique, étaient natifs de Savoie et de l'ancienne république italienne de Gênes.

Nombreuses sont aussi les associations régionales qui pour diversifier et compléter les sources de recherches se sont attelées à des relevés de minutes notariales. Ainsi, le Centre Généalogique de Saône-et-Loire (C.G.S.L.) a édité sous forme de dossiers spécialisés les actes des notaires de la région chalonnaise de 1573 à 1820. Le plus souvent, ces relevés se limitent aux contrats de mariage et aux testaments qui intéressent au premier chef, et pour cause, les passionnés de l'histoire des familles.

Et ce n'est pas tout : d'aucuns dressent région par région la liste des insurgés de la commune de Paris à Rochefort-sur-Mer et dans différents forts de Charente-Maritime sur la côte atlantique (avec dates et lieux de naissance, filiations et alliances)[4] ; d'autres indexent les questions / réponses publiées dans la revue nationale *Héraldique et Généalogie* qui en est, en juin 1996, à sa 28e année de parution et à son 139e numéro trimestriel, d'autres encore donnent les noms et l'état civil des hommes qui participèrent à la prise d'Alger en 1830, dressent des listes des blessés, des malades et des morts d'origine française et européenne dans les hôpitaux militaires lors des campagnes de l'Ancien Régime, de la Révolution et de l'Empire, etc.

Le besoin de globaliser et de mondialiser les données s'est fait également de plus en plus sentir lorsque les recherches généalogiques se sont spécialisées et affinées. Pardonnez-moi de faire à nouveau appel, pour étayer mon propos, à deux études que je mène actuellement depuis plusieurs années :

• la première est relative à la migration helvético-franc-comtoise massive après la guerre de Trente Ans[5],
• la seconde consiste à indexer toute la population de la ville de Besançon au XVIe siècle, à partir des registres paroissiaux, mais aussi des minutes notariées, des comptes municipaux, des procès, des fondations et donations, de l'épigraphie (pierres tombales, inscriptions sur les maisons, taques de cheminées, etc.) et de l'ensemble des archives disponibles.

À ce jour, cette banque de données comprend 8 548 noms (avec dates de naissance et de décès, parrain et marraine, ascendance et descendance, alliance(s), profession, adresse dans la cité, origine géographique pour les immigrés (venus des villages environnants mais parfois aussi de pays fort éloignés), testaments, procès, titres, armoiries, fonctions électives et administratives, détails biographiques les plus divers) et 1 726 fiches renvoyant aux différentes variantes graphiques des patronymes (certains noms de famille s'écrivant parfois sous près de 20 formes différentes et parfois insoupçonnées jusqu'à la création du fichier, ce qui conforte encore davantage l'idée de l'absolue nécessité d'entreprendre des études familiales globales et ce, *a fortiori*, lorsque les registres paroissiaux commencent à faire défaut ou sont incomplets).

Or, dans ces deux exemples, la nécessité d'une coopération internationale est vite apparue indispensable : dans le premier cas, pour identifier les lieux-dits en Suisse et étudier l'ascendance des migrants avant leur traversée des montagnes du Jura dans les années 1650 et suivantes ; dans le second cas, pour connecter les familles byzantines de la Renaissance avec la Belgique et les Pays-Bas actuels où certaines familles comme les Perrenot de Granvelle et les Chifflet firent carrière tandis que d'autres comme les d'Emskerque (appelés ensuite d'Anvers) en étaient originaires, ou encore avec la Suisse où nombre de familles durent émigrer pour sauver leur vie, après leur conversion au protestantisme.

Imaginer, par exemple, un fichier genevois du XVIe siècle identique à celui en cours d'élaboration pour la même période à Besançon est un rêve qui devra bien, un jour prochain, devenir une réalité, pour le plus grand bonheur des généalogistes et des historiens qui savent bien que, pour retracer la trajectoire des familles, il convient de faire abstraction des frontières, simples accidents de l'histoire.

On pourrait aussi évoquer l'intéressante étude présentée à ce même congrès par M. Pierre Le Clercq, vice-président de la Société Généalogique de l'Yonne, portant sur 45 Bas-Bourguignons établis au Canada avant 1730. Parmi les familles étudiées, citons les Lepage, fondateurs de la ville de Rimouski, dans la province de Québec, sur le fleuve Saint-Laurent, et la famille d'Ailleboust qui a donné Louis d'Ailleboust, gouverneur de la Nouvelle-France. Ces recherches en généalogie ascendante n'ont pu être entreprises que grâce à la rédaction préalable par les généalogistes canadiens de dictionnaires exhaustifs et détaillés,

mentionnant, chaque fois que cela était possible, les localités ou les provinces d'origine.

Aussi, depuis mon élection à la présidence de la Fédération française de généalogie en 1993, ai-je toujours plaidé pour la constitution de banques de données nationales et internationales, ce qui s'est déjà concrétisé sous deux formes :

- des relevés d'inscriptions dans les cimetières car la plupart de ceux-ci ne disposent pas de registres d'inhumations et, en outre, parce que les actes de décès ne précisent jamais où les défunts sont enterrés (parfois fort loin de leur résidence ou même de leur lieu de décès). Depuis le début de cette année, grâce à un logiciel commun conçu par M. Alain Morineau et publié dans *La Vie Généalogique*, organe de presse de notre Fédération, l'informatisation de ces relevés a pu commencer (à titre d'exemple, une vingtaine de cimetières de Franche-Comté et d'autres régions françaises sont ainsi déjà « entrés » sur ordinateur, avec des méthodes précises qui permettent de retrouver toutes les indications portées sur les pierres tombales). Cette action est une priorité absolue car les pierres tombales anciennes disparaissent inexorablement et à une vitesse toujours croissante pour faire place à de nouvelles sépultures. Il est grand temps de sauver ce qui peut encore l'être.

- la création d'un fichier national de migrants intradépartementaux, interdépartementaux et internationaux : chaque association, chaque généalogiste amateur a la possibilité, lorsqu'a été relevé un acte d'état civil concernant une de ces catégories de personnes, de l'adresser à la Fédération qui en confie l'informatisation — selon une grille définie au niveau national — au Centre Généalogique Midi-Provence (C.G.M.P.). Dans un avenir proche, cette banque de données sera consultable sur Minitel, réseau national de télématique qui a eu l'avantage de pénétrer très tôt et en profondeur la société française, mais aussi le relatif inconvénient de freiner quelque peu l'irruption dans notre pays du phénomène mondial d'Internet.

Depuis plusieurs années, les unions régionales de généalogistes ont utilisé le réseau Minitel pour diffuser leurs relevés d'actes d'état civil informatisés. Ne disposant pas de moyens financiers étatiques pour constituer leurs banques de données et acquérir leurs propres serveurs, elles ont dû signer des contrats avec des sociétés commerciales spécialisées dont elles perçoivent des dividendes au prorata des heures de consultation du public. Toutes les régions françaises ou presque sont actuellement présentes sur ces serveurs, mais sans interconnexion des données qui permettraient aux généalogistes et aux chercheurs de les interroger à partir d'une banque d'information nationale. L'exemple des bases regroupant les migrants et les inscriptions dans les cimetières devrait avec le temps avoir raison de certaines réticences, dans le plus grand respect — bien évidemment — du travail et des spécificités régionales.

Si l'on peut estimer à 20 ou 25 millions le nombre d'actes d'état civil déjà transcrits en France par les membres des associations, les trois quarts ont déjà fait l'objet d'une informatisation et près de huit millions sont d'ores et déjà consultables sur Minitel. C'est en Auvergne-Bourbonnais (1,5 million d'actes), en Lorraine (1,25 million d'actes), en Normandie, en Bourgogne, en Champagne-Ardenne, en Picardie, en Bretagne (900 000 actes avec même des listes de conscrits et de marins), en Aquitaine, en Alsace, ainsi que dans le Haut-Berry que les transcriptions ont le plus progressé. Les Nantais complètent leurs recherches en y incluant même des listes de passagers de bateaux dont beaucoup appareillèrent de France pour l'Amérique du Nord.

Sur les quelque 36 000 communes que compte la France, 9 000 à 10 000 ont déjà fait l'objet de transcriptions totales ou partielles (actes de mariage seuls) de leur état civil. La Fédération française de généalogie a entrepris depuis un mois de recenser les communes ayant déjà fait l'objet d'études en y incluant la codification de celles-ci, la nature des actes et les dates extrêmes des documents analysés. À terme, cette liste, sans cesse remise à jour, est appelée à être consultable sur Minitel[6] et Internet.

Ces transcriptions ont été effectuées soient à partir des originaux, soit grâce aux microfilms réalisés depuis des décennies par les Mormons ou les services départementaux d'archives. Parfois, comme dans le Haut-Berry, ce sont les associations elles-mêmes qui ont fait l'acquisition du matériel de microfilmage pour faire avancer toujours plus vite la recherche généalogique.

En outre, le Minitel offre à la consultation du public le catalogue de grands dépôts publics comme la Bibliothèque publique d'information du Centre Pompidou (B.P.I.)[7] qui — bien que non spécialisée — possède néanmoins 200 à 300 ouvrages généalogiques et héraldiques de base. Il vient, en 1996, de s'enrichir d'un nouveau serveur[8] où le lecteur peut avoir accès dans des délais records à l'ensemble des fichiers (par noms d'auteurs ou des familles étudiées, par localités et par thèmes) de la Bibliothèque généalogique, fondée le 31 juillet 1986 et installée dans le premier arrondissement de Paris, au 3, rue de Turbigo. Celle-ci abrite, en particulier, tout le fonds de la Fédération française de généalogie avec une collection complète des bulletins des associations, des monographies, des travaux de transcription des registres d'état civil, des microfilms, des microfiches, des collections de faire-part (environ 400 000 dont 250 000 déjà classés) et d'ouvrages généalogiques, héraldiques, onomastiques et archivistiques. La Bibliothèque généalogique a mis aussi en chantier deux banques de données en cours d'informatisation :

- les cartes de sûreté de Paris, documents d'identité délivrés à tous les hommes français ou étrangers résidant dans la capitale française pendant la Révolution en 1793-1794, avec âge, lieu d'origine et de résidence, profession, etc. Plus de 200 000 documents avec de nombreuses indexations établies à partir du programme ISIS de l'Unesco, et quelque 200 000 fiches de pensionnaires de l'État en 1817.
- L'existence du Minitel ayant partiellement retardé la familiarisation des généalogistes français (pourtant fort rompus à l'utilisation de l'informatique) avec le réseau Internet, il a paru urgent de combler cette lacune. S'est alors créé, avec des responsables de la Fédération, un Institut de documentation sur l'histoire des familles, appelé aussi KAROLUS. Cet Institut est d'abord et avant tout un serveur de données généalogiques, héraldiques et archivistiques, destiné à diffuser ces informations sur Internet où il est accessible depuis le 5 août 1996, pour une période de remplissage, jusqu'à son lancement officiel le 1er janvier 1997. Ses données représentent d'ores et déjà 600 pages de documentation.

Le menu de KAROLUS comporte en particulier les adresses et toutes informations sur les associations généalogiques, les bibliothèques spécialisées et les archives du monde entier, les cadres de classement et les répertoires des services d'archives, des informations sur les logiciels de généalogie, des lignées ascendantes et descendantes avec des listes de mariages famille par famille, offertes par des chercheurs, des bibliographies avec analyses d'ouvrages, des créations d'armoiries (avec numérisation en couleurs), un dictionnaire illustré des termes du blason permettant de visualiser les pièces honorables et des centaines de meubles, et même un service d'identification d'armoiries anonymes, des rubriques questions / réponses, des propositions d'échanges et des annonces ouvertes à tous, etc.[9]

Au sein de la Fédération française, certaines unions géographiques se sont elles aussi branchées sur le *cyberspace*, à l'instar de celles de la Caraïbe (regroupant les îles des Antilles appartenant ou ayant appartenu à notre pays, c'est-à-dire les *West Indies*) ou de la Normandie dont on connaît, pour l'une comme pour l'autre, les liens privilégiés avec l'Amérique du Nord. De son côté, l'association « Ancêtres Italiens » s'apprête à brancher sur le *Net* une bibliographie comportant 3 957 notices par mots-clés thématiques et géographiques dont la localisation précise de 59 695 lieux-dits, hameaux et communes d'Italie, les épicentres de certains patronymes, des registres de baptêmes, de mariages et de sépultures région par région, des arbres généalogiques comme celui de la famille Agnelli, des listes de personnes nées dans les États pré-unitaires italiens recensées dans tous les actes français du XVe siècle jusqu'en 1830[10].

Internet et le Minitel sont également appelés à accueillir les banques de données relatives aux inscriptions dans les cimetières et aux migrants interdépartementaux et internationaux. D'autres fichiers, onomastiques et héraldiques, récemment ouverts au siège de la Fédération, ont été créés dans le but d'alimenter ces sources d'information. Quant à la Fédération française de généalogie, elle est prête à étudier dans les meilleurs délais toutes les possibilités de collaboration afin de faire progresser la mondialisation des données généalogiques et héraldiques, thème proposé pour le Congrès en France de l'an 2000.

Déjà, avec le professeur Yves Landry, du Canada, détaché en France à l'université de La Rochelle pour quelques années, nous avons mis à l'étude depuis juin 1996 la possibilité d'établir des contacts et des échanges généalogiques des deux côtés de l'Atlantique, via Internet. Un projet commun a été adressé conjointement aux plus hautes autorités françaises et j'ai été reçu, voici un mois, par M. Erlande-Brandenburg, directeur des Archives nationales de France, et ses principaux collaborateurs, pour leur en présenter de vive voix les éléments appelés à être transmis au Ministre de la Culture, auprès duquel le Président de la République, par un courrier du 2 août 1996, m'a également conseillé de m'adresser. C'est dire tout l'intérêt que portent les responsables politiques à l'éclosion de ce mode de communication à l'échelle mondiale, surtout lorsqu'il s'agit de faire progresser une discipline humaniste comme la nôtre.

Comme le soulignait déjà avec force en 1674 l'oratorien philosophe français Nicolas de Malebranche, dans son ouvrage traitant *De la recherche de la Vérité* : « De toutes les sciences humaines, la science de l'homme est la plus digne de l'homme ». Voici un *leitmotiv* que nos collègues chercheurs peuvent scander dans toutes les langues du monde, y compris à travers le maillage géant d'une toile d'araignée à l'échelle de notre planète. Comme pour toutes les autres sciences, la constitution de banques de données internationales va servir de formidable levier pour la croissance et l'expansion des sciences héraldique et généalogique.

## NOTES

1. *Souvenirs d'enfance et de jeunesse, IV, le Séminaire d'Issy.*

2. Adresse de l'Association : Ancêtres Italiens, 3, rue de Turbigo, 75001 Paris. Tél. : 01.46.64.27.22 (21h-22h), Fax : 01.46.65.60.13 — Marc Margarit, président.

3. Paris, Archives nationales, E//3706/12.

4. « Insurgés de la Commune de Paris (1871) emprisonnés à Rochefort-sur-Mer (17) », *Généalogie franc-comtoise, bulletin du centre d'entraide généalogique de Franche-Comté*, (no. 66, 2e trimestre 1966), p. 59-61.

5. Déjà publiée partiellement en Suisse dans les *Mémoires de la Société Jurassienne d'Émulation.*

6. 36-15 GENEFEDE.

7. 36-15 BPI.

8. 36-17 BIBGEN.

9. L'adresse de KAROLUS sur Internet est : *http:/www easynet.fr/karolus/*.

10. Voir également sur ce sujet les comptes rendus de la table ronde animée par Mme LOIS K. YORKE, responsable du département des manuscrits des *Public Archives of Nova Scotia* à Halifax, Canada.

# BORDER RELATIONS

Anne K. Toohey

"Border Relations" suggests that not only are Canadian and U.S. families interrelated because of long-term migration across the U.S./Canada border, but also that certain families followed an intergenerational family migration pattern in which descendants of original migrants to Canada tended to migrate back and forth across the border for several generations. Although this pattern was first noticed in the case of a particular family, the Kipps of New York, Nova Scotia, Montreal, Ontario, Illinois, and various parts of the western-United States, as published genealogies of similar and then not so similar families were read, it became apparent that this intergenerational family migration pattern between the United States and Canada was actually quite common.[1]

Intergenerational migration between the United States tended to begin with an American colonist—with a New England Planter or a Loyalist emigrating to Canada, and then continued each generation or so through three or four moves back and forth across the U.S./Canada border. In some sense, each generation of these families followed the migration routes and patterns of their own generation. But while historians have previously studied migration patterns based on the statistical analysis of individuals in each specific migration, what distinguishes the migration pattern described today is that it is an intergenerational family pattern. It is intended to show the movement of migration over time in one family, and then to compare the pattern of migration to that in other families.

The topic of U.S./Canada migration is not new. Canada and the United States share a long border, and political and social historians have always been interested in U.S./Canada migration. Some historians have emphasized that an "undefended" border has allegedly existed since the conclusion of the War of 1812, and argue that a special friendship or relationship links the two countries.[2] This relationship is based on a mingling of Canadian and American people, and has been described "as one of those great natural phenomena which are taken for granted in the lives of the two nations."[3] This migration between the

two countries has taken place over a long period of time:

> Ever since French Canadians settled in the Illinois country and Louisiana during the last quarter of the seventeenth century, and New Englanders supplanted the Acadians in Nova Scotia about the middle of the eighteenth, the populations of the regions which are now the U.S. and Canada have been spilling great waves of men and women into each other's territories. . . [with the mixing of] basic American stock of the Maritime provinces and Ontario in Canada, the millions of French Canadians in New England and New York, the traces of the Canadian in the American Middle West and of the American on the Canadian prairies, and the persistent to and from movement of both stocks along the Pacific coast from Mexico to the Bering Strait. Here is a continent where international boundaries have been disregarded for almost two centuries.[4]

Certain periods in history have generated more intense migrations between the U.S. and Canada. Intense migrations have been summarized in the chart which follows the text, and may serve as a useful historical framework for the analysis of U.S./Canada migration. A few generalizations add to the framework: Canada takes up more space on the map, but since its population tended to cluster within a hundred miles of the border, Canadian population has consistently been 1/10 of that of the United States. The direction of the migration has often been toward the south, "with the U.S. acting as a not-so-distant magnet pulling Canadians south."[5] However, there have been periods which have reversed this general trend—such as the aftermath of the American Revolution, the Fraser and Yukon gold rushes, the opening of the Canadian West, and the Vietnam War resistance.[6] At the same time, at least during the 18th and 19th centuries, there has been a general trend westward. Remember that, in addition, certain families have participated in the movement back and forth across the border in several of these migrations.

As can be seen, several of these periods of intense migration have quite a bit to do with the contemporary political situation in one or both countries. However, it is often difficult to capture the fluidity of migration history with the abstract concepts of political history. Part of the problem with political borders is that they imply a stasis: the border defines the political allegiance of the citizens on either side of it, when the truth is many Canadians that crossed the border in either direction may have been one or less generations removed from family roots in the United States, and vice versa. One historian of migration has stated that in understanding the fluidity of migration patterns, it is better not to be deceived by political frontiers. Better evidence of migration patterns may be uncovered if the migration patterns of North Americans on the march are analyzed in continental terms.[7]

Social history emphasizes that there are multiple reasons for migration that may have little to do with politics. The historian James Shotwell states that "the migration across the 'imaginary boundary' known as the U.S./Canada border may have had little if any political significance, at least in the eyes of the migrants themselves. While they were loyal citizens of either country during their residence in it, their decisions to migrate were determined for the most part by the same kind of non-political considerations as had brought them or their ancestors overseas from Europe."[8] Part of the problem may be that in a political sense "the world today can hardly understand this kind of nationalism, strong in its loyalties to community life and proud of citizenship in a free country, but basing both pride and loyalty upon an intimate personal sense of the dignity of man himself."[9]

After the War of 1812, most migration between Canada and the U.S. was motivated by non-political factors that affected individual opportunity—often economic, but also religious, or social opportunity based on community or family ties. Religious dissenters, especially Mennonites and Quakers from Pennsylvania, and Quakers from New York, disenchanted by their communities' insistence on oath-taking and on contributing to the wars from the Revolution to the War of 1812, followed the paths west of Albany to Niagara and on to Ontario. After the mid-19th century, the main factor influencing migration was economic opportunity. As land opened in the west, be it in Canada or the United States Midwest, easterners followed paths into or through Canada.

The paths they followed were predictable: Most of the routes took full advantage of the natural pathways of stream and river. Other routes were hewn out of the wilderness by earlier explorers or settlers or armies following paths made by the Indians. The second chart gives a verbal description of the most important travel routes to Canada in the early 19th century: The "path" to the Maritime Provinces was up the Atlantic seaboard following shipping lanes long used to transport people and goods. From the Maritime Provinces, some traveled up the St. Lawrence River to Quebec.

There were several routes from the Hudson River to Ontario and Quebec, which are described on the chart. Rather than repeat what is written there, I would like to quote a description based on memories written later in life by the Ryerse children, about their trip with their Loyalist family from New York to Long Point on Lake Erie, Ontario, in the 1790s:

> . . . great supplies of groceries were purchased, farm utensils were gathered, and tools, pots, boilers, etc. were assembled. It would be much easier for a family to go from Canada to China now then it was to come from New York to Canada then . . . . As there were no wagon roads from New York to the Canadian border, families had to travel by boat. And so, the Ryerse family started out by Sloop to Albany, NY, thence by land to Schenectady where they procured a flat bottomed boat into which the family and their baggage was loaded. Then with poles and oars, and against a strong current, they made their way up the Mohawk River a long distance until they came to a place called Wood Creek which they navigated for a long distance toward Lake Ontario, until they approached a stream called the Oswego. To enter this, they had to draw their boat by hand across a portage of some two miles, then down this stream to Lake Oswego, up the lake in

this boat westward to the Niagara River, then up the Niagara as far as Queenstown where again they had to portage a distance of nine miles around the Falls to Chippewa. As it was now drawing towards the close of summer, they would soon have to get up a shanty and prepare for winter. Consequently, arrangements were made immediately for continuing their journey. Supplies were added to those brought form New York and they started once more on their journey, bidding good-bye to the last vestige of civilization. Up the river they went 18 miles to Lake Erie and then along the shore of the Lake nearly 100 miles. It took them 12 days, not bad traveling in those days, taking the current of the river and lake, adverse winds and an unknown coast into consideration. When they came within the bay formed by Long Point, they watched the coast for a favorable impression and after a scrutiny of many miles, the boat was run into a small creek, the high banks sloping gradually on each side.[10]

Historians have noted the difficulties of capturing the fluidity of migration history. In fact, there was a time when historians doubted whether a whole history of the continental migration with its integration and reintegration of Canadians and Americans back and forth across the border could be written. Historians surmised that migration history would be hard to write because:[11]

*the source materials upon which an investigator must depend were practically unobtainable* . . . for great areas along the migration routes. How could the Americans who poured into what is now Ontario after 1783 be distinguished from the Loyalists of the American Revolution whom they had submerged numerically before the War of 1812: *Who had taken the trouble to sort out the Canadians from the waves of North Americans and Europeans* which broke over the pine forests of the Lakes region and the fat farm lands of the American Middle West?[12]

The problem in determining how many arrivals in British North America remained there was

acknowledged early in the 19th century. In 1831, Governor Aylmer reported to Lord Goderich, the colonial secretary in London that:

it would be extremely difficult if not impossible to ascertain the number of emigrants who actually settled in the Canadas: as to those who arrive at Quebec many pass into the United States, some of whom return from thence, and establish themselves in Canada, others return from Canada to the United Kingdom and some of those who emigrate to the United States from the United Kingdom come to settle in Canada.[13]

"Unfortunately, the government statistics in both countries furnish only moderately revealing information and that for only part of the long story."[14] Aggregate records, collected by both the Canadian and U.S. governments about migration are of relatively recent vintage, and therefore of little use in the time period under discussion. The United States government collected "Canadian Border Crossing Records" which contain useful personal information about American and Canadian citizens who crossed the U.S./Canada border, however, the government did not begin to collect these records until 1895. In practice, during the period under consideration, with the exception of the War of 1812, the border was wide open to travel or commerce, and transborder travel was heavy enough that one Burlington, Vt. tavern keeper painted George Washington's portrait on the south side of his sign and Admiral Horatio Nelson's likeness on the north.[15]

Similarly, before the collection of ship passenger records by national governments, the existence of such lists is incomplete. The U.S. federal government began collecting ship passenger records in 1820, long after the mass exodus of Loyalists. The Canadian government began collecting ship passenger records in 1865. In any case, most migration from Canada to the United States was overland, or by inland water routes, and therefore did not generate records. Therefore, other records must be substituted to place individuals (e.g., land, census, tax, military, and religious —such as Quaker removal certificates).

The stumbling block for the social historian writing migration history is that social historians are trapped by their own emphasis on counting individuals to form a statistical analysis, with a peculiar lack of attention to following those same individuals further through time. According to the historian David Russo, overgeneralization, or the "widespread practice of rendering all kinds of evidence statistically" reduces human beings to "faceless averages that don't describe or explain real individuals who have actually lived and died" in a real social setting.[16] Therefore, the social historian may find it difficult to identify separate social groups after the migration has taken place. For instance, the historian may find to his surprise that the Anglo-Canadian emigrant settling in the U.S. joined in with the members of his new community in so intimate and natural a way as to make it difficult to keep track of ex-Canadians in the United States. This principle seems equally true on both sides of the border despite the assertion that U.S. immigrants in Canada are less likely lost sight of because in its smaller population the individual necessarily plays a more distinctive part.[17]

It is for these reasons I think that tracing the more distinctive individual, or family, might give us a more fruitful handle on the issue of U.S./Canada migration. In order to grab this handle, the best secondary works about individual families are those by genealogists. And who better than genealogists can keep track of individuals through time? Who better than a genealogist can identify the source materials upon which a genealogical researcher must depend to place an individual in time and place and which some historians bemoaned "were practically unobtainable?" Who better can take the trouble to sort out the Canadians (or Loyalists or specific individuals) from the waves of North Americans and Europeans that migrated to Canada—family by family, if necessary? And the statement that: "Indeed, would it have been at all possible to sort them out," should definitely serve as a challenge to the genealogist's particular research skills in sorting out specific individuals and families by using primary records.

What I would like to propose, then, is that we look at the term "border relations" from an entirely different historical perspective: that of genealogical, biographical and historical studies. In this case, the term "border relations" now refers to families whose members migrated back and forth across the U.S./Canada border. I hope the concept of families with migrating members over several generations can add a dimension of fluidity to the discussion of U.S./Canada migration.

## The Kipps

I would like to turn now to my own family, the Kipps of New York, to provide a case study for intergenerational family migration in the U.S. and Canada. These Kipps were descendants of the early Dutch immigrant Hendrick Henderson Kipp, who immigrated to the New World in 1637. The story of three Loyalist Kipp brothers provides an excellent example of intergenerational family migration across the U.S./Canada border, which went from Westchester County, New York, to Nova Scotia, in 1783.

When I first began compiling the genealogy of my own branch of the Kipp family of New York, I began with the family genealogy, *History of the Kip Family in America*, by Frederic Ellsworth Kip. This genealogist states that my own four-times-great-grandfather James Kipp was "compelled to emigrate to Nova Scotia because of his outspoken loyalty to King George, and there accidentally drowned."[18] With this comment, discussion of his life and family substantially ends, though the author does explain that his wife and young children came back to New York, and then in the next generation, his son, John, emigrated to Canada. The author gives no specific place in Canada to which John emigrated, nor does he mention that James's grandson, Caleb, repatriated himself by moving to Illinois. This is common in compiled genealogies: they often start or end at the border. Sometimes this is because the genealogist does not know how or where to search. In earlier American genealogies, this problem is compounded by the fact that the American family often was ashamed of the unpatriotic behavior of an ancestor, and disowned him in print, even though he may be one of the United Empire Loyalists so praised by Canadians.

The Kipp genealogy[19] traces the Kipp family back to Brittany, France to one Ruloff de Kype, the great-grandfather of the immigrant Hendrick Hendrickson. During the Wars of Religion, Ruloff fought with the Ducs de Guises. In 1562, upon the triumph of the Protestants, he fled with his sons to Holland, and, in 1569, returned to France, fought with the army of the Duc d'Anjou, and fell in battle on the banks of the Charante, near Jarnac. As history will show, Ruloff was not the first Kipp to cross the border in an attempt to ensure his own safety.

Ruloff's son, also named Ruloff (born in 1544), remained in Holland and became a Protestant. His grandson, Hendrick, became involved in the "Company of Foreign Countries" that funded the voyage in which Henry Hudson discovered the Hudson River in New York. His great-grandson, Hendrick Hendrickson Kip, the immigrant, married and had several children in Amsterdam before coming with his family to New Amsterdam (now New York City) about 1637.

Hendrick, a tailor by trade, owned a number of lots on Manhattan Island. He was a member of the governing Board of Nine Men, and admitted to the rights of a great burgher—that is to a group of about 20 families from whom public office-holders were chosen.

Hendrick's son, Jacob Kip, also owned valuable land and held many offices in New Amsterdam. He was also a brewer and a storekeeper, and he built a house on Kip's Bay that was destined to play an important part in the Revolution. You can see in this 20th-century map why I wish the farm was still in the family: Jacob's house formed the centerpiece of Kip's Bay Farm, which eventually comprised all the land north of 26th St. and south of 42nd St. and east of Lexington Ave., Third Ave. and 2nd Ave. to the East River. The Empire State Building can be seen at the left of the map about three blocks from the property line; the United Nations Building can be seen just north of the property line along Kip's Bay on the East River. Jacob Kip's house stood just where the present 2nd Ave. now crosses 35th St. The house was torn down in 1851.

During the American Revolution, the British landed at Kip's Bay. The Kip's Bay house, which had been the headquarters of General George Washington, now became the headquarters of the British General George Howe. At that point, Washington's troops were pushed north. Following the withdrawal of both British and rebel forces from Westchester County after the Battle of White Plains (October 28, 1778), the American troops were stationed north of the Croton River. The British occupied all of New York City and Long Island. The British line extended from the Hudson River to the Long Island Sound, across the lower part of Yonkers and Eastchester, about two miles above King's Bridge. This made Westchester

County a no-man's land, where much guerilla warfare was practiced between adherents of patriot militia and Loyalist troops.[20]

Jacob's grandson Benjamin and great-grandsons Thomas, Samuel and James were all Loyalists from Westchester County. Jacob's son Jesse, a miller, had migrated from New Amsterdam to Newtown Long Island in about 1710. Jesse's son, Benjamin, moved across the Long Island Sound to Westchester County, New York, and before the Revolution, Benjamin owned a 400-acre farm in North Castle, and held numerous community offices. In the town records, he is called Benjamin Kipp, Esquire, and on this early map and in a later record, when he performed a marriage at Morrisiana, Westchester Co. in 1782, he is called "Squire Kipp." Squire Benjamin Kipp was an active Loyalist during the Revolution. Benjamin's lands were confiscated by the Committee of Forfeiture in 1789, and he was forced to go behind British lines at Morrisiana in 1780. He died May 24, 1782 at Morrisiana, age 79.

Benjamin's three youngest sons also were Loyalists. Although of Quaker background, these three sons nonetheless fought on the British side. Thomas Kipp was a lieutenant in a regiment of Loyalist volunteers in the regular royal troops under the superior officer, Col. Isaac Hatfield, his brother-in-law.

Samuel and James Kipp were officers in the "Westchester Light Horse," also known as "DeLancey's Raiders." DeLancey's Raiders had its camp at King's Bridge, at Morrisiana, then at West Farms, on the land owned by James DeLancey along the Bronx River. Its chief field of operations was the "Neutral Ground" that part of Westchester County situated between the lines, between the Croton River in the North, and the Long Island Sound in the South. The regiment was formed by James DeLancey, nephew of Brigadier General Oliver DeLancey. James DeLancey was the sheriff of Westchester County before the Revolution, and was well known in the county. He delegated his long-time friend Samuel Kipp to recruit a company. Many of the soldiers Samuel recruited from North Castle were his own relatives or tenants from his own farm. Among them were his brother, James Kipp, Captain Gilbert Totten (related to his first wife, Freelove Totten), Captain Moses Knapp of Yorktown (brother-in-law of Samuel's brother Thomas, and father of Samuel's second wife).[21]

The historian, Hufeland, who chronicled Westchester County during the American Revolution in the 1920s explains:

> A number of DeLancey's most active officers as well as men under them were born and brought up in the vicinity. Captains Totten and Kipp came from North Castle just South of [the patriot Col. Christopher] Greene's post [at the house of the Davenport family, probably relatives of Samuel's mother Dorothy] and Knapp [lived] just north of it, and all of them knew every foot of the ground and all the Loyalists living there.[22]

This knowledge made them extremely effective in their mission to keep the lines of supply and communications open to New York City for the British troops, supplying the British army with beef, forage and other provisions (which they often stole from the families of patriot neighbors, just as the patriots did from the Loyalists for the American army), recruiting and scouting for the British army, and taking prisoners for exchange.[23]

## Migration

At the end of the American Revolution, many Loyalists emigrated. Their land had often already been confiscated before the end of the war and redistributed (often sold) to patriot neighbors. The British removal of Loyalists from the former American colonies was fairly well organized. The Loyalists congregated with their families in New York in 1783 and 1784 and shipped out by military regiment and company. About 35,000 Loyalists took advantage of the British government's support, including free transportation and material support (tents, blankets and food), and eventually, land. Loyalists tended to go to four British-governed places; the very wealthy tended to go to Britain. Southerners were evacuated to several islands in the West Indies, including the Bahamas, Turks and Caicos, and Jamaica. Some Loyalists followed the Hudson to Albany, and then wended their way by river tributaries, creeks and old Indian paths to what is now Ontario, and some were transported by ship to Nova Scotia, including that area that became New Brunswick. The three Loyalist Kipp brothers emigrated to Nova Scotia.

The trip to Nova Scotia was not without its dangers. John Caldwell of Westchester County, New York, for instance, arrived in Digby County, Nova Scotia in the Spring of 1784 as a widower with three children. He had sailed on the *Prince of Wales* with a company of other Loyalists from Westchester County. This vessel was driven by a gale to Bermuda, and wrecked. When news reached Digby, the *Joseph* was sent to Bermuda to transport the 35 survivors to Nova Scotia.[24]

John Kennedy, Loyalist, and brother-in-law to Thomas Kipp, sailed on the transport ship, the *Martha*, that struck a reef on the southwest coast of Nova Scotia and sank. The ship had sailed along with others from Sandy Hook in September, and had on board 174 persons. Of these, 99 perished, including half of the Maryland Loyalists, who comprised most of the passengers. Only 75 were saved by fishing vessels. Captain Patrick Kennedy of the Maryland Loyalists stated that neglect on the part of the master of the ship played a large part in the disaster. According to Kennedy, the ship had left New York with a set of old sails and only a dozen men and boys as crew. When the *Martha* reached Nova Scotian waters, night was coming on just as land was sighted. It was thought that the captain would anchor the ship until morning. Instead, the captain allowed the vessel to continue. His meager crew were attempting to rig and erect a new main topsail to replace one that had been ripped apart by strong winds. The ship struck a ledge, and the mainsail fell and smashed the long boat. The captain announced that he would be the last to leave the boat, but when the little jolly boat was put over the side, he jumped in, and rowed away.[25]

In addition to the hardship of getting to Nova Scotia, late-18th-century Nova Scotia and New Brunswick have been described as places "with capricious weather, miserly soil and geographical loneliness."[26] When entreated by old friends to return home, that "all had been forgiven," some Loyalists sold their land in the Maritime Provinces and returned to New York. Sometimes this was a decision that was soon regretted as animosity still lingered from the Revolution, making return most uncomfortable. Therefore, in the 1790s, many Loyalists (some formerly residents in the Maritime Provinces) moved from New York to Ontario, Canada, where Governor John Graves Simcoe was promising land in lavish quantities to disbanded soldiers.[27]

The three Loyalist Kipp brothers migrated from New York to Nova Scotia at the end of the

American Revolution, but none of the Kipps stayed in Nova Scotia for a whole generation.

Thomas Kipp returned to the United States in 1811. Thomas, the youngest son of the Loyalist Squire Benjamin Kipp, was 26 when he removed to Nova Scotia. The Muster List of 1784 at Digby lists Thomas, a wife and four children.[28] Thomas was married to Abigail Hatfield, not only the daughter of a Loyalist, but also the sister of Thomas's superior officer Col. Isaac Hatfield. The Hatfields were a cohesive Loyalist family: four of the Hatfield brothers were Loyalists, and five of the Hatfield sisters married Loyalists. All of these Hatfield Loyalists went to Nova Scotia, where one of them, Elizabeth Hatfield Kipp, was the mother of Thomas's brother Samuel's second wife.[29]

Thomas Kipp resided at Marshalltown, Parish of Digby. Thomas petitioned for recompense due to losses suffered as a Loyalist, but his claim to one-quarter part of the farm confiscated from his father in North Castle, to horse and cattle, and to unremunerated service to the British army was denied.[30] He also testified about his brothers Samuel and James Kipp in 1786. He was taxed in the Parish of Digby in 1789.[31]

In 1790, one of Thomas Kipp's neighbors, George Wood of Marshalltown, departed for Ontario, where he had relatives residing near Brockville. The very favorable comments sent by Wood to his friends in Digby, coupled with the uncertainty of economic conditions in Nova Scotia during this period, led a number of families to migrate to Upper Canada. Among them, Thomas Kipp of Marshalltown "bade adieu in 1811 to their adopted home and proceeded by way of Boston and New York to the western prairies."[32]

Despite what the local history of Digby says, Thomas does not seem to have gone to Upper Canada (or at least for long). He returned to New York City with his family. His will was dated 1818 in New York City, and probated there on September 5, 1823.[33]

## Samuel Kipp

Samuel Kipp left New York in June 1783 with a group of "Westchester Light Horse" under the direction of Captain Moses Knapp and himself. He probably sailed on the *Thetis,* which left in the June fleet carrying Westchester Loyalists bound for Cumberland.[34] Samuel appears on the Muster Roll at Digby on May 29, 1784, but he, Knapp and various other members of the company on board were granted land at Remsheg (now called Wallace, and formerly called Fanning's Bay) in Cumberland County, Nova Scotia.[35]

Samuel's wife, Freelove Totten, and his four children by this marriage, never followed him to Nova Scotia. Although the Totten and Kipp families had seemed very close before the Revolution (Samuel Kipp's father, Squire Benjamin, witnessed the making of Freelove Totten's father's will), Freelove's father stated that he had always backed the Revolutionary side, and he may have influenced his daughter not to follow her Loyalist husband into exile.[36] In addition, Freelove and her children remained in a Quaker congregation, and may not have approved of Samuel's active military role in the Revolution.

As was fairly common when wives of Loyalists refused to follow them into exile, Samuel Kipp took advantage of an English law of 1760 that allowed remarriage after three years of desertion, and he married Mary Knapp, the oldest daughter of Moses and Elizabeth Hatfield Knapp, in Nova Scotia.[37]

Samuel settled on the Westchester grant in Cumberland County. He states in his petition of March 25, 1796, that "the corps migrated to Nova Scotia and settled in the wilderness of Cumberland, where no provision [by the British government] has ever been made for their subsistence."[38] He owned a sawmill. He became a delegate to the Provincial Parliament.[39] In 1789, the birth of Samuel's first child was registered at the Anglican Church in Quebec, and by 1796, Samuel seems to have settled in Montreal. His old comrade in arms (and also his father-in-law after his second marriage to Mary Knapp), Moses Knapp, who went back to New York for awhile, also settled in Montreal. Samuel Kipp died February 23, 1805 at the comparatively young age of 52. Apparently, he had never fully recovered from the bayonet wound he received fighting on the Neutral Ground in Westchester County during the Revolution.[40]

Samuel and Mary Knapp Kipp had four children. All of Samuel's children married French-Canadian Catholic spouses. One son, Samuel Kipp, became a merchant in Kingston, providing provisions for the War of 1812 on the Great Lakes, and then for the westward movement. James and his nephews Joseph Desautels and Théophile Brugière, sons of his sisters, Elizabeth and Charlotte Kipp, migrated to the United States, where they became known figures in the saga of building the American West.

James Kipp (baptized in the Anglican Church in Quebec City in 1789, and died in Missouri in 1880) led a long and adventurous life as a fur trader, factor in charge of forts, Indian trader and fort builder for the American Fur Co., and as a sometimes river boat captain on the Missouri River. By the age of 20, James had left home in Montreal to seek his fortune as a trapper with the Northwest Fur Company on the Red River, which flows between Winnipeg and North Dakota. During the War of 1812, James came back to Canada, where he married Elizabeth Rouchelou in Kingston in 1813. During the war, he and his brother Samuel were both merchants in Kingston. In 1818, he transacted some legal affairs in Montreal, and left Canada again. In 1818, having traveled through Minnesota, he engaged himself to the Columbia Fur Company, which sent him to a trading post near the Mandan Indians. This company sold out to the American Fur Co. in 1827, and James remained with American Fur for the rest of his working life.[41]

James Kipp was a well-known figure along the Missouri River for over four decades. Nearly all the well-known travelers on the river met Kipp, and described him in their journals. Kipp accompanied George Catlin, the well-known Indian artist, to the Mandan, Hidatsa and Arikara villages, and interpreted for him and helped him with his observations of those tribes that subsequently appeared in his famous paintings. He entertained the German visitors Maximilian, Prince of Wied, and Charles Bodmer, the artist at Fort Clark in the winter of 1833-1834. Maximilian described the close quarters in which the Germans lived with their host and his Indian wife and half-Indian children. Once again, Kipp helped the Germans to understand the customs of the Indians, while allaying the Indians' suspicions of the Germans. Kipp also appears in the writings of the Swiss artist Rudolph Friederich Kurz, who spent a brief period in 1851 at Fort Berthold. Kipp and his Mandan wife, the only persons purportedly at that time who could speak both Mandan and English, gave Kurz a great deal of help on the dictionary that Kurz was compiling on the Mandan language.

Father Pierre-Jean de Smet, a Catholic missionary, met Kipp at Fort Union in 1841, and described him as a "gentleman well worthy of his station."

The naturalists John Audubon and Edward Harris met Kipp and described him in 1843. He provided Audubon with many of the specimens for his collections. Thaddeus Culbertson, the scientist, met Kipp when the trader was in charge of Fort Berthold in 1850. He appears in the journals of Charles Larpenteur and other traders. He appears in the letters exchanged by other factors in the American Fur Company. John Palliser met Kipp in 1847, when he visited his farm near Independence, Missouri, where James Kipp lived with his white wife and family.[42]

James's half-Indian son by Earth Woman, Joe Kipp, became a fur trader and fort factor like James. Joe befriended the famous western writer, James Schultz, and they had many adventures together. Joe thereby ensured himself an immortal place in western writing since he appears in Schultz's highly autobiographical writing as the figure Berry. The following story illustrates how easily Joe Kipp moved back and forth across the Canadian border as it suited him. It is also a fine literary illustration of a story from the American West:

In 1870, Fort Benton was the only settlement of any importance on the Upper Missouri River. Though small, it was headquarters for that part of the country and was the center of the great fur trade. The steamboats that came every spring from St. Louis with goods for the traders and supplies for Helena and other mountain camps went back with tremendous tarpaulin-covered bales of buffalo robes and pelts of beaver, wolf, deer, elk and antelope.

Until the appointment of the new marshal, Harding, liquor was an important part of the trade. Once he confiscated several cases of liquor, the traders realized their trade with the Indians would disappear if they could not find some way to outwit him. The Blackfeet, the Gros Venture and other tribes demanded liquor along with trade articles. They would switch their trade to the Hudson's Bay Co. if the American Fur Co. traders could not supply it.

Joe Kipp proposed to his partner Charles Thomas that they cross the international boundary and build a post in Canada. Kipp slipped away to Helena and bought 75 cases (750 gallons) of liquor and loaded it onto rafts, eluding the marshal. At Sun River, Thomas was waiting for him with wagons and teamsters, and they loaded the liquor for the trip north to Canada via the Red River cart trail.

Three days later Harding caught up with them. "Well Joe, I've got you at last," he said. "Turn around and head for Fort Benton."

"Harding, you are just 20 min. too late," said Kipp. "You are no more marshal here than I am, for right here we are in Canada; the north fork of the Milk River is the line."

Harding knew that the boundary line had not been surveyed. He said, "You have no proof that we are in Canada. I'll take chances that we are south of the line. I arrest you for having liquor in your possession in Indian territory. Turn around for Fort Benton."

Kipp laughed and said that the marshal had no proof that they weren't in Canada, and pointed out that they had five men to his one self. "Here we stand you off," said Kipp.

The marshal turned around and headed south.

Later Kipp founded Fort Standoff just north of the Belly River. And it turned out that later, surveyors revealed that the very spot where the marshal had tried to make the arrest was just about 300 yards south of the border.[43]

In the last quarter of the 19th century, Joe Kipp returned to Montana, and became a rancher. He died in 1913, and is buried in Browning, Montana.

**James Kipp**

We have come a long way from Nova Scotia in 1783, but it is to that place and time that we must return to pick up the thread of James Kipp, the third Loyalist brother. This James Kipp was my four-times-great-grandfather. James died at Cumberland, Nova Scotia in October of 1785,

leaving his widow (Zipporah) and four children (John, David, Charlotte and Elizabeth), "in distress."[44] Thomas testified that after James died, Zipporah took the children back to New York. She came back without them to testify in 1786. She estimated her loss at £272 sterling, but received £150 sterling.[45] She did not receive compensation in land for herself or her son because she no longer intended to settle in Canada.

Zipporah subsequently remarried her cousin, Caleb Carpenter, in a second marriage for both, in a Quaker ceremony in Chappaqua, New York in 1796. Caleb and Zipporah were Quakers; James Kipp's parents, Benjamin and Dorothy Davenport Kipp, had been Quakers. In addition, James had two brothers who, as Quakers, remained neutral during the Revolution. It is not surprising then, that when James and Zipporah's son, John Kipp, married Caleb's daughter, Ruth Carpenter, they retained their Quaker background. When they moved to Canada (probably after Zipporah's death in 1816), they went with other Westchester Quakers to the Quaker community of Sparta, Ontario. Since Canada was part of the New York yearly meeting of Quakers, the Kipps did not move outside the political sphere of their religious group. This may have seemed more important to them than the fact that they were emigrating to another country.

Among the settlers that the local history of Sparta named as coming back from Pennsylvania to Sparta with Jonathan Doan, the Quaker land agent, were John Mills and John Kipp. The local history of Sparta acknowledges, however, that "John Mills, however, migrated with his family from New York State."[46] John Mills is my three-times-great-grandfather on the maternal side. John Kipp, my three-times-great-grandfather, also migrated from New York, from Westchester County. Mills and Kipp, with their families, and the families of William Harvey, Samuel Scott and Joseph Albertson of Pennsylvania, "made a party of eighteen persons. Having arrived at the Niagara frontier, some of the men drove cattle through bush trails to the prospective settlement, while others shoved and pulled a scow along the shore of Lake Erie from Buffalo to Port Stanley. It took several weeks to make even this latter journey."[47] No doubt, the trip of the Kipps and the Mills from Westchester County, New York, to Niagara, Ontario, paralleled the trip of the Ryerse family in the 1790s.

Other families that ended up in Sparta from Westchester County include the family of Reuben Haight, whose wife, Sarah, was the famous pioneer minister of the Friend's meeting at Sparta. She was the member of an Old Quaker family, whose great-aunt had been whipped through the streets of Boston for professing her belief.[48] Reuben Haight was also a cousin of John Kipp, being the son of a brother-in-law of the three Loyalist brothers. In 1822, a son, James Haight, worked on shares with a neighboring farmer, sold his wheat at York, and took the money back to Westchester County, New York. When he came back, he had a horse, a light wagon and a box of second-hand clothing, all gifts from their friends in Westchester County. These manufactured goods were welcome in the wilderness, where, in the words of another son, Ephraim Haight, he could "stand at night in the old log house and look over the half-door and see the wolves's eyes shining in the darkness," and where the daily work was to chop down trees to clear the forest for pasture, and where Ephraim says "we went away in the morning while the stars were still shining and didn't come home until the stars were out again."[49]

Sparta was also peopled by the families of several settlers who came from Nova Scotia, including John and Elias Moore, from Digby, Nova Scotia. Most of the early settlers in Sparta were Quakers. In 1819, there were enough co-religionists so that the Friends of Yarmouth applied to the Norwich monthly meeting for permission to establish a preparatory meeting at Sparta. Thereafter, until 1821, the meetings were held on first-days alternately at the homes of John Kipp and Elias Moore. In 1821, the first Quaker meeting-house was erected.[50]

Sons of early Sparta Quaker pioneers were especially active in the Rebellion of 1837, despite the Quaker emphasis on the principles of peace and non-violence. Many frontier communities in the 1830s were dissatisfied with the monopolization of government offices by the Family Compact and with laws enacted by the more conservative Tories regarding such things as the designation of more Crown and Clergy reserves of land than other settlers thought necessary. In addition, Quakers perceived that pressure was put up on them to abandon their principles of peace and attend the annual military drill on training day. Quakers who refused to do so were "taxed" as "officers raided their houses and barns, carrying off a fat hog here, a watch there . . . a cheese, a pair of blankets, books, clothes or anything else valuable."[51] Shades of penalties born in the Westchester "Neutral Ground" for some of them. In addition, the Friends were indignant because they were often summoned before a magistrate for little or no reason (there was a case of a hired man's striped shirt being hung to dry, and being mistaken for the American flag).[52] Also, coming from the northern states, they were perceived as having a more democratic spirit than was present in Upper Canada.[53]

After the abuses of the election of 1836, when Reform candidates lost, Reformers began to think that the only method for obtaining reform was armed rebellion.[54] By the election of 1836, Reformers had begun to meet regularly in Sparta. These Reformers eventually became participants in the Rebellion of 1837: John's son, Caleb Kipp, several of Caleb's brothers-in-law, and many neighbors, in a company of about 50 men, left Yarmouth to join Duncombe's forces at Scotland in Brant County, Ontario. On December 13, the company arrived at Scotland, where about 300 rebels from Norwich and Burford had already gathered. Almost immediately after arrival, alarming reports came in that the rebels were in danger of being trapped between two converging forces. Duncombe retreated to Norwich, and gave the order to disband the following morning.[55] For this participation as member of the "Spartan Rangers" in the "Duncombe Rising," Caleb Kipp was jailed in London, Ontario, on December 17, 1837. He was bailed out on January 11, 1838, recommitted, petitioned, ordered freed and banished from Canada for life on August 13, 1838.[56]

Caleb Kipp left Canada with his wife and young family in a covered wagon. Traveling across Ontario to Detroit, he went across Michigan and up into Illinois, where he settled near the Fox River in the town of Elgin, Kane County, Illinois. He did not go empty handed: several pieces of furniture in the wagon had come all the way from England, and he had money to buy land in Illinois. According to the 1850 United States census, three children had been born in Canada by 1838; the fourth child, my great-grandfather, Melbourne Kipp, was born in 1840 in Illinois. Caleb held $345 in personal property in the Kane County Personal Property list in 1848. He became a respectable citizen, and sent three sons off to fight for the Union Army in the Civil War (the only one that did not go was too young to serve). His son's father-in-law, William Panton, maintained a stop on the Underground Railroad that helped African Americans escape to Canada. While three of the four sons went out west for awhile after the Civil War, three of them eventually came back in their middle age to settle in Kane County, Illinois.

In addition, Caleb's family did not lose touch with its Canadian relatives in Sparta. In Canadian remembrances collected late in the 19th century, Caleb Kipp's wife, Phoebe Mills Kipp is remembered, as is her daughter, Alma, who came back to visit her grandfather, John Mills.[57] In addition, my family has inherited family pictures of the Canadian side of the family, as well as some of the furniture that had traveled by covered wagon from Canada to Illinois.

## Migration patterns

I have read a lot of Canadian and American genealogies that have contained families that followed the same intergenerational, international migration patterns as the Kipps. In fact, the topic that I shared with you today, "Border Relations," could not have been done without the benefit of an extensive collection of Canadian and American history, local history and genealogy such as the one that has been collected over almost two centuries at the Library of Congress.

Many Canadian and American genealogies describe families that followed the same intergenerational migration patterns as the Kipps: the Hatfields,[58] the Knapps,[59] the Underhills,[60] the Lands,[61] the Willets,[62] the Fowlers, the Purdys,[63] the Outhouses,[64] the Powells,[65] the Seelys,[66] the Ryerses,[67] the DeLongs,[68] the Fayerweathers,[69] the DeLanceys[70] and others. Descendants of more than one German mercenary that fought for the British and received land in Nova Scotia followed this pattern: for instance the Dukeshires (Tuchsherers).[71] The descendants of Scottish or other British Isle families that were more recent immigrants to the colonies and therefore stayed loyal to the king also followed this pattern: for instance, the Livingstons[72] and the Sutherlands.[73]

Not all of the genealogies I read were perfect sources: some stopped at the Canadian border by lacking knowledge of—or even perhaps refusing to acknowledge—the continuing life of a Loyalist in Canada. Some started at the Canadian border because the researcher had not found the American colonial roots of a family. Sometimes, because of my knowledge of Westchester County, I was able to figure this out—sometimes I am sure I missed families involved in this pattern. If one had infinite time, the family lines and migration pattern of many of these families could be fleshed out by doing extensive genealogical research such as I did about the Kipps. However, reading genealogies as secondary sources, even when they may not follow all the family lines involved in this intergenerational migration pattern, still often describe enough about family migration to make this migration pattern clear.

If you map the moves of the families whose migration histories I collected, you will see a distinct pattern of westward movement, which supports the westward migration patterns on this continent that were previously described by historians.

Some early emigrants to Nova Scotia and Ontario came from families that had been in the colonial United States for at least four generations before the American Revolution. Many of these families tended to have been religious dissenters in Europe: Pilgrims, Huguenots, Quakers, Mennonites. The Pilgrims and the Huguenots had often emigrated from England and France to spend a generation or so in Holland, sometimes intermarrying with the Dutch. The Dutch emigrated to New Amsterdam in the New World; the Pilgrims emigrated to the Massachusetts Colony.

Several generations later, these two streams of emigration to the New World came together again, through migration, in Westchester County, New York, and in 1776, individuals were forced to take sides in the American Revolution. The Dutch had migrated from the earliest colony at New Amsterdam to Long Island, and then to Westchester County (and often on to Dutchess County and Albany). The Massachusetts settlers migrated to Rhode Island (usually because they were religious dissenters against the Pilgrims), or to Connecticut for land. Quakers from Rhode Island moved down to Long Island, and followed another Quaker migration path from Long Island to Westchester County. Connecticut settlers moved west into New York, particularly the adjacent New York counties of Westchester and Dutchess.

After the Revolution, many Loyalists moved to Nova Scotia. Of those who went to Nova Scotia, some returned to the United States; some returned, but went from the U.S. to Ontario, while some went to Quebec, and then on to Ontario. Another strong migration of Loyalists took place between New York, New Jersey and Pennsylvania to Ontario.

From Ontario, families moved west back into the United States—especially to Michigan, Illinois and other points in the Midwest. In addition, some families moved to the Far West, and sometimes settled on both sides of the U.S./Canada border.

In following a number of these families through several generations of migrations back and forth across the U.S./Canada border, we find evidence to support the statement that "there are North American families today . . . some of whose members have changed political allegiance back and forth about once a generation since 1750, as the continental migrations have crossed and recrossed the international boundary."[74]

## BIBLIOGRAPHY

BREBNER, JOHN BARTLET, "Forward" in HANSEN, MARCUS LEE, *Mingling of Canadian and American Peoples* (New York: Russell & Russell, 1970); BROWN, DOROTHY I., *A Loyalist's Legacy: The Family of Robert Land* (Mississauga, Ont.: D.I. Brown, 1985); BUCK, CHARLES S., *Old Sparta and Its Neighborhood, Elgin County, Ontario* (St. Thomas, Ont: Elgin County Library Board, 1979); CALLAHAN, NORTH, *Flight from the Republic: The Tories of the American Revolution* (Westport Conn.: Greenwood Press, 1967); COLDHAM, PETER, *American Loyalist Claims* (Washington, D.C.: National Genealogical Society, 1980); CRARY, CATHERINE, "Guerilla Activities of James Delancey's Cowboys in Westchester County: Conventional Warfare or Self-Interested Freebooting," in ROBERT A. EAST and JACOB JUDD, *The Loyalist Americans: A Focus on Greater New York* (Tarrytown, N.Y.: Sleepy Hollow Restorations, Inc. 1975); DUTTON, WILLIAM LEONARD, *The Dotten (.10) Family in the U.S.A. and Canada: A Genealogical Compilation: or the Descendants of Ensign James Dotten, U.E.L. (1751-1831) of the Westchester N.Y. Disbanded Corps and His Wife Abigail (ODell)* (New Brunswick: by the compiler, 1970); FANJOY, HAROLD, *The Seeleys of New Brunswick* (Saint John, N.B.: Fanjoy and Ward, 1992); FROST, JOSEPHINE C., (ed.), *Underhill Genealogy: Descendants of Captain John* (Underhill, Underhill Society of America, 1932); HANNA, WARREN LEONARD, *Stars Over Montana: Men Who Made Glacier National Park History* (West Glacier, Mont: Glacier Natural History Association, 1988); HATFIELD, ABRAHAM, *The Hatfields of Westchester: A Genealogy of the Descendants of Thomas Hatfield of New Amsterdam and Mamaroneck, Whose Sons Settled in White Plains, Westchester County, New York* (New York: New York Genealogical and Biographical Society, 1935); HOUSTON, CECIL J. and SMYTH, WILLIAM J., *Irish Emigration and Canadian Settlement: Patterns, Links, and Letters* (Toronto: University of Toronto Press, 1990); HUFELAND, OTTO, *Westchester County during the American Revolution, 1775-1783* (Harrison, N.Y.: Harbor Hill Books, 1974, c. 1926); KIP, FREDERICK ELLSWORTH, *History of the Kipp Family in America* (Boston: Hudson Printing Co., 1928); LEWIS, VERNE B., *Pryor, Smith, Tidd and Powell—and Other Loyalist Ancestors of My Grand-parents, Charles and Susan Plummer* (Mercer Island, Washington: V.B. Lewis, 1982); LIVINGSTON, EDWIN A., *Family History and Genealogical Record of Daniel Livingston U.E. and Some of his Descendants* (Prescott, Ont.: E.A. Livingston, 1983); MATTISON, RAY H. in LE ROY R. HAFEN (ed.) *The Mountain Men and the Fur Trade of the Far West: Biographical Sketches of the Participants by Scholars of the Subject* (Glendale, Ca.: The Arthur H. Clark Co., 1965); "Memoirs of Mrs. Rundle," in *Material re: Messrs. Doan, Zavitz, etc.* London, Ontario: 1943)[75]; OUTHOUSE, DONALD E., *Robert Outhouse, 1750-1849, and His Wife Sarah (Caldwell) Outhouse, United Empire Loyalists* (Yarmouth Nova Scotia: D.E. Outhouse, 1988); PRIKLER, VERDA DUKESHIRE, *Tuchscherer: History and Genealogy of the Dukeshire Family in North America* (Middleton, N.S.: Black Print Co., 1978); PURDY, CLAYTON C., *Gabriel Purdy: His Ancestors and Descendants* (Baton Rouge, La.: Oracle Press, 1986); PURDY, CLAYTON C., *Henry Purdey: His Ancestors and Descendants* (Baton Rouge, La.: Oracle Press, 1985); READ, COLIN, *The Rising in Western Upper Canada, 1837-8: The Duncombe Rebellion and After* (Toronto: University of Toronto, 1982); RICHARD, LOUIS, *Samuel Kipp (1753-1803) et ses descendants : une étude biographique et généalogique* (Ottawa, Ont.: 13 Ave. Woodlawn, 1950); RUSSO, DAVID J., *Clio Confused: Troubling Aspects of Historical Study from the Perspective of U.S. History* (Westport Conn.: Greenwood Press, 1995); RYERSE, PHYLLIS A. and RYERSON, THOMAS A., *The Ryerse-Ryerson Family* (Ingersoll, Ontario: Ryerse-Ryerson Family Association, 1994); SABINE, LORENZO, *Biographical Sketches of Loyalists of the American Revolution* (Westport Conn.: Mecklor, 1984); SAVARY, A. W., *Supplement to the History of Annapolis* (Toronto: William Briggs, 1913); STORY, D. A., *The De Lanceys: A Romance of a Great Family* (London: T. Nelson & Sons, 1931); SHOT-WELL, JAMES T., "Introduction," in HANSEN, MARCUS LEE, *Mingling of Canadian and American Peoples* (New York: Russell & Russell, 1970); SUTHERLAND, CONN HARKNESS, *The Sutherlands and Westchester, Nova Scotia* (Agincourt, Ont: Generation Press, 1986); THOMPSON, JOHN HERD and RANDALL, STEPHEN J., *Canada and the United States: Ambivalent Allies* (Athens, Ga.: University of Georgia Press, 1994); WALKER, WAYNE W., *Simon DeLong: Loyalist of Nova Scotia, Canada* (Ottawa, Ont.: W. W. Walder, 1992); WILLIAMS, DONALD E., *Fayerweather Friends: The Fairweather Genealogy* (Riverview, N.B.: D. Williams, 1992); WILLITS, GEORGE D., *The Willits Families of Upper Canada and Their Descendants with Other Kin of Daniel Eugene Willits* (Woodstock, Ont.: G. D. Willits, 1993); WILSON, ISAIAH W., *A Geography and History of Digby, Nova Scotia* (Belleville, Ont.: Mika Studio, 1972); WRIGHT, ESTHER CLARK, *Loyalists of New Brunswick* (Hantsport, Nova Scotia: Lancelot Press, 1981).

## NOTES

1. I hope to bring several of my own academic perspectives to this topic. My academic training is in history and librarianship. I am also a genealogist by subject specialty, and I work as a Reference Librarian in the Local History and Genealogy Section at the United States Library of Congress in Washington, D.C. In addition, I have a special interest in Canadian studies, as I am also the Recommending Officer for acquiring Canadian publications at the Library of Congress.

2. JOHN HERD THOMPSON and STEPHEN J. RANDALL, *Canada and the United States: Ambivalent Allies* (Athens, Ga.: University of Georgia Press, 1994), p. 1.

3. JAMES T. SHOTWELL, "Introduction," in HANSEN, MARCUS LEE, *Mingling of Canadian and American Peoples* (New York: Russell & Russell, 1970), p. v.

4. JOHN BARTLET BREBNER, "Forward," in HANSEN, MARCUS LEE, *op. cit.*, p. ix.

5. JOHN HERD THOMPSON and STEPHEN J. KENDALL, *op. cit.*, p. 5.

6. *Ibid.*, p. 5.

7. JOHN BARTLET BREBNER, *op. cit.*, p. x.

8. JAMES T. SHOTWELL, *op. cit.*, p. v.

9. *Ibid.*, p. v.

10. PHYLLIS A. RYERSE and THOMAS A. RYERSON, *The Ryerse-Ryerson Family* (Ingersoll, Ontario: Ryerse-Ryerson Family Association, 1994).

11. Italics in the following passages are the addition of the present author in order to emphasize certain ideas.

12. JOHN BARTLET BREBNER, *op. cit.*, p. ix-x.

13. CECIL J. HOUSTON and WILLIAM J. SMYTH, *Irish Emigration and Canadian Settlement: Patterns, Links, and Letters* (Toronto: University of Toronto Press, 1990), p. 25.

14. JAMES T. SHOTWELL, *op. cit.*, p. vii.

15. JOHN HEARD THOMPSON and STEPHEN J. RANDALL, *op. cit.*, p. 17.

16. DAVID J. RUSSO, *Clio Confused: Troubling Aspects of Historical Study from the Perspective of U.S. History* (Westport Conn.: Greenwood Press, 1995, p. 109-112), *passim.*

17. JAMES T. SHOTWELL, *op. cit.*, p. vii.

18. FREDERICK ELLSWORTH KIP, *History of the Kipp Family in America* (Boston: Hudson Printing Co., 1928), p. 399.

19. Much of the material in the genealogy part of this speech is taken from the same genealogy (see note 17), and will not be cited each time.

20. CATHERINE CRARY, "Guerilla Activities of James Delancey's Cowboys in Westchester County: Conventional Warfare or Self-Interested Freebooting," in ROBERT A. EAST and JACOB JUDD, *The Loyalist Americans: A Focus on Greater New York* (Tarrytown, N.Y.: Sleepy Hollow Restorations, Inc. 1975), p. 16.

21. LOUIS RICHARD, *Samuel Kipp (1753-1803) et ses descendants : une étude biographique et généalogique* (Ottawa, Ont.: 13 Ave. Woodlawn, 1950), *passim.*

22. OTTO HUFELAND, *Westchester County during the American Revolution, 1775-1783* (Harrison, N.Y.: Harbor Hill Books, 1974, c. 1926), p. 381.

23. CATHERINE CRARY, *loc. cit.*, p. 18.

24. DONALD E. OUTHOUSE, *Robert Outhouse, 1750-1849, and His Wife Sarah (Caldwell) Outhouse, United Empire Loyalists* (Yarmouth Nova Scotia: D. E. Outhouse, 1988), p. 7-8.

25. NORTH CALLAHAN, *Flight from the Republic: The Tories of the American Revolution* (Westport Conn.: Greenwood Press, 1967), p. 47.

26. PHYLLIS A. RYERSE and THOMAS A. RYERSON, *The Ryerse-Ryerson Family* (Ingersoll, Ontario: Ryerse-Ryerson Family Association, 1994).

27. *Ibid.*

28. A. W. SAVARY, *Supplement to the History of Annapolis* (Toronto: William Briggs, 1913), p. 122.

29. ABRAHAM HATFIELD, *The Hatfields of Westchester: A Genealogy of the Descendants of Thomas Hatfield of New Amsterdam and Mamaroneck, Whose Sons Settled in White Plains, Westchester County, New York* (New York: New York Genealogical and Biographical Society, 1935), *passim.*

30. Public Record Office (Great Britain), in AO (Audit Office) 13/24/299-300, cited in PETER WILSON COLDHAM, *American Loyalist Claims, Abstracted from the Public Record Office, Audit Office Series 13, Bundles 1-35 and 37* (Washington, D.C.: National Genealogical Society, 1980), p. 275.

31. ISAIAH W. WILSON, *A Geography and History of the County of Digby, Nova Scotia* (Belleville, Ont.: Mika Studio, 1972), p. 386.

32. ISAIAH W. WILSON, *op. cit.*, p. 387.

33. FREDERIC E. KIP, *op. cit.*, p. 400-401.

34. ESTHER CLARK WRIGHT, *Loyalists of New Brunswick* (Hantsport, Nova Scotia: Lancelot Press, 1981), p. 78.

35. WILLIAM LEONARD DUTTON, *The Dotten (.10) Family in the U.S.A. and Canada: A Genealogical Compilation: or the Descendants of Ensign James Dotten, U.E.L. (1751-1831) of the Westchester N.Y. Disbanded Corps and His Wife Abigail (Odell)* (New Brunswick: by the compiler, 1970), A-K.

36. LOUIS RICHARD, *op. cit.*, p. 17-18.

37. *Ibid.*, p. 47.

38. PETER WILSON COLDHAM, *op. cit.*, p. 275.

39. LOUIS RICHARD, *op. cit.*, p. 40.

40. LOUIS RICHARD, *op. cit., passim.*

41. LOUIS RICHARD, *op. cit., passim.*

42. RAY H. MATTISON, in LE ROY R. HAFEN (ed.), *The Mountain Men and the Fur Trade of the Far West: Biographical Sketches of the Participants by Scholars of the Subject* (Glendale, Ca.: The Arthur H. Clark Co., 1965), p. 202-205.

43. WARREN LEONARD HANNA, *Stars Over Montana: Men Who Made Glacier National Park History* (West Glacier, Mont: Glacier Natural History Association, 1988), p. 83-84.

44. PETER WILSON COLDHAM, *op. cit.,* p. 274.

45. AO 13/14, 27-29. In LORENZO SABINE, *Biographical Sketches of Loyalists of the American Revolution* (Westport Conn.: Mecklor, 1984), p. 465.

46. CHARLES S. BUCK, *Old Sparta and Its Neighborhood, Elgin County, Ontario* (St. Thomas, Ont: Elgin County Library Board, 1979), p. 7-8.

47. *Ibid.*

48. *Ibid.,* p. 15.

49. *Ibid.,* p. 14-15.

50. *Ibid.,* p. 10.

51. *Ibid.,* p. 24.

52. *Ibid.,* p. 25.

53. *Ibid.,* p. 33.

54. *Ibid.,* p. 29-33.

55. *Ibid.,* p. 36-38.

56. COLIN READ, *The Rising in Western Upper Canada, 1837-8: The Duncombe Rebellion and After* (Toronto: University of Toronto, 1982), p. 226.

57. "Memoirs of Mrs. Rundle," in *Material re: Messrs. Doan, Zavitz, etc.* (London, Ontario: 1943). This book is a bound typescript in the collections of the Library of Congress that collects memories by and about the Zavitz, Haight, Chase, Vail, Rundle, Kipp and Mills families in Sparta, Ontario in the mid-19th century.

58. ABRAHAM HATFIELD, *op. cit.*

59. Although there are Knapp genealogies in the Library of Congress, these genealogies do not discuss the Loyalist Knapps in any depth. Most of what I know about the Knapps comes from their intermarriages with Kipps and other Westchester Loyalist families (and therefore their appearance in the published genealogies of these families).

60. JOSEPHINE C. FROST (ed.), *Underhill Genealogy: Descendants of Captain John Underhill* (Underhill Society of America, 1932).

61. DOROTHY I. BROWN, *A Loyalist's Legacy: The Family of Robert Land* (Mississauga, Ont.: D. I. Brown, 1985).

62. GEORGE D. WILLITS, *The Willits Families of Up-per Canada and Their Descendants with Other Kin of Daniel Eugene Willits* (Woodstock, Ont.: G. D. Willits, 1993).

63. CLAYTON C. PURDY, *Gabriel Purdy: His Ancestors and Descendants* (Baton Rouge, La.: Oracle Press, 1986), and CLAYTON C. PURDY, *Henry Purdey: His Ancestors and Descendants* (Baton Rouge, La.: Oracle Press, 1985).

64. DONALD E. OUTHOUSE, *Robert Outhouse, 1750-1849, and His Wife Sarah (Caldwell) Outhouse, United Empire Loyalists* (Yarmouth, N.S.: D. E. Outhouse, 1988).

65. VERNE B. LEWIS, *Pryor, Smith, Tidd and Powell—and Other Loyalist Ancestors of My Grandparents, Charles and Susan Plummer* (Mercer Island, Washington: V. B. Lewis, 1982).

66. HAROLD FANJOY, *The Seeleys of New Brunswick* (Saint John, N.B.: Fanjoy and Ward, 1992).

67. PHYLLIS A. RYERSE and THOMAS A. RYERSON, *op. cit.*

68. WAYNE W. WALKER, *Simon DeLong: Loyalist of Nova Scotia, Canada* (Ottawa, Ont.: W. W. Walder, 1992).

69. DONALD E. WILLIAMS, *Fayerweather Friends: The Fairweather Genealogy* (Riverview, N.B.: D. Williams, 1992).

70. D. A. STORY, *The De Lanceys: A Romance of a Great Family* (London: T. Nelson & Sons, 1931).

71. VERDA DUKESHIRE PRIKLER, *Tuchscherer: History and Genealogy of the Dukeshire Family in North America* (Middleton, N.S.: Black Print Co., 1978).

72. EDWIN A. LIVINGSTON, *Family History and Genealogical Record of Daniel Livingston U.E. and Some of His Descendants* (Prescott, Ont.: E. A. Livingston, 1983).

73. CONN HARKNESS SUTHERLAND, *The Sutherlands and Westchester, Nova Scotia* (Agincourt, Ont: Generation Press, 1986).

74. JOHN BARTLET BREBNER, *op. cit.,* p. xi.

75. This book is a bound typescript in the collections of the Library of Congress that collects memories by and about the Zavitz, Haight, Chase, Vail, Rundle, Kipp and Mills families in Sparta, Ontario in the mid-19th century.

## APPENDIX 1: Kipp family chart

**Ruloff de Kype**
(ca. 1520, Alençon, Brittany, France-
†March 13, 1569, in battle, Jarnac, France)

**Ruloff Kype**
(1544-†1596, Holland)

**Hendrick Kip**
(1576-†?), m. Margaret de Marneil, Holland

**Hendrick Henderson Kip**
(1600, Niewenhuys, Holland-
†New Amsterdam, New York)
m. 1624 Tryntie Lubberts, Amsterdam, Holland

**Jacob Kip**
(May 16, 1631, Amsterdam, Holland-
†December 24, 1690, New Amsterdam, New York)
m. 1654, Maria de la Montagne, New Amsterdam, New York

**Jesse Kip**
bap. December 16, 1660
m. 1695 Maria Stevens
(†April 1722, Long Island, New York)

**Benjamin Kipp**
bap. May 24, 1714
(†May 24, 1782)
m. Dorothy Davenport

**James Kipp**
(April 6, 1751-
†1784, Cumberland Co,. Nova Scotia)
m. Zipporah Carpenter

**Thomas Kipp**
(July 14, 1756-
†December, 1823, New York, New York)
m. Abigail Hatfield

**Samuel Kipp**
(Dec. 16, 1753-†Feb. 23, 1805, Montreal)
m. (1) Freelove Totton
(2) Mary Knapp

**John Kipp**
(1773-†Sparta, Ontario)
m. Ruth Carpenter

**Caleb Kipp**
(March 7, 1809, New York-
†December 23, 1885, Rockford, Illinois)
m. Pheobe Mills, Yarmouth, Ontario, 1834

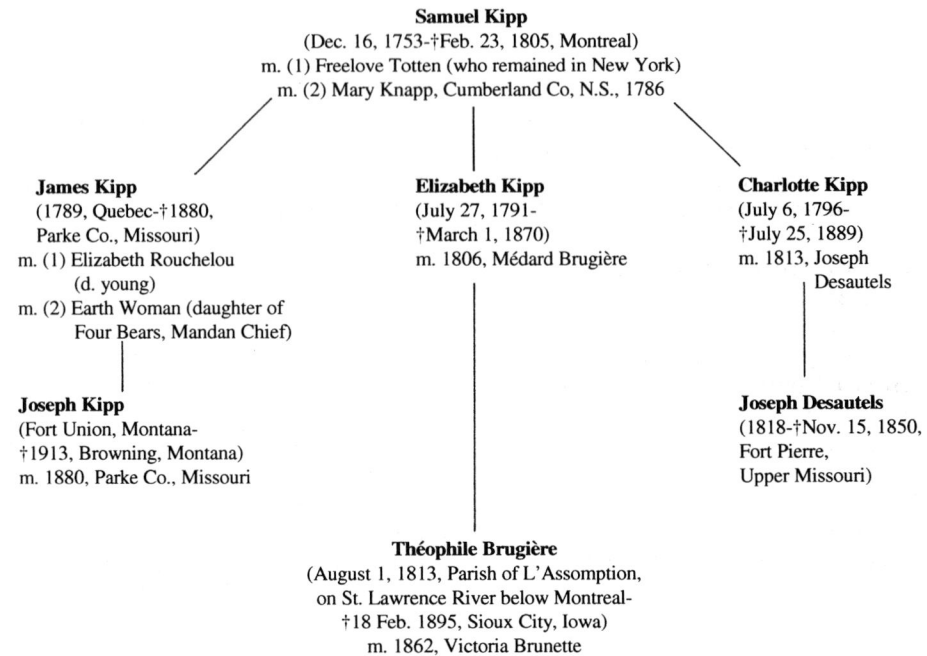

**Samuel Kipp**
(Dec. 16, 1753-†Feb. 23, 1805, Montreal)
m. (1) Freelove Totten (who remained in New York)
m. (2) Mary Knapp, Cumberland Co, N.S., 1786

**James Kipp**
(1789, Quebec-†1880,
Parke Co., Missouri)
m. (1) Elizabeth Rouchelou
(d. young)
m. (2) Earth Woman (daughter of
Four Bears, Mandan Chief)

**Elizabeth Kipp**
(July 27, 1791-
†March 1, 1870)
m. 1806, Médard Brugière

**Charlotte Kipp**
(July 6, 1796-
†July 25, 1889)
m. 1813, Joseph
Desautels

**Joseph Kipp**
(Fort Union, Montana-
†1913, Browning, Montana)
m. 1880, Parke Co., Missouri

**Joseph Desautels**
(1818-†Nov. 15, 1850,
Fort Pierre,
Upper Missouri)

**Théophile Brugière**
(August 1, 1813, Parish of L'Assomption,
on St. Lawrence River below Montreal-
†18 Feb. 1895, Sioux City, Iowa)
m. 1862, Victoria Brunette

---

**APPENDIX 3:** Periods of intense migration between the U.S. and Canada

**Early Fur Traders:** French Canadians, trapping and trading with the Indians, sometimes settled in the U.S. and Canadian Midwest and Far West.

**French Acadian Expulsion:** Some Acadians went back to France, but many ended up in New England, Louisiana and in the Mississippi River area. Some went to other parts of Quebec or Ontario, or even back to the Maritimes.

**New England Planters:** New England colonists who were encouraged to settle on lands, especially in Nova Scotia, vacated by the Acadians.

**American Loyalists:** American colonists who were loyal to Britain during the American Revolution fled to Canada for political asylum and were given land by the British government in Canada. This relocation took place over a period of years. The first wave was in 1783, right after the Revolution. The migration, continued until the War of 1812, as Canadian government opened land to UEL and UEL sons and daughters.

**War of 1812:** Migration slowed, but the War of 1812 gave impetus to the migration of religious dissidents and land seekers after the War was over.

**The Revolution of 1837:** Many families of U.S. origin in Canada were in favor of democratic reform of the Canadian government according to principles espoused by MacKenzie.

**The 19th-Century Fur Trade (Opening of the Canadian and American West)**

**The Underground Railroad**

# PROBLEMS IN ACADIAN GENEALOGICAL RESEARCH

Stephen A. White

Obviously, the upheavals of Acadian history translate into difficulties for researchers who wish to retrieve genealogical information from surviving documentation. Unlike the French Canadians, the Acadians lost a great many of their records. To understand exactly what happened in this regard, it is useful to review briefly the first two centuries of the history of the Acadian people, before examining some of the steps taken to facilitate research despite this loss. For genealogical purposes, one may conveniently divide Acadian history into four periods:

I.  French colonisation (1636-1713);
II. development under British rule (1713-1755);
III. deportation and dispersion (1755-1785);
IV. resettlement (after 1785).

Because of its strategic situation between Canada and New England, Acadia became a military objective even before it had a permanent civilian population. Despite French colonisation as early as 1604, families only came to it beginning with the arrival of the *Saint-Jehan* from La Rochelle in 1636. Unfortunately, the church registers prior to 1679 and the notarial archives prior to 1687 were all destroyed, and many later records are likewise missing, so very little is known regarding the colony's earliest families, particularly concerning their precise origins. It is thus exceptional to be able to pursue research beyond the ancestors named in Acadia's first census, taken in 1671. Fortunately, the French authorities took many subsequent censuses, and it is through them that the first several generations of Acadian families can be reconstructed.

During the decades of the Acadians' ill-fated neutrality under the British, parish registers were regularly kept, and parts of those for three, out of about a dozen parishes, still survive. Meanwhile, no minutes of the several notaries who practiced in Acadia during this period have been preserved, notwithstanding Longfellow's immortalisation of one of their number. No genealogically useful enumerations of the population were generated in British-controlled territory through these years. On the other hand, there are many census records and a rich collection of notarial documentation extant for the islands retained by the French after the Treaty of Utrecht, particularly concerning the fortress-city of Louisbourg.

The dispersion of the Acadians was a far more complex series of events than the often-encountered popular misconception of mass transplantation from Nova Scotia to Louisiana. Acadian settlements were systematically eradicated, and considerable quantities of documentation disappeared with them, including both parish records and notarial minutes. The deportation of 1755 scattered those Acadians who were considered British subjects among seven American colonies and four English ports, while the evacuation of 1758 sent those who had taken refuge on Île Royale and Île Saint-Jean back to France. Hundreds of other Acadians who succeeded in evading these forced removals fled to Quebec, while many who got only as far as Chaleur Bay were captured and brought back to Beauséjour, Pisiguit, and Halifax. Only a handful of missionary or parochial registers contain records for the families who remained in Atlantic Canada, or for those in England and the American colonies, but such records are relatively plentiful for those who went to France and Quebec, or who eventually reached Louisiana. Nevertheless, much of what occurred during this period to individual families may be reasonably well understood from study of an astonishing array of lists, beginning with the enumeration made by the spy Thomas Pichon in the winter of 1754-1755 and the one copied by Col. John Winslow into his journal in the tragic autumn of 1755, and ranging through lists of families arriving in South Carolina (1755), surviving in Pennsylvania and New York (1756), arriving in Saint-Malo (1758), being redistributed in Massachusetts (1760) or enumerated around Chaleur Bay (1760, 1761) to the Quebec census of 1762, the lists of refugees in France (annually drawn up from 1762 to 1773), and the lists appended to the responses to the French minister's circular letter offering repatriation in 1763. There then follow censuses in Quebec and Belle-Île-en-Mer (1765) and Louisiana (1766, 1769, 1770, etc.), lists of arrivals in Brittany (1763, 1766) and Louisiana (1767, 1768, 1769), and censuses in Saint-Pierre and Miquelon (1767, 1776, 1784-1785). Thanks to these and many less comprehensive records, the principal stages in the peregrinations of most families may be followed, once one can satisfactorily establish their identities. Indeed, one may even presume from the absence of certain individuals and families from some of these records, that their deaths occurred during specific intervals. Taking, for example, the family of Charles Granger and Françoise LeBlanc, one learns from Winslow's list that, on the eve of their expulsion, their family included seven boys and five girls and was in relatively comfortable circumstances, having about 130 head of livestock. The family was sent to Virginia and transshipped to Falmouth in England, as may be inferred from the appearance of the widow Granger and her five surviving sons and one surviving daughter in the listings eight years later. The Grangers went to Brittany in 1763 and appear in the census of Belle-Île-en-Mer in 1765. The *Déclaration* at Belle-Île of the widow shows that her husband had died at Falmouth on October 12, 1756, but it does not mention the deaths of the six children who perished between 1755 and 1763. Because of a gap in the Grand-Pré registers, the given names of all of these are not available, but they exemplify the high rate of mortality among younger children during the Deportation, for one may conclude that five of them had been aged 12 or under in 1755. The registers of Belle-Île permit one to follow the family's subsequent history. Françoise LeBlanc died at Bangor on February 1, 1793, 37 years after her life at Grand-Pré had been so irrevocably disrupted.

The resettlement of the Acadians was slow and arduous, particularly in Atlantic Canada. The rich land they had cultivated prior to their dispersion had been given to others; few were able to return to the tidal marshes they or their compatriots had dyked and drained; instead many had to take up new, poorer land along the coasts. The first permits for resettlement date from 1761, but landowner status was nowhere obtained until 1772. The reorganisation of parishes was particularly slow, few being founded before 1800, and of those, several (e.g., Arichat, Church Point, and Memramcook) are missing substantial portions of their early records due to fires and other mishaps. It is often necessary to rely at least in part on secondary sources, such as the unpublished compilations of Placide Gaudet (1850-1930), to reconstruct many family units who existed during this period. Subsequently, tracing 19th-century Acadian families in Atlantic Canada is much like tracing other groups; the same groups of census materials, land and probate records may be consulted for any of them. One distinction remains to be pointed out: unlike many people of other origins, the Acadians rarely erected long-lasting burial markers until relatively late in the last century.

In France, Quebec, and Louisiana, information concerning Acadian refugees is relatively plentiful. All three places had well-established parochial systems, from which nearly all the records are preserved, and consequently vital statistics are readily obtainable, provided one can identify the parishes in which the Acadians lived. In all three, the notarial archives have been preserved as well, and thus marriage contracts and other documents may be available to provide additional information. In France and Louisiana, there are also quite a few nominal enumerations of the population.

A small number of families remained in the American colonies, particularly in Maryland, after the departure of the great majority of their compatriots. The descendants of many of these families altered their names over time, becoming Gold, Wells, and White, for example, instead of Doiron, Dupuis and LeBlanc. Research may be further complicated concerning the descendants of these exiles where they tended to leave the Roman Catholic Church. And even the records kept by the latter do not always themselves conform to the standards maintained elsewhere. In the cathedral parish in Baltimore, for example, there is a period during which the priests did not record the names of the parents of the children they baptized.

The leading problem encountered by enthusiasts of Acadian genealogical research is thus the lack of records, especially for the period of the colonisation of Acadia and that of the subsequent dispersion of its inhabitants. Those records that did survive the *Grand Dérangement* were often dispersed as widely as the Acadians themselves. The pre-1755 parish records of Port Royal (from 1702), for example, wound up in two repositories in Nova Scotia; those of Beaubassin in Quebec (1679-1686) and La Rochelle (1712-1748); those of Grand-Pré in Saint-Gabriel d'Iberville. In the latter case, one learns with dismay that many of the earliest (before 1707) and latest (after 1748) records in the set that had safely been transported to Louisiana were destroyed in a flood in 1893. Additionally, some registers, as they were originally kept, do not include all the data one would desire to find in them.

The founders of the Centre d'études acadiennes at the Université de Moncton addressed the first of these problems by determining to collect together all the documentation that could be identified as containing useful genealogical information. Thanks to modern technology, this objective was relatively easy to attain with respect to the material pertaining to the first three periods of Acadian history described above. Hundreds of reels of microfilm have been acquired, catalogued, and made available to researchers. Some of the same material, and numerous other documents, have been photocopied. The result is generally believed to be the most complete collection of information concerning the Acadians of the 17th and 18th centuries that exists anywhere. It is additionally the mandate of the Centre d'études acadiennes to collect all relevant data concerning the Acadians of Atlantic Canada. This has likewise been done, and the Centre's collections include copies of substantially all the parish records of the Acadian regions through the 19th century (with the exception of some records in the dioceses of Antigonish and Halifax), as well as copies of the provincial and federal censuses down to 1901. An extensive collection of New Brunswick land records is very helpful for those whose ancestors lived in this province. The Centre's holdings are rounded out by its collection of secondary sources. The notes of Placide Gaudet are particularly important because Gaudet had occasion to interview many of the children and grandchildren of individuals who had been involved in the dispersion itself. Other manuscript sources include similar, although less plentiful, genealogical gems. The Centre also has a large collection of published source materials. For the Acadians in Louisiana this is quite comprehensive, because so much has been put into print, notably by Father Donald Hébert. Several others are also responsible for the transcription and publication of

a great deal of data concerning their forebears before they reached Louisiana. Besides Father Hébert, Albert J. Robichaux Jr. and Mr. and Mrs. Milton Rieder were particularly active in this area, the former in publishing abstracts and copies of records from France (1758-1785) and the latter in publishing abstracts of pre-Deportation parish records. A full bibliography of such works would require more space than is available here. Similarly, genealogical publications in Quebec are extremely numerous. The Centre has a significant, albeit incomplete, collection of *répertoires de mariages*, a copy of the *Fichier Loiselle*, and copies of the genealogical compendia, from Tanguay to Jetté, but only for the years 1750 to 1765 and not the full series of the *répertoire* of the *Projet de recherche en démographie historique* of the Université de Montréal. Additionally, it has microfilm copies of selected Quebec parish records, mostly from the period 1755 to 1780, and only from the areas from Quebec City westward. It also possesses a number of published inventories, especially those compiled by P.-G. Roy, and some inventories of the minutes of the early notaries. Among the more useful of the latter are those prepared by Frère Éloi-Gérard Talbot for Maîtres Michon and Rousselot, who had many Acadians from the rivière du Sud among their clients.

Once one collects such a large quantity of documentation, one must of necessity find someone to put order into it. Besides trained archivists, the Centre d'études acadiennes has always had on its staff, since its foundation in 1968, one or more genealogical specialists. The first of these, Father Hector Hébert, s.j., undertook a new compilation of data from the original parish registers and census records. Much research had previously been conducted in an unscientific manner, inadequately documented, and may have been based on faulty transcriptions and even rife with speculative hypotheses. A return to the original sources was thus deemed advisable. Father Hébert's original plan, formulated under the direction of the Centre's founder, Father Clément Cormier, c.s.c., was to abstract information from individual records on file cards dubbed "fiches satellites," to be used in reconstituting entire family units on larger cards called "fiches maîtresses." The latter comprise a substantial part of Father Hébert's collection at the Centre. While Father Hébert was still at this task, Father Patrice Gallant was hired to begin preparation of a compendium of genealogical knowledge entitled the *Dictionnaire généalogique des familles acadiennes*. This has long been the dream of Acadian genealogists, to have a comprehensive work comparable to the one published by Mgr. Cyprien Tanguay between 1871 and 1890. Placide Gaudet set about to compile such a compendium, but lacked access to many documents necessary to bring such a project to fruition. His information nevertheless provided part of the base for the new work. It would appear, however, that Father Gallant drew his chief inspiration from the manuscript *Dictionnaire des Acadiens* by Father Archange Godbout, o.f.m. In addition to keeping close track of his sources, Father Godbout offers his readers occasional explanatory notes showing his reasoning in reaching certain conclusions. Father Gallant borrowed heavily from Father Godbout, and then expanded upon the result. The present writer has been employed at the Centre since 1975 to make further expansions, extending the reach of the *Dictionnaire* to encompass additional families, and completing the data compiled. The great bulk of his work has been concentrated on broadening the analysis and amplifying the explanations, so that the *Dictionnaire généalogique des familles acadiennes* may truly be considered an exhaustive work.

The *Dictionnaire* marks a significant departure from the ordinary work-product of an archival centre. The staff of the Centre d'études acadiennes has prepared finding aids and indexes that facilitate consultation of source materials, such as the parish registers of the archdiocese of Moncton and various censuses, particularly of selected parts of the three Maritime Provinces. As suggested above, the *Dictionnaire* is much more than a mere finding aid. It amounts to a distillation of all that is known concerning Acadian genealogy. It is organised on the same plan as Mgr. Tanguay's work. Family names are arranged alphabetically, and then each family unit is treated in chronological order, according to their dates of creation (usually the date of marriage of the spouses). The offspring are listed in order of birth. Dates of birth and baptism, of marriage, and of death and burial are all provided where available, along with reference to the register in which they have been found. Where precise dates are missing, approximate birth dates are calculated from census entries or ages at the time of death. No date is given without some kind of documentary support.

Baptismal sponsors and witnesses at marriages and burials are noted, as are dispensations for consanguinity and affinity. After the listing of the children, a summary of the sources used is provided, along with abstracted data from any relevant censuses, and explanatory and biographical or historical notes.

The most important element that must be established in Acadian genealogy is the affiliation. Moreover, it must be made clear what basis exists for believing that a certain person was indeed the child of certain parents. Where the baptism and marriage records exist, this is quite straightforward. Where the family appears in a census the connections may be quite plain. If some or all of these records are missing, other proofs of affiliation must be found. Mention of the relationships of witnesses, for example, may prove that an additional child belonged to a given family; this is noted in the *Dictionnaire* parenthetically, with reference to the register entry. In other cases connections may be proved by analysis of dispensations for consanguinity or affinity; these proofs are laid out in complementary notes. Other connections may only be suggested by circumstantial evidence, such as a particular grouping of families in a census; these deductions are also outlined in explanatory notes. Where the opinions of Placide Gaudet, Father Archange Godbout, or others have been relied upon, this is noted parenthetically, and the precise reference is given among the secondary sources. The category of secondary sources is also used to guide the reader to potentially useful biographical material. The guiding principle in all this is the desire to inform the user of the weaknesses as well as the strengths of the information. Many things can be proved, but many others are merely believed to be as they are portrayed on the basis of certain evidence, and it is incumbent on the compiler to make that distinction known. In some cases other researchers may find better evidence, whether in favour or against the proposition advanced, but in all cases it should be relatively easy to understand just what point has been reached in the work that has been accomplished up to this time. In these respects the *Dictionnaire* differs from most works in Acadian genealogy, whether published or manuscript, for few have shown such rigour in the citation and expatiation of their sources.

The laudable endeavour of compiling a definitive work is unfortunately an enormously time-consuming one. The many years of effort that have gone into the *Dictionnaire* have not yet resulted in its publication, although the first segment of its information, covering the period from 1636 to 1714, will soon appear. In order to make, not only that, but a second part covering the years 1715 to 1780, more quickly available, even in a relatively incomplete form, recourse has been had to computerisation. Understanding that large numbers of the participants in the World Acadian Congress of 1994 would wish to consult its genealogical documentation, the administration of the Université de Moncton secured a grant to begin work on the *Banque de données généalogiques acadienne*. During the 1994 Congress, the unfinished *Banque* was copied, and the copies were lent to those families holding reunions who requested them. The *Banque* is still in the process of being compiled, from the information in the manuscript of the *Dictionnaire*. It currently is about four-fifths complete, and contains about 75,000 names. It may be consulted by special arrangement at the Centre d'études acadiennes. In the near future it will be made more widely accessible, either through reproduction on compact disk, or through the Internet, or both. It must be mentioned that the *Banque* does not at this point include all the *Dictionnaire*'s information. Notably absent are the explanatory and biographical notes, as well as some data concerning sources.

The *Dictionnaire* and the *Banque* both contain information of great value to researchers who are interested in the Acadians of the 17th and 18th centuries. For those who seek more contemporary data concerning Acadian families in Atlantic Canada, the Centre d'études acadiennes has a number of research tools available. For the period after 1780, it is proposed to extend the *Dictionnaire* on a regional basis. A manuscript has already been prepared for the Acadians of Prince Edward Island, following them to 1840. A similar compilation has been begun for the Acadians of southeastern New Brunswick. The present writer has already compiled the genealogies of most of the Acadian families of Richmond, Antigonish, and Guysborough Counties in Nova Scotia. Father Patrice Gallant began a series of notebooks and card files on the Acadians of Saint-Pierre and Miquelon, the Magdalen Islands, Inverness County, and Pomquet, N.S. In addition, abstracts have been made of all entries for the French in some of the federal censuses in Cumberland, Digby, and

Yarmouth Counties in Nova Scotia, Victoria County in New Brunswick, and all of Prince Edward Island. The Centre possesses copies of published, indexed census transcriptions for various censuses of Albert, Gloucester, Kent, Northumberland, Restigouche, Victoria, Westmorland, and York Counties, New Brunswick. It also has indexes to many of the parish registers of the dioceses of Bathurst and Moncton. Currently in preparation is a *répertoire de mariages* for the Moncton diocese, including all records found in the registers through 1900.

While the foregoing is merely a partial listing of available materials, the reader may derive some assurance from it that considerable advances have been made in Acadian genealogy since the opening of the Centre d'études acadiennes in 1968. Indeed, in many cases, members of the general public who know no more than two or three generations of their ancestry may find, provided their information brings them back into the 19th century, that an hour or less will suffice to trace their lineage all the way back to their first ancestor on record in 17th-century Acadia. And this may be done with full assurance of the information's accuracy, and with complete documentation. It nevertheless remains that, in most cases, the first ancestor cannot be traced to his or her origin in Europe. The origins of many of Acadia's founding families have long been an enigma. Geneviève Massignon may have been close to a solution to this, for her thesis argues quite persuasively that, to the extent that the Acadian patois reflects the dialect of Poitou, the early Acadians must have been of Poitevin origin. Unfortunately, in the 30 years since Ms. Massignon published her findings, no one has been able to identify more than the handful of colonists she herself located. There is increasing interest, particularly among certain groups in France, in pursuing further research, but the problem is still the question of where to look. Just this summer, a new project has been undertaken that might prove helpful in suggesting certain possibilities, while it should surely open up new vistas with regards to some later arrivals in Acadia, for whom we have much better documentation. This is a *Recueil des origines des Acadiens des 17e et 18e siècles,* compiled from the data in the *Dictionnaire généalogique des familles acadiennes*. All the available information has been entered into a data base, and presently it will be possible to print out lists sorted according to parishes, dioceses, or provinces of origin. It is hoped that publication of this information will encourage additional collaboration between researchers in the New and Old Worlds.

Acadian genealogy continues to be a dynamic field of research. The Centre d'études acadiennes has collected together the great bulk of existing documentation and has employed, since its foundation, professional genealogists to compile from this data a tolerably complete, well-reasoned and painstakingly supported reconstruction, not just of the genealogies of certain families, but of the entire population of 17th- and 18th-century Acadia. This corpus of information is continually in the process of refinement, as analysis proceeds, and corrections are still often made to it, as new connections come to light through the study of dispensations for consanguinity and affinity, or through the occasional discovery of hitherto unknown documents. The next stage in the process is the dissemination of the information, through publication of the *Dictionnaire généalogique des familles acadiennes*, the *Banque de données généalogiques acadienne*, and the *Recueil des origines des Acadiens des 17ᵉ et 18ᵉ siècles*. The appearance of these materials will mark a turning point in Acadian genealogical research.

# ARCHIVAL METHODOLOGY AND GENEALOGICAL RESEARCH IN THE INFORMATION AGE: TWO SOLITUDES OR CONVERGING DISCIPLINES?

Lois K. Yorke

Not so many years ago, archives were welcoming and non-threatening environments where historical research was encouraged and flourished. The holdings were finite, the visitors relatively few; staff were accommodating and research pathways, for the most part, simple and direct. Like many another golden memory, of course, much of this is myth. In fact, archives were often viewed as enclaves focusing exclusively on scholarly historical research; genealogy was tolerated, but as a specialized antiquarian interest. The general public sometimes drew near, but were not encouraged; and staff were regarded as research assistants, the "handmaidens of history," fortunate indeed to be the servants of historians.

Over the past quarter-century a fundamental "paradigm shift" has occurred. Archives have been democratized by changing attitudes regarding information, both its technology and management, and the right of access to it. In turn, genealogy has been "commodified" by shifting demographics, the ephemeral nature of the family unit, and the nostalgia of the search for "roots." Archives have also experienced the advent of a new, professional methodology that is both part and product of the Information Age; and by this convolution, in particular, the genealogical research community has been significantly alienated.

These are strange new worlds for both the archivist and the genealogist, fraught with confusion, frustration and a very real potential for misunderstanding and estrangement. This paper will examine the fundamental changes brought about by the new methodology and by automation, viewed against the challenges and constraints of the Information Age. Particular emphasis will be placed on the functional requirements of modern archival work; the conflicting expectations of user groups and resource allocators; and the special challenges posed by the increasingly articulate and politically aware genealogical research community. Lastly, the presentation will address how the two disciplines can work together more closely to guarantee convergent paths of interest and accountability, as they approach the frontiers of the coming century.

In the continuing upheaval of the "paradigm shift," the old familiar archival landscape has been forever altered and displaced. Research tools long beloved by researchers are disappearing with alarming frequency: subject-based arrangement systems for holdings, item-level descriptions, surname indexes and sometimes even the card catalogues themselves, have been either discontinued or relegated to the far corners of the reading room. Archives are moving increasingly to automated databases and/or to access systems based on inventory indexes, which lead in turn to hierarchical finding aids. These modern access-and-retrieval tools provide vital information about context, internal arrangement and external relationships between holdings; but they are recent innovations, and to the uninitiated they are often forbidding. Under this new regime the holdings have also, in many instances, lost their old identities. No longer "papers" or "records" or "collections," they have instead become "fonds d'archives"—records kept together under the name or office of their creator and retained in their original order.

A further change is that access to holdings now often proceeds via altered routes and in time-consuming steps; this in turn creates the impression that the research path is difficult and labourious, everywhere strewn with impediments to progress. Even getting as far as the reading room has become a challenge in many institutions. Archivists are increasingly concerned over the security and long-term preservation of holdings, most of which are undeniably unique and physically fragile. Users are often alienated, however, by what appear to be unreasonable and unnecessary restrictions: registration procedures, embargos on personal belongings, limits on the use of original records, restrictions on photocopying, etc. As a final insult, even the archivist—the former "walking, talking finding aid"—has disappeared. The replacement is a kind of information analyst, attempting to cope with the modern-day reality of "too many masters, too many tasks."

Having examined the fundamental changes brought about by the new methodology, let us move next to the nature of archival work. Modern archival methodology is built upon the basic functions of acquisition, accessioning, appraisal and selection, arrangement and description, preservation and public service. These activities determine the shape of institutional holdings, the rhythm of the workplace and the patterns of access and use. After a quarter-century spent in both disciplines, it is apparent to me that almost without exception, genealogists—including those professing and practising a scientific methodology—have neither knowledge, nor understanding, nor appreciation of these fundamental processes which define the archival world. If any one factor can be identified as responsible for the growing divergence of the two disciplines, this is it—the increasing professionalization of archives, the failure of archivists to adequately convey this shift in perspective and practice, and the obvious confusion and misunderstanding emanating from the genealogical community.

The potential for friction has been further exacerbated by the changing dynamics of record-keeping in the Information Age. For example, probably the single most significant development in archives over the last quarter-century has been the exponential growth of primary source materials, chiefly those generated by government. Researchers, whatever their subject interest, once had a choice of perhaps half a dozen basic and limited sources to review—usually in paper form. Now awaiting them is a staggering array of complex and structured holdings, in a variety of media formats. The fact that there is so much more to chose from is both exciting and discouraging. Government records, for example, are being used in new, imaginative ways to yield genealogical data; at the same time, protection-of-privacy legislation frequently introduces new impediments to access. Just perusing the finding aids and designing a research strategy can take up as much time today as it did 25 years ago to conduct a complete review of all the available sources themselves.

Processing this accelerating influx of material is an overwhelming challenge. Regardless of user expectations, new acquisitions do not magically appear the day after arrival—arranged, described, boxed, reference-coded and neatly supplied with all the appropriate access points. Instead, providing this physical and intellectual control is a complex and time-consuming exercise. New material must be examined in order to determine its original order—if any—and archival value; files or items lacking archival value will be culled; preservation work may be required; final arrangement will be determined; and then the descriptive work can begin. Here the archivist must keep in mind the needs of various user groups. The new acquisition may contain, for example, information valuable to genealogists, demographers and political scientists; each group will approach the holding from a different perspective or direction, and the archivist must therefore create interpretive tools that address and accommodate these variables. In general, researchers remain blissfully unaware of this highly structured activity and fail particularly to understand its importance to the success of their work.

The most invigorating development within the Canadian archival community over the last ten years has been the advent of library-based cataloguing standards. These procedures—for example, those required by the *Rules for Archival Description* now in general use nationally—are supposed to result in finding aids and access systems of a uniform nature and appearance throughout the country. There is a long learning curve in such endeavours, however, and most archives have yet to accomplish this basic goal within their own institutions. While archivists struggle to implement the new standards, moreover, researchers are left to ponder some less-than-user-friendly end-products.

Several projects are now underway nationally as well to create electronic databases of holdings at regional or provincial levels. These efforts are harbingers of the future with respect to providing contextual linkage and network access. Nevertheless, they rarely provide the indexing or depth of detail sought by genealogists—and if not carefully designed and managed, they can also drain institutional time and resources. Faced with these many and various demands, archivists are left with little opportunity or energy to develop customized access tools that might facilitate genealogical research.

On average, most mid- to larger-sized archives are now reporting that annually, 60% to 70% of their clientele are there to research the family tree. Of these, however, only a minority practise "scientific genealogy," namely research based upon the scrupulous examination, collation and documentation of primary source materials, resulting in a verifiable family reconstitution that acknowledges historical change over time. Instead, most family researchers are primarily interested in names, dates and family relationships; as well, those who are hobbyists are often willing to rely on secondary sources of questionable accuracy. These researchers show little interest in social history or in the records-creation process, failing to understand that a rudimentary knowledge of both is the key to successful archival research of any kind.

In addition, we live now in an electronic universe and are well-accustomed to the immediacy of information and product delivery: think of the television news, the Internet, lunch at McDonald's. Within this context, many users of archives can now tolerate and absorb information only if it is delivered in two-minute packages, with the most important details clearly visible, "up front," or mouse-controlled. The archival records-creation process has traditionally run counter to this. Documentation is frequently complex and multilayered, sometimes archaic in format or terminology, and almost always bureaucratic in context; such holdings require concentration, dexterity—and just plain patience—in order to "tease out" the relevant data. Add to this the new emphasis on archival methodology, with its provenance-based holdings, original order, and internal structure based on hierarchical levels of arrangement—and you have the ingredients for one very disaffected and disgruntled client community.

Within this user-*un*friendly landscape, archivists are frequently suspected—and are just as frequently guilty—of holding genealogists and their work in low esteem. This conflict is fuelled by the growing divergence between the two fields of endeavour. On the one hand, archivists deal on a daily basis—and sometimes to the limits of their endurance—with genealogical hobbyists who are resistant to the most basic reference and research procedures, but who are nevertheless aware of their own strategic importance as a demographically significant user group or client constituency. On the other hand, genealogists have been alienated both by archival information technology—which they frequently perceive to be neither responsive nor adaptive to their research needs—and by the new-model archivist, who in many instances refuses on principle to take any interest whatever in family history.

The genealogical community, in turn, displays a quid pro quo disinterest in the formal nature and purpose of archives. For even the most professional genealogist, archives are still an information resource centre for family history. Nothing could be further from the truth for most modern archives. Cultural heritage institutions they are indeed, but family history centres they are not—which in turn highlights the second fundamental issue of this paper, namely the conflicting expectations of those who use archives and those who fund them.

The reality is that modern archival institutions, whether government sponsored or privately endowed, function under specific formal mandates—frequently embodied in enabling legislation—and have acquisition policies that define and regulate the kinds of material they acquire. Most genealogists are unaware of this, failing especially to understand that the accumulation of genealogical source materials and family history case files may be only an incidental activity for the institution, provided as a courtesy service. Indeed, the fundamental rationale of any formal archives is the long-term preservation of records and papers appraised as having archival value. Within this raison d'être, archival material must display legal, fiscal, evidential and/or informational value before its retention can be justified. Informational value alone is significant, but by no means the sole determinant for preservation; nevertheless, it has become a benchmark by which researchers measure the quality of the holdings within archives.

In these days of financial restraint, funding agencies everywhere are demanding increased accountability from the archives which they sponsor, be they government, corporate or community-based. These demands are normally expressed through reduced funding; this, in turn, is translated into fewer staff, decreased operating hours and reductions in user services. In extreme cases, institutions are now being told to rationalize their holdings and exclude certain kinds of material—private-sector records and genealogical files are particularly vulnerable to this exercise. Another new feature is the user-pay system, whereby archives—traditionally non-revenue-generating institutions—are now expected to help pay their way. Admission fees, processing and storage charge-backs for donors, and even a service fee for every box retrieved, are a few of the strategies being contemplated. Too frequently, however, users blame the institutions themselves —and not the funding agencies—for decisions leading to reduced levels of service, or to altered institutional priorities.

Irreparable damage is being done to archives and their holdings by these conflicting expectations. Moreover, since nine-tenths of archival activity lies hidden from the public gaze, user interest is inevitably drawn to the one function that is visible, namely public service. While this activity typically constitutes less than one-quarter of an institution's mandated responsibilities, its directness ensures that it has become another benchmark by which the institution will be measured.

The majority of users experience public service through its most obvious component—reference service. Because good reference service is vital to successful archival research—and thus to an institution's public image and reputation— this function often becomes "the tail that wags the dog." This is especially true of the genealogical community, since their sheer numbers, frequent unfamiliarity with archival procedures, and potential value as a client constituency dictate that every effort should be made to accommodate them. In extreme cases, the internal functioning of an institution can be seriously impaired through the imbalance thus created: hours, user services, processing work, automation projects—all are cut back, deferred or jettisoned in hard times, but reference service goes on forever.

This brings us to the third issue identified in this paper, namely the dynamics of the genealogical research community. Over the past 25 years, genealogists have emerged as an organized, articulate, computer-literate and highly motivated special-interest group. They make up the largest single component within the "client profile" of any major archives. In their ability to exploit automation and electronic networking for research and data-gathering purposes, they have become major players in the traditionally conservative and underfunded world of archives. No longer mere hobbyists, genealogists wield considerably more "political" power in the cultural heritage arena than they are aware of—or have thought to harness effectively. As both disciplines approach the frontiers of the new century, it is important not only to examine the points of difference between them, but also to investigate those areas of mutual interest where enhanced cooperation will promote convergence.

First, some suggestions for the genealogists. Genealogical organizations, with their extensive community contacts and high "recognition factor," are ideally suited to developing and carrying out lobbying strategies on behalf of archives. Resource allocators need to be reminded constantly that the archives that they fund are neither dumps nor warehouses, yielding no immediate or measurable profit. Instead, archives are among the intrinsic building blocks of national heritage and identity, one of the great untapped "natural resources" for promoting both cultural diversity and national unity. Who better than family researchers to help promote this?

When developing strategies for direct political lobbying, genealogical organizations should not be concerned—as some have been—that their activities will somehow alienate or harm those institutions that they are attempting to assist. They should bear in mind, however, that because of funding relationships, most archives will have to assume a disinterested or arm's-length position towards public advocacy. For example, archivists cannot organize or participate in letter-writing campaigns directed to their own funding agency —for obvious reasons. Nevertheless, the usual strategy of letter-writing—to elected politicians, government officials, corporate sponsors, etc.—combined with meetings, interviews and media coverage, is still an effective tool for marshalling opposition to budgetary cutbacks. In the past five years alone, concerted efforts by user groups have prevented reduced services and/or the elimination of some half-dozen archives across Canada. In the latest instance, one provincial government had to beg for the flood of protest letters to stop.

Genealogical organizations should also promote the practice of scientific genealogy and the development of a more rational and scholarly approach to their own discipline. Through such efforts, genealogists and archivists will be able to collaborate more effectively in future, particularly in the design of automated systems compatible with the needs of both professional communities. In general, the more that the two groups can work together to achieve similar ends, the more opportunities will become available to both. In the United States, for example, sustained activity in developing a sophisticated professional infrastructure for genealogy is leading gradually to the recognition of "family reconstitution" as an academic sub-discipline of historical sociology—with accompanying vocational recognition and access to institutional and grant agency funding. In Canada, the development of professional certification and regulatory bodies is seen as integral to the recognition of genealogy as a scholarly pursuit within the cultural heritage sector.

Genealogical organizations should also work more closely with archives to develop volunteer services or "Friends of the Archives" interest groups. The use of volunteers in larger institutions is often precluded by union-management collective agreements, but "Friends of the Archives" initiatives lie under no such constraints and are becoming increasingly popular. Such efforts require close cooperation between the two participating bodies, in the development of mutual objectives and realistic time-frames, then in working together to sustain momentum. In return, "Friends" organizations offer diverse opportunities, including genealogical workshops, fund-raising projects and public relations experience. More significantly, they provide an atmosphere of open communication, in which both the institution and its users can identify areas where cooperation and consultation are needed and can be provided.

At another level, individual genealogists should take an aggressive interest in learning about the organization of holdings and the structure of access systems within their own local archives. Reference staff are more than willing to provide this guidance, particularly if the knowledge can then be disseminated within a larger user group. Allied to this, genealogists contemplating specialized projects such as transcriptions or computerized indices of primary source materials should consult with archives' staff before starting out. Such projects will almost never duplicate any effort that the archives itself might undertake, but the institution will appreciate being informed that the work is in progress. In turn, qualified volunteers may be given access to original holdings rather than microform copies, thus improving the quality of their work. In addition, end-products can sometimes be customized or formatted to meet certain archival standards, which will in turn enhance the research value of the completed project—particularly if it will be available electronically.

Several genealogical organizations across Canada have, within the last decade, established their own information resource centres. Usually these facilities are located within a community museum or museum-archives, and are staffed by volunteers. For everyone concerned, these are tremendously challenging ventures, offering great potential for cultural tourism, revenue generation and sometimes even local employment. Most significantly, they are opportunities for genealogists to accomplish what archivists can no longer do: transcription and collation of nominal data, personal-name indexing, customized research assistance, etc.

In general, archivists are enthusiastic about these local initiatives, and more than willing to provide start-up assistance or advice. There is potential for conflict, however, if the facilities are promoted as "archives" and the staff as "archivists"—particularly if there is competition for funding. Unless genealogical organizations hold material of unquestioned archival value, in unique or original form—for example, family correspondence, church registers, business records—their holdings do not constitute archives and should not be described as such. Instead, their reliance on family history case files, gravestone inscriptions and microform copies of material held elsewhere identifies these facilities as documentation centres—vital within the local network of cultural-heritage information resources, but not an archives.

Next, some suggestions for the archival community on reaching out to genealogists. In general, archivists must become more aggressive in "selling" themselves and their institutions through public awareness activities. The president of the Association of Canadian Archivists has recently observed that archivists work within "a profession that is at best misunderstood, and at worst ignored as another cultural frill." It need not and should not be so! Imaginative public relations exercises can do much to remove the misconception that archivists are glorified file clerks, pedigree compilers or closet-historians. Portable exhibits and astute media coverage are obvious vehicles for developing an informed awareness of archives within the wider community. A more recent innovation is the "open house" exercise, whereby visitors are invited in to observe what really goes on in an archives. This is a golden opportunity to learn how materials are sorted, arranged and described, why the finding aids are structured as they are, which automation projects are underway, and the extent of the institution's processing backlog.

Organizing a "Friends of the Archives" group may be overambitious for smaller institutions; if so, they should instead consider establishing a researcher committee, whereby senior staff and/or management regularly consult a panel of frequent users, including genealogists, for constructive criticism and advice. In smaller communities, having a representative from the genealogical sector on the board of the local museum or archives provides a similar line of communication. In my home institution, a recent Strategic Planning Initiative included a day-long session with three dozen researchers, predominantly genealogists; their input was invaluable in identifying core services to be maintained, possible new directions to be explored, and areas of common concern requiring further consultation.

Archivists also have a responsibility to develop finding aids, research tools and access pathways designed to assist users, not to impress fellow-archivists. The new standards being implemented will go a long way towards achieving this objective, but until they are fully operational there will be a period of adjustment. During the interim there is ample opportunity for cooperation with the genealogical community, in order to facilitate access to and retrieval of information as quickly and efficiently as possible.

Archivists must also become more active in developing automated access, through on-line catalogue systems and networking services. Users now expect automation in archives, and frequently cannot understand why it has not yet arrived. Genealogists have been much more successful in utilizing automation as a research tool, particularly with respect to database creation and management. Document imaging technology will no doubt be the next significant tool that they will seize upon. Here again, however, the genealogist's need for item-level description and access runs counter to the archival principle of provenance-based subject indexing. As well, advocates of document imaging are only beginning to grasp the anomalies of paper-based records and the immensity of holdings in a modern archival institution. Once more, there is ample opportunity for cooperation between archivists and genealogists, especially in designing systems that will take users' needs into account.

In their efforts to reach out to the wider community, archivists will be increasingly constrained by the realities of the workplace. No longer are they merely struggling to balance "too many masters, too many tasks"; these days they are fighting for their very jobs. The genealogical community, on the other hand, is strategically situated to recognize and assume the initiative for many of the challenges identified in this discussion. Technologically sophisticated, economically advantaged, politically aware, goal-oriented and articulate: these are the advantages that render genealogists the ideal partner-stakeholders in the modern archival community. I would argue that as we become more inured to the Information Age, archivists and genealogists are perilously close to taking divergent paths of interest and accountability. Yet these paths can and should converge—and I challenge the genealogical community to take the first steps towards integration.

# GENEALOGY ON THE INTERNET:
# SOME HELPFUL HOME PAGE ADDRESSES (URLS)

Judith P. Reid

## 1. General resources

Afrigeneas
*http://www.msstate.edu/Archives/History/afrigen/*

Cyndi's List of Genealogy Sites on the Web
*http://www.oz.net/~cyndihow/sites.htm*

The Genealogy Gateway to the Web
*http://www.polaris.net/~legend/genalogy.htm*

Genealogy Home Page
*http://www.genhomepage.com*

Genealogy Resources on the Internet
*http://www-personal.umich.edu/~cgaunt/gen_int1.html*

Genealogy SF
*http://www.genealogysf.com/*

Genealogy Toolbox
*http://genealogy.tbox.com/genealogy.html*

JewishGen
*http://www.jewishgen.org/*

Online Genealogy Resources
*http://www.cooklib.org/gene.html*

RAND Genealogy Club
*http://www.rand.org/personal/Genea/*

ROOTS-L Home Page
*http://www.rootsweb.com/roots-1*

Vital Records State Index
*http://www.inlink.com/~nomi/vitalrec/staterec.html*

## 2. Genealogical resources by country

**Worldwide**
World Genealogy Web Project
*http://www.dsenter.com/worldgenweb/index.html*

**Australia**
Australian Family History Compendium
*http://www.cohsoft.com.au/afhc/*

Genealogy in Australia
*http://www.pcug.org.au/~mpahlow/welcome.html*

**Benelux Countries**
Genealogy and Family History in the Benelux
*http://www.ufsia.ac.be/genealogy/genealog.htm*

The Holland Page
*http://ourworld.compuserve.com/homepages/paulvanv/homepage.htm*

**Canada**
Acadian Genealogy Homepage
*http://www.freespace.net/~cajun/genealogy*

Canadian Genealogy Resources
*http://www.iosphere.net/~jholwell/cangene/gene.html*

National Archives of Canada
*http://www.archives.ca/*

National Library of Canada
*http://www.nlc-bnc.ca/*

**East Europe**
Federation of East European Family History Societies
*http://feefhs.org*

## Europe

Genealogy Resources in Europe
*http://www.tc.umn.edu/~pmg/Europe.html*

## France

American-French Genealogical Society
*http://users.ids.net/~afgs/afgshome.html*

Genealogy of French-speaking people and areas (FRANCETRES)
*http://www.cam.org/~beaur/gen/welcome. html*

## Germany

German Genealogy Home Page
*http://www.genealogy.com/gene/*

Internet Sources of German Genealogy
*http://www.bawue.de/~hanacek/info/edatbase .htm*

## Ireland

Grenham's Irish Recordfinder
*http://indigo.ie/~rfinder/*

IRLGEN
*http://www.bess.tcd.ie/roots_ie.htm*

National Archives of Ireland
*http://www.kst.dit.ie/nat-arch//*

## Italy

Italian Genealogy
*http://www.italgen.com*

Resources & References (Italian Genealogical Research)
*http://homepage.interaccess.com/~arduinif/ tools01.htm*

## Latin America/Hispanic

Compuserve Hispanic Genealogy
*http://ourworld.compuserve.com/homepages/ Aflred_ Sosa*

The Puerto Rican/Hispanic Genealogical Society
*http://www.linkdirect.com/hispsoc/*

## Scandinavia

Genealogical Resources in Denmark
*http://www.sn.no/disnorge/danmark.htm*

Genealogy Finland Home Page
*http://www.mediabase.fi/suku/genealog.htm*

Swedish Genealogy Page
*http://www.ts.umu.se/~petersj/swegen.html*

## Switzerland

Swiss Genealogy
*http://www.mindspring.com/~philipp/che.html*

## United Kingdom

U. K. + Ireland Genealogy
*http://midas.ac.uk/genuki*

## United States of America
## Libraries and Archives

Allen Co. Public Library, Ft. Wayne, Indiana
*http://www.acpl.lib.in.us/Genealogy/genealogy. html*

Library of Congress
Local History and Genealogy Reading Room
*http://lcweb.loc.gov/rr/genealogy/*

LDS Family History Library
*http://www.lds.org/Family_History/How_Do_ I_Begin.html*

The Library of Virginia, Richmond
*http://leo.vsla.edu/lva/lva.html*

National Archives
*http://www.nara.gov/*

New York Public Library. US History, Local History and Genealogy Division
*http://www.nypl.org/research/chss/lhg/genea. html*

Newberry Library
*http://www.newberry.org/isc341*

## Societies

Federation of Genealogical Societies
*http://www.fgs.org/~fgs/*

National Genealogical Society Home Page (Arlington, Virginia)
*http://www.genealogy.org/~ngs/*

New England Historic Genealogical Society
(Boston)
*http://www.nehgs.org*

**Publishers**
Everton Publishers Home Page
*http://www.everton.com*

## 3. Searchable genealogical resources

The Books of Remembrance
Memorial database for Canadian war dead
*http://www.schoolnet.ca/books/remember.htm*

Cemetery Listing Association (CLA)
Database of U.S. cemetery records
*http://mininet.systems.smu.edu/cla/*

Census of Norway, 1801
*http://www.uib.no/hi/1801page.html*

Danish Surname Database
*http://www.danbbs.dk/~jensg*

1871 Census of Canada for Ontario
*http://stauffer.queensu.ca/docsunit/searchc
71. html*

GENDEX—WWW Genealogical Index
Index of names for all U.S. GenWeb sites
*http://www.gendex.com/gendex/*

Genealogist's Index to the World Wide Web
Index to queries and databases for GenWeb
*http://members.aol.com/genwebindx/index.htm*

Genealogy Toolbox Surname and Family
Data Index. Keyword searches of multiple
family web sites
*http://genealogy.tbox.com/genealogy/surnam
es/ sigen.html*

GenServ.
Search GEDCOM files by surname
*http://www.genserv.com*

Lacy's Genealogy Gateway Databases on the
Web
*http://www.polaris.net/~legend/database.htm*

Library of Virginia Digital Collections in-cludes
the Virginia Colonial Records Project
*http://image.vtls.com/*

Maine Marriages
Index to Maine Marriages, 1892-1966
*http://www.state.me.us/sos/arc/archives/
genealog/marriage.htm*

National Archives of Ireland
Irish Records on Transportation of Convicts
from Ireland to Australia, 1788 to 1868; also,
Archives of the Ordnance Survey of Ireland
*http://www.kst.dit.ie/nat-arch*

National Park Service U.S. Colored Troops
Database
*http://www.itd.nps.gov/cwss/usct/html*

Online Genealogical Database Index
Access to many searchable GenWeb databases
*http://www.gentree.com/*

Ontario Cemetery Finding Aid. Database of
over 1.1 million interments in Ontario, Canada
*http://www.islandnet.com/ocfa/homepage.html*

PERSI (Periodical Source Index)
*http://www.ancestry.com/home/library/
abtpersi.htm*

Roots Location List Name Finder
*http://www.rootsweb.com/rootsweb/searches/*

Roots Surname List Finder. Database of
persons researching specific surnames
*http://www.rootsweb.com/rootsweb/searches/*

Rootsweb Genealogical Data Cooperative
Variety of databases in addition to surname and
location lists
*http://www.rootsweb.com*

Scott McGee's GenWeb Page
*http://www.genealogy.org/~smcgee/genweb/*

Social Security Master Death Index
Records from the U.S. Social Security system
*http://www.ancestry.com/ssdi/advanced.htm*

U.S. GenWeb Project
*http://www.usgenweb.com*

Virginia Colonial Records Project, Library of Virginia
*http://image.vtls.com/colonial/*

## 4. Heraldry, royalty, and nobility

The American College of Heraldry
*http://users.aol.com/ballywoodn/acheraldry. html*

The College of Arms (London, England)
*http://www.kwtelecom.com/heraldry/collar ms/*

François Velde's Heraldry Site
*http://128.220.1.164/heraldry/intro.htm*

Hapsburg Home Page
*http://h-net.msu.edu/~habsweb/*

Heraldry Links (Shield and Crest Guide to Heraldry Sites)
*http://anansi.panix.com/userdirs/wlinden/ heraldry.shtml*

Rand Genealogy Club Links (Historical Information Medieval and Royal Genealogy)
*http://www.rand.org/personal/Genea/other. html#HI*

Royal and Noble Genealogical Data on the Web
*http://www.dcs.hull.ac.uk/public/genealogy/ GEDCOM.html*

WW-Person
A database of the higher nobility in the Holy Roman Empire
*http://www8.informatik.uni-erlangen. de/html/ww-person.html*

# WHAT GENEALOGICAL RESOURCES ARE OFFERED BY THE SCANDINAVIANS VIA THE INTERNET? THE CASE OF SWEDEN: CRITICAL ASSESSMENT AND PRAGMATIC ADVICE [1]

Marianne Sandels

Every morning here in Ottawa, I pick up the complimentary newspaper that is delivered outside my door in the *Quality Hotel* and read the latest news and weather report. Has it been nice and sunny in Europe? It is easy to check what it has been like in Brussels, Rome and Vienna, but Copenhagen, Helsinki, Oslo, Reykjavik and Stockholm never appear. Have the Scandinavian countries disappeared from the face of the earth?

We do exist, we are part of Europe and we do have computers. In fact, Sweden boasts a high degree of familiarity with computers and new technical gadgets. Surfing on the Internet is fashionable. However, when it comes to creating resources on the Internet, making them available, free of charge, and in English, I am afraid that in Sweden's case things are rather discouraging. We are not bilingual by any means, but English is widely spoken especially by professional people in the world of archives, libraries and learning. In addition, English is the only language we really have in common with the other Scandinavian countries, as Finnish does not even belong to the family of Indo-European languages. Thus we should realize that making information available in English, to people all over the world, is our first priority.

Let us now be matter-of-fact and look at a few examples. The first one is taken from the library world, which is certainly integrated into international scholarship and technical advancement. Uppsala University Library, the most important research library in Sweden, provides generally excellent information in Swedish as well as in English. Its guide to on-line public access library catalogs (OPACS) is to be recommended (http://www.ub.uu.se/bibkat3.html#norden). Please notice that the National Library catalogs of Denmark and Norway, for example, are already accessible on the Internet, free of charge. Sweden has been lagging behind, but is now planning to offer free WWW access to its Union Catalog LIBRIS later this year or next year.

The world of research libraries is interesting for genealogists, not only because many institutions, especially the older ones, feature manuscript collections, but also for other reasons. LIBRIS, for example, contains not only the names of Swedish authors, but also their year of birth and death—even if their publications are minor ones.

What about the archives? The National Archives in Stockholm (*Riksarkivet*) offer just basic information—in Swedish only—about collections, activities and other archives. As a matter of fact, there is just a minimal notice, in Swedish, about the major event this year: the release of a CD-ROM, *Nationell Arkivdatabas* (NAD, for short), a national database of a great number of archives. This major resource, to be updated annually, has been created under the auspices of the National Archives and features multiple search facilities, general information about different kinds of archives, directories etc. It is not accessible via the Internet.

Although we do not live in the best of worlds where all information is stored on-line and accessible via the Internet, I think we should endeavor to create the *second-best* of worlds in which *at least* the basic information about vital resources is made available: (1) immediately; (2) in English; (3) free of charge, of course; and (4) updated regularly.

All around the world, institutions and individuals will then be able to find out for themselves what collections, compilations, databases, etc. are useful in their particular case. The price of the CD—ROM I just mentioned is not prohibitive, only a few hundred dollars, so major archives and libraries will be able to subscribe.

To pursue this line of creating at least the second-best of worlds, I would like to mention two good examples, one from Sweden and another from Norway. Any Internet enthusiast will be able to judge very quickly, whether these two databases are worth further investigation for a specific research problem. Needless to say, it would have been desirable to have all these millions of entries available on the Internet, but let us hope this problem will be solved at another phase.

The first example, the Swedish Demographic Database (http://www.ddb.umu.ddb/en/) was created two decades ago under the auspices of the National Archives. The aim was simply to computerize parish registers of the 19th century and make them available for research. As of today there are more than 1.6 million entries in the sources.

The second example, the Norwegian Historical Data Centre (http://www.uit.no/rhd/nhdc/nhdc.html) (http://www.uit.no/rhd/nhdc/nhdcgen.html# intro), was established a few years later at the University of Tromsö and was modeled on the database I previously mentioned. Chronologically, however, it embraces a longer period of time, both the 18th and 19th centuries.

Who offers the best Internet guide to the bewildering archival landscape of Sweden? Not surprisingly, perhaps, he is the type of enthusiast one finds all over the world, a passionate genealogist, who is familiar with both traditional and modern research methods. His pages on the Internet are *Håkan Skogsjö's* Swedish Genealogy Site (http://www.aalnet.aland.fi/Cloudia/hskogsjo/econtent.htm). Significantly, this person lives in the geographical centre of the Scandinavian countries, in Mareihamn, Åland, a conglomeration of islands that belong to Finland but linguistically and culturally remain close to Sweden. His pages will soon become the official information of the Federation of Swedish Genealogical Societies, *Svenska Släktforskarförbundet*, a most important organization founded in 1986. In addition to general information, his pages provide a number of links to archives, sources, etc. in the other Scandinavian countries as well. Undoubtedly, these hypertext pages are the best introduction for any non-Swedish speaking person. They also contain useful bibliographic and historical information.

Please note, however, that for the Swedish-American heritage, for Swedes who emigrated from the Old World, there are wonderful resources created here in the New World. This being a special field of genealogy, I will avoid discussing it here. The same applies for the LDS Centre in Salt Lake City.

Another interesting site, created by Hans Ahlborg, is Svensk släktforskning (http://www.abc.se/~m6921/genealx.html). Although he does not provide information in English, one should try his links because they are quite good, despite their limited number. This URL may inspire you to take your first Swedish lesson.[2]

To conclude this overview and rapid glance, I would like to express my general feeling that the government sector, which runs so much of Sweden, could do much better in making more information readily available on the Internet. (And in English, please! Or at least with short summaries in English!) And let us hope that all those who are responsible for updating information really do this at regular intervals. During the summer months activity is traditionally low, so this may explain why I have seen so many "old" pages during the last few weeks. Has the weather been nice and sunny in Scandinavia?

## NOTES

1. For the panel discussion, screen printouts and copies were distributed to the audience. To save space, the relevant URLs are indicated here instead.

2. I am afraid to say, though, that the Scandinavian Genealogy Page, in English, which he refers to at the top of his page, does not seem to be accessible at the present.

# FRENCH GENEALOGY AND THE INTERNET

Jean-Marie Thiébaud

During the last 20 to 25 years, French genealogy has made use of computerization. At first limited to certain specialists, it has rapidly spread to organizations and to many individuals who, frequently, discovered computers because of the genealogical data they wished to archive, classify, and computerize.

The French Federation of Genealogy created an information commission, following the Congress of Istres in 1981, in an effort to harmonize methods of classification and programming. This was still the period when amateur researchers were blaming computers for "taking the poetry out of genealogy."

Then France discovered the Net, but only after a long experience with very responsive servers, thanks to a specialized French telecommunications network: Minitel.

Many organizations started putting their transcribed civil records (births, marriages, and burials) on Minitel (nearly 10 million documents at this time, from the 16th to the end of the 19th century, with figures doubling every two years).

The creation of these services, which are complex to put in place, is not at the level of ordinary persons, but do provide organizations with appreciable financial remuneration to offset the costs of computer equipment and the operating costs to manage the collection of genealogical data.

There has resulted a certain reticence on the part of organizations to use the Internet since it does not offer, or offers only with great inconvenience, a system of compensation.

The first organization to use the Web was Généalogie et Histoire de la Caraïbe (Genealogy and History of the Caribbean), a member of the French Federation of Genealogy that studies the French Antilles. Its leader is Philippe Rossignol, who created the information commission of our Federation. This organization has a monthly bulletin and worldwide correspondents. Because of the scope of his genealogical work, it became nearly indispensable to use the network offered by the Internet. This experiment was started in May 1996 and each bulletin is put on the Web. At the present time, it has been visited by more than 1,000 people.

This first experiment has led the French Federation of Genealogy to also become involved in the experiment on a much larger scale. Thus was born KAROLUS, a server for genealogical, heraldic, archival, and other data put in place to disseminate information worldwide via the Internet.

It has been accessible on the Internet since August 5, 1996, for a period of development, until its official launching on January 1, 1997. Most notably, it includes:

- addresses and other information about federations and associations, archives, and libraries
- classification schemes and indexes of archival services
- articles and information about genealogical practice
- ascending and descending genealogies
- indexes of specialized journals in genealogy and heraldry and reviews of works
- listings of research instruments
- works of researchers: transcriptions, tables, indexes
- highly complete information about contemporary heraldry with coloured armorial drawings
- an illustrated dictionary of the terms of blazon
- an identification service for unknown arms
- a question and answer section
- a section for announcements
- European museums useful for family history
- events, shows, regional, national, and international meetings
- addresses of professional genealogists
- specialized libraries
- publishers of genealogical software, etc.

Access to KAROLUS is free. The service is managed by the Institute for documentation on family history. The address of KAROLUS, which includes information on the genealogical research of all countries worldwide, from Afghanistan to Zimbabwe, is: http://www.easynet.fr/karolus/ and the e-mail address of Alain Morineau, Founding President of KAROLUS and former Secretary General of the French Federation of Genealogy, is: morineau@easynet.fr.

Besides this service put in place by the Federation, organizations and individuals have begun to use the network. Let us note first Genealogy and History of the Caribbean, which I have already mentioned, for which the address is: http:// members.aol.com/GHCaraibe.

This server currently includes only text, which makes it a little dry, even for genealogists who are constantly seeking data, and still more data . . . Besides the monthly bulletins of the association published since January 1996, and the index of names described in 1995, one will find there:

- a list of towns, parishes and registers of Guadeloupe (including La Désirade, Marie-Galante, St. Barthelemy, St. Martin, Les Saintes), Guyana, Martinique, but also the former French islands: Santo Domingo (Haiti), St. Christophe (St. Kitts), St. Lucia, Granada, Dominica
- a bibliography
- addresses of servers and associations

Other French genealogical associations on a regional level also opened Internet addresses, such as the Genealogical Union of Normandy, whose address is: http://www.aol.com/uchgn/. In particular, one finds there a list of the activities of associations in Normandy and a table of the transcriptions of marriage records undertaken in each department in that region.

Individuals, as well as French genealogical and heraldic professionals, also use the Web.

One could mention also an address pertaining to Saint-Pierre and Miquelon likely to interest Canadians and Americans: http://www.io.org/~socrates (however, more oriented to history than genealogy).

Despite these openings and the desire of the French Federation of Genealogy to develop its activities on the Internet with KAROLUS, it is not foreseeable—in the short term—to obtain, via modem, direct access to all the data computerized by genealogical associations:

- birth, marriage, and burial records
- rubbings of inscriptions on headstones (data bank started on a national scale in 1995)
- analyses and indexes of notarized minutes, of which certain associations have made a specialty
- ships' passenger lists from the major French ports
- lists of wounded soldiers from the 17th and 18th centuries who fought in French regiments coming from all countries of Europe
- security cards (identity cards) for all male Parisians aged 15 to 60 who lived in Paris during 1793-1794 (400,000 documents)

The Internet, however, does allows us to know where to write to get more detailed information.

The goal of the French Federation of Genealogy is also to disseminate the files of migrants it has begun to set up, in order to actively help break down the frontiers among researchers the world over.

# ARCHIVES AND THE INTERNET: RECENT DEVELOPMENTS IN CANADA AND IMPLICATIONS FOR THE FUTURE

Lois  K.  Yorke

The impact of electronic technology on the archival landscape in Canada has accelerated over the last decade, from barely imaginable "future world" to an immediate reality directly confronting the Canadian Archival System. Within this panel discussion, I wish to identify the most visible aspects of the interface between archives and the Internet in Canada; and to suggest various implications and opportunities that exist, especially for genealogical research, within this new landscape.

First of all, a few general observations on the nature of archives, vis-à-vis the electronic universe—and these are by no means confined to the Canadian experience. Unlike the library book, neither the archival fonds nor the archival collection (the basic building blocks of archival holdings) is a discreet item easily reducible or amenable to electronic manipulation. Instead, archival units are complex, hierarchically structured entities, with multiple internal and external linkages that cannot be easily captured or controlled.

The nature of archival work thus conspires against the significant returns that information technology supposedly promises the researcher, particularly with respect to genealogical data. Archival work is concerned with the physical and intellectual control of holdings, primarily through indexes and descriptions conveyed in thematic or repository guides and institutional finding aids (e.g., inventories, box or file lists and, occasionally, key-word indexes). When brought together comprehensively in an information retrieval system, either hard copy or on-line, these research tools present a top-down panorama of institutional holdings. Rarely, however, do these modern systems offer item-level description, surname indexes or integrated relational databases constructed from and across various holdings—all of which, of course, are the staples of traditional genealogical research.

In response to the demands of family historians for more detailed descriptions and item-level

access, archivists point to budget cuts, staff reductions, changing professional methodologies and a lack of support from sponsoring bodies. The days of the old-style research tools designed specifically to cater to user demands are gone—forever.

How does all this relate to the apparently limitless potential offered by the Internet? At present, most archives in Canada are to some extent automated internally with respect to administrative functions and, with increasing frequency, in the provision of automated catalogues and/or integrated databases. The more progressive and economically advantaged repositories are now linked and/or networked externally as well, via the Internet, a Wide Area Network (WAN), or some similar electronic infrastructure.

The potential for delivery of information and services normally associated with the Internet, however, has not yet been well defined or utilized within the Canadian Archival System. Nor has there been a proliferation of electronic source materials specifically developed for the genealogical community. Again, the time-lag results largely from the complex nature of archival work, combined with the hard reality of economic constraints. Technological impediments are also an important consideration: scanning of original documents, for example, has produced less-than-satisfactory results, and the sheer volume of archival holdings defies retroconversion into any electronic format for which recognized preservation standards have been developed and approved.

Given these dynamics, what progress has been made in Canadian archives towards realistic participation in the Internet? The answer is, more than might be expected, but less than the genealogist's day-dream. With increasing rapidity, archives across Canada are achieving an electronic presence, most frequently through websites or home pages used to advertise their address, hours and services, programs and publications. Holdings catalogues, relational databases, subject and name indexes, graphic materials collections, on-line client services and other researcher adjuncts are also appearing, albeit more slowly and with mixed results.

One of the most recent and more innovative approaches is SchoolNet, the demonstration of which has proved to be a popular exhibit during this International Congress. Sponsored primarily by the National Library, SchoolNet encourages partnerships intended to train secondary school students in informatics, while at the same time fostering national and multicultural identity. Projects to date have included the digitization of selected archival documents, textual subject and case files, photographic and cartographic holdings. Though still in its infancy, SchoolNet offers interesting possibilities, both to Canadian youth and to researchers interested in our documentary and graphic heritage.

Of more interest to genelogists, however, are projects such as the British Columbia Archival Union list (BCAUL) (http://library.ubc.ca/www.0.archbc/select), an electronic inventory that provides descriptions of holdings at the fonds/collections level for over 150 repositories throughout B.C. In other words, an on-line catalogue for the archival holdings of an entire province—not the personal-name index of the genealogist's daydream, but nevertheless an invaluable reference and researcher service. Similarly, the British Columbia Archives and Records Service (BCARS) website (http://www.bcars.gs.gov.bc.ca/bcars.html) has, among other features, a digitized collection of heritage photographs available on-line. This project had proven immensely popular with net-surfers eager to browse, or to download items for their own files.

These British Columbia initiatives are well-regarded nationally with respect to systems and project design, funding partnerships and implementation strategies. As well, their emphasis on the integrity of information-resources management—vis-à-vis the constantly changing landscape of information technology—marks them as prototypes for standards development in data structure and data content. The BCAUL project is deservedly being examined at present as a template for a proposed electronic National Union List of archival holdings.

Other notable Canadian ventures to date include the National Archives' *ArchiVia* database of selected institutional finding aids, marketed on CD-ROM and now in its second edition. This is complemented by the multi-layered National Archives' website (http://www.archives.ca/) and by appropriate linkages across the Internet. A much smaller, but no less innovative project, is that launched recently by the Beaton Institute, University College of Cape Breton (UCCB), in Sydney N.S. Utilizing both the UCCB website (www-http://eagle.uccb.ns.ca/beaton.html) and the database design of the university's on-line library catalogue, the Institute —which is a university/ regional archives—has uploaded its digitized findings aids to the Internet.

In conclusion, what are the implications for the future of Canadian archives on the Internet? Genealogists will understandably want on-line catalogues, indexes, databases and other familiar library-type services—immediately, if not sooner. Archivists, however, approach these issues from a different methodological perspective and with considerable restraint. Economic determinants, training requirements and information management imperatives are the real and immediate priorities driving archival participation in the electronic universe.

Archives must obtain adequate and secure funding before attempting to develop and implement sophisticated automation projects. As well, human resources allocation must expand beyond the traditional "stand-alone" archivist to include information technologists and systems designers. Perhaps most importantly, Canadian archives have already learned that, as in the library world, protocols and standards in information resources management are absolutely essential. An old adage about premature automation reminds us that "garbage in = garbage out"; archivists learned this lesson a long time ago and are determined not to repeat it.

Lastly, in order to succeed in the electronic universe, Canadian archives are quickly learning cooperative strategic planning with other archives and with information management agencies. The Canadian Archival System has come a long way in the last decade; by developing electronic partnerships focusing on the Internet and its seemingly endless potential, it will go even further in the next.

# SLOVAK CIVIC FLAGS AND BANNERS[1]

Z d e n k o  G.  A l e x y

The Heraldic Commission established by the Slovak Ministry of the Interior in 1975 has consultative functions in connection with the legal capacity of town and community parliaments to assume heraldic and vexillological symbols. Fortunately, the law in force contains a provision requiring that any draft resolution presented to the local parliament should always be accompanied by approval of the respective Regional Archives director. However, the Archives, being under the control of the Ministry of the Interior, were directed to consult the Heraldic Commission before giving such approval. Consequently, the final responsibility for changes to arms or the assumption of arms was vested with the Heraldic Commission. As we shall see later, this proved to be of capital importance with respect to the procedures adopted in vexillological matters.

By 1988 the revision and approval of newly assumed civic arms of all the 135 Slovak towns were completed and work on codification of civic arms by publishing the results of these activities had started. At that stage, the author succeeded in persuading the Commission that purely heraldic symbols (i.e., arms, shields) were not the only and appropriate means or visual media to fulfil the function of symbols of the civic community and to be daily seen and used both indoors and outdoors. It was consequently accepted that arms, along with civic flags and banners, should be codified and published. The results of a search covering the territory of the then Czechoslovak Federation, made by the Prague Vexillological Club, revealed that only 25 towns in Slovakia possessed civic flags and that only a few of them were in actual use. In some instances, the same colour composition and partitions were used by more than one town.

The ad hoc vexillological group within the Commission accepted the author's proposal that, for practical reasons, the Commission should not be required to consult the 135 towns with respect to the confirmation of existing civic flags and the creation of new ones. It was further accepted in principle that the flags of the 135 towns would have to be designed and codified by the Ministry

of the Interior in order to ensure that the contents of a given flag would be assigned to one town only. Applying this principle of exclusivity of design proved difficult and special measures were taken as outlined below.

We assumed that the new flags had to be as simple in construction as possible, one reason being that a simple flag can be manufactured easily and inexpensively. It was also decided not to allow armorial shields (containing town arms) to be placed on these flags. To further draw a clear distinction between these civic flags and country (state) flags, the author's suggestion was accepted to introduce in all town flags a simple rectangular incision (indentation) called a swallow-tail. Later, when communities without township status applied to the Heraldic Commission for arms and flags, the decision was taken that a double swallow-tail (two incisions in the fly) should constitute the distinctive mark of community flags as opposed to town flags.

As we shall see, the interconnection between arms and flags (as far as colours are concerned) was respected and the decision was taken to follow heraldic practices and to limit flag colours to the basic seven heraldic tinctures only.

The task of creating new flags for 110 towns involved analysing the composition of existing town flags and the following types were chosen to serve as guidelines for new flags to be created and codified.

A. When flags represented simply the contents of arms, e.g., BANSKÁ BYSTRICA [FIGURE 1], the inherited patterns were accepted and reconfirmed.

B. Monocoloured ones such as that used since 1550 by NITRA [FIGURE 2] were reconfirmed.

C. Monochrome ones of ancient origin and with a bordure in another colour, such as BANSKÁ ŠTIAVNICA (1739) [FIGURE 3] were also reconfirmed. That composition was also applied to GELNICA [FIGURE 4] when a flag for that ancient town was created by the Commission.

D. As mentioned above, the Commission encountered several situations where the same flag was used by more than one of the 25 towns. Here the principle of seniority (ancientness) of the arms or flag was applied with the following results :

- the yellow-green flag of LEVICE [FIGURE 5] was reconfirmed, whereas ŽILINA, using hitherto the same colour composition, was granted another flag [FIGURE 6], the contents of which will be discussed later;

- the yellow-blue flag borne by KOŠICE for several hundred years [FIGURE 7] was reconfirmed, whereas ŽIAR NAD HRONOM [FIGURE 8] was granted a new four-striped flag bearing in the upper half the arms' tinctures and, in the lower half, its ancient flag colours.

E. Our research led to an exciting surprise when, in LEVOČA, a flag composition evidently having mediaeval roots was discovered. The main armorial charge being the double cross of Slovakia [FIGURE 9], the burghers decided to adopt the three cuts symbolizing this double cross. An artefact with this symbol was found by the author in the LEVOČA Town Museum. The Commission has used it as a model for the flag of LEVOČA itself and for all six Slovak towns, where a double cross appears in their respective civic arms, e.g., ZVOLEN [FIGURE 10] and ŽILINA, shown earlier.

F. As to the partition of the flag field by stripes, there are two extreme positions in Slovakia:

- For two-striped flags, the colours are usually the tincture of the arms' charge and that of the shield (field). This is the case of BRATISLAVA [FIGURE 11]. In SABINOV [FIGURE 12], the two flag colours are those appearing in the arms' field. The ancient flags of PEZINOK [FIGURE 13] always consisted of two colours and the actual arms' tinctures were derived from these colours—a rather unusual procedure.

- The ancient flag of KREMNICA [FIGURE 14] displays seven stripes, and can therefore be considered the opposite extreme as to number of stripes (appearing in all four mediaeval arms' colours). In line with this complicated composition, the Commission decided to create a nine stripe flag when codifying the flag for SPIŠSKÁ STARÁ VES [FIGURE 15].

G. Between these extreme compositions, we find flags of different age composed of:

- three stripes, viz. BREZNO [FIGURE 16], RUŽOMBREROK [FIGURE 17] granted in 1938;

- four stripes, e.g., HNÚŠŤA [FIGURE 18];

- five stripes for KRÁĽOVSKÝ CHLMEC [FIGURE 19] and SPIŠKÉ PODHRADIE [FIGURE 20], both created by the Heraldic Commission.

H. Quartered flags were used by one town only in Slovakia, TRENČÍN [FIGURE 21], and their origin evidently derives from the Lamb's cross banner of the town arms. Similarly, as demonstrated above for LEVOČA, quartering of the banner field of TRENČÍN represents a classical and highly heraldic approach. For nearby TRENČIANSKE TEPLICE, the Commission approved a flag with similar content [FIGURE 22]. In the case of VRÚTKY [FIGURE 23], the quartered flag corresponds to the quartered town arms.

I. In my study presented at the 16th International Congress of Genealogical and Heraldic Sciences (Helsinki, 1984), I draw attention to the fact that the most frequent charge in Slovakia's civic arms is hammers in saltire as symbols of mining, an industry of first importance in Slovakia during the Middle Ages, more than 50 towns and communities having this charge in their arms. The Heraldic Commission had to take these facts into consideration and finally decided to invent and introduce the saltire, a heraldic charge hitherto unused in flags. Instruments typical of mining and related industries appear in numerous arms, and the corresponding saltire flag was derived from them: LIPTOVSKÝ HRÁDOK [FIGURE 24], MEDZEV [FIGURE 25], NOVÁ BAŇA [FIGURE 26] and ROŽŇAVA [FIGURE 27].

The Commission found the saltire flag composition suitable for devices other than mining and related instruments appearing in civic arms. Halberds crossed in saltire in the arms of STRÁŽSKE [FIGURE 28], and keys appearing in the arms of ZLATÉ MORAVCE [FIGURE 29] induced the Commission to choose the saltire flag in these instances also. In the latter case, the saltire itself consists of two colours corresponding to the two metals of charges in the town arms of ZLATÉ MORAVCE.

J.  An unusual composition of a town flag is that of DUNAJSKÁ STREDA [FIGURE 30]. A heraldic artist (Püspöki-Nagy) designed both the new arms and flag for this town and although far from local traditions, the Commission confirmed this creation.

As mentioned earlier, the first task of the Commission was to deal with the heraldic and vexillological symbols of all the 135 towns in Slovakia. When the above-mentioned colour-illustrated book was published under the authority of the Ministry of the Interior, communities not having township status started contacting the Heraldic Commission. They expressed the wish to have their arms duly examined and the Commission did this along with suggestions and proposals for community flags, so that there are at present more than 100 community flags codified by the Commission. The double swallow-tail is common to all of them and plays the role of a significant distinction between town and community flags. Almost all of these new flags are composed of different numbers of stripes [FIGURES 33 to 38] and it proved necessary to introduce the use of stripes of more than one width value in the same flag to ensure that the same flag composition was not used by more than one town or community. The saltire type of flag appears here as well [FIGURE 39], a new creation of arms and flag for CHMEĽNICA.[2]

There is a fortnightly periodical *Verejná správa* (Public Administration) published by the Ministry of the Interior separately in two languages (Slovak and Hungarian) and each issue contains the description and illustration of both heraldic and vexillological symbols of a community, as approved by the Heraldic Commission. FIGURES 33 to 39 are flag depictions published on the back covers of *Verejná správa* issues over a period of time.

Due to the number of new community arms and flags that are approved and the periodicity of *Verejná správa*, it will take some time before all of them are published. Nevertheless, this publication method certainly proved to be the proper marketing device for the Commission's purpose.

This outline of the situation in Slovakia shows the importance of meaningful cooperation between the protagonists of heraldry, on the one hand, and of vexillology, on the other, and the author encourages them to work together at enhancing the quality of the symbols of civic entities, whether presented in stone, metal or textile.

**NOTES**

1.  The author has previously published this paper in Polish and Slovak. It is published here for the first time in English.

2.  The illustrations of arms and flags appearing with this paper were taken from a book published by the Slovak Ministry of the Interior in 1991: *Erby a vlajky miest v Slovenskej republike*/Arms and Flags of Towns in the Slovak Republic. The accompanying text (in Slovak) is published in full in the German translation of that book. In it, all possible variants of use of the basic form that were envisaged for the town of MYJAVA appear on p. 308-311 [FIGURE 31]. Several types of town banners designed by the author are being published [FIGURE 32]. The proposed banner of the mayor of MYJAVA is no. 6.

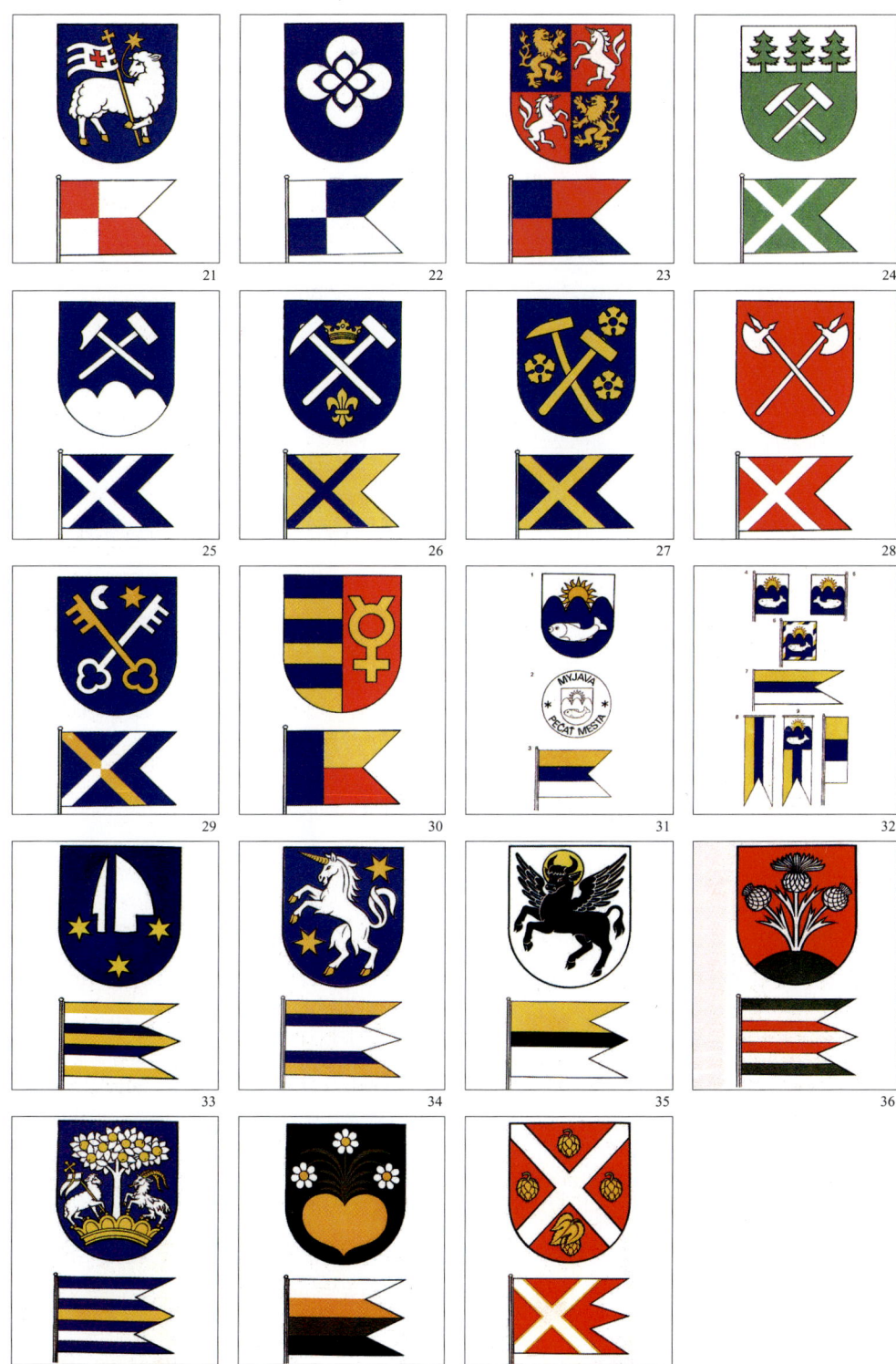

21  22  23  24

25  26  27  28

29  30  31  32

33  34  35  36

37  38  39

# THE DEVELOPMENT OF NAVAL AND MILITARY SYMBOLISM IN BRITISH HERALDRY

Peter L. Allpress

The object of this paper is to try to discern the development of naval and military symbols in British heraldry and to make a brief survey of similar symbolism in Continental heraldry. Heraldry itself developed from the need to identify combatants in the primitive warfare dating from the Crusades. The charges in coats of arms remained fairly simple throughout the Middle Ages and any references to specific military engagements were not very frequent.

The most significant manner in which deeds of naval and military valour were recognised were by augmentations of honour granted by the sovereign. However, such augmentations did not by any means cover all the developments in armorial bearings adopted by individuals to commemorate their own participation in naval and military events and careers. Up to the 18th century, probably most naval and military achievements were commemorated by augmentations that were of fairly normal heraldic significance; it was later in the 18th century and particularly dating from the Napoleonic wars that naval and military symbols in heraldry became more explicit. However, it is worth examining a few of the earlier augmentations.

One of the earliest and probably legendary augmentations, was made to Sir Richard Fowler, a Crusader, by Richard Cœur de Lion, for his vigilance in saving the Christian camp from a surprise attack and is a crest consisting of *an owl Argent ducally crowned Or* [FIGURE 1]. The Pelham buckles are still seen in the arms of descendants of John de Pelham, granted after the Battle of Poitiers in 1356, the buckles representing those of the surrendered sword of King John of France, Pelham being charged with his custody after the battle. Several augmentations were granted by Henry V after the Battle of Agincourt. Sir John Trelawny received the addition of three oak leaves to his family arms [FIGURE 2] and Sir Richard Waller was granted an unusual one consisting of the following addition to the crest *on a mount Vert a walnut tree proper* on the sinister side *an escutcheon charged with the arms of France with a label of three points Argent.* This was the shield of the Duc d'Orléans taken prisoner by Sir Richard Waller at the battle.

Henry VII is said to have granted Sir John Cheney a bull's head as a crest after the Battle of Bosworth Field where Henry defeated Richard III. The valiant knight, after combat with Richard himself, is said to have replaced his shattered helmet with the skull and horns of an ox, which he severed from a nearby animal. Richard III was a much maligned sovereign whose most useful act in his short reign was the establishment on a permanent basis of the College of Arms in London.

After the Battle of the Spurs took place in France in August 1513 at Guingate, Sir John Clerke, who with Sir William Stamford, was credited with the capture of Louis d'Orléans, Duc de Longueville, was granted a peculiar augmentation still seen in the arms of members of the Clerke family, it was *on a sinister canton Azure, a demi-ram salient Argent, and in chief two fleurs-de-lis Or, the whole debruised by a baton* [FIGURE 3].

A well-known augmentation was that granted by Henry VIII after the Battle of Flodden Field against the Scots in September 1513 to Thomas Howard, Earl of Surrey (later Duke of Norfolk). The correct blazon *on the bend between six cross crosslets fitchee* of the Howard arms is *an escutcheon Or, charged with a demi-lion rampant, pierced through the mouth by an arrow, within a tressure flory counter flory of the first* (this is the tressure of the Scottish Royal Arms).

The lion of Scotland suffered much under the Tudors as later in 1543, after the defeat of the Scots at the Battle of Solway Moss in which Sir Thomas Wharton as governor of the Town and Castle of Carlisle took part. Sir Thomas was granted by Edward VI an augmentation to his arms *Sable a maunch Argent* consisting of *on a bordure engrailed Or, eight pairs of lion's gambs erased saltirewise Gules.* So, after Flodden the Scottish lion was cut in half and its throat pierced by an arrow for the Howards, now it lost its legs to the Whartons.

Coming now to the period of the Civil War, a great deal of heraldry came about in connection with some of the battles fought by the Royalists and the escape of Charles II after the Battle of Worcester.

A magnificent augmentation directly connected with the Battle of Edgehill in 1642 was granted by Charles I to Dr. Edward Lake for his valour in the fight, in which he received 16 wounds and, when shot in the left arm, held the horse's reins in his mouth to continue the fight. The augmentation and a baronetcy were granted on December 30, 1643, the augmentation to occupy the first and fourth quarters being *Gules, a dexter arm embowed in armour, issuing from the sinister base of the shield holding in the hand a sword erect all proper, thereto affixed a banner Argent, bearing on a cross between 16 escutcheons* (for the wounds) *of the first, a lion passant guardant Or.* The crest of augmentation is also very interesting: *a cavalier in complete armour on a horse courant Argent, bridle and trappings all proper, in his dexter hand a sword embrued, holding the bridle in his mouth, the sinister arm hanging down useless, round his body a scarf in bend Gules.* The arms of his descendant Sir Atwill Lake show well the details of the augmentations. These arms, which relate personally to an event, may perhaps be a foreshadowing of some of the elaborate augmentations that occurred much later in the Napoleonic wars.

Sir Edward Walker (1611-1677) holds a very important position in heraldry during the middle part of the 17th century as he was appointed Garter King of Arms and knighted by Charles I in 1645 and, after the King's execution, went into exile with Charles II and continued to grant arms on the King's authority during the exile and after the Restoration until his death in 1677. His grants of arms therefore included many to those people who assisted Charles II in his escape from England after the Battle of Worcester on September 3, 1651. Most of the grants consisted of the addition of crowns or lions to the arms of those concerned. Two grants are of special interest, that to Colonel Careless, who accompanied Charles into the famous oak at Boscobel, consisting of *an oak tree with three Imperial crowns on a fess* [FIGURE 4], and similar arms that were granted to the Penderel family, the five brothers who lived

on the estate that belonged to the Catholic Gifford family, having been particularly helpful in saving the King [FIGURE 5]. The other arms of note are those granted to the son of Colonel Lane, whose daughter, Jane, made the famous journey with Charles riding pillion behind her on a strawberry roan. The augmentation consisted of *a canton of the Royal Arms of England* and a crest being *out of a wreath Or and Azure, a demi-horse Strawberry colour, bridled Sable and garnished Or, supporting an Imperial crown Gold.*

A period now begins when a great deal of naval activity took place and signs of charges of a more specifically nautical character started to appear. It is now appropriate to list the different ways in which such nautical and military symbols were introduced into armorial bearings. They were often, but not always, augmentations of honour. Those ennobled or appointed Knights of the Bath up to 1815 or after that to the Grand Cross of an order of chivalry often took supporters of a naval or military character. Landscape heraldry was introduced showing sea battles or fortifications. The badges of various orders and decorations and medals were included within the armorial shield or suspended below it. Crests of naval officers were often placed on a naval coronet or crown, which is a curious figure composed of the sail and stern of a ship repeated and alternating on the rim of a circlet. It is sometimes entirely gold, but usually sails are argent. The name of a ship or battle could be inscribed on the circlet. One of the earliest users of a naval crown was in the crest granted to Admiral Sir Robert Holmes in 1668 for his services in the war against the Dutch. Out of the naval crown was an arm in armour holding a trident. This crest together with the augmentation in the arms are now held by Lord Heytesbury, a descendent in the female line. Mottoes with a naval or nautical significance were also sometimes adopted by naval commanders.

An example of a completely new coat of arms being granted to a naval officer is that of Admiral Sir Cloudesley Shovell (1650-1707) who achieved victories in the Mediterranean over the Turks and the French. He was granted arms including two crescents and a fleur-de-lis. He is doubly famous: first, as the *Dictionary of National Biography* points out, his Christian name was known to be spelt in at least 25 different ways; and second, on his return from the Mediterranean, he came to an untimely end when his ship, the *Association*, and three others of the fleet ran onto rocks off the Scilly Isles. Washed ashore half dead, he was despatched by an islander who coveted his emerald ring. The woman confessed to the crime 30 years later on her death bed and the ring was handed over to an old friend, the Earl of Berkeley. A few years ago his striking clock-watch was put up for sale at Christie's in London. This had also been stolen from him after the wreck; and it was blamed for the squadron's wreck as his navigational calculations were based upon it with lamentable results. The disaster persuaded the government of the day to offer the considerable reward of £20,000 for a timekeeper that could accurately measure the east-west position, and a chronometer was developed in due course that led to Greenwich Mean Time and much greater efficiency in naval operations.

An early naval exploit later commemorated in armorial bearings was the Battle of La Hogue, fought in May 1692 between English and Dutch fleets against the French. A special medal was for "Officers, Marines and Seamen who shall be found to have done any signal or extraordinary service." One of these in gold, showing the conjoined busts of William and Mary, and a massive chain, was presented to Captain Tupper of Guernsey, who gave warning that the French fleet under Admiral Tourville was in the Channel. In 1826, Tupper's grandson, John Elisha Tupper, applied to the College of Arms for confirmation, and was granted arms to include the medal on a canton and in the crest [FIGURE 6]. The name Tupper is of special interest to Canadians as Sir Charles Tupper (1821-1915) was a prominent statesman and was prime minister of Canada for a short time. However, he was from a different branch of the family and did not have the Tupper medal in his arms.

Perhaps the earliest example of supporters with a nautical flavour was Sir Edward Montagu (1625-1672), youngest brother of the first Earl of Manchester, who after having supported Cromwell, was instrumental in bringing back Charles II from the Continent. He was appointed admiral of the Narrow Seas and lieutenant admiral to the Duke of York, the Lord High Admiral. Montagu was created Earl of Sandwich in 1660 and took as one of his supporters: *a triton crowned with an eastern crown holding a trident in his right hand* [FIGURE 7]. He died in a sea battle with the Dutch off Southwold Bay in 1672.

Another early example of naval attributes is that of Admiral Sir George Byng created Baron Byng and Viscount Torrington in 1721. He was an eminent naval commander noted for the defeat of a Spanish fleet off Cape Passaro in 1718. He had one of his supporters as a sea-horse and both supporters standing on ships' guns [FIGURE 8]. His fourth son, Admiral John Byng, was court-marshalled and shot in 1757 for his failure to relieve Minorca.

Most of the more famous admirals of the mid-18th century commemorated their naval service by supporters granted to them on their elevation to the peerage. Lord Hawke had, dexter, a figure of Neptune and sinister, a sea-horse, while his arms included three boatswains' whistles. The Boscawens had two sea-lions [FIGURE 9]. Rodney's eagle supporters hold staves enfiled with naval coronets and holding the banner of St. George. The Hoods, Viscount Hood and Viscount Bridport both have nautical supporters, the former a merman and a mermaid, the latter Neptune and a sea-lion. Another admiral, William Hotham (1736-1813), was created baron in 1797 and had two sailors for his supporters.

Up to this time, there were few prominent naval leaders and they were usually rewarded by titles or appointments to the Order of the Bath, their resultant arms often showing the naval references already mentioned. The extension of warfare after 1793, however, involved many more leaders who had to be rewarded and more battles to be commemorated. This was accomplished by the award of gold medals and armorial innovations. The wars' period coincided with the appointment of Sir Isaac Heard as Garter King of Arms (1784-1822), of whom it is said that "as a herald he was largely responsible for the landscape and similar coats of arms and augmentations conspicuous in the grants to Lord Nelson and the heroes of the Napoleonic Wars." Heard was himself in the navy, 1745-1751, and his arms granted in 1762 and amended in 1774 included *a Neptune with an Eastern crown Or, his trident Sable headed Or, issuing from a stormy ocean, the left hand grasping the head of a ship's mast appearing above the waves as part of the wreck all proper* with such arms, he was perhaps sympathetic to the embellishment of the arms of naval and military commanders.

The first "landscape" arms granted seem to have been to Sir Roger Curtis (1746-1816), a naval officer at the siege of Gibraltar 1779-1783, created knight bachelor in November 1782 for his services at the siege there, later created baronet for his part as Captain of the Fleet under Lord Howe at the "Glorious First of June" 1794. The Curtis arms include *in chief the Rock of Gibraltar surrounded by fortifications and the sea* and *in base three fleurs-de-lis and on a canton a sword erect proper, hilted and pommelled Or entwisted with a palm branch Vert*. The arms were extant until the recent death of the fourth baronet.

Symbols of military significance have not up to this time been as evident as those naval. The Siege of Gibraltar was also commemorated by the commander-in-chief General Sir George Augustus Eliott, who was created Lord Heathfield with arms including *on a chief the arms of Gibraltar* which were *Azure between two pillars a castle Argent from the gate a golden key pendent, the words* PLUS ULTRA *inscribed under*. However, this is always shown as a fairly normal heraldic charge rather than as a landscape like in the Curtis arms.

Naval battles in the last decade of the 18th century and up to Trafalgar in 1805, were rather more important than land battles, which did not have great significance, apart from some action in Egypt, until the Peninsular War, beginning in 1808.

The first important sea battle was that of the "Glorious First of June" 1794, after which large gold medals were issued to admirals and small gold medals to captain of ships involved in major engagements. These gold medals appear in the arms of some participants. Knighthoods of the Bath were sparingly awarded until 1815 when the order was reconstituted into three classes and greatly increased in numbers, over 50 knights Grand Cross and nearly 200 knights commanders being appointed on the January 2, 1815. All existing knights of the Bath were appointed knights Grand Cross at that time.

Gold medals and gold crosses were also issued to military commanders up to 1815. After the end of hostilities, it was realised that no recognition was given to those below post rank in the navy and field rank in the army, who bore the burden of the fighting. Eventually Queen Victoria, years later in 1847, approved the award of Naval General Service Medals to cover actions from 1793 to 1840, and Military General Service Medals for actions up to Waterloo in 1815. These medals, which had numerous bars or clasps to indicate the actions in which the participants took part, were issued to those surviving in 1848 to claim them. Mention is made of these medals as they are sometimes found within the shield of arms or pendent therefrom.

The next major action was the Battle of Cape St. Vincent in 1797, after which the commander-in-chief, Admiral Sir John Jervis, was created baron and later Earl St. Vincent. His arms show his motto as THUS, which has a special nautical significance described by Burke as follows: "This motto is a graceful and seamanlike allusion implying perfect rectitude. THUS is the word of direction given to the steersman by the quartermaster when the ship is going in a perfectly correct course." His supporters also have special significance, the dexter being an eagle holding a thunderbolt representing the *Foudroyant* or Thunderer, while in command of which he took the French man-of-war *Pégase*, and the sinister being a Pegasus representing his prize. Vice-admiral the Hon. William Waldegrave was created Baron Radstock after this action and kept ST. VINCENT as his motto. The Waldegrave arms are some of the simplest known being just *Per pale Argent and Gules*.

For this action Commodore Horatio Nelson was created knight of the Bath, which involved the assumption of arms with a crest representing the stern of the San Josef, one of the ships he captured. His arms underwent further changes when he was granted an augmentation after the battle of the Nile in 1799 of *a chief wavy Argent, thereon waves of the sea from which a palm tree issuant between a disabled ship on the dexter and a battery in ruins on the sinister* and an additional crest *on a naval crown Or, the chelengk or diamond plume of triumph presented to Horatio Viscount Nelson by the Grand Signior, sultan Selim III*. The arms were further augmented after Trafalgar for his brother who was created Earl Nelson, by the addition of the word TRAFALGAR *on a fess wavy Azure*. The second augmentation was later dropped from the arms by the second Earl Nelson in order to comply with the terms of the annuity. The supporters are dexter *a sailor habited and armed with a cutlass with a pair of pistols in his belt proper, his right hand supporting a pike also proper, thereon hoisted a commodore's flag Gules, and his left holding a palm branch: sinister, a lion reguardant, in his mouth*

318

*two broken staffs and flowing from one the Spanish and from the other the French ensigns and in the dexter paw a palm branch all proper.*

But to go back in time a few years, after the Battle of Camperdown in 1797, Admiral Adam Duncan added his large Naval Gold Medal and the word CAMPERDOWN to his arms. This is perhaps the first time that a gold medal of the Napoleonic war period was incorporated into armorial bearings. A similar augmentation of a small gold medal with the word NILE was granted to the brother of Captain Henry D'Esterre Darby of the Bellerophon some years after that battle.

Another captain to commemorate the Battle of the Nile was Sir Benjamin Hallowell Carew (1760-1834). He added Carew to his name late in life after inheriting some Carew property. His arms show Carew quartering Hallowell on the dexter shield, the Hallowell arms having in chief the small naval gold medal won at the Nile and the badge of the Order of St. Ferdinand and of Merit awarded him by the king of the Two Sicilies. This Order was granted to a number of British naval and military officers and occurs in several coats of arms. According to Nicholas Carlisle in his book on the several foreign orders of knighthood, about 40 members of the British services were awarded the various grades of the Order. Hallowell is remembered for sending Nelson a coffin entirely of wood and iron from the wreck of *L'Orient's* mainmast with the note, May 23, 1799: "My Lord, herewith I send you a coffin made of part of *L'Orient's* mainmast, that when you are tired of this life you may be buried in one of your own trophies, but may that period be far distant is the sincere wish of your obedient and much obliged servant, Ben Hallowell." *L'Orient*, the flagship of the French fleet, blew up in a great explosion. Hallowell in the *Swiftsure* was later engaged along Italy's coast and he was made a commander of the Royal Sicilian Order of St. Ferdinand and of Merit for his services in the reconquest of Naples in 1799, he was also later made knight commander of the Bath and Grand Cross of the Bath in 1831, the badge of the Order of the Bath together with that of the Sicilian Order being shown pendent from the shield of arms.

The Battle of Trafalgar in 1805 naturally gave rise to much commemoration in the arms of various participants: Nelson, his second in command Collingwood and third in command William Carnegie, 7th Earl of Northesk, as well as some eight of the 27 captains of ships all added some reference to Trafalgar in their arms. Rear-admiral the Earl of Northesk's augmentation consisted of *a naval crown pendent from a riband Gules beneath the word* TRAFALGAR and a second crest *on the waves of the sea, the stern of a French man-of-war in flames proper.* The supporters, leopards reguardant, were augmented by a representation of the Trafalgar medal suspended by a gold chain around the neck of the leopards who were now to support banners charged with the cross of St. George and thereon in letters of gold the words BRITANNIA VICTRIX. It is interesting to note that many of Northesk's Trafalgar documents were sold at auction in London in December 1994 for high prices, his large naval gold medal reaching £95,000. Captains Bullen (*Britannia*), Eliab Harvey (*Téméraire*), Tyler (*Tonnant*) and Duff (*Mars*) all added the Trafalgar medal to their arms. The case of Captain John Pilfold of the *Ajax* is particularly interesting as he was granted arms for the first time on March 29, 1808 and then an augmentation to these very arms on April 14 following. The augmentation consisted of adding the Trafalgar medal suspended from a naval crown to the neck of the sea-horse crest, and again the medal suspended from a naval crown on a canton in the shield of arms [FIGURE 10].

A sea battle off Santo Domingo in 1808 led to some interesting heraldry. Admiral Sir Alexander Cochrane received an augmentation of a crest, including a flag of Rear-Admiral of the White on which are inscribed the words SANTO DOMINGO. He also had an augmentation to his arms of a sphinx on a chief wavy in honour of his services in Egypt in 1801. This Admiral Cochrane was uncle to an even more famous Admiral Lord Cochrane, who served under the governments of Chile and Peru, and by his naval assistance largely contributed to the independence of these countries from Spain. He later commanded the Greek navy in Greece's struggle for independence. Another admiral at Santo Domingo was Thomas Louis. He was a great friend of Nelson and was with him at the Nile, where he received the small gold medal. Louis was granted a baronetcy for distinguished service in the ship *Canopus* and his arms are remarkable for their supporters, which deserve full description: *Dexter: a British sailor habited proper his exterior hand supporting a staff, thereon hoisted a flag Argent charged with a cross Gules surmounted by a pair of wings Or, and inscribed with the words* SANTO DOMINGO *in base Sable: sinister: an allegorical figure representing the Nile, the head and upper part of the face concealed by a veil Argent the mantle Vert, inscribed with hieroglyphics, wreathed about the waist with bullrushes proper and in the exterior hand the ancient rudder Or.* The curious motto IN CANOPO UT AD CANOPUM is translated by Elvin as "on board the *Canopus* (which he commanded) as at *Canopus* (i.e., Aboukir, where was the Canopic mouth of the Nile)," whereas in Debrett's Peerage it is thought the reference is to the star Canopus and it is translated as "In the ship *Canopus* in order to go to heaven," which is most apt as Louis died in his ship *Canopus* off Egypt's coast in 1807. The captain of the *Canopus* at Santo Domingo was Francis William Austen, brother of the novelist Jane Austen.

Two actions in the East Indies resulted in place names appearing on pennons in crests. Captain Christopher Cole in 1810 in a very daring attack captured Neira, the chief of the Banda Islands from the Dutch. The citadel Belgica was carried by escalade under cover of a tempest and that accounts for the scaling ladder in the arms and a representation of the fortress Belgica on a canton [FIGURE 11]. The other action was that by Captain (later Admiral Lord) Edmund Lyons when he captured Fort Marack in Java in 1811. A banner in the crest bears the name Marack and pendent from the shield are three decorations from left to right: the French Order of St. Louis, the Hanoverian Guelphic Order and the Greek Order of the Redeemer (Lyons was Ambassador to Greece for several years).

Admiral Booty Harvey's arms show ROSARIO on a banner in the crest and the motto DIEPPE, as in an engagement off Dieppe in the *Rasario* in 1812 he captured three enemy ships.

An unusual augmentation was that granted to Captain (later Admiral) William Henry Smyth, who was mainly noted for carrying out hydrographical surveys in the Mediterranean in 1814-1815 and later. Apart from receiving the Order of St. Ferdinand and of Merit from the King of the Two Sicilies, which appears within his arms and suspended from the shield, he received the augmentation of *a chief Argent thereon a mount Vert inscribed with the Greek letters* KYPA *Gold, and issuant therefrom a representation of the silphium plant proper.* A botanical dictionary states that

the silphium is called the compass plant "because it presents the edges of its radical leaves nearly due north and south, whilst their faces are turned east and west." Presumably it was because of this peculiarity of the silphium that Smyth adopted it in his arms, it being appropriate to an hydrographer and astronomer. Elvin states that KYPA represents an abbreviation of *Kypana,* the Doric form of Cyrene and is found on a celebrated coin of that colony.

Another case of the name of a ship appearing on the circlet of a naval crown is that of Captain Toup Nicolas. Actually it is a case of father and son sharing arms as his father Captain John Harris Nicolas (1758-1844) was granted arms in 1816 including *on a chief wavy* (in allusion to the services of Captain Nicolas and his eldest son Captain Toup Nicolas C.B.) *Ermine a trident Or, surmounting in saltire a flagstaff proper, thereon hoisted a pennant Gules both passing through a chaplet of laurel Vert.* The son received an augmentation including the word PILOT on the rim of the naval crown "in commemoration of his distinguished services in H.M. sloop *Pilot* on the east and west coasts of Calabria during the years 1810-1812 and also in allusion to the gallant action fought near Toulon between the said sloop and the French national ship *La Légère* on June 17, 1815" (The day before Waterloo) [FIGURE 12].

So far, in the realm of naval symbols, supporters, naval crowns or coronets and the name of a ship or battle on the rim thereof, medals in the crest and within or pendent from the shield and some mottoes have been dealt with. It remains to consider the landscape heraldry, so derided by pure heraldists. One must, however, concede that such heraldry does perpetuate noteworthy historical events and since heraldry in modern times had deviated to a great extent from its original practical purpose, one should not criticise it too harshly.

The next landscape augmentation, after Nelson's for Trafalgar, was a particularly involved one to the highly unusual figure of Admiral Sir Sidney Smith. He had a remarkably colourful life serving for a time in 1789 under King Gustaf III of Sweden during the war against Russia, for which he was appointed a knight Grand Cross of the Order of the Sword of Sweden. In 1796 he was captured by the French and spent two years imprisoned in the Temple in Paris. He escaped, however, and acted prominently in the siege of Acre in 1799, the relief of which caused Napoleon to retire to Egypt. For his services in the siege of Acre, Sidney Smith received the following augmentation in 1803: *On a chief the interior of an ancient fortification in perspective proper; in the centre a breach, and on the dexter side of the said breach the Union flag of Great Britain, and on the sinister side the standard of the Ottoman Empire, being, Gules within an increscent an estoile of eight points Argent displayed. Crests: First: The Imperial Ottoman Chelengk, or plume of Triumph, proper, upon a turban Argent; the cap Gules. Second crest: A leopard's head proper, gorged with a plain collar, therefrom a line reflexed, issuant out of an eastern crown Or. Supporters: Dexter, a lamb murally crowned Argent, in his mouth an olive branch proper, supporting the banner of Jerusalem, viz. Argent a cross potence between four plain crosses Gules. Sinister, a tiger guardant proper, navally crowned Or, in his mouth a palm branch proper, supporting the Union flag of Great Britain, with the inscription* JERUSALEM 1799 *in fess, upon the cross of St. George.* In the illustration the badge of the Swedish Order is shown pendant from the shield.

Two other commanders received augmentations of naval battle scenes—Sir Charles Brisbane for an action off Curaçao against the Dutch in the West Indies and Captain George Nicholas Hardinge for cutting out a Dutch ship *Atlante* and a French ship *Piedmontaise* off Ceylon. The two ships' names are inscribed on flags in the crest and a chief in the arms shows two damaged ships.

A final naval story concerns a very famous naval officer Admiral Edward Pellew, Viscount Exmouth, and the naval bombardment of the corsair stronghold of Algiers in 1816. A rather scratch British fleet together with some Dutch warships bombarded the town causing great damage as well as receiving considerable damage and casualties from the Algerine batteries. The Dey of Algiers finally surrendered and 1,642 Christian slaves of various nationalities were freed, of whom 1,110 were Sicilian and Neapolitan and 18 English.

Pellew was created Viscount Exmouth and received arms including on a chief a view of Algiers with his ship *H.M.S. Queen Charlotte* [FIGURE 13]. His crest consisted of the wreck of the *Dutton*, a troopship that had foundered off Plymouth in 1796, when Pellew happened to be on shore in the vicinity. He single-handedly organised the rescue of all the crew and troops on board, who had panicked in the absence of most of their officers on shore at the time. The second-in-command at Algiers, Admiral Sir Alexander Milne, received a similar augmentation. The flag in his crest bears the word IMPREGNABLE the name of his ship during the battle.

Apart from the Battle of Navarino in 1827, in which Admiral Sir Edward Codrington commanded a mixed British, Russian and French fleet that destroyed the Turkish fleet, no serious naval battles took place until the Great War of 1914-1918. Codrington showed his gold medal for Trafalgar, where he commanded the *Orion*, in his arms, and in his crest showed the flags of the three nations who took part, as well as inscribing NAVARINO on the circlet of the naval crown.

From then on, naval officers who reached high rank, if appointed Grand Cross of the Bath would adopt supporters and perhaps suspend the badge of the order from their shield of arms. A last example is Admiral of the Fleet Earl Beatty of Great War fame, who adopted as supporters a sailor of the Royal Navy and a Royal Marine and suspended from his arms the badges of the Orders of Merit, Bath, Royal Victorian and Distinguished Service Order [FIGURE 14].

Looking at the navy from a social point of view, the early naval commanders were often drawn from the nobility, and the Duke of York, Charles II's brother and later James II, as Lord High Admiral, took to the sea himself in fights against the Dutch. Later officers came from the minor nobility or gentry and quite a lot of naval and military officers seem to have been sons of clergymen and many came from Irish families. They started life at sea at a very early age, about 11 or 12, usually under the patronage of a captain known to the family and the naval and military tradition was very strong in certain families, generation after generation going into the services.

A puzzling question is how some commanders who were ennobled from fairly modest beginnings, came to be owners of considerable estates. The answer must be prize money. From the time of Drake or even earlier, there seems to have been a sort of free-for-all on the oceans and anyone who could arm a ship could prey on ships less well-armed. In time of war, the capture of enemy ships to obtain prize money often took priority over the more strategic requirements of the war. Nelson was critical of this attitude, although his own prize agent, Alexander Davison, appointed after the Battle of the Nile to deal with the prizes then taken, became very rich, but this was rather as a contractor to the army to supply stores and uniforms. He was, however, generous enough to present medals to all those who took part in the Battle of the Nile and those in Nelson's flagship the *Victory* at Trafalgar. An example was Captain Philemon Pownall R.N. under whom Pellew started his career. Pownall in 1762 captured off Cadiz a Spanish treasure ship with a cargo of silver and his share of the prize money amounted to £64,872. Pellew's eldest son, the second Viscount Exmouth, was named Pownall after him.

Turning now to the military side, preceding the war in the Peninsula, which gave rise to much new heraldry, there had been various campaigns in India. One of the most famous was the capture of Seringapatam in 1799 to end the fourth Mysore War. George Harris, son of a Kent clergyman, was the general who led the campaign and was rewarded in due course with a barony and an augmentation to his arms that is worth quoting in full: A chief depicts *the fortress and gates of Seringapatam, the drawbridge let down, and the Union flag of Great Britain and Ireland hoisted over the standard of Tipu Sahib, all proper.* The crest is *on a mural crown Or, the royal tiger of Tipu Sahib passant guardant Vert, striped Or, spotted of the first, pierced in the breast with an arrow of the last, vulned Gules, charged on the forehead with a Persian character for Hyder, and crowned with an Eastern coronet both of the first.*

In the same way as naval officers, military commanders showed battlements and captured castles as well as the names of battles and places taken. The numbers of the regiments engaged were sometimes shown on flags or banners. A fine selection of supporters also begins to occur with soldiers of different regiments and some truly beautiful examples of mounted cavalry.

After Nelson's victory at Aboukir Bay in Egypt, General Abercromby was appointed to deal with Napoleon's army and succeeded in doing so at Alexandria in 1801, but was himself badly wounded and died shortly after. His arms were augmented by, *on a chief Argent, a fess embattled Gules, a dexter arm issuant in chief embowed in armour, proper, garnished Or, encircled by a wreath of laurel, the hand supporting the French standard in bend sinister also proper.*

The war then turned to the Peninsula where various battles were commemorated in arms, either by a view of the battlements, such as those of Lieutenant-General Sir John Hamilton with Alba de Tormes, or the name of the place of the battle or regiment involved. General John Byng, later field-marshal and first Earl of Strafford had the colour of the 31st Regiment added to his arms, as he seized the colour from the officer holding it when attacking the French position at Mougerre near Bayonne in 1813.

Lieutenant-General Sir Richard Hussey Vivian (1775-1842) has arms full of military lore as a result of long campaigning in the Peninsular War and later service at Waterloo. He was created a baronet in 1828 and first Baron Vivian in 1841. His arms included *on a chief embattled Gules, a wreath of oak Or, between two medals* that on the dexter representing the gold medal and clasp given to the first baron for his services in the action of Sahagun, Benevente and Orthes, and that on the sinister, the silver Waterloo medal. The crest is *issuant from a bridge of one arch embattled, and having at each end a tower, a demi-hussar in the uniform of the 18th Regiment holding in his right hand a sabre, and in his left a pennon flying to the sinister Gules, and inscribed with gold letters,* CROIX D'ORADE. The supporters are, *dexter, a grey horse caparisoned, thereon mounted a hussar of the 7th Regiment of Light Dragoons (Hussars) habited armed and accoutred, his sword drawn proper; sinister, a bay horse guardant, caparisoned, thereon mounted a lancer of the 12th Regiment of Lancers, habited armed and accoutred, supporting his lance also proper* [FIGURE 15].

Lord Vivian had a natural son, Sir Robert John Hussey Vivian, Grand Cross of the Bath, who was a general in the Madras Infantry and he also had military supporters awarded on his appointment as Grand Cross of the Bath. His arms show the badge of the Order of the Bath and the motto of the Order, TRIA JUNCTA IN UNO. They also show the custom of having two shields *accolé,* the dexter containing his arms and the symbols of the Order of the Bath and the sinister containing his arms impaling those of his wife.

Some unusual examples of the use of medals suspended from the shield are connected with the campaign in the Peninsula. Colonel Thomas Peacocke served with the Portuguese forces and received the Portuguese Campaign Gold Cross and was appointed a knight of the Portuguese Order of the Tower and Sword. He shows the helmet of a knight in his arms although he was not appointed a knight of a British order [FIGURE 16]. He was, however, granted a royal licence by the king of England to wear his Portuguese decoration.

We must inevitably now come to Waterloo where, like Trafalgar, many officers included the Waterloo Medal and other symbols in their arms. It is worth mentioning that Waterloo was the first time that a medal was awarded to all ranks who took part in the battle and some 39,000 were issued. The naval and military General Service Medals were not approved until 1847 and the Army of India medal for the period 1799-1829 was not issued until 1851.

The most interesting arms from Waterloo are those of Lieutenant-Colonel Alexander Clark-Kennedy (1782-1864) of the first or Royal Regiment of Dragoons, who had the distinction of capturing the eagle of the 105th Regiment of French Infantry during the battle. His arms included *on a chief of honourable augmentation Ermine, the eagle and colours of the 105th Regiment and a sword crossed proper and above them the word* WATER-LOO. The crest of augmentation is *a soldier of the first Royal Dragoons holding in his right hand a sword proper and in his left a French eagle with a tricoloured flag having thereon the number 105.* The flag has the following inscription L'EMPE-REUR NAPOLÉON AU 105ᵉ RÉGIMENT D'INFANTE-RIE DE LIGNE. The badges suspended from the shield are of a knight of the Royal Hanoverian Guelphic Order, commander of the Order of the Bath and the Waterloo Medal. The motto around the shield is that of the Guelphic Order. Colonel Kennedy was later promoted lieutenant-general and aide-de-camp to Queen Victoria and knight commander of the Bath in 1862. An officer of the same regiment who greatly assisted Kennedy in the capture of the eagle was Lieutenant George Gunning whose arms show a good representation of the Waterloo Medal [FIGURE 17].

The arms of Sir Henry Allen Johnson include references to a father and son's services during the Napoleonic War period. Sir Henry Johnson (1748-1835) served in America and was inspector general of recruiting in Ireland when rebellion broke out. In 1798, he was detached with 3,000 men to occupy New Ross and he defeated the rebels when they attacked. He was made governor of Ross Castle and general in 1801, and a baronet in 1818. His son saw much service in the Peninsula and was appointed aide-de-camp to the Prince of Orange, for which he was appointed knight of the Military Order of William of the Netherlands. The arms show supporters, the dexter being a grenadier and the sinister a light infantryman *supporting with his sinister hand a banner Gules inscribed* NEW ROSS *in letters of gold.* The dexter shield is surrounded by the motto of the Netherlands Order and shows the badge of the Order suspended below.

Finally, a good example of how a knight Grand Cross marshalled his arms with supporters and various orders is shown in the arms of Sir Frederick Adam, a major-general at Waterloo where his troops were instrumental in attacking the "Old Guard" towards the end of the day and may have been decisive in the victory. He later commanded the troops in Malta from 1817-1822 and was high commissioner of the Ionian Islands from 1824-1831. His supporters appear to be a British soldier and probably a Greek soldier of the Ionian Islands. The shield is surrounded by the motto and chain of the Order of St. Michael and St. George, of which Adam was one of the earliest knights Grand Cross, the order having been founded in 1818 and he having been appointed in 1821. The badges shown below are those of the Orders of the Bath, St. Michael and St. George, Maria Theresa of Austria and St. Anne of Russia.

During the many years of hostilities, campaigns took place in many parts of the world. A rather unusual place to give rise to its special mention in armorial bearings is Ternate Island in the East Indies. This is a volcanic island of the Moluccas 25 square miles in area just off the west coast of Halmerhera and it was captured from the Dutch on June 21, 1801 by troops under the command of Lieutenant-General Daniel Burr. The crest granted was *out of a mural crown Argent inscribed with the word* TERNATE *Sable, a demi-Malay soldier habited and armed with a kreese, the dexter arm supporting a Standard intended to represent that taken at the capture of the aforesaid Island of Ternate by the said Lieutenant-General Burr all proper, the sinister hand resting on the mural crown.*

That the mural crown was a privilege reserved to army officers is shown in the arms of Lieutenant-General Sir Rufane Donkin (1775-1841), who had a long and varied career, receiving the Army Gold Medal for Talavera and an augmentation including a representation of that gold medal, an elephant and the word INDIA. The medal also appears on the crest consisting of a plough and anchor on a mural crown. Donkin was for a time acting governor of the Cape and during this time named Algoa Bay, Port Elizabeth after his wife who had recently died in India. The badges of the Order of the Bath and Hanoverian Guelphic Order are suspended from the shield with the Talavera Gold Medal in the centre. The inscription BONA SPE is also to be seen in the form of a motto above the crest.

Mention must be made of Major-General Sir Isaac Brock, the "Hero of Upper Canada," who was killed at Queenston Heights three days after being appointed a knight of the Bath on October 10, 1812 for his victory at Fort Detroit on August 16 of that year. He was, of course, unaware of his appointment as knight of the Bath or of his subsequent grant of arms being: *Gules an eagle displayed Or, on a chief embattled Argent, a lion passant guardant of the field.* Crest: *out of a mural crown Argent, a demi-Canadian Indian, the dexter hand supporting a Tomahawk erect proper.* Supporters: Dexter, *a Grenadier of the 49th Regiment of Foot,* sinister *a soldier of the same, both armed and habited proper.* Motto: CANADA [FIGURE 18]. The Indian refers to the assistance received from Tecumseh and his warriors in the capture of Detroit.

Other arms showing the name of a regiment concerned were those relating to one of the more disastrous campaigns during the war period. One may well wonder what the representation of a fortress entitled MONTE VIDEO is doing in the arms of a British army officer. The story of why British troops should be storming Monte Video in 1807 is too complicated to relate, but in storming that city, Lieutenant-Colonel Spencer Vassall lost his life leading his regiment, the 38th Foot (South Staffordshire Regiment). His son later obtained arms commemorating the event with the following augmentation: *a fess Or, on which is represented the breached bastion of fortress above which occur the words* MONTE VIDEO *and a canton Argent with the number 38 within a branch of cypress and another of laurel, the stems united in*

*saltire.* The crest also consists of the fortress flying a flag with the words MONTE VIDEO and the unusual motto EVERY BULLET HAS ITS BILLET.

A small coat of arms for Captain Percy Shawe Smith is interesting as he was a member of the 13th Light Dragoons, which took part in the Charge of the Light Brigade at Balaclava, and he shows all the medals it was possible to obtain for service in the Crimean War (1854-1856), namely from left to right—the Turkish Crimea Medal, the British Crimea War Medal with clasps for the battles of Alma, Balaclava, Inkerman and Sebastopol, the Turkish Order of the Medjidie and the Sardinian War Medal.

Perhaps the most extreme example of the augmentation of arms by the introduction of references to several military campaigns is that of Field Marshal Hugh Viscount Gough (1779-1869), whose service covered the Peninsular War and later service in India and China. The first augmentation of 1816 for service in the Peninsula includes *a representation of the Spanish Order of Charles III* and *on a chief a representation of the fortress of Tarifa with a breach between two turrets and the British flag flying from the dexter turret all proper.* In 1843, a further augmentation recognised service in India with an additional quartering including the words CHINA and INDIA. Two crests of augmentation were granted, *on a mural crown Argent, a lion passant guardant Or, holding in the dexter paw two flag staves in bend sinister proper, the one bearing the Union flag of Great Britain and Ireland surmounting the other, the staff broken, with a triangular banner flowing therefrom to represent a Chinese flag, having thereon a dragon and in an escroll above the word* CHINA, the other crest is *a dexter arm embowed in facings of the 87th Regiment (Gules faced Vert), the hand grasping the colour of the said regiment displayed and a representation of a French eagle reversed and depressed the staff broken proper, in an escroll above the word* BAROSSA. Even the supporters bear names of campaigns, the dexter lion being *gorged with an Eastern crown inscribed* PUNJAB *and the sinister dragon gorged with a mural crown inscribed* CHINA.

An example of an officer on being promoted Grand Cross of the Bath not adopting supporters of his regiment is that of Field Marshall Sir William Maynard Gomm whose supporters granted in 1851 were on the dexter side *an ancient warrior in armour proper, mantle and surcoat Argent, resting the exterior hand on a sword also proper, and on the sinister side, a female figure vested Argent, holding in the dexter hand a Passion Cross and in the sinister a book, both Or.* Gomm is, however, of particular interest to philatelists as, while he was governor of Mauritius, his wife organised a fancy dress ball and wished to send out the invitations by post. The first issue of stamps were being engraved by a local half-blind watchmaker and on being pressed by the Postmaster to get the stamps ready in time, he just succeeded in having them ready in time for Lady Gomm's ball on September 30, 1847. These were the famous Post Office Mauritius stamps of which only 14 of the 1d. and 12 of the 2d. are believed to exist now.

To finish the account to how military officers introduced military symbols into their arms, two recent examples from the First World War can be quoted—Field Marshall Earl Haig and General Lord Horne. Both show regimental supporters, Haig's being very fine cavalrymen—a private of the 7th Queen's Own Hussars and a lancer of the 17th (Duke of Cambridge's Own) Lancers, while Horne's are more ordinary "Tommies" being a Gunner of the Royal Horse Artillery and a Private of the Seaforth Highlanders.

It remains to see if any parallels can be found in the heraldry of other countries involved in the wars of the 18th and 19th centuries. In France, before the Revolution, arms seldom seem to have shown more than the badges of the orders to which the owners belonged. The Royal Military Order of St. Louis named after St. Louis IX, was instituted in 1694 by Louis XIV and confirmed by Louis XV in 1719. It was to be awarded only to Catholic officers of the army and navy for service in the royal armed forces. This Order was suppressed during the Revolution and reinstated by Louis XVIII in 1816, and was in fact awarded to about 11 British Naval officers for their service at the Battle of Navarino. The other two orders that are usually found together were that of St. Michael, founded in 1469 by Louis XI, and that of the Holy Ghost (Saint-Esprit), founded by Henry III in 1578. They were known as "Les Ordres du roi." One had to be a member of the Order of St. Michael before entering that of the Holy Ghost.

During the French Revolution all heraldry and orders were suppressed until Napoleon introduced the Legion of Honour in 1802 and a completely new system of heraldry. The Legion of Honour was maintained throughout all the succeeding changes of government up to the present day. Apart from the three orders mentioned, which are found pendent from shields of arms or from chains surrounding the shield, there are few cases where specifically military or naval symbols appear in arms. One J. L. H. d'Alphonse and the Duc de Brissac show some military signs, but they are not part of the armorial bearings.

Some Spanish arms display orders and medals. The egregious Manuel Godoy, who entered court as a young guardsman and rose, through the favours of the queen, to become commander-in-chief of the army and more or less dictator of Spain and Principe de la Paz (Prince of the Peace), shows on his arms the Order of the Golden Fleece and the Order of Charles III of Spain.

The arms of the Duque de Infantado, an admiral, show his arms against anchors and those of the Duque de San Carlos are decorated with some ten orders and medals. There is an interesting engraving of arms of General Don Miguel Ricardo de Álava, a Spaniard who fought with Wellington in the Peninsula and at Waterloo. In 1834, he was Spanish ambassador in London. The arms shown on a mantle have five orders or medals suspended below, being the Order of the Bath, the Order of St. Ferdinand, the Order of St. Hermenegilde, the Waterloo medal and the Army Gold Cross, which he earned for being present in nine general actions. De Álava, then described as Lieutenant-General Miguel de Álava, was appointed an honorary knight commander of the Bath on October 20, 1815.

To sum up, I think one is safe in saying that English heraldry is unique in the way that it has incorporated symbols representing specific historical events from throughout the world into armorial bearings.

## BIBLIOGRAPHY

BURKE, *General Armory;* DE LA MOTTE, *Historical and Allusive Arms;* J. F. HUXFORD, *Honour and Arms. The Story of Some Augmentations of Honour;* A. C. FOX-DAVIES, *The Art of Heraldry;* JOSLIN, LITHERLAND and SIMPKIN, *British Battles and Medals;* D. E. IVALL, *Cornish Heraldry and Symbolism;* R. PERKINS and CAPT. K. J. DOUGLAS-MORRIS, *Gunfire in Barbary;* ELVIN, *Mottoes Revised;* W. A. SHAW, *The Knights of England,* 2 vols.

1

2

3

4

5

6

7

8

9

10

11

12

13

14

15

16

17

18

# THE EVOLUTION OF A DISTINCTIVE SOUTH AFRICAN HERALDIC IDIOM, 1963-1996

Frederick G. Brownell

For much of the past two centuries, South Africa has been within the broad sphere of British influence, with London as its hub. Thus, when the South African Bureau of Heraldry came into being on June 1, 1963, the principal outside influence was that of the College of Arms. While retaining cordial relations with the College, the Bureau of Heraldry has, however, also looked further afield, seeking advice, inspiration and guidance from colleagues and other heraldic practitioners in Scotland, Ireland, the Netherlands, Germany, Scandinavia and elsewhere.

My predecessor, Norden Hartman, spent some six months in the British Isles and Europe on a study tour during 1964 and our former principal heraldic artist Johan Coetsee spent four months overseas in 1969. In my own case, I was fortunate to be able to spend two months visiting heraldic and genealogical establishments in the British Isles, Scandinavia and Europe in 1979, ending up with the 8th International Congress of Vexillology in Vienna. It was at that congress that I realised what an important vehicle these congresses are for the interchange of ideas, especially for those of us who are geographically isolated from our colleagues.

The broader perspective that we have gained from interaction with overseas friends and colleagues over the past generation has certainly proved invaluable to our development in the heraldic and allied fields.

Taken in combination with the multi-cultural composition of the South African population and the rich diversity of our flora and fauna, this has led to the evolution of a distinctive South African heraldic idiom that will undoubtedly evolve even further as the years pass.

As you are aware, the political face of South Africa changed substantially on April 27, 1994 and questions have indeed been asked as to the relevance of heraldry, with its Eurocentric origins, in the "New South Africa." Faced with the challenges of a complex and changing society, South African heraldry strives to be vibrant, innovative and rele-

vant, enriching but remaining within the main stream of international heraldic practice. We obviously need to be receptive to changing needs and, where necessary, be prepared to adapt to suit the circumstances. I am sure we will continue to do so.

In the first few years after the establishment of the Bureau of Heraldry in 1963, there was little to distinguish our heraldry from that of the older heraldic authorities. In many cases this is still so, but the needs of our unique Southern African situation, with its diverse population that encompasses the full spectrum from the Stone Age to the Atomic Age has, from time to time, dictated the need for adaptation and a dynamic new approach.

I do not propose dwelling on our early heraldic designs, most of which were prepared by persons outside the Bureau of Heraldry. Suffice it to say that they tended to be rather prosaic. Since I shall be trying to illustrate an evolutionary process, the images that I will present are very largely in chronological sequence.

The arms of the MUNICIPALITY OF GLENCOE [FIGURE 1], which date from 1968, give a fair indication of the type of design we were then producing. Glencoe is in a coal-mining area and it was there that one of South Africa's first coal-fired power stations was erected, hence the colour *Sable* and Jupiter's thunderbolt.

The arms of the DIVISIONAL COUNCIL OF ALBANY [FIGURE 2] in the Eastern Cape, where most of the British Settlers who went to South Africa in 1820 were settled, have a clearly British flavour in the shield, with South African fauna as supporters. We had no cut and dried policy on supporters at that stage, but since Divisional Councils had almost County status, they were appropriate in this case.

In both these coats of arms the crests are, to my mind, somewhat too large.

The arms of MARK SHUTE [FIGURE 3], which, like those of Albany, date from 1975, are once again entirely conventional. They are based, in part, on the arms of Shute of Hollington, County

Cambridge, with whom there is a genealogical link.

It was really only in the mid-1970s that a distinctive South African heraldic tradition started to take shape. Certainly, South African flora and fauna had by then found their way into our arms, but it is only once the Bureau of Heraldry took the initiative in devising arms, rather than expecting the prospective armiger to submit a completed design, that we began to come into our own.

One of the main sources of inspiration has been the simple, strong and superbly stylized modern Finnish designs. It is simply a case of their style of heraldic design being suited to the message we wish to convey. Certainly, the late Olof Eriksson has had a more profound influence on my approach to heraldic design than anyone else.

Many of our clients, particularly schools and clubs, require simple arms comprising a shield only. The arms of GLENSTANTIA PRIMARY SCHOOL [FIGURE 4] are an example of a distinctively South African chief embodying a Cape-Dutch gable, with a thistle, which alludes to the first part of the school's name. These arms were devised in 1981.

The arms of the DIVISIONAL COUNCIL OF KAFFRARIA [FIGURE 5], which were devised a year later, combine both European and African shield forms, since it is in Kaffraria that the Black man and White man first met in the 18th century. Previous contact had been with San and Khoi tribes. You will note that although the crest has a full-face orientation, the helmet was then still placed in 3/4 profile, as was the practice in England. This was one of the last registrations in which the orientation of the helmet was not determined by that of the crest.

In the early 1980s a *demi-cogwheel trefly* was devised to ensure a clear family relationship between the arms of technical colleges, of which there were then already more than 50. In each case it is used in conjunction with another charge appropriate either to the name or locality of the College.

In the arms of the TECHNICAL COLLEGE OF SOUTH AFRICA [FIGURE 6], which serves the whole country by distance education, the Protea cynaroides, our national flower, appears in chief.

The arms of the KLERKSDORP TECHNICAL COLLEGE [FIGURE 7], which is situated in one of the major maize producing areas, bears in chief a stylized cob of maize. Arms of the other technical colleges follow the same general pattern.

I could not come to Canada without showing that we have also incorporated maple leaves into South African registered arms. One example is that of the arms of ERNEST LAWRENCE HARRIS [FIGURE 8], who was born in Toronto and came to South Africa as a young man. The hedgehogs or "hérissons" are, of course, a play on the surname.

So far I have dealt with arms depicted on European type shields. Where appropriate we also register arms on a variety of traditional African shields. Where such shields are used, one would obviously not dream of depicting a helmet.

One example is the arms of the MOLEFE TRIBAL AUTHORITY [FIGURE 9]. The Molefe tribe are ethnic Basothos who, during the 19th century, moved from their original lands in the Free State, over the Drakensberg, and settled in Zulu territory, where they have since adopted many of the local customs, while retaining their original home language. In their case we have made use of a Zulu shield, but ensigned this with a representation of a traditional conical Basotho grass hat, which also appears in the shield as ordinary charges. The leopard occupies an important place in Zulu culture, while the Springbok links this tribe to its original territory.

I shall now move to two examples of a group of civic arms, all of which have only a mural crown as the crest. This basic pattern evolved as a result of the passing of the Black Local Authorities Act in 1982. This Act saw the creation, in a short space of time, of a large number of new local authorities.

The reorganisation of existing local authorities and the creation of new ones is nothing new. We have seen it happen in Britain, Scandinavia, Europe and elsewhere, to meet the needs of changing societies and changing conditions. In South Africa we are experiencing a similar evolutionary process as a result of massive urbanisation spurred on by constitutional and other political changes.

A local authority can obviously function without a heraldic identity, but one cannot ignore the human factor. The mayor of a local authority is traditionally invested with a chain of office, pendant from which there is customarily a representation of the civic arms. Logically then, if the mayor is to be properly dressed, then the local authority he or she represents must bear arms! In the design of arms for certain of these newly established local authorities, we found ourselves faced with the task of trying to reconcile divergent traditions and views. On the one hand there are those who, while recognising heraldry as an acceptable system of identification, nevertheless argue that the helmet is foreign to African culture and consequently has no place in African arms. There are others who feel that the helmet is an anachronism that should in any event be dropped.

The strict application of this view would have meant that arms would have to be devised without either helmet, mantling or crest since it is our view in South Africa that the traditional crest cannot exist without the helmet to which it is, and was, physically attached.

The mural crown, widely used in various forms to ensign civic arms seemed to offer a possible alternative to accommodate these viewpoints. The solution has been to register these arms with a helmet and mantling, but in place of the traditional crest, to ensign the helmet with a mural crown that is decorated in some way.

At a glance these arms are hardly distinguishable from those with a traditional crest, but if the local authority so wishes, they may equally be used in an abbreviated form consisting of the shield and mural crown alone, which is in line with international practice. Although this category of civic arms evolved as a solution to a specific problem area that had been identified, its acceptance in its own right has now also led to its quite general use in the arms of civic authorities. The following two figures are examples of civic arms devised on this basis.

The MUNICIPALITY OF KUISEBMOND [FIGURE 10] is situated at the mouth of the Kuiseb River in what was the South African enclave of Walvis Bay on the South West African coast. It is a rich fishing area with large flocks of pelicans. The shield has been so partitioned as to represent the Kuiseb River flowing into the sea from the adjacent desert. This river, in fact, seldom flows but it is the thought that counts.

The MATWABENG TOWN COMMITTEE [FIGURE 11] controls a local authority situated near Senekal in the eastern Free State. This is an area of distinctive conical sandstone koppies or hills with flat tops, to which the design of the chief alludes. The head of a steenbok, a shy gazelle still found wild in the area, is in base. As you will note, the principal colours of the shield have been carried through to these mural crowns.

In other civic coats of arms mural crowns are ensigned of, or have charges *issuant*. One example is the arms of the BOGGOMS BAY LOCAL COUNCIL [FIGURE 12]. This local authority on the Southern Cape coast takes its name from the most common call of baboons, troops of which are still found in the nearby mountains. The arms, which are *per pale serpentine* to give the illusion of the sweep of a bay, are charged with two whales in reference to the annual visit of these large sea mammals to the bay. *A baboon's head erased* seemed to be a logical addition to the crest.

African tribal tradition has also inspired a number of charges that are not found in European heraldry. One of these will be found in the arms of the GAZANKULU COLLEGE OF NURSING [FIGURE 13]. Gazankulu is the traditional home in South Africa of the Shangaan tribe whose lands also extend over the national borders into Mozambique. Spoons attached to one another by means of a chain, all of which is carved out of a single block of wood, are unique to Shangaan culture and symbolic of peace, harmony and co-operation. The candle, in turn, is the principal source of light in rural homes not yet supplied with electricity. This candle is symbolic of the light of knowledge and in this case replaces the more customary nurses' lamp. Aloes, which are also found in profusion in Gazankulu, have long been recognised as having medicinal properties, hence the wish of the College that one be depicted for the crest.

We now move to another category, namely the arms of Regional Services Council. These Councils, which are now known as District Councils, replaced the former Divisional Councils in 1986. Their main function is to provide services—for example, the bulk supply of electricity and water—the co-ordination of transport and other facilities, and expertise in the broad sense to all the local authorities in their respective regions.

We were faced with the challenge of creating a distinctive pattern that would not only identify this particular category, but also be acceptable to the residents of all the local authorities served by these Councils, irrespective of their colour, creed or culture.

Fortunately we were able to start from scratch since Regional Services Councils were an entirely new concept. There are two elements in common to all Regional Services Council coats of arms.

The first is that the shield is ensigned of a distinctive coronet and the second is that birds are used as supporters. We have dispensed entirely with a helmet and mantling.

The distinctive coronet consists of a mural crown encircling three towers, instead of having towers rising from the rim as in the case of Spanish and Portuguese civic arms. The design of this crown thus alludes to the Councils' function of supporting and serving the needs of the local authorities in their region. As far as the supporters are concerned, these are always birds indigenous to the region.

The first coat of arms devised in this category was that of the WESTERN CAPE REGIONAL SERVICES COUNCIL [FIGURE 14]. The Western Cape, with its Mediterranean type climate, is South Africa's principal wine-growing area, hence the bunch of grapes. It is also the home of the Cape-Dutch gable and of the Malgas or Cape Gannet. You will note that all three towers are of the same height. We narrowed and heightened the central tower in subsequent representations of this crown.

The KALAHARI REGIONAL SERVICES COUNCIL [FIGURE 15] serves an arid area north of the Orange River, with rich mineral deposits, in particular iron ore, hence the use of the old chemical symbol for iron. It is also home to Southern Africa's remaining Stone Age inhabitants, the San or Bushmen, who are represented by a bow-and-arrow cross. The supporters are two Kori Bustards, an endangered species found in the Kalahari Desert.

Moving to the coastal area north of Cape Town, we have the territory served by the WEST COAST REGIONAL SERVICES COUNCIL [FIGURE 16]. South Africa's richest crayfish beds lie off this coast, while the hinterland is rich in succulent plants. The supporters are black-backed seagulls.

Innovative charges, within an otherwise conventional heraldic representation, will be found in the arms of the TRANSVAAL MUSEUM in Pretoria [FIGURE 17]. In these arms the charge in chief is a tree cladogram, a symbol of the evolutionary process and thus well known in the natural history museum context. It is shown in conjunction with a DNA spiral, the key of life. The martial eagle chosen for the crest is displayed in the foyer of the Transvaal Museum, which is well known for its ornithological collection.

A unique South African charge will be found in the arms of the WATERBERG SKI BOAT CLUB [FIGURE 18]. The Waterberg district is a largely bushveld region where warthogs, our local "wild boars," are still found in the wild. Despite living hundreds of kilometres from the coast, the Waterberg has an ardent group of fishermen who regularly take their ski boats down to the coast for some sea fishing. For them, we created a sea-warthog with which they are delighted.

As part of the "grand apartheid" philosophy applied by the previous government in South Africa, ten ethnic "homelands" were created, each with its own national coat of arms. These were comparatively well-known, but it is little known that the Republic of Venda intended to extend official coats of arms to government departments as well.

Of these the VENDA DEPARTMENT OF POSTS AND TELECOMMUNICATIONS [FIGURE 19] was the only department to register arms. Its primary function, namely communication, was represented by the charges in the shield. The traditional Venda shield is ensigned with a headring that supports a Venda tribal drum similar to that in their national arms, but charged with an *elephants' head caboshed*. We proposed using a similar crest for the arms of other departments, but with the demise of the African "homelands" and the re-incorporation of Venda into the Republic of South Africa, nothing further came of this idea.

Also with a distinctively African flavour are the arms of the LINGELETHU WEST CITY COUNCIL [FIGURE 20]. Situated on the Cape Flats near Cape Town, Lingelethu West is one of the most populous of the new local authorities in South Africa. Its inhabitants are with few exceptions Xhosas from the former Ciskei and Transkei who retain strong bonds with their ancestral culture. In principle, we are not too keen on the human figure as a charge, but in this case the local authority put up a strong case for a representation of a Xhosa woman in traditional dress, smoking a distinctive clay pipe. The shield is ensigned with a headring, a traditional African symbol of authority, which in this case supports the type of turban worn by Xhosa matrons. Both the leopard and lion occupy an important position in Xhosa culture.

The former Republic of Bophuthatswana was the only former "homeland" to make a concerted effort to have arms registered for its urban councils. Most of these were devised as a group and in each case we employed a specially designed mural crown with a spear-head issuant from each crenellation. The arms of the MOTHIBISTAT URBAN COUNCIL [FIGURE 21] show this crown, while the charges in the shield are Tswana totem animals associated with the region.

Seals are an integral part of heraldic evolution and that of the ORDER OF ETHIOPIA [FIGURE 22] bears the arms of the Order, depicting an African mother with her baby on her back, kneeling and grinding corn, with a dove descending in dexter chief. The Order of Ethiopia is an exclusively African branch of the Anglican Church in South Africa. Its head is consecrated as a Bishop of the Church of the Province of Southern Africa.

Moving from seals to badges, I felt I had to include the badge of the AMERICAN CHAMBER OF COMMERCE IN SOUTHERN AFRICA [FIGURE 23]. In practice their name appears on the rim. We do not normally register any wording (other than a motto), as part of a badge.

Signs of the Zodiac have also found their way into South African arms, a case in point being the arms of the CANCER DEPARTMENT OF THE NATIONAL HOSPITAL IN BLOEMFONTEIN [FIGURE 24]. Here the crab holds two flowers in allusion to "Bloem," while the fountain completes the name of the city.

To end this paper, I would like to present the arms for two of our nine new provinces. The first of these is that of the PROVINCE OF GAUTENG [FIGURE 25] or "Place of Gold" in Sesotho, of which Johannesburg is the provincial capital. This, our richest and most westernized province, opted for an African-type shield. The pick is appropriate to both mining and agriculture, while the supporters allude to the province controlling the lion's share of the economy. The lion also links these arms to those of the former Transvaal, out of which it was taken, and by extension to those of the old *Zuid-Afrikaansche Republiek*, the first version of which was devised in 1857. The coronet is taken from the head of the Provincial Legislature's Mace.

The last illustration is of the arms of the PROVINCE OF MPUMALANGA [FIGURE 26], a Swazi word for "where the sun rises." The partition of the shield is reminiscent of the continuum of the highveld, escarpment and eastern lowveld, while the Barberton daisy can be seen as alluding to the sun which rises over the province. The kudu supporters are indigenous to the province, which is adjacent to the southern part of the world famous Kruger National Park. The coronet which rests on the upper edge of the shield has alternating rays and Barberton daisies. The rays refer to both the rising sun and to the peaks of the Drakensburg mountain range which is known in the vernacular as the "barrier of spears."

We have also registered arms for the Province of the Eastern Cape, and have prepared a draft design for the North West Province, but the other provinces are being somewhat tardy. They are probably still trying to find their political feet and will, no doubt, react to my offer of assistance in due course.

I have tried to give you an indication of how South African heraldry is evolving. We are all trying to find our feet in the new political dispensation which came into being on April 27, 1994 and in the heraldic field we will make every effort to continue adapting to changing requirements.

1

2

3

4

5

6

7

8

NTJA PEDI HA-E-HLOLWE-KE SEBATA

9

PRO BONO PUBLICO

10

11

EXCOLE ET CONSERVA

12

335

13

14

15

16

17

18

19

20

21

22

23

24

25

26

# THE EXPORT OF SCOTTISH HERALDIC SYMBOLISM

Charles J. Burnett

The ancient realm of Scotland has a variety of distinguishing symbols that singly, or in combination, give the nation and her people an identity among the world community. These symbols were not adopted together at one time, the oldest has been in use for over 700 years, the most recent is only 294 years old, yet all are now synonymous with Scotland.

The Royal Arms of Scotland, "the ruddy lion ramping on his field of tressured gold," has been the sovereign's ensigns armorial since the middle of the 13th century. The shield was given a crest lion holding a sword by 1380; from the middle of the 15th century, the shield was supported by unicorns; around 1470 a royal motto had been adopted, IN MY DEFENS GOD US DEFEND, now usually shortened to IN DEFENS. From 1502, the shield was encircled by a collar of thistles, and the crest lion also had to hold the saltire flag of Scotland; finally, by 1542, the crest lion had the saltire flag replaced by a sceptre and the unicorns were given banners to carry. One hundred and fifty years later, a second royal motto was incorporated into the arms, NEMO ME IMPUNE LACESSIT. This gradual development over some 400 years provided an armorial display that reflected the dignity of an old independent kingdom and brought together four of our national symbols —the royal arms, St. Andrew, his cross, and the thistle.

The unicorn supporters have never become so popular as another national symbol, probably because they are not uniquely Scottish. However, it is a remarkable coincidence that this congress is in right of a Scottish grant of arms, dating from 1962, when the congress met in Edinburgh. The fourth quarter bears a unicorn's head in allusion to Scotland. There are other examples of the Scottish unicorn, one from Canada, and one from the United States of America, which I will feature in a moment.

Andrew, the first of Christ's apostles, had been adopted as the patron saint of Scotland before 1250. One of the first visual records of the Saint on his distinctive cross is the seal of the Guardians of Scotland, in use between 1286 and 1292. The Saint's saltire cross was a recognisable national symbol by 1385 because, in that year, the Scottish Parliament decreed that Scots and their French allies should wear:

> a sign before and behind, namely a white St. Andrew's cross, and if his jacket is white, or his coat white, he shall bear the same white cross in a piece of black cloth round or square,

in order to distinguish them from their English enemies. Thereafter the saltire appears as a national symbol on Scottish coins, and on military and naval flags.

The figure of St. Andrew with his cross has formed part of the Royal Arms of Scotland since 1502. The pendant badge that hangs from the collar of a knight of the Thistle also features our patron saint. As a result of these uses, St. Andrew gradually became a feature in the badges used by certain Scottish regiments.

There is no evidence in Scotland for the use of the thistle as a plant badge before 1470. Soon after that year, during the reign of James III, King of Scots, a low-value coin was struck bearing two thistles. We also know from a royal inventory that King James slept in a bed that had a cover embroidered with thistles. The plant very quickly became a well-loved decorative device that appears in architecture and on furnishings. In 1500 an official document detailing the marriage contract between James IV, King of Scots, and Margaret Tudor, daughter of Henry VII, King of England, was drawn up in Scotland and decorated by the king's limner. On one side of the document is a panel enclosing the Royal Arms of Scotland, which is surrounded by Scottish thistles and English roses—the first time the two countries had been symbolised together with plant badges.

During the reign of the next sovereign, James V, King of Scots, two of our national symbols underwent change when used in strictly royal circumstances. The thistle was crowned and the saltire was given an encircling open crown round the intersection of the cross arms. These two new devices first appeared on a coin struck ca. 1540. The regal thistle is still the royal badge used in Scotland by the sovereigns of the United Kingdom of Great Britain.

The last symbol to gradually assume prominence is the star devised for the Most Ancient and Most Noble Order of the Thistle, Scotland's premier order of chivalry. The star consists of a thistle encircled with the motto of the order—the second royal motto, NEMO ME IMPUNE LACESSIT—surmounting a saltire with rays between the cross arms. This particular star design was devised on December 31, 1703. The sovereign was then Queen Anne, who had an especial interest in her Scottish kingdom and Stewart ancestry. During her reign Scotland and England were joined to form the United Kingdom. In 1712 the Queen redesignated the Scots Regiment of Guards as the Third Regiment of Foot Guards and gave the regiment a new name, the Scots Guards. New colours were devised for the regiment. It was the custom of the period for the regimental colonel, lieutenant colonel, and major each to have distinguishing flags so that their presence could be recognised on the battlefield. The new colours given by Queen Anne contained the following devices: the colonel had the Royal Arms of Scotland, the lieutenant colonel had the combined rose and thistle plant badge of the United Kingdom, and the major received the star of the Order of the Thistle.

By the end of the 18th century, the Scots Guards had adopted the thistle star as their regimental badge and this appeared on buttons, belt plates, and other items of uniform. During the Napoleonic campaign, another Scottish regiment, the Royal Scots, was granted a motif from the Order of the Thistle. This occurred in 1812 when the collar of the order was incorporated into the regimental badge by express authority of the Prince Regent, later King George IV.

Gradually during the 19th century, other Scottish regiments adopted Order of the Thistle motifs as a means of identifying their Scottish origin.

The different Scottish symbols have been employed in a variety of ways at various times. The saltire is, of course, one of the heraldic ordinaries and cannot be claimed exclusively for Scotland. Within our country the saltire performs the dual role of an ordinary in the arms of many families, but when rendered argent on an azure field it becomes a national symbol. The earliest known use of the saltire as an ordinary in Scotland occurs in the arms of the Bruce family. A privy seal impression survives from 1218 bearing the arms of Robert Bruce, fourth laird of Annandale. Other Scottish families show the plain saltire (such as the Maxwells), or the saltire between different charges. The Johnstones, Haldanes, Andersons, and the Napiers have the latter.

The national saltire first appears in the Arms of Scotland's one and only North American colony, appropriately named Nova Scotia. A reversal of tinctures is used for difference, coupled with an inescutcheon of the Royal Arms of Scotland. These arms were adopted ca. 1625. The national saltire is also used as part of the arms of the Scottish office of arms granted in 1672, and then appears in an exported version created for the Company of Scotland trading to Africa and the Indies, which were granted in 1696.

The thistle has always been exploited as a decorative device, but was first granted as a heraldic charge to a Scot in 1565 when Sir James Sandilands, Lord Torphichen, received an imperial crown and a thistle as an augmentation to his own arms. After 1660 the thistle appeared as a charge of augmentation granted to two men who had helped to save the Scottish crown jewels during the civil war, and in 1672 it also appeared as part of the arms for the Scottish office of arms.

I have already mentioned briefly the use of the thistle star by Scottish regiments in the British army. Many of these were raised in the Highlands and as a result wore Highland dress, namely the kilt. The standard British military red coat was adapted for wear with the kilt. Because the kilted regiments were so distinctly different from the rest of the British army, they were always recognised and noticed on the field of battle. Their reputation as fighting soldiers was thus enhanced wherever they appeared in action throughout the British Empire. The Black Watch, The Seaforth Highlanders, The Cameron Highlanders, The Gordon Highlanders, and the Argyll and Sutherland Highlanders became renowned during the 19th century. A major reform of the British army took place in 1881, many regiments were amalgamated, and at the same time no doubt encouraged by Queen Victoria, who had fallen in love with all things Scottish, the non-kilted Scottish regiments adopted tartan trousers and emphasised their Scottish origins by using some of the national symbols on their regimental badges and uniform. The Royal Scots, the Royal Scots Fusiliers, the King's Own Scottish Borderers, the Cameronians, and the Highland Light Infantry all began to wear tartan.

When emergencies arose within the British Empire, or when a dominion or colony was threatened by internal or external agencies, regiments of volunteer soldiers were raised locally to meet the threat. Scots and their descendants were a prominent group amongst the immigrant population of Canada, Australia, New Zealand, South Africa, and in Far Eastern colonies. Several of the local regiments consisted entirely of Scots and they wished to be recognised as a distinctive unit. Many of the units modelled themselves on the home-based Scottish regiments within the British army, and these local regiments established links by adopting the tartan and regimental device of the parent regiment.

Here in Canada during 1964, out of 75 infantry regiments in the Canadian army, 19 were distinctly Scottish in both uniform and regimental device. I shall show a selection of 10 Canadian regimental badges:

1. The Cameron Highlanders of Ottawa
2. The Cameron Highlanders of Canada
3. The Black Watch of Canada
4. The Toronto Scottish (Unicorn)
5. The Scots Fusiliers of Canada
6. The Highland Light Infantry of Canada
7. The Argyll and Sutherland Highlanders of Canada
8. The Nova Scotia Highlanders
9. The Perth Regiment
10. The Essex and Kent Scottish

Similarly, in South Africa there were, and still are, regiments that were initially raised from immigrant Scots: the Capetown Highlanders, the Pretoria Highlanders, and the Transvaal Scottish.

Here are two examples from Australia: the New South Wales Scottish Regiment and the Cadet Corps of the Scots College, Warwick, Queensland.

The British had a settlement on the Chinese mainland at Shanghai. Between 1914 and 1930, there existed a volunteer force known as the Shanghai Scottish. In Burma, the Rangoon battalion of volunteers had a Highland Company.

These examples are sufficient to show how the national symbols were used by the military overseas to identify Scottish units.

Finally, since the end of the Second World War, the growing interest in genealogical origin has affected Scotland and her scattered people to a remarkable degree. Scottish societies, family groups, and public institutions have realised how heraldry can be used to provide a colourful visual symbol to identify the Scottish connection. Here are eight examples of arms, from across the world, granted by the Lord Lyon King of Arms in Edinburgh, to groups wishing to show their Scottish link:

1. St. Andrew's College, Grahamstown, South Africa, 1952
2. The Caledonian Society of Aden, Saudi Arabia, 1955
3. St. Andrew's College, University of Sydney, Australia, 1966
4. Salmond Hall, Knox College, New Zealand, 1969
5. The American-Scottish Foundation Inc., 1969
6. St. Andrew's Society of Florida, 1970
7. St. Andrew's Society of Tuscaloosa, Alabama, 1984
8. St. Andrew's Society of San Francisco, California, 1989

Considering the size and small population of Scotland, the impact of her heraldic symbolism on the rest of the world has been out of all proportion to her place in the community of nations.

# LES INFLUENCES DE L'ART HÉRALDIQUE FRANÇAIS SUR L'ART HÉRALDIQUE ROUMAIN [1]

Dan Cernovodeanu

L'art héraldique français, l'un des plus anciens de l'Europe, a connu un développement important à travers les siècles et a rayonné non seulement dans les pays voisins de la France, mais aussi dans des régions plus éloignées. Son influence sur les États avoisinants (le Brabant et les pays flamands, l'Angleterre, les pays rhénans etc.) [2] s'est exercée du XIIIᵉ au XVᵉ siècles alors que, dans les contrées plus éloignées, son action remonte au XVIIIᵉ siècle seulement. Le cachet spécifique de l'art héraldique français se retrouve dans l'armorial de la Russie de Pierre le Grand et de Catherine II [3] et dans celui des boyards des principautés roumaines de la Valachie et de la Moldavie [4].

L'héraldique moldo-valaque a d'abord subi l'influence de la symbolique de Byzance et des Asénides et, ensuite, de leur héraldique de brève durée [5]. À partir de la fin du XIVᵉ siècle et du début du XVᵉ siècle, l'art du blason moldo-valaque, issu de la fusion d'éléments autochtones, byzantins et balkaniques fut soumis, pendant les siècles qui suivirent, à de multiples influences provenant d'États voisins : d'abord des royaumes de Hongrie et de Pologne et ensuite du Saint-Empire romano-germanique [6]. C'est ainsi que la libre adoption des armes caractéristique de l'héraldique byzantine s'implanta chez les boyards de la Valachie et de la Moldavie [7]. Seuls les Princes issus des dynasties nationales de ces deux pays [8] et quelques rares dignitaires possédaient des armoiries octroyées par les souverains des États voisins précités et leur usage demeura partiel, sinon facultatif [9]. D'ailleurs, ces mêmes princes ne concédèrent jamais d'armoiries à la noblesse de leur pays.

Ainsi, l'armorial des boyards moldo-valaques, subissant des influences de l'héraldique centrale-européenne dans la première période de son existence, appelée *classique* (du XIVᵉ au XVIᵉ siècle), a connu, du XVIIᵉ au XVIIIᵉ siècle, une seconde époque, durant laquelle on constate une certaine décadence de l'art du blason dans les deux pays concernés, cette décadence étant causée par la domination ottomane, devenue de plus en plus contraignante. En effet, les dirigeants turcs n'avaient pas intérêt à favoriser le développement de l'art héraldique dans les principautés danubiennes. D'une part, ils considéraient — et à juste titre — que les insignes armoriés incarnaient les coutumes des peuples chrétiens d'Europe et, d'autre part, que l'usage de tels insignes pouvait inciter leurs titulaires à secouer le joug ottoman pour se rallier à un système politique de type occidental, caractérisé par l'usage généralisé d'emblèmes héraldiques distinctifs et appréciés [10].

Enfin, pendant la troisième et dernière étape de l'héraldique nobiliaire moldo-valaque appelée *moderne*, l'usage des armoiries se répand chez les boyards de tout rang et ces armoiries ressemblent de plus en plus à celles de l'Occident européen. Cette influence se manifeste d'abord chez les princes phanariotes qui ont régné sur la Valachie et la Moldavie à partir du XVIIIᵉ siècle et adopté un certain style, d'influence surtout française, dans la représentation de leurs propres armes et de celles des principautés soumises à leur autorité [11]. Les boyards, sujets de ces pays, ont imité ce style qui renforçait leur tendance à utiliser des insignes héraldiques d'inspiration occidentale, plus précisément provenant de la France de l'Ancien Régime [12]. Cette nouvelle vague d'influence provenait de Constantinople et plus précisément des princes phanariotes qui s'étaient ouverts aux modes occidentales. Cette ouverture avait eu lieu après la paix de Karlowitz de 1699 (marquant le début de la décadence du pouvoir des Sultans d'Istamboul) et durant tout le XVIIIᵉ siècle, lorsque les gouvernants turcs, cessant leur opposition à toute coutume européenne et chrétienne, avaient permis la pénétration grandissante dans l'Empire ottoman de la culture et de la civilisation françaises, arrivées alors à un très haut degré d'éclat et de raffinement qui se faisait remarquer par la cour impériale et les grands dignitaires istanbuliotes. Signalons à titre d'exemple, l'apparition dans les arts décoratifs turcs du style lalé (le rococo ottoman), résultant d'une alliance d'éléments ornementaux du style Louis XV avec l'art du Proche et du Moyen Orient. On constate aussi que l'héraldique rococo a également pénétré Constantinople, non pas par la voie des dirigeants ottomans qui ne connaissaient pas l'usage des armoiries, mais par le biais des dignitaires grecs et chrétiens du quartier du Phanare qui l'ont adopté avec beaucoup d'empressement. C'est donc par la filière phanariote que l'art du blason français a pu influencer, assez timidement d'abord, puis d'une manière plus prononcée, l'armorial des boyards moldo-valaques de la fin du XVIIIe siècle.

L'art héraldique français de l'époque a aussi pénétré indirectement chez les boyards roumains de la seconde moitié du Siècle des lumières et du début du XIXe siècle par le biais de la noblesse militaire russe entrée en contact avec les dirigeants des deux principautés danubiennes pendant les nombreuses campagnes russo-turques. Cette noblesse militaire n'hésitait pas à étaler devant ces dirigeants toute une gamme d'objets armoriés (bagues, sceaux, breloques, argenterie, gardes d'épée, harnais etc.) gravés de compositions héraldiques inspirées de l'art du blason français de l'Ancien Régime (qui avait pénétré en Russie pendant le règne de Catherine la Grande) et du blason de l'Empire napoléonien introduit pendant le règne d'Alexandre Ier [13].

Par la suite, les contacts directs beaucoup plus fréquents et plus étroits de l'aristocratie européenne avec les boyards moldo-valaques ont incité ces derniers à faire usage d'armoiries de plus en plus conformes aux canons classiques de l'art héraldique occidental. Et, à partir de la troisième décennie du XIXe siècle, la noblesse de ces deux principautés danubiennes a manifesté une préférence marquée pour l'art du blason français de la Restauration, allant jusqu'à adopter le style et la forme de l'écu français moderne et à la meubler, dans la plupart des cas, dans le style usuel des compositions héraldiques de l'époque de Louis XVIII, de Charles X puis de Louis-Philippe [14].

Les rapports de plus en plus serrés entre la France et les deux principautés danubiennes, favorisa dès le début du XIXe siècle la pénétration de l'influence française même si les premières relations diplomatiques directes entre ces deux pays, ne datent que de la fin du XVIIIe siècle [15]. Ces rapprochements franco-roumains permirent à de nombreux jeunes boyards moldo-valaques de se rendre à Paris pour parfaire leurs études universitaires. Sous l'influence des mœurs de la noblesse française et de la mode parisienne, ces jeunes nobles roumains arrivés sur les rives de la Seine iront faire graver leurs armoiries familiales sur leurs bagues, sceaux de poche ou de bureau, sur leur argenterie et d'autres objets usuels ou d'apparat, par des graveurs parisiens, fins connaisseurs de tous les canons de l'art du blason français. C'est de cette période que date la réglementation précise de la plupart des armoiries de la noblesse moldo-valaque qui prit la forme d'une « héraldisation » des emblèmes sigillaires utilisés à travers les siècles par les divers membres d'une même maison noble. Soumis à une sélection et à un choix final, ces éléments emblématiques seront inclus comme meubles héraldiques dans ces armes de libre adoption recréées par leurs possesseurs modernes, en les soumettant maintenant aux exigences de l'art héraldique français contemporain [16].

Mais les influences de cet art ne se sont pas limitées au domaine de l'héraldique boyarde de type privé, elles ont aussi influé sur l'héraldique d'État. Pendant le règne du prince Barbe Stirbey (1849-1853 et 1854-1856), l'aigle valachique, symbole ancestral du pays, a été quelquefois représentée (sur la manchette d'un grand quotidien bucarestois, ou sur des en-têtes de diverses autorités publiques) de façon très ressemblante à l'aigle napoléonienne, c'est-à-dire parée des attributs (les foudres) de ce réputé oiseau héraldique français [17]. Après l'union de la Valachie à la Moldavie en 1859 (pour former ensemble les Principautés-Unies sous le règne du prince Alexandre-Jean Cuza), le cabinet princier de Bucarest, dirigé par le français Arthur Baligot de Beyne [18], contactera, par l'entremise de l'Agence diplomatique des Principautés-Unies à Paris [19], plusieurs héraldistes parisiens de renom dans le but de concevoir de nouvelles armoiries pour le pays roumain.

À partir du mois d'avril 1863 jusqu'au début de l'année suivante, de nombreuses missives entre Paris et Bucarest portent sur les divers projets d'armoiries pour les Principautés-Unies et ces projets sont soumis à l'examen et à l'approbation du prince Cuza [20]. On confia finalement le projet à trois héraldistes français de l'époque du Second Empire dont la compétence était reconnue, à savoir : Tronson du Coudray [21], Froyez [22] et le bien connu d'Hozier [23], peut-être descendant direct d'Ambroise-Louis-Marie d'Hozier (1767-1846), le dernier généalogiste et héraldiste de la Cour royale de France, ou du frère du précédent, le colonel comte d'Hozier (1775-

1846). Grâce au travail de ces héraldistes français, les armes des Principautés roumaines, en usage jusqu'alors, *parti, au 1 à l'aigle valachique et au 2 au rencontre d'aurochs moldave*, devaient être remplacées par *écartelé, au 1 et 4 l'aigle valachique, au 2 et 3 un rencontre d'aurochs, et sur le tout l'écusson, tiercé en fasce* des armes du prince Cuza. Ce projet approuvé par le Prince Régnant, mais reçu avec beaucoup de réserve par les gouvernants du pays[24], n'a jamais pu être légiféré et sanctionné par le Parlement des Principautés-Unies. Cet empêchement était dû, d'une part, à l'opposition de quelques hommes politiques très influents (parmi lesquels, le réputé Michel Kogălniceanu)[25] et, d'autre part, à l'abdication forcée du prince Cuza, survenue en février 1866. Néanmoins les armoiries proposées furent utilisées officieusement de 1864 à 1866 sur les en-têtes, la vaiselle[26] et l'argenterie de la cour princière de Bucarest, et sur les en-têtes de quelques hautes autorités du pays, le Conseil d'État par exemple. Elles furent aussi utilisées par les agences diplomatiques des Principautées-Unies étant accréditées auprès de certaines cours souveraines d'Europe : France, Autriche, Italie, Serbie, *et al*. Cette utilisation à l'extérieur du pays a entraîné l'inclusion de ces armes officieuses dans différents armoriaux français de l'époque[27].

Ces armoiries de source française et constituées d'un écartelé et d'un écusson sur le tout ont servi de base pour les armoiries de la principauté de Roumanie sous le règne suivant de Charles Ier de Hohenzollern. Ce nouveau souverain conserva l'écartelé aux armes du pays, remplaçant seulement l'écusson en cœur les armes du prince Cuza par celles des Hohenzollern : *écartelé d'argent et de sable*. Ces armoiries d'État ont été officiellement légiférées en 1867[28] et sanctionnées en 1872[29] par le Parlement bicaméral roumain.

Les armes du royaume de Roumanie de 1881 s'inspirent directement des précédentes, l'écartelé et l'écusson en cœur étant maintenus tout comme les modifications effectuées en 1872. Ces modifications faisaient que le rencontre d'aurochs moldave et l'aigle valachique des quartiers 3 et 4 étaient remplacés par le lion de l'Olténie et les deux dauphins affrontés des régions maritimes de la Moldavie, devenus, par un transfert de signification à partir de 1878, le symbole de la Doubroudja[30].

Revenant à l'influence de l'art du blason français sur les armoiries de la noblesse roumaine, il faut encore préciser que cette influence s'est perpétuée sans interruption tout au long du XIXe siècle jusqu'à la quatrième décennie du siècle présent. Signalons dans ce sens les riches trophées accompagnant comme ornements extérieurs les armes de beaucoup de familles boyardes moldo-valaques. Ces trophées inspirés de l'héraldique du Premier Empire napoléonien étaient parvenus dans les pays roumains par l'entremise de la noblesse militaire russe. Cette influence d'ordre héraldique a été grandement facilitée par la suite par le Tsar Nicolas Ier et son gouvernement qui souhaitaient au niveau politique l'infiltration des familles les plus notables des deux principautés danubiennes grâce aux mariages d'officiers de l'armée impériale russe à des jeunes filles nobles. Initialement, le but de cette politique visait une domination psychologique menant à l'annexion éventuelle de ces pays à la Russie des Tsars[31]. Les officiers concernés, tous d'origine noble, possédaient des armoiries familiales dont le style, inspiré de l'armorial français de l'Empire ou de la Restauration, a pu faire l'envie des divers membres des familles de grands ou de moyens boyards et les inciter à adopter des insignes héraldiques semblables à celles de leurs nouveaux parents russes. En même temps, l'influence de l'art héraldique français a été renforcée par les contacts directs, dont on a fait mention plus haut. Ultérieurement, l'« héraldisation » de l'armorial moldo-valaque a enteriné définitivement le style de provenance française qui s'était implanté dans le blason roumain. Une preuve évidente en ce sens nous est fournie par l'apparition, en 1918, de l'unique armorial de Roumanie, œuvre du regretté Emmanuel Hagi-Mosco, où les 90 armoiries représentées sont figurées sur des écus *de type français moderne* issu du XIXe siècle[32]. Il faut toutefois remarquer que cette influence ne s'est presque pas exercée sur l'armorial ecclésiastique et a peu touché l'héraldique des districts et des municipalités, restée beaucoup plus fidèle aux traditions héraldiques autochtones[33].

En conclusion, le rôle de l'art héraldique français a été prépondérant dans l'évolution et le développement de l'art du blason roumain à partir du XVIIIe siècle et ce, tant dans le domaine de l'héraldique privée que dans celui de l'héraldique d'État. S'ajoutant aux puissantes influences politiques et culturelles exercées par la France depuis plus de deux siècles sur les pays roumains puis sur la Roumanie, le rayonnement de l'art du blason français a donné à la Roumanie l'occasion de s'inspirer du génie créateur de la France en matière d'armoiries.

## NOTES

1. Cette communication est une reprise, révisée et augmentée, de l'article abordant le même sujet paru dans la revue *Hidalguía* [Madrid], 31, no. 180 (1983), p. 693-701.

2. M. PASTOUREAU, *Traité d'héraldique*, Paris, Picard, 1979, p. 62 (note 16) et p. 63 (note 23).

3. I. N. MĂNESCU, « Stemele lui Dimitrie Cantemir și rolul lor în heraldica țărilor române » [Les armes du prince Démétrius Cantemir et leur place dans l'héraldique des pays roumains], *Revista Arhivelor*, L, vol. 35, no. 3 (1973). p. 465-480, 14 ill. ; *idem*, « Stema cu deviza *Non solum armis* » [Les armoiries accompagnées par la devise « Non solum armis »], *Târgoviște, cetate a culturii românești* [Târgoviște, cité de la culture roumaine], Bucarest (1974), p. 225-233, 6 ill. ; *idem*, « Éléments d'héraldique roumaine dans l'armorial russe », *Actes du XVe congrès international des sciences généalogique et héraldique*, Madrid, t. 2 (1983), p. 5-13, ill.

4. D. CERNOVODEANU, *Știința și arta heraldică în Români*a [La science et l'art héraldiques en Roumanie], Bucarest, 1977, p. 173-174.

5. *Idem*, « Contributions à l'étude des origines lointaines de l'héraldique (Moyen Orient) et son développement du XIIe au XVe siècles à Byzance et dans le Sud-Est européen », *Genealogica et Heraldica, Actes du XIVe congrès international des sciences généalogique et héraldique*, Copenhague (1982), p. 339-358 ; *idem*, « L'Apparition des armoiries dans le Sud-Est européen », *Actes du IIe colloque de l'Académie internationale d'héraldique*, Paris (1983), p. 49-54 ; *idem*, « Les armoiries des souverains du Sud-Est européen dans les rôles d'armes français, anglais et allemands du XIIIe au XVe siècles », *Genealogica et Heraldica. Actes XVIIe congrès international des sciences généalogique et héraldique*, vol. 2, Lisbonne (1990), p. 187-225.

6. *Idem*, *Știința și arta ...*, p. 166-168 ; 172.

7. *Ibid.*, p. 16 et p. 39-40 ; *idem*, « Le processus de la libre adoption dans l'espace Sud-Est européen (XIIIe-XIXe siècles) », communication présentée au IIIe colloque de l'Académie internationale d'héraldique, Montmorency, (19-23 sept. 1983).

8. *Idem*, « Les émissions monétaires armoriées des princes de Valachie aux XIVe et XVe siècles et leurs implications dans l'histoire de cette principauté », *Actes du IXe congrès international de numismatique*, Louvain-la-Neuve (1982), p. 891-903.

9. *Idem*, *Știința și arta...* p. 66-67 et p. 119-120 ; *idem*, « Les reflets des armes royales de Hongrie sur les armes dynastiques des princes de Moldavie (XIVe-XVIe siècles) », *Actes du XVe congrès international des sciences généalogique et héraldique*, t. 1, Madrid (1982), p. 391-428.

10. C. MOISIL, *O pagină de heraldică veche* [Une page d'ancienne héraldique roumaine], Bucarest, 1949, p. 10-

12 ; D. CERNOVODEANU, *Știința și arta...*, p. 41 et p. 165-175.

11. E. RIZO-RANGABÉ, *Livre d'or de la Noblesse phanariote...*Ire édit., Athènes, 1892 et 2e édit., Athènes, 1904. En plus des généalogies de ces familles, l'auteur présente leurs armoiries, dont l'aspect trahit les influences de l'art héraldique français des XVIIIe et XIXe siècles ; D. CERNOVODEANU, *Știința și arta...*, p. 173.

12. *Ibid.*, p. 173-174.

13. *Ibid.*, ainsi que G. BUZDUGAN, « Din activitatea unui vechi atelier de gravură fondat în București în perioada regulamentară » [Sur l'activité d'un ancien atelier de gravure fondé à Bucarest pendant la période du Règlement Organique], *Buletinul Societății Numismatice Române* [Bucarest], 72-73, nos. 126-127 (1978-1979), p. 14-19, 20 ill.

14. D. CERNOVODEANU, *Știința și arta...*, ainsi que G. BUZDUGAN, *op.cit.*

15. D'abord des consuls (à Bucarest à partir de 1796, à Jassy, de 1797), ensuite des agents diplomatiques (à l'époque des Principautés-Unies), enfin des ministres plénipotentiaires à Bucarest depuis le début de 1880. G. A. PORDEA, *Les relations franco-roumaines à travers les âges*, Paris, Poirier-Bottreau édit., 1976, p. 29-30, 47, 69 et 78.

16. D. CERNOVODEANU, *Știința și arta...*, p. 174-175.

17. *Ibid.*, p. 60 et 62, ainsi que la pl. 16, no. 1.

18. G. A. PORDEA, *Les relations franco-roumaines...*, p. 61 et 69.

19. Le chef de cette Agence était à l'époque le colonel Jean Alecsandri, frère de Basile Alecsandri, le grand poète roumain et ministre des Affaires étrangères de Moldavie (janv.-nov. 1859), puis de Valachie (oct. 1859-mai 1860), voir D. BERINDEI, « Guvernele lui Alexandru Ioan Cuza (1859-1866). Liste de miniștri » [Les cabinets ministériels durant le règne d'Alexandre-Jean Cuza. Liste des ministres], *Revista Arhivelor*, Bucarest, II, no. 11 (1959), p. 149-151.

20. Bucarest, Bibliothèque de l'Académie roumaine, mss. roumains, *Archives du prince A.-J. Cuza, cartes II et IX*, contenant la correspondance échangée par le Cabinet princier de Bucarest avec l'Agence diplomatique des Principautés-Unies à Paris pendant les années 1860-1866 ; voir aussi D. CERNOVODEANU, « Contributions à l'étude de l'héraldique d'État des Principautés-Unies roumaines (1859-1866) », *Revue roumaine d'histoire*, tome 16, no. 2 (avril-juin 1977), p. 329 et note 35 ; *idem*, *Știința și arta...*, p. 148.

21. Bucarest, Bibliothèque de l'Académie Roumaine, mss. roumains, *Archives du prince A.-J. Cuza, cartes II*, p. 228-229 et 430.

22. *Ibid.*, p. 236 et 318.

23. *Ibid.*, p. 239.

24. Ces gouvernants craignaient que, par son aspect et par les attributs qu'elles affichaient, les nouvelles armoiries des Principautés-Unies projetées par le cabinet du prince Cuza, ne soient interprétées par les adversaires de l'extérieur du pays roumain, comme une manifestation

(par le langage cryptique de l'art du blason) des velléités d'indépendance complète de ce territoire, encore à l'époque sous la suzeraineté de l'Empire ottoman. Voir en ce sens D. CERNOVODEANU, « Contributions à l'étude de l'héraldique d'État... », p. 329 ; idem, *Ştiinţa şi arta...*, p. 149.

25. *Idem*, « Contributions à l'étude de l'héraldique d'État... », p. 324 et note 19, puis p. 325 ; idem, *Ştiinţa şi arta...*, p. 144-145.

26. Voir au Musée d'histoire de la ville de Bucarest, Section contemporaine, porcelaines, no. inv. 47504, le service en porcelaine de Sèvres, commandé à cette réputée manufacture par le prince Cuza en 1864. Voir aussi D. CERNOVODEANU, *Ştiinţa şi arta...*, p. 344 et pl. 69, no. 5.

27. \*\*\* *Armorial des Souverains*, Paris, Hervé, 1864, 2e série, pl. 110, ainsi que l'*Almanach de Paris. Annuaire général de Diplomatie, de Politique, d'Histoire et de Statistique pour tous les États du globe*. 1re année, Paris, Amyot, 1865, p. 887 ; 2e année, 1866, p. 889 ; 3e année, 1867, p. 875 ; 4e année, 1868, p. 580 ; 5e année, 1869, p. 520. Voir aussi le général P. V. NĂSTUREL, *Stema României* [Les armoiries de la Roumanie], Bucarest, 1892, p. 179-180 ; D. CERNOVODEANU, *op. cit.*, p. 152.

28. Voir la Loi du 30 mars 1867 (conçue et approuvée par la Chambre des députés à cette date), *Monitorul, Jurnal Oficial al României*, no. 75 (2/14 avril 1867) ; Loi du 12/24 avril 1867, sanctionnée, à son tour, par le Sénat de la Roumanie, Ministère des Affaires étrangères (roumain), Service des archives, rôle 67, dossier 55/1872 ; Général P. V. NĂSTUREL, *op. cit.*, p. 185-204 ; S. D. GRECIANU, *Eraldica română. Actele privitoare la stabilirea armeriilor oficiale...* [L'Héraldique roumaine. Les Actes concernant l'établissement des armoiries officielles...],

Bucarest, 1900, p. 11-39 et p. 43-67 ; C. MOISIL, *Stema României* [Les armoiries de la Roumanie], Bucarest, 1931, p. 18-19 ; D. CERNOVODEANU, *op. cit.*, p. 159-160.

29. Voir le projet du Sénat du 11 novembre 1871, adopté par la Chambre des députés le 6 mars 1872, la loi étant promulguée le 11 mars de cette même année, *Monitorul Oficial*, no. 57 (11 mars 1872) ; Général P.V. NĂSTUREL, *op. cit.*, p. 219-221, S. D. GRECIANU, *op. cit.*, p 81-99 ; C. MOISIL, *op. cit.*, p. 19 ; D. CERNOVODEANU, *op. cit.*, p. 161.

30. *Idem*, « Emblematica şi heraldica dobrogeană » [L'emblématique et l'héraldique de la Dobroudja], *Actes du IIe colloque international d'écologie*, Constanţa (1978), p. 267-275, 4 ill.

31. P. CERNOVODEANU, « Strategii matrimoniale ruse în societatea românească a perioadei regulamentare » [Stratégies matrimoniales russes dans la société roumaine de la période du Règlement organique], *Actes du VIIe symposium d'études généalogiques (Jassy 9-12 mai 1996)*, en cours d'édition.

32. E. HAGI-MOSCO, *Steme boiereşti din România* [Armoiries des boyards de Roumanie], Bucarest, 1918, p. 1, 10f. illustrées.

33. D. CERNOVODEANU et I. N. MĂNESCU, *Noile steme ale judeţelor şi municipiilor din R.S. România. Studiu asupra dezvoltării istorice a heraldicii districtuale şi municipale româneşti. Les nouvelles armoiries des districts et des villes municipales de la R.S. de Roumanie. Étude sur le développement historique de l'héraldique de district et de municipalité roumains.* (Texte bilingue, roumain et français), Bucarest, 1974, 218 p., 12 pl. couleurs, 100 ill. noir et blanc.

# TRANSCENDING THE FRONTIERS OF REALITY: THE SIGNIFICANCE OF HERALDIC LEGENDS

Luc Duerloo

During one particularly fierce encounter, an ancestor of the barons van Ittersum made a dreadful tactical mistake. Upon seeing this his liege lord, the count of Holland, cried: "You're an ass!" Ittersum agreed: "Hay my lord, I am a treble ass."[1] Hence he adopted the arms *Argent, three asses' heads caboshed Gules*, which his descendants, living in Overijssel, have borne ever since.[2] It is a bit difficult (to say the least) to believe that this event ever happened. Medieval warfare hardly employed any tactics, and lieges showed a tendency to bash in their lord's brains rather than echo their verbal abuse. Yet the older heraldic literature is full of such stories. One of the most popular handbooks ever published on the subject, Pierre Palliot's *La vraye et parfaite science des armoiries*,[3] is littered with legends and stories relating to the origins of particular coats of arms. Alexander Nisbet's *A System of Heraldry* likewise abundantly proves that Scots have always been great storytellers.[4]

Heraldists of previous generations were not the only ones to take these legends seriously. At the Council of Trent (1545-1563), the French deputation tried to secure precedence over the other delegates by pressing France's claim to be the eldest daughter of the Church. One of the arguments they put forward to impress their fellow prelates was that it was common knowledge that Clovis, the first French king, had received his coat of fleurs-de-lis straight from heaven. By this token God had expressed his pleasure at the king's conversion to Christianity.[5] Similar arguments were still being tabled a century later. Juan Caramuel y Lobkowitz, a Cistercian monk, sometime a titular abbot of Melrose in Scotland[6] and a zealous champion of the Counter Reformation,[7] claimed in his ἩΣΠΑΝΟ ΣΘῶΜΑ that the combined arms of Castile and Leon formed the true image of the first vision of the prophet Ezekiel.[8] One year before the treaty of the Pyrenees (1659), Jean-Jacques Chifflet, physician at the court of Brussels, was still attacking the sacred origins of the fleur-de-lis in his *Lilium Francicvm*. His prin-

cipal argument for denying that the French fleurs-de-lis had anything to do with heavenly things, rested upon the bee-shaped objects recently recovered from Childeric's tomb in Tournay. Adding insult to injury, the book further stated that, given the way the French fleurs-de-lis were traditionally represented, any comparison with the Virgin's lilies was nothing less than an obscenity.[9]

Probably the most bizarre instance in point occurred in Lisbon between 1582 and 1588, when the prioress of the Dominican convent of the Annunciation, sister Maria da Visitacão, claimed to have received stigmata in the shape of the five escutcheons that constitute the principal charge in the arms of Portugal.[10] The association was not unfounded since the legends surrounding the origins of the Portuguese arms interpret the escutcheons as representations of the wounds of Christ.[11] The nun's claim to outward signs of sanctity proved to be political dynamite, when she used her newly acquired reputation as a platform to speak out in favour of the pretensions of Antonio, Grand Prior of Crato, to the Portuguese throne and against the accession of Philip II. In December 1588 the Spanish viceroy-cum-inquisitor-general, cardinal-archduke Albert, and his collaborators at the Holy Office exposed her stratagem and dispatched her to a lifelong exile in Brazil. The severity of the sentence precluded the risk of her making an unwanted come back.

Considering this and other evidence on how seriously heraldic legends used to be taken, it is curious that modern heraldists have paid little if any attention to this aspect of the noble art of arms. Only a handful of scholars have devoted a separate study to the subject. Among the more scholarly heraldic literature of the previous century, only Lower's *Curiosities of Heraldry*[12] and the royal Saxon *Hofrat* Graesse's *Geschlechts-, Namen- und Wappensagen des Adels deutscher Nation* come to mind. For the present century, there is very little outside Winfrid Scott-Giles' *The Romance of Heraldry*. In an effort to complement and enrich what is provided by these three works, the present contribution has been based on a collection of some 200 legends and fanciful stories gathered from heraldic treatises, armorials, antiquarian tracts, local histories and occasionally guidebooks. Although this collection is a limited sample of the legends that have been woven around armorial bearings, it does allow the formulation of a number of considerations and conclusions regarding heraldic legends.

Upon analysing this documentation one is struck with the ease with which the basic plot of one heraldic legend is adapted to the needs of another. A fine example of such a recurring and reusable *topos* is associated with the arms of Aragon. According to tradition King Charles the Bald of France came across the dying Count of Barcelona after one bloody battle against the Normans. Observing that the man simply used a plain golden shield and eager to record his valour for posterity, the King dipped the fingers of his right hand into the moribund's wounds and smeared four bloody stripes on the count's shield. Even though such behaviour would nowadays be reckoned a war crime, it is reputed to have been taken as a mark of esteem and is supposed to have given rise to the well-known arms of Aragon: *Or, four pales Gules.* [13] All this sounds grand, yet any Welshman will tell you that it was Llewellyn ap Ynyr, Lord of Yale in county Denbigh, who was granted the arms *paly of eight Argent and Gules* by his Prince, Gryffyd ap Madoc, Lord of Dinas Bran, for the former's contribution to the battle of Corwen or Crogen or whatever. The Prince struck upon the design of these arms when "Llewellyn accidentally drew his left hand, smeared with blood, across his sword, leaving four bloodstains upon it." [14] However, Italians will assure you that the Neapolitan house of Caraffa that gave pope Paul IV to the Church, derives its coat of arms, *Gules, three bars Argent,* from yet another similar incident. [15] Alongside the more mystique interpretations that were put forth, [16] the most common explanation for the origins of the arms of Austria goes along similar lines. As the story goes, Margrave Leopold II came home one day after a terrible battle in which he had killed so many infidels that his originally white surcoat looked to have been entirely soaked in blood. Upon untying his sword-belt however, he found that a narrow white band had been preserved underneath. Seeing this as a mark of divine protection, he

decided that his arms would henceforth be *Gules, a fess Argent.* [17] The Styrian counts and later princes of Starhemberg sported their variation on the theme by claiming that the bottom half of their original arms, *per fess Argent and Gules, in chief a panther issuant Azure, crowned and incensed Or,* recalled an encounter with a band of unfortunate Saracens. [18] The adaptation of these *topos* come full circle with the legend that relates the origin of the coat born by the dukes of Arenberg: *Gules, three medlar flowers Or.* In this version emperor Henry I came across the wounded Hartmann von Arberch after one grisly fight against Hungarian invaders. Noticing that the knight's shield was wholly tainted with blood and that three flowers from the medlar tree under which he lay dying had fallen unto it, the emperor decreed that henceforth Hartmann's descendants would use this device as a mark of distinction. [19] One may simply dismiss these stories by stating that Emperor Henry I, Charles the Bald and Margrave Leopold II lived before heraldry had been invented. But that would be missing the point. The moral to be drawn from the different variations on this theme is that truly honourable arms are acquired by shedding one's blood in battle, or that of one's adversaries, while fighting for one's lord and sovereign.

This message was certainly echoed when Edward Lake was granted a genuine augmentation of arms for the distinguished conduct he displayed when defending the king's cause against the supporters of Parliament at the battle of Edge Hill (1642). According to his letters patent "he received sixteen wounds to the extreme hazard of his life, and his left arm being then disabled by a shot, he held his bridle in his teeth." [20] The grant added a first quarter *Gules, a dexter arm in armour embowed, the hand holding a sword erect all proper, thereto affixed a banner Argent, on a cross between sixteen escutcheons Gules, a lion passant guardant Or,* and an additional crest showing the grantee sallying towards the enemy while biting the bridle of his horse. [21]

The battlefield is certainly the place where heraldic fact and fiction meet. The overwhelming majority of heraldic legends are set in a martial environment. The stock in trade is more or less as in the following story. A member of the House of de Soissons-Moreul or Morel had served the French king well in an encounter. Eager to reward him for his services, the king asked the knight which favour he should grant him. The valiant knight refused to accept a material reward and, instead, prayed the king for the privilege to bear a single fleur-de-lis in his arms. "Nay," replied the king, "you shall have a million." In commemoration of this event, the family bore *Azure, semy of lis Or, a demi-lion Gules* as its coat of arms, the *mi-lion* providing a rather pleasant pun on the *million* of lilies awarded by the king.[22] Just as middle-of-the-road is the legend surrounding the name and arms of Tripp of Huntspill in the county of Somerset. Their blazon reads: *Gules, a scalding ladder in bend between six cross-crosslets Or.* Authoritative writers have it that:

this atchievment was given unto my Lord Howard's fifth son at ye siege of Bullogne. King Harry ye Vth being there, ask'd how they took ye town and castle. Howard answered: 'I tripp'd up ye walls'. Saith the king: 'Tripp shall be thy name and no longer Howard' and honoured him with ye scalding ladder for his bend.[23]

Taking things at face values, both knight, seemed particularly inspired by the virtue of modesty. Still these are strange manifestations of modesty, as one of the knights lays claim to a grand lineage and both are seen as valuable and esteemed lieges, rubbing shoulders with their princes at crucial junctures of their reigns.

The latter element features in almost every heraldic legend. The credibility of the story is enhanced by putting it in a historical context that can be easily recognized. A small squadron of valiant knights gained the right to bear a particular coat of arms during the pre-heraldic days of wandering nations. The instances of Aragon and Arenberg have already been mentioned. The Medicis pretended that their original six torteaus recalled the imprints left by the mace of the Langobardic giant Mugel on the shield of Sir Everard de Medici, a paladin of Charlemagne.[24] The chief of the Scottish House of Dalzell or Dalziell is reputed to bear *Sable, a naked man with his arms extended proper*, in recognition of the recovery of the corpse of King Kenneth III after he had been killed by the Picts.[25] The same king fights off the Danes in what is probably the most complete heraldic legend on record. This

story, which is cherished by the Earls of Errol, merits to be quoted as it offers a full explanation of the Hay name, arms, crest, supporters, motto and property:

In the reign of Kenneth III, about 980 the Danes, having invaded Scotland, were encountered by that king near Loncarty in Perth shire. The Scots at first gave way and fled through a narrow pass, where they were stopped by a countryman of great strength and courage and his two sons with no other weapons than the yokes of their ploughs. Upbraiding the fugitives for their cowardice, he succeeded in rallying them. The battle was renewed and the Danes totally discomfitted. It is said that after the victory was obtained, the old man lying on the ground, wounded and fatigued, cried 'Hay, Hay', which word became the surname of his posterity. The king, as a reward for his signal service, gave him as much land in the Carse of Gowrie as a falcon should fly over before it settled. And a falcon being accordingly let off, flew over an extent of ground six miles in length, afterwards called Errol, and lighted on a stone still called Falconstone. The king also assigned three shields or escutcheons for the arms of the family to intimate that the father and the two sons had been the three fortunate shields of Scotland.[26]

The Crusades presented another great opportunity to secure a dashing coat of arms. One story tells how Godfrey of Bouillon, Duke of Lorraine and leader of the First Crusade, created new arms for his duchy by piercing three eagles with just one arrow while hunting underneath the walls of the besieged Jerusalem. As a result, his successors to the duchy have borne *Or, on a bend Gules, three allerions Argent*. While pursuing the Christian war effort, his brother Baldwin, Count of Boulogne and Auvergne, is said to have adopted a gonfalon in his arms in remembrance of the ensign the pope had sent to prop up the crusading army.[27] Legend has it that, shortly after, a major row had erupted between the Count of Flanders and Count of Jülich, the former had killed the king of Albania en route to Palestine and had taken over his arms: *Or, a lion rampant Sable, armed and langued Gules.*

The son of the deceased King, however, had managed to wrest the arms from the Count of Flanders, only to be disposed of by the Count of Jülich, who accordingly felt empowered to bear the same arms. In the end he is reported to have settled for: *Or, a lion rampant Sable, armed and langued Argent.*[28] The shield of the noble House of d'Anglure is said to refer to the terms upon which one crusading ancestor was released from captivity,[29] while the crest of Sir Isaac Newton proclaimed that one of his predecessors had captured an eastern prince at the battle of Ascalon.[30] Other heraldic legends pertaining to English families and set in the Near East are those of the Houses of de Vere, Earls of Oxford,[31] and Fowler of Foxley in Buckinghamshire.[32]

A third great way to pick up a dazzling shield is by participating in one of the battles that changed the course of history. Ancestral deeds performed at the battle of Hastings (1066) are supposed to be recalled in the arms of Fortescue, Ferrers and Saint John.[33] The no-less dramatic encounter of Bouvines (1214) has left a mark on the arms of de Montmorency[34] and d'Estaing.[35] Some of the caltraps used to cripple the English cavalry at Bannockburn (1314), still lie scattered upon the Earl of Perth's compartment.[36] Not only the legend surrounding the feathers of the prince of Wales,[37] but also the crest of de la Bere[38] and the augmentation granted in 1575 to Sir Peter Legh of Lyme[39] hark back to the Battle of Crécy (1346). The capture of King John II of France at the Battle of Poitiers (1356) is commemorated in the achievements of de la Warr[40] and Pelham,[41] while the blood spilt at Agincourt (1415) stuck to the arms of John de Wodehouse.[42] A rather late, yet almost unbelievable story, concerns the bull's scalp crest of Cheney and is set amidst the turmoil of Bosworth (1485).

> Tradition records that this crest was granted by Henry VII to Sir John, afterwards baron Cheney, KG, in remembrance of his having, on the field of Bosworth, after a personal encounter with king Richard, cut the skull and horns of the hide off an ox which chanced to be near, and fixed them upon his head to supply the loss of the upper part of his helmet.[43]

The moral intended in this story is probably that one should never sally forth without having an ox's hide close at hand.

Other heraldic legends prefer to shun these well-known and amply documented events and go for rather more *flou artistique* by staging the action in one of the endemic conflicts that festered on the fringe of medieval Europe. The endless wars between Scots and Englishmen are the setting of the legend explaining the coat of Binning of Easter Binning, *Argent, on a bend engrailed Sable, a waggon of the field.* "One of this family is said to have, *temp.* David II, gone in a waggon covered with hay and surprised and taken from the English the castle of Linlithgow."[44] On the other side of the border, the unremitting service performed by one forebear in the campaigns against John Balliol, King of Scots, won the family of Dodge of Stopford in Cheshire the right to exhibit in their arms *a woman's dugge or breast distilling drops of milk proper.*[45] The Lloyds of Plymog in county Denbigh claim the three Englishmen's heads in their arms stand for the three Sassenach commanders slain by their ancestor Ednyfed Vychan, lord of Bryngenigle.[46] Centuries of strife for the reconquest of Spain are reflected in the legends explaining the origins of the arms of Navarre, Leon, Castile and Portugal.[47] It is perhaps hazardous to add to this category the story elucidating the arms of Douglas, *Argent, a human heart Gules, regally crowned Or, on a chief Azure, tree mullets of the field.* Some zealous clansmen will certainly rise and point out that Froissart mentions the story in his chronicles. To them this mention provides ample proof that Sir James Douglas did indeed set out on a pilgrimage to the Holy Land at the death of King Robert Bruce (1329), with the intent of depositing the King's heart in the church of the Holy Sepulchre. They will maintain that he decided to interrupt his journey in Spain and assist the beleaguered Castilians in their campaigns against the Moorish king of Grenada. In one encounter his party of dauntless Scotsmen was isolated and surrounded. Realizing that his position was desperate, Sir James fulfilled King Robert's lifelong ambition of leading an army against the infidel, by throwing the casket that contained the King's heart into the Moorish ranks. By some mysterious contrivance, the heart was later returned to Melrose Abbey, where it has recently been excavated. Any Douglas would agree that the Lockharts, who bear duly differenced versions of *Argent, a human heart Gules, within a fetter lock Sable, on a chief Azure, three boar's heads erased of the first,* have tried to gatecrash their coat of arms into the story by claiming a lineal descent from the man who bore the casket. However, they would be much less eager to grant that Froissart was not a contemporary witness to the events.[48]

In the legend attached to the arms of Walcot of Walcot in Shropshire, *Argent, a chevron between three chess rooks Ermine*, a mock duel is staged. The main actor is one John Walcot, of whom an old parchment relates that "playinge at the chesse with Henry the Fifth, kinge of Englande, he gave hym the checke matte with the rouke, whereupon the kinge changed his coate of armes, which was a crosse with flower de lures, and gave him the rouke as a remembrance."[49] The Anglo-French war of *cuisines* is treasured in the tale explaining the arms of Leche of Chatsworth county Derby, *Ermine, on a chief indented Gules, three ducal coronets Or*. Here yet another old parchment in slightly more readable spelling reveals that:

> one of this auncient family living in Berkshire near Windsor, in ye time of King Edward III, entertained and feasted three kinges in his house: one ye king of England, ye king of France and ye king of Scots; which two kings were at that time prisoners to king Edward. Which king Edward, to requite his good entertainment and other favours, gave him three crowns on his chief indented Gules, ye field Ermine.[50]

The black leg that features in the arms of the 4th noble tribe of Wales alludes to yet another form of contest. Cilmin Troed-ddu or Cilmin Black Foot, founder of the tribe, is believed to have cheated a group of wizards out of their book of magic. They chased him across the mountains of Snowdonia, but could not hurt him unless he touched running water. While jumping over a brook, one of Cilmin's feet accidentally touched the surface and immediately turned black. For the remainder of his days, he could show his blackened foot as token of his prowess and his descendants have done so ever since.[51]

Amidst all this open or thinly veiled strife, women hardly ever appear. When they do, they tend to be as sinewy and bellicose as their male counterparts. The curious crest of Dudley of Clapton in Northamptonshire, *on a ducal coronet Or, a woman's head wearing a helmet, the hair dishevelled and, throat latch loose proper*, tends to

prove this. Sir Bernard Burke's view on this is based on yet another unidentified manuscript:

> The father of Agnes Hotot, the great heiress who married Dudley, having a dispute with one Ringsdale about the title to a piece of land, the competitors agreed to meet on the debatable ground and decide the affair by combat. Hotot, on the day appointed, was laid up with illness, but his daughter Agnes, rather than the land should be lost, armed herself cap-a-pie and mounting her father's steed, went and encountered Ringsdale, whom, after a stubborn contest, she unhorsed. And when he was on the ground, she loosened her throat latch, lifted up her helmet and let down her hair about her shoulders, thus discovering her sex. In commemoration of this exploit, the crest of the female head was ever afterwards used.[52]

None other than Otto von Bismarck, the Iron Chancellor, was wont to tell his guests that the rather unusual composition of his coat of arms, *Azure, on three nettle-leaves in pall Argent, a trefoil Or*, was similarly due to a bellicose great-great-aunt of his. The woman was wooed by a prince of the Wends, but rejected his overtures. Angered by this, the prince swore that he would have the flower of her virginity (trefoil in the text), if need be by force. One day when her father was out, the prince sneaked into the castle and took the maiden captive. Holding her in his arms, the prince cried: "Your trefoil will not hurt me." The maiden thereupon stabbed him in the heart with the dagger she always kept close at hand and replied: "Then feel the sting of my nettle-leaf."[53]

In the realm of heraldic legends, the adversary need not be human, nor does man need to be victorious. Adversial confrontation is by itself the main ingredient. "Thus a second son of Struan Robertson, for killing a wolf in Stocket Forest by a dirk in the king's presence, got the name of Skene, which signifies a dirk in Irish, and three dirk points in pale for his arms." That is at any rate what a number of his heirs, bearing *Gules, three skenes or daggers paleways in fess Argent, hilted and pommelled Or, on the point of each a wolf's head couped Or*, wanted people to believe.[54] Percival Cresacre, ancestor of the Cresacres of Barnborough county York, is supposed to have been slain by a wild cat and this incident is said to have inspired the family crest.[55] In what could be a medieval version of Chaplin's Modern Times, the heraldic legend of the Brandenburg von Wedells pits man against contemporary technology. The story relates that, in the course of a hunt, the daughter of the then king of Brandenburg was caught in the wheel of a mill. Apprehending the danger, the miller's man stopped the wheel with his bare hands in the nick of time, losing both his arms in the process. Utterly grateful that the man had saved his beloved daughter, the king allowed him to marry her, ennobled him and granted him a coat *Or, a millwheel Sable and an armless man issuant* as a crest. It is not without irony that the poor man lost his arms to get a coat of arms in return.[56]

In a number of instances animals help man in overcoming a hostile environment. The crest of the Lathoms of Lathom county Lancaster, which was subsequently taken up by their heirs the Stanleys Earls of Derby, consists of an eagle holding a swaddled infant between its claws. According to the records of the visitation of Lancaster, this odd combination commemorates the baby that was adopted into the family after it had been found in an eagle's nest on the estate.[57] The Dukes of Leinster are said to have chosen monkeys for their crest and supporters as a tribute to the monkey that rescued a young Fitzgerald from a fire in one of their castles.[58] The arms and crest attributed to Celynin of Llwydiarth in Montgomery shire display a goat and an infant beneath a holly tree and likewise refer to the nigh mythological rescue of one of his ancestors.[59] The Scots go even further by pretending that their kingdom was once rescued by an even pricklier plant. Trying to surprise King Malcolm I in Stains Castle, a party of Danes approached the walls barefooted and under the cover of darkness. While attempting to swim across the moat, they discovered to their dismay that it was dry and full of thistles. Their shrieks and yells alarmed the defenders, who had no trouble chasing them away.[60]

In this case, one readily understands that the Scottish thistles were a highly cost-effective version of the vigilant geese the Romans kept at the Capitol. Nor will anyone who is acquainted with classical mythology fail to see that Celynin's goat was borrowed from the myths surrounding the youth of Zeus on Crete. And everyone knows that

infants found and fostered by otherwise wild animals have been quite fashionable since the days of Romulus and Remus. The treasure-house of antique myths and stories is certainly one of the principal sources of *topoi* for heraldic legends. The kings of Poland in any case proved they knew their classics when devising an explanation for their arms. Drawing upon Roman techniques of predicting the future, they stated that a nest of white-feathered eagles, a highly potent omen, was uncovered as the foundation-stone of the first Polish city was laid. Recognizing the importance of this omen, the kings adopted a white eagle in their arms.[61] Even old Germanic mythology is found in these legends. The Franconian noble House of Stein von Altenstein, and its Belgian branch Stein d'Altenstein, has claimed that their arms, *Gules, three hammers Or*, prove their descent from Thor, the god of thunder.[62] Drawing from similar sources, the Borgia pope delighted in spreading the rumour that the bull in his arms represented Apis and denoted kinship with the Egyptian god Osiris.

Christian traditions are a second major source of inspiration. In a series outnumbering Rambo movies, the apparition of the Cross to Constantine gives rise to numerous sequels. The saltire of Saint Andrew was sighted in the skies during a battle between Scots and Picts (818). While besieging Jerusalem (1099), the knights of Lorraine caught the first glimpse of what was to become the famous cross of Lorraine.[63] The battle of Ourique (1139) is said to have given rise to the escutcheons in the arms of Portugal.[64] In their fight against the heathen Estonians (1219), the Danish army took courage from seeing the apparition of the Danebrog.[65] Atmospherical conditions at the battle of Bayonne (1451) are reputed to have provided the white cross that was to become so typical for French military standards.[66] And as late as 1641, the Spanish army in the Netherlands claimed to have seen a white cross transform itself into the red ragged saltire that traditionally adorned the regimental flags of the *tercios*.[67] In a curious variation on this theme, the dukes of Brittany claimed that their plain ermine coat derived from the ermine mantle worn by the Virgin Mary during an apparition.[68] Both the Montmorencys[69] and the O'Donnells[70] claim to have received the crosses that adorn their arms when their forbears converted to Christianity. The latter even managed to have this feat recorded in some versions of the life of

Saint Patrick. The legends surrounding the life of Saint Elizabeth provided the topic for the story relating to the arms of the House of Lalaing, *Gules, ten lozenges conjoined 3,3,3, 1 Argent*. One particularly devout ancestress had to conceal the alms she gave the poor from her thrifty husband. One day during the Christmas-season, however, he noticed how she sneaked away from the table with an apron full of brown biscuits. He stopped her en route to the parish poor and demanded that she show him the content of her apron. While doing so, it was discovered that the biscuits had miraculously turned white. The thrifty husband thereupon repented his lack of humanity. In commemoration of the miracle and so as to exhort his descendants to show compassion to those less fortunate, he furthermore decided that ten white biscuits would henceforth adorn the arms of the family. [71]

Folklore and popular beliefs have also provided heraldic legends with several *topoi*. Like in the case of Cilmin Troed-ddu, a great many deal with various confrontations with the supernatural. The swan crests and badges adopted by medieval knights to denote their supposed descent from the Swan Knight are well documented. [72] The heraldic legend sported by the scions of the Dutch House of Arkel are a peculiar variation on this theme. [73] Descendants of Moreiddig Warwyn or Moreiddig Fair Neck bear *Sable, three boys' heads couped at the shoulders proper, having snakes wreathed around their necks Vert*. They are supposed to have chosen this device because their forbear was born with an odd birthmark that was ascribed to the unfortunate encounter of his pregnant mother with an adder. [74] The Provençale family de Porcelet, whose arms are *Or, a boar passant Sable*, claims it has a similar origin. One of their kin had the imprudence to turn away an old beggar-woman and was cursed by the witch. As she was pregnant at the time, the curse made her give birth to as many children as the first animal that came her way. As it turned out she met a pig and was consequently delivered of a no less than nine sons, [75] which must have made her think twice before refusing alms to anyone else.

It is most revealing that, in spite of bearing obviously canting arms, a family such as the de Porcelets felt the need to device a heraldic legend that would enhance the respectability of their straightforward and rather rustic coat of arms. After all, enhancing prestige and reputations is what heraldic legends are all about. Drawing upon *topoi* taken from antiquity and Christian traditions and folklore, dynasties and families that had risen to prominence contrived stories that pretended to explain the significance of their armorial bearings. Even if a grain of truth can be discerned in some of these stories, their purpose is not to enlighten but to shroud. Their hidden message is in nearly all cases either a claim to divine election or an assertion of old lineage by pretending to princely favour in some distant past. As these two purposes roughly coincide with the divide between sovereign dynasties and non-sovereign noble houses, it is safe to assume that the majority of heraldic legends came into circulation in the course of the establishment of the dynastic state. In this process they underscored the dynasties' claims to rule by divine right and the grandees pretence to stand well above the recently risen gentry or lesser nobility. By setting the heraldic legends in almost exclusively martial surroundings, they indicate how crucial the theme of conflict was in the value systems that underlaid the process of heraldic design in the late Middle Ages and early modern period.

## NOTES

1. H. W. M. J. KITS NIEUWENKAMP, *Encyclopedie van de Heraldiek* (Amsterdam: Elsevier pocker, A37, 1961), p. 92.

2. HOGE RAAD VAN ADEL, *De Nederlandse Adel, Besluiten en Wapenbeschrijvingen* (The Hague: 1989), p. 126.

3. PIERRE PALLIOT, *La vraye et parfaite science des armoiries ov l'indice armorial de feu maistre Lovvan Géliot* (Dijon: 1660).

4. ALEXANDER NISBET, *A System of Heraldry, speculative and practical with the true art of blazon according to the most approved heralds in Europe* (London: 1816).

5. W. SCOTT-GILES, *The Romance of Heraldry* (London: 1957), p. 99.

6. D. IMHOF (ed.), *De Boekillustratie ten tijde van de Moretussen* (Antwerp: 1996), p. 134-135.

7. R. J. W. EVANS, *The Making of the Habsburg Monarchy 1550-1700, An Interpretation* (Oxford: 1979), *passim.*

8. LUC DUERLOO, "Caramuel in Defence of the Spanish Monarchy," in *Rebelión y Resistencia en el Mundo Hispánico del Siglo XVII*, WERNER THOMAS AND BART DE GROOF, ed., *Avisos de Flandes, I. Leuven, 1992*, p. 305-306; JUAN CARAMUEL Y LOBKOWITZ, 'HΣΠANOΣΘὼMA, *Declaración mystica de las armas de España* (Brussels: 1636).

9. D. IMHOF (ed.), *op. cit.*, p. 169-170; JEAN-JACQUES CHIFFLET, *Lilium Francicvm, veritate historica, botanica et heraldica illustratvm* (Antwerp: 1658).

10. RICHARD L. KAGAN, *Lucrecia's Dreams. Politics and Prophecy in Sixteenth-Century Spain* (Berkeley: n.d.), p. 7.

11. PIERRE PALLIOT, *op. cit.*, p. 49-50.

12. M. A. LOWER, *Curiosities of Heraldry* (London: 1845).

13. CLAUDE F. MÉNESTRIER, *La méthode royale, facile et historique du blason, avec l'origine des armes de plus illvstres états et familles de l'Europe* (Paris: 1671), p. 231.

14. BERNARD BURKE, *The General Armory of England, Scotland, Ireland and Wales* (2nd ed., London: 1884), p. 613.

15. CLAUDE F. MENESTRIER, *Origine des armoiries* (Paris: 1679), p. 65.

16. ELISABETH KOVÁCS, "Der heilige Leopold und die Staatsmystik der Habsburger," in: RÖHRIG, FLORIDUS and STANGLER, GOTTFRIED, (ed.), *Der heilige Leopold. Landesfürst und Staatssymbol* (Vienna: 1985), p. 80. [PAKOSTA, KARL], *Die Herkunft des rotweißroten Bindenschilden*. Vienna, 1976.

17. PIERRE PALLIOT, *op. cit.*, p. 53.

18. JOHANN SCHWERDLING, *Geschichte des uralten und seit Jahrhunderten um Landesfürst und Vaterland höchst verdienten theils fürstlich, theils gräflichen Hauses Starhemberg* (Linz: 1830), p. 33-34.

19. *Die Arenberger. Geschichte einer europäischen Dynastie.* I: *Die Arenberger in der Eifel* (Koblenz: 1987), p. 4.

20. W. SCOTT-GILES, *op. cit.*, p. 181.

21. BERNARD BURKE, *op. cit.*, p. 578.

22. PIERRE PALLIOT, *op. cit.*, p. 429.

23. BERNARD BURKE, *op. cit.*, p. 1031.

24. CLAUDE F. MÉNESTRIER, *La méthode royale . . .*, p. 244.

25. ARTHUR CHARLES FOX-DAVIES, *A Complete Guide to Heraldry* (2nd ed., London: 1929), p. 165.

26. BERNARD BURKE, *op. cit.*, p. 470.

27. PIERRE PALLIOT, *op. cit.*, p. 50, 358.

28. E. WARLOP, "Oud Vlaenderen en de zwarte leeuw op gouden veld," in *Miscellanea archivistica*, XXVIII (1980), p. 7.

29. D. L. GALBREATH and LÉON JÉQUIER, *Manuel du blason* (2nd ed., Lausanne: 1977), p. 78.

30. BERNARD BURKE, *op. cit.*, p. 731.

31. W. SCOTT-GILES, *op. cit.*, p. 63-64.

32. BERNARD BURKE, *op. cit.*, p. 372.

33. W. SCOTT-GILES, *op. cit.*, p. 38.

34. PIERRE PALLIOT, *op. cit.*, p. 19.

35. CLAUDE F. MÉNESTRIER, *La méthode royale . . .*, p. 209.

36. W. SCOTT-GILES, *op. cit.*, p. 82.

37. CECIL R. HUMPHERY-SMITH, "Feathers," in: *Genealogica & Heraldica, Report of the 14th International Congress of Genealogical and Heraldic Sciences in Copenhagen*, SVEN TITO ACHEN (ed.) (Copenhagen: 1982), p. 299.

38. W. SCOTT-GILES, *op. cit.*, p. 104.

39. THOMAS WOODCOCK and JOHN MARTIN ROBINSON, *The Oxford Guide to Heraldry* (Oxford: 1988), p. 69.

40. W. SCOTT-GILES, *op. cit.*, p. 104-105.

41. THOMAS WOODCOCK and JOHN MARTIN ROBINSON,

*op. cit.*, p. 70.

42. W. SCOTT-GILES, *op. cit.*, p. 106.

43. BERNARD BURKE, *op. cit.*, p. 189.

44. *Ibidem*, p. 83.

45. RODNEY DENNYS, *The Heraldic Imagination* (London: 1975), p. 131.

46. BERNARD BURKE, *op. cit.*, p. xxx-viii.

47. PIERRE PALLIOT, *op. cit.*, p. 45-50.

48. W. SCOTT-GILES, *op. cit.*, p. 83-85.

49. BERNARD BURKE, *op. cit.*, p. 1063.

50. *Ibidem*, p. 592.

51. FRANCIS JONES, "The Royal and Noble Families," in WAGNER, ANTHONY, A.O., *Royal and Princely Heraldry in Wales* (London: [1969]), p. 11-12.

52. BERNARD BURKE, *op. cit.*, p. 303.

53. J. G. T. GRAESSE, *Geschlechts-, Namen- und Wappensagen des Adels deutscher Nation* (Dresden: 1876), p. 15-16.

54. BERNARD BURKE, *op. cit.*, p. 930.

55. *Ibidem*, p. 242.

56. J. G. T. GRAESSE, *op. cit.*, p. 178.

57. BERNARD BURKE, *op. cit.*, p. 586.

58. ARTHUR CHARLES FOX-DAVIES, *op. cit.*, p. 215.

59. FRANCIS JONES, *loc. cit.*, p. 16-17.

60. W. SCOTT-GILES, *op. cit.*, p. 175-176.

61. PIERRE PALLIOT, *op. cit.*, p. 53.

62. J. G. T. GRAESSE, *op. cit.*, p. 160.

63. JEAN LE FÉRON, *Le simbol des armoiries de France, d'Escoce et de Lorraine* (Paris: 1555), 33-34.

64. HERVÉ PINOTEAU, "Un difficile problème, celui de l'origine des armes de Portugal," in *XV Congreso internacional de las ciencias genealógica y heráldica* (Madrid: [1983]), III, p. 350-356.

65. WITHNEY SMITH, *Spectrum vlaggenboek* (Utrecht: 1976), p. 64.

66. JEAN LE FÉRON, *op. cit.*, 35.

67. JULES CHIFFLET, *Crux Andreana victrix sev de cruce burgundica coelitus in Ariensi obsidione visa commentarius* (Antwerp: 1642), p. 10-12.

68. PIERRE PALLIOT, *op. cit.*, p. 43.

69. CLAUDE F. MÉNESTRIER, *La méthode royale . . .*, p. 202.

70. BERNARD BURKE, *op. cit.*, p. 747.

71. J. SCHYRGENS, *Berlaymont, Le cloistre de la Reyne de tous les Saints* (Brussels: 1928), p. 3-4.

72. ANTHONY WAGNER, "The Swan Badge and the Swan Knight," *Archeologia*, 97 (1959), p. 127-188.

73. KL. SIERKSMA, *De Gemeentewapens van Nederland* (Utrecht: Prisma, DI., 1968), p. 165-166.

74. FRANCIS JONES, *loc. cit.*, p. 17.

75. CLAUDE F. MÉNESTRIER, *La méthode royale . . .*, p. 213.

# FALLING LEAVES [1]

Cecil R. Humphery-Smith

The pages of Siebmacher[2] and of Rietstap[3] abound with blazons of coats of arms with leaves in them. The former has its own splendid illustrations in the several editions and the latter is illustrated in Rolland[4] and accompanied by later supplements. Scanning the earlier illustrated works of Petra Sancta[5] one finds leaves of strawberry, poplar, plane, stinging-nettle, *nenuphar* and oak, apart from the formal trefoils, quatrefoils and so on [FIGURE 1]. Invariably these are in threes sometimes pall-wise.

The English rolls of arms of the 13th century[6] provide their clutch of foils and undesignated leaves, of which many of the species can be determined by applying the pun. Can John Lisle's *Or, a chevron between three leaves Gules* allude to any but lime in autumn colours [FIGURE 2]?[7] Adam Emerrug's chief can only bear elm leaves[8] and Hugh Morieus's perhaps mulberry [FIGURE 3].[9] But, no others appear at this period. By the 16th and 17th centuries, however, the picture has changed; leaves fall on and around the ordinaries. A single aspen leaf for ASPINALL, a betony leaf for BETTY, a rose leaf for BENDLISE, two leaves of laurel or perhaps tansy for TANSLEY and two of oak for JACK. Three apple leaves for APLETON, of aspen for COGAN, burdock for NOBLE, fern for VERNAI, fig for GREVES, holly for IRWIN and vine or ground wort for WORTFORD, with *Azure, three woodbine leaves Argent* for BROOME.

William Linwood, Bishop of St. David's is remembered in glass at Caius College, Oxford, bearing *Argent, a chevron between three linden leaves Vert*; Thomas Waller, commemorated in hall glass at Grays Inn, had three walnut leaves in bend [FIGURE 4]. The Leveson tomb at St. Bartholomew the Great in Smithfield bears the arms *Azure, three bay leaves Or* [FIGURE 5]; Thomas Hollingsworth (temp. Edward V) and John Hollingsworth a century later each had three holly leaves [FIGURE 6]; Hezilrigg had three presumably hazel leaves and Foulis, for whom any leaf would have been appropriate, usually had holly or bay [FIGURES 7-8].

A multitude of leaves then appears with four pairs of lime leaves pendant for GROVE, five holly leaves in saltire for WOODWARD, six oak leaves in pairs for BALDWN and ten elm leaves for ELMES. And here comes the fall.

While the delightful coat for the Reverend Dr. William Beloe, F.S.A., Rector of All Hallows and Prebendary of Lincoln, the translator of Herodotus, *Argent semy of laurel leaves proper and fretty Sable within a bordure Azure charged with nine mullets of six points Or* seems to be good heraldry, record of a grant has not been discovered. Perhaps I have missed it as not being the easiest to trace through the ordinaries. If so, I must apologize to him, for his motto declares his good sentiments and clear conscience: VITA ET PECTORE PURO. Heralds were ever bad Latinists, but I suspect they would have known not only how to distinguish *pectus* from *cor* or animus, but also that this quotation derived from Horace.

As for the rest of those cited, they were apparently all the product of the stationers, coach painters, amateur armorists, hatchment makers, engravers and silversmiths, effectively bucket-shop heraldry from before 1700. How are the mighty fallen?

Several attempts have been made to catalogue sources for the study of the records of the heralds' visitations of the 16th and 17th centuries, which, at least in principle, did much to try to bring order back into heraldic usage in England and Wales. Some account of how the process failed has been demonstrated recently by John Beddels, Howard Pursuivant Extraordinary.[10] The records of the visitations represent the most important source of genealogical information on English and Welsh families for one of the most difficult periods of history when research into family histories is confused by loss of records, migrations, changing fortunes and allegiances. They also provide a remarkable account of heraldic design during a period when class structures were being intermingled and *nouveaux riches* of Tudor mercantile families were rising into the arena of the gentry and nobility. The heralds showed their sense of fun and heraldry is a subject for amusement as well as serious scholarship. They used many devises to lampoon the upstarts of those times.

While it is assumed that the visitations made by the heralds were only concerned with those having coats of arms and landed estates and, therefore, unlikely to be of assistance to folk tracing the ancestries of "ordinary people" (whatever that may mean), this is largely an erroneous belief. The origins of the Common Man in English society so impinge upon all walks of life that every student of genealogy is bound to discover a wealth of fact and valuable clues within these sources.

As well as the notes of evidence, sketches of coats of arms, seals and monuments, church windows, banners, brasses, and vivid descriptions of topography and social life, this remarkable collection contains an important body of genealogical material and pedigrees for families of the 16th and 17th centuries taken down contemporaneously before and after the Reformation and before the Civil War and after the Restoration. Those are significant times when Catholic, Protestant, Reformer, Puritan, Cavalier or Roundhead, Kingsman or Parliamentarian, might be regarded as treacherous. Such individuals might therefore find themselves excluded from official lists, the pedigrees of the heralds' visitations included.

With previous listings[11] on the subject incomplete and new material emerging over the past 30 years, I have collected material to produce a new and comprehensive catalogue of the visitations, which includes a comprehensive guide to all manuscript and printed sources, an index to all names in the visitation records giving a pedigree of two or more generations and coats of arms, a transcript of the rare Phillips manuscript of disclaimers and a complete index of disclaimers and those respited for proofs of right to bear and use arms. This becomes an invaluable guide for those tracing ancestry covering all the family trees and related data for the period 1530-1690 and also an important source for localisation of surnames as well as for heraldic studies.

Genealogists, demographers, local and family historians should read Squibb's work for the greater detail, but need only be aware of the briefest facts about the origins of these visitations. Heraldists may care to make deeper studies.[12]

In essence, during the French wars, Henry V had received reports of the misuse of armory by battle leaders. It was clear that there was much abuse of arms, and the first Garter King of Arms, Sir William Bruges, was commanded to survey and record the bearings and genealogies of the increasing numbers of those who made use of arms in order to correct irregularities. Henry issued writs to the sheriffs of Sussex, Hampshire, Wiltshire and Dorset in 1417 allowing the continuance of the use of armorial ensigns by those who had assumed arms while at Agincourt with him and by those who had borne such insignia since time immemorial, but forbidding the use of coats of arms except by right of ancestry or a valid grant. There is some evidence of visitations by heralds in the 15th century.

The Tudors had come to the throne of England impoverished and in the aftermath of the wars of the Roses, barely a year after King Richard III had given the heralds of the royal household a permanent home in Coldharbour near Blackfriars' steps by the river Thames in London. Tudor monarchs were certainly unable to afford to keep the heralds and the accoutrements of ceremony and court life. They did, however, find them to be necessary.

As a result of the Charter of 1484, it is not improbable that all the heralds were unfavourable to the Tudors in any event. Ultimately they were made use of not only in their accustomed duties in ceremony and as messengers and ambassadors but also in recording the survivors of the internal wars along with the new men who had profited from them.

In 1530 Henry VIII took advantage of the writs of his predecessor to send out his heralds on visitations of the counties to discover who thought themselves to be gentlemen. The first surviving warrant, dated April 6, 1530, was issued to Thomas Benolt, Clarenceux King of Arms (1511-1534). He was commissioned to travel throughout his southern province with authority to enter all dwellings and churches "to put down or otherwise deface at his discretion whatever arms he might find wrongly used . . . in plates, jewels, paper, parchment, windows, gravestones and monuments and elsewhere wheresoever they may be set or placed."

The writ was repeated by Henry VIII in 1555 and again in 1558, compelling county sheriffs and their officers to assist the heralds in carrying out their survey. The bailiff of each hundred, upon display of the royal commission, was to prepare a list of all persons using titles or arms, who were then summoned to appear before the herald or his deputy, a time and place being given. Each person was to bring with him his authority for the bearing and use of arms. This often consisted of a pedigree prepared by local antiquaries or professional genealogists showing this use of arms from ancient times, along with evidence from seals, deeds, family muniments, papers, oral record, monuments and the like. The heralds recorded and confirmed the use of arms that were in order, along with notes of evidences and the pedigrees.

Defective arms were corrected; those without crests might be persuaded to have grants confirming the ancient use of arms and granting a new crest, and, if no authority for the use of arms could be found, the usurper disclaimed. He signed a disclaimer renouncing any right to bear arms and his name was added to a list, which was subsequently published at the cross in the county town.[13] Those who refused to answer the summons were warned to appear before the Earl Marshal under penalty of £10 and stubborn cases were brought before the Earl Marshal's Court of Chivalry. The leaves fell—not a maple among them!

Some of those who disclaimed later received grants of arms. These might be entirely new designs, but often the coat that they had improperly borne or else a variant of it would be the subject of a new grant. The heralds also registered pedigrees whether arms were being recorded or not, and many pedigrees entered were not accompanied by coats of arms. The heralds were empowered to "remove all false arms and arms devised without authority . . . to take note of descents." One is tempted to recommend the continuance of the visitations today. It would provide employment and revenue and bring an end to the gross misuse, scandalous misappropriation of arms and heraldic trespasses we witness throughout the world today.[14]

It is perhaps necessary to realise the conditions and lack of facilities, amenities and services in those times to appreciate fully the enormous value of these records and the difficulties under which they were compiled. Original note books made by heralds, their deputies, and submitted by local genealogists to the visiting heralds were not generally retained among the records or collections of the College of Arms, but only the final approved records of the visitations. Such notes, along with many copies and augmented versions of the

records, fell into private hands, if they survived. The majority, apart from those held by the heralds, is now among the Harleian and Additional collections of manuscripts in the British Library and in the libraries of Caius College, Cambridge and Queen's College, Oxford. Many others are widely dispersed in private collections.

A number of the heralds of those times were scholars and antiquaries of eminence and expertise in research and judgement. Others were less careful and their genealogical skills and presentation would not stand up to present-day scrutiny. There can be little doubt but that there were younger sons of the ancient nobility and gentry of England and Wales who had left issue which had fallen on hard times, but from whom descended some of those who had recovered their fortunes as provisioners, merchants, craftsmen and cum-brothers of the guilds. Many were new families yet the heralds and the local antiquaries and professional genealogists were prepared to produce fanciful ancestries for them, in a few cases backed up by "evidence" consisting of downright forgeries. Fortunately, such travesties are not frequent.

Nearly all the original records of these surveys are kept at the College of Arms in London and, because the heralds are not recipients of public funds and receive salaries that were reduced under King William IV (currently £49.07 per annum for Garter King of Arms, £20.25 for each of the other two kings, £17.80 for each herald and £13.95 for pursuivants, paid quarterly!), it is only right and proper that they should charge fees for access to the records and collections that they maintain. There are, however, some of the original and many copies and augmented versions of the visitation records in other collections together with original notes made by heralds and contemporary copyists. Several county archaeological and record societies and, in particular, The Harleian Society, have published copies of visitation records from a variety of these sources in excellent, good and indifferent editions.

## NOTES

1. Presented by Richard Baker B. Sc., Ph.D., D.I.C. Fellow, Secretary and Tutorial Superintendent of The Institute of Heraldic and Genealogical Studies.

2. J. Siebmacher, *Grosses und allgemeines Wappenbuchen*, 1605-1961.

3. J. B. Rietstap, *Armorial général* (1884).

4. V. and H. V. Rolland, *Illustrations and Supplements to Rietstap's Armorial général* (1967-1979).

5.  SILVESTRO PETRA SANCTA, S.J., *Tesserae Gentilitiae* (1638).

6.  C. R. HUMPHERY-SMITH, *Anglo-Norman Armory Two* (1984).

7.  *Nativity Roll* ca. 1300, *Parliamentary Roll* ca. 1312.

8.  *St. George Roll* 1285, *Charles Roll* 1285.

9.  *Parliamentary Roll* ca. 1312.

10.  *Family History*, no. 148 (July 1996).

11.  *Family History*, no. 1 (Oct. 1962); G. D. SQUIBB, *Visitation Pedigrees and the Genealogist* (1964, 1978).

12.  A. R. WAGNER, *Heralds of England* (1987); GRAZE-BROOK AND RYLAND, *Visitation of Shropshire* (Harleian Society vol. 27 and 29).

13.  *Armigerous Ancestors* (1997) is the short title of a Catalogue and index to Heralds' visitation sources that fully discusses disclaimers.

14.  In England, recent legislation of the Theft Act and the Trades Descriptions Act (1968) provides some protection against misuse of arms.

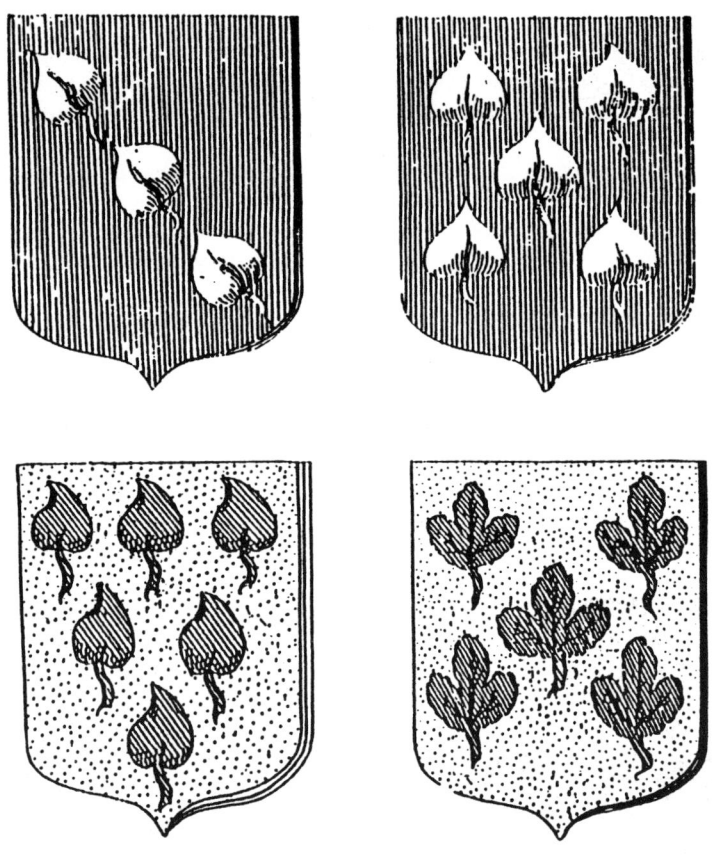

**FIGURE 1**: Examples from Petra Sancta's *Tesserae Gentiliae* (1638)

**FIGURE 2:** John Lisle

**FIGURE 3:** Hugh Morieus

**FIGURE 4:** Waller

**FIGURE 5:** Leveson-Gower

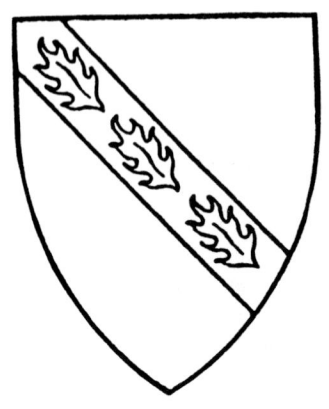

**FIGURE 6:** Hollingsworth

**FIGURE 7:** Hezilrigg

**FIGURE 8:** Foulis and Liston-Foulis

# WHEN DID THE IRISH CHIEFS ADOPT HERALDRY?

John J. Fitzpatrick Kennedy

Boundaries can be cultural as much as geographical. Such cultural boundaries are evident when we examine how heraldry, part of feudal culture, was adopted by the Gaelic Irish chiefs in medieval Ireland.

## The negative thesis

In 1913, E. C. R. Armstrong, Keeper of Irish Antiquities in the National Museum, Dublin, and later (1923) Bluemantle Pursuivant of Arms, wrote the article "A Note as to the Time Heraldry Was Adopted by the Irish Chiefs."[1] He was, then, in a most advantageous position to speak on the matter, because he had access to a growing collection of medieval Irish seals, on which he was something of an authority. Seals were then considered the best "hard evidence" for determining when heraldry arose and how it spread to various levels of medieval society, so Armstrong was in tune with the preferred methodology of his time and even in the vanguard of its study in Ireland.[2] In short, he was a research pioneer in the study of Irish heraldry and sigillography.

Yet, both in his articles and in his book, *Irish Seals and Seal Matrices*, Armstrong's account suffers from serious problems. One problem was the size of the sample of Gaelic Irish seals he presented and still more specifically the number of Gaelic Irish armorial seals. To this day, there is no complete published catalogue of Irish seals, many of which are scattered among private (e.g., the Ormonde Archives) and foreign collections for anyone patient enough to recollect them.

Armstrong provided a sample of about 15 Gaelic Irish seals and only about five Gaelic Irish armorial seals dated prior to the 16th century. On the negative side, despite the small sizes of his samples, Armstrong was bold enough to draw some rather sweeping historical conclusions about the Gaelic Irish chiefs and aristocrats and their presumed attitudes toward feudalism, primogeniture and heraldry—this despite his unfamiliarity with the Irish language and its literary sources. Indeed, he ventured to pronounce that insofar as the extant evidence admitted, the Gaelic Irish did not seem to have used heraldry very extensively prior to the 16th century (largely when, under Henry VIII's policy of Surrender and Re-Grant, many Gaelic chiefs adopted arms and were ennobled as earls, barons or feudal lords). I think this reflects his Cambrensian viewpoint.

Having noted Gaelic Irish armorial seals are still scattered and unedited, we must also admit that Armstrong might be correct when all the evidence is in, at least about some Gaelic chiefs. But, we must also recognize that extant evidence has a way of increasing with further research so we ought not put all our money on the first hypothesis enunciated.

Yet, Armstrong thought there were good historical grounds for this sparsity of Gaelic Irish armorial seals, e.g., (1) the Gaelic chiefs were hostile to feudal culture, resisting primogeniture in favour of their native *derb fine* inheritance patterns. For Armstrong, it followed that since heraldry was tied to feudalism, which the Gaelic chiefs only adopted in the 16th century, when forced to, they did not use heraldry to any extent in medieval times; (2) the Gaelic bards rejected heraldry as a foreign importation, never mentioning it in their poems; and (3) that the Irish Gaels were uniformly hostile to the "foreigners" (*Gall* in Gaelic). Yet, today, Armstrong's negative thesis about the adoption of heraldry by the Gaelic Irish chiefs appears a classical case of drawing a very large scale conclusion from too little evidence. This becomes apparent when we realize that the critical editions of Gaelic bardic poetry still remain to be accomplished. Armstrong would thus appear premature in his pronouncements on what the most bardic poets wrote about until they have all been critically examined. It is also apparent when we look carefully at Gaelic attitudes toward feudalism. For Armstrong appears ante-diluvian compared to modern Irish and Anglo-Irish historians, who have begun to appreciate how adaptable and intertwined were Gaelic and Anglo-Norman feudal cultures in many parts of the medieval Irish lordship. Far from being hostile, the Gaelic chiefs borrowed freely what they believed was useful from the Anglo-Norman colonists, for example, their harness, armour and military tactics, castles and tower houses. Gaelic and Anglo-Normans regularly intermarried throughout the medieval period. Thousands of examples of cross-cultural exchange could be given.

It is important to appreciate that Armstrong probably relied on the historical scholarship of Goddard H. Orpen, who in 1911 had just published the first two volumes of his classic *Ireland Under the Normans 1169-1216*, with its strong pride in Anglo-Norman culture and the belief that the Anglo-Normans came to Ireland as conquerors to extend a quasi-mythic *pax Normannica*. Orpen characterized the Gaelic Irish polity, prior to the coming of the Anglo-Normans as one of tribal anarchy, an unrelieved and senseless warfare among tribal groups, perpetually devoid of rhyme or reason. In short, political and barbaric chaos.[3]

This view of the Anglo-Normans and their alleged "conquest" of Celtic Ireland owes a great deal to the writings of Geraldus Cambriensis, a 12th-century Anglo-Norman churchman and close relative of the so-called "invaders." But, recent historical research has dramatically changed our view of the Anglo-Normans, who came to Ireland neither as independent invaders nor conquerors, but as allies of a disgruntled and dethroned Gaelic provincial king who aspired to establish a national monarchy with their alliance. Moreover, the coming of the Anglo-Normans, largely as land-hungry individuals, was scarcely less chaotic, greedy and haphazard than the alleged chaos of the Gaelic tribes, though it may have been feudal. Most of the Anglo-Normans who came to Ireland had been supporters of King Stephen, and under a cloud with Henry II, king of England. They sought the promise of land and its wealth in Ireland rather than poverty and disgrace in Wales.

Nor can we with justice claim they sought mystically to extend a *pax Normannica*, for they proved as grasping, perfidious and self-serving as any of the Gaelic kings who competed for power, wealth and influence in those very harsh times. Moreover, they were professional warriors, who after grasping the divisions among the Irish themselves, sought their own best self-interest in the obtaining of land, wealth and power, not that of the Crown or some great cultural *pax Normannica*.

Further, we know the Gaelic kings themselves in the 12th century were not behaving chaotically. Quite consistently they had, since the 10th century, under such monarchs as Brian Boru Maelsechlainn *et al.*, been attempting to establish a stable national monarchy. Their leading churchmen had been attempting to reform the Irish church and the people's semi-pagan marriage mores and to bring them more into line with the universal Church's reforms. Some of these Gaelic Irish kings were not only abreast of political and religious developments on the continent, but had succeeded dramatically, though not permanently in unifying Ireland. Far from being chaotic, their political struggles steadily tended toward creating a stable national unity. Various Irish provincial kings (e.g., the Ui Briain and the MacCarthaig) were both politically shrewd and cultured, with major court centres and contacts not only with the archbishops of Canterbury and the popes, but were already feudalizing their realms with the help of various Anglo-Normans. Moreover, many of the Gaelic aristocrats were not particularly inimicable to the appearance of Henry II in Ireland or to feudalism, for they hoped he would check the greed, rapine and unruliness of those independent Anglo-Normans who had come in the service of Dermait MacMurrough Kavanagh, king of (south) Leinster. And Henry II did so, for a time, precisely because he feared the aspirations of Strongbow, the son-in-law and declared heir apparent of MacMurrough Kavanagh, as king of Leinster, to set up a rival monarchy in Ireland.

I have not the space to adduce all the historic evidence with which it is possible to rebut Armstrong's position, but I believe he misinterpreted a great deal. Crudely, we can summarize Anglo-Norman involvement in medieval Ireland as follows:

Phase I (1169-1269): Anglo-Normans are invited in, and begin colonizing, especially in south Leinster, Meath, Dublin, Waterford, Wexford. For about a century or more, their feudal colony expands whether by means of piecemeal military extension at the cost of the native Gaelic dynasts (e.g., de Courcy's conquest of parts of Down and Antrim, de Burgh's rather treacherous treatment of O'Connor in Connacht, the FitzGerald invasion of Desmond, etc.) or more peaceful intermarriage and alliance. At no point, however, are all the Gaelic royal provincial dynasts conquered, nor is the entire land subject to feudal law. Henry II and John are the only monarchs to visit Ireland in this time.

Phase II (1260-1541): Increasingly pushed to the limit, the Gaelic dynasts push back, helped by several factors: (1) the importation of Scots warriors from the Hebrides—the galloglas—of the Irish annals; (2) their own adoption of harness and castles from their Anglo-Norman cousins and their ability to fight full-fledged battles, not only their traditional cattle raids; and (3) some inspired leadership on the part of a number of Irish chiefs, the Gaelic resurgence begins reclaiming substantial amounts of allodial land. This is assisted in the 14th century by the Bruce Invasion (1315-1318), which devastated the Anglo-Norman feudal colony, the Black Plague (1345), which affected the feudal colony more than the Gaelic tribes, and the English Crown's involvement in Welsh, Scots and French wars, during which Ireland was left to its own devices. Lack of Crown involvement left the Anglo-Norman magnates and colony wrestling with a better-armed and more effective Gaelic adversary, with whom relations have to be more carefully managed. Ireland becomes a Lordship of shifting spheres of influence as Gaelic dynasts and Anglo-Norman magnates intermarry, change alliances or fight blood feuds with one another. The Lordship remains nominally one of the Angevin realms, but increasingly beyond the effective control of the Crown, which alternately neglects, attempts to militarily subdue and neglects.

Hence, Irish medieval history does not significantly support Armstrong's interpretation. Armstrong's negative thesis about the Gaelic Irish chiefs's adoption of heraldry owes too much to an insupportable Cambrensian bias. Yet, despite Armstrong's weaknesses, such Irish heraldists as the late J. G. Barry[4], have rather uncritically accepted his conclusions. This is blindness compounded.

## A more positive view

Yet after Armstrong's death, in 1922, his small sample was expanded. In the 1930s, Edmund Curtis, in his edition of *The Calendar of Ormond Deeds*, and in several later articles, drew attention to seals that were either inaccessible or unknown to Armstrong. Since then, still other Gaelic Irish seals have come to light, some indeed, armorial. While these seals supplement Armstrong's sample to about 30 Gaelic seals and eight Gaelic armorial seals prior to the 16th century, these numbers still do not promote extrava-

gant confidence in any major supposition about the adoption of heraldry by themselves.

Moreover, the fact that there are many non-armorial seals does not exclude the possibility that their owners nonetheless used heraldic arms in real life, though not on their seals. In feudal society, many armigerous knights and squires, employed non-armorial seals, even though they, in great likelihood, used heraldry on their shields and a wide variety of other artifacts. So, the simple use of a non-armorial seal is far from conclusive proof, even within thoroughly feudal cultures, that their user was not employing heraldry elsewhere. Hence, the scarcity of Gaelic Irish armorial seals hardly proves, as Armstrong seems to think, that Irish chiefs did not employ heraldry. In short, apart from the lack of confidence in the numbers, Armstrong's evidence is inconclusive, not negative. This same conclusion was reached by Dr. Michael Powell Siddons writing on the development of Welsh heraldry:

> Although this seal evidence is negative it cannot in itself be taken as conclusive proof that heraldry was not used by Welshmen at this time, for non-armorial seals were sometimes used in later centuries by definitely armigerous families without the use of heraldry.[5]

Here, I will simply assert that there are samples of such Gaelic Irish medieval armorial seals, and other armorial artifacts, there are bardic poems that appear to describe heraldic banners, and there are many Gaelic chiefs who were not inimicable to feudalism nor to feudal inheritance patterns. So, by Modus Tollens, Armstrong is very likely wrong in his argument respecting the adoption of heraldry. Furthermore, Barry is wrong to follow Armstrong uncritically, because one blind fellow leading another will fall into a pit.

For the bulk of the medieval period, Ireland was a land of two distinct cultures and what one modern Anglo-Irish historian has called "not so much a Lordship, as a patchwork of lordships," co-existing with series of uneasy compromises and alliances that often broke down, shifted and gradually re-established themselves in new patterns. We can distinguish generally three major spheres of influence: (1) the Anglo-Norman feudal Pale, which varied in size—in the 12th century sizable, but from 1260 until 1540 shrinking to within a few counties surrounding Dublin and a few outposts around Waterford, Dundalk, Limerick and Galway; (2) the Marches in the Liberties and counties, originally granted by the Crown for as much as various feudal magnates could conquer and hold, these "Liberties" were run and subinfeudated by various Anglo-Norman barons. While vassals of the Crown, Crown writ was loosely enforced within such lands. Often they claimed Gaelic lands and incorporated entire Irish septs (lineages), which effectively ruled themselves according to their traditional "Brehon" law. Such "March" lands could be volatile, but often blended English feudal law for colonists and Brehon law for Gaelic lieges. It is in such Marcher areas where Gaelic Irish chiefs and Anglo-Normans lived near one another that cross-cultural evidences of heraldry become apparent; (3) the unconquered Gaelic Irish kingdoms such as Thomond, Tyrconnell and major parts of Connacht and Ulster. All these areas were nominally granted to some Anglo-Norman conquerer (e.g., the Earl of Ulster, the de Clare's lordship of Thomond, etc.). But often by the late 13th century, the land had effectively been re-conquered by various Gaelic aristocrats, and the Anglo-Norman lineages had either evacuated completely or become themselves so intermarried and gaelicized as to have adopted Gaelic surnames and lifestyles. In these areas, cattle-droving was the basis of the economy and the Gaelic lifestyle persisted, irrespective of whether a family was Gael or Gall (foreigner). This situation persisted down into modern times, the real conquest of Ireland only taking place in the late 16th and 17th centuries, well after the Reformation, when religious divisions added the distinctively zealous element known only too well today in Northern Ireland.

I shall argue that those Irish chiefs who used armorial seals had regular and enduring interactions with the Anglo-Normans. I surmise that heraldry appealed to them as a visual and decorative "ensign" in battle, which initially transcended its feudal role as an indicator of "primogeniture" in Gaelic circles. In feudal heraldry, after all, brisures were only adopted late, and for most of the medieval period followed no particular system. Feudal marriage customs were scarcely more canonical than Gaelic ones and illegitimacy was not the social taint that it became later.

An uncritical Cambrensian attitude has kept alive a cultural gulf in Irish historiography much wider than the Irish sea. For example, in heraldic scholarship it can be seen in S. M. Collins's essay.[6] Collins is surprised by the numerous instances of Irish arms in such continental rolls as von Grunenburg's *Wappenbuch*. He writes, "It would be unsafe to place any great confidence in Grunenberg over a foreign coat [i.e., English, Scots, Welsh or Irish], or for that matter in any continental armorist."[7] Grunenburg appears to have relied for these coats on Richenthal, who relied in turn on the 14th-century Uffenbach Roll. Collins goes on to blason the coats of the four "Grafs von Lagonie, von Conaxien, von Ultonigen and von Ultonigen (this repetition probably intending Munster)" from the 14th-century Uffenbach Roll more or less to illustrate how fanciful these are. But, as Collins blasons these four coats, we can see that one corresponds precisely to the medieval arms of the O'Neills of Ulster (admittedly their title confused there with the Grafs von Lagonie), another corresponds closely to the arms of the MacCarthys Mór, formerly Gaelic kings of Munster, then Desmond (south Munster), a third corresponds to the de Burgh, Earls of Ulster, while the fourth referring to Connacht shows: *Gules three fishes naiant in pale Argent*, which may fancifully reflect the continental knowledge that many Flemish, English and Hanseatic ships fished herring off the coast of Connacht. Galwaymen to this day are known as "Herring-chuckers."

Collins, misled by the modern arms of the four provinces, misidentifies them and seems unaware of Gaelic Irish familial heraldry when it is found in a 14th-century continental Roll. Yet, 1350-1399 falls well within the medieval period used by Armstrong, and here we have continental evidence of the correct arms of the O'Neills of Ulster and the MacCarthys Mór of Munster. According to Collins, continental armorists probably know nothing of Ireland and are fantasizing about Irish arms.

Yet, Collins seems utterly unaware of the *Schottenkloster*, a Benedictine *paruchia* of southern Germany, Switzerland and Austria, founded by Gaelic Irish monks, who maintained their presence in this very location (Grunenburg lived in Constance, where there was a *Schottenkloster*) from the 11th century (prior to the coming of the Anglo-Normans) down to the Reformation, drawing regular recruits from Ireland. The German *Schotten* translates the early medieval Latin word for a Gaelic Irishman, *Scottus*. Modern Scotland derives its name from the fact that Argyll was settled and dominated culturally by the Irish Gaels or *Scotti* of the Dalriata in Ulster. In the early Middle Ages, Scotland was uniformly known as Alba. It was not until the 12th century that Ireland began to be referred to exclusively as Hibernia and Scotland slowly began to be called Scotia. In many of the continental rolls such as Grunenburg's, the Irish arms are referred to as the arms of the *Kunig von Hibernie seu Scotia* to clarify which nation is being indicated.

As if to highlight the Irish connection and the use of the MacCarthy arms, we might note that the Abbot of the Vienna *Schottenkloster* Monastery *Unser leibe Frau zu Schotten* from 1392 to 1399 was an Irishman, known in German as Abbot Heinrich. We have his seal, which shows him mitred, seated with staff, hand held in blessing within a Gothic niche, below which is a shield with the stag. Is this once again the seal of a MacCarthy abbot of the Schottenkloster in Vienna? We know the MacCarthys had long and enduring connections with the *Schottenkloster*. Thus, there appears to be some evidence for the MacCarthys Mór having adopted their arms well before the 1542 creation of the earls of Clancarty under Henry VIII's policy of "Surrender and Re-Grant."

I conclude, Collins unwittingly displays all the commonplaces of the Cambrensian bias against the possibility of Gaelic Irish influence on continental heraldry. But, if this is true of the MacCarthys, it is even more obvious for the O'Neills of Ulster, for there are three medieval seals of considerable interest, two of which replicate the arms mentioned by Grunenburg, Richenthal and the Uffenbach Roll. The first is the equestrian seal of Brian "of the Battle of Down" O'Neill (†1260), which shows him "In armour, with flat helmet, sword and shield, with uncertain heraldic charge thereon. Riding to the r(ight) on a pacing horse."[8] Brian, king of Keneleoghain, rose in rebellion against the English, having obtained the loyalty of one of the O'Briens and O'Connor, but was killed in battle in 1260 (not 1276 as Armstrong states). Can the uncertain charge on his shield be the dexter hand of the O'Neills that appears on the armorial seal of his grandson, Aodh Reamhar O'Neill (fl. 1337-1364), son of that Donal O'Neill who addressed the famous Remonstrance of 1318 to

Pope John XXII, denouncing the treachery of some feudal barons in medieval Ireland? This ancient device, presumably symbolic of the *derb fine* itself, and the ancient inheritance pattern of Gaelic Ireland, or possibly the *Dextra Dei*, presumably continues until we next meet it in the quartered arms of the first earl of Tyrone, Conn Baccach O'Neill in 1542.

Let us not forget that the O'Neills themselves divided into two rival branches, the O'Neills Mór and the O'Neills Clann Aodha Buidhe. Among these later rivals of the O'Neills Mór, we find the seal of Muircheartach Ceannfhada O'Neill (1369-1392), again with the dexter hand erect. These were identical to the arms depicted in the Uffenbach Roll and later in the Wappenbuch!

### Bards, primogeniture and Gaelic genealogy

Yet, Armstrong maintains that the Gaelic Irish chiefs were hostile to heraldry and to feudal primogeniture and feudal culture. But, both Edward I and II summoned a large number of Gaelic kings and chiefs, including that Domnall O'Neill of the Remonstrance of 1318 and Aodh Reamhar to war in Scotland. The O'Neills appear to have adopted heraldry and approached the required feudal inheritance pattern of primogeniture. What now of Armstrong's argument that they were hostile to both, which has bewitched so many Irish armorists and poisoned the study of Irish heraldry for far too long?

It would be natural to assume that the Gaels were reluctant to abandon a thousand-year-old culture, simply because the Anglo-Normans expanded into their land and set up a colony. It would even be natural to suppose they opposed the conquest of their allodial territories and peoples. Yet, despite this, the Gaels were not necessarily hostile to feudal culture and this is reflected in the large number of borrowings they took from it and the several attempts various Gaelic kings and aristocrats made to obtain feudal rights and laws for themselves.[9] For, as Robin Frame, a recent historian of the medieval Irish Lordship has commented, "The truth probably is that the feudal and Gaelic worlds were from the start closer to each other than their respective sources, with their dissimilar languages and conventions, readily disclose."[10]

A glance through the historical scholarship in the Cambridge *A New History of Ireland*, vol. 2, *Medieval Ireland*, makes one realize just how involved with feudal culture the Gaelic Irish chiefs were. They regularly participated in feudal levies when the king addressed them as lords who had taken fealty to him, in the Scots, Welsh and French wars. Like their Anglo-Norman neighbors, they sometimes rebelled when their territories or rights were threatened. But, they also served as allies and vassals to Anglo-Norman lords in enforcing feudal law in other parts of Ireland. They armed themselves in haketons, shirts of mail, camails and conical helmets just as did their Anglo-Norman neighbors. They also intermarried with them. But, more importantly, their own culture was close enough to and had sufficient flexibility to accommodate feudal mores, through adaptation. As Robin Frame continues:

> If the Anglo-Normans adjusted quickly to Irish styles of warfare, by about 1300 there had been significant, though by no means revolutionary, changes among the Irish themselves; adaptation in the military as in other areas of life was not all on one side. Perhaps the most significant development was the diffusion among the Gaelic nobility of defensive armour. Its spread seems to have been accompanied by an increased capacity, when need be, to stand and fight.[11]

Need I remind you that defensive armour head to toe appears as the prerequisite of heraldry's rise? Kenneth Nichols, a scholar of medieval Gaelic Irish society, points out that Gaelic Irish inheritance patterns were varied. The common terms used in historical sources are Tanistry and Gavelkind, but there were many local variations. In Gaelic Irish circles, lords held sway not so much over territory as over people. A kinship group, the *derb fine*, claiming descent from a common ancestor, in an assembly, ideally selected the "brightest, strongest and best" from among the five generations descending from their ancestral king. So, it was quite possible for a chief to be succeeded by his brother or uncle, rather than his eldest son. Yet, the system of Tanistry varied from place to place. Often in Munster, in imitation of Anglo-Norman primogeniture, long-lived chiefs would have their eldest sons nominated as *Tanists* (Successors) failing kin of their immediate relatives being

"brightest, strongest and best," with the result that among the MacCarthys Mór, between 1359 and 1508, son succeeded father for six generations. Lordship of a territory (*Oireacht* or *Iraght*, the assembly of people of a given territory) could be chaotic because of conflict over succession between rivals in a sept, or it could be fairly orderly and well organized. So, we again must beware the stereotype and pay more attention to local detail when proclaiming Gaelic "hostility" to primogeniture.

Apart from seals, I think that historical accounts speak quite directly to the process by which Gaelic chiefs adopted heraldic shields, banners and insignia. Listen to the following quote from the *Calendar of the Justiciar's Rolls Ireland* for September 1309, complaining about an Anglo-Norman baron, "Maurice Cauntetoun and his accomplices . . . having combined with Douling O'Bryn [O'Byrne] and other Irishmen from the mountains of Leinster, openly put themselves at war with the king *with standards displayed* . . ."[12] Here, both an Anglo-Norman baron and his Gaelic Irish ally both displayed their banners in open rebellion against the king. There are hundreds of similar citations that could be multiplied.

Or, again we read of Domnall MacMurrough Kavanagh, who is recorded at different times as having displayed his banner in rebellion against the Crown outside Dublin in 1328, but is found later as a knight banneret in Edward III's expedition against the Scots from Ireland in 1335! Could he have led a contingent from Ireland without all the panoply and trappings of heraldry as a knight banneret? But, in the 1370s, Art Mór MacMurrough Kavanagh, Domnall's second cousin, resisted King Richard II, and narrowly escaped capture. His seal, styling him "king of Leinster", was found in his camp, though unfortunately what it depicted is not described! But, his grandson Donal Reagh MacMurrough Kavanagh's elaborate heraldic regal seal is extant from 1475. I am tempted to speculate that the unknown device on Art's seal was probably identical to those arms used by his grandson in 1475. It would make perfect sense. These are the traditional arms of the MacMurrough Kavanaghs, though unknown to Armstrong. So once again, one of the royal bloods of Gaelic Ireland appears armigerous, possibly in the late 14th century, but definitely in the late 15th.

Further north, in Connacht in 1201, we find the bardic poem of Giolla Brigdhe *Albanach,* a great bard, who describes the fierce wolf on the banner of Cathal Crovderg O'Connor's fortress. While the bard may not have the language of heraldic blason, what have we here but a banner with a significant charge, functioning for all intents as a heraldic battle banner? Between 1293 and 1309, we find another poem, entitled *Coir Connacht ar Chath Laigen,* to another O'Connor of Connacht named Aedh macEoghan, king of Connacht (1293-1309), where we read:

> About his body he had a bright woven coat of mail, a dark branching helmet upon the descendant of Conn . . . He takes his blue sword . . . white shield before him, dragons upon it and golden branches . . . [13]

Are these a poetic attempt to describe a blason? I would suggest that they are. They appear to me to strike a note that may just refer to the oak tree with spreading branches that is still borne by the O'Connor Don.

Lastly, I cannot fail to mention that in 1336, Ruadhri Mór O'Cinnéidigh, a chief, who would appear to be the head of the line of Clangillekevin Buidhe, and an ancestor of the chiefly line of the O'Kennedys Foinn of Lackeen Castle, [14] sealed with a single lion passant, on a charter with the then Earl of Ormond. The Earl acknowledged O'Kennedy's sway in north Tipperary, agreeing not to invade O'Kennedy's territory provided he respected the earl's territory. In 1356, this Ruadhri Mór sealed with an armorial seal, showing a shield divided *per pale* with what appear to be *two lions* (beasts) *rampant combatant.* The tinctures are unknown, and these arms do not appear to resemble the latter *Sable, three helmets in profile proper,* borne by the O'Kennedys Fionn of Lackeen Castle in the 16th century. Moreover, Ruadhri's son also used a seal, which unfortunately is not extant, so we cannot say conclusively if this example precisely meets Sir Anthony Wagner's definition of true heraldry. Yet, it comes very close, just on its own!

There are still other examples that could be cited here, but perhaps the point to draw from all this is already made. Among the Gaelic lineages known colloquially as the "royal bloods," that is the provincial kings: the O'Neills Mór and

Clannaboy, the MacCarthys Mór, the O'Connors of Connacht, the MacMurrough Kavanaghs of south Leinster and the O'Briens of Thomond (though I have not had space to show the evidence here for them) heraldry seems already to have been in use in the medieval period. Even in certain other prominent lineages, such as the O'Kennedys of Ormond, there appears to be evidence for the use of armorial seals. In some cases, these armorial seals are identical with the arms later used by these very lineages when the Ulster's Office was established, so there is a strong presupposition that they continued in use throughout the medieval period. In other cases, we may be dealing with proto or early heraldic devices or charges on shields described by bards, who were not especially conversant with the conventions of blason. Either way, however, there seems to be strong evidence of an interest in and usage of symbols on shield and banner, many of which became hereditary from the mid-14th century. Some are known, surprisingly, from continental sources, likely due to the influence of the Schottenkloster community of Irish Benedictines, who formed a source of much information on things Irish for Switzerland, southern Germany and Austria from the 11th to the 16th centuries. Armstrong's Cambrensian bias in his interpretation of Irish medieval history does not hold up to critical investigation whether with seals or still other evidence, such as bardic poetry, crown records or objets d'art!

## NOTES

1. E. C. R. ARMSTRONG, "A Note as to the Time Heraldry Was Adopted by the Irish Chiefs," *Journal of the Royal Society of Antiquaries of Ireland,* 42 (Dublin: 1913), p. 66-72.

2. *Idem, Irish Seals and Seal Matrices* (London: 1914).

3. GODDARD H. ORPEN, *Ireland Under the Normans 1169-1296,* vols. 1 and 2 (Oxford: 1911).

4. J. B. BARRY, "Guide to Records of the Genealogical Office, Dublin, with a Commentary on Heraldry in Ireland and on the History of the Office," *Analecta Hibernica,* 26 (Dublin: 1976), p. 3-43.

5. MICHAEL POWELL SIDDONS, *The Development of Welsh Heraldry,* vol. 1 (Aberystwyth: 1991), p. 5.

6. ART COSGROVE (ed.), *A New History of Ireland,* vol. 2, *Medieval Ireland 1169-1534* (Oxford, Clarendon Press: 1987).

7. S. M. COLLINS, "Some English, Scottish, Welsh and Irish Arms in Continental Rolls," *The Antiquaries Journal,* 21 (London: 1941), p. 203-210.

8.  *Ibid*, p. 206.

9.  W. De G. BIRCH, *Catalogue of Seals in the Department of Manuscripts in the British Museum,* vol. 4 (London: 1895), p. 695.

10.  J. OTWAY-RUTHVEN, "The Request of the Irish for English Law," *Irish Historical Studies,* 6 (1948-1949), p. 261-270; and "The Native Irish and English Law in Medieval Ireland," *Irish Historical Studies,* 7 (1950-1951), p. 1-16.

11.  ROBIN FRAME, "War and Peace in the Medieval Lordship of Ireland," in J. F. LYDON (ed.), *The English in Medieval Ireland* (Blackrock: 1981), p. 125.

12.  JAMES. LYDON, "A Land of War," chapter 9, in ART COSGROVE (ed.), *A New History of Ireland,* vol. 2, *op. cit.,* p. 263.

13.  *Ibid.,* p. 247-250 for biographical data on Aedh. The quote comes from PETER HARBISON, "Native Irish Arms and Armour in Medieval Gaelic Literature, 1170-1600," *The Irish Sword,* part. 1, vol. 12, 48 (Dublin: 1976), p. 176.

14.  SEAMUS PENDER (ed.), "The O'Clery Book of Genealogies," *Analecta Hibernica,* 18 (Dublin, 1950-1951), p. 150-151. The seal of Rotheric O'Kennedy was preserved in the Ormond Archives until the seal was given by the Irish Government to the family of late U.S. President, John Fitzgerald Kennedy.

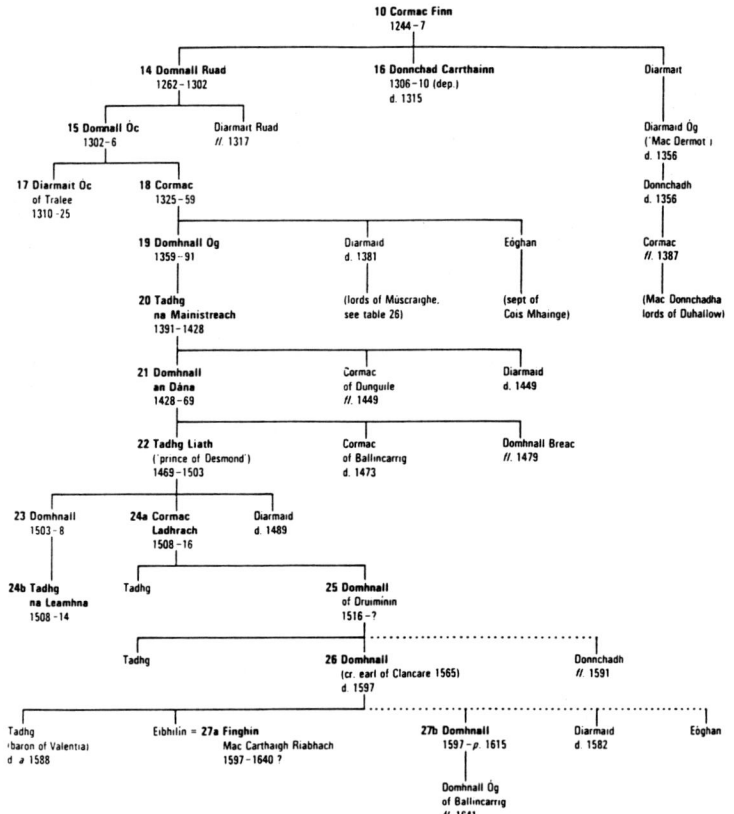

**TABLE 1:** MacCarthys of Desmond: Mac Cartaigh Mór, Kings of Desmond and Earl of Clancare, 1262-ca. 1640.

# TABLE 2: O'Neills of Tyrone: Ó Néill, Kings of Tír Eógain and Earls of Tyrone, 1166-1616.

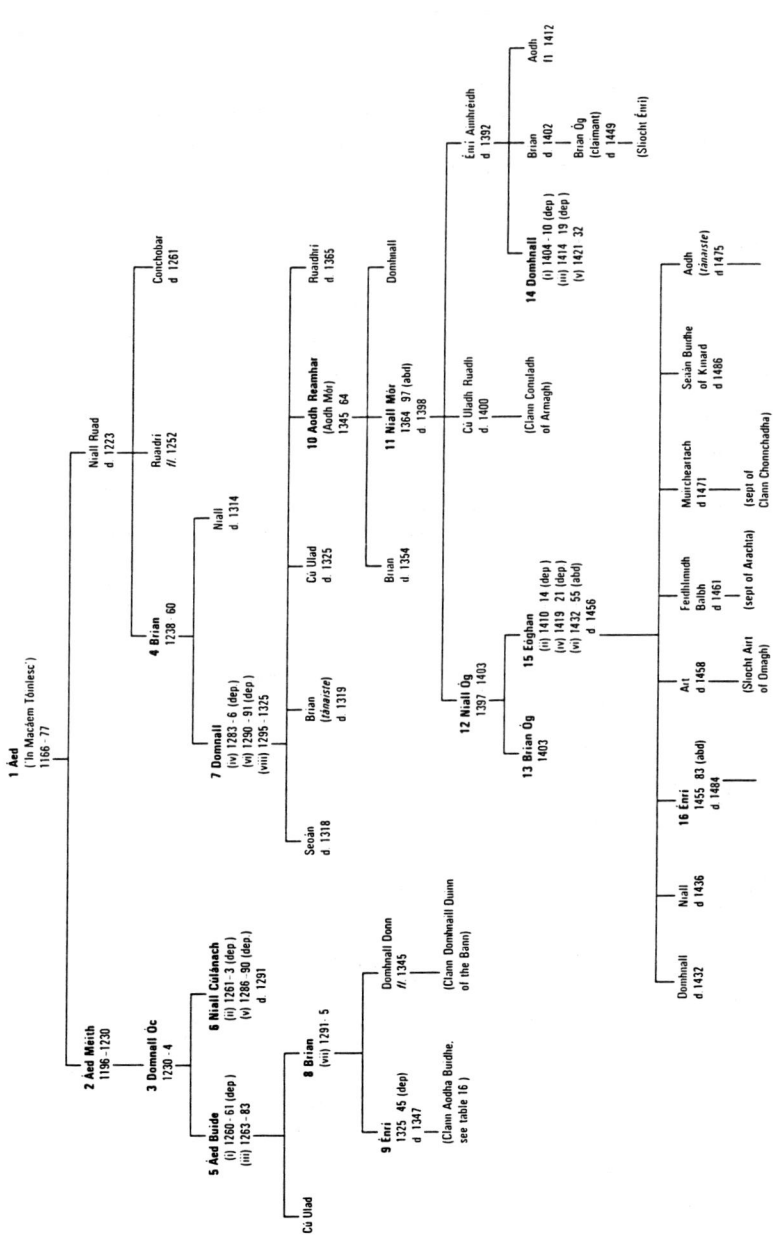

**MacCARTHY**

1                                        2                          3

**FIGURE 1:** Modern rendering of arms of the MacCarthys Mór from MacLysaght (by Nora Maguire, artist to the Genealogical Office); **FIGURE 2:** Arms of the MacCarthys Mór mistakenly attributed to "Graff von Ultingen" from Richenthal's *Das Konzil zu Konstanz*, ca. 1465, but based on the Uffenbach Roll (mid-14th century); **FIGURE 3:** Arms of the Earl of Clancarty, ca. 1542.

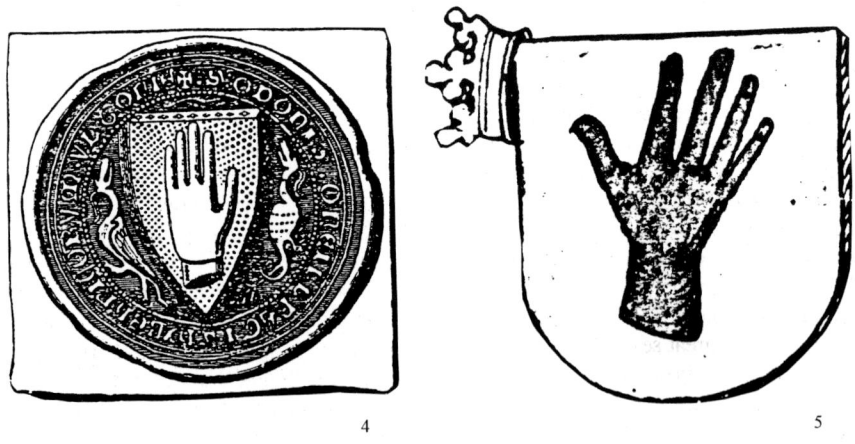

4                                                  5

**FIGURE 4:** Armorial seal of Aedh Reamhar O'Neill, with the dexter hand erect couped aupaumée of the O'Neills Mór; **FIGURE 5:** Arms of the "Graff von Lagonie." Again, no such title existed. It is nonetheless the dexter hand of the O'Neills Mór, but shown not aupaumée and reversed, from Richenthals, *op. cit.*, based on the Uffenbach Roll (mid-14th century).

# IMPRESSIONS OF STATE AUTHORITY

Patricia L. Kennedy

Surveying the impression of the royal arms in wax and in print on public documents in British North America, from the 1760s to the 1860s, illuminates our understanding of how the symbols of Crown or state authority were used, and their visibility to the populace at large. The explanations for variations in practice, the similarities and differences, are complex and elusive. The field of study lies on the boundaries of heraldry, sigillography, bibliography and printing history—which may explain its being so long overlooked. Expertise is needed from those disciplines and others. The author draws on her familiarity with manuscript records of the colonial era to study how the great seal deputed was used in the several colonies, while exploring the relationships between the *public instruments* issued under that seal and their printed counterparts. Further exploration is planned, to study how symbols of state authority were depicted on documents printed for public distribution in the colonies that were to become Canada. [1]

My study had its origins in questions that arose, but could not be addressed, when Daniel Cogné and I collaborated as curators of the exhibition, and authors of the catalogue, *Lasting Impressions: Seals in Our History / Les Sceaux: empreintes de notre histoire* (1991-1992). My attention has been drawn more to sigillography than to heraldry. Dedicated bibliographers [2] have increased my interest in and understanding of the printing of government documents. Out of seemingly disparate research threads has coalesced a new understanding of how symbols of state authority came to be impressed upon their viewers.

Let us first consider how the royal coat of arms and other heraldic symbols of state authority are depicted in wax—as the great seal deputed for a colony—and their metamorphosis when impressed on paper to accompany copies of the documents to which the wax seal was initially affixed, pendant or *en placard*. What was done, and who saw it?

The choice of great seal, privy seal or *cachet* 1reflected the degree of authority being exercised or delegated by the state. Governors received their authority through commissions issued under the Great Seal of the United Kingdom and delegated authority to subordinates within a colony through letters patent issued under the great seal deputed for that jurisdiction. Documents embodying lesser delegations of powers received lesser seals. The medium used emphasized the significance of the document: letters patent were engrossed on parchment, lesser documents were written out on paper. Viceregal assent to statutes was symbolized through the great seal deputed affixed to the parchment original, but the recognition accorded to proclamations varied: not all were on parchment, some were on paper under the governor's privy seal or *cachet*. Letters patent transferring title to lands from the Crown to individuals, granting pardons or privileges over inventions were issued under the great seal deputed; licences to practice the law or medicine were issued on paper with the governor's privy seal or *cachet*. Despite occasional divergences, the standard practices exhibit strong patterns, common to all colonies in British North America. [3] The intent of symbolizing authority, the concern to economize on expensive parchment and wax, problems with defective matrices, and other motivations for these patterns of usage merit further study.

The first question to address is this: what heraldic symbols of state authority might the populace of British North America have had opportunity to see, whether as seals affixed to documents or in other formats? Escutcheons illustrating the royal arms were carved [4] and mounted in court houses, on the Government House portals, and at other locations where state authority was exercised in judicial processes and similarly theatrical displays of power. How many people lived in the capital and had opportunity to view these symbols? Were the details visible? Were those present in a court house in fit state to observe? Little evidence has been found to indicate that the few constables and other enforcers of authority exhibited insignia, and again one must ask whether observers would have noticed heraldic detail.

While the Great Seal of United Kingdom, the monarch's signet and numerous lesser seals used by imperial authorities would have been familiar to the upper echelons of colonial officials, they would have virtually been unknown to ordinary persons. The same might be said of the great seal deputed for a colony when affixed to the original (copy of record) for statutes and proclamations, writs for elections, or commissions appointing men to public office. On deeds for land grants, pardons, or letters patent granting privileged control of an invention, they would have been seen "once in a lifetime" by ordinary men and women. The privy seal (signet) or *cachet* of governors were more common, being used on militia commissions, warrants of survey, licences authorizing civil marriage or the practice of medicine and the law, the sale of liquor, and trade in the Indian territories.

The seals used by senior government officers, the legislatures, the courts and officers of the law[5] incorporated symbols from the royal arms, broadening the opportunities for exposure to the general public. How good was the impression, either to a wafer under paper or directly on colored sealing wax? Whether affixed *pendant* from a ribbon or directly to the parchment *en placard*, the great seals deputed for British colonies were *papered*. Lining the matrices with (waste) paper prevented adherence of the wax, but tended to obscure the fine details in the seal design. Signets impressed into paper over a wafer might suffer equally from a diminution of detail, depending on wear of the matrices, thickness of the paper, and skill of the seal press operator. The *cachets* applied directly to red or black sealing wax exhibited distortions resulting from uneven pressure or irregularities in the wax. Thus, even when holding a sealed document, the common man might not be able to make much of the heraldic or other symbols portrayed on it.

Did printing documents of public interest, and adorning them with symbols of state authority, render those symbols more accessible? The answer is yes and no. Much depended on the printers,[6] their choice of graphics and their skills in impressing them on paper, and the equipment available to them.[7]

Analysis of the printed texts will answer some of the questions to be posed about how and why symbols of state authority were reproduced thereon. Government records may contain answers to others, concerning the instructions given to printers, the protocols determining when and in what format types of documents would be printed, and less obvious matters such as the economic factors guiding choices. Holdings at the National Archives of Canada offer some exceptionally informative records: not only the audited public accounts documenting the government side of official publication, but also the account books of the firm that produced the *Quebec Gazette* and served as government printer throughout the 18th century. For the widest range of government printing, these accounting records tell us not only how many copies were printed, but also how and to whom they were distributed. Investigation has as yet revealed no evidence found of any written general protocol, beyond a few tenders for printing that specify paper quality and size. Variations found in usage implies there was no written protocol, but specific directions were given on occasion.

Let us consider what documents were printed, in what formats, and for distribution to whom; plus the likelihood of their survival. Proclamations were produced both as broadsides,[8] for posting up in public places and in gazettes. Statutes were printed in the official *gazette,* making them immediately available both to the officials responsible for enforcing them and to the population at large. Reprinting in book format was usually directed toward the judicial establishment, in shorter press runs. A wide range of official notices were printed both in the official *gazette* (and any other available newspapers) and as broadsides. The demand for blank forms kept a printer well-occupied. The civil administration and judicial establishment demanded printed warrants of several types, licences and permits for various functions, bonds, certificates, subpoenas, receipts; commissions, election writs, and deeds —at a premium rate for work on parchment. Private enterprises demanded bills of lading, bills of exchange, receipts, labels and price lists. Graphic elements are incorporated into examples of all types, ranging from elaborate royal arms on statutes and proclamations to charming nautical scenes on bills of lading,[9] or simple borders composed of standard printers' ornaments.

Considering the quantity of information needed for future reference that was contained in gazettes, the probability of their being retained is high. Scattered issues can indeed be found amongst surviving personal papers of the era. Broadsides, by nature intended for posting, have survived in smaller numbers, most commonly when enclosed with a governor's despatch to his superiors in London or kept on file by an official concerned with it. Printed forms, when submitted as evidence of some activity, survive in large numbers while those issued to individuals (notably permits and licences) were less likely to be preserved.

For the moment, let us assume that the surviving examples are representative of both the range and the frequency that ordinary people might have seen such items—and thus of the populace's exposure to impressions of state authority in print. The nature of those impressions is demonstrated in the illustrations. The most common were the gazette masthead incorporating the royal coat of arms, or the arms alone on a broadside; smaller examples of the royal arms heading specific items in the gazettes, and the ornamental *factotums.*[10] The same blocks were used by the printers when ornamenting particular types of forms, either the royal arms heading the sheet or an ornamental capital opening the text immediately following the recitation of the governor's titles.[11]

Judging from original imprints, the quality of the printers' wood-blocks must have been very good; details are quite precise and the average impression is clear—some are superb. The size of the plate seems not to be a factor, except for very small *factotums.* The paper quality, the unsized surface and occasionally uneven texture, appears to have presented more problems. The variations resulting from the printer's skill in inking might also be a significant factor. Cracked blocks enable us to assess whether inking was the sole variant when an impression was clear in one issue and blurred in the next. Deterioration of blocks may be the chief determinant of blurred images, whether that degradation resulted from abrasive wear or corrosion.[12]

Bibliographers have investigated the source of printers' ornaments as well as their regular type fonts. Suppliers' catalogues have not only been found, but also associated with purchases by specific printers. These merit study in relation to the replacement of blocks, to determine when and why it was done and to speculate on why it might have been delayed. The blocks for the royal arms ought to have been replaced when changes occurred, as when Ireland was united with England and Scotland or when Hanover was raised from an electorate to a kingdom (see below). What degree of wear or severity of cracking merited replacement might depend on ease of carrying that out: the length of time necessary to order new blocks and their cost. To the extent that the printers' accounts survive, or the government subsidized purchases, the acquisition of new or replacement type fonts, ornaments and presses can be studied in detail.

Who controlled the printer in his work for the government? The variations evident in surviving imprints—be they gazettes, broadsides or books—argue that no written protocol governed the style of presentation in general. If the printer worked in the absence of specific or general instructions on how to lay out texts for the state, then his ideas of how a text should be presented, the ornamenting of it, may be presumed to derive from his training, his observation of practice elsewhere, the availability of ornaments, and specific instructions—or any combination of these factors. Even when custom and training inspired the printer, lack of ornaments would have restrained his work. Louis Roy, first printer in Upper Canada, had been trained in the *Quebec Gazette* shop, but appears to have had few ornaments available. His American-born successor, Gideon Tiffany, may have been as restrained by that as by any republican sentiments.[13] The costs of paper and the design of broadsides to occupy half-sheets or full sheets (notably the classic doubles in Quebec, setting English and French texts in parallel blocks) could have played a role. Should heading space be used for a title or salutation in a larger font, or for ornamentation?

The role played by aesthetics is even more difficult to assess. The *Royal Gazette and Nova Scotia Advertiser* exhibits quite random patterns in use of ornamental blocks. The symmetry of placement observed in the *factotums* ornamenting the *Quebec Gazette* may result more from the presentation of bilingual texts in parallel columns than any aesthetic sense of the printer. The *factotums* are not all perfectly aligned in the *Gazette*—the printer would want to use all possible space for commercial purposes. However, when statutes were reprinted from the *Gazette* typesetting, but without the commercial texts, the alignment is more regular, with occasional blank spaces. Nonetheless, it must be noted that Brown & Gilmore and their successors the Neilsons had a remarkable range of ornaments and used them in borders and rules, scattering the *factotums* widely through the public notices and commercial notices in the *Quebec Gazette* and in other products—if with little evident artistic sensibility. So much for being dour Scots!

Proclamations and other texts printed as broadsides show more balance in layout, perhaps because the format allowed more freedom in the use of the paper. There was space to play with, when the job might be billed per page rather than per line. The characteristic double broadsides, presenting bilingual texts to the people of Quebec and Lower Canada, often have the royal arms in pairs, centred above the left and right-hand text blocks, where one centred on the sheet ought to suffice. This usage may have a technical origin —the need to balance text blocks on the press— or resulted from whim, when the brevity of a text left substantial blank space on the paper. Indeed, the size of the block and its absence exhibit a strong correlation to the length of the texts.

Evidence of written instructions—for specific printing jobs rather than as general protocols— can be found. The public accounts of Upper Canada[14] include statements from the government printer supported by the spiked drafts of texts he had printed. Analysis of these shows a distinct pattern: proclamations and statutes were supplied to him as formally structured texts, with some indication of titles to be assigned and layout; regulations and official notices were supplied as in precisely worded texts, but without guidelines on format; while general announcements were delivered informally through letters, from which the key details might be extracted and given a new format. Orders for printed forms were occasionally sent to him with a copy of the text to be reprinted, marked with any changes needed such as the name of a new governor and the date. The presence or absence of an ornament must have exerted an influence on his set-up of the new form.

The printer worked not from the original "copy of record" text bearing the great seal or any other symbol of state authority, but rather from a certified copy of the statutes, proclamations and other formal documents. He would not have known whether the governor's privy seal had been used instead of the great seal deputed. A representative sample of broadside proclamations for Quebec, Lower Canada and Upper Canada

were found to have been printed as often without as with the royal arms. Some double broadsides were ornamented with both paired royal arms and heraldic *factotums*! The paired royal arms were not always a perfect match. While the mortised blocks for capitals were on occasion set upsidedown, no example of the royal arms has been found in that state.

Usage in the official gazettes, which in the 18th century were produced by printers who wished to market a newspaper as well as fulfil their contracts to government, the royal coat of arms is almost invariably featured centrally in the masthead, occupying 40% or more of the page width. Indeed, the printer of the official gazette had motive to insert symbols of state authority, to distinguish his work as a superior publication, to highlight his connection with the government. The masthead was left standing, so that only the date and issue number needed to be changed for the next printing. Smaller blocks might be inserted at the head of proclamations, statutes and other official communications printed in the gazette, to distinguish their status, but enormous variations in usage are evident. Some consistency in the presentation of specific texts may have resulted from type being left standing from issue to issue, official communications being customarily repeated thrice. Through the 18th century, the gazettes were printed in a four-page format (with two- or four-page supplements on special occasions), weekly or semi-weekly. While official documents and government notices generally appeared on the first page(s) of the *Quebec Gazette* and *Upper Canada Gazette*, substantial variation was evident in other colonies.

News in general appeared unornamented. A correlation is evident between the use of common ornamental blocks such as ships, rural scenes and houses next to commercial notices with the use of heraldic/symbolic blocks for texts emanating from the government. Indeed, on occasion, the frequency of ornaments being used for the commercial notices outweighs that for the official ones. This suggests that availability of printers' ornaments in general may have been the single most influential factor in their use. When the printer could afford blocks, he acquired a selection to satisfy the whims and interests exhibited by all his clients—not just the government. The commercial market may indeed have influenced the official, by demonstrating that ornamentation drew attention to a text and was worth paying for—even if of specious relevance. The relevance of the ornament to a commercial notice was frequently tenuous: a brig next to the announcement of a schooner arrived or ready to sail, the black boy next to the notice of a runaway apprentice, the three-window house next to a description of a villa for sale or lease. The number of players in this game is so great and the evidence so slight, however, that speculation on their motivations, and on who influenced whom, may lead nowhere. The relation between the symbols in royal arms and heraldic *factotums* and the government communications they ornamented was direct and unequivocal: they were symbols of the state and used only for state business—if in a rather "one size fits all" fashion.

One of the intriguing features revealed in the examination of gazettes and broadsides was that the printers clearly had some heraldic awareness, if not specific knowledge. When changes to the royal coat of arms following the Union of England, Scotland & Ireland were announced by proclamation, January 1, 1801, authorization was also sent for continued use of the existing great seal deputed in each colony. No new matrices were prepared, so the old heraldic symbols continued to be impressed in wax. The implementation of instructions for changes to ensigns armorial, flags and banners merits study. When another change came in 1817, on Hanover being raised from an electorate to a kingdom, each colony was in due course supplied with the matrices for a new great seal deputed. Printers, relying on English type founders for their blocks, soon obtained and displayed the altered royal arms of 1801 while the government continued to impress the old image on wax for two more decades!

The next incident is more intriguing. Victoria succeeded her uncle William IV to the throne of the United Kingdom, but not to that of Hanover, in June 1837. Authorization was duly sent to the governors for continued use of William's Great Seal Deputed in each colony, pending the design and production of matrices for new seals in the new queen's name. Whether the initiative came from the governor's office or the printer, we may never know, but when broadside proclamations were printed at Quebec in November 1837, a block depicting the royal arms as they stood in 1800 was used. Within a few months, the printers had a new, corrected block available and in use.

From the earliest issues, the printers ornamented the *Quebec Gazette* with *factotums*. Within a very short period, the use of any but heraldic *factotums* for government notices ceased. The heraldic *factotums* are consistent in design, if not in detail. The opening is surmounted by a crown and encircled by the garter and flanked by the lion and the unicorn, whose feet rest on a banner inscribed with the motto DIEU ET MON DROIT, and either lances and pennants or the thistle and rose (emblems of Scotland and England) filling in the upper corners of the block. Variations in the crown design offer an easy means for identifying the several versions of both the *floral* and the *martial* heraldic *factotums* used at Quebec. These heraldic *factotums* were used extensively to ornament not only the statutes, proclamations and other official publications in the *Quebec Gazette*, but also broadsides, licences and permits, warrants authorizing payment and other work done from the printing house for government officers.

Throughout the 18th century and for the first decades of the 19th century, strong patterns are evident in the printers' use of ornaments. In the *Quebec Gazette*, the royal arms appear in the masthead but rarely below it. Official communications appear in parallel columns, English to the left, French to the right. News reports and commercial notices exhibit no such pattern, with English and French versions in either column, not necessarily on the same page. The first rank of official communications—notably proclamations and statutes —are distinguished by insertion of a *factotum* at the head of each. One soon notices a distinct pattern in usage of the heraldic *factotums*: the *martial* version appears with English texts and the *floral* with French texts. Was this a private joke of the printers? The exceptions may be telling: while the *martial* version has been found heading French texts, the *floral* was not found on the English—with one notable exception. A message from Governor Frederick Haldimand to the Oneida was printed in 1779 in parallel columns (gazette style) with a *floral factotum* heading the English text and a *martial factotum* heading the Oneida text—perhaps in honor of these important Indian allies in a time of war.

The contract as government printer at Quebec was monopolized by Brown & Gilmore and Brown's nephews Samuel and John Neilson for much of the period under study. They ran a substantial, sophisticated office. The number of *facto-tums* and other ornaments used in a single issue of the gazette suggests they had six or eight sets at hand, and could have several pages of type set up at one time. Variations in such details as the crown, the density of the floral and martial details, the fineness of lines and other features over the decades suggest that the stock was acquired gradually and replaced on occasion. At least three distinct designs are evident. The length of time that cracked or flawed ornaments were kept in use in other colonies suggests that their printers were less well endowed with ornaments and were obliged to move a single block from page to page while producing a four-page gazette. The reasons for shifting from use of the *factotums* to "miniature" royal arms at the head of an official text early in the 19th century may relate to the gradual deterioration of the *factotum* blocks, or to the labor (and thus extra costs) involved in setting the initials within the mortice.[15]

As the population grew and government activities increased, many civil and military officials had notices published in the gazettes or as broadsides. The extensive use of printed symbols of state authority on documents generated by military officials—notably general orders from the commander of the forces and on commissions to officers in the Militia—may reflect ideas of patriotism, or have arisen from a desire to lend a sense of authority to the document being issued. The inclusion of the royal arms or an heraldic *factotum* on notices relating to the civil or judicial administration may have been a deliberate choice, intended to emphasize their link to the state. The work of the chief emigrant agent is a good example: he had to compete with many commercial rivals in managing the influx of immigrants, to guard them against unscrupulous passenger agents and the like. The emblems in their office seals merit a closer, fuller study. Preliminary investigation suggests the adoption of many elements from the royal arms. Again, the question will arise as to whether the official suggested a design to the engraver or vice-versa. Regulatory agencies with less obvious links to the Crown adopted symbols appropriate to their jurisdiction, such as the Trinity House,[16] whose notices were ornamented with an anchor, emblematically linked to its corporate seal.

Another factor to consider is the heraldic awareness and knowledge of the type founders and block makers in England—the suppliers from whom the colonial printers obtained their stock. The type founders were supplying the English market as well, a more discerning audience, exposed to more use of heraldic emblems on a daily basis. They also had relatively easy access to officials, and to specialists in the subject. Engravers, painters and other artists who depicted heraldry in precious metals (for seal matrices or to decorate silver or gold plate) and on other media might well have been hired to prepare designs for the founders.

## Conclusions

This commentary results from preliminary investigations. Many questions await a fuller study, in particular the surprisingly strong influence of the printer in the acquisition and use of ornaments, whether to symbolize state authority or to decorate his work. I hope this little foray (transcending boundaries between research disciplines) will stimulate thought and investigation, elsewhere in the British Empire and in other empires.[17] Books, gazettes and broadsides penetrated where officials and institutions might not travel. Reading materials were relatively rare and treasured, frequently recycled and reread. They carried ideas and impressions through non-verbal means as well in their texts. Let us seek to learn more about the impressions they made.

## Illustrations

For each item listed below, the first sentence/line describes the item and (within brackets) provides the formal citation of its location. The citation may be omitted. The second line provides the minimum credit required by the National Archives of Canada.

1. *Signet* of William IV at the head of the royal instructions to Lord Durham, 1837 (MG 24, A 27, vol. 6). Courtesy of the National Archives of Canada, Neg. C-124568.

2. Reverse of the Great Seal Deputed of George III for Quebec, appended to a proclamation of July 23, 1793 (RG 4, B 7, vol. 1). Courtesy of the National Archives of Canada, Neg. C-131486.

3. Great Seal Deputed of Queen Victoria for the Province of Canada, affixed *en placard* at the head of the letters patent appointing the attorney general February 13, 1841 (RG 4, B 9, vol. 3). Courtesy of the National Archives of Canada, Neg. C-131485.

4. Tax stamp impressed into paper supplied to the British colonies in 1765, to be used for legal documents (RG 4, B 16, vol. 1). Courtesy of the National Archives of Canada, Neg. C-83435.

5. Privy seal of Sir George Prevost, governor of Lower Canada, at the head of a proclamation of August 22, 1814 (RG 4, B 3, vol. 4). Courtesy of the National Archives of Canada, Neg. C-137139.

6. Privy seal of Frederick Haldimand, governor of Quebec, at the head of a proclamation of May 17, 1779 (RG 4, B 3, vol. 1). Courtesy of the National Archives of Canada, Neg. C-102048.

7. *Cachet* of Frederick Haldimand, governor of Quebec, at the foot of a warrant to discharge four pardoned prisoners, August 15, 1778 (RG 4, B 20, vol. 1, p. 12). Courtesy of the National Archives of Canada, Neg. C-102045.

8. *Cachet* of Sir William Johnson, superintendent of Indian affairs in the northern district of North America, at the foot of a treaty concluded at Niagara with the Hurons of Detroit, July 18, 1764 (MG 19, F 31). Courtesy of the National Archives of Canada, Neg. C-135294.

9. Double broadside illustrated with mismatched impressions of the royal coat of arms: proclamation by Sir George Prevost, January 12, 1814 (RG 4, D 9, vol. 29). Courtesy of the National Archives of Canada, Neg. C-93278.

10. Proclamation by Hector Theophilus Cramahé, lieutenant governor of Quebec, published in parallel columns ornamented with *martial* and *floral factotums* in the *Quebec Gazette* of November 16, 1775 (RG 4, D 1). Courtesy of the National Archives of Canada, Neg. C-80103. Alternative: proclamation by Alured

Clarke, lieutenant governor of Quebec, November 19, 1791, printed in parallel columns ornamented with *martial* and *floral factotums* in the *Quebec Gazette* (RG 4, D 1), Neg. C-80103.

11. Broadside of a proclamation by Christopher Billopp, administrator of New Brunswick, April 21, 1823, ornamented with the royal coat of arms (Archives Library). Courtesy of the National Archives of Canada, Neg. C-54708.

12. Broadside of a proclamation by Peter Russell, administrator of Upper Canada, December 15, 1798 (Archives Library). Courtesy of the National Archives of Canada, Neg. C-54635.

13. Licence for a pedlar, issued by authority of Sir George Prevost, July 29, 1814—on a printed form ornamented with the royal coat of arms (RG 4, B 28, vol. 116). Courtesy of the National Archives of Canada, Neg. C-140675.

14. Notice of May 6, 1834 from the chief emigrant agent for Upper and Lower Canada, published in the *Quebec Gazette* under an impression of the royal coat of arms. Courtesy of the National Archives of Canada, Neg. C-54722.

15. Notice of June 26, 1820 from the Trinity House of Quebec, published in the *Quebec Gazette* with a block illustrating an anchor, emblematic of the corporation. Courtesy of the National Archives of Canada, Neg. C-22175.

## NOTES

1. This is a report on work in progress: an exploration of the relationships between manuscript documents bearing seals of public authorities and the corresponding printed texts, many of which bear the royal arms and other symbols of state authority illustrated through various printing methods. Awareness of this relationship has crept up on me during a lengthy career at the National Archives of Canada. Spending three decades in the archives has given me exceptional opportunities both to recognize and observe the overlapping of research disciplines and topics while exchanging ideas that occasionally inspired new lines of study, and to explore many hidden treasure troves.

   Archives hold much that is unrecognized and hence unexplored. What has not been catalogued appropriately is not truly accessible. Automation compounds this denial of access, for certain key words have never been incorporated into the descriptive catalogues and guides, so cannot be found through a computerized search.

2. Thanks are due to Dr. Joyce Banks, Michel Brisebois

and Dr. Liana vander Bellen of the Rare Books Division, National Library of Canada, and to Dr. Patricia Fleming of the University of Toronto for their generosity with advice, information and encouragement.

3. The term "British North America" is generally applied to those colonies that came to form the Dominion of Canada (1867-1873), as distinct from the colonies to the south that had achieved independence in 1783 through a revolutionary war. Constraints on time and opportunity to travel narrowed the central time frame for this study of printed expressions of state authority during the British Regime to the 1770s through 1820s.

4. The carving of escutcheons in Quebec and Lower Canada is documented through the accounts submitted by their sculptors to the government (see National Archives of Canada, RG 1, E 15 A).

5. The public accounts of the colonies and the personal accounts of individual officials—such as Edward William Gray, sheriff of Montreal, 1765-1810—demonstrate that seal matrices and presses were amongst the first equipment to be acquired when offices were set up. Whether the matrices were produced by local engravers or ordered from England might affect the heraldic knowledge expressed in the design and the quality of its execution.

6. While the colonial governments wished access to a printing press, their desires for equipment and qualified operators were often frustrated. Nova Scotia's press arrived in 1751, but the death of the printer delayed operations until the next year. Quebec's press and printers arrived in April 1764, before the inception of civil government. Similarly, New Brunswick's first press was brought into operation before the first governor was sworn in. Cape Breton, though a separate jurisdiction 1784-1820, lacked a press. Prince Edward Island was separated from Nova Scotia in 1769 but waited until 1786 for a press and printer. Newfoundland was to wait half a century longer. Upper Canada, separated from Quebec in 1791, obtained a press the next year but experienced difficulties in hiring and keeping a qualified printer.

7. The Canadian Institute for Historical Micro-reproduction (CIHM) has catalogued and prepared microfiche for literally thousands of imprints scattered through the National Archives of Canada's holdings, and in other archives—items that archivists do not customarily highlight in their cataloguing of manuscript materials. Using the automated CIHM catalogue greatly speeds the task of locating government documents.

My investigation of available examples of imprints was directed to a rather random selection, based on ease of access (in holdings of both National Archives and the National Library of Canada) to the original printed texts.

The study of readily accessible originals in Ottawa results in a certain bias towards the printers of Quebec/Lower Canada and Upper Canada. Future research in the Colonial Office records at the Public Record Office (London) should provide the ideal balance, given that governors sent copies of gazettes, broadside proclamations and a wide range of other printed works home for the information of the imperial authorities and these have been preserved in large quantities at a single archival location.

While the imprints examined may have been limited, my discussions with the bibliographers mentioned above have confirmed the supposition that the general impressions or practice drawn from that selection are valid for Nova Scotia, New Brunswick and other colonies.

Travel and time are essential for a full-scale study. Microfilm copies are a frustrating substitute; inadequacies of the film, poor resolution and other technical features of the reproduction compound with blurring and other imprecisions of the images to render them illegible. Only examination of the original imprints can answer many questions, but finding them may be a challenge. Bibliographic descriptions only rarely include any details of royal arms in mastheads, decorative capitals, *factotums* and other printers' ornaments —but they do tell us where the texts are located, a very substantial narrowing of the field to be investigated.

The term *factotum* is used to identify mortised initial blocks: printing blocks having a blank or mortised space into which leters or numbers can be inserted. The decoration of such blocks falls into several broad categories, including geometric, floral and heraldic. Initial blocks on which the decoration was interwoven with the letter were a costly investment; mortised initial blocks offered a sustantial economic advantage to the under-funded printing house. For a fuller discussion of *factotums* and illustrations of decorative blocks used in North America, see ELIZABETH C. REILLY, *A Dictionary of Colonial American Printers' Ornaments and Illustrations* (Worcester, Mass.: American Antiquarian Society, 1975).

8. The term *broadside* is applied to single-sided imprints, occupying half or full sheets of paper, intended for posting on church doors or other public spaces where the populace might see and read them. A double-sided imprint is properly termed a *handbill*; intended for general distribution, it offers substantial text on a single sheet of paper, but without the costs inherent in complex layouts and folding for a pamphlet.

9. The range of nautical illustrations on various documents submitted to the Vice Admiralty Court of Nova Scotia astonishes as much as it delights. Determining which of the surviving imprints (in RG 8, Series IV at the National Archives of Canada) were printed at Quebec, Halifax and other ports of British North America remains to be investigated. Printers routinely advertised having such blank forms in stock.

10. The practice of printing the letters LS [for *locus sigilli*], alone or within a circle, to denote where the seal was affixed to the original document, was not commonly followed in all colonies at all times.

11. By using photocopies on mylar in the next phase of this investigation, it should be possible to identify common sources for particular blocks—following the example set by ELIZABETH CARROLL REILLY, *op. cit.*

12. Thanks to distinct cracks or flaws in blocks, we can trace their usage with greater certainty from page to page of one issue, or through several issues, and determine whether the printer might have had more than one example of a particular block.

13. When John Bennett replaced Titus Simons as government printer in Upper Canada, an inventory of

materials belonging to the government was compiled on its transfer in July 1807. The list included the press, chases, type fonts and composing sticks, but specified no ornaments (see National Archives of Canada, Civil Secretary's letterbook, RG 7, G 16 C, vol. 1).

14. Statements of account supported by vouchers (receipted invoices) were submitted by government officials, including the official Printer, for audit; those for Upper Canada have survived in great numbers (see the National Archives of Canada, RG 1, E 15 B).

15. On seeking advice from Lower Canada in 1802, officials in Upper Canada learned that an increase of nearly 50% in prices quoted by two printers (Desbarats and Neilson) was attributed to the cost of paper and labor (National Archives of Canada, Civil Secretary's letterbook, RG 7, G 16 C, vol. 2).

16. Incorporated at Quebec in 1805, with a branch at Montreal, Trinity House managed the licensing of pilots and the establishment and operation of navigational aids in the St. Lawrence River and Gulf.

17. The first press in the Americas was operating at Mexico City by 1534.

1

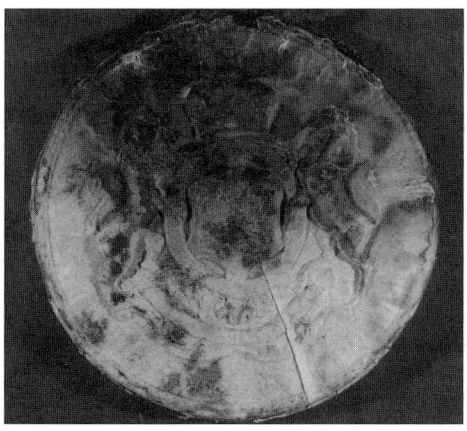

2

3

4

5

6

7

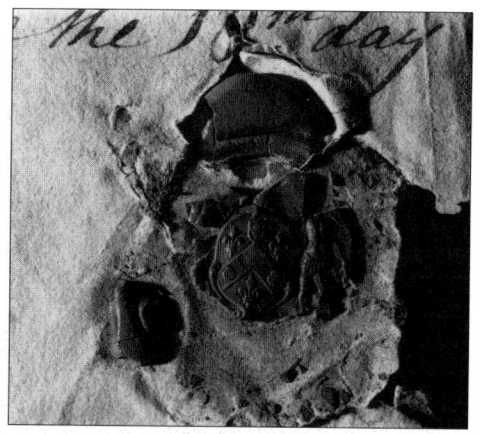

8

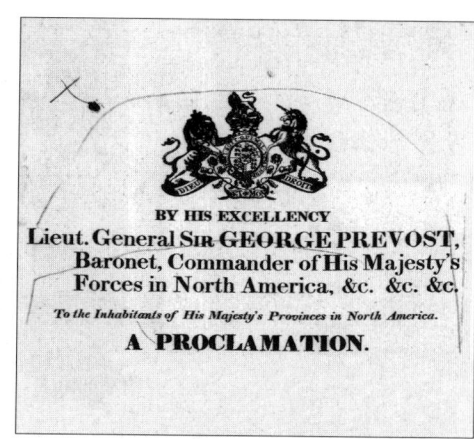

BY HIS EXCELLENCY
Lieut. General SIR GEORGE PREVOST,
Baronet, Commander of His Majesty's
Forces in North America, &c. &c. &c.

*To the Inhabitants of His Majesty's Provinces in North America.*

## A PROCLAMATION.

9

## THE QUEBEC GAZETTE.    LA GAZETTE DE QUEBEC.

Nᵒ. 566.

THURSDAY, NOVEMBER 16, 1775.    JEUDI, le 16 NOVEMBRE, 1775.

BY THE HONORABLE
HECTOR THEOPHILUS CRAMAHE, Esq;
*Lieutenant-governor of the Province of Quebec, &c. &c.*

A PROCLAMATION.

PAR l'HONORABLE
HECTOR THEOPHILE CRAMAHE, Ecuier,
*Lieutenant-gouverneur de la Province de Québec, &c. &c.*

PROCLAMATION.

H. T. CRAMAHE.

GOD Save the KING.

H. T. CRAMAHE.

VIVE LE ROI.

10

By the Honorable **Christopher Billopp**, Esquire, Administrator of the Government, and Commander-in-Chief
of the Province of New-Brunswick, &c. &c. &c.

(L. S.)

## A PROCLAMATION.
### CHRISTOPHER BILLOPP.

WHEREAS by Proclamation under my Hand and Seal, bearing date at Saint John, the seventeenth day of April, one thousand eight hundred and twenty-three, I did make known to all concerned, that by virtue of His Majesty's Royal Instructions, the Administration of the Government of this Province has of right devolved on me; And Whereas sundry Proclamations and Notices have appeared in the Public Papers since the demise of the Lieutenant-Governor, purporting to have been issued in the name and under the authority of the Honorable WARD CHIPMAN, as President of the Province, in whom no legal authority is vested for that purpose. I do hereby, for the due preservation of the public Peace, and of the rights of all His Majesty's liege Subjects within this Province, publish and make known that all Proclamations, Civil Appointments, and Public Acts whatsoever, done and issuing in the name and by the authority of the said Honorable WARD CHIPMAN, as President, or Administrator of the Government, are absolutely illegal and of no effect.

Given under my Hand and Seal at the City of Saint John, this twenty-first day of April, in the Year of our Lord one thousand eight hundred and twenty-three, and in the fourth year of His Majesty's Reign.

11

## PROCLAMATION.

**Peter Russell,** *esq. President, administering the government of Upper-Canada.*

WHEREAS by *letters* received from his Grace the Duke of Portland, one of his Majesty's principal secretaries of state, since the issuing the proclamation of the *thirty-first* of October last, it appears that, in consequence of a *Representation* made by the EXECUTIVE GOVERNMENT of THIS PROVINCE, to his Majesty's MINISTERS, on the *Exemption* of the U. E. LOYALISTS and their CHILDREN from every expence attending the grants of land made, or to be made to them, his Majesty has been graciously pleased to signify his Royal Pleasure that the FIRST *LOYALISTS*, and their SONS and *DAUGHTERS* shall continue to receive his Majesty's BOUNTY of Two HUNDRED ACRES EACH as heretofore, *free from any expence whatever.* And that it is to be understood, that this MARK of the Royal Munificence is expressly confined to those LOYALISTS only, who were actually resident in the province on, or before the TWENTY-EIGHTH of JULY LAST.

*Be it therefore known,* that, notwithstanding what has been declared to the contrary in the proclamation *aforesaid*, all LOYALISTS coming within the above description, whose names have been enrolled upon the U. E. lists, *previous* to the date of this proclamation, and their SONS and DAUGHTERS when of AGE, or MARRIED, to whom the King's bounty in lands has not been already extended, may continue to consider themselves entitled to receive from this government, TWO HUNDRED ACRES OF LAND *free* from the payment of fees and all other charges; but that, except to the extent allowed by his Majesty's INSTRUCTIONS, neither U. E. loyalists, nor their children, can be considered as exempted from the STANDING FEES, it having been ordered that they shall be annexed to every further grant of land, to them as well as to others, be its extent what it may.

GIVEN under my hand and seal at arms, in council at York, this fifteenth day of December, in the thirty-ninth year of his Majesty's reign, and in the year of our Lord one thousand seven hundred and ninety-eight.

PETER RUSSELL.

*By Command of the President in Council,*
**John Small,** C. E. C.

YORK: Printed by WILLIAM WATERS and TITUS G. SIMONS.
1798.

12

---

Nᵒ 51.

PROVINCE OF Lower-Canada. His Excellency Sir George Prevost Baronet, Captain General and Governor in Chief, in and over the Province of Lower Canada, Vice Admiral of the Same &c. &c. &c.

To all whom these Presents may concern:

WHEREAS according to the form of the Statute of the Provincial Parliament of Lower Canada, made and passed in the thirty-fifth year of His present Majesty's Reign, intituled "*An Act for granting to his Majesty, Duties on Licences to Hawkers, Pedlars and Petty Chapmen, and for regulating their trade, &c.*" A Certificate under the hand of *Neff, Perrault & Green* — Clerks of the Peace for the District of *Quebec* — in the said Province, hath been produced by *Abraham Morrency* — of the parish of *Beaumont* in the said District, Hawker, and now remains on File in the Office of the Secretary of the Province in the said District of *Quebec* — setting forth that he, the said *Abraham Morrency* — hath complied with the regulations prescribed by the above said Statute, for the purpose of obtaining a Licence to be a Hawker, Pedlar or Petty Chapman.

I DO THEREFORE hereby Licence and Allow the said *Abraham Morrency* to be a Hawker, Pedlar or Petty Chapman, and as such within this Province, to travel and trade conformable to the Provisions, in the said abovementioned Statute set forth and contained.

THIS LICENCE to be in force until the Fifth day of April, One thousand eight hundred and *fifteen* — and no longer.

Given under my Hand and Seal at Arms, at the Castle of St. Lewis, in the city of Quebec, this *twenty ninth* — day of *July* — 1814, in the *fifty fourth* — year of His Majesty's Reign.

By His Excellency's Command,
*Jno. Taylor Sy. Secy.*  George Prevost

[Licence for a Hawker, Pedlar or Petty Chapman.]

13

---

## NOTICE.

*Office of His Majesty's Chief Agent for the superintendance of Emigrants in Upper and Lower Canada,*
Quebec, 6th May, 1834.

CONDUCTORS of public and private works in Upper and Lower Canada in want of Artificers, Mechanics, or Labourers, are requested to transmit to this Office, an account of the number of persons required, specifying the rate of wages to be paid, probable period wanted, also the nearest landing place and Post Office.

Private proprietors who have for sale Land or Farms in Upper and Lower Canada, are also informed that they may transmit to this office, for the free inspection and information of Emigrants arriving from the United Kingdom, the particulars of such Lands or Farms, specifying accurately the terms, description of soil, timber, situation, nearest landing, and Post Office.
*All Letters must be Post paid.*
A. C. BUCHANAN.
d-2  Chief Agent.

14

---

**NOTICE TO PILOTS AND OTHERS CONCERNED.**
TRINITY-HOUSE, QUEBEC,
Monday, 26th June, 1820.

THE proceedings of the Trinity-House, Quebec, against JOSEPH PARANT, Pilot for and below the Harbour of Quebec, for the loss of the Ship Alligator, on the twelfth day of May last, and against JEAN GODBU, Pilot for and below the Harbour of Quebec, for the loss of the Brig Minerva, on the fourteenth day of May last, having been submitted, according to law, to His Excellency the Governor in Chief, and His Excellency having signified by Warrant under his Hand and Seal, his approbation of the said proceedings, whereby the said Joseph Parant and the said Jean Godbu are declared to have forfeited their respective Branches, it is hereby notified that their names are erased from the list of Pilots for and below the Harbour of Quebec.

By Order,
33d6  WM. LINDSAY,
Registrar T. H. Q.

15

# LES PIERRES TOMBALES DES COMTES DE LANNOY À CLERVAUX AU GRAND-DUCHÉ DE LUXEMBOURG

Jean-Claude Loutsch

## Petit historique de la seigneurie de Clervaux

Avant de nous consacrer à l'étude des pierres tombales des comtes de Lannoy-Clervaux, il convient de donner un aperçu historique sommaire de la seigneurie de Clervaux située au nord du Grand-Duché de Luxembourg, en plein cœur de l'Ardenne, dans un site particulièrement enchanteur[1].

Clervaux apparaît avec Gérard, comte de Clervaux, frère de Frédéric, comte de Vianden, en 1129 et 1132. Son successeur, Simon, comte de Clervaux est cité en 1157, puis nous trouvons en 1198 Henri, comte de Sponheim et en 1240 Simon, comte de Sponheim, tous deux intitulés comtes de Clervaux. Il est impossible de savoir si Clervaux était un comté à l'époque. Aussi bien les Vianden que les Sponheim sont des grandes familles comtales et leurs titulatures peuvent s'expliquer de cette façon[2]. De toute manière, l'historien allemand Johannes Moetsch estime que les Vianden et les Sponheim sont vraisemblablement issus d'une même famille à l'origine[3]. En tout cas, à partir de 1300 apparaît à Clervaux une famille chevaleresque, donc d'un tout autre milieu social, issue de la famille de Meysembourg. Ses archives[4], conservées avec un soin tout particulier depuis 1145, ne concernent Clervaux qu'après 1300. Tout se passe comme si aucun seigneur n'avait résidé à Clervaux entre 1240 et 1300 et qu'une nouvelle seigneurie avait été créée pour les Meysembourg-Clervaux, vassaux des comtes de Luxembourg. Ils portaient *d'or au chef de gueules chargé de trois merlettes d'argent*[5].

Vers 1400, Marie de Clervaux, fille unique et héritière, fut mariée à Frédéric de Brandenbourg, issu d'une branche cadette des comtes de Vianden[6]. Leurs descendants portèrent un écartelé de Brandenbourg (*De gueules à l'écusson d'argent*) et de Meysembourg-Clervaux[7]. En 1492 Marguerite de Brandenbourg-Clervaux épousa Nicolle de Heu, chevalier, seigneur d'Ennery, un des plus riches citains de la ville de Metz. Sa famille, du paraige du Commun, c'est-à-dire à l'origine non patricienne, était alliée à tout le patriciat de la

république messine et surtout avait accumulé depuis le début du XIVe siècle une fortune considérable[8]. Outre leur métier de changeur, les Heu n'avaient fait qu'augmenter leur richesse en exerçant tous les négoces possibles. L'hôtel de Heu, à Metz, est conservé, et est encore de nos jours un sompteux palais. Les armes portées par cette famille étaient *de gueules à la bande d'argent, chargée de trois coquilles de sable*[9].

Leur fils aîné, Nicolle de Heu (1498-1547), épousa Anne de Failly, d'une famille de noblesse barroise[10]. La fille unique de ces derniers, Elisabeth de Heu (†1599), mariée à Godefroy d'Eltz, seigneur de Wolmerange et d'Ottange en partie (†1614), laissa entre autres une fille, Claudine D'Eltz, dame de Clervaux, mariée à Claude de Lannoy, comte de la Motterie, gouverneur de Maastricht, chevalier de la Toison d'Or en 1638. C'est ainsi que l'illustre famille de Lannoy arriva à Clervaux[11].

Le cinquième fils des Heu-Clervaux, Gaspard I de Heu, chevalier, seigneur de Buy, Flévy, d'un cinquième de Clervaux, etc. se convertit à la religion luthérienne et livra une lutte politique active en faveur des réformés, tant et si bien qu'il finit par être emprisonné, puis exécuté à Vincennes en 1558. Il avait épousé Jeanne de Louvain, fille de Jean, seigneur de Rognac, dont la sœur avait été mariée à Jean du Barry, seigneur de la Renaudie. Il semblerait que ce soit pour venger son beau-frère que ce dernier se soit mis à la tête de la conjuration d'Amboise[12] qui visait à capturer le roi François II et surtout les Guise. Le fils de Gaspard, aussi prénommé Gaspard, époux de l'héritière de Beaufort au Luxembourg, fit de son château de Beaufort un repaire de « reformés ». En fait il y rassembla des brigands, luttant ouvertement contre les troupes régulières. Il fut capturé le 17 janvier 1593 et fut accusé « d'homicide, assassinats, rapines, enlèvements et emprisonnements de marchands passant sous la sauvegarde du roi », etc. et finit par être décapité le 15 avril 1593 à Luxembourg. Ces deux Gaspard père et fils méritent mention, car ils pourraient être à l'origine de certaines irrégularités que nous trouverons dans la disposition des quartiers des pierres tombales.

## Les sépultures des seigneurs de Clervaux

Jusqu'au début du XVII⁰ siècle les seigneurs de Clervaux furent enterrés dans une chapelle construite en 1470 comme annexe de l'église de Munshausen, église paroissiale de Clervaux jusqu'en 1803. Sept pierres tombales armoriées y sont conservées, entre autres celle du jeune Gaspard III de Heu († 1573), fils de Gaspard II. Parmi ses quartiers figurent les armes des Louvain-Rognac, famille de Guyenne [13].

En 1630 Godefroy, baron d'Eltz et de Clervaux donna à l'ordre de St. François la chapelle construite par ses ancêtres à Troisvierges pour qu'ils puissent y fonder un couvent. Par son testament de 1631, il leur légua une grosse somme, précisant néanmoins que les seigneurs de Clervaux devraient dorénavant être enterrés dans l'église des Franciscains [14]. Les deux pierres tombales que nous allons décrire y furent installées en leur temps. Elles y restèrent jusqu'à la fin du XVIII⁰, puis furent déplacées en la chapelle Notre-Dame de Lorette située dans le parc du château de Clervaux, construite en 1762 sur l'emplacement d'un ancien ermitage et restaurée en 1786 par le comte Adrien-Jean-Baptiste de Lannoy-Clervaux [15], et son épouse Constance-Polyxène-Reine-Stanislas de Wignacourt, d'une famille originaire d'Artois. Le portail d'entrée de la chapelle est surmonté des armes d'alliance Lannoy et Wignacourt (*d'argent à trois fleurs de lis au pied coupé de gueules*) placées sous la Vierge Consolatrice des Affligés, patronne du Luxembourg.

## Les pierres tombales des Lannoy à Clervaux

Il s'agit de deux larges plaques de marbre noir (env. 2 x 1 m.) ornées de marbre blanc pour l'épitaphe et les écus qui la surmontent [16].

La première, pour Albert-Eugène, comte de Lannoy, est ornée de 16 quartiers, les écus disposés en deux colonnes (de huit) de chaque côté de l'épitaphe et accompagnés des cimiers respectifs. Il s'agit des huit quartiers d'Albert-Eugène de Lannoy et des huit quartiers de son épouse Anne-Marguerite, fille d'Adrien de Reede de Saasfeld et de Marie de Wyhe. Les armes d'alliance Lannoy-Rheede sous une couronne, et supportées par deux griffons surmontent le tout [17].

## Description des armes

### À gauche [FIGURES 1-3] :

**Lannoy :** *D'argent à trois lions de sinople, couronnés d'or, armés et lampassés de gueules. Casque couronné. Cimier : Tête et col de licorne d'argent, accornée d'or* [18]. Famille originaire de Lannoy près de Lille (Nord).

**Ongnies :** *Écartelé : aux I et IV de sinople à la fasce d'hermine* (Ongnies), *aux II et III d'argent à trois lions de sable, armés, lampassés et couronnés d'or* (Halewyn). *Cimier : Deux têtes et cols de chiens braque adossés de gueules, colletés d'argent* [19]. Famille d'Artois.

**Noyelles :** *Écartelé : aux I et IV contre-écartelé d'or et de gueules, aux II et III d'or à trois maillets de sinople* (Mailly), *et sur le tout d'argent au lion de sable* (Fiennes). *Cimier : Une tête de lévrier de gueules, colletée du même bordée et bouclée d'or* [20]. Famille de Picardie.

**Lille :** *De gueules au chef d'or. Cimier : un cygne issant* [21]. Il s'agit ici des armes portées par les châtelains de Lille, en principe éteints depuis le début du XIV⁰ siècle. Ce quartier reste donc douteux. Il est vraisemblable qu'il s'agisse d'une autre famille homonyme, également originaire du Nord de la France.

**Eltz :** *Coupé de gueules et d'argent, au lion d'or issant de la partition. Casque couronné. Cimier : Le lion issant* [22]. Branche luxembourgo-lorraine de cette famille originaire du pays de Trèves.

**Bemelburg :** *Écartelé d'argent et d'azur. Cimier : Deux proboscides aux armes* [23]. Famille originaire du pays de Hesse.

**Huy :** *De gueules au lion d'or, l'épaule chargée d'un écusson à trois losanges. Cimier : Le lion issant.* Il s'agit ici d'armes inventées de toutes pièces. Le véritable nom, Heu, est remplacé par Huy, ce qui peut encore s'expliquer. Il est possible que les Heu aient été à l'origine des marchands venant de Huy et installés à Metz à la fin du XII⁰ siècle. Les personnes de ce nom sont très nombreuses dans cette ville au XIII⁰ siècle, et seule une branche arriva à sortir rapidement et brillamment de la médiocrité pour accéder au patriciat par le paraige du Commun, groupant les familles peu anciennes [24].

**Heu portait :** *De gueules à la bande d'argent, chargée de trois coquilles de sable.* Cimier : *Un anneau d'argent sur un bonnet plat de gueules* [25]. En revanche, il est peu vraisemblable que leurs armes n'aient pas été connues par les Lannoy ou le fonctionnaire chargé de commander la pierre tombale. Elles figurent sur les épitaphes de l'église de Munshausen, et c'est par les Heu que la baronnie de Clervaux était parvenue aux Lannoy. On doit donc admettre que ces armes déplaisaient, soit par l'origine bourgeoise de la famille, soit par les activités criminelles des deux Gaspard de Heu évoquées plus haut.

**Ennery :** *D'argent au lion de sable.* Cimier : *Le lion issant.* Sans doute, pour mieux brouiller les pistes, ici aussi une fausse famille a été placée. Devrait être Failly. *D'argent au rameau arraché de houx de gueules de trois ou de cinq feuilles, à la bordure engrêlée de sable.* Cimier : *Une tête et col de lévrier d'argent colleté de gueules, bouclé d'or* [26]. En fait, la seigneurie d'Ennery (Moselle) appartenait à la famille de Heu, achetée par Thiébaut de Heu en 1323 [27] aux anciens seigneurs du nom d'Ennery qui portaient, en effet, un lion [28].

### À droite [FIGURES 4-7] :

**Rheede :** *D'argent à deux fasces vivrées de sable.* Casque couronné. Cimier : *Un vol de sable* [29]. Originaire du duché de Gueldre, mais aussi province d'Utrecht.

**Nyenrode :** *Écartelé d'argent à la fasce de gueules et d'argent à trois fasces d'azur.* Casque couronné. Cimier : *Un écureuil issant* [30]. Province d'Utrecht.

**Duras :** *De sable semé de fleurs de lis d'argent.* Cimier : *Une tête et col de chien braque de sable* [31]. Province de Liège.

**Immersele :** *D'argent à trois fleurs de lis au pied coupé de sable, à l'écusson en abîme d'argent à trois pals de gueules.* Cimier : [32]. Marquisat d'Anvers.

**Wyhe :** *Coupé-ondé, en chef un lion couronné issant, en pointe diapré-ondé.* Cimier : *Le lion issant* [33]. Originaire du duché de Gueldre.

**Doegeren :** *D'argent à une aigle sans griffes, la tête de front, de sinople.* Cimier : *Un chien issant de sable, colleté* [34]. Originaire du duché de Gueldre.

**Bogarde :** *De gueules au chevron d'argent.* Cimier : *Un buste d'homme aux armes* [35]. Originaire du duché de Juliers.

**Dasvsyn :** *D'argent à cinq cotices de gueules.* Casque couronné. Cimier : *Un renard issant de gueules posé de front, empoignant de chaque patte une boule d'or* [36]. Originaire du duché de Gueldre.

La deuxième plaque funéraire, pour Adrien-Gérard, comte de Lannoy, fils du précédent est ornée de trente-deux quartiers, les écus disposés en deux colonnes de chaque côté de l'épitaphe, à gauche les 16 quartiers d'Adrien-Gérard de Lannoy, déjà décrits. À droite figurent les 16 quartiers de son épouse Isabelle-Thérèse-Claire, fille de Jean-Guillaume, baron de Bocholtz et d'Anne de Hoensbroeck. Les armes d'alliance Lannoy-Bocholtz sous une couronne, et supportées par deux griffons surmontent le tout [37].

### Quartiers de droite [FIGURES 8-12] :

**Bocholtz :** *De sinople à trois têtes de léopard d'argent* [38]. Originaire du duché de Gueldre. Une branche à Liège début XVIIe siècle.

**Vinck :** *D'or au chevron abaissé de sable sommé d'un pinson de gueules* [39]. Originaire du duché de Gueldre.

**Cortenbach :** *D'or à trois bandes de gueules* [40]. Comté de Fauquemont, principauté de Liège.

**Hanxeler :** *D'azur à deux pièces en forme de C affrontées et entrelacées d'or, les quatre extrémités en forme de tête d'oiseau* [41]. Duché de Gueldre, duché de Limbourg.

**Boedberg :** *D'azur, au chef d'argent chargé de trois merlettes de gueules* [42]. Originaire du duché de Clèves.

**Amsterade :** *De gueules à la croix gringolée d'argent* (Huyn). *En cœur un écusson d'argent à trois tourteaux de gueules* (Printhagen) [43]. Rhénanie.

**Bocholtz** : *De sinople à trois têtes de léopard d'argent*[38]. Originaire du duché de Gueldre.

**Merwyck** : *De sinople au chef d'hermine*[44]. Originaire du duché de Gueldre.

**Hoensbroeck** : *Fascé de huit pièces d'argent et de gueules, au lion de sable, armé, lampassé et couronné d'or, brochant*[45]. Originaire du duché de Gueldre.

**Dave** : *De gueules à la bande d'argent*[46]. Comté de Namur, principauté de Liège.

**Scheiffart de merode** : *D'or à quatre pals de gueules*[47]. Aix-la-Chapelle, puis principauté de Liège.

**Hompesch** : *De gueules au sautoir engrêlé d'argent*[48]. Juliers, Limbourg.

**Bocholtz** : *De sinople à trois têtes de léopard d'argent*[38]. Originaire du duché de Gueldre.

**Vinck** : *D'or au chevron abaissé de sable, sommé d'un pinson de gueules*[39]. Originaire du duché de Gueldre.

**Wittenhorst** : *D'or à deux fasces de gueules*[49]. Originaire du duché de Clèves.

**Wees** : *D'argent à une fasce de sinople*[50]. Originaire du duché de Gueldre.

En analysant les familles figurant sur ces tableaux de quartiers, on peut constater plusieurs groupes familiaux. Les quatre premiers quartiers Lannoy appartiennent tous au Nord de la France, Flandre française, Artois et Picardie. Les quatre quartiers suivants, qu'on peut considérer comme « luxembourgeois », sont en fait composés de familles tréviroise, lorraine, barroise et messine, ayant toutes des ascendances luxembourgeoises. Les quatre quartiers Reede sont en partie néerlandais (province d'Utrecht), en partie anversois et liégeois, actuellement royaume de Belgique, alors que les quartiers Wyhe sont tous issus du duché de Gueldre, donc néerlandais.

Il y a donc là des familles très internationales, bien que toutes originaires de pays situés entre la Manche et le Rhin, mais soumises à des souverainetés très différentes.

En revanche, parmi les 16 quartiers Bocholtz, à l'exception de trois quartiers liégeois, toutes les familles sont originaires des bouches du Rhin, du duché de Gueldre, alors Provinces-Unies, actuellement royaume des Pays-Bas, des duchés de Juliers et de Clèves, actuellement République fédérale d'Allemagne. On y retrouve même une certaine endogamie : trois quartiers Bocholtz, deux quartiers Vinck. On peut donc considérer que les Bocholtz, bien que d'une famille importante, étaient beaucoup plus provinciaux que les Lannoy.

Dans le cadre du sujet de ce congrès, il nous a paru intéressant de présenter les pierres tombales de Clervaux qui n'ont jusqu'à présent fait l'objet d'aucune étude.

**NOTES**

1. Voir JOSEPH GOEDERT, *Bio-Bibliographie du canton de Clervaux. La cité et la commune de Clervaux*, Luxembourg 1987.

2. Voir CAMILLE WAMPACH, *Urkunden- und Quellenbuch zur Geschichte der altluxemburgischen Territorien bis zur burgundischen Zeit*, vol. 1 et 2.

3. JOHANNES MOETSCH, « Die Grafen von Vianden und Clervaux, Verwandte der Grafen von Sponheim », dans *Annuaire de l'Association Luxembourgeoise de Généalogie et d'Héraldique* (1991).

4. M.-F.-X. WURTH-PAQUET et N. VAN WERWEKE, *Archives de Clervaux. Analysées et publiées*, Luxembourg 1883.

5. JEAN-CLAUDE LOUTSCH, *Armorial du pays de Luxembourg*, Luxembourg, Ministère des Arts et des Sciences, 1974, p. 292, 577.

6. JULES VANNÉRUS, *La famille de Brandebourg*, Bruxelles, Dewitt, 1926-1934, 5 vol., (Extr. de *Annuaire de la noblesse de Belgique*, 1924, 1926, 1929-1930, 1931-1932, 1934).

7. JEAN-CLAUDE LOUTSCH, *op. cit.*, p. 431.

8. BARON D'HANNONCELLES, *Metz ancien*, vol. 2, Metz, 1856, p. 128-137 ; *Annuaire de la noblesse de Belgique* (1885), p. 145 ; MUSEBECK, *Beiträge zur Geschichte der Metzer Patrizierfamilie de Heu*, Metz, 1905 ; GEOFFROY DE FAILLY, *Histoire d'une famille de Lorraine*, tome 2, p. 16-21 (inédit, incomplet, n'existe que sous forme d'un jeu d'épreuves).

9. JEAN-CLAUDE LOUTSCH, *op. cit.*, p. 431.

10. GEOFFROY DE FAILLY, *op. cit.*, t. 1.

11. *Annuaire de la noblesse de Belgique* (1852), p. 192 ; HERCKENRODE, *Nobiliaire des Pays-Bas et du comté de Bourgogne par M. De Vegiano, seigneur d'Hovel et neuf de ses suppléments, rédigés et classés en un seul ouvrage...*, Gand, 1870, vol. 3, p. 1178.

12. GEOFFROY DE FAILLY, *op. cit.*, t. 2, 19-21.

13. LUCIEN KOHL et NORBERT THILL, *Munshausen Aus der Geschichte der Ortschaft*, Heimat und Mission, 1990-1992, p. 233-249.

14. PIERRE PINT, *Das alte und das neue Ulflingen (Troisvierges)-und sein ehemaliges Franziskanerkloster*, Ons Hémecht, 1911, p. 343-346 (donne référence à tous les

documents publiés par WURTH-PAQUET et VAN WERWEKE, *op. cit.*, note 4).

15. EMILE PRÜM, *Die neue Pfarrkirche von Clerf*, vol. 2, 1916, p. 69-73 ; DOM BERNARD-JACQUES THIEL, O.S.B., *La vie érémitique au duché de Luxembourg au XVII$^e$ et XVIII$^e$ siècle*, t'Hémecht, 1954, p. 60-68.

16. Voir ANNEXE 1 : Tableau des quartiers généalogiques Lannoy.

17. Voir ANNEXE 2.

18. JEAN-CLAUDE LOUTSCH, *op. cit.*, p. 500 ; J.-B. RIETSTAP, *Armorial Général*, rééd. Lyon, Sauvegarde Historique, 1950 ; JEAN-THÉODORE DE RAADT, *Sceaux armoriés des Pays-Bas et des pays avoisinants*, Bruxelles, Société belge de Libraire, 1898, vol. 2, p. 314. Louis de Lannoy, seigneur de la Motterie (†1565) portait une brisure, un écusson en abîme de Cordes-Watripont (*D'or à deux lions adossés de gueules, les queues passées en sautoir, armés et lampassés d'azur*). Voir GEORGES DANSAERT, *Le blason de la maison de Lannoy à travers les siècles*, Bruxelles, Dewitt, 1928.

19. J. B. RIETSTAP, *op. cit.* ; MICHEL POPOFF, *Marches d'armes I*. Artois et Picardie. Paris, Léopard d'Or, 1981, p. 85.

20. JEAN-THÉODORE DE RAADT, *op. cit.*, vol. 3, p. 43 ; MICHEL POPOFF, *op.cit.*, p. 64.

21. JEAN-THÉODORE DE RAADT, *op. cit.*, vol. 2, p. 352 ; E E. WARLOP, *The Flemish Nobility before 1300*, Courtrai, Desmet-uysman, 1976, vol. 3, no. 130.

22. JEAN-CLAUDE LOUTSCH, *op. cit.*, p. 336.

23. JEAN-CLAUDE LOUTSCH, *op. cit.*, p. 220 ; J. B. RIETSTAP, *op. cit.*, verbo Bömmelberg alias Boineburg. Branche de cette famille, dite de Hohnstein, dont un rameau s'était fixé au comté de Vianden, portait l'écartelé décrit. Les autres branches portaient *un écartelé de sable et d'argent*. Voir JOHANN MAXIMILIAN HUMBRACHT, *Die höchste Zierde Teutschlands...*, Frankfurt am Mayn, Knoch, 1707, p. 234.

24. Voir JEAN SCHNEIDER, *La ville de Metz aux XIII$^e$ et XIV$^e$ siècles*, Nancy,1950.

25. JEAN-CLAUDE LOUTSCH, *op. cit.*, p. 431.

26. JEAN-CLAUDE LOUTSCH, *op. cit.*, p. 350.

27. WURTH-PAQUET et VAN WERWEKE, *op. cit.*, no. 118, 138, 142.

28. GILBERT CAHEN, *Catalogue des sceaux des archives départementales de la Moselle*, I, 1981, p. 193 ; WURTH-PAQUET et VAN WERWEKE, *op. cit.*

29. (Reede.) J. B. RIETSTAP, *op. cit.* ; JEAN-THÉODORE DE RAADT, *op. cit.*, vol. 3, p. 201.

30. (Nyenrode.) J. B. RIETSTAP, *op. cit.* : *Écartelé, aux I et IV d'or à la fasce de gueules, aux II et III fascé d'or et d'azur, les fasces d'or chargées de 4-3-2 flanchis de gueules*. Casque couronné. Cimier : *Un renard issant de gueules*.

31. J. B. RIETSTAP, *op. cit.* ; JEAN-THÉODORE DE RAADT, *op. cit.*, vol. 1, p. 405 ; RENÉ WATTIEZ, *Sceaux armoriés de Hesbaye*, Liège, Bibliophiles liégeois, 1985, p. 180.

32. En fait Lierre, sgr. d'Immersele. J. B. RIETSTAP, *op. cit.* ;

JEAN-THÉODORE DE RAADT, *op. cit.*, vol. 2, p. 344.

33. J. B. RIETSTAP, *op. cit.* ; JEAN-THÉODORE DE RAADT, *op. cit.*, vol. 4, p. 239.

34. (Egeren.) En fait : *D'argent à une chauve-souris de sable*. J. B. RIETSTAP, *op. cit* .; JEAN-THÉODORE DE RAADT, *op. cit.*, vol. 1, p. 410.

35. JEAN-CLAUDE LOUTSCH, *op. cit.*, p. 248. J. B. RIETSTAP, *op. cit.* ; JEAN-THÉODORE DE RAADT, *op. cit.*, vol. 1, p. 282, vol. 4, p. 396.

36. (van Aeswijn.) J. B. RIETSTAP, *op. cit.*

37. Voir ANNEXE 3.

38. Casque couronné. Cimier : *Un cygne issant d'argent*. A. FAHNE, *Geschichte der Dynasten, Freiherren und Grafen von Bocholtz*, Cologne, Heberle, 1856-1863, vol. 1-3 ; J. B. RIETSTAP, *op. cit.* ; JEAN-THÉODORE DE RAADT, *op. cit.*, vol. 1, p. 77.

39. Casque couronné. Cimier : *Une tête et col d'aigle de sable entre un vol d'or*. A. FAHNE, *op. cit.*, vol. 1$^2$, 274 ; J. B. RIETSTAP, *op. cit.*

40. Cimier : *Un buste d'homme aux armes coiffé d'un chapeau de cardinal de gueules, galonné d'or*. A. FAHNE, *op. cit.*, vol. 1$^2$, 28 et TABL. III ; J. B. RIETSTAP, *op. cit.* ; JEAN-THÉODORE DE RAADT, *op. cit.*, vol. 2, p. 258.

41. Ou Hanxleden : *D'azur à l'anille à l'antique d'or, les quatre bouts terminés en tête d'oiseau ou de serpent, posée en bande ou en barre*. Cimier : *Un vol aux armes*. J. B. RIETSTAP, *op. cit.*

42. Casque couronné. Cimier : *Une tête et col de loup (ou d'âne) collété, aux armes du chef*. A. FAHNE, *op. cit.*, vol. 1$^2$, p. 11-12, 201-202. J. B. RIETSTAP, *op. cit.* ; JEAN-THÉODORE DE RAADT, *op. cit.*, vol. 1, p. 344.

43. (Huyn d'amstenraedt.) Casque couronné. Cimier : *Une tête et col de paon au naturel*. J. B. RIETSTAP, *op. cit.*

44. Cimier : *Un vol coupé d'hermine et de sinople*. A. FAHNE, *op. cit.*, vol. 1$^2$, 242 ; J. B. RIETSTAP, *op. cit.*

45. Cimier : *Le lion issant*. A. FAHNE, *op. cit.*, vol. 1$^2$, 109-110.

46. Généralement brisé d'un *lambel d'azur*. J. B. RIETSTAP, *op. cit.* ; JEAN-THÉODORE DE RAADT, *op. cit.*, vol. 1, p. 372.

47. JEAN-CLAUDE LOUTSCH, *op. cit.*, p. 568 ; J. B. RIETSTAP, *op. cit.* ; JEAN-THÉODORE DE RAADT, *op. cit.*, vol. 2, p. 465 ; E. RICHARDSON, *Histoire de la maison de Merode* (traduit de l'allemand et mis à jour par la princesse Jean de Merode, née princesse de Bauffremont Courtenay).

48. Cimier : *Un bonnet de gueules retroussé d'argent, soutenant deux jambes cuirassées du même, coupées à la cuisse, les genoux affrontés, les chevilles (les pieds ne sont pas visibles) posées sur le bonnet*. J. B. RIETSTAP, *op. cit.* ; JEAN-THÉODORE DE RAADT, *op. cit.*, vol. 2, p. 101-102.

49. Casque couronné. Cimier : *Deux plumes de faisan aux armes*. A. FAHNE, *op. cit.*, vol. 1$^2$, 200 ; J. B. RIETSTAP, *op. cit.* ; JEAN-THÉODORE DE RAADT, *op. cit.*, vol. 4, p. 277.

50. Cimier : *Un lévrier assis d'argent, colleté et bouclé d'or*. J. B. RIETSTAP, *op. cit.* ; JEAN-THÉODORE DE RAADT, *op. cit.*, vol. 4, p. 217.

7

8

9

10

11

12

**Tableau des quartiers (Annexe 1)**

Génération la plus ancienne (colonne de droite, de haut en bas) :

- Louis de LANNOY, s. de la Motterie (†1565) — Louise-Michèle d'OGNIES
- Adrien de NOYELLES — Françoise de LILLE
- Bernard d'ELTZ (†1550) gouverneur de Thionville — Marguerite de BEMELBURG
- Nicolle de HEU (1498-1547) sgr. de Clervaux — Anne de FAILLY (†1561)
- Godart de REEDE de SAASFELD — Gertrude de NIEVRODE
- Guillaume de DURAS — Marguerite de LIERE
- Bernard de WYHE — Marguerite van EGEREN
- Floris van den BOGAERDE — Agnès van HESSWYN
- Arnoul de BOCHOLTZ — Françoise de VINCK-LA NGENFELD
- Guillaume de CORTENBACH (†1549) — Anne de HANXLIER
- Corneille de BOIDBERG, maréchal héréditaire du duché de Gueldre — Agnès de HOEN D'AMSTERODE
- Arnoul de BOCHOLTZ — Jeanne de MERWICK
- Herman de HOEN de H. — Marie de DAVE
- Ulric SCHIEFFART de MIRODE — Ursule de HOMPESCH
- Arnoul de BOCHOLTS — Françoise de VINCK-LA NGENBURG
- Jean de WITTENHORST — Marie-Jossine de WEES

Deuxième colonne :

- Jacques de LANNOY, sgr. de la Motterie, de Wasnes, etc. (†1587)
- Suzanne de NOYELLES, dame de Ponchel (†1590)
- Godefroy d'ELTZ, sgr. de Wolmerange et Ottange en partie (†1614)
- Elisabeth de HEU (†1599) dame de Clervaux, d'Ennery et de Failly en partie
- Adrien de REEDE de SAASFELD
- Anne de DURAS
- Joachim de WYHE
- Joachime van den BOGAERDE
- Guillaume de BOCHOLTZ (1523-1595)
- Ode de CORTENBACH (1531-1616)
- Adrian de BOIDBERG (†1565) maréchal héréditaire du duché de Gueldre
- Elisabeth de BOCHOLTZ (†1584)
- Gothard de HOENSBROECK (†1584)
- Gertrude SCHIEFFART de MIRODE
- Gothard de BOCHOLTZ
- Alexandrine de WITTENHORST

Troisième colonne :

- Claude de LANNOY, comte de la Motterie (1578-1643) gouverneur de Maëstricht puis de Namur, 1638 chevalier de la Toison d'Or
- Claudine d'ELTZ, dame de Clervaux en partie et d'Ennery (1577-1640)
- Adrien de REEDE de SAASFELD — x.p.c. 8-VIII-1609 — Marie de WYHE, dame de Herme
- Godefroit, baron de BOCHOLTZ (1570-1638) grand mayeur de Liège — Marguerit de BOIDBERG, dame de Breberen (†1600)
- Herman, baron de HOENSBROECK — x.p.c. 14-V-1585 — Anne de Bocholtz (†1601)

Quatrième colonne :

- Albert-Eugène, comte de LANNOY, baron de Clervaux et d'Ennery, etc. (1622-1697) Ambassadeur pour le roi d'Espagne, colonel d'un régiment d'enfanterie, lieutenant-gouverneur du duché de Luxembourg
- A-Marguerite de REEDE de SAASFELD dame de Bolland, Julémont et Trembleur veuve de Robert d'Argenteau, sgr. d'Ochain
- Jean-Guillaume, baron de BOCHOLTZ (1599-1682) — p.c. 2-II-1627 — Anne de HOENSBROECK chanoinesse de Munsterbilsen

Cinquième colonne :

- Adrien-Gérard comte de Lannoy et de Clervaux (1648-1730) justicier des nobles du Luxembourg, gouverneur du comté de Namur
- Marie-Thérèse de BOCHOLTZ (1633-1735)

**ANNEXE 1 : Tableau des quartiers**

392

LANNOY REEDE

Sous une couronne à trois fleurons
et deux fois trois perles
Supports : Deux griffons

CI GISSENT

| | | |
|---|---|---|
| | MESSIRE ALBERT EUGENE COMTE DE | |
| | LANNOY ET DU S.E.R., BARON DE CLER- | |
| LANNOY | VAUX, SEIGNEUR D'ENNERY, VAL- | RHEEDE |
| | MERANGE, BLETANGE, DU HAUT BAN | |
| OGNIE | DE TREMBLEUR, JULEMONT, &, &, | NVENRODE |
| | AIANT ETE AMBASSADEUR DE SA MA- | |
| NOYELLE | IESTE CATHOLIQUE EN DIFFERENTES | DVRAS |
| | COURS D'ALLEMAGNE ET COLONEL | |
| LILLE | D'UN REGIMENT D'INFANTERIE AU | IMERSELLE |
| | MÊME SERVICE QUI TREPASSA LE | |
| ELTZ | 25 D'AOUST 1697 AGE DE 82 ANS. | WYHE |
| | | |
| BEMELSBERG | ET TRES NOBLE DAME MADAME ANNE | DOEGEREN |
| | MARGUERITE BARONNE DE REED DE | |
| HUY | SATSFELDT, HERITIERE DE BOLLAND | BOGARDE |
| | SA TRES CHERE EPOUSE QUI TREPASSA | |
| ENNERY | LE | DASVSYN |

LANNOY BOCHOLTZ
Sous une couronne à trois fleurons
et deux fois trois perles
Supports : Deux griffons

CI GISSENT

MESSIRE ADRIEN GERARD
COMTE DE LANNOY ET DU
ST. E. R ; BARON DE CLER-
VAUX, SEIGNEUR DE BOUSSE
ECH, HUPPERDANGE, STOLZEM-
BOURG, OURN, DE LA LIBRE
TERRE DE BOULAND, DU HAUT

| | | | | |
|---|---|---|---|---|
| LANNOY | RHEEDE | BAN DE TREMBLEUR, JULE-<br>MONT, JUSTICIER ET CHEF | BOCHOLT | HOENSBROVEK |
| OGNJES | HVENRODE | DES NOBLES DU DUCHE DE<br>LUXEMBOURG ET COMTE DE | VINCK | DAVE |
| NOYELLE | DVRAS | CHINI, GENERAL LIEUTE-<br>NANT, MARECHAL DE CAMP | CORTEMBACK | MERODE |
| LJLLE | IMERSELLE | DES ARMEES DE S. M. I. ET<br>C., GOUVERNEUR CAPITAINE | HANXELER | HOMPESCH |
| ELTZ | WYHE | GENERAL DES PAIS ET COMTE<br>DE NAMUR, ADMINISTRATEUR | BOETBERG | BOCHOLT |
| BEMELOBERG | DOEGEREN | GENERAL DES VILLE ET CHÂ-<br>TEAU DUDIT NAMUR, SOUVE- | AMSTERACD | VONCK |
| HUY | BOGARDE | RAIN BAILLY GRAND VENEUR<br>ET BAILLY DU BOIS D'ILLEE | BOCHOLT | (WITTENHORST) |
| ENNERY | DASWYN | QUI TREPASSA LE 19 DE CE<br>M.. 1730. | MERWIJCK | (WEES) |

ET MADAME LA BARONNE DE
BOCHOLTZ SA TRES CHERE
ET HONOREE EPOUSE QUI
TREPASSA LE

R.I.P.

# SEARCHING FOR HERALDIC ROOTS IN SWITZERLAND

Günter Mattern

Switzerland, in the heart of Europe, was for many centuries a country from which people often found themselves forced to emigrate. After the Thirty Years' War (1618-1648) Swiss people, either farmers or craftsmen, settled in Alsace, the Rhine Palatinate, Prussia, or even as far away as Poland and Russia. They settled in Lombardy and worked as confectioners and chocolate dealers. In Germany, the word "Swiss" is synonymous with "dairyman," a person responsible for dairy cows and for the preparation of cheese.

Many Swiss served as mercenaries in the armies of other European states and kingdoms, mainly in France but also in the German states, in Austria, in the Netherlands, under the British Crown or in the Italian states. Even today the Holy See engages Swiss soldiers for the Papal Guard.

Later, the Swiss began to emigrate to Africa and to the Americas.

Emigrants, or their succeeding generations, now ask us to find their genealogical and heraldic roots. We often receive letters with such questions as:

- We are of Swiss origin; which arms did we use?
- My mother comes from the German-speaking area, what was her coat of arms?
- My ancestors fought in the battle of Morgarten (1315); which arms did they use?
- My name is Smith, Taylor or Miller; which arms belong to my family?

The first part of our answer is fairly easy: "You should first find the origin of your family."

The Swiss citizen tends to refer not to his birthplace, but to the Heimatort or place of origin of his family or tribe. This is a medieval tradition which is still in use today. The origin of my wife's family Cuendet is at Sainte Croix (in the Canton of Vaud) but the family had left this town by the 18th century. However, in the town's civic book, the Cuendets are still listed and the lists are regulrly updated.

Your place of origin was and is responsible for the financial support you received if you were poor or if you became an undesirable person in other Swiss communities, e.g., for criminal reasons. Every Swiss citizen may claim his Heimatort (place of origin) in a maximum of three places, unless he wishes to cancel any of them.

Now, you can imagine how difficult it is to find the personal coat of arms in Switzerland, especially since the Cantons (states) that joined the Confederation have altered over the centuries. Some allied towns or areas joined the Confederation, while others left it through force majeure between 1789 and 1815. Within the Confederation, states were also created, such as Basel Land (1833) or Jura (1978).

Unlike the citizens of other countries, each Swiss is a citizen of a Canton and a member of a community. The Confederation has no right to confer citizenship on someone unless that person is already a citizen of a community. Citizenship is historically inherited by a family. Until recently, a married woman took the citizenship of her husband; nowadays she can keep her own citizenship. Consequently the children inherit the citizenship of both their father and their mother. This makes it much more difficult to find the roots we are seeking. [1]

The Federal Office of Statistics and the Swiss Genealogical Society have published an important book, entitled *The Family Names of Switzerland*. This contains, in alphabetical order, all family names that have held citizenship in each community. For each community, it gives the period during which each name is found (before 1800, 1800-1900, after 1900). Extinct families are not listed, however. [2]

Another helpful book is the *Historical Biographic Encyclopaedia of Switzerland* (HBLS). In it, all persons or families who have worked in public life are listed and their arms are shown. [3]

The Swiss genealogist, Mario von Moos, recently published the *Bibliography of Swiss Genealogies* (of which there is an English edition), listing publications about Swiss families but not about nobles. [4]

Nobles are included in the HBLS or in the publications of the Swiss heraldry society: *Genealogical Handbook of Swiss History.*[5]

The Swiss heraldic system is not a specific or single one. As Switzerland contains four different cultures (Italian, French, German and Romansch), its heraldic system is heavily influenced by neighbouring countries.

In the Italian-speaking regions of Ticino or Grisons, armorial bearings are based on the Lombardic style. Many families use the chief charged with the Imperial eagle of the Ghibelins or the towers and other elements of the Guelfs.

In the French-speaking area, the heraldic system is largely that of France or the Savoyard territories, though the German system is also used, since many families have migrated into that part of Switzerland. For instance, descent through the bastard line is well recognised in medieval arms. Even today, the form of the shield tends to be based on the Italian or French style, while the components of the arms are similar to those found in Italian or French heraldry.

The German-speaking part of Switzerland follows Germanic patterns: simple, clear ordinaries and charges, often based on the origin, geography or occupation of a family. Many of them are canting arms. In rural areas, it is common to find the triple-mount in base (*sommet à trois coupeaux*) in peasant arms, a characteristic symbol of people living in the mountains that is also found in Alsace (The Vosges); Baden-Württemberg (Black Forest) or in Vorarlberg and the Tyrol.

As in the whole of Europe, Swiss society is structured in social classes. During the Middle Ages, the Swiss obtained their Letters Patent from the Emperor of the Holy Roman Empire or from the Hofpfalzgrafen (the Palatinate), i.e., from officials given the right to grant arms by the emperor or by princes. These ennobled families used coronets or quartered their arms, although titles of nobility had been abolished in Switzerland. Later some of them received titles from the French kings or other European rulers. Social status was shown by augmentation of the personal arms with the arms of territories that belonged to the family estates.

Some families were vassals (*ministériaux*) of the emperor or of certain bishops (Basel, St. Gallen, Geneva, etc.). In the course of time, they reached high rank and established themselves as the patriciate or nobility in the government of free cities. As in the Holy Roman Empire, these families did not belong to the high nobility, but had a strong economic influence in the free or imperial towns and possessed, or held in fee, territories with high or low jurisdiction. They considered themselves noble or at least fitted into the noble class. Even today, these families have much influence on both the culture and the economy of Switzerland. Their arms can be found in churches, churchyards and stained-glass windows as well as on houses, portals and in books.

It should not be assumed that the prefixes "von" or "de" are clear indicators of nobility. Families such as von Planta, von Salis, de Diessbach, de Graffenried, von Mülinen or von Sury belong to the nobility, whereas von Arx, von Aarburg or von Lanthen are farmers using the place name or house name as a family name (as is true in Northern Europe).

Other families were members of trade guilds or craftsmen's corporations and may still belong to them today by ancient right, tradition or social rank. These guilds show the arms of their members on heraldic tables, one for the dead members, the other for the living. The famous Roll of Arms of Lucerne dates from the 15th century. Many panels of heraldic stained-and painted-glass show the arms of the guilds and also the military organisations (rifle associations and ordinance societies) and of their respective members. Such documents form the basis for research into the families living in imperial towns (*Reichsstädte*) such as Zürich, Basel, Bern, Solothurn, Lucerne, Zug, Fribourg, Geneva or Lausanne, or in certain towns that had passed through a period of independence.

Other towns did not have the right to form corporations and semi-military organisations, but in some you will find arms in the church and on its pews and benches. In Zürich, there is a central committee of the Guilds (*Zentralstelle Zürcher Zünfte*) that is responsible for the creation of new arms for the members.

In other towns, or in the countryside, where there was no right to form guilds and corporations, the creation of personal arms was considered of less importance. People used "house-marks" to protect and distinguish their property, such as animals, house and tools. Originally these house-marks could be "inherited" by a person who took over the farm. Later the marks were set in shields and became a family ensign.

Some families, on changing their social status, also changed their arms. For example, the Lusser family of Altdorf (Canton Uri) were farmers and used a house-mark. Eventually they became mayors of Altdorf and changed their arms. In the 18th century, some branches of the Lusser family served as officers in the French and Portuguese armies, or in Swiss units serving in those countries. As they were often decorated or ennobled by the respective kings, they adopted the French or Portuguese heraldic system. Thus, one family could bear several coats of arms or change them because of a change in their social circumstances. Similarly, the Basel family of Wieland, which obtained a baronetcy from the King of Bavaria, changed their crest.

The Swiss heraldic system does not resemble in any way the English or Scottish systems; it is based on the German, French or Italian systems, depending on the area from which the family originates. Its only speciality is the three mounts or mounds in base. This feature can be used to find ancestors in Switzerland or the neighbouring territories.

## How to find your family arms in Switzerland

Some publications dealing with family arms are issued by corporations, guilds, communities or cantons. Unfortunately, not all the regions of Switzerland have yet published such books.

There are some compendia, such as *Monumenta Helvetica* (Winterthur)[6] or *Heraldica Helvetica*[7] (Geneva), but they cover only a part or a certain period of time.

The best approach is to consult the State Archives of the community or communities from which you come. These are competent offices that will give you—on payment of an appropriate fee—both information and advice.

If you have established your family tree, you should ask the community from which your ancestors are known to originate. You should also consult the State Archives of the relevant canton. Some of the archival departments have competent heraldic departments that can tell you from which branch you are descended. The Genealogical Society of Switzerland can also help locate the arms (see address below).

Please note, however, that not all Swiss families have established the right to bear arms. It may be that some of them did have and use distinguishing signs or marks, but these have been lost or forgotten, or are no longer traceable.

One difficulty—as I have tried to explain—is that some of the families used arms that were, over the course of the generations, forgotten, and new ones were created. In other words, a family that had a historical coat of arms could create new ones because of the ignorance of succeeding generations. In some cases, however, the new arms served to identify several branches of the same family. Furthermore, some arms have survived only in the form of seals, and as a result we can know the charges but not the tinctures.

Unfortunately, some archives were burned during the French Revolution and the occupation (1789-1806) or destroyed by Swiss citizens rebelling against their former Sovereigns. Other documentary evidence, such as that found in epitaphs or on gravestones, was destroyed through neglect, including family arms.

For many well-known coats of arms in Switzerland, no crest or badge exists. For others, the crest is three *plumes d'autruche*—ostrich feathers. In my opinion, this shows that crests did not exist in the past and that families later completed their achievement in this rather boring form.

Swiss family arms are not protected by law, and unscrupulous traders often try to sell prospective clients coats of arms that do not belong to their family name. American, German and Swiss merchants have found that there is a lucrative business in serving people's vanity this way. Representatives may ring at your door, traders and exhibitors at craft and technical fairs will also try to convince you of the authenticity of an invented coat of arms. You will meet them even at agricultural shows and cattle markets. There is an American company, operating in Europe, that will try to sell you "your family tree" and "your own coat of arms." The products sold by these traders all have one thing in common: the genealogical tree and, therefore, the arms are false and valueless. The texts may be compared with those from the Middle Ages, in which traders tried to trace your genealogy back to Adam and Eve, or to Venus or Jupiter.

The famous "European Roll of Arms," Milano, which is often quoted, does not exist.

## Swiss emigrants to Canada[8,9]

1633: Two Swiss citizens from Solothurn (Soleure) with the names *Rutac* and *Jean Terme* lived in French Canada, on the Île d'Orléans.

1655: People from the Canton of Fribourg emigrated to the French-speaking part of Canada (*François Tissot, François Rime, Pierre Miville*).

1665: M. de Tracy, Lieutenant General of the Americas, offered a tract of land to Swiss immigrants, to be known as the "Canton des Suisses fribourgeois." The offer was not, however, taken up.

1672: *François Miville's* son became liege lord of the territory of Bonne-Rencontre, near the river Chaudière, and the ancestor of the *Deschênes* family.

1677: *Jacques Bizard* became burgomaster (mayor) of Montréal.

1721-1745: The Swiss Regiment "Karrer" served at Louisbourg, Nova Scotia, and some of the soldiers stayed in Canada.

Under British sovereignty, the word "Swiss" in the French-speaking area became synonymous with "protestant," as French-speaking, protestant Swiss were hired as ministers (pastors) or as administrators.

1768-1794: *David-François de Montmollin* (1721-1803) was pasteur in Québec. During the American Revolution and the War of 1812, two Swiss held the office of governor general in Canada: *François-Louis-Frédéric Haldimand* (1718-1791) from Yverdon (Vaud), administered the British Colony from 1777 to 1784; *Georges Prévost* (1767-1816) from Geneva, administered the Colony from 1811 to 1816.

The Swiss regiments "de Meuron" and "von Wattenwyl" (de Watteville) were placed in the British service and protected the Canadian border against the United States. In 1815, more than 500 Swiss soldiers remained in Canada, settling in the Eastern area of the country.

In the late 18th century, the Swiss family Gugy exerted a certain influence on the political life of Canada. In 1763 *Conrad Gugy* (1730-1786), a Swiss officer in Dutch service, bought some land in Canada, as he had formerly been an officer under British rule. His brother, an officer in the Swiss Royal Guard in France, succeeded him, and his son Louis (1770-1840) and his grandson *Conrad August* (1796-1876) were both active in the political and military scene in Canada.

In 1891 the Swiss priest *Paul Benoît* founded a settlement called Notre-Dame-de-Lourdes, 130 kilometres south of Winnipeg, where 15 Swiss families settled, mainly as farmers.

In 1903 *Carl Stettler* (1861-1929), from Eggiwil (Bern), founded a community south of Edmonton called Stettler and, in 1950, it had 1,500 inhabitants.

After the First World War, possibly because of the insistence of immigration officers, many German and Swiss names were changed to approximate English equivalents, so citizens of the United States or Canada may have problems in tracing their original names. Some examples of such changes that have been traced are given here:

| Swiss Name | North American English version |
|---|---|
| Aebi | Eby; Aby |
| Baumann | Bouma |
| Blaser | Blosser |
| Brechbühl | Brakebill |
| Brodbeck | Broadback |
| Brupacher | Brubaker |
| Bürki | Bergey |
| Burkhalter | Burkholder |
| Egli | Egle; Egley |
| Glättli | Gladley |
| Gerster | Castor |
| Grob | Grove |
| Hersche | Herschey |

| | |
|---|---|
| Hodel | Huddle |
| Huber | Hoover |
| Jöhr | Year |
| Kaufmann | Coffman |
| Kneubühler | Knewbill |
| Krähenbühl | Greybill |
| Leibundgut | Longneck |
| Meili | Miley; Meylin |
| Nägeli | Negley |
| Neukomm | Newcome |
| Öchslin | Axeline |
| Pfeif(f)er, Pfyffer | Phifer |
| Ramseier | Ramsey |
| Rieser | Reesor |
| Rubli | Rublee |
| Schäfer | Shaver |
| Scheebeli | Schnebele; Snively |
| Schneider | Snyder; Sneider; Taylor |
| Stauffer | Stoufer |
| Tschanz | Johns |
| Tschudy | Judy; Schudi |
| Wyss | White |
| Zimmerman | Carpenter |

## Addresses of Swiss societies

*Zentralstelle für genealogische Auskünfte*
(Genealogical Information Centre)
Manuel Aicher,
*Vogelaustrasse* 34, CH-8953 *Dietikon.*
(Post giro account: Zürich 80-38'473-3)

Library of the Swiss Genealogical Society
(for information concerning family arms):
Edgar Kuhn,
*Schweizerische Landesbibliothek,*
CH-8706 Bern.

*Schweizerische Heraldische Gesellschaft /*
Société Suisse d'Héraldique:
Gregor Brunner
Burgstrasse 32
CH-8706 Meilen.

## NOTES

1. MANUEL AICHER, *"Genealogische Forschungen in der Schweiz,"* Herold, vol. 14 (Berlin: 1995), p. 233-241; *Idem, "Die Zentralstelle für genealogische Auskünfte,"* Herold, vol. 14 (Berlin: 1995), p. 242-250.

2. *Familiennamenbuch der Schweiz / Noms de Familles de la Suisse* (Zürich: 3rd edit., 1989).

3. *Historisch Biographisches Lexikon der Schweiz,* 7 vols. (Neuchâtel: 1921-1934).

4. MARIO VON MOOS, *Familiengeschichtliche Bibliographie der Schweiz* (Zürich: 1993); English version: *Bibliography of Swiss Genealogies* (Camden ME: Picton Press, 1993).

5. *Genealogisches Handbuch zur Schweizer Geschichte,* 4 vols., 1908-1987.

6. *Monumenta Heraldica,* Winterthur.

7. *Heraldica Helvetica,* Genève.

8. LEO SCHELBERT, *"Einführung in die schweizerische Auswanderungsgeschichte der Neuzeit,"* Schweiz. Zeitschrift für Geschichte / Revue suisse d'histoire, Suppl. no. 16, Zürich (1976), p. 182-183, 192-193, 226-230. See also: L BOVAY, *Le Canada et les Suisses* (Fribourg: 1976).

9. KARL LÜÖND, *Schweizer in Amerika; Karrieren und Misserfolge in der Neuen Welt* (Zürich: 1981).

# THE ARMS OF THE KING OF SCOTS AND SELECTED HERALDRY

Robert A. McColgan

## What heraldry? What heraldry!

Before heraldry as a science came into being, there were designs on shields, flags and so on that identified a leader, clan, army, legion, sovereignty, etc. These, however, lacked clarification and regularization through the use of the scientific nomenclature of heraldry to replicate by blazon these pictorial or three-dimensional representations; neither was there a system for hereditary transmittal. Also lacking was a central authority to create and amend rules, grants, records, to settle disputes and generally to administer these honours. Where honours are concerned mighty disputes and even wars do arise.

There are a number of heraldists who claim that heraldry evolved out of the military necessity of recognition. From the time closed helmets were introduced into warfare, the faces of friend and foe alike were blinded from view. Yet other heraldists claim an illiterate society required unique, heraldic and hereditary symbols on seals for legal purposes such as the sale or transfer of land and other matters legal. It would seem that demographic and socio-economic imperatives of the time cried out for heraldry. It had to be invented! To say, however, that heraldry was invented by blind illiterates, based solely on the foregoing, would not seem very likely.

Heraldry as we know it today is a scientific, unique hereditary means of identification by design and blazon, which appeared in the first half of the 12th century. If one allows 20 years for a generation, by 1190 or so it had happened.

## Pre-heraldic history and Celtic oral tradition

Heraldist and non-heraldists alike are familiar with the imperial double eagle of Rome. This bicephalous or double-headed eagle symbolized the Western Roman Empire of Rome and the Eastern Roman Empire of Constantinople (Byzantium). Long after Rome and its Western Empire had fallen, the emperors of the East used the bicephalous eagle as a symbol of their sovereignty.

It should be remembered that in the 12th century, Byzantium had yet to adopt heraldry. We are fortunate indeed to have in the possession of Prince Raymond-Alexis Comnène a seal-ring dating from the 12th century, showing at the end of each of the four arms of a cross, two of the letters of "KOMNENOS" in Greek characters. This served as a cognizance for the Comnène Emperors of the Eastern Roman Empire. The Comnène Emperors of Byzantium were Isaac I Comnène (reigned 1057-1059); Alexis I (reigned 1081-1118); John II (reigned 1118-1143); Manuel I (reigned 1143-1180); Alexis II (1180-1183) and Andronicus I (1183-1185). These sovereigns displayed the bicephalous eagle to symbolize their earthy power extending from the Orient to the Occident and the Cross as a symbol of the spiritual power of the state religion, Christianity.

Prince Raymond-Alexis Comnène, now living in Ottawa, Canada, approved a much simplified version of his arms in 1982. Quarterings, bicephalous eagle and regalia have been removed, save for the imperial crown, which in itself has been much simplified as well. These strikingly simple and beautiful arms are blazoned: *Azure three bells Or on a chief Argent a cross Gules, the shield ensigned by an imperial crown proper and accompanied by three Comnène crosses of the second one on the dexter of the shield one on the sinister and one above the imperial crown.*

Having just mentioned the Eastern Empire, it would be remiss not to relate a most interesting and noble episode of Scottish history regarding the Holy Land. This takes us to the first quarter of the 14th century and explains how the Douglases added a king's heart to their shield blazoned: *Argent a human heart Gules ensigned by an imperial crown proper on a chief Azure three molets of the first.*

King Robert I (Robert the Bruce) reigned from 1306 to 1329 and spent a great part of his life trying to wrest his kingdom from the clutches of the English by warfare, treaty and diplomatic manoeuvre. Years before his death, the King had told Bishop Lamberton that to expiate his sins, and should the crown be regained and the kingdom restored, he would go on a crusade to the Holy Land. The herculean task of freeing the kingdom for this venture and then putting it back in order took all the time he was given, and at 55 years he died from a life of hard campaigning and rough outdoor living. However, before his death, the king had his friend and comrade-in-arms "The Good Sir James" give a solemn oath that he would take the heart of the Bruce to Jerusalem.

In witness whereof the Bruce presented a great sword to Sir James Douglas and engraved on the blade was the King's charge: "I wil ye charge efter yat I depart to a holy grafe and thair bury my hart." Note that the "y" was an engravers abbreviation for "th;" therefore, the inscription reads: I will thee charge after that I depart to a holy grave (Jerusalem, in the Holy Land) and there bury my heart. Also engraved on the blade is the hand of Bruce advancing his heart with his finger to the cradling hand of Douglas. The initials RBR standing for Robert Bruce Rex (King) and JD for James Douglas are also on "ye" blade.

Sir James Douglas and the Scottish knights escorting the heart of their late king joined Castile's crusade against the Moors. In 1330 in Andalusia the Scottish contingent was cut off from the main column and attacked by a numerically superior force of Moors. The "Good Sir James" was killed leading the arrowhead charge of his knights. Nonetheless, fortune favoured Scotland as a knight "with the heart of a king" namely Sir Simon Lockheart survived the field of battle and returned to Scotland. The Heart of the Bruce is now at rest in Melrose Abbey.

The wonderful oral tradition of the Celtic race relates that prior to William the Lion, or Alexander II, assuming the Arms of the King of Scots, as we know them, Scottish kings showed *Argent a boar Sable* (on a silver background a black boar). This would have been quite appropriate for Scotland, as at that time boars were the most furious and feared creatures in the land. They could grow to a quite an astounding size and their fearsome tusks could down and gore a horse and rider with lightning speed. These qualities of size, power, speed and ferocity seemed to be well suited to kings of the time. All in the land knew of these creatures' power from first hand experience, not as some mythical or far-off beast such as the dragon or the lion.

Yet another Celtic tradition has it that this symbol royal came down to the leader through battle; for example, the complete destruction of the 9th Roman Legion. Hundreds of years previously, this Roman Legion entered Scotland never to be

heard from thereafter. It just vanished without a trace! And its "colours" consisted of a black boar. Considering the immense oral tradition of the Celtic peoples, many hundreds of years constitute very little.

Nevertheless, however much we enjoy these most plausible of Celtic tales, they are not to be discounted out of hand. Now let us turn to the intriguing topic of the origin and development of the Scottish Royal Arms.

### The Arms of the King of Scots

The Arms of the King of Scots are blazoned: *Or a lion rampant Gules armed and langued Azure within a double tressure flory-counter-flory of the second.* That is to say: on a gold shield a red lion standing on its hind legs with blue claws and tongue and two red lines going round to edge of the shield with red half fleurs-de-lis set thereon the tops alternately pointing towards the shield and away from the shield.

Early writers attribute the lion in the Scottish Arms to "William the Lion," King of Scots, who reigned for 49 years from 1165 to 1214, well into heraldic time. Many of the King's nobles had adopted coat armor and one can be reasonably sure that the king himself had also adopted such armory even though this has yet to be proved. Of course those items that might survive, such as wax seals and the metal seal matrix, were made at the time of his coronation, before heraldry burst on the scene.

Furthermore, William the Lion's reign was marked by peace in the kingdom and therefore not given the Lion characteristic in battle. Again, it would seem to hold that the name came from his new coat of arms. This, however plausible, has not been proved; therefore, one must turn to his son King Alexander II.

The Arms of the King of Scots, in their present form, first appeared on the equestrian side of the Great Seal of King Alexander II, who reigned from 1214 to 1248. The lion and the tressure florycounter-flory show most clearly on the king's very large saddle cloth (not yet a trapper), which goes almost to the ground. The lion itself can be discerned on the shield. These arms (the tressured lion) again appear most clearly on the shield and horse trapper shown on the Great Seal of King Alexander III, who reigned from 1249 to 1286.

This single unquartered coat of arms remained thus on the equestrian side of the great seal of each successive sovereign to the end of the reign of King James V (who reigned 1513-1542).

The marriage contract between Mary Queen of Scots and the Dauphin in 1557 required the Arms of the Dauphin to be quartered with those of the Queen; however, when he became King of France, the Arms of France and Scotland were to be conjoined under one crown.

After the death of King Francis II, and previous to her two subsequent marriages, Queen Mary dimidiated France, whilst retaining the integrity of Scotland to the sinister. Neither of the arms of the Queen's two successive husbands were included in the great seal. Queen Mary I's last heraldic intervention consisted of quartering England 1 and 4 with Scotland 2 and 3 with an escutcheon of pretence of the Arms of England. The sinister half of the escutcheon was shown worn or unclear. Such a lack of clarity and the arms themselves alluded to, as Mary Queen of Scots deemed it, Elizabeth I of England keeping her from her rightful place on the English throne. This heraldic sojourn did not reach either the head privy seal or that of the great seal, but would have contributed to Queen Mary's ultimate fate.

James VI King of Scots (reigned 1567-1625), after the death of Elizabeth I, ascended to the throne of England in 1603 as James I of England (reigned 1603-1625). Nonetheless, both of James' kingdoms remained separate and independent from each other, but with the two crowns vested in the person of one sovereign. This necessitated two uniquely quartered coats of arms, one for each of his two independent kingdoms. Therefore, the Arms of James VI, in Scotland, showed for the first and fourth quarters Scotland (*Or a lion rampant Gules armed and langued Azure within a double tressure flory-counter-flory of the second*) and for the second grand quarter France modern quartering England (1 and 4 *Azure three fleurs-de-lis Or*, and England 2 and 3 *Gules three lions passant guardant in pale Or*) and for the third quarter Ireland (*Azure a harp Or stringed Argent*). More simply put, first Scotland; second England (France Modern quartering England); third Ireland and fourth Scotland.

The Arms of King James as James I of England showed for the first and fourth grand quarters France modern quartering England; the second quarter Scotland; the third quarter Ireland.

At the time of the Act of Union in 1707, Mary II was using the arms as for James VI; however,

her husband, William III, being an elected sovereign, bore an escutcheon of his paternal arms of Nassau overall blazoned: *Azure billety a lion rampant Or*.

At this point it will, I think, be most useful to clearly set out the progression of the kingdoms, as much for my reference as anyone else's. Prior to 1603 Scotland and England were two separate and independent kingdoms, each with their own and separate sovereign. In 1603 James VI King of Scots also became King James I of England and thereafter ruled his two separate and independent kingdoms as James VI in Scotland and James I in England. This arrangement of two kingdoms continued until 1707 when, due to extreme economic pressure applied by England, the Act of Union combined the two kingdoms under one parliament, creating the Kingdom of Great Britain, which remained as such until the 1801 Act of Union with Ireland, in turn creating the United Kingdom of Great Britain and Ireland. This remained in effect until, when in 1922, the United Kingdom of Great Britain and Northern Ireland came into being. There is no such thing as a single coat of arms for the United Kingdom of Great Britain and Northern Ireland. However, there are Arms of the United Kingdom of Great Britain and Northern Ireland for use in Scotland and there are Arms of the United Kingdom of Great Britain and Northern Ireland for use in England and in Northern Ireland.

Due to the scope and subject matter intended for this publication, the heraldry of those monarchs who reigned after the Kingdom of Great Britain came into being in 1707 cannot be dealt with.

It must be noted that during the parliamentary "Reign of Terror" under Oliver Cromwell and the "Puritan Horde," who so foully murdered King Charles I (House of Stuart), Scotland, England and Ireland lost their royal heraldry. Happily, after the death of the tyrant, Charles II was beseeched to return home to an oppressed and pillaged land to set things right. Upon the king's return, in 1660, he occupied the throne of his late father, King Charles I.

It is most important, in this modern time of haste, for those Scots and those of Scots ancestry wishing to honour Scotland, her history and tradition to remember that the Royal Arms and Crest of Scotland have retained their quite separate and official status as a sovereign coat of arms. This is the property of the Sovereign. In Scotland, the keeper of the great seal and others, on certain occasions, are required to fly the Royal Banner of Scotland. This must never be flown at Highland games, gatherings of clans or tattoos. Just as there are laws to protect the royal banner for use in England (wrongly referred to as the Royal Standard), so Scottish Law protects its tressured lion. Of course, these have no effect overseas, but one would think that, out of respect, the national flag of Scotland, that is, the white X-shaped cross on a blue background, would be flown. This is known as the saltire of Saint Andrew and can (and should) be flown on occasions as previously mentioned. Saint Andrew is the patron saint of Scotland and also of Russia and the Ukraine.

## The saltire of Saint Andrew as the national flag of Scotland

Another oral tradition handed down intact and eventually recorded is that of Athelstane Ford as the birth place of Scotland's national flag. It came to pass that the saltire of Saint Andrew appeared with dramatic results above a field of battle in Scotland during the Dark Ages.

An army of Scots, under King Achaius, and Picts, under King Hungus, found itself surrounded by a great host led by King Athelstane, King of England. The vastly outnumbered Scots prayed for divine guidance and intervention and were blessed by a vision of white clouds, in the form of the saltire of Saint Andrew against the blue of the sky. Upon seeing this mighty omen the King swore a mighty oath that, if Saint Andrew would grant him victory, he (Saint Andrew) would then be proclaimed patron saint of Scotland, and his (Saint Andrew's saltire) badge would evermore go into battle with them. The outcome is clear, as today the saint's banner waves proudly over Scotland as the national flag.

The Bishop of Ross, John Leslie, claims this vision of the saltire of Saint Andrew appeared to both King Achaius and King Hungus during the night previous to the battle, whilst on their knees at prayer—a good interpretation for a cleric.

## The Crown

The present Crown of Scotland was commissioned by James V in 1513 and in the main consists of material from the Crown of King Robert I, which was crafted in 1314 to celebrate his great victory of Bannockburn. This battle finally re-established the sovereignty of the Kingdom of Scotland.

As a point of interest, the Scottish Regalia consisting of the Crown, Sceptre, Sword of State and Ring is the most ancient of all the royal regalia of the United Kingdom, save for the Ampulla, which has been embellished over time.

## The crest

King Robert II (reigned 1371-1390) is the first King of Scots to have borne a crest on his helm, and from this first occurrence it has incorporated a lion. A lion crest is displayed both on his great seal and his armorial bearing.

Furthermore, the crest borne on the helm, as displayed on the equestrian side of his great seal, is that of *a lion statant guardant*. From this first rendering of the king's crest, it was displayed as a *lion statant guardant* on the equestrian side of the great seal to the end of the reign of King James V (reigned 1513-1542).

A most interesting instance of royal prerogative reveals itself when the crest on the great seal is compared with the crest of the armorial achievement. The crest, as it appears in the kings' coat of arms, is *a lion sejant affronte Gules imperially crowned holding in the dexter paw a sword and in the sinister paw a sceptre Or*. There would seem to be a number of plausible explanations for these two renderings, varying from the king's will to the skill of seal engravers of the time. Here ends the speculation.

This is but another example of royal heraldry's not being required to follow the conventional rules of non-royal heraldry.

## The armorial supporters

The first appearance of supporters, or more precisely, a single supporter, in conjunction with the king's arms occurred on coinage during the reign of King James I (reigned 1406-1437) and consisted of a single unicorn sejant. We next find two lions supporting the shield of James I on his privy seal.

Each successive king or queen used, for different purposes, a unicorn and/or unicorns and/or lions as royal supporters.

Another fine example of royal heraldry following no convention or rule other than the rule of the sovereign is that of Mary Queen of Scots, who used two distinct sets of supporters concurrently, unicorns on her great seal and lions on her privy seal.

James VI King of Scots, before ascending the throne of England, had as his royal supporters two unicorns. Upon his ascent to the English throne, he took one unicorn from his Scottish arms and one lion from his English arms to become his royal supporters in each of his two kingdoms.

## The Canadian application of the Royal Arms of Scotland

Having shown but a glimpse of this immense Scottish tradition and heraldic presence, we must now look to Canada, where "The Scottish Way" far outweighs the actual number of Scots.

However, it first must be mentioned that a gap exists in Scotland's Register of Arms between 1621 and the undertaking of the present Lyon Register, begun in 1672. Again the vile and pungent sulphur of Oliver Cromwell cannot be expunged (even yet) from the nations. These records are believed to have been part of a cargo carried off to London for Cromwell and lost at sea.

Notwithstanding the aforegoing, the fact that the Arms of Nova Scotia existed in 1625 is clear from their being referenced by other sources, including Letters Patent of Baronets of Nova Scotia. We therefore see in Canada the heraldic Royal Arms of Scotland and the pre-heraldic device of Saint Andrew combined to form the Arms of Nova Scotia, which are indeed the oldest outside the United Kingdom, emanating from the United Kingdom.

An amusing aside to all of this is that in 1868, when the original provinces were granted arms by the College of Arms in London, the said College seemed to be unaware of the original grant by King Charles I and granted new arms such as: *Or on a fess wavy Azure between three thistles proper a salmon naiant Argent*. This error was eventually obliterated by a royal warrant of King George V that restored the original and rightful arms of Nova Scotia.

This strange episode is all the more baffling as the Arms of Nova Scotia were re-entered in the New Register of the Court of the Lyon between 1805 and 1810. At the time of Canadian Confederation, arms were assigned to each o f the four founding provinces individually (Ontario, Quebec, Nova Scotia and New Brunswick), with the Dominion Government using these arms as quarterings to become the national coat of arms. As other provinces joined the confederation, their arms were incorporated in the same way until the Dominion

Arms appeared as a cauldron of bubbling toil and trouble. Finally in 1921, the Arms of the United Kingdom of Great Britain and Ireland (as used in England and Ireland), but with France modern in the fourth quarter and *a base Argent three maple leaves conjoined in one stem proper* for Canada were assigned by royal warrant of King George V, dated November 21, 1921. This Achievement almost, but not quite, achieved the status of a Saint Andrew's Day Grant, lacking but nine days. Had Garter only realized what might have been. The badge of the Baronets of Nova Scotia and the Arms of Nova Scotia itself are a combination of the Royal Arms of Scotland and the saltire of Saint Andrew.

Another most interesting case of the Royal Arms of Scotland and the saltire appearing in a Nova Scotian context occurred during a meeting of the Privy Council at the Palace Holyrood on March 18, 1628, when a Seal of the Office of Admiralty of New Scotland was agreed to be struck. The seal would show a ship with the mainsail bearing the Arms of Nova Scotia: *Argent a cross of Saint Andrew with an escutcheon of the Royal Arms of Scotland*. The head of the ship would consist of a unicorn sitting bearing the saltire of Saint Andrew and standing upon the stern a savage man also holding Saint Andrew's saltire.

## Scottish heraldry and the Canadian army

There are now in Canada 48 infantry regiments in the Reserve Army of which 18 or 38% are either Highland or Scottish. These units appear in every region of the country such as The Black Watch (Royal Highland Regiment of Canada) in Quebec; The Cameron Highlanders of Ottawa (M.G.) in Ontario; The Seaforth Highlanders of Canada in Vancouver, British Columbia; and The Nova Scotia Highlanders, with detached companies, in Nova Scotia. Also of great import is the recreated regiment of the "Old 78th Fraser Highlanders," with garrisons or outposts all over North America. This historic unit, under the patronage of Lord Fraser of Lovat, allows Canadians and Americans alike to celebrate our common heritage as it existed before the terrible upheaval of revolution.

When one looks at the bonnet badges of these regiments, one notes without exception that wreaths of thistle, some with maple leaves intertwined; the figure and/or the saltire of Saint Andrew; the crests of noble Scottish Houses; and indeed, the Royal Arms of Scotland are ancient components of these new devices.

The badge of my former unit, The Cameron Highlanders of Ottawa (M.G.), is described as: *within a wreath of thistles and maple leaves the figure of Saint Andrew with Cross standing on a mount charged with a plaque inscribed* ADVANCE: on the lower level of the wreath two scrolls, the upper inscribed THE CAMERON HIGHLANDERS, the lower OF OTTAWA (M.G).

The badge of The Seaforth Highlanders of Canada, the unit of which my old friend the Hon. John Fraser, former speaker of the House, is Honorary Colonel, is described as: *a stag's head caboshed* above a scroll bearing the motto GUIDICH'N RIGH (Help the King). Below the ducal coronet and cipher of the Duke of Albany.

The 78th Frasers, on the other hand, were formed in 1757 before the advent of bonnet, shako or cap badges. Therefore, a strip of black bear skin running from the balmoral band to the toorie was used. Knowing Davie Crocket's prowess of "killing a complete bear when he was only three," one is awed by these chaps who took a strip off, on the fly, as it were.

No work or series of works could possibly encompass this all-intriguing subject, let alone a paper of this size. My desire throughout has been to inform, in a most readable and entertaining way, without, I hope, a hint of the dry and wizened.

# THE TOWEL AS A BADGE OF WENCESLAS, KING OF GERMANY AND BOHEMIA, AND ITS TRANSFORMATIONS

Mikhail Medvedev

The towel badge of King Wenceslas of Luxembourg, which can also be defined as a scarf or headband badge, is especially interesting because of its heraldic echo in different regions of Europe of the time.[1] The history of emblems derived from the original royal towel reflects both different heraldic practices and the unity of these practices within the international culture of heraldry.

With Wenceslas of Luxembourg, King of Germany and Bohemia (1361-1419), grandson of the "great romantic" King John the Blind and son of the "great pragmatic" Emperor Charles IV, we have a brilliant example of an unlucky and disappointing monarch. But his badge had a fate of its own. Inspired most probably by French examples and being a rarity for the heraldry of central Europe, this emblem made a special impression on contemporary observers. Among the outstanding historical monuments bearing this badge is the famous illuminated copy of the Golden Bull of Charles IV, made for his son in 1400 and now preserved in the National Library in Vienna.[2] The manuscript is richly adorned with heraldic emblems, such as the Imperial Arms of Wenceslas, in his capacity as *Imperator coronandus*, his royal arms and his personal badge, formed by a towel or kerchief bent in the form of a circle, with a specific knot and two large dangling (or flying) ends [FIGURE 1]. On the same page of the manuscript are depicted, side by side: the badge in its usual form (several times repeated), the badge within the imperial achievement, and a free interpretation of the same badge within a scene of lasses bathing [FIGURE 2]. This scene, or rather scenes, being full of beauty, erotism and even irony, also reveals the main symbolic significance of the badge. It is a towel of spiritual ablutions, a sign of purity; whence, the later legend, according to which Wenceslas was delivered from imprisonment by a beautiful female bath attendant.

In its more complicated form, the badge consisted of a towel as such and a kingfisher or halcyon surrounded by the towel and sitting on its knot. This form of the badge can be found on the façade of the Old Town's Tower of Charles' Bridge in Prague, again as a part of a large and impressive heraldic composition [FIGURE 1] that offers further explanation of the towel's meaning. The kingfisher in it stands for Halcyone, queen of Thessalia. According to Ovid, she refused to survive her husband, who had died in a shipwreck, and attempted to drown herself. The gods saved Halcyone, turning her into a bird.[3] The halcyon carries important connotations: fidelity, chivalrous true love, regal status, and, more importantly, death and revival in water, a striking parallel with the theme of spiritual bathing.[4]

However, these symbolic characteristics of the towel badge must not overshadow its essential role as a personal emblem. The kerchief or band, added to the arms of the Empire in the form of a banderole, is not a sign of virtue—it is not even a towel: it is the mark of King Wenceslas, which makes the achievement strictly personal.

One can follow the well-known British tradition of differentiating between personal and livery badges. However, this approach seems rather questionable both for British heraldry and for the general badge tradition throughout Europe.

Livery badges, as well as groups identified with liveries, could not be other than personal, being the mark of a specific master. No wonder then that the personal towel badge played a livery role, being conferred by Wenceslas upon the first Duke of Milan in 1395.[5] However, the same personal nature of the badge prevented it from being inherited by Sigismund, the rival half-brother and successor of Wenceslas. Neither did Sigismund adopt a new badge for himself, so that, unlike its master, the towel remained without a rival and its usage continued without any direct connection with Wenceslas himself.

In Milan the towel received a new role and significance. The Italian use of the royal scarf was studied by Gastone Cambin and Carlo Maspoli, so I shall discuss it only briefly. It became an object of special respect, being a mark of the sovereign's supreme attention, *divixia Imperialis*, as it was called, but at the same time it was reinterpreted as a personal badge—or *impresa*—of the Viscontis (and later of the Sforzas) [FIGURE 3]. This time it was bestowed by the dukes upon their retainers, used for armorial augmentations (such as that of the Borromeos), and appeared in combination with other family badges: the dove *en soleil*, the crown transfixed with two branches, or with partitions nebuly.

Let us note some further formal changes. The band/towel in Italy was clearly defined as a headband, *capitergium cum gassa*, whose iconography was sometimes slightly modified by the omission of the knot. There is an impressive version of this *impresa*, dated 1478, with a lovely sad face appearing within the headband's circle. This was published by Gastone Cambin, who saw it as a moon within the *capitergium*,[6] but maybe the ghostly face belonged to the personified headband itself.

The *capitergium cum gassa* could be placed on escutcheons with or without a crest, preserving its non-armorial significance, or possibly forming a shield for peace.

So the right to wear the royal badge, the *divixia Imperialis*, resulted in the adoption of this badge by the grantee himself. This is a rather typical Italian situation that can also be illustrated with the adoption of the Ferrarian rings by the Sforzas, or with the usage of Lancastrian livery emblems by the Gonzagas. Does this mean that the *imprese*, as they existed in Italy, are essentially different from badges? This is not an easy question to answer. Most probably the real difference between the two is rather socio-political than heraldic. The Viscontis, Gonzagas, Borgias and Medicis, as well as other powerful princes, received royal badges and other heraldic emblems not in the capacity of simple retainers but not as equals either. Italian princes provided well for their social position but this had to be reinforced by recognition, confirmations and concessions from the grand sovereign. No wonder then that some of them used emblems of royal origin to mark their environment and retainers.

If the *capitergium* flourished in Italy, it was not absent in German lands.

In 1440, following international fashion, Margrave Frederick II of Brandenbourg founded the *Selschapp Onnser Liuen Frowen* (Society of Our Lady), well known to modern readers as the Order of the Swan.[7] In founding the Society, besides responding to the fashion and to purely religious rea-

sons, Frederick evidently tried to establish closer connections with the local nobility. The Society was designed to involve numerous noble families. The structure of the corporation was amorphous and more horizontal than vertical and was open to friendly nobles of all ranks and even to wives and daughters. The membership was hereditary. According to the foundation deed (1440) and the statute (1443), members were linked by the special veneration of Our Lady, not by politics.

The collar of the Society consisted of instruments of torture (cogged clamps) clutching human hearts. The main pendant represented the Virgin with Child within the apocalyptical sunshine. However, it was the auxiliary pendant attached below the holy image that gave the popular name to the Society: a swan displayed, surrounded by a towel (Dwele) with a long fringe, almost certainly inspired by the old badge of Wenceslas.

An explanation of the symbolism is given in both the foundation deed and the statute. The instruments of torture symbolize the bitterness of earthly life. The swan symbolizes death: each Society member having to be prepared to sing his last song praising the Lord. The statute also comments on the swan (which foresees its death) as being a christological symbol. Finally, the towel of chastity is present to the pious members of the Society beyond the grave.

The regal towel is here combined with another—and much more important—great international entity of medieval heraldry: the swan. The theme of the swan-song is rather traditional in heraldry. One can recall the famous swan badge of John, Duke of Berry, adopted by this prince for the Duchy of Boulogne, and thus reflecting the legend of the Swan Knight. This swan was sometimes represented with a wound. Another wounded swan (this time pierced with an arrow) served as a badge to Claude of France, the Queen of Francis I. Originally it was the swan of the Duchy of Brittany. In the Armorial of the Golden Fleece, it formed the ducal crest (instead of the more known lion/leopard) and was represented unwounded. Most probably these are *mortal wounds*, signs of a near death and such attributes that are proper to a swan just like a horseshoe is proper to an ostrich.

So, the swan pendant of the Society's collar contains all the principal motifs of the original royal badge: the iconography of a bird within a circle formed by a scarf, the theme of spiritual bath, the theme of death and everlasting life.

It was not unusual for Frederick II to use the towel to show his legitimate right of succession to the Luxembourgs, in Brandenbourg, which belonged to this house for several generations and was transferred to the Hochenzollerns by Sigismund only in the 1410s (the definitive investiture occurring in 1417). In fact, Brandenbourg never belonged to Wenceslas himself, so that the royal towel was interpreted as an emblem of the entire family and as a means of claiming a part of the latter's moral (and territorial) legacy. But this was an unwritten tradition. Both the foundation deed and the statute underlined the vertical rather than the horizontal features of the Society and, accordingly, not the seignorial symbology, but the general symbolism of the Society's insignia.

Actually, these corporate insignia not only reproduced much of the personal and livery badge of King Wenceslas, but also belonged to the same emblematic genre within heraldry, which unity was clearly reflected in the contemporary German term *Gesellschaft* ("*Selschapp*"). This wide term was applicable to corporations (such as German political and tournament leagues); temporal orders, with their declared, but almost non-existing, corporative status; and non-corporative (but well-centralised) groups of retainers marked with a livery badge or collar.[8] The term indicated also the good relations with the Society's master—whether it be incorporated nobility of a province, or several united lords, or a powerful monarch. Thus the collar of the Order of the Jar of Aragon and the Lancastrian collar of esses were called, respectively, *Gesellschaften* of the kings of Spain and England.[9]

Here again, as for the Italian heraldic peculiarities, one can presume that this wide usage of a term point, to a simple misunderstanding between local "heraldries," a wrong interpretation of livery emblems by a German observer. But more probably, livery badges and insignia of noble corporations show here their underlying primitive unity. Both in the culture of badges and of orders, we find a specific blend of seignorial symbology and the symbolism and attributes of saints with robes of orders and liveries of corporations, numerous collars and pendants and a great variety of social practices present in all these emblems—is it actually possible to find exact borders and specifications?

An entire emblematic system of heraldry still existed at the time: a kind of empire ruled by armory. By the end of renaissance, this empire was divided into numerous parts and numerous sys-

tems. But dealing with the monuments of the 15th century, we face not only interlaced forms and meanings but a common emblematic culture that effectively reflects local peculiarities.

It is possible that the Society of Our Lady with the swan had a close emblematic predecessor: the *Gesellschaft* of "Tusin." The origin, appearance and meaning of the latter's name are not clear,[10] although it is known that King Albrecht of Habsburg had in his right of Bohemia, such *Gesellschaft* from 1438 until his death in the next year. Some authors link its foundation (as a corporation or as a badge) with the times of Wenceslas.[11] Was it a version of the towel? An erudite compilation gives a cross of red for the "Tusin", which could be a confusion with the badge of the Bohemian Order of the Star.

Besides that of Italy and Germany, the badge of Wenceslas influenced the heraldry of Poland, where there existed and still flourishes, the "clan" arms Nalęcz (Headband). Originally, these arms were: *Gules, a scarf or band Argent forming an annulet, its ends crossed in saltire in base*. But before the end of the 15th century, a new version appeared and became predominant: the same scarf, but with its ends tied.[12] I believe this to be the result of the towel's influence, and a perfect example of the natural love of heraldic forms already in use (the subject so profoundly studied by Don Faustino Menendez Pidal de Navascués).

Finally, let us recall the later romantic legend about adventures of Wenceslas, already mentioned here, which is the base for the arms of the Bath Attendants' Guild of Prague: the towel in which attendance a kingfisher is introduced as a charge. The Guild claimed to have obtained a corresponding concession from Wenceslas himself.

Now we can observe the influence of badges on arms, which can serve as another example of the *inner* links between heraldic cultures. The regal towel, with its specific forms, symbolism and political value, offers an occasion to trace such links and thus to study the life of medieval heraldry in its natural circumstances.

## NOTES

1. Most likely the towel itself echoed other similar emblems. The rich context that could predetermine the towel's adoption seems to be a subject for a separate study.

2. Wien, Nationalbibliotek, ms. 338.

3. *Metamorphoses*, XI, 270-748.

4. When this paper was being presented in Ottawa, Dr. Duerloo noted in the course of discussion that both the kingfisher's symbolism (fidelity, death in water, new life) and the historical significance of the towel link the bird with St. John of Nepomuk and his martyrdom for which Wenceslas was responsible. By joining the halcyon and the towel, Wenceslas probably made a kind of rhetorical gesture of repentance or self-justification.

The royal kingfisher's connection with *Metamorphoses* was discussed by Prince Karel Schwarzenberg. It is to be noted also that within the above-mentioned manuscript, the towel is present with numerous birds of rich, and sometimes of clear, symbolic meaning (i.e., goldfinch). However, none of the birds therein are part of a badge.

5. G. CAMBIN, *Le rotelle milanesi* (Fribourg: 1987), p. 222.

6. *Idem*, tav. XIII.

7. The main works: R. STILLFRIED, *Graf von. Die Schwanen-orden* (Halle: 1845); S. HÄNLE, *Urkunden und Nachweise zur Geschichte des Schwanen-Orden* (Ansbach: 1876); R. STILLFRIED and S. HÄNLE, *Das Buch vom Schwanen-orden* (Berlin: 1881); TH. DÄSCHLEIN, Die Schwanen-orden . . . (Ansbach: 1927). See also such modern works as: H. KRUSE, W. PARAVICINI and A. RANFT, *Ritterorden und Adelsgesellschaften im spätmittelalterlichen* Deutschland. *Ein systematisches Verzeichnis*, t. 1 (Kieler Werkstücke. Reihe D., Frankfurt/Main: 1991), the Order is listed there under no. 69; D'A. J. D. BOULTON, *The Knights of the Crown* (Woolbridge: 1987), p. XVIII, 397, 400, 486.

8. H. KRUSE *et al.*, *op. cit.*; D'A. J. D. BOULTON , *op. cit.*; B. HEIDENREICH, *Ritterorden und Rittergesellschaften* (Wurzburg: 1960); A. RANFT, *Adelsgesellschaften* (Sigmaringen: 1994).

9. R. STILLFRIED and S. HÄNLE, *op. cit.*, p. 29-30.

10. See D'A. J. D. BOULTON, *op. cit.*, p. 345; H. KRUSE, W. PARAVICINI and A. RANFT, *op. cit.*, no. 67.

11. A. RANFT, *Adelsgesellschaften* (Sigmaringen: 1994), p. 30.

12. J. SZYMAŃSKY, *Herbarz średniowiecznego rycerstwa Polskiego* (Warszawa: 1993), p. 192-195.

**FIGURE 1:** The towel alone from the *Golden Bull of Charles IV*, and with a kingfisher (on the façade of the Old Town's Tower of Charles' Bridge in Prague)

**FIGURE 2:** The badge within the imperial achievement and as a part of an allegorical composition (from the *Golden Bull of Charles IV*, fol. 1)

411

**FIGURE 3:** The Visconti's *imprese* of the dove, the *soleil* (*Radia Magna*)
and the headband (*Capitergium*)

**FIGURE 4:** The arms of Florian Waldauf von Waldenstein, by Dürer, ca. 1520. Three *Gesellschaften* are
included: the collars of the Order of Temperance (or of the Jar) of Aragon, and of the Society of Our
Lady (or of the Swan) of Brandenbourg, and the Lancastrian livery collar of esses.

# INTERACTION IN HERALDRY BETWEEN NORWAY AND SWEDEN

Clara  Nevéus

Modern Norwegian heraldry has certain well-defined characteristics—in particular where heraldry of a "geographical" kind is concerned. A number of heraldic principles are applied quite strictly: the most striking of these prescribes that only two tinctures, one metal and one colour, may be used in the shield of a coat of arms. Another principle states that there shall be only one type of charge, used singly or in multiple. Last but not least, a coat is to be depicted in planar style (Norw. *flatestil*) without perspective or shading, which might give an impression of volume [FIGURE 1].[1]

The originator of these rules was the grand old man of Norwegian heraldry, Hallvard Traetteberg (1898-1987), whose influence extended from the first years of the 1920s up to his death. He worked in the Norwegian National Archives from the mid-1920s until 1966. From the 1930s on, he was, in effect, if not in name, the State Heraldic Officer of Norway, by dint of his scientific mind and artistic talent. Despite his valuable work as artist and archivist, it may be said that his most lasting achievement has been in the field of armory.[2]

Through his contacts with Harald Fleetwood, Swedish National Herald (1931-1953), and C. Gunnar U. Scheffer, the latter's successor with the title of State Herald (1953-1974), Traetteberg was in a position to influence heraldry in Sweden. My aim here is to establish how this influence was applied and to what extent Swedish armorists have been inspired by Norwegian praxis, especially as regards the design and depiction of newly created arms. Correspondence to and from Traetteberg, from 1930 onwards, is preserved among the documents of the National Heraldic Office.[3] Some correspondence, dated from 1953 and later, is also to be found in the office records of the National Archives.[4]

At first the letters are predictably concerned with official matters, but gradually take on a more personal tone. In the autumn of 1939, Harald Fleetwood made use of his contacts in the Department for Foreign Affairs to obtain a Swedish decoration for his Norwegian colleague; Traetteberg's letter of thanks to him is dated on the eve of the German invasion of Norway in April 1940. Only when the war had ended was the official correspondence resumed. Unfortunately, there is reason to believe that many letters have disappeared or found their way into the gentlemen's private archives, to which I have not had access.

From Scheffer's time there are a number of policy declarations among the papers of the State Heraldic Board, of which he was secretary. Correspondence with the Norwegian lawyer Hans Cappelen, A.I.H., is also preserved in the records of the National Archives Office from 1965 onwards.

Since my investigation is principally concerned with the content and depiction of coats of arms, the scarcity of written documentation is perhaps not too serious: more important is to examine municipal arms, which came into being during the period in question, and to see how they appear in drawings prepared for approval.

Another matter that must be borne in mind is the differences between Swedish and Norwegian legislation and practice. Without going into detail, it is apparent that the position that Traetteberg had adopted in Norway from 1937 onwards, the year in which new laws were enacted concerning the national arms of Norway, was without equivalent in Sweden. From that time on, the Norwegian praxis has been that new arms for towns and rural districts should comply with the norms of heraldry and blazonry, and that no such arms should be confirmed at the highest level without the approval of the National Archives.[5]

According to a royal decree of 1936,[6] the Swedish National Herald could perform heraldic research and make his views known concerning municipal arms, but nowhere was it stated that municipal arms could not obtain royal sanction without the herald's support. As far as I can see, however, this was not enforced. Subsequent to the reorganisation of 1953, the situation was altered. That year, the responsibilities of the National Heraldic Office were transferred to the National Archives with their newly established heraldic section, initially headed by State Herald Scheffer. To assist in more important questions, such as those concerning municipal arms, the State Heraldic Board was set up, with legal, artistic and antiquarian experts among its members.[7] For municipal arms to achieve official recognition, it was laid down that an official ruling must be obtained from the Board. Consequently, royal approval was in fact not given in a number of cases where the Board's ruling had been unfavourable. But after a change in the law in 1974, royal approval was replaced with registration at the Patent and Registration Office and arms were allowed to be registered despite a negative ruling. Thus far this has occurred in ten instances or so, all of them after Scheffer's retirement that same year.

Since the early 1950s, a private foundation known as the Swedish Institute for Municipal Heraldry (*Svenska kommunalheraldiska institutet*, SKI) has also been in operation, to some extent in competition with the National Archives. Several coats of arms emanating from this foundation were not approved officially: the decision of the borough concerned was in itself considered to afford sufficient protection. (The arms have most often been of high quality—if not in accordance with Norwegian ideals.[8]) These circumstances have had an inhibiting effect on official heraldry in Sweden, due no doubt to the stronger position of municipal authorities in Sweden in comparison to Norway. A feeling prevailed that one was obliged to reach agreement with the municipalities, since these had the alternative of settling their heraldic usage without recourse to the National Archives. It cannot be ruled out that this has contributed to certain Swedish coats acquiring a more conventional content— or a poorer design—than would have been the case had the central heraldic authorities been in a position of greater strength.

In 1938 Traetteberg published in the (Swedish) National Heraldic Office's *Information*[9] a fundamental treatise on the rules governing heraldic tincture. He initially worked with extant mediaeval armorials and the work of continental heraldic theoreticians, notably G. Seyler (1884). He finally arrived at six rules of tincture for an heraldic shield:

1. Heraldry recognises six tinctures, the metals gold and silver and the colours red, blue, black and green. (Green should seldom occur.)
2. A coat of arms should be of two tinctures only, except for special reasons.
3. One of the tinctures must be gold or silver.
4. Metal should not border on metal nor colour on colour wherever a relatively long common boundary is concerned.
5. Certain details in conventional figures, such as beasts' claws, may have a tincture distinct from that of the figure itself. Details which are not part of the main figure, such as a crown on a lion's head, must be of another tincture.
6. It must be possible to depict arms with complete clarity by means of areas of tincture, avoiding all use of lines within the shield (or flag).

It must be made clear that, up to that moment, Traetteberg himself had not observed these rules in all their rigour, and that the second principle mentioned in my introduction, on unity of charge, does not appear here—but it is, of course, not a rule of tincture. (I have not found this rule formulated in writing earlier than in Traetteberg's preface to the exhibition "Public Heraldry in Norway 1921-1975," Oslo, 1975).

One might reasonably imagine that a Swedish armorist—particularly National Herald Fleetwood —would have commented on this important article in *Information*, but one seeks in vain for any response. As it happens, the correspondence of 1937 shows that Traetteberg and Fleetwood take very different views with respect to a coat for the Norwegian municipality of Arendal, in which a ship argent is shown sailing upon a river of the same metal. Moreover, Traetteberg takes a much more severe view of the respect that is due to arms. This can be seen from the correspondence of 1932 on the presentation of Swedish and Norwegian coats, together with an advertisement in the publications of Kaffe Hag. No obvious change in the choice of charges or use of tinctures can be discerned in Swedish heraldry over the years that followed [FIGURE 2]. In 1939 there appeared in *Information* a very laudatory article by Arvid Berghman concerning the contemporary heraldic artists Hupp, Britze and Busch. The first two of these were inspired by 15th- and 16th-century models; the third is more modern in style, but by no means approaches the strict ideals of Traetteberg.

Clearly Fleetwood has not allowed himself to be influenced by Traetteberg to any great degree, but they apparently remained friends. However, in revising certain coats containing human figures,

414

Fleetwood has seen to it that the unheraldic "proper" or natural colouring of faces and hands was replaced by approved tinctures. Fleetwood was actually more interested in sigillography than in armory.

The first printed reaction to Traetteberg's tincture rules came from the pen of Scheffer in an essay written in 1958 on some recently approved arms for rural areas (hundreds) in the administrative province of Skaraborg.[10] His essay comments and elaborates on Traetteberg's article of 1938. A key sentence is: "The heraldic aim of achieving the strongest possible effects of colour rules out detail of design and fine tonal nuances." For heraldic painting a basic principle is laid down, that only a "setting-out of plane areas of tincture" is admissible. In agreement with Traetteberg, he thinks that laws of tincture should be drawn from the age in which they were observed, i.e., the early Middle Ages. Perspective drawings with shadows and effects of light, he further states, belong to a later period and are foreign to heraldic art, which cannot develop as it ought unless it returns to its original principles [FIGURE 3].

We can adduce a case in point to demonstrate the Swedish Heraldic Board's reaction to a coat produced by the above-mentioned Swedish Institute for Municipal Heraldry, i.e., the arms of Gnosjö, a rural municipality in southern Sweden, famous for its early small-scale industrialisation. The arms, in green and silver, contain two narrow ribbons, alluding to wiremaking, and five waterwheels—five because of the five parishes making up the municipality. In its minutes, the Board approved the choice of charges and the proposed blazon, but rejected the attached drawing, which, like many more of the Institute's coats of arms, was the work of Sven Sköld, the illustrator of Arvid Berghman's publications.[11] The Board's criticisms have to do with the laws of tincture, which were now to be adhered to as laid down by Traetteberg, mentioned here by name. Uno Lindgren, the Institute's secretary, rushed to the artist's defence, pointing out that shading was customary in continental heraldry, as well as in the work of recognised artists, and had previously been allowed and sanctioned in Sweden. Lindgren's defence was rejected by the Board with the argument that it had not been possible to break with previous attitudes all at once, even though there had been a desire to

do so. The task of the newly established Board was to serve as a forum to deal with questions of heraldic principle. The outcome in this case was that Gnosjö adopted the arms, but decided not to apply for recognition by royal decree. After the 1974 change in the law, the arms were registered at the Patent Office with the same design [FIGURE 4].

Scheffer returned to the subject of heraldic theory in 1966 in a short contribution to the magazine *Heraldisk Tidsskrift*. He discusses "prevailing contemporary style" in painting and concludes that "not since the birth of heraldry in the Middle Ages have the flat surface and uninterrupted effects of colour been such significant factors on the painter's agenda as they are today, despite all their chopping and changing 'isms'." The fact that modern heraldry, nevertheless, often appears mediocre to him is ascribed by Scheffer to the tendency to distort the flat surface by shading, highlighting and shadows. This practice would leave the way open for a return to naturalism. He draws examples for comparison from the Kaffe Hag Armorials from Germany and Switzerland, illustrated by Otto Hupp and Paul Ganz respectively. Hupp's work, with its relief-like style deriving from late mediaeval and renaissance precedents, seems to approach actual genre-painting. In the same article Scheffer refers to Traetteberg by name. In small exhibitions during the 1960s and a larger one on the occasion of his retirement in 1974, Scheffer continued his campaign in favour of planarity.

In his obituary of Scheffer,[12] Olof Eriksson, the Finnish heraldic artist, rightly draws attention to Scheffer's contribution to the development of modern, stricter heraldic design in Sweden, and its significance for modern Finnish heraldry. As Eriksson's first contacts with Scheffer were made while the latter was Fleetwood's assistant, it is probable that he had already absorbed Traetteberg's principles during the 1940s, but that it was only when he had become State Herald that he felt free to work actively for compliance with the new trend coming from Norway [FIGURE 5]. It is nonetheless a pity that heraldic design was used as a weapon in the battle between Scheffer and his antagonists in the Institute.

Heraldic expertise was to a degree brought back from Sweden to Norway through the young Hans Cappelen's contacts with Scheffer; he worked, for example, as an amanuensis in the heraldic department of the National Archives for nearly six months during 1967. These contacts continued over the years, and Scheffer was in a position to examine Cappelen's heraldic work at an early stage, doing so, it is reported, in a friendly and constructive manner. I do not know, however, whether he expressed an opinion on Cappelen's essay on the planar style of heraldic illustration, published in *Heraldisk Tidsskrift* in 1970; it does contain a number of critical observations—but to go into these is beyond the scope of the matter at hand.

## Conclusion

Scheffer thus enthusiastically accepted and tried to promulgate Traetteberg's ideas on the planar style in heraldic painting. It is evident that he gave new instructions to the department's artist, Brita Grep, who had done most of the heraldic painting during Fleetwood's regime. However, with respect to the number of tinctures and types of charges, he has not applied his mentor's rules with the same consistency. We also note that the colour green is *not* unusual in municipal heraldry, whether Norwegian or Swedish! Jan von Konow, A.I.H., Scheffer's successor from 1975 to 1981, mostly adhered to his predecessor's practices. In a few cases he accepted dubious compositions, e.g., two coats of arms in "rock-carving" style, clearly because of the pressure from inflexible municipal representatives. A few ill-conceived coats were also registered *against* the advice of the heraldic department, during both von Konow's and my own term in office. As for military arms, which remarkably enough are at present the liveliest sphere of heraldic development in Sweden, it is now the practice to simultaneously create two versions: one quite detailed in colour, intended for large format use on ceremonial occasions; another considerably simplified in black and white, intended for use on stationery, etc. [FIGURE 6].

It is not always easy to gain acceptance for the level of excellence one strives for although this level may be lower than Traetteberg's. I cannot resist offering as a *bonne bouche* a quotation cited by Traetteberg in the heraldic context of a letter to Fleetwood in 1938; its author is Sir Robert Vansittart:

"It's not as easy as you think"
the nettled poet sighed,
"It's not as good as I could wish,"
the publisher replied,
"It might," the gently critic wrote,
"have easily been worse."
"We will not read it anyhow,"
the public said, "it's verse."[13]

## NOTES

1. HANS CAPPELEN and KNUT JOHANNESSEN, *Norska kommunevåpen* (1987).

2. *Heraldisk Tidsskrift* (1987), p. 313.

3. The archives of the *Riksheraldikerämbetet* in the National Archives.

4. The archives of the heraldic section of the National Archives.

5. See HANS CAPPELEN and KNUT JOHANNESSEN, *op. cit.,* p. 40.

6. SFS (Swedish Constitutional Documents) 1936: 57.

7. SFS 1953:529. Later reorganised according to SFS 1983: 415. At this time, the State Heraldic Board was abolished and replaced by a National Archives consultative heraldic board with similar composition and functions.

8. More on this subject in *Ny Svensk Vapenbok* (1992), p. 44 and *passim*, see the index under Idégivare/Konstnärer, SKI, p. 184.

9. *Meddelanden från Riksheraldikerämbetet* (1938), p. 27-49.

10. First published in *Västergötlands fornminnesförenings Tidskrift* [The Magazine of the Västergötland Antiquarian Society], vol. 1, (1958). Also—but without references—in SCHEFFER's *Heraldisk Spegel* (1964).

11. 1954-09-07—In the minutes there is also a reference to a declaration of principle in a similar matter in the minutes of 1954-01-21 and 04-09.

12. *Heraldisk Tidsskrift* (1981), p. 232.

13. The text of this paper has been translated by Stephen Coombs. The pictures have been compiled by Vladimir A. Sagerlund.

**FIGURE 1:** Some modern Norwegian coats of arms: Borge (1980), Varteig (1979), Eidskog (1986), Hedmark (1987). From *Norske Kommunevåpen*, 1987.

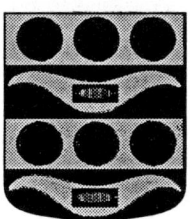   

**FIGURE 2:** Some Swedish municipal coats of arms, approved by Harald Fleetwood: Kinna (1934), Munkfors (1945), Saltsjöbaden (1944), Lappland (1949).

**FIGURE 3:** Three coats of arms for "hundreds" in Skaraborg, all approved by Gunnar Scheffer in 1957: Skåning, Vilske, Kålland.

**FIGURE 4:** Coat of arms of Gnosjö, designed by Sven Sköld in 1954.

**FIGURE 5:** Some interrelated coats that came into existence during Fleetwood's and Scheffer's terms of office: Ånge (as urban district 1948 and as municipality 1971), Strängnäs (cathedral town in 1937 and 1976).

**FIGURE 6:** Coats of arms of the navy base Muskö, design by Vladimir A Sagerlund.

418

# TRENDS IN UNIVERSITY HERALDRY:
# THE BRITISH EMPIRE AND BEYOND

Bruce Patterson

To begin this paper I will look at armorial bearings granted to universities and colleges by the English Kings of Arms, extending to Lord Lyon and Ulster King of Arms, and into the independent Commonwealth heraldic authorities in Canada and South Africa. I am thus beginning with British and colonial university heraldry, but will move beyond the period of Empire in time. I shall also occasionally go beyond in terms of geography.[1]

## Beginnings

Many of the very ancient universities of Europe, arising as they did around the advent of heraldry, represented themselves by the use of seals, although some would later adopt arms. Corporate heraldry developed somewhat later than personal heraldry, and arms did not come to represent universities until the 15th century. The earliest English universities were Oxford and Cambridge, whose arms were recorded at the visitations of 1575-1576. Cambridge's arms were granted in 1573, and Oxford dates the use of its arms from approximately 1429 [FIGURES 1-2].[2] The first grant made to a corporate entity in England, the Drapers' Company, had been made in 1438,[3] and interest by universities in matters armorial would follow. A number of colleges at Oxford and Cambridge had been using arms, although these were primarily the arms, differenced and undifferenced, of their founders. Many were recorded at the visitations of 1575, although I note that the arms of King's College Cambridge were granted by its founder, King Henry VI, in 1449.[4] I shall examine the use of founders' arms presently.

Outside of the two original universities, the first grant of arms made by the English Kings of Arms was to one in far-off America, the College of William and Mary in Williamsburg, Virginia, on May 14, 1694: *Vert a college Or edifice Argent masoned proper, in chief the rising sun Or the hemisphere of the third* [FIGURE 3].[5] These arms continue to be used. Surprisingly, the College was the only one of the pre-revolutionary

foundations in America to have been granted arms, although a number of them have since acquired excellent heraldic systems, the further development of which was usually due to the efforts of an outstanding figure in their midst: in the case of Harvard (and other institutions), Pierre de Chaignon la Rose,[6] and in the case of Yale, its "Pursuivant of Arms," Theodore Sizer.[7] Prof. D'Arcy Boulton appears to be fulfilling a similar role for the University of Notre Dame.[8] Harvard's original design dates from 1643, while Yale's is from 1740. Most other American universities with arms date theirs from the late 19th or early 20th century. Although a number have adopted armorial bearings—almost always just the shield—most still use seal designs as official symbols.

We now turn to Scotland, which enjoys not only its own heraldic authority, but also boasts several ancient universities. The first of these to have been granted arms was the University of Edinburgh in 1789 [FIGURE 4]. It would be 99 years before the next Scottish university, Aberdeen, received a grant, followed by Glasgow in 1900 and St. Andrew's in 1905.

Trinity College, Dublin, had arms that appeared on a seal as early as 1612, although these were not granted, but rather recognised later by Ulster King of Arms [FIGURE 5].[9] There were three grants to Irish universities in the latter half of the 19th century, and three immediately before the Great War.

The University of London received its arms in 1838 [FIGURE 6], and Durham in 1843. Both have many constituent colleges and other bodies that would themselves gain arms in the following years. The University of Manchester's grant came in 1871, and then we pause until Reading in 1896, which initiated a busy few years until the First World War, with grants to five English universities, reflecting the growth of the "red brick" universities. Greater activity was taking place in the Dominions and colonies, however. Shortly after its foundation in 1856, the University of Bombay became the first legitimately armigerous colonial university, and Madras followed in 1898. The University of Sydney received its arms in 1857, Melbourne in 1863, and Queensland in 1912. The University of the Cape of Good Hope (now the University of South Africa) was granted arms in 1903, the University of Wales in 1910, and the University of Hong Kong in 1913 [FIGURE 7].

Curiously enough, Canadian universities felt free to adopt ungranted arms. This happened quite early on, an example being Queen's University in Kingston, adopting arms in 1850 very similar to the ones eventually granted [FIGURE 8]. Judge Matheson told me these had been designed, but never granted, by the Lord Lyon. The present arms of the University of Toronto were designed in 1857 by its first president, but not granted until 1917. Canadian universities began the cautious steps to armorial legitimacy with the grant to the newly formed University of British Columbia in 1915, followed by the older University of Toronto and its University College in 1917. In general, however, grants to Canadian institutions were few until the mid 1950s.

The first grant to a New Zealand university did not take place until 1948, being the University of Otago.

Grants—of all kinds—around the Commonwealth began to dry up in the 1930s and 1940s, due to the Depression and the War. The early and mid-1960s were a particularly energetic period of granting, and an inevitable falling-off occurred in the late 1960s and 1970s, perhaps due to the end of a wave of post-war expansion, and perhaps due to a climate that increasingly favoured logos to armorial bearings. Grants continue to occur at a pace somewhat slower than the heyday 30 years ago; nevertheless, there are still challenges to be met, which I shall be covering later.

## Armorial components

Like all early grants, universities used a shield alone, although some colleges used crests. The first grant of a crest was to the University of Leeds in 1905. The first grant of supporters was to the University of Western Ontario in 1931, and was not followed again until the University of New England, in Australia, in 1955 (the first English university grant with supporters was the University of Sussex in 1962). The correspondence regarding the University of Western Ontario grant contains nothing in which justification is given for

this innovation.[10] The Lord Lyon, who formerly was reluctant to grant crests and supporters, now does so occasionally, such as to British Columbia's Trinity Western University. The State Herald of South Africa has not granted supporters to a university, but usually grants a crest. A small majority of the grants made by the Chief Herald of Canada include supporters.

There are, however, indications that the ancient universities sometimes added supporters without authority—I have seen examples of the arms of both Oxford and Cambridge using angels as supporters [FIGURES 9-10]. Cambridge combined its "alma mater" emblem with its arms making the woman a sort of crest.[11] When Daniel Wilson designed the arms of the University of Toronto in 1857, he included supporters, although these were never depicted and were not included in the grant of the rest of the design 51 years later.[12]

Crests and supporters are generally the favoured armorial presentation today, although some universities opt for a simpler approach. The use of armorial accoutrements does add to the flexibility of the use of arms, although if this flexibility is not employed it can become a great disadvantage. I hope I am not ungracious to our host University of Ottawa in remarking that the use of its shield alone—an excellent design—would serve much better as identification than the constant repetition of the complete achievement. My undergraduate college, Trinity College, Toronto, had, until recently, also been guilty of this, having reproduced the achievement of (impaled) arms, crest, motto, supporters and compartment down to the size of a microchip.

## Common symbols

By far the most prevalent symbol of education is that of the open book, which, of course, is featured in the arms of Oxford University. Cambridge has a closed book, which has not proved to be nearly as popular: I know of Memorial University of Newfoundland, which has three closed books in its arms, as does York University in England. The crest of Trinity College Cambridge's 1573 arms has one, as does that of the University of Otago in New Zealand. Trinity College, Toronto, contains a closed book resting below a mitre. The crest of the University of Warwick has it both ways: an open book resting on a closed one.

There are other variations: the University of Sussex has its supporters standing on open books: I am not sure about the symbolism there! The crest of Bond University in Australia has an open book with the pages "riffled." Harvard used to have the book in base flipped around, but in 1885 it was placed in the more usual position. [13] An evangelical Christian publication claims that "the overturned book symbolizes that which can only be known through the illumination of the Holy Spirit" and that this alteration was due to the "emerging philosophy of Humanism." [14]

After books, the use of flames is the most evident example of educational symbolism. This often takes the form of torches, or as flames set in different ways. Irradiated charges often result, such as with Massey University in New Zealand, which has a mullet irradiated, and its crest arises from flames. The lamp of learning, usually styled an antique lamp, is also a very popular charge, mainly in England. It is also associated with nursing, and in Canada it has appeared in this way in the arms of the University of Ottawa's Faculty of Nursing and the Victorian Order of Nurses. There are other flame-related charges in heraldry: I particularly like the arms of University of Bath in England, which have two faces of Sul, a Celtic god of wisdom [FIGURE 11]. [15] Rand Afrikaans University has a flint with two fire-steels.

The owl, a classical symbol of wisdom, has found its way into several university arms, such as the 1994 grant to Nipissing University in North Bay, Ontario. An owl (between two lamps) appears on the chief of the arms of Birbeck College, London, and there is one in the crest of the University of Alberta. A Canadian innovation has been the use of the raven in educational heraldry, a "symbol of sagacity in some first nations traditions." [16] This has occurred twice, in the arms of the University of Northern British Columbia, and as the supporters of the arms of Carleton University in Ottawa.

In South Africa, several more uses have been made of classical symbolism and its association with the scholarship of the ancients, such as the porticoes in the arms of the University of the Western Cape [FIGURE 12] and the University of the North.

Technical and technological universities have appropriate charges related to their subjects of study. The most popular, although perhaps the least exciting, is the cogwheel. University College Swansea has a hammer, pickaxe, and anchor. Calipers and bridge masonry are charges used by Brunel University. The Technical University of Nova Scotia has a miner's pick, a mechanic's hammer, a surveyor's bob, and an electromagnet.

Symbols of advanced technology, as well as charges from the other sciences, are increasingly favoured in university arms. This is to be encouraged, as long as the new charges are simple and can be easily identified. The University of Warwick has particularly "scientific" arms, part of which are *representations of the two isotopes of lithium, that in the second quarter having six, and that in the third seven protons and neutrons in its nucleus, with electrons in orbit, Argent . . . on a chief Argent a representation of a DNA double helix, spirals Azure lined Gules, with connecting lines Gold.* Nanyang Technical University in Singapore also has atomic isotope charges. The 1971 arms of the Open University in England read *Azure an open book proper bound Gules and irradiated Or thereon a television screen and on a chief Or two spools of recording tape proper,* with supporters each *a lion rampant Or holding a television mast proper.* Moreover, this university uses its logo as its badge and crest, namely *a round based escutcheon Azure round pierced in the canton.* [17] In Scotland, the University of Strathclyde has on its chief a *wave packet Sable between two open books* [FIGURE 13]. Australia's Bond University's 1987 arms have a field of *ten computer pixels barwise*—plus the inevitable southern cross [FIGURE 14]. The pixel, or picture element, is the smallest dot that can be displayed on a computer screen. [18]

Keys appear in the armorial bearings of the University of Surrey and (irradiated) in those of the Loughborough University of Technology; in Canada, it is used as a symbol for museums. The University of Central Lancashire combines many educational symbols: supporters holding torches, their forelegs resting on closed books, and a crest of *a lion's foreleg holding a scroll.* One of my particular favourites is the crest of the University of Keele: *In front of a laurel Vert a representation of Rodin's statue Le Penseur Or* [FIGURE 15].

There are also national and local symbols in university arms, and the use of beavers, maple leaves, southern crosses, roses, shamrocks, and so forth, are evident enough. Several colleges at the University of Wales include dragons or green and red tinctures, and the College of North Wales uses the arms of the Principality with an additional pale. A clever use of a national symbol is the boomerang division in arms of the Australian National University [FIGURE 16].

Of the ten provinces in Canada, all but two, Nova Scotia and Ontario, have what are essentially "provincial universities," and six of the remaining eight (the Universities of Quebec and Prince Edward Island do not bear arms) use significant parts of the provincial arms in their arms. This type of reference is also found in provincial and state university arms in South Africa and Australia. The University of Sydney rearranges the arms of New South Wales [FIGURE 17], and the University of New South Wales adds a chief to them [FIGURE 18]. In South Africa an anchor of hope can be found in the arms of the University of Cape Town and the University of South Africa, a Voortrekker wagon in the arms of the University of Pretoria, bugles in those of the University of Orange Free State, and wildebeests in the University of Natal's [FIGURE 19]. Local or civic symbols are also common, such as the mullets of Leeds or the cormorants of Liverpool. The University of Bristol obtained the mayor's permission to include the municipal arms in their own [FIGURE 20], [19] while the City University of London uses as a chief the arms of the City.

As I note elsewhere, with the University of Bombay as an example, early grants were cautious in including local fauna, but such charges gradually found their way into university heraldry, as can be seen in the crests of the University of the West Indies, a pelican [FIGURE 21]; La Trobe University in Australia, a wedge-tailed eagle; and the University of Bophuthatswana, a chanting goshawk.

Universities, of course, use appropriate religious symbolism, and occasionally cultural references are also made. The University of Durban-Westville in South Africa refers to its Asian constituency with a Sanskrit motto and a crest of the Lion Capital of Asoka's column. Items from the mythology of the culture can also be found, such as the Chinese University of Hong Kong, which uses the mythical *feng* bird, a symbol of southern China. [20]

**Founders and cadency**

Universities, of course, have founders, and lucky founders sometimes have their arms used by the institution. The 1575 grant of arms to Queen's College Cambridge uses the arms of Queen Margaret of Anjou, all within a bordure vert. Gonville and Caius also uses a bordure. Other colleges whose arms were confirmed at the visitations are nevertheless undifferenced versions of the founder's arms, such as Christchurch Oxford using the arms of Cardinal Wolsey, and St. John's Cambridge using the Beaufort arms. The use of a founder's arms continues to the present day: at the University of Toronto the Anglican and Roman Catholic colleges, Trinity and St. Michael's, both use adaptations of the arms of their episcopal founders. Massey College in Toronto adds a bordure charged with flames to the arms of its benefactor, a former governor general. In the case of the University of St. Andrew's, we see a successful armorial combination of its founders, with a reference to the see of St. Andrew's, the red lion of King James I, the crescent of Pope Benedict XIII, and the mascles of Henry Wardlaw [FIGURE 22]. [21] Other universities are named after prominent individuals, and use their namesakes' arms in various ways: Brock University in Canada and Rhodes University in South Africa are among those that adapt the arms of their inspiration. Churchill College, Cambridge, adds an open book to the arms of Sir Winston Churchill.

Forms of armorial tribute have also been made to older universities. The arms of the University of Saskatchewan, granted in 1978, but assumed in 1909, are inspired by Oxford's, the field changed to green and the crowns to garbs to mark it as the provincial university [FIGURE 23]. A less appropriate form of tribute was used by the University of King's College in Halifax, the oldest Anglophone university in this country, which quartered the arms of the University of Oxford with four other arms to which they were not entitled: the royal arms, the arms of the Province of Nova Scotia, and the assumed arms of the Diocese of Nova Scotia—plus the royal crown: perhaps the most ambitious example of armorial piracy one could imagine [FIGURE 24]. This was corrected in 1964 with the grant of arms, the tribute to their Oxonian inspiration remaining in the ancient crown in chief [FIGURE 25]. Unfortunately, they still top off the shield with a royal crown, incorrectly claiming that their royal charter entitles them to do so. [22]

For a while, Trinity University, Toronto, used (ungranted) arms similar to Cambridge University, whence a number of its important scholars had come: the four lions became stags and the ermine cross was made semy of maple leaves, and other small changes were made. [23]

Other bodies also get armorial nods. Queen Mary College at the University of London shows its ties with the Drapers' Company by adding a chief to the arms of the Company. Grants to Montreal's Sir George Williams University, and to its successor body, Concordia University, both include an inverted triangle, indicating association with the Y.M.C.A. Huron College at the University of Western Ontario adds a bordure to the arms of the Anglican diocese of Huron.

In some cases, a new university is the offspring of another, and pays armorial tribute to this fact. An example is the University of Dundee in Scotland, once a college (Queen's College, revised arms granted 1955) of the University of St. Andrew's. Its arms contain the same per saltire and chief divisions and colours, but with new charges [FIGURE 26]. Charges may also be used to show inspiration and derivation, such as the red martlets of McGill University, Montreal [FIGURE 27], found in the chief of the arms of the University of Victoria, British Columbia [FIGURE 28], McGill having aided the younger institution. [24]

The creation of a university from two previous institutions is another matter, and sometimes it is shown armorially in the combination of charges, as with Concordia University, Montreal, or in the unique dimidiation for Heriot-Watt University in Edinburgh, combining the arms of the Watt Institute with those of George Heriot's hospital [FIGURE 29]. [25]

Sometimes a constituent college is able to pay armorial tribute to its mother university. University College Toronto rearranges slightly the charges of the University's arms, changing the chief to a chevron and the blue field to red. In New Zealand, Otago's University College adds a gold bordure to the University arms, while the Otago University Students' Association adds a bordure counter-compony of university colours. Other examples of armorial imitation are the similarity between the arms of the University of New Brunswick and its constituent Neill House, and the ermine cross on red arms for the University Reader in Divinity at Cambridge.

An interesting example of corporate cadency can be found at the University of Otago. Its residences are controlled by the Stuart Residence Halls Council, which was granted arms in 1949. The two halls of residence also wanted distinctive arms, and the solution found was to add a label to one (Arana Hall) and a crescent to the other (Carrington Hall). [26]

Rarely do a university and its constituent bodies co-ordinate to receive grants at the same time; however, there have been two interesting multiple-grant documents: in 1590, to the Readers at the University of Cambridge, and in 1957, to six colleges and societies at the University of Durham, some using variations on the University's cross. [27]

## Granting powers

The bulk of grants of which I have spoken have been made by the English Kings of Arms. Obviously, Scottish universities have been granted arms from the Lord Lyon. Lyon grants have also been made to the University of Calgary, Trinity Western University, the University of Waterloo, and Simon Fraser University in Canada; St. Andrew's College, Sydney, Australia; the University College of Pius XII, Basutholand; and the University of Otago in New Zealand and some of its dependent bodies. In the cases of McGill and Queen's Universities in Canada, a matriculation from the Lord Lyon has followed a College of Arms grant. Responsibility for grants to Canadian universities has fallen to the Canadian Heraldic Authority since 1988.

An interesting development from earlier this year concerns a new example of a grant received from the heraldic authority of a former colonial power—that made to the University of Namibia by the State Herald of South Africa.

A handful of universities have been honoured with royal warrant grants: Royal Military College in Kingston, Ontario; the Royal University of Malta; Nuffield College, Oxford; and the University of South Africa (formerly the University of the Cape of Good Hope). In 1909, the Imperial College of Science and Technology in London received a royal warrant grant that includes the royal arms themselves.

## The use and misuse of arms

Some universities can be quite creative with the use of their arms—in Canada perhaps the best practitioner of this is McGill University, Montreal—and this, in turn, results in popular affection for the arms. There are also universities that use their arms rarely, if ever, and then only in an inappropriate way, being unable to depart in the slightest from the artwork of the letters patent.

We have seen, in addition to the old challenge of assumed arms, the introduction of logos. Some of these are excellent and serve the purpose of ready identification, albeit being useful for a limited amount of time. All too often undistinguished logos are enforced with the same lack of creativity that marks the use, in some cases, of arms. Sometimes universities that want to be different opt for logos to break free of the strictures of an "ancient" system. In a conversation I had recently with someone involved in a symbols project at an Ontario university, I suggested that the university petition to have its present assumed arms granted. The reply was that the administration was favouring a logo, to make a statement that they are not a regular university. Fair enough—perhaps a good logo is better than a shoddy assumed arms design, although I hope they will one day consider the appropriateness of arms.

A mistaken pursuit of modernity is not the only threat to legitimate heraldry. Past associations can also endanger its use. The University of Bombay has arms from the 1850s [FIGURE 30]; however, after independence it decided that the London-granted arms were a colonial relic, and should be replaced. While I can understand their desire to use something with more Indian symbolism than the presence of an eastern crown on the lion, I am less ready to excuse what they adopted instead [FIGURE 31]. [28]

The Irish have also turned to lion hunting. The arms granted to University College, Cork, by Ulster King of Arms in 1889 included a lion [FIGURE 32]. This beast was eliminated by the faculty in 1950 in favour of a Jesuit symbol [FIGURE 33]. The old arms were restored by a subsequent president, who, although no less an Irish nationalist, thought it petty to alter the arms in this way. [29] At present there is a debate going on in Canada over a proposal by the Royal Military College to alter its arms, which include an augmentation of the royal Union badge. [30]

Should all universities have granted arms? I would say yes, for they are corporate bodies contributing to the community. All need a form of identification, and at least in the countries hitherto mentioned, armorial bearings are the most appropriate form. We have seen time and again that uni-

versities will resort to a form of armorial achievement to represent themselves, and far better it is that such bearings be granted by a legitimate authority. In a speech reprinted in *The Coat of Arms*, Sir George Bellew, former Garter King of Arms, states that an armorial grant should be pursued only by institutions that have reached a certain maturity and respectability. [31] I would argue that such a precondition is quaint and unnecessary: all universities should obtain granted arms, and the sooner into their history the better, otherwise assumed arms will arise. Post-secondary institutions are regulated strictly enough so that we may be assured that all are centres of genuine scholarship, and not degree mills. Incorporation of a new institution of learning should satisfy any heraldic officer of the state's confidence in it.

**The future**

Although grants in England and Scotland have slowed down in recent years, there is a new challenge to be met, namely the transformation of 34 polytechnical institutions into university status in 1992. [32] Many of them do not bear arms at present, although there has been increased granting activity.

University grants have also slowed down in Australia. The only recent grants to Australian universities that I have so far discovered were to the private Bond University and to Charles Stuart University. Many Australian universities use logos or assumed arms, some of which are actually quite appealing. Five out of the seven universities in New Zealand, plus several of their constituent colleges, use legitimate arms.

Under its own heraldic authority, Canada has enjoyed a gentle acceleration in the number of grants, and at least two-thirds of our degree-granting institutions bear arms. We still have a way to go; however, the word seems to be spreading about the benefits of legitimately granted arms. The holdouts will be not so much those that prefer logos—for the passing nature of these devices will bring universities to heraldry sooner or later—but rather universities that have long used inappropriate heraldry.

Particularly worthy of praise is the success of the Bureau of Heraldry of the Republic of South Africa, which can boast that an amazing 100% of South African universities are armigerous.

Is there not a similarity between universities and heraldry? At their best they are a lively combination of a desire to preserve the past with a constant seeking out of future direction, and the frontiers in both directions will always expand. Universities will always use a variety of symbols, and this is something we should not fear. However, as they are centres of truth, creativity, and even beauty, we must ensure that particular care (and lively care, at that) is paid to the way in which heraldry is used, a consideration all too often ignored. Universities will continue to arise, and a proportion of them will seek granted arms. We must see that such a proportion is high.

## NOTES

1. I illustrated some of my observations with slides, about half of them taken from the painted arms of the universities of the British Empire and its First World Allies found in the Great Hall of Hart House, at the University of Toronto. These were done in 1919 by the great heraldic artist Alexander Scott Carter.

I have made a study of university calendars and histories, and BRIGGS' *Civic and Corporate Heraldry*, LOW'S *Roll of Australian Arms*, PAUL'S *Ordinary of Arms*, and CAMPBELL'S *The Identifying Symbols of Canadian Educational Institutions* have been particularly helpful. I acknowledge the help of the Canadian Heraldic Authority in providing me with examples of recent grants, and am grateful to the State Herald's having supplied me with information on South African university arms. Other thanks are due to Roger Gardiner, Robert Laing, Gregor Macaulay, Jon Good, John Kennedy, and John Matheson.

This paper is perhaps best described as an armorial safari, a series of observations I have made while collecting university heraldry. My collection is by no means complete, and I would be grateful for any further information. Some time in the future I hope to publish a roll of arms booklet of university arms granted from heralds in London, Edinburgh, Dublin, Ottawa, and Pretoria.

2. *The Heraldry Gazette*, New series 52 (June 1994), p. 1.

3. GEOFFREY BRIGGS, *Civic and Corporate Heraldry* (London: Heraldry Today, 1971), p. 13.

4. *Ibid.*, p. 218.

5. Taken from a College publication. I have seen elsewhere a different blazon with a parted field of green and blue; however, the one I am using seems closer to the illustrations I have seen.

6. See *The Tercentenary of Harvard College* (Cambridge: Harvard University Press, 1937).

7. See *The Arms of Yale University and Its Colleges at New Haven* (New Haven: Yale University Press, 1963).

8. See *Heraldry in Canada*, vol. 31, no. 3 (June 1997).

9. *The Book of Trinity College Dublin 1591-1891* (Belfast: Marcus Ward, 1892), p. 9.

10. This material from the Archives of the University of Western Ontario was brought to my attention by Mr. Roger Gardiner.

11. See examples in H. P. STOKES, *The Emblem, The Arms, and the Motto of the University of Cambridge: Notes on Their Use* (Cambridge: C.U.P., 1928), p. 33.

12. University of Toronto Archives, *Senate Minutes 2* (Oct. 1, 1857): 429.

13. SAMUEL ELIOT MORISON, "Harvard Seals and Arms," *The Harvard Graduates' Magazine* (September 1933), p. 12.

14. "300 Years of Change at Harvard," *The Forerunner* (October 1991), p. 11.

15. *The Heraldry Gazette*, vol. 2, no. 40 (October 1966), p. 2.

16. Booklet of the Presentation of Coat of Arms ceremony, University of Northern British Columbia, May 14, 1994.

17. *The Heraldry Gazette*, New series 51 (March 1994), p. 5

18. GREGOR MACAULAY, "The Arms of Bond University," *The New Zealand Armorist*, no. 47 (Winter 1993), p. 17.

19. G. BRIGGS, *op. cit.*, p. 74.

20. The Chinese University of Hong Kong, *Calendar 1970-71*.

21. CHRISTOPHER GREEN, "The Heraldry of the University of St. Andrew's," *The Coat of Arms*, vol. 3, no. 22 (April 1955), p. 210.

22. IAN CAMPBELL, *The Identifying Symbols of Canadian Educational Institutions*, 2nd ed. (Waterloo: Canadian Heraldry Associates, 1990), p. II-3, 14.

23. ROBERT M. BLACK, *The Arms of Trinity College* (unpublished manuscript, 1987), p. 7.

24. ALAN BEDDOE and STROME GALLOWAY, *Beddoe's Canadian Heraldry* (Belleville: Mika, 1981), p. 104.

25. *The Heraldry Gazette*, vol. 1, no. 8 (October 1958), p. 3.

26. GREGOR MACAULAY, "The Arms of Arana and Carrington Halls," *The New Zealand Armorist* (date unknown), p. 17.

27. ANTHONY WAGNER, "The Armorial Bearings of Certain Colleges and Societies of Durham University," *The Coat of Arms*, vol. 5, no. 33 (January 1958), p. 365.

28. AROON TIKEKAR, *The Cloister's Pale: A Biography of the University of Bombay* (Bombay: Somaiya, 1984), p. 118.

29. JOHN A. MURPHY, *The College: A History of Queen's/ University College Cork* (Cork: Cork University Press, 1995), p. 386-387.

30. For some correspondence on this matter see *Canadian Monarchist News*, vol. 1, no. 4 (Winter 1995-1996), p. 6.

31. SIR GEORGE BELLEW, "Modern Heraldry," *The Coat of Arms* (April 1963), p. 237.

32. As a result of the Higher and Further Education Act, 1992.

1

2

3

4

5

6

7

8

9

10

11

12

13

14

15

16

17

18

19

20

21

22

23

24

427

25

26

27

28

29

30

31

32

33

# L'HÉRALDIQUE HAÏTIENNE SOUS LE RÈGNE DU ROI HENRY Ier

Robert Pichette

Le premier janvier 1804 naissait la République d'Haïti constituée par la partie française de la colonie de Saint-Domingue. Il s'agissait de la première république noire au monde. Jean-Jacques Dessalines, ancien esclave, en devint le premier président avant de se proclamer empereur le 22 septembre 1804. Il se fit couronner sur le Champ de Mars de Port-au-Prince sous le nom de Jacques Ier, le 8 octobre 1804. La proclamation de l'Empire par Bonaparte, en mai 1804, aura sans doute incité Dessalines à créer la première monarchie dans le Nouveau Monde depuis les Aztèques et les Incas. Bien que plusieurs de ses sujets aient réclamé la création de titres de noblesse, Jacques Ier refusa d'en créer, déclarant : « Moi seul, je suis noble ![1] ».

Le sanguinaire et tyrannique empereur fut assassiné en 1806. La république fut proclamée et l'un des plus remarquables noirs de l'histoire nord-américaine, Henry Christophe, en fut élu président[2]. En 1807, le pays se scinda en deux républiques ; celle du Nord et celle de l'Ouest où Alexandre Pétion exerça la présidence jusqu'en 1818. La république du Nord fut transformée en royaume en mars 1811 et, de président, Henry Christophe devint le roi Henry Ier « par la grâce de Dieu et la Loi constitutionnelle de l'État ».

Bien qu'analphabète, le roi était un organisateur exceptionnel et s'était entouré de conseillers hautement compétents. Gouvernement et cour furent créés rapidement et aucun détail n'échappa à l'œil du nouveau souverain qui aimait le faste et le grandiose comme en témoignent encore aujourd'hui les imposantes ruines de son palais de Sans Souci, du site des Ramiers et de la chapelle royale de Millot mais surtout de la citadelle Laferrière — œuvre cyclopéenne — qualifiée par Georges Duval, architecte en chef des Monuments historiques de France, d'« une des plus extraordinaires forteresses de notre temps, premier monument de la race noire enfin libérée[3] ».

Tout fut réglé minutieusement, avec un luxe de détails, même les uniformes. Les moqueurs prétendaient que l'article premier du Code Henry spécifiait que nul ne devait paraître à la cour sans uniforme et que l'article deux précisait que chaque uniforme serait différent[4] !

Le sacre et le couronnement du roi et de la reine eurent lieu au mois de juin 1811 mais dès le 5 avril, un édit du roi créait une noblesse héréditaire dans le but exprès de conférer de la splendeur au trône. Trois jours plus tard, un autre édit créait quatre princes, sept ducs, 22 comtes, 39 barons et 14 chevaliers. À l'instar de la noblesse napoléonienne, Henry Ier créa des princes mais aucun marquis ni vicomte.

Les titres correspondaient à des majorats car Henry Ier avait concédé d'immenses plantations à ses nobles militaires à qui il faisait obligation de résider sur leurs terres afin qu'ils servent de guides sociaux aux cultivateurs. Grand admirateur des institutions anglaises, le roi avait modelé son système sur une sorte de féodalisme anglais[5].

À ces premiers titres s'ajoutèrent de nouvelles créations et des promotions au cours du règne. Ainsi, le maréchal de camp Guerrier, aide de camp du roi et commandant le premier arrondissement de la province de l'Ouest, fut titré initialement comte de Mirebalais. Il devait être promu, plus tard, duc de l'Avancé.

Depuis Chateaubriand on s'est gaussé, avec un brin de racisme et beaucoup de condescendance, du comte de la Marmelade, du comte du Dondon, du comte de Limonade, du comte du Trou et du baron de Latortue[6]. En réalité, ces titres nobiliaires décernés à d'anciens esclaves par un souverain légitime et dûment reconnu correspondent à des désignations territoriales et ne sont guère plus comiques que d'innombrables noms inscrits à l'Armorial général de France.

Ainsi Aimé Césaire, dans sa *Tragédie du roi Christophe*, fait dire au baron de Vastey[7], secrétaire du roi Henry :

> Homme de peu de foi ! Allons ! Le rire des Français ne me gêne pas ! Marmelade, pourquoi pas ? Pourquoi pas Limonade ? Ce sont des noms à vous remplir la bouche ! Gastronomiques à souhait ! Après tout les Français ont bien le duc de Foix et le duc de Bouillon ! Est-ce plus ragoûtant ? Il y a des précédents, vous voyez ![8]

DIEU MA CAUSE ET MON EPÉE.

*Armes du Roi.*

RENAIS DE MES CENDRE

DIEU PROTÉGE LE ROI.

*de la Reine*

1

MALGRÉ LES FLOTS

LES VENTS ET

*Armes de la Capitale*

JE SEME LA TERREUR

*du Prince de St Marc*

2

FIDÉLITÉ AU ROI.

A DIEU ET

*du Duc de l'Anse*

IL S'ÉLÈVE PAR SA VALEUR.

5

6

430

QUI S'Y FROTTE S'Y PIQUE.

Duc de l'Avancé

7

LA FLAMME EST MON ÉLÉMENT.

Comte de Ste. Suzanne

8

EN TOUT TEMPS EN TOUT LIEUX.

Comte de Vallière

9

POUR MA CAUSE ET MON ROI.

Comte de Jérémie

10

HONNEUR. FIDÉLITÉ.

Comte d'Ennery.

11

AMOUR. PATRIE. ET GLOIRE.

Comte de Léogane

12

*Comte de la Pasquite.*

13

RETRAITE — DE — MONT-ROUX.

*Baron de Barth. Choisy.*

14

IL BRAVE — LES VENTS ET — LES FL.COTS.

*Baron de Bartieu Fabien.*

15

NEPTUNE — ET LA — FORTUNE.

*Baron de Cadet Antoine*

16

AMÉNITÉ — DEVOUEMENT.

*Baron de Célestin Cap*

17

PREUX — ET — LOYAL.

*Baron de Moupoint*

18

*Comte de Terre-neuve*

19

GUERRE AUX REBELLES.

*Baron de Bazile Jaillans*

20

RIEN NE RÉSISTE A SES EFFETS.

*Baron d'Ambroise*

21

UTILE EN PLUS D'UN GENRE.

*Baron de Béliard*

22

PROBITÉ.

*Baron de Petit*

23

PERSÉVÉRANCE EXACTITUDE

*Baron de Sévelinge*

24

MENTOR GUIDE.
EST MON

*Baron de Bazin*

25

CONSTANCE LA VERTU.
FONDEE SUR

*Baron de Delon*

26

SINCÉRITÉ FRANCHISE

*Baron de Lastey.*

27

IL TRIOMPHE D'ANGERS.
DES

*Chevalier de Félix.*

28

À Londres où il se trouvait, en 1822, « magnifique ambassadeur » après y avoir vécu pauvrement en émigré durant la Révolution, Chateaubriand dédaignera cette nouvelle noblesse du Nouveau Monde et se moquera avec ingratitude du journaliste Jean-Gabriel Peltier, « ambassadeur du roi nègre Christophe auprès de George III, correspondant diplomatique de M. le comte de *Limonade*, et buvant en vin de Champagne les appointements qu'on lui payait en sucre[9] ».

Or, le comte de Limonade était un jeune mulâtre intelligent du nom de Julien Prévost qui tenait son titre d'un territoire de la province du Nord d'Haïti. Ayant reçu son éducation en France et considéré comme l'un des plus compétents conseillers du roi Henry Ier, il en fut le secrétaire d'État et le ministre des Affaires étrangères[10].

C'est à lui que nous devons une relation de l'accession au trône et du sacre d'Henry Ier publiée au Cap-Henri (l'actuel Cap-Haïtien), en 1811. Par lui également que nous connaissons cette noblesse indigène calquée dans une très large mesure sur le système nobiliaire et héraldique instauré dans l'Empire français par Napoléon. La publication de la *Relation* fut bientôt suivie par l'*Almanach Royal d'Hayti* qui donne une profusion de détails sur l'organisation de la cour, du gouvernement et de la noblesse[11].

Le 15 avril 1811, soit sept jours après l'édit de création de la noblesse, Henry Ier signait l'« Édit du roi qui détermine les armoiries des princes, ducs, comtes, barons et chevaliers du royaume »[12]. On y trouve 86 blasonnements. Les barons n'étaient désignés dans l'édit de nomination que par leurs patronymes alors que les princes, ducs et comtes y étaient désignés par leur prénoms, patronymes et désignations nobiliaires. Dans l'édit qui leur assigne des armoiries, les barons sont titrés de noms de terre et les chevaliers portent tous la particule, ce qui n'était pas le cas dans l'édit de création.

Henry Ier, qui s'était doté d'un grand chambellan, d'un grand maréchal du palais, d'un grand écuyer, d'un grand veneur, d'un grand maître de cérémonies et d'un grand aumonier[13], avait naturellement eu soin de se donner un roi d'armes assisté de pas moins de 13 hérauts. Selon sir George Bellew, ancien roi d'armes Jarretière, le roi d'armes s'appelait Baraquet. C'est, pour l'instant, tout ce que l'on sait de ce personnage[14]. On ne sait pas non plus s'il est l'auteur des armoiries concédées ni quel rôle l'imposant collège de hérauts jouait.

Les concessions d'armoiries ont été recueillies et peintes dans un véritable armorial intitulé *Armorial Général du Royaume d'Hayti*[15]. L'ouvrage relié compte 31 pages, la page de titre étant imprimée. Le papier utilisé semble très ancien car son filigrane est une variante du pot ou vase à fleur sommé d'une couronne et surmonté d'un fleuron, le vase portant le sigle PO. Ce filigrane se retrouve surtout dans le papier fabriqué dans le nord de la France au XVe siècle[16]. L'armorial comprend 90 armoiries dont les armoiries du roi, de la reine Marie-Louise, du prince royal Jacques-Victor Henry[17].

Les armes du roi se blasonnent : *d'azur semé d'étoiles d'or au phénix du même sommé d'une couronne royale, entouré d'un listel d'argent portant la devise « Je renais de mes cendres ».* *Supports : deux lions d'hermine armés, lampassés et couronnés d'or. La devise sur un listel sous l'écu : Dieu, ma Cause et mon Épée.* L'écu, sommé de la couronne royale, est entouré du collier de l'ordre royal et militaire de Saint-Henry nouvellement créé [FIGURE 1].

Les armes de la reine diffèrent de celles du roi, l'écu étant semé d'abeilles au lieu d'étoiles. Il est entouré de deux rinceaux fleuris qui soutiennent la couronne royale et la devise est : *Dieu protège le roi* [FIGURE 2]. Par ailleurs, le frère de la reine Marie-Louise, le prince Noël, titré duc de Port-de-Paix avec le prédicat d'Altesse Royale, portait *d'or, au pavillon d'Hayti, accompagné de trois abeilles en chef, au naturel, sur les plis flottans de l'étendart ce moto* [sic] : *Il est beau de mourir pour son roi ; l'écu sommé et timbré d'un casque à visière levée, taré et posé de front, assorti de ses lambrequins pris des émaux des armes, pour supports deux autruches d'argent, onglées et couronnées de gueules à l'antique*[18].

Quant au prince royal, l'écu est brisé d'un lambel d'argent de trois pointes. La couronne et le collier de l'ordre sont identiques mais la devise est différente : *Les jeux de l'enfance annoncent les grands hommes.* Viennent ensuite les armes de la capitale Cap-Henry qui se blasonnent : *de pourpre au navire habillé entrant dans le port.* *Tenants : deux Hercules de sable armés de massues d'or. Devise : Malgré les vents et les flots.* La couronne royale surmonte l'écu [FIGURE 3].

L'héraldiste qui a conçu les armoiries assignées ou concédées à la noblesse du roi Henry Ier avait un sens étonnamment aigu de l'héraldique à son meilleur. À une époque où l'art et la science héraldique avaient atteint le sommet de la décadence, celles-ci sont de fort belle facture. Elles ont toutes le mérite d'être simples, exception faite des armes du cardinal-archevêque duc de l'Anse et des armes de la capitale qui sont tout à fait dans le goût de l'époque.

Elles sont en outre originales à plus d'un titre. Par exemple, on n'y trouve aucune couronne et, si Henry I$^{er}$ a été influencé par Napoléon I$^{er}$, il n'a pas retenu les toques de l'héraldique impériale. Par contre, on trouve des heaumes tarés de front ou de profil selon le rang du titulaire et neuf sont surmontés d'un chapeau militaire dont le nombre de plumets semble indiquer le rang militaire. Ces chapeaux ne se retrouvent que dans les armes des barons et sont d'ailleurs spécifiquement nommés « chapeau de baron » dans l'édit de concession. Henry I$^{er}$ n'a pas retenu non plus les chefs et les francs-quartiers de l'héraldique impériale française.

Dans beaucoup de cas, les meubles semblent inspirés par la devise. D'autres sont une allusion directe à la fonction du titulaire. C'est le cas du baron de Béliard, directeur et intendant des jardins et des eaux et forêts des palais du roi, et du baron de Sévelinge, bibliothécaire du roi. Dans le premier cas, les armes, telles que blasonnées dans l'Armorial, se lisent : *de sable, au rateau et à l'arrosoir d'argent, posés en sautoir ; l'écu sommé et timbré d'un casque à visière levée, taré et posé de profil, surmonté du chapeau de baron, assorti de ses lambrequins pris des émaux des armes, pour supports deux caméléons de sinople, rampans ; moto [sic] : Utile en plus d'un genre* [FIGURE 22].

Les armes du baron de Sévelinge sont tout aussi simples : *de pourpre, à la bibliothèque d'or ; l'écu sommé et timbré d'un casque à visière levée, taré et posé de profil, surmonté du chapeau de baron, assorti de ses lambrequins pris des émaux des armes ; pour supports deux pintades de sable, becquées et membrées d'or ; moto [sic], Persévérance, exactitude* [FIGURE 24].

La faune héraldique de l'Armorial n'est pas exclusivement indigène car il n'y a ni licornes, ni lions, ni tigres, ni autruches, ni zèbres en Haïti ! Par contre, des animaux typiques des Antilles ou d'Amérique ne déparent pas l'Armorial. C'est le cas du caïman du blason du maréchal de camp Louis Achille, comte de Laxxvon, et de nombreux supports : les condors des armes du chevalier de Prézeau, les castors de vair des armes du

baron de Louis Pierreault, les veaux marins des armes du baron de Bastien Fabien [FIGURE 15] et les lamantins de vair des armes du baron de Cadet Antoine qui d'ailleurs portait comme écu *d'argent à la baleine d'azur* [FIGURE 16].

Les blasonnements officiels ont tendance à être quelque peu simplistes et à manquer de précision. Quelques-uns sont carrément erronés par rapport à l'illustration qu'ils veulent décrire et on y trouve huit armoiries à enquerre. Le roi d'armes Baraquet, s'il est l'auteur de ces créations héraldiques, avait une prédilection marquée pour le pourpre, émail peu utilisé dans l'héraldique continentale et que l'on retrouve 21 fois dans l'Armorial.

Si l'exécution artistique des blasons est bien dans le goût du temps et démontre une tendance naturaliste qui est aussi de l'époque, il n'en reste pas moins que ce premier armorial du Nouveau Monde s'inspirait d'un solide axiome héraldique : qui porte le moins est le plus.

Le règne d'Henry I$^{er}$ finit mal. Frappé d'apoplexie en l'église de Limonade le 15 août 1820, faisant face à une révolte et abandonné par sa garde, le roi se suicida d'une balle au cœur le 8 octobre 1820. Selon la légende, elle était d'or. Le prince royal Victor Henry fut assassiné par les mutins, mais la reine et ses deux filles, les princesses Améthyste et Athénaire, eurent la chance d'être rescapées par la marine britannique et trouvèrent initialement refuge en Angleterre[19]. La reine Marie-Louise vécut jusqu'en 1850[20]. Un autre fils, le prince Ferdinand, mourut dans la misère à Paris[21].

L'Armorial général se retrouva en Angleterre, on ne sait comment. Ce qui est certain, c'est qu'il fut acquis par James Pulman, roi d'armes Clarenceux et légué par testament en date du 29 mars 1858 au chapitre du *College of Arms*. Henry I$^{er}$, anglophile convaincu, aurait approuvé.

Si l'exemplaire qui se trouve dans les collections du *College of Arms* est le manuscrit original, il en existe également un autre, semblable mais non identique, appartenant à M. Guy A. Béliard, ancien fonctionnaire des Nations-Unies et descendant du baron de Béliard. Ce manuscrit, incomplet et endommagé, aurait appartenu au roi en propre selon une tradition de famille[22]. Son existence était connue en 1941[23] et le *College of Arms* en possède une photocopie[24].

Si la noblesse créée par Henry Christophe, devenu Henry I$^{er}$ est bien connue, celle créée par un autre souverain d'Haïti l'est moins bien. Faustin Soulouque, président de la République en 1847, se fit proclamer empereur d'Haïti le 29 août 1849 sous le nom de Faustin I$^{er}$. Durant son règne, il créa quatre princes, 59 ducs, 90 comtes, 300 barons et 46 chevaliers. On ignore tout jusqu'à présent de l'héraldique de cet éphémère empire mais, comme dans le cas de la noblesse du roi Henry I$^{er}$, il existe certainement des descendants de ces créations. Sir Harry Luke écrivait en 1945 qu'il avait un ami, évêque catholique irlandais, dont le cuisinier était originaire des Antilles et qui portait le très authentique titre de Marquis Toujours-Vert. Faustin I$^{er}$ régna jusqu'au 15 janvier 1859 date où il fut déposé après un règne marqué par la terreur, la corruption et l'inefficacité administrative.

Il y avait au contraire de la grandeur et du génie chez Henry Christophe. L'éducation fut au cœur de ses préoccupations. Ainsi, ayant rendu l'enseignement obligatoire, il avait créé des écoles particulières dans chaque arrondissement et une école centrale dans chaque district militaire. De plus, il fonda une Académie royale et des écoles professionnelles qui privilégiaient l'enseignement technique. Le politicologue haïtien, René-A. St-Louis, précise :

> Dans son système d'éducation, la priorité fut accordée à la technique. Tout élève, à quelque degré d'enseignement qu'il pût appartenir, devait connaître un art manuel. Voulant à tout prix promouvoir l'éducation, il n'hésita pas à faire appel à des professeurs et techniciens anglais, français, américains [25].

Sur sa tombe, dans son extraordinaire citadelle Laferrière, on inscrivit : LE CIVILISATEUR. Au moment de mourir, Aimé Césaire lui fait dire à son page, Afrique : « Défais moi [...] de mes nobles, de ma noblesse, de mon sceptre, de ma couronne. Et lave-moi ! Oh, lave-moi de leur fard, de leurs baisers, de mon royaume ! [26] ». Et le rideau tombe sur la *Tragédie du roi Christophe* après que le fidèle baron de Vastey, s'adressant à la dépouille du souverain, demande « aux oiseaux essaimeurs de pollens » de lui dessiner ses armes non périssables : le phénix couronné.

## BIBLIOGRAPHIE SOMMAIRE

« L'Art haïtien avant 1930 » *Conjonction*, Revue franco-haïtienne, Port-au-Prince, Institut Français d'Haïti ; BEAUBRUN ARDOUIN, *Études sur l'histoire d'Haïti*, Paris, 1865, 11 vol. ; EUGÈNE AUBIN, *En Haïti*, Paris, Armand Collin, 1910 ; G. R. BELLEW, Somerset Herald, « Strange Heraldry for a Negro Aristocracy: The "Register of Arms" of King Henry Christophe's Haitian Court », *The Illustrated London News* (16 juin 1934), p. 964-965 ; JOHN CANDLER, *Brief Notices of Hayti*, Londres, Thomas Ward and Co., 1842 ; AIMÉ CÉSAIRE, *La tragédie du roi Christophe*, Paris, Présence Africaine, 1963, réédition revue par l'auteur, 1970 ; JOSEPH WILKIE DARISMÉ, « Structure agraire et classes sociales de St-Domingue à Haïti 1793-1900 », mémoire de maîtrise, Université Laval, Québec, 1975 ; J.-C. DORSAINVILLE, *Histoire d'Haïti, cours supérieur*, Port-au-Prince, Éditions Henri Deschamps, édition de 1924 rééditée en 1934 ; EARL LESLIE GRIGGS et CLIFFORD H. PRATOR, *Christophe Henri and Clarkson Thomas: A Correspondence*, Berkley, University of California Press, 1952 ; W.W. HARVEY, *Sketches of Hayti from the expulsion of the French To the death of Christophe*, Londres, L. B. Seeley and Son, 1827 ; VERGNIAUD LECONTE, *Henri Christophe dans l'Histoire d'Haïti*, Paris, Éditions Berger Levrault, 1931 ; YVAN LOSKOUTOFF, « L'héraldique sous les tropiques : l'armorial du roi Henry-Christophe I$^{er}$ d'Haïti » (décembre 1995), conférence à paraître dans la *Revue française d'héraldique et de sigillographie* ; COMTE de LIMONADE [JULIEN PRÉVOST], *Relation des glorieux événements qui ont porté leurs Majestés Royales sur le trone d'Hayti, Suivie de l'Histoire du Couronnement et du Sacre du Roi HENRY I$^{er}$ et de la Reine MARIE-LOUISE*, Imprimé au Cap-Henry, Chez P. ROUX, imprimeur du Roi, 1811, l'An 8$^e$ ; SIR HARRY LUKE, « Monarchy in Haiti », *Jamaican Historical Review*, vol. 1 (1945), p. 125-136 ; ALBERT MANGONÈS, *La Citadelle le Palais de Sans Souci le Site des Ramiers Monuments à l'indépendance d'une nation et à la liberté de son peuple*, Port-au-Prince, Institut de Sauvegarde du Patrimoine (assistance de l'UNESCO), 1980 ; MAJOR G. H. OSTERHOUT, U.S.M.C., « The Fortress-Citadel of King Christophe of Haiti, The Negro Napoleon: A Monument to his Tyranny and Genius », *The Illustrated London News* (31 mars 1934), p. 488-490 ; ROLAND I. PERUSSE, *Historical Dictionary of Haiti*, Metuchen, N.J., The Scarecrow Press, Inc., 1977 ; SELDEN RODMAN, *Haiti: The Black Republic*, Old Greenwich, Connecticut, The Devin-Adair Company, 1978 ; ENOCH TROUILLOT, *Le gouvernement du roi Henri Christophe*, Port-au-Prince, Imprimerie Centrale, 1974 ; J. VERSCHUEREN, *Panorama d'Haïti*, Paris, P. Le Thiellleux éditeur, 1948, t. 1 (très riche bibliographie).

## NOTES

1. SIR H. LUKE, « Monarchy in Haiti », *Jamaican Historical Review*, vol. 1 (1945), p. 125, et S. RODMAN, *Haiti: The Black Republic* (1$^{re}$ éd. Devlin-Adair, Old Grennwich, Conn., 1954), 4$^e$ édition révisée, 1978, p. 15.

2. Les historiens ne s'accordent pas sur le lieu de naissance d'Henry Christophe. Certains le font naître sujet britannique, fils d'esclaves de Grenade. D'autres le font naître sujet français né à Saint-Christophe, aujourd'hui St. Kitts. Il se serait enfui à Haïti à l'âge de 12 ans où il serait devenu le domestique d'un officier de la marine française. Il aurait pris part à la guerre d'Indépendance américaine et aurait combattu, notamment, à Savannah.

3. A. MANGONÈS, *Les monuments du roi Christophe : la Citadelle le Palais de Sans Souci le Site des Ramiers*, Institut de Sauvegarde du Patrimoine National, Port-au-Prince, 1980.

4. G. R. BELLEW, « Strange Heraldry for a Negro Aristocracy: The "Registrer of Arms" of King Henry Christophe's Haitian Court », *The Illustrated London News* (16 juin 1934), p. 964-965.

5. R.-A. ST-LOUIS, *La présociologie haïtienne ou Haïti et sa vocation nationale*, Deneau, Montréal, 1970, p. 95.

6. Respectivement le maréchal de camp Pierre Toussaint ; le maréchal de camp Jasemain, gouverneur de la citadelle Henry et grand veneur ; le maréchal de camp Julien Prévost, secrétaire d'État et ministre des Affaires étrangères ; le maréchal de camp Toussaint Dupont, inspecteur général des cultures; les barons Stanislas Latortue, intendant des finances de la province du nord et Joseph Latortue, intendant des finances de la province de l'Ouest.

7. Pompée Valentin, baron de Vastey, était un mulâtre qui avait reçu son éducation en France. Conseiller loyal et intime du roi Henri, il fut un ardent défenseur de la monarchie haïtienne et écrivit plusieurs ouvrages. Il portait *de gueules à une épée et à une plume d'or posées en sautoir, au chef d'argent*. Supports : *à dextre un renard d'or, à senestre une licorne d'azur colletée d'or*. Devise : Sincérité, Franchise.

8. A. CÉSAIRE, *La tragédie du roi Christophe*, Présence Africaine, Paris, 1963, réédition de 1970. Hors ces deux illustres exemples cités par l'écrivain Antillais, mentionnons Louis de Trémignon, Antoine de Rigollot, Cir-Yves de Jambon, Jean-François-Eustache de Chéri, Pierre de Coquet, Nicolas-Jean de Taillefumier, Anatole du Scex, Blaise de Troussebois, Charles-Antoine de Poussemothe, Gilles Le Fessier du Fay, Pierre Belon Lapisse ou, perle des perles, Jean-Louis-Victor Le Vacher, seigneur de la Tour aux Pommiers, de la Rocheculdebœuf et de l'Eschigné de la Chaise. Tous ces messieurs — pour ne rien dire de Louise de Fouilleuse, épouse d'Alexandre de Tracy, vice-roi de la Nouvelle France — ont ceci en commun qu'ils sont militaires, chevaliers de Malte ou de Saint-Louis et, bien entendu, ils sont Européens et blancs.

9. *Mémoires d'outre-tombe*, texte de l'édition originale de 1849 annotée par Pierre Clarac, t. 1, p. 411. Ghislain de Diesbach trace de Peltier le portrait suivant : « pittoresque énergumène du monde des lettres et des affaires, réplique affaiblie de Beaumarchais, avec moins de talent et presque autant d'entregent ». (G. DE DIESBACH, *Chateaubriand*, Perrin, 1995, p. 96).

10. R. I. PERUSSE, *Historical Dictionnary of Haiti*, The Scarecrow Press, Inc., Metuchen (N.J.), 1977, p. 64. Le maréchal de camp Julien Prévost, comte de Limonade, portait : *de sinople à l'épée d'argent et à la plume d'or posées en sautoir*. Supports : *deux lévriers d'argent, colletés d'or, bouclés et lampassés de gueules*. Devise : Amour et Fidélité.

11. SIR H. LUKE, *op. cit.*

12. *Au Cap-Henry, chez P. Roux, imprimeur du Roi.*

13. Corneille Brelle, créé par *motu proprio* du roi archevêque d'Haïti, duc de l'Anse, et fait cardinal sans bénéfices de bulles papales.

14. G. R. BELLEW, *op. cit.*

15. Londres, *College of Arms*, ms JP 177. L'armorial fut en montre à Londres en juin 1936 à l'occasion de l'exposition commémorative du 450ᵉ anniversaire de fondation du *College of Arms*. L'auteur tient à exprimer ses vifs remerciements aux membres du *College of Arms* de Londres et à M. Robert D. Watt, Héraut d'armes du Canada, qui ont aimablement et efficacement facilité ses recherches et permis la reproduction photographique des armoiries.

16. R. PAQUOT, *Dictionnaire encyclopédique des marques et monogrammes*, t. 2, Henri Laurens éditeur, Paris, s.d.

17. Parmi les princes du sang, il y avait le prince Noël, duc de Port-de-Paix, frère de la reine, marié à Son Altesse Royale Célestine-Joseph, et Son Altesse Royale Marie-Augustine Chancey, veuve du prince des Gonaïves.

18. Le baron de Barthélemy Choisy portait lui aussi le drapeau d'Haïti sur champ d'argent.

19. Par les soins du contre-amiral sir Hugh Popham et d'un Français, le colonel Vincent.

20. La reine et les princesses sont inhumées à Pise.

21. J.-C. DORSAINVILLE, *Histoire d'Haïti, cours supérieur*, éditions Henri Deschamps, Port-au-Prince, 1924, réédition de 1934, p. 185.

22. Photocopie du manuscrit Béliard faite au *College of Arms* lors d'une visite de M. Guy A. Béliard, le 24 septembre 1976.

23. A. E. GROPP, *Libraries and Archives of Haiti, with Information on Private Libraries*, New Orleans, 1941.

24. Lettre de R. C. Yorke, archiviste du *College of Arms*, à Robert D. Watt, Héraut d'armes du Canada, Londres, le 28 avril 1996.

25. R.-A. ST-LOUIS, *op. cit.*, p. 95.

26. A. CÉSAIRE, *op. cit.*

**Illustrations,** ms Londres, *College of Arms,* JP 177

(1) fol. 1 ; (2) fol. 2 ; (3) fol. 4 ; (4) fol. 10 ; (5) fol. 11 ; (6) fol. 15 ; (7) fol. 17 ; (8) fol. 20 ; (9) fol. 21 (10) fol. 24 ; (11) fol. 26 ; (12) fol. 33 ; (13) fol. 34 ; (14) fol. 36 ; (15) fol. 50 ; (16) fol. 51 ; (17) fol. 53 ; (18) fol. 58 ; (19) fol. 60 ; (20) fol. 61 ; (21) fol. 63 ; (22) fol. 67 ; (23) fol. 72 ; (24) fol. 73 ; (25) fol. 74 ; (26) fol. 75 ; (27) fol. 76 ; (28) fol. 80.

# FLEURS DE LIS DE FRANCE ET D'AILLEURS

Hervé baron Pinoteau

La royauté française fut une royauté liliacée. Du XIIᵉ siècle à 1830, avec l'interruption de 1792-1814, l'État français posséda des armes fleurdelisées et tout le décor étatique fut semé de fleurs de lis. Ainsi, les magistrats des cours souveraines comme le parlement de Paris étaient réputés « siéger sur les lis ».

La profusion des fleurs de lis est un fait typiquement français et il nous faut aller y voir de plus près, ce que j'ai déjà expliqué lors du congrès international de Madrid tenu en 1955, mais il est bon de préciser que l'étude de ce phénomène m'a entraîné sur des voies bien curieuses depuis cette époque. Voies et découvertes qui m'ont empêché de rabâcher les mêmes idées ou les mêmes approximations. Depuis cette époque, j'ai quand même fait quelques progrès et, à la suite de la rédaction d'un vaste livre à paraître, sur la symbolique de la France, j'en suis arrivé à des conclusions qui me permettent de faire une synthèse impossible à bâtir lorsque j'ai tout commencé en 1954, il y a donc 42 ans.

Il est curieux de constater que les fleurs de lis ont été le sujet de nombreuses explications et dissertations du XIIIᵉ siècle à nos jours. Que n'a-t-on pas dit à leur sujet ! On vit même un ennemi du roi de France au XVIIᵉ siècle, le Franc-Comtois Jean-Jacques Chiflet, « démontrer » que la fleur de lis dérivait graphiquement des abeilles trouvées dans la tombe de Childéric Iᵉʳ, père de Clovis Iᵉʳ, qu'on venait de découvrir par hasard en 1653. Plus près de nous, nombreux furent les auteurs qui virent en cette fleur un dérivé d'un fer de pique franque dite angon. On ne s'y arrêtera point.

Alors d'où vient la fleur de lis?

La solution du problème est fort simple : la fleur de lis est la fleur du lis des jardins. En français, le terme de fleur de lis apparaît comme fleur de rose autour des années 1160-1170 dans une littérature de cour, disons le *Lai de Lanval* de la mystérieuse Marie de France et le *Erec et Enide* de Chrétien de Troyes, mais il faut aussi ajouter le *Roman de Thèbes* vers 1150. En latin, Guillaume le Breton nous décrit l'étendard de Philip-pe II Auguste vu à Bouvine : « *vexillum videlicet floribus lilii distinctum* », mais j'ai trouvé une fois dans une œuvre de saint Grégoire de Tours[1] le terme de « *flores liliorum* » au sujet de véritables fleurs. De toutes façons, les gens du XIIIᵉ siècle qui nous parlent des fleurs de lis en savent plus que nous sur le nom, et c'est tout naturellement que Giraud de Barri, un poète gallois qui admirait la France, s'étonne vers 1216 que notre roi orne ses écus et ses étendards d'armes comportant de petites fleurs, « *gladioli flosculis* », qui mettent en fuite les bêtes féroces des autres souverains[2]. Ours, panthères, lions et autres bêtes terribles déguerpissaient à l'odeur de ces fleurs... Ces « florets » ou « florettes » ou « flurettes » d'or sont ainsi nommées dans les armoriaux de la fin du XIIIᵉ siècle.

Il faut l'admettre, ce sont bien des fleurs qui paraient les armes de nos rois, armes dites « de France » par Joinville et que l'on nomme « de France ancien » en opposition avec celles « de France moderne » quand les fleurs de lis sont réduites à trois.

Nous n'avons pas de représentation de ces armes au XIIᵉ siècle si on exclut un étendard fleurdelisé en bordure d'un manuscrit provenant de Saint-Victor de Paris, découvert par Michel Pastoureau, et pouvant être attribué au roi qui était des plus bienveillants pour cette proche abbaye. L'écu fleurdelisé apparaît un moment au centre de l'écu de Pierre II de Courtenay, petit-fils de Louis VI le Gros et disparaît quand le prince Louis prend ces armes en 1209, date à laquelle il reçoit la chevalerie et où il a un sceau équestre avec contre-sceau héraldique. Ces armes furent gardées par lui au contre-sceau du sceau de majesté quand il devint le roi Louis VIII, mais on les voit en couleur sur un vitrail de Chartres nous montrant le prince à cheval vers 1219.

Je l'ai expliqué en 1980 lors d'une communication à la Société nationale des antiquaires de France[3], il existe de nombreux indices prouvant que Louis VII portait déjà ces armes. Inutilement balayés par un héraldiste connu, ces indices concordent cependant pour qu'on ait la certitude de telles armes avec Louis VII dont les descendants seront seuls à porter cette composition liliacée. Les frères et les cousins de Louis VII assumeront des armes sans fleurs de lis : Dreux, Bretagne, Courtenay avec ou sans Romanie, Bourgogne, Dauphiné de Viennois, Vermandois, Portugal... La chose était évidente aux auteurs du XVIIe siècle. Mais Louis VII est le premier de nos rois à prendre des fleurs de lis sur des monnaies de Dreux trop souvent attribuées à Louis VI le Gros et ce au nom d'une mauvaise compréhension de la date d'attribution de ce « comté » à Robert Ier, frère de Louis VII.

Dans la communication citée ci-dessus, j'ai expliqué que le jeune Louis VII fut sacré par le pape Innocent II à Reims en 1131, peu après la mort de son frère aîné Philippe qui avait été sacré au même endroit en 1129. Tout montre que Louis VII, âgé de 10 ans, avait dû revêtir des vêtements du genre de ceux de son aîné, âgé de 12 ans lors de son sacre.

Ces vêtements devaient être naturellement cosmiques. Dès Charles II le Chauve, la tunique royale était couverte d'étoiles et l'on sait que les empereurs saxons avaient des manteaux de même nature. Il s'agissait là du cosmos visible, la livrée du Créateur qui nous est évoquée dans le livre de la *Sagesse* (18,24) au sujet de la tunique talaire du grand prêtre d'Israël. Femme d'Hugues Capet, la reine Adélaïde offrit à Saint-Denis un ornement cosmique différent de celui de Charles II le Chauve et les empereurs saxons utilisèrent le manteau cosmique dont un exemplaire, celui de saint Henri II, est encore visible au trésor de la cathédrale de Bamberg.

Or, devenu seul roi à la mort de son père Louis VI le Gros en 1137, Louis VII dut se faire faire de nouveaux vêtements pour son mariage à Bordeaux avec Aliénor d'Aquitaine, les multiples couronnements des cours couronnées et l'assistance aux sacres de ses trois femmes successives. C'était l'époque, fort longue, où saint Bernard de Clairvaux dissertait sans fin sur le *Cantique des cantiques*. Qu'on en juge : 86 sermons commençant en 1135 et n'ayant point épuisé le sujet quand saint Bernard mourut en 1153 ! C'est dans ces textes que le roi et ses gens purent entendre l'apologie du lis. En effet, le Christ est un lis et tous ceux qui lui sont semblables, la Vierge, les saints, sont aussi des lis. Or, comme le dit saint Bernard, il y a deux mondes, le matériel et le spirituel, le premier étant celui du soleil, de la lune, des astres et de la terre, le second étant celui du ciel

des élus, ce qui entraîne, sans que saint Bernard l'ait dit, que c'est un ciel de lis. Roi pieux, Louis VII dut changer de cosmos sur ses vêtements de cérémonie et c'est tout naturellement qu'il partit pour la deuxième croisade en 1147 après avoir entendu la prédiction de saint Bernard à Vézelay en 1146, en arborant des « connaissances » fleurdelisées, je veux dire des armes *d'azur semé de fleurs de lis d'or*, le bleu étant le hyacinthe donné par la *Vulgate* pour la couleur de la tunique « super humérale » d'Aaron, ou manteau de l'éphod (*Exode* 28,31), mais aussi la couleur de nos rois et même de pas mal de descendants par femmes des Carolingiens, ce qui est évidemment une notion à voir de plus près.

Dans la cohue féodale et internationale de la croisade, le roi par excellence, pouvant éventuellement s'opposer à un autre roi prestigieux, Conrad III, roi des Romains que nos Français appelaient l'empereur d'Allemagne, ce roi assuma des armes assez extraordinaires, montrant l'aide de l'univers tout entier dans cette pieuse entreprise. En effet, comme le dit la *Sagesse* (5,20 ; 16, 17 et 24), l'univers va au combat avec le juste contre les insensés ; il s'emploie à fond pour le châtiment des méchants !

Un roi qui pensait à la Jérusalem céleste si l'on croit ses actes et qui fut triomphalement accueilli comme le Christ à Jérusalem en 1148, sans doute le dimanche des Rameaux 4 avril, portait aux yeux du monde des armes atypiques et superbes.

En véritable héritier des Carolingiens et de leur monde disparu, Louis VII bénéficiait d'une symbolique et d'études portant sur le grand prêtre d'Israël et le Temple de Jérusalem. La *Vulgate* avait orné de lis certains éléments de ce Temple et cette fleur seule ou en rinceaux peuplait les manuscrits carolingiens. On sait par Sédulius Scottus, donc en plein milieu du IXe siècle, toute l'importance du lis ornant les sceptres étincelants et l'opposition qui était faite entre le lis blanc de la paix et la rose rouge de la guerre, opposition de couleurs qui ira loin puisque la loi martiale de 1789 annoncera la possible ouverture du feu sur des manifestants par un drapeau rouge, la fin de l'application de cette loi étant annoncée par un drapeau blanc... C'est ici la source du drapeau rouge de la Révolution universelle, symbole de la loi martiale du peuple révolté contre son maître. Il y aurait trop à dire en la matière, mais que de conséquences pour des méditations symboliques remontant aux Carolingiens !

La fleur de lis qui fut au sommet des sceptres et même des couronnes carolingiennes, semblait obligatoire pour signifier l'origine divine du pouvoir. Fleur indiquant la divinité et même le Dieu trinitaire, le lis me paraît finalement découler de la vision trinitaire de l'univers et de la société selon des idées issues du fond des âges, mais aussi de la foi chrétienne. Il se peut que cette fleur trinitaire nous soit venue de Lombardie, avant même Charlemagne. La Pseudo-Donation de Constantin est d'ailleurs un hymne à la Sainte-Trinité. L'architecture et le décor du Tempietto de Cividale dans le Frioul sont là pour baliser nos réflexions. Tout montre aussi que Charlemagne reçut à la Noël 800 une couronne impériale du genre diadème orné d'une aigrette trifide au-dessus du front, couronne d'or avec le signe de sainteté comme nous le disent ultérieurement les *Annales de Xanten* faisant implicitement référence au diadème du grand prêtre qui était orné d'une fleur ou fleuron d'or où était gravé « consacré au Seigneur » (*Exode* 28,36 et 39,30), donc « saint diadème » si l'on croit le *Lévitique* (8,9).

La multiplication par quatre sur la couronne impériale et royale de cette fleur divine eut sans doute lieu dès Charlemagne, proclamant ainsi le dogme trinitaire dans les quatre directions de l'espace, les quatre vents dont parle la Bible. Couronnes et sceptres liliacés étaient donc bien établis dans le monde carolingien. Les successeurs des empereurs, à l'Ouest comme à l'Est s'en souviendront. À l'Ouest, alors que nous avons très peu de « monuments » sur nos rois, je veux dire ceux de France, on peut observer la conservation du lis de façon bien discrète. Le « V » inscrit dans le losange central (et capital) des monogrammes royaux se transforme en un « V » aux lignes courbes enfermant un point dès Lothaire et Louis V puis sous Robert II le Pieux, Henri I$^{er}$ et Philippe I$^{er}$. Le buste de Louis VII sera orné d'une couronne à trois fleurons sur une monnaie de Bourges et je ne fais qu'évoquer ici les sceaux de majesté des premiers Capétiens où sceptres et couronnes sont fleurdelisés.

Superbe fleur au sommet d'une tige bien droite, le lis des jardins fut réputé fleur royale et féconde depuis l'Antiquité grecque et romaine. C'est donc bien naturellement que de nombreux souverains l'utilisèrent dans leur symbolique, puisque les souverains germaniques tiennent encore le sceptre au lis en plein XIII$^e$ siècle. Frédéric I$^{er}$ Barberousse est parfois figuré tenant une

fleur de lis ou accompagné d'une fleur de lis sur des monnaies. À la place d'un astre, la fleur de lis sacralise l'espace et le souverain.

Il n'en reste pas moins que la solution héraldique de nos rois fut telle que la fleur de lis semble à tous une expression de la nation française. Les dynastes issus de Louis VII en furent nommés fleurs de lis puis princes des fleurs de lis aux XIV$^e$ et XV$^e$ siècles, même dans des actes officiels. Les armes de France brisées furent ainsi obligatoires pour tous ces princes issus de ce qui reste la plus illustre et ancienne « race » de l'Occident puisque sa lignée remonte au VIII$^e$ siècle et même avant, ses premiers membres existant visiblement au VII$^e$ siècle, donc sous les Mérovingiens.

C'est ainsi qu'une multitude de dynastes du sang de France ayant la nationalité française ou étant étrangers, ont perpétué le souvenir héraldique de leur prestigieuse ascendance vers Louis VII en passant, pour beaucoup, par saint Louis. C'était (et c'est encore) « la sainte et sacrée lignée par hoir mâle » comme la nommait Jean Golein en son *Traité du sacre* écrit sous Charles V et dont la loi de succession, par voie purement masculine était alors réputée avoir saint Charlemagne pour auteur, ce qui fit que Charles V plaça une statuette de l'empereur au sommet du sceptre royal dont la partie supérieure est au Louvre. La lignée en question était aussi réputée descendre de Charlemagne et de Clovis par voie féminine, ce qui était expliqué dans de nombreuses chroniques officielles. Or, Charlemagne fut crédité des armes parti d'Empire et de France ancien, ou le contraire, dès les *Enfances Ogier* d'Adenet le Roi vers 1275. Au début du XIV$^e$ siècle commencèrent à apparaître les légendes poétiques sur la naissance des armes fleurdelisées données par le ciel à Clovis ; ce roi barbare fut obligé de les porter pour être vainqueur de ses ennemis, ce qui lui fit abandonner des armes aux crapauds ou aux croissants, puis aller vers le baptistère de Reims.

Il paraissait normal aux érudits de parer les grands ancêtres des Capétiens directs et des Valois de ces fleurs de lis véritablement magiques ou apotropaïques. De Clovis, premier roi de France catholique et dont nous allons célébrer bientôt le 1500$^e$ anniversaire de baptême, au roi contemporain, en passant par saint Charlemagne, toute la lignée était fleurdelisée à l'image de la couronne et du sceptre, véritable axe du royaume par lequel tombaient du ciel les grâces bénéfiques et fécondes.

Il n'est pas inutile que vous sachiez que le chef du nom et des armes de France, qui prend le titre de duc d'Anjou et la qualité de chef de la maison de Bourbon, a été jugé seul capable de porter les pleines armes de France, et ce par un arrêt de la première chambre de la cour d'appel de Paris datant de 1989, déboutant un Orléans et un Bourbon Parme. Il est curieux de constater que ce signe de nos rois a été confirmé à leur légitime successeur par la justice contemporaine qui rend ses jugements et arrêts au nom de l'actuel souverain, le peuple français. Il est vrai que les armoiries sont protégées par les tribunaux en mon pays, étant considérées comme l'image, une extension de la personne.

Il est évident que l'absence de fleurs de lis dans les armes de cadets issus de Louis VI le Gros, comme les Dreux (éteints à la fin du XVI<sup>e</sup> siècle) et les Courtenay (éteints au début du XVIII<sup>e</sup> siècle) fut fort préjudiciable à ces dynastes que le roi ne voulait pas reconnaître comme princes du sang. Il est vrai qu'ils ne descendaient pas de Louis VII et surtout de saint Louis, ce qui entraîna une certaine injustice pour les très modestes Courtenay qui en arrivèrent à écarteler leurs tourteaux d'un issu de France qui ne leur était point concédé par le roi, lequel, par le parlement de Paris, leur nia la qualité princière.

Sans fleur de lis au XIII<sup>e</sup> siècle, les Courtenay ne purent en mettre sur leurs armes impériales de Romanie, nom de l'Empire latin de Constantinople. Il faudra attendre les Anjou, princes de Tarente, descendants par femme de ces Courtenay pour voir au XIV<sup>e</sup> siècle l'union des armes impériales (la croix accompagnée de 20 croisettes et de quatre annelets) aux armes de Sicile brisées de la bande d'argent des Tarente.

Nous voici donc à pied d'œuvre pour aborder les Angevins de Naples. Charles I<sup>er</sup> comte d'Anjou, du Maine et de Provence, frère de saint Louis, fut roi de Sicile puis roi de Jérusalem. Jusqu'en 1435, date de la mort de la reine Jeanne II, les rois de Sicile (à vrai dire de terre ferme) et de Jérusalem joignirent leurs armes de France ancien au lambel de gueules avec celles, prestigieuses, de Jérusalem, commémorant en champ d'argent la fameuse croix reliquaire qui servait d'enseigne au roi de cette ville dès la troisième bataille de Ramlah en 1105, en compagnie de son étendard blanc.

Ceux qui connaissent l'héraldique italienne sont familiers avec l'invasion de nos fleurs de lis,

en particulier à travers le chef d'Anjou. Nombreuses sont les familles italiennes qui ont montré leur attachement au roi angevin avec un chef de France ancien au lambel de gueules. De plus, la domination angevine ne s'étendait pas que sur l'île de Sicile puis sur la seule terre ferme. Il suffit d'entrer dans la salle des lis du palais de la Seigneurie à Florence pour voir de vastes murs couverts des armes de France ancien avec un lambel de gueules qui court tout en haut ceux-ci. La commune de Florence fut en effet sous la protection de Robert I<sup>er</sup>, mais il est vrai que ce roi fut aussi maître de Gênes et de Rome où des traces de son pouvoir seraient à rechercher.

Les fleurs de lis étaient sans doute précieuses à bien des cadets de cette illustre lignée angevine quand on voit des Tarente et des Duras se dire « de France », nom évidemment touchant, encore qu'ici illégal puisque réservé aux enfants du roi, du dauphin et du fils aîné du dauphin.

Les armes de France ancien souvent privées du lambel de gueules, chose curieuse, furent mêlées aux armes de Hongrie dans la branche aînée des Angevins, ce qui a laissé une trace d'intérêt en dehors des sceaux : c'est l'écu émaillé qui figure sur le globe d'or du roi apostolique ; il est écartelé de France ancien au lambel de gueules et du fascé d'argent et de gueules des Arpads, ce qui en met la fabrication au début du règne de Charles I<sup>er</sup>-Robert (1301/1310?).

Les fleurs de lis d'or en champ d'azur passèrent dans les armes de villes hongroises et de nos jours encore, des villes de Slovaquie conservent le lointain souvenir du règne de Capétiens angevins. Ceux-ci allèrent aussi régner en Pologne, premier contact entre l'aigle blanc et les lis !

La deuxième maison d'Anjou qui prétendait à Naples et toujours à la Sicile ainsi qu'à Jérusalem, continuera la tradition des armes fleurdelisées unies à la croix du royaume de Terre Sainte perdu depuis le XIII<sup>e</sup> siècle.

N'oublions pas Jacques des Baux, mort en 1383, qui était issu des Tarente par sa mère : son tombeau de San-Cataldo de Tarente montre l'écu en bannière tiercé en pal de Tarente (d'Anjou-Sicile avec la bande d'argent), des Baux (l'étoile) et d'une aigle éployée, souvenir des prétentions sur Constantinople mis au goût du jour.

J'ai cité un tiercé en pal : il fut aussi courant chez les derniers rois de la première maison d'Anjou issus des Duras. Ce tiercé en pal de Hongrie (le fascé), de France ancien (avec ou sans lambel) et de Jérusalem, assumé par Ladislas et Jeanne II fut pris par les Aragon-Sicile ayant enfin conquis Naples !

Les ducs de Lorraine issus d'une fille du roi René d'Anjou, donc de la deuxième maison, se déclarèrent héritiers des prétentions de ce roi *in partibus*. Comme il avait assumé, lui aussi, un tiercé en pal de Hongrie, d'Anjou-Sicile et de Jérusalem, on vit les Lorrains, ducs et cadets s'emparer de ces armes prestigieuses en compagnie de celles de l'Anjou, de France ancien à la bordure de gueules. C'est ainsi que le dernier duc effectif de Lorraine, François III, marié a Marie-Thérèse d'Autriche, transmit ces armes à la nouvelle maison d'Autriche. La convention de Vienne entre l'Empereur et le Roi très chrétien, datant du 28 août 1736, en l'article 6, assurait la transmission des titres ducaux de Lorraine et de Bar, ainsi que les armes correspondantes aux descendants du duc François III, cette conservation de titres, armes etc, ne pouvant en rien affaiblir la souveraineté du roi.

Au début de l'empire d'Autriche en 1804 et jusqu'en 1866, les grandes armes impériales comporteront un quartier de France ancien au lambel de gueules pour symboliser Naples ou si l'on préfère la terre ferme.

Jusqu'en 1918 les lettres patentes « autrichiennes », mais en français, nommant les chevaliers de la Toison d'or de la branche autrichienne, étaient scellées d'un sceau aux armoiries de Philippe le Bon, duc de Bourgogne, fondateur de l'ordre en 1430. Autrement dit, l'issu de France à la bordure componée avait encore droit de cité à Vienne sur la fin de la Première Guerre mondiale.

L'influence angevine s'étale encore de nos jours sur les armes et le drapeau de la République de Bosnie-Herzégovine qui s'est inspirée des monnaies et de sceaux des souverains Kotromanic du XIVᵉ siècle qui montrèrent avec l'écu à fleurs de lis et une bande leur fidélité aux Angevins de Hongrie[4].

Autre trace, bien discrète, des Angevins, le voile de la Vierge de Czestochowa : en souvenir de sainte Hedwige de Hongrie, reine de Pologne, ce voile de la sainte icône est peint en bleu fleurdelisé d'or et doublé de rouge, tout comme un vêtement de sacre royal français.

Il est évident que le rayonnement de la maison de France, nom officiel depuis vers 1300, entraîna la présence de fleurs, de lis en Navarre : les trois fils de Philippe IV le Bel et de Jeanne Iʳᵉ de Navarre-Champagne furent pleinement rois de Navarre comme le furent les comtes d'Évreux, ce qui entraîna la présence de quartiers fleurdelisés en ce royaume pyrénéen et même dans les armes de Jean II d'Aragon qui épousa la reine Blanche de Navarre de la branche d'Évreux[5].

Les Génois ayant demandé à Charles VI d'être leur seigneur, on vit longtemps sur les monnaies de Gênes un écu parti des armes de France (les trois fleurs de lis) et de la porte du château de cette ville. Plus tard, récoltant l'héritage des Angevins, Charles VIII et Louis XII mêleront à nouveaux les fleurs de lis aux croix de Jérusalem. La branche ducale d'Orléans ayant hérité du duché de Milan, on vit le poète Charles, Louis XII, François Iᵉʳ et des cadets arborer la guivre des Visconti, ce qui entraîna, en sens inverse, des fleurs de lis à Milan.

Notre François II devint roi d'Écosse et il serait d'intérêt de trouver des traces de ses armes liant fleurs de lis et lion autrement que sur les sceaux, armes augmentées de celles d'Angleterre à la mort de Marie Tudor pour l'effarement de l'ambassadeur d'Élisabeth à Paris et la fureur de celle-ci. Notre futur Henri III plaça quant à lui son écu de France au lambel de gueules sur le tout de l'écartelé de Pologne et de Lithuanie, puis devenu roi de France il préféra adjoindre un écu parti de Pologne et de Lithuanie à senestre des armes de France.

La fin du Moyen Âge vit la deuxième maison de Bourgogne s'installer dans les Pays-Bas. Le duc de Brabant et de Limbourg, comte et seigneur de nombreux fiefs théoriquement de l'Empire, fit connaître les fleurs de lis, symbole très français qui ne fut guère aimé des Flamands.

Dans cette direction du nord, commémorons François de France, duc d'Anjou, etc., frère cadet d'Henri III, qui fut duc de Brabant, de Limbourg, de Lothier, etc. bref candidat à tous les Pays-Bas si l'on en croit sa longue titulature en 1580-1582 : ses armes furent complexes mais éphémères. Il fut inhumé en 1584 avec les armes de France à la bordure de gueules, fin d'un rêve belge !

C'est beaucoup plus au sud que nous trouvons les Orléans, ducs de Longueville, comme princes de Neuchâtel du XVIᵉ siècle au tout début du XVIIIᵉ. Les armes fleurdelisées des descendants du fameux bâtard d'Orléans, comte de Dunois furent mises en écartelé avec celles de ce territoire suisse, *d'or au pal de gueules chargé de trois chevrons d'argent*.

Au XVIᵉ siècle encore, les armes de France furent vues dans le Nouveau Monde. Tout d'abord au Canada où elles furent attachées en haut d'une croix, prise de possession symbolique à une époque où l'on ne hissait pas un pavillon de marine en haut d'un mât planté en terre, encore que la chose pouvait être à la limite possible, mais il est assuré qu'un pavillon hissé doit pouvoir être changé, ce qui sous-entend une occupation permanente. Sous Louis XIV, la prise de possession de la Louisiane sera faite de même façon par Cavelier de la Salle. Encore au XVIᵉ siècle, la présence française se manifestera par un pilier de pierre érigé en Floride : il était orné des armes du roi et on en a une image dans un ouvrage bien connu. Il est évident que les Français s'inspirèrent là des fameux *padrões* portugais. Je crois que les Américains ont remis un tel pilier aux armes fleurdelisées à l'endroit où les Français vinrent il y a tant de siècles.

Une des grandes extensions des armes fleurdelisées dans le monde advint avec l'héritage d'Espagne. Les rois catholiques avaient déjà deux quartiers bourguignons dans leur écu, dont celui qu'on nomme de Bourgogne moderne, l'issu de France à la bordure componée, mais la composition fut augmentée des armes propres de Philippe V, ex-duc d'Anjou : *de France à la bordure de gueules*. Une bonne partie des Amériques et les îles les plus lointaines comme les Philippines virent ainsi nos fleurs de lis à partir de 1700-1701, énorme compensation à la perte des Pays-Bas catholiques où les souvenirs héraldiques bourguignons, donc liliacés, furent longtemps présents.

Par les Bourbons d'Espagne, les fleurs de lis essaimèrent à nouveau vers Naples et Palerme jusqu'en 1861, date de la disparition du royaume des Deux-Siciles. Encore en Italie, les duchés de Parme, Plaisance et Guastalla, le royaume d'Étrurie, le duché de Lucques, à nouveau les duchés de Parme et de Plaisance auxquels furent adjoints quelques territoires, arborèrent nos fleurs de lis jusqu'à la fin de la souveraineté des Bourbons à Parme en 1859. Un prince de cette lignée, Félix, époux de la grande-duchesse de Luxembourg Charlotte mit l'écu des Bourbon Parme (*de France à la bordure de gueules chargée de 8 coquilles d'argent*) sur le tout de l'écartelé de Luxembourg et de Nassau, sa femme étant théorique duchesse du Nassau perdu en 1866. Leur fils, S.A.R. Mᵍʳ le grand-duc et duc Jean n'a pas senti la nécessité d'indiquer qu'il avait un père dans le domaine des symboles et ne garde curieusement que le seul écartelé Nassau-Luxembourg

de sa mère. C'est l'un des trois cas d'abandon des armes fleurdelisées par un Capétien.

De nos jours, les Orléans Bragance prétendants au Brésil portent ou non l'écu d'Orléans (*de France au lambel d'argent*) en cœur des armes impériales brésiliennes.

Cependant, l'autre souverain capétien sur un trône est S.M. le roi d'Espagne, Jean-Charles Iᵉʳ, qui a l'écu *de France à la bordure de gueules* sur les quartiers de ce royaume. C'est la brisure de Philippe V, le souverain étant cadet dans la maison de Bourbon, autre nom officiel de la maison de France depuis le traité de Montmartre en 1662. Les fleurs de lis sont donc omniprésentes en Espagne, les armes de l'État figurant même sur le drapeau et le pavillon des autorités. Cette incursion espagnole me fait d'ailleurs penser à de nouveaux titrés de ce royaume qui se mettent à arborer des chefs de France sans aucune brisure, ce qui est évidemment une usurpation des droits du roi, le mien. Il leur faut une bordure de gueules.

Mettons de côté les concessions des armes de France à des étrangers, ainsi à César Borgia « de France » (*sic*), adopté par Louis XII, aux Visconti, aux Este, aux Médicis pour n'évoquer que les plus illustres d'entre eux. Parlons plutôt de la plus longue usurpation des armes de France, celle qui fut faite en Angleterre.

Se considérant roi de France, comme petit-fils de Philippe IV le Bel, Édouard III d'Angleterre voulut ignorer que sa filiation passait par sa mère et que ses pseudo-droits étaient primés dans l'ordre de primogéniture par ceux, évidents si on parle de femmes, de Jeanne II de France, reine de Navarre, fille de Louis X le Hutin, morte en 1349 : elle fut mère de Charles II le Mauvais, roi de Navarre et comte d'Évreux, Capétien de père et de mère, ouvertement candidat au trône lors de la crise de 1357-1358.

Négligeant le serment de fidélité qu'il avait prêté en tant que duc de Guyenne et de comte de Ponthieu à Philippe VI de Valois en 1329, Édouard III revendiqua le royaume de France dès 1337. C'est au tout début de février 1340 que ce roi d'Angleterre prit le titre et les armes de roi de France. Le grand sceau de majesté fut modifié et l'on assista à la naissance d'un écartelé de France ancien et d'Angleterre. Le royaume de France étant celui du roi très chrétien et étant environ cinq fois plus peuplé que celui d'Angleterre, il fut évident que ses armes devaient être mises à l'honneur aux quartiers 1 et 4. À partir de ces armes et de cette époque, une multitude de princes, de personnes issues des princes, de personnes physiques et morales ont assumé les fleurs de lis sans l'accord de leur légitime possesseur. Il serait bien impossible à un Britannique de dresser la liste de toutes ces armes illégitimes pour un Français. Le plus curieux est que des ducs britanniques issus des Stuarts sont venus chez nous avec des armes fleurdelisées et que les ducs de Fitz-James ne se sont éteints qu'en 1967.

N'accordant finalement que peu d'importance à cette question, étant restés maîtres du terrain de par la volonté de Dieu manifestée par sainte Jeanne d'Arc et tant de bons soldats à la fin de la guerre de Cent ans, les Français admirent que la reine Marie, troisième épouse de Louis XII, arborât son écartelé de France et d'Angleterre dans le 2 du parti, armes éphémères comme on sait. De même, Madame, duchesse d'Orléans, née Henriette-Anne de Grande-Bretagne, eut ainsi les armes de son père Charles Ier au 2 de son parti : on y voyait donc les armes de France en écartelé avec celles d'Angleterre. Plus pittoresque encore : le couple Philippe II d'Espagne et Marie Ire Tudor eut des sceaux où les armes d'Espagne-Autriche furent jointes à celles d'Angleterre, etc., donc avec les lis de France (1555-1558), composition éphémère, elle aussi, et qui eut sa réplique quand Marie Stuart se déclara reine d'Angleterre et d'Irlande après la mort de cette Marie Ire.

Notons qu'au tout début du XVe siècle, en tout cas dès 1408 (et probablement dès 1403), Henri IV de Lancastre se mit au goût du jour et prit les armes de France moderne (*d'azur à 3 fleurs de lis d'or*) dans ses quartiers 1 et 4, copiant ainsi la révolution héraldique opérée par Charles V et Charles VI. Les membres de la famille royale firent de même. Je ne résiste pas au plaisir de dire qu'Henri IV de Lancastre avait une sœur, Philippa, qui fut l'épouse de Jean Ier roi de Portugal. Leur père commun, Jean de Gand, duc de Lancastre, brisait les armes écartelées de France et d'Angleterre d'un lambel d'hermine et parfois d'un lambel de France. C'est ce dernier lambel qui brisa les armes de Portugal chez l'infant Henri le Navigateur, duc de Viseu, fils de Philippa et de Jean Ier. C'est ainsi que cet illustre Capétien assuma les fleurs de lis que sa lignée n'arborait point.

En 1800, les choses avaient changé. Il n'y avait plus de roi de France en France, Louis XVIII vivant péniblement exilé, souvent comme simple comte de l'Isle (Jourdain en Armagnac). La Grande-Bretagne voulait faire la paix avec la République française et on s'apprêtait à créer un Royaume-Uni de Grande-Bretagne et d'Irlande en mettant le parlement de Dublin à Londres. C'est alors qu'un acte royal britannique énonça le nouveau titre de Georges III et créa de nouvelles armes : ce fut la fin du titre bien vain de roi de France à Londres et la fin des fleurs de lis dans les armes du roi britannique et de toute sa famille, la date précise de cette révolution étant le 1er janvier 1801.

Le plus curieux de l'affaire fut que le roi Stuart conserva les quartiers fleurdelisés dans ses armes de prétention : il s'agit du cardinal duc d'York, alias Henri IX, qui mourut en 1807. Vous savez que ce prétendant au trône britannique fut très mécontent en 1804 car Napoléon Ier l'invita au sacre en lui donnant du « Mon cousin » alors qu'il estimait avoir droit à « Monsieur mon frère »...

De ces prétentions françaises restent plusieurs traces comme la combinaison azur et or de la Jarretière et de la devise « Dieu et mon droit » ; comme les curieuses fleurs de lis blanches qui parsèment le manteau royal de drap d'or fait en 1821 et qui sert encore pour le couronnement dans Westminster (roses, chardons et trèfles accompagnent ces fleurs) ; comme enfin les fleurs de lis d'or qui alternent avec les croix pattées sur les couronnes de la souveraine, de son mari et de leurs enfants, ces croix ayant la prééminence sur les fleurs de lis qui ne passent d'ailleurs point aux générations suivantes, donc chez les princes cadets.

Puisque j'aborde le domaine des couronnes, ne sont fleurdelisées que deux couronnes en dehors de celles dont je viens de parler et de celles, évidentes des Capétiens français : roi et reine, dauphin et dauphine, fils de France et leur conjoints, filles de France, petits-fils de France et leurs conjoints, petites-filles de France, princes du sang et leurs conjoints, princesses du sang de France. Ces deux couronnes sont tout d'abord celle des ducs de Parme dans la deuxième moitié du XIXe siècle et de nos jours, puis celle de Bulgarie. Ferdinand de Saxe-Cobourg-Gotha devint en effet prince de Bulgarie en 1887 et se proclama roi des Bulgares en 1908. Fils de Clémentine d'Orléans et l'époux de Marie-Louise de Bourbon Parme, ce roi arbora une couronne fleurdelisée qui est encore portée par S.M. Siméon II, mais cette couronne, comme celle de Parme est sommée d'un globe crucifère et non pas de la double fleur de lis en carré des Capétiens. Dans leurs armoiries personnelles, les rois des Bulgares purent prendre celles de leurs quatre quartiers, ce qui entraînait les armes Orléans et Bourbon Parme (sans coquilles) chez Ferdinand I<sup>er</sup> et Bourbon Parme (avec coquilles) chez S.M. Siméon II.

Une des plus curieuses survivances des armes de France est le quartier de France moderne attribué au Canada par le roi du Royaume-Uni George V en sa proclamation du 21 novembre 1921 afin de symboliser la communauté française. Aux yeux des Français c'est évidemment une solution impossible pour leur droit héraldique. Il y a de la gêne à voir nos armes royales si mal placées et une bannière de France tenue par une licorne ! On aurait aimé une solution plus originale et sortant des vieilles prétentions. Le chef de France dans les armes de la province de Québec est tout aussi contestable, mais le drapeau bleu à croix blanche cantonnée de quatre fleurs de lis du même est assez remarquable. Il est dérivé du pavillon de notre marine marchande depuis les XVI<sup>e</sup> et XVII<sup>e</sup> siècles.

Dans le même genre est la bannière de l'Association française de l'ordre hospitalier de Saint-Jean de Jérusalem, dit de Rhodes, dit de Malte. On peut y contempler un *tiercé en pal de Jérusalem, du Dauphiné d'Auvergne et de France sous le chef de Religion, de gueules à la croix d'argent*. Ces armes du tiercé sont là, paraît-il, pour rappeler les anciennes langues de Provence, d'Auvergne et de France, mais c'est la preuve que les Français qui ont composé cette bannière n'ont plus aucun sens de l'héraldique et de l'honneur des armes de leur anciens rois, des anciennes armes de leur nation. Or ces armes qui sont réputées représenter la Sainte Trinité depuis Charles V, sont là humiliées d'abominable façon et cette bannière est arborée par cette association dans la chapelle du château de Versailles pour ses cérémonies de la Saint-Jean... Qu'aurait dit Louis XIV qui n'aimait pas l'ordre !

Autre signe de nos temps troublés, je dirais même déboussolés, les compas et boussoles ont leur nord souligné d'une étoile à cinq rais alors qu'une fleur de lis y régnait autrefois.

Nous n'oublierons pas pour conclure que la fleur de lis n'était pas toujours signe de paix. Elle pouvait être chez nous signe de justice, expression sanglante de la souveraineté, car c'est avec une telle fleur métallique et chauffée au rouge que le bourreau marquait le signe royal sur la chair des criminels.

Évocation bien triste me direz-vous ! Mais n'y a-t-il pas mieux à dire sur cette fleur si royale ? Or, il faut le constater, la fleur de lis devint prénom en italien, sous l'influence des armes des Angevins de Naples ou plus simplement de celles de Florence.

Nous tenons-là une curieuse extension de cette fleur. En effet, Fiordiligi est un personnage de l'*Orlando innamorato* écrit en 1486 par Matteo Maria Boiardo qui nous conte ses amours tragiques avec Bradamante, et nous retrouvons ce couple dans l'*Orlando furioso* de Ludovico Ariosto, en l'an 1532.

Plus près de nous, si j'ose dire, Wolfgang Amadeus Mozart mit de la musique sur le livret de *Così fan tutte* écrit par Lorenzo da Ponte. Nous sommes alors en 1790 et la belle Fiordiligi se sent devenir volage, jusqu'à tromper son fiancé Guglielmo qui n'hésite alors point à la qualifier de « *La mia fior, fior di diavolo...* Ma fleur, fleur du diable ! ».

Allons, me direz-vous, l'orateur s'égare avec des fleurs de lis bien loin de l'héraldique ! Aussi je vous quitte en vous remémorant les airs d'une femme troublée qui, d'une voix de soprano, nous décrit ses angoisses devant son infidélité. Mais, en réalité, vous le savez bien, les femmes ne sont heureusement pas toutes des Fiordiligi, loin de là !

**NOTES**

1. *De gloria confessorum,* chap. 50.

2. *De principis instructione liber.*

3. « La création des armes de France au XII<sup>e</sup> siècle », *Bulletin de la Société nationale des antiquaires de France 1980* (Paris, 1982), p. 87-99.

4. Je renvoie à l'article de mon ami le d<sup>r</sup> GÜNTER MATTERN, « Wappen und Flagge von Bosnien-Herzegowina », *Archives héraldiques suisses,* no. 1 (1995), p. 54-55.

5. Je renvoie au magnifique ouvrage publié sous la direction de mon ami FAUSTINO MENÉNDEZ-PIDAL DE NAVASCUÉS, *Sellos medievales de Navarra,* Pampelune, 1995.

# UNE FAMILLE GÉNOISE ÉMIGRÉE À LYON : LES PIANELLI (XVIe-XVIIIe SIÈCLES), HÉRALDIQUE ET GÉNÉALOGIE

Michel Popoff

La ville de Lyon en France a abrité durant tout le Moyen Age une importante colonie italienne, ce mouvement migratoire, pour des raisons dynastiques et politiques évidentes, s'est accéléré au XVIe siècle. Le Cabinet des manuscrits de la Bibliothèque nationale de France conserve, sous la cote *fr. 8716-8717* deux manuscrits héraldiques concernant l'alliance de Battista Pianello, citoyen génois installé à Lyon, avec une lyonnaise : Marie Besset ; à partir de là sont répertoriées les alliances de leurs descendants (et nombreux collatéraux) avec armoiries peintes et esquisses généalogiques de 1582 à 1742. Ce document, extrêmement riche d'un point de vue héraldique, généalogique et même psychologique, n'a jamais été étudié à notre connaissance, et à plus forte raison publié.

Le premier volume, relié aux armes des Pianelli (*coupé de gueules et de sable, à la fasce écotée d'or brochant sur le trait du coupé*) cimées d'une aigle couronnée, contient 110 armoiries peintes (deux à la page), retraçant les alliances de la famille Pianello depuis l'année 1582 jusqu'à l'an 1742. Il est plus que probable que la rédaction de ce volume a été commencée sous l'impulsion de Baptiste Pianello, écuyer, trésorier de France à Lyon en 1636, chevalier de l'ordre de Saint-Michel, qui épousa Marie Besset en 1638, et mourut vers l'an 1685 : leurs armoiries occupent les deux premiers feuillets du manuscrit. Ce premier volume décrit méticuleusement, dans une première partie, l'intégration d'une famille arrivée de Gênes à Lyon pour faire de la banque et certainement aussi pour rejoindre d'autres familles alliées ou issues de la même « *albergo* ». Génération après génération les Pianelli se trouvent ainsi alliés aux principales familles (issues le plus souvent de la robe) du Lyonnais, Forez et Dauphiné : Joseph-Claude de Planelli de La Valette est, vers 1750, chevalier d'honneur de la Cour des Comptes du Dauphiné. L'ascension sociale de cette famille suit un schéma classique : l'argent de la banque permet d'acheter des charges anoblissantes, charges qui permettent des alliances prestigieuses et l'intégration dans un réseau social fort. Cette intégration, durant à peu près un siècle (1560-1660), n'efface pas le souvenir des attaches génoises. C'est seulement dans la première moitié du XVIIIe siècle qu'un membre de la famille, certainement Laurent Pianello, chevalier, baron de Maubec, conseiller à la Cour des Monnaies de Lyon, qui un siècle après son aïeul, conscient du fait que son lignage est en train de perdre la « mémoire » de ses origines et de ses alliances, entreprend une démarche de recompilation — dont la vanité n'est pas toujours exclue — afin de reconstituer un semblant d'archives généalogiques. Notes et annotations sont à lire avec attention car l'ensemble est révélateur : fierté des origines (dont la noblesse est souvent à tort exagérée), sélection des alliances les plus prestigieuses. Le second volume est totalement consacré à l'illustration et à la célébration de l'antiquité et de la haute noblesse du lignage : le rattachement à la maison de Savoie et surtout à Charlemagne et donc aux Carolingiens, ce qui permet de faire figurer sur les grandes armes peintes au fol. 2 à côté des armoiries Pianello, les quartiers de Savoie, de Dauphiné, de l'Empire, et sur le tout le semé aux fleurs de lis de France.

## BnF ms fr. 8716

Fol. 1 : un écu en pleine page. *Coupé de gueules et de sable à l'écot d'or brochant sur le trait du coupé. Cimier : une aigle de sable couronnée d'or. Supports : deux aigles de sable couronnées d'or, la tête contournée.*

Fol. 2 : un écu en pleine page. *Coupé de gueules et de sable à l'écot d'or brochant sur le trait du coupé. Cimier : une aigle de sable couronnée d'or. Supports : deux aigles de sable couronnées d'or, la tête contournée.* L'écu est entouré du collier de l'ordre de Saint-Michel.

Fol. 3 : un écu en pleine page. *Écartelé au 1 et 4 d'or à l'aigle de sable, au chef d'azur chargé de trois étoiles d'or ; au 2 et 3 d'azur à trois fleurs de* lis d'or, au chef du même chargé d'un lion issant de gueules. L'écu entouré d'une cordelière.

Fol. 4 à 6 : *blancs*

Fol. 7 : deux écus côte à côte. (a) *coupé de gueules et de sable à l'écot d'or brochant sur le trait du coupé.* (b) *coupé de gueules et de sable à l'écot d'or brochant sur le trait du coupé* parti *d'azur au chef d'or à l'arbre au naturel brochant sur le tout, posé sur un tertre de sinople et soutenu par deux lions couronnés d'or affrontés.* « Laurent Pianello cytoyen de Gennes mary de Sperancine d'Onetto. »

Fol. 8 : deux écus côte à côte. (a) *coupé de gueules et de sable à l'écot d'or brochant sur le trait du coupé.* (b) *coupé de gueules et de sable à l'écot d'or brochant sur le trait du coupé* parti *d'argent à la bande de sinople formée de feuillages d'où isse une tige du même fleurie de gueules, accompagnée en pointe d'une étoile d'azur.* « Baptiste Pianello, bourgeois de Lyon, mary d'Elizabeth d'Agnola. C'étoit un riche banquier gênois, il vint à Lyon en 1560 où il exerça la banque sans déroger à la noblesse. »

Fol. 9 : deux écus côte à côte. (a) *coupé de gueules et de sable à l'écot d'or brochant sur le trait du coupé.* (b) *coupé de gueules et de sable à l'écot d'or brochant sur le trait du coupé* parti *d'un parti au I d'azur au lyon contourné d'or ; au 2 d'argent à la croix latine d'or.* L'écu est entouré d'une cordelière. « Baptiste Pianello, bourgeois de Lyon, mary en secondes noces d'Elizabeth Ventriste. »

Fol. 10 : deux écus côte à côte. (a) *coupé de gueules et de sable à l'écot d'or brochant sur le trait du coupé.* (b) *coupé de gueules et de sable à l'écot d'or brochant sur le trait du coupé* parti *d'or à l'aigle de sable, au chef d'azur chargé de trois étoiles d'or.* L'écu est entouré d'une cordelière. « Baptiste Pianello, conseiller du roy et président au bureau des finances de la généralité de Lyon, mary de dame Marie Besset dame de La Valette et de Saint-Étienne de Furay. Il étoit fils de noble Laurent Pianello né à Lyon en 1564 et de dame Marguerite Dénot ; et petit-fils de noble Baptiste Pianello ou Planelli citoyen de Gênes, lequel vint s'établir à Lyon en 1560 et d'Elizabeth d'Agnola sa première femme. »

Fol. 11 : deux écus côte à côte. (a) *écartelé, au 1 et 4 coupé de gueules et de sable à l'écot d'or brochant sur le trait du coupé ; au 2 et 3 d'or à l'aigle de sable, au chef d'azur chargé de trois étoiles d'or.* Cimier : *une aigle de sable couronnée d'or.* (b) *écartelé, au 1 et 4 coupé de gueules et de sable à l'écot d'or brochant sur le trait du coupé ; au 2 et 3 d'or à l'aigle de sable, au chef d'azur chargé de trois étoiles d'or*, mi-parti *d'un burelé-vivré de gueules et d'argent.* L'écu entouré d'une cordelière. « Laurent Pianello-Besset, conseiller du roy, trésorier de France et général des finances en la généralité de Lyon, mary de dame Laure Mascranny La Verrière. »

Fol. 12 : un écu *coupé de gueules et de sable à l'écot d'or brochant sur le trait du coupé* brochant sur un bourdon et cimé d'un chapeau ecclésiastique de sinople à deux houppes. « Baptiste Pianello prestre et prothonotaire apostolique, chanoine d'honneur à Aisnay. »

Fol. 13 : deux écus côte à côte. (a) *coupé de gueules et de sable à l'écot d'or brochant sur le trait du coupé, au lambel d'argent.* Cimier : *une aigle de sable couronnée d'or.* (b) *coupé de gueules et de sable à l'écot d'or brochant sur le trait du coupé, au lambel d'argent, parti d'argent au rosier de sinople fleuri de trois roses de gueules.* L'écu entouré d'une cordelière. « André Pianello, conseiller du roy et magistrat en la sénéchaussée de Lyon, mary de Marie Quiron ou Chiron. »

Sur ce même folio est collé une fiche de papier, portant le numéro 14, sur laquelle on lit :

Mr André Pianelli doyen du présidial de Lyon, mort en 1698, ou 1699 âgé de 88 ans ou environ, maria N. Pianelli sa fille par contrat du 15 septembre 1689 à Mr de Bonnel mort doyen de la cour des monnoyes en Xbre 1732, laissant pour fils unique Mr de Bonnel cy-devant maître des requêtes.

[Pas de fol. 14 : voyez la note au fol. 41]

Fol. 15 : deux écus côte à côte. (a) *d'azur à la guivre d'or ondoyant en pal, au chef de gueules chargé de deux flèches d'or passées en sautoir.* b) *d'azur à la guivre d'or ondoyant en pal, au chef de gueules chargé de deux flèches d'or pas-*

sées en sautoir, parti d'un *coupé de gueules et de sable à l'écot d'or brochant sur le trait du coupé.* L'écu entouré d'une cordelière. « Jean Bertrand, seigneur du Mey, conseiller du roy et trésorier général de France en Dauphiné, mary de Marguerite Pianello. »

Fol. 16 : deux écus côte à côte. (a) *d'azur au chevron d'or accompagné en chef de deux colombes d'argent et en pointe d'un serpent volant d'or.* (b) *d'azur au chevron d'or accompagné en chef de deux colombes d'argent et en pointe d'un serpent volant d'or,* parti d'un *coupé de gueules et de sable à l'écot d'or brochant sur le trait du coupé.* L'écu entouré d'une cordelière. « Henry Austrein, seigneur de Jarnosse, conseiller du roy et lieutenant particulier au présidial de Lyon, mary de Marguise Pianello. »

Fol. 17 : deux écus côte à côte. (a) *d'argent à la bande de sinople formée de feuillages d'où isse une tige du même fleurie de gueules, accompagnée en pointe d'une étoile d'azur.* (b) *d'argent à la bande de sinople formée de feuillages d'où isse une tige du même fleurie de gueules, accompagnée en pointe d'une étoile d'azur,* parti *d'argent à l'arbre arraché de sinople.* « Sebastiano d'Agnola, citoyen de Gennes, mary de Pelegrina Fachinetti. »

Fol. 18 : deux écus côte à côte. (a) *écartelé, au 1 contr'écartelé au 1 et 4 palé de six pièces d'or et d'azur au chef de gueules chargé de trois hydres d'or* [qui est Joyeuse], *au 2 et 3 d'azur au lion d'or, à la bordure de gueules chargée de huit fleurs de lis d'or* [qui est Saint-Didier] ; *au 2 fascé de six pièces d'or et de sable* [qui est Vausèche] ; *au 3 de gueules au lion d'or, au chef d'hermine ; au 4 de gueules* [sic pour azur ?] *à la tour d'argent accompagnée de six roses d'or* [qui est La Tourette] ; *et sur le tout d'or au lion de gueules* [qui est Ginestoux]. (b) *écartelé, au 1 contr'écartelé au 1 et 4 palé de six pièces d'or et d'azur au chef de gueules chargé de trois hydres d'or* [qui est Joyeuse], *au 2 et 3 d'azur au lion d'or, à la bordure de gueules chargée de huit fleurs de lis d'or* [qui est Saint-Didier] ; *au 2 fascé de six pièces d'or et de sable* [qui est Vausèche] ; *au 3 de gueules au lion d'or, au chef d'hermine ; au 4 de gueules* [sic pour azur ?] *à la tour d'argent accompagnée de six roses d'or* [qui est La Tourette] ; *et sur le tout d'or au lion de gueules* [qui est Ginestoux], mi-parti d'un *coupé de gueules et*

de sable à l'écot d'or brochant sur le trait du coupé. L'écu entouré d'une cordelière. « Just-Henry de Ginestoux, marquis de La Tourette et de Durfort, baron de Chaleron, mary de dame Antoinette Pianello. »

Fol. 19 : deux écus côte à côte. (a) *d'azur au chevron d'or accompagné de trois trèfles du même.* (b) *d'azur au chevron d'or accompagné de trois trèfles du même* parti d'un *coupé de gueules et de sable à l'écot d'or brochant sur le trait du coupé.* L'écu entouré d'une cordelière. « Mathieu Barthelot, chevalier, sieur d'Ozenay, cy-devant capitaine au régiment Dauphin, mary de Marie Pianello. »

Fol. 20 : deux écus côte à côte. (a) *d'azur à trois fasces ondées d'or accompagnées en chef de trois fleurs de lis du même.* (b) *d'azur à trois fasces ondées d'or accompagnées en chef de trois fleurs de lis du même* parti *d'or au lion de gueules.* L'écu entouré d'une cordelière. [Pas de texte]

Fol. 21 : deux écus côte à côte. (a) *d'azur au chevron accompagné en chef de deux étoiles et en pointe d'un croissant, le tout d'or.* (b) *d'azur au chevron accompagné en chef de deux étoiles et en pointe d'un croissant, le tout d'or,* parti d'un *coupé de gueules et de sable à l'écot d'or brochant sur le trait du coupé, à la bordure engrêlée du même.* L'écu entouré d'une cordelière.

Fol. 22 : deux écus côte à côte. (a) *d'argent à un bateau à trois mâts de sable.* (b) *d'argent à un bateau à trois mâts de sable* parti *d'or à la guivre de sinople ondoyant en pal, au chef d'argent chargé de deux flèches de gueules, empennées de sinople, passées en sautoir et liées aussi de gueules.* L'écu entouré d'une cordelière. « Jean-Baptiste du Vivier, seigneur de Saint-Jean de Pied Barles, conseiller secrétaire du roy maison et couronne de France et greffier de la cour du Parlement de Dauphiné, mary de Françoise Bertrand. »

Fol. 23 : deux écus côte à côte. (a) *d'argent à l'aigle bicéphale de sable.* (b) *d'argent à l'aigle bicéphale de sable,* mi-parti *d'or à la guivre de sinople ondoyant en pal, au chef d'argent chargé de deux flèches de gueules, empennées de sinople, passées en sautoir et liées aussi de gueules.* L'écu entouré d'une cordelière. « François du Mas, sieur de Charconne et de Baudiné, capitaine au régiment lyonnois, mary de Marie Bertrand. »

Fol. 24 : deux écus côte à côte. (a) *d'or à la guivre de sinople ondoyant en pal, au chef d'argent chargé de deux flèches de gueules, empennées de sinople, passées en sautoir et liées aussi de gueules.* (b) *d'or à la guivre de sinople ondoyant en pal, au chef d'argent chargé de deux flèches de gueules, empennées de sinople, passées en sautoir et liées aussi de gueules* parti de gueules au mont d'or de six coupeaux accompagné en chef d'une couronne du même. L'écu entouré d'une cordelière. [Pas de texte]

Fol. 25 : deux écus côte à côte. (a) *écartelé au 1 et 4 d'or à l'arbre arraché de gueules ; au 2 et 3 d'argent à deux lions affrontés d'or tenant un anneau de sable, à la bordure d'azur chargée de dix fleurs de lis d'or et d'un lambel de gueules.* (b) *écartelé au 1 et 4 d'or à l'arbre arraché de gueules ; au 2 et 3 d'argent à deux lions affrontés d'or tenant un anneau de sable, à la bordure d'azur chargée de dix fleurs de lis d'or et d'un lambel de gueules,* mi-parti *d'or à trois fèves de sinople rangées en pal.* L'écu entouré d'une cordelière. « Guillaume d'Andrea, mary de Marguerite Favard. »

Fol. 26 : deux écus côte à côte. (a) *d'argent à deux lions affrontés d'or tenants un anneau de sable, à la bordure d'azur chargée de dix fleurs de lis d'or et d'un lambel de gueules.* (b) *d'argent à deux lions affrontés d'or tenants un anneau de sable, à la bordure d'azur chargée de dix fleurs de lis d'or et d'un lambel de gueules,* mi-parti *d'un échiqueté de gueules et d'or.* L'écu entouré d'une cordelière. « Dominique d'Andrea, Sr de Venellea, mary de Françoise de Vento. »

Fol. 27 : deux écus côte à côte. (a) *d'or au sautoir de gueules.* Cimier : *femme nue de carnation, de face, les bras croisés tenant un [???]* (b) *d'or au sautoir de gueules* parti d'un *écartelé au 1 et 4 d'or à l'arbre arraché de gueules ; au 2 et 3 d'argent à deux lions affrontés d'or tenants un anneau de sable, à la bordure d'azur chargée de dix fleurs de lis d'or et d'un lambel de gueules.* L'écu entouré d'une cordelière. « Henry de Jerente, capitaine d'une galère, mary de Magdelaine d'Andrea. »

Fol. 28 : deux écus côte à côte. (a) *d'azur au chevron d'or chargé de trois palmes de sinople, accompagné de deux roses aussi d'or en chef, et d'une grenade du même en pointe.* (b) *d'azur au chevron d'or chargé de trois palmes de sinople, accompagné de deux roses aussi d'or en chef, et d'une grenade du même en pointe* parti d'un *écartelé au 1 et 4 d'or à l'arbre arraché de gueules ; au 2 et 3 d'argent à deux lions affrontés d'or tenants un anneau de sable, à la bordure d'azur chargée de dix fleurs de lis d'or et d'un lambel de gueules.* L'écu entouré d'une cordelière. « Jean-François de Paumier, conseiller du roy et trésorier de France en Provence, mary de Marquise d'Andrea. »

Fol. 29 : deux écus côte à côte. (a) *d'or au chevron d'azur accompagné de trois têtes de léopard de sable, à la bordure de gueules.* (b) *d'or au chevron d'azur accompagné de trois têtes de léopard de sable, à la bordure de gueules* mi-parti d'un *écartelé au 1 et 4 d'or à l'arbre arraché de gueules ; au 2 et 3 d'argent à deux lions affrontés d'or tenants un anneau de sable, à la bordure d'azur chargée de dix fleurs de lis d'or et d'un lambel de gueules.* L'écu entouré d'une cordelière. « Jean de Fourbin, seigneur de La Marthe, mary de Marguise d'Andrea. »

Fol. 30 : deux écus côte à côte. (a) *d'azur au lion d'or.* Cimier : *un lion d'or assis et issant de face tenant un listel d'argent portant les lettres F F F de gueules.* (b) *d'azur au lion d'or* parti d'un *écartelé au 1 et 4 d'or à l'arbre arraché de gueules ; au 2 et 3 d'argent à deux lions affrontés d'or tenants un anneau de sable, à la bordure d'azur chargée de dix fleurs de lis d'or et d'un lambel de gueules.* L'écu entouré d'une cordelière. « Lazarin de Felix, conseiller du roy et trésorier général de France en Provence, mary de Luonesse d'Andrea ; sa fille nommée Françoise de Felix épousa en 1627 Antoine de Valbelle, seigneur de Montfuron, d'où est sortie la branche de Valbelle, marquis de Montfuron. »

Fol. 31 : deux écus côte à côte. (a) *d'argent à trois feuilles d'ortie (?) de sinople.* (b) *d'argent à trois feuilles d'ortie (?) de sinople,* mi-parti d'un *écartelé au 1 et 4 d'or à l'arbre arraché de gueules ; au 2 et 3 d'argent à deux lions affrontés d'or tenants un anneau de sable, à la bordure d'azur chargée de dix fleurs de lis d'or et d'un lambel de gueules.* L'écu entouré d'une cordelière. « Nicollas de Calvet, conseiller du roy en la sénéchaussée de Montpellier, mary de Jeanne d'Andrea. »

Fol. 32 : deux écus côte à côte. (a) *d'argent à trois feuilles d'ortie (?) de sinople.* (b) *d'argent à trois feuilles d'ortie (?) de sinople,* parti *de gueules au taureau passant d'or accompagné en chef de deux branches du même passées en sautoir et cantonnées en chef d'une étoile aussi d'or.* L'écu entouré d'une cordelière. « Guillaume de Calvet, conseiller du roy et maistre des comptes à Montpellier, mary d'Elizabeth de Bossuges. »

Fol. 33 : deux écus côte à côte. (a) *écartelé au 1 et 4 d'azur au lion d'or ; au 2 et 3 de gueules à deux bandes d'or ; à la croix d'argent brochant sur le tout.* (b) *écartelé au 1 et 4 d'azur au lion d'or ; au 2 et 3 de gueules à deux bandes d'or ; à la croix d'argent brochant sur le tout,* mi-parti *d'argent à trois feuilles d'orties (?) de sinople.* L'écu entouré d'une cordelière. « Marcelin de Manifacier, conseiller du roy et visitteur général des gabelles de Languedoc, mary de Marguerite de Calvet. »

Fol. 34-39 : blancs

Fol. 40 : deux écus côte à côte. (a) *d'or à l'aigle de sable, au chef d'azur chargé de trois étoiles d'or.* (b) *d'or à l'aigle de sable, au chef d'azur chargé de trois étoiles d'or,* parti *d'azur au croissant renversé d'argent accompagné en chef de deux étoiles d'or.* L'écu entouré d'une cordelière. « Guillaume Besset, mary de Marguerite Champt. »

Fol. 41 : deux écus côte à côte. (a) *d'or à l'aigle de sable, au chef d'azur chargé de trois étoiles d'or.* (b) *d'or à l'aigle de sable, au chef d'azur chargé de trois étoiles d'or,* parti *d'azur au mont d'argent accompagné en chef de deux étoiles d'or surmontées d'une croisette du même.* L'écu entouré d'une cordelière. « Jean Besset, seigneur de La Valette, mort en 1650 doyen du présidial de Lyon, ne laissa qu'une fille unique, Marie Besset, héritière de La Valette, qui épousa en 1638 messire Baptiste Planelli dit Pianello, trésorier de France à Lyon. Ledit Jean Besset étoit fils aîné de Léonard Besset, seigneur de La Valette, dont la feuille a été coupée je ne sçay pourquoy. Jean Besset, seigneur de La Valette, conseiller du roy au présidial de Lyon, mary d'Anne Micollier. »

Fol. 42 : deux écus côte à côte. (a) *d'or à l'aigle de sable, au chef d'azur chargé de trois étoiles d'or.* (b) *d'or à l'aigle de sable, au chef d'azur chargé de trois étoiles d'or,* parti *d'or à la fasce de gueules chargée de trois croissants tournés d'argent.* L'écu entouré d'une cordelière. « Jean Besset, seigneur de La Valette, conseiller du roy au présidial de Lyon, mary en secondes noces de Marie Strossy. »

Fol. 43 : deux écus côte à côte. (a) *d'or à l'aigle de sable, au chef d'azur chargé de trois étoiles d'or.* (b) *d'or à l'aigle de sable, au chef d'azur chargé de trois étoiles d'or,* parti *d'azur au soleil d'or accompagné de six étoiles du même en orle, et d'un croissant d'argent en pointe.* L'écu entouré d'une cordelière. « Louis Besset, seigneur de Montchaud, conseiller secrétaire du roy maison et couronne de France, mary de Claire Staron. »

Fol. 44 : deux écus côte à côte. (a) *d'azur à trois étoiles d'or, au chef d'argent chargé de trois bandes de gueules.* (b) *d'azur à trois étoiles d'or, au chef d'argent chargé de trois bandes de gueules,* parti *d'or à l'aigle de sable, au chef d'azur chargé de trois étoiles d'or.* L'écu entouré d'une cordelière. « Mathieu Mazenot, mary de Marguerite Besset. »

Fol. 45 : deux écus côte à côte. (a) *d'azur à trois étoiles d'or, au chef d'argent chargé de trois bandes de gueules.* (b) *d'azur à trois étoiles d'or, au chef d'argent chargé de trois bandes de gueules,* parti *d'or à l'arbre de sinople fruité de gueules, sur un tertre aussi de sinople, au chef d'azur chargé de trois étoiles d'or.* L'écu entouré d'une cordelière. « Marc-Anthoine Mazenot, mary d'Estiennette Breton. »

Fol. 46 : deux écus côte à côte. (a) *d'azur à trois étoiles d'or, au chef d'argent chargé de trois bandes de gueules.* (b) *d'azur à trois étoiles d'or, au chef d'argent chargé de trois bandes de gueules,* parti *d'argent à trois fasces de gueules.* L'écu entouré d'une cordelière. « Marcelin Mazenot, mary de Marie Pecoil. »

Fol. 47 : deux écus côte à côte. (a) *écartelé au 1 et 4 d'or au lion de sable ; au 2 et 3 d'or à trois fleurs de lis de sable ; sur le tout d'or au lion de sable.* (b) *écartelé au 1 et 4 d'or au lion de sable ; au 2 et 3 d'or à trois fleurs de lis de sable ; sur le tout d'or au lion de sable,* mi-parti *d'azur à trois étoiles d'or, au chef d'argent chargé de trois bandes de gueules.* L'écu entouré d'une cordelière. « Joachim Vanscort, mary de Marie Mazenot. »

Fol. 48 : deux écus côte à côte. (a) *écartelé au 1 et 4 d'or au lion de sable ; au 2 et 3 d'or à trois fleurs de lis de sable ; sur le tout d'or au lion de sable, au lambel d'argent sur le tout.* (b) *écartelé au 1 et 4 d'or au lion de sable ; au 2 et 3 d'or à trois fleurs de lis de sable ; sur le tout d'or au lion de sable, au lambel d'argent sur le tout*, mi-parti *d'azur à trois étoiles d'or, au chef d'argent chargé de trois bandes de gueules.* L'écu entouré d'une cordelière. « Mathieu Vanscort, mary de Marguerite Mazenot. »

Fol. 49 : deux écus côte à côte. (a) *d'or à la bande d'azur chargée de trois étoiles d'or, accompagnée de deux trèfles de sinople.* (b) *d'or à la bande d'azur chargée de trois étoiles d'or, accompagnée de deux trèfles de sinople*, parti *d'or à l'aigle de sable, au chef d'azur chargé de trois étoiles d'or.* L'écu entouré d'une cordelière. «Marcelin Gajot, mary d'Anthoinette Besset. »

Fol. 50 : blanc.

Fol. 51 : deux écus côte à côte. (a) *d'or à la bande d'azur chargée de trois étoiles d'or, accompagnée de deux trèfles de sinople.* (b) *d'or à la bande d'azur chargée de trois étoiles d'or, accompagnée de deux trèfles de sinople*, mi-parti *de gueules à trois fasces vivrées d'argent, au chef de gueules chargé d'une aigle d'argent couronnée d'or accompagnée en pointe d'une clef d'argent posée en pal, à dextre d'un casque aussi d'argent de profil ; à l'écusson d'azur à la fleur de lis d'or brochant sur le trait du chef.* L'écu entouré d'une cordelière. « Louis Gajot, trésorier de France, mary de Marie Mascranny. »

Fol. 52 : blanc.

Fol. 53 : deux écus côte à côte. (a) *d'azur au chevron d'argent accompagné de trois losanges du même, au chef de gueules au lion issant d'or.* (b) *d'azur au chevron d'argent accompagné de trois losanges du même, au chef de gueules au lion issant d'or*, parti *d'or à la bande d'azur chargée de trois étoiles d'or, accompagnée de deux trèfles de sinople.* L'écu entouré d'une cordelière. « Jean Carrette, mary de Jeanne Gajot. »

Fol. 54 : deux écus côte à côte. (a) *de gueules à la gerbe d'or, au chef du second chargé de trois flammes du premier.* (b) *de gueules à la gerbe d'or, au chef du second chargé de trois flammes du premier*, parti *d'or à la bande d'azur chargée de trois étoiles d'or, accompagnée de deux trèfles de sinople.* L'écu entouré d'une cordelière. « François du Faure, conseiller du roy, trésorier général des Ponts et chaussées, mary de Marie Gajot. »

Fol. 55 : deux écus côte à côte. (a) *d'azur à la roue d'or clouée de gueules.* (b) *d'azur à la roue d'or clouée de gueules*, parti *d'or à la bande d'azur chargée de trois étoiles d'or, accompagnée de deux trèfles de sinople.* L'écu entouré d'une cordelière. « Jean Charrier, seigneur de La barge, baron de Sandrans, conseiller du roy, trésorier de France et général des finances à Lyon, mary de dame Marie Gajot. »

Fol. 56-57 : blancs.

Fol. 58 : deux écus côte à côte. (a) *d'azur au dauphin d'or couronné du même, au chef aussi d'azur chargé de trois étoiles d'or.* (b) *d'azur au dauphin d'or couronné du même, au chef aussi d'azur chargé de trois étoiles d'or*, parti *d'or à la bande d'azur chargée de trois étoiles d'or, accompagnée de deux trèfles de sinople.* L'écu entouré d'une cordelière. « Gaspard Beget, mary d'Heleyne Besset qu'il épousa en 1616. »

Fol. 59 : deux écus côte à côte. (a) *d'azur à trois étoiles d'or rangées en fasce, accompagnées en pointe d'un croissant d'argent.* (b) *d'azur à trois étoiles d'or rangées en fasce, accompagnées en pointe d'un croissant d'argent*, parti *d'or à la bande d'azur chargée de trois étoiles d'or, accompagnée de deux trèfles de sinople.* L'écu entouré d'une cordelière. « Marcelin Charbonnel, seigneur du Baye, mary d'Heleyne Besset en 2e noces en 1626. »

Fol. 60 : deux écus côte à côte. (a) *d'azur à trois pals d'argent, au franc-canton de gueules à la croix pattée d'or.* (b) *d'azur à trois pals d'argent, au franc-canton de gueules à la croix pattée d'or*, parti *d'or à la bande d'azur chargée de trois étoiles d'or, accompagnée de deux trèfles de sinople.* L'écu entouré d'une cordelière. « Gaspard de Saint-Pol, seigneur de Chazelletz, troisiesme mary d'Eleine Besset. »

Fol. 61 : deux écus côte à côte. (a) *d'or à trois quintefeuilles d'azur.* (b) *d'or à trois quintefeuilles d'azur,* parti d'un *tranché d'argent et d'azur chargé de trois tourteaux d'azur et de trois besants d'argent en orle.* L'écu entouré d'une cordelière. « Jean Croppet, grossier ez coure de Lyon, mary de Marguerite Bullioud. »

Fol. 62 : deux écus côte à côte. (a) *d'or à trois quintefeuilles d'azur.* (b) *d'or à trois quintefeuilles d'azur,* parti *d'azur à la bande bretessée et contre-bretessée d'or, accompagnée de deux croissants d'argent et de deux têtes d'aigle d'or en chef, et d'une étoile du même en pointe.* L'écu entouré d'une cordelière. « Odet Croppet, conseiller du roy au présidial de Lyon, mary en premières nopces de Marguerite Chomat. »

Fol. 63 : deux écus côte à côte. (a) *d'or à trois quintefeuilles d'azur.* (b) *d'or à trois quintefeuilles d'azur,* parti d'un *écartelé d'argent et d'azur, à la bande de gueules.* L'écu entouré d'une cordelière. « Odet Croppet, conseiller du roy au présidial de Lyon, mary en secondes nopces de Marguerite de Saint-Prie Fontaine. »

Fol. 64 : deux écus côte à côte. (a) *d'or à trois quintefeuilles d'azur.* (b) *d'or à trois quintefeuilles d'azur,* parti *d'azur à la bande d'or accompagnée en chef d'une étoile du même, et d'un lion d'argent en pointe.* L'écu entouré d'une cordelière. « Jean-Pierre Croppet, seigneur d'Irigny et Lucenay, conseiller du roy, maistre de porte à Lyon, mary d'Anne du Coing. »

Fol. 65 : deux écus côte à côte. (a) *d'azur à la montagne d'argent accompagnée en chef d'une croisette accostée de deux étoiles, le tout d'or.* (b) *d'azur à la montagne d'argent accompagnée en chef d'une croisette accostée de deux étoiles, le tout d'or,* parti *d'or à trois quintefeuilles d'azur.* L'écu entouré d'une cordelière. « Justinian Micollier, conseiller du roy au présidial de Lyon, advocat général au Parlement de Dombes, mary de Méraude Croppet. »

Fol. 66 : deux écus côte à côte. (a) *d'azur à la montagne d'argent accompagnée en chef d'une croisette accostée de deux étoiles, le tout d'or.* (b) *d'azur à la montagne d'argent accompagnée en chef d'une croisette accostée de deux étoiles, le tout d'or,* parti *d'argent à trois plantes de sinople*

à une fleur de gueules (rosiers) sur un tertre aussi de sinople, au chef d'azur chargé d'une croisette d'or accostée de deux étoiles du même.* L'écu entouré d'une cordelière. « Mathieu Micollier, seigneur de Belair, mary de Marie Dumas. »

Fol. 67 : deux écus côte à côte. (a) *d'azur au chevron d'or accompagné de trois moutons d'argent, et d'un croissant d'argent en chef.* (b) *d'azur au chevron d'or accompagné de trois moutons d'argent, et d'un croissant d'argent en chef,* parti *d'azur à la montagne d'argent accompagnée en chef d'une croisette accostée de deux étoiles, le tout d'or.* L'écu entouré d'une cordelière. « Jean de Loaille, mary de Marie Micollier. »

Fol. 68 : deux écus côte à côte. (a) *d'argent au chevron d'azur accompagné de trois trèfles de sinople, au chef d'azur au lion passant d'or.* (b) *d'argent au chevron d'azur accompagné de trois trèfles de sinople, au chef d'azur au lion passant d'or,* parti *d'azur à la montagne d'argent accompagnée en chef d'une croisette accostée de deux étoiles, le tout d'or.* L'écu entouré d'une cordelière. « Hierosme Lentillon, secrétaire du roy maison et couronne de France, mary en secondes nopces de Marie Micollier. »

Fol. 69 : deux écus côte à côte. (a) *d'azur à la montagne d'argent accompagnée en chef d'une croisette accostée de deux étoiles, le tout d'or.* (b) *d'azur à la montagne d'argent accompagnée en chef d'une croisette accostée de deux étoiles, le tout d'or,* parti *d'or au chevron d'azur chargé de trois fleurs de lis d'or, accompagné de trois roses de gueules.* L'écu entouré d'une cordelière. « François Micollier, seigneur de Belair, mary de Lucie Bertrand. »

Fol. 70 : deux écus côte à côte. (a) *d'azur à la fasce d'or accompagnée en chef d'une aigle d'argent, et de trois croissants d'argent en pointe.* (b) *d'azur à la fasce d'or accompagnée en chef d'une aigle d'argent, et de trois croissants d'argent en pointe,* parti *d'or à trois quintefeuilles d'azur.* L'écu entouré d'une cordelière. « Jean-Baptiste Sarde, conseiller du roy et président et trésorier général de France à Lyon, mary d'Anne Coppet.»

Fol. 71 : deux écus côte à côte. (a) *d'azur au chevron d'argent accompagné de deux besants d'or en chef, et d'un trèfle du même en pointe.* (b) *d'azur au chevron d'argent accompagné de deux besants d'or en chef, et d'un trèfle du même en pointe*, parti *d'or à trois quintefeuilles d'azur.* L'écu entouré d'une cordelière. « Philippe-Emanuel Faure, conseiller et advocat du roy au présidial de Lyon, mary de Louise Croppet. »

Un folio non chiffré portant trois pièces collées numérotées 72, 73 et 74.

Nº 72 : les armoiries Pianello avec supports, cimier et lambrequins, le tout rehaussé à l'or.

Nº 73 : *écartelé au 1 et 4 d'argent à deux lions affrontés d'or tenant un anneau de sable, à la bordure fleurdelisée d'or au lambel de gueules ; au 2 et 3 d'or à l'aigle de sable, au chef d'azur à trois étoiles d'or ; et sur le tout coupé de gueules et de sable à l'écot d'or brochant sur le trait du coupé.* Cimier : *une aigle de sable couronnée d'or.* Supports : *deux aigles de sable couronnées d'or, la tête contournée.*

Nº 74 : les armoiries Pianello gravées en taille douce (125 x 97 mm). En haut la devise ROBORE ET CELERITATE. Cette vignette porte en bas à droite la signature : *J. de Fornazeris delineavit et sculpsit*, signature d'un artiste lyonnais réputé, qui travailla pour le roi de France de 1570 aux premières années du XVIIᵉ siècle, et qui séjourna à Lyon entre 1601 et 1619.

Folio non chiffré sur lequel est collé une bande de papier portant le nº 75, expliquant la parenté avec le chevalier de Forbin :

Guillaume Dandrea x Marguerite de Favard
Dominique Dandrea x Françoise de Vento
Marquise d'Andrea x Jean de Forbin
Le chevalier de Forbin
Marquise d'Andrea x Raymond de Not
Marguerite de Not x Laurent Pianello
Baptiste Pianello x Marie Besset

Un folio non chiffré sur lequel est collé, portant le nº 76, le certificat d'enregistrement d'armoiries suite à l'édit de novembre 1696 :

### Armoiries

Je soussigné, directeur pour la Régie & Recette des droits d'enregistrement des armoiries, ordonné être fait par Edit du mois de Novembre 1696. Soussigné, reconnois que Me *Jean-Baptiste Pianello protonotaire apostolique, & chanoine d'honneur d'Esnay*, a ce jourd'huy apporté en ce bureau & présenté ses armes, pour être enregistrées à l'Armorial Général, & qu'il m'a payé, sçavoir, pour les droits d'enregistrement, suivant le Tarif, la somme de *vingt livres*, pour les deux sols pour livre *deux livres* & trente sols pour les frais du brevet & du Blason, & autres reglez par l'arrest du Conseil du 20 novembre 1696, promettant luy délivrer ledit brevet dudit enregistrement, en me rapportant le présent recepissé. Fait à *Lyon* jour d'*huy 8 octobre* mil six cens quatre-vingts-*dix-huict.*

Récépissé *de la somme de vingt trois livres et dix sols.*

Registre *second pour le clergé & la noblesse.*

article *nº 292* [signé : *illisible*]

Un folio non chiffré, portant collée et chiffrée 77, une feuille portant le crayon généalogique suivant :

Notes remises par Monsieur du Bessy, de Saint-Estienne, en 7bre 1762

**Gaspard de Beget**, né le 8 mars 1582, fils de Marcellin et de Margueritte des Sauvages, épousa le 22 octobre 1616 Hélène Besset, [*dont*] Jacques de Beget, épousa Antoinette Boyer, fille de Jean, et d'Anne de Vindre, [*dont*] Marcellin de Beget, épousa Louise de Saignard, fille d'Antoine baron de Quevievez, et de Isabelle de Cremeaux, [*dont*] Armand de Beget, épousa Françoise de Layois des Ponchets, fille de Nicolas, et de Eléonore de Launay d'Antraigues, [*dont*] (1) Marcellin de Beget, baron de Saussac, sans postérité ; (2) Armand de Beget, doyen à Notre-Dame du Puy ; (3) Louise, mariée à François du Charbonnel du Bet ; (4) Marguerite, mariée à Claude de Jullien Villeneuve.

**Marcellin Charbonnel du Bestz**, épousa 1°, le 2 décembre 1617 Antoinette de Bronac, fille de Charles, et de Jeanne du Verger ; 2° épousa le 7 octobre 1626 **Hélène Besset**, fille de Léonard [seigneur de La Valette], veuve de Gaspard de Beget, [*dont, de ce second lit*] 1°) Léonard de Charbonnel de Jussac, épousa N... [*dont*] Gaspard de Charbonnel de Jussac, épousa Catherine Veron, fille de Jean, et de Catherine Piquet, [*dont*] Jacques de Charbonnel de Jussac, épousa en 1742 ... Pourrat du Cluzel, [*dont*] de Charbonnel de Jussac, lieutenant d'infanterie. 2°) Charles Charbonnel du Betz, épousa le 5 juin 1638 Anne de Beget, fille de Gaspard de Beget, et de Hélène Besset, [*dont*] Jacques de Charbonnel du Betz, épousa Thérèse de Colomb de Chambaud, fille de Jean, et de Lucresse de La Rochette, [*dont*] François de Charbonnel du Betz, épousa Louise de Beget, fille d'Armand et de Françoise de Layois des Ponchetz, [*dont*] Armand de Charbonnel du Betz.

N° 77 v°

**Louis de Murat Lestang de Murat**, seigneur de Sablons, épousa le ... Catherine Béraudier, fille d'Antoine, secrétaire du roy, et de Margueritte de Soleiral, [*dont*] Antoine de Murat de Lestang de Murat, président à mortier au Parlement de Dauphiné, épousa le ... Virginie Daviti, [*dont*] Claude de Murat, président à Grenoble, marquis de Lestang, épousa le 18 janvier 1724 Louise Gabrielle de Falcoz de La Blache, fille de Victor, comte d'Anjou, brigadier des armées du roy, [*dont*] (1) Laurent de Murat, capitaine dans le régiment de Royal Dragons en 1757 ; (2) Victor de Murat, marquis de Lestang, président à mortier au Parlement de Grenoble ; (3) Louise Gabrielle Scolastique de Murat, mariée le 13 avril 1744 à Jean-François de Rousse de Gaubert, comte de Lavie.

N° 78

Mon grand père (Laurent) de La Valette mourut à Lyon le dimanche 9 octobre 1718 sur les neuf heures du matin âgé de 74 ans et demy, étant né le ... may 1644. Il avoit reçu ses sacrements la veille ou l'avant-veille, et il ne s'étoit allité que depuis quatre ou cinq jours, étant sorty le lundy précédent, ce fut une fièvre continue, accompagnée de rhûme, qui l'emporta. Il avoit déjà eu une maladie semblable vers les fêtes de la Pentecôte, et ses longues infirmitez l'avoient fort affoibly.

Mon père et ma mère étoient à Paris lors de sa mort. J'y étois aussy depuis près d'un mois.

Il faut voir dans le *Journal de Verdun* de décembre 1718, page 441, ce qui y est dit de la mort de mon grand père [1].

Ma grand mère de La Valette [*Claude de Mascranny*] mourut le jeudy 7 février 1743 sur les cinq heures et demie du soir après une maladie de 12 jours. Elle auroit eu le 16 de ce mois 92 ans accomplis, étant née en 1651.

Ma tante [*Marie Planelli de La Valette*] mourut le Vendredi saint 19 avril 1737 sur les 6 heures du matin dans la 60ème année de son âge.

N° 79

Marcellin Gayot, fils de Gérard Gayot de la ville de Saint Chaumont, et de demoiselle N. Rochette, vint s'établir à Lyon, rue Mercière, et fit une fortune très considérable dans le commerce.

Il épousa en avril 1614 demoiselle Antoinette Besset, fille du sieur Léonard Besset de la ville de Saint-Etienne, et de demoiselle Jeanne Chauvin.

Il mourut en 1642, riche de 800 000*lt*, étant trésorier de la Charité, et fut enterré aux Jacobins dans la chapelle des Besset. Sa femme ne mourut qu'en 1664.

De Marcellin Gayot descendent tous les messieurs Gayot de La Bussière, Gayot d'Amarcins, et Gayot de la cour des aydes à Paris, qui jouissent tous de la noblesse depuis cent ans.

Ledit Marcellin avoit deux frères, Pierre et Michel Gayot dont la postérité est éteinte depuis le commencement de ce siècle.

Il étoit fils de Gérard Gayot, lequel avoit des frères, d'où vient M. Gayot de

La Rejasse et Gayot de Pittaval. Gérard étoit, dit-on, fils d'Antoine, et Antoine fils de Jean Gayot, qui le premier vint s'établir à Saint-Chaumont, et y apporta l'art de la soye vers l'an 1540, mais ces deux derniers degrés ne sont pas établis sur titres, mais seulement par une généalogie manuscritte soutenue de la tradition.

N° 80

Cette feuille coupée contenoit les armes de noble Laurent Pianello ou Planelli, né à Lyon le 20 juillet 1564, fils de noble Baptiste Pianello et d'Elizabeth d'Agnola. Il épousa le 4 octobre 1600 demoiselle Margueritte Dénot, fille de noble Raymond Dénot, et de Marquise d'Andrea, d'une famille distinguée de Provence.

Laurent Pianello mourut à Lyon le 29 septembre 1648 et fut enterré au grand couvent des R.P. Capucins dont il avoit été le Père Temporel depuis l'année 1606.

La note cy-derrière a été tirée d'une autre que j'ay vue écritte de la main de mon grand père, Laurent Pianello, seigneur de La Valette, mort en 1718.

N° 81

Marquise d'Andrea, femme de noble Raymond Dénot, étoit fille de noble Dominique d'Andrea, écuyer de la ville de Marseille, et de dame Françoise de Vento. D'autres disent qu'elle sœur, et non fille, dudit Dominique d'Andrea, seigneur de Venelles. Je n'ay pas vu les titres, et je me suis conformé aux notes de mon grand'père de La Valette.

Quoiqu'il en soit, cette famille d'Andrea, qui étoit venue d'Italie, et anciennement établie à Marseille, est éteinte depuis longtems. Celle de Vento subsiste encore.

Il y a eu une Magdelaine d'Andrea, mariée à Henry de Gerente, capitaine de galère ; et une Marquise d'Andrea, qui fut femme de Jean de Fourbin, seigneur de La Marthe. Nous avons perdu de vue tous ces parents là avec lesquelz mon grand'père et mon bisayeul avoient encore conservé des relations.

Marguerite Denot, veuve de noble homme Laurent Pianello, mourut à Lyon le 15 janvier 1657 sur les six heures du matin, elle étoit âgée de 76 ans et 10 mois. Elle fut enterrée le lendemain aux Minimes dans la chapelle de la famille.

Baptiste Pianello, père dudit Laurent, vint s'établir en France en 1560, il n'avoit alors que 22 ans. Il testa à Lyon en mars 1604, étant sur le point de partir pour Avignon, où il mourut. D'autres mémoires disent à Gênes, sa patrie. Son testament fut ouvert le 14 janvier 1606, quelque tems après son déceds. Le testament, qui est en italien, contient des legs très considérables en faveur des hôpitaux de Lyon.

### BnF ms fr. 8717

Les deux plats intérieurs sont ornés d'une vignette gravée aux armes : *écartelé au 1 et 4 d'argent à deux lions affrontés d'or tenant un anneau de sable, à la bordure fleurdelisée d'or au lambel de gueules ; au 2 et 3 d'or à l'aigle de sable, au chef d'azur à trois étoiles d'or ; et sur le tout coupé de gueules et de sable à l'écot d'or brochant sur le trait du coupé .*

Pièce n° 1

Laurent Pianello, *fils de* Baptiste Pianello et de Marie Besset, *fille de* Jean Besset et d'Anne Micolier, *fille de* Justinian Micolier et de Méraude Croppet, *fille de* Jean Croppet et de Marguerite Bullioud, *fille de* Pierre Bullioud et de Méraude de La Porte, *fils de* Aubert Edoart Bullioud et d'Antoinette Paterin, *fils de* Claude Bullioud et de Grégoirette de Bellieure, *fils de* Pierre Bullioud et de Louise de Saconins de Pravieu, *fille de* Pierre de Saconins de Pravieu et d'Huguette de Thureio, *fille de* Guichard de Thureio et d'Isabeau de Coligny, *fille de* Estienne de Coligny et de Léonor de Villars, *fille de* Humbert de Villars et de Léonor de Beaujeu[2], *fille de* Louis de Forest (†1295), dit de Beaujeu, et de Léonor de Savoye, *fille de* Thomas de Savoye (†1259), et de Beatrix de Fiesque[3], *fils de* Thomas (1177-†1223) de Savoye et de Béatrice de Genève[4], *fils de* Humbert (1136-†1188) de Savoye et de Béatrix de Vienne[5], *fils de* Amé de Savoye (1080-†1149) et de Marthe de Vienne[6], *fils de* Humbert de Savoye (1048-†1103) et de Gisèle de Bourgogne comté[7], *fille de* Guillaume de Bourgogne et de Gertrude de Limbourg, *fils de* Renaud de Bourgogne et d'Alix de Normandie, *fils de* Otte Guillaume de Bourgogne et d'Ermentrude de Rheims, *fils de* Albert, roy d'Italie, et de Gerberge de Bourgogne, *fils de* Bérenger, roy d'Italie et empereur, et de Gisle de Toscane, *fils de* Adalbert, marquis d'Ivrée, et de Gisle d'Italie, *fils de* Bérenger, roy d'Italie, *fils de* Evrard, duc de Frioul, et de Gisle de France, *fille de* Louis le Débonnaire, et d'Ermentrude de Hasbain, *fils de* Charlemagne, empereur et roy de France, et d'Ildegarde de Suaube

Fol. 2 : grand écu coupé de trois et parti de cinq, ce qui fait 24 quartiers :

(1) *Coupé de gueules et de sable à l'écot d'or brochant en fasce sur le trait du coupé.*

(2) *Ecartelé au 1 et 4 d'or à l'aigle de sable, au chef d'azur chargé de trois étoiles d'or ; au 2 et 3 d'azur à trois fleurs de lis d'or, au chef du même au lion issant de gueules.*

(3) *D'azur au mont d'argent accompagné en chef d'une croisette d'or surmontée de deux étoiles du même rangées en fasce.*

(4) *D'or à trois quintefeuilles d'azur.*

(5) *Tranché d'argent et d'azur à six besants de l'un et de l'autre.*

(6) *De gueules à la croix d'or.*

(7) *D'azur à la bande d'or accompagnée en chef d'une étoile du même.*

(8) *D'azur à la fasce d'argent accompagnée de trois trèfles d'or.*

(9) *De gueules billeté d'or au bâton d'argent brochant.*

(10) *De gueules au sautoir d'or.*

(11) *De gueules à l'aigle d'argent membrée, becquée et couronnée d'azur.*

(12) *Bandé de six pièces d'or et de gueules.*

(13) *D'or au lion de sable, au lambel de gueules.*

(14) *De gueules à la croix d'argent, à la cotice d'azur.*

(15) *Bandé de six pièces d'argent et d'azur.*

(16) *Palé de six pièces d'or et de gueules.*

(17) *De gueules à l'aigle d'or.*

(18) *D'or au dauphin d'azur.*

(19) *D'azur au lion billeté d'argent.*

(20) *D'argent au lion de gueules à la queue fourchée passée en sautoir.*

(21) *De gueules à deux léopards d'or.*

(22) *D'or au lion de sable.*

(23) *D'or à l'aigle de sable.*

(24) *D'or à l'aigle bicéphale de sable membrée, becquée et nimbée de gueules, à l'écu d'azur semé de fleurs de lis d'or brochant sur la poitrine.*

Et sur le tout un écu *d'azur semé de fleurs de lis d'or.*

Fol. 3 : quatre écus, deux à deux, l'un sous l'autre. [Laurent Pianello, fils de :]

(1) Baptiste Pianello, *coupé de gueules et de sable à l'écot d'or brochant en fasce sur le trait du coupé,* [et de :]

(2) Marie Besset, *écartelé au 1 et 4 d'or à l'aigle de sable, au chef d'azur chargé de trois étoiles d'or ; au 2 et 3 d'azur à trois fleurs de lis d'or, au chef du même au lion issant de gueules.,* fille de :

(3) Jean Besset, *écartelé au 1 et 4 d'or à l'aigle de sable, au chef d'azur chargé de trois étoiles*

d'or ; *au 2 et 3 d'azur à trois fleurs de lis d'or, au chef du même au lion issant de gueules*, [et de :]

(4) Anne Micolier, *d'azur au mont d'argent accompagné en chef d'une croisette d'or surmontée de deux étoiles du même rangées en fasce*, fille de :

Fol. 4 : quatre écus, deux à deux, l'un sous l'autre.

(5) Iustinian Micolier, *d'azur au mont d'argent accompagné en chef d'une croisette d'or surmontée de deux étoiles du même rangées en fasce*, [et :]

(6) Méraude Croppet, *d'or à trois quintefeuilles d'azur*, fille de :

(7) Jean Croppet, *d'or à trois quintefeuilles d'azur*, [et de :]

(8) Marguerite Bullioud, *tranché d'argent et d'azur à six besants de l'un et de l'autre*, fille de :

Fol. 5 : quatre écus, deux à deux, l'un sous l'autre.

(9) Pierre Bullioud, *tranché d'argent et d'azur à six besants de l'un et de l'autre*, [et de :]

(10) Méraude de La Porte, *de gueules à la croix d'or*, fils de :

(11) Aubert-Edoard Bullioud, *tranché d'argent et d'azur à six besants de l'un et de l'autre*, [et de :]

(12) Antoinette Paterin, *d'azur à la bande d'or accompagnée en chef d'une étoile du même*, fils de :

Fol. 6 : quatre écus, deux à deux, l'un sous l'autre.

(13) Claude Bullioud, *tranché d'argent et d'azur à six besants de l'un et de l'autre*, [et de :]

(14) Grégoirette de Bellièvre, *d'azur à la fasce d'argent accompagnée de trois trèfles d'or*, fils de :

(15) Pierre Bullioud, *tranché d'argent et d'azur à six besants de l'un et de l'autre*, [et de :]

(16) Louise de Saconins de Pravieu, *de gueules billeté d'or au bâton d'argent brochant*, fille de :

Fol. 7 : quatre écus, deux à deux, l'un sous l'autre.

(17) Pierre de Saconins, *de gueules billeté d'or au bâton d'argent brochant*, [et de :]

(18) Huguette de Thurey, *de gueules au sautoir d'or*, fille de :

(19) Guichard de Thurey, *de gueules au sautoir d'or*, [et de :]

(20) Isabeau de Coligny, *de gueules à l'aigle d'argent membrée, becquée et couronnée d'azur*, fille de :

Fol. 8 : quatre écus, deux à deux, l'un sous l'autre.

(21) Estienne de Coligny, *de gueules à l'aigle d'argent membrée, becquée et couronnée d'azur*, [et de]

(22) Léonor de Villars, *bandé de six pièces d'or et de gueules*, fille de :

(23) Humbert de Villars, *bandé de six pièces d'or et de gueules*, [et de]

(24) Léonor de Beaujeu, *d'or au lion de sable, au lambel d'azur*, fille de :

Fol. 9 : quatre écus, deux à deux, l'un sous l'autre.

(25) Louis de Forest, dit de Beaujeu, *écartelé au 1 et 4 de gueules au dauphin d'or ; au 2 et 3 d'or au lion de sable, au lambel d'azur*, [et de]

(26) Léonore de Savoye, *de gueules à la croix d'argent à la cotice d'azur*, fille de :

(27) Thomas de Savoye, *de gueules à la croix d'argent à la cotice d'azur*, [et de]

(28) Béatrix de Fiesque, *bandé de six pièces d'ar-gent et d'azur*, fils de :

Fol. 10 : quatre écus, deux à deux, l'un sous l'autre.

(29) Thomas de Savoye, *d'or à l'aigle de sable* [et de]

(30) Marguerite de Foucigny, *palé de six pièces d'or et de gueules*, fils de :

(31) Humbert de Savoye, *d'or à l'aigle de sable* [et de]

(32) Béatrix de Vienne, *de gueules à l'aigle d'or*, fils de :

Fol. 11 : quatre écus, deux à deux, l'un sous l'autre.

(33) Amé de Savoye, *d'or à l'aigle de sable* [et de]

(34) Mahaut d'Albon, *d'or au dauphin d'azur*, fils de :

(35) Humbert de Savoye, *d'or à l'aigle de sable* [et de]

(36) Gisle de Bourgoigne comté, *d'azur au lion billeté d'argent*, fille de :

Fol. 12 : quatre écus, deux à deux, l'un sous l'autre.

(37) Guillaume de Bourgoigne, *d'azur au lion billeté d'argent,* [et de]

(38) Gertrude de Limbourg, *d'argent au lion de gueules à la queue fourchée et passée en sautoir*, fils de :

(39) Renaud de Bourgoigne, *d'azur au lion billeté d'argent* [et de]

(40) Alix de Normandie, *de gueules à deux léopards d'or*, fils de :

Fol. 13 : quatre écus, deux à deux, l'un sous l'autre.

(41) Otte-Guillaume de Bourgoigne, *d'azur au lion billeté d'argent* [et de]

(42) Ermentrude de Rheims, *d'or au lion de sable,* fils de :

(43) Albert roy d'Italie, *d'or à l'aigle de sable*, [et de]

(44) Gerberge de Bourgogne, *d'azur au lion billeté d'argent*, fils de :

Fol. 14 : quatre écus, deux à deux, l'un sous l'autre.

(45) Bérenger roy d'Italie et empereur, *d'or à l'aigle de sable*, [et de]

(46) Gisle de Toscane, *de sable au lion d'or*, fils de :

(47) Evrard duc de Frioul, *d'or à l'aigle de sable*, [et de]

(48) Gisle de France, *d'or à l'aigle bicéphale de sable, membrée et nimbée de gueules, la poitrine chargée d'un écu d'azur semé de fleurs de lis d'or*, fille de :

Fol. 15 : quatre écus, deux à deux, l'un sous l'autre.

(49) Louis le Débonnaire, roy de France, *d'or à l'aigle bicéphale de sable, membrée et nimbée de gueules, la poitrine chargée d'un écu d'azur semé de fleurs de lis d'or*, [et de]

(50) Ermengarde de Hasbain, *coupé d'or et de sable au lion de l'un en l'autre*, fils de :

(51) Charlemagne empereur et roy de France, *d'or à l'aigle bicéphale de sable, membrée et nimbée de gueules, la poitrine chargée d'un écu d'azur semé de fleurs de lis d'or*, [et de]

(52) Ildegarde de Suaube, *d'or à trois léopards de sable.*

Soit 26 générations !

## BIBLIOGRAPHIE

E. BÉNÉZIT, *Dictionnaire critique et documentaire des peintres, sculpteurs, dessinateurs et graveurs...* Nouv. éd. Paris, 1976 ; article Fornazeris ; P.-M. DIOUDONNAT, *Dictionnaire des vanités*, Paris, 1972 ; t. 2, p. 149 ; *idem, Encyclopédie de la fausse noblesse et de la noblesse d'apparence*, Paris, 1976 ; p. 275 ; H. JOUGLA DE MORENAS, *Grand armorial de France...* t. 5, Paris, 1948, p. 274, article Pianelli alias Planelli de La Valette ; G. DE RIVOIRE DE LA BATIE, *Armorial du Dauphiné...* Lyon, 1867 ; E. DE SÉREVILLE et F. DE SAINT-SIMON, *Dictionnaire de la noblesse française*, Paris, c. 1975, t. 1, p. 793 ; J. TRICOU, *Armorial et répertoire lyonnais*, Paris, 1965-1976 ; (les sept fascicules publiés [A-Das] contiennent des renseignements concernant les familles alliées).

Cette bibliographie doit beaucoup à la gentillesse et à l'érudition de notre ami Hervé Pinoteau qu'il m'est très agréable de remercier ici.

## NOTES

1.  Voici la retranscription de ce texte paru dans la « Suite de la clef ou Journal historique sur les matières du tems », plus connu sous le nom de « Journal de Verdun » : *Le 9 du même mois, la mort enleva à Lyon un autre magistrat d'un sçavoir et d'un mérite distingué : c'est messire Laurent Pianelli, chevalier seigneur de La Valette. Il étoit premier président du Bureau des trésoriers de France de la généralité de Lyon ; il avoit aussi rempli avec distinction la charge de Prévost des Marchands de cette riche ville. Son corps fut enterré chez les Minimes, fondez par ses ancêtres, où le clergé de l'église d'Aisnay, sa paroisse, l'accompagnèrent. Il est mort à l'âge de 74 ans, universellement regretté dans Lyon, et partout où son mérite étoit reconnu. On lui doit l'établissement de la nouvelle Académie de Lyon, puisque l'hôtel de LaValette a servi, pour ainsi dire, de berceau à cette académie naissante pendant plusieurs années, laquelle en a tiré de fort grands secours par la belle et nombreuse bibliothèque de livres et manuscrits choisis dont elle étoit remplie. M. le président de La Valette avoit épousé demoiselle de Mascranny ; il a laissé de ce mariage un fils, conseiller en la Cour des Monnoyes de Lyon, et une fille encore plus distinguée par son mérite et par sa vertu que par sa naissance. Cependant la famille de Pianelli, dont son père est sorti, s'est toujours signalée par une grande probité de justice, d'équité, et par toutes les vertus morales, qui semblent lui être héréditaires. Cette ancienne famille de Pianelli est originaire de la ville épiscopale de Bitonte, dans la terre de Bari, au royaume de Naples, environ à trois lieues des côtes du golfe de Venise. C'étoit autrefois un marquisat qui appartenoit à la maison d'Aquaviva.*

2.  PARADIN, *Alliances généalogiques*, p. 1012.

3.  Voir *Histoire de Savoye*, p. 66.

4.  *Ibid.*, p. 64.

5.  *Ibid.*, p. 57.

6.  *Ibid.*, p. 54.

7.  *Ibid.*, p. 47.

# SCOTTISH HERALDRY FURTH OF SCOTLAND

Elizabeth A. Roads

This paper will not cover the migration of Scots to what might be termed the New World, i.e., Canada, South Africa, Australia and New Zealand. Those countries were largely settled by people of British extraction or, in the case of Quebec, by those of French extraction and, in parts of South Africa, those of Dutch extraction. Leaving that aside, much of the heraldic tradition, particularly of New Zealand and Australia and the English-speaking parts of North America and South Africa, is of British origin. One could produce a paper in itself on the links between Scotland and the English-speaking New World. The migration of Scots to these countries has been immense. There are more native Gaelic speakers in Cape Breton than there are now in Scotland. Needless to say, those Scots who settled in new countries far overseas have often looked back to Scotland when seeking to establish an armorial identity and there are numerous examples of coats of arms for those of Scottish extraction in Canada, Australia and New Zealand and other parts of the world that show their Scottish antecedents.

This paper concentrates on the armorial links between Scotland and the rest of Europe partly as this is an area that has not yet been discussed in any great detail. In times when travel was far less possible than it is nowadays, when communications took a great length of time and there were no such machines as telephones or faxes, Scots long settled abroad still held on to their Scottish identity and introduced among other items Scottish heraldry to those countries which already had, in many cases, a well-established heraldic tradition of their own.

One of the countries that had the closest of links with Scotland was, of course, France. There were numerous marriages between the Scottish and French royal families, as well as between others of note. Many Scots went to live in France as part of the Garde Écossaise and, of course, many of those with French origins settled in Scotland, some having come in the train of King David I, who for long forcibly lived in England.

The many alliances between the French and Scots and the now long familiar Auld Alliance have gone to strengthen the ties between our two countries. There were numerous Scottish Acts of Parliament that concerned France, and letters of Louis, son of the King of France, are mentioned in Scottish Acts of Parliament as early as 1282. There are many records of the commissioners concluding treaties with France; France standing by Scotland in the hostilities between Scotland and England. In 1326 Charles, King of France, entered an alliance, offensive and defensive, with Scotland against England. In the mid-16th century there were letters granted naturalising all Frenchmen in Scotland and Scots in France. Scotland was one of the principal importers of Burgundy and that wine is still very much enjoyed in Scotland. These long links between the two countries have meant that many Scots have settled in France. As early as the 13th century there were those that were described as *L'Escot* or *L'Escote*. While many of the families' names became somewhat unrecognisable from their Scottish origins, many did not. Equally, many of the names that now strike one as entirely Scottish had, in fact, a French origin. The surname of Bruce comes from the town of Brix in Normandy. But the theme that interests us is the armorial link between these families. We can look at many coats found in France and see that those coats clearly had a Scottish origin. One of the most famous French families, that of Colbert, was very much thought to be of Scottish origin. In 1771 a pedigree was recorded in Scotland on behalf of John Cuthbert of Castlehill tracing the origins of that family to very early times, back to 700. In the course of this pedigree, mention is made of the family settling in or around Edinburgh and also in France, where representatives of the family continued to flourish. The pedigree talks of the descent of John Baptiste Colbert, Marquess of Seignelay, from the family of Edward Colbert, a descendant of Cuthbert of Castlehill, and this is mentioned in an Act of the Scottish Parliament of 1686. This descent is well supported by the fact that the French family of Colbert have on their shield a serpent or snake and this closely allies them with the family of Cuthbert of Castlehill in Scotland, which also includes a snake.

Letters of naturalisation were granted to many people, for example, a Robin Carre. Subsequently, there was a family called Carre de Luzancay, of Carreville de la Hautière de Brilly et de Coulanges. The interesting thing about this family is that the arms show a chevron with thereon three pierced stars. This is clearly a direct quotation from the Scottish arms of Ker. In France, the arms of the ancestral Scottish family were often quoted or alluded to rather than repeated without difference. This is not so apparent in other countries, but it shows that France had a very well-established heraldic tradition of its own. Those who went to live there wished to quote from their Scottish arms, but to give them a French flavour so that their adoption of a new country was clearly shown.

Another example is the arms of the family of Blair. Blair of Balthayock was a long-established Scottish landed family. But when a scion of the family left Scotland in about 1590 he established himself in Béarn. The arms, when they were used in France, were not precisely the same as those used in Scotland, but the Blair link between the two families is clearly continued in the design of the arms, which in France show a shield of *Sable, a fess between three roundels with thereon an escutcheon*. The shield showing the fess and roundels is the shield of Blair of Angus as it appears in the 1542 Armorial of Sir David Lindsay of the Mount [FIGURE 1].

Another family that might not seem to be of particularly Scottish origin was the family of Coqueborne du Berry. However, the name Coqueborne looks very similar to the Scottish name Cockburn. Both families showed such very closely linked arms that one realises the family indeed descends from George Cockburn, Captain of 100 Scots in the guard of the king. His son, John or Jean, married into a French family and from this marriage descended a family that became entirely French. The name was not always Coqueborne, but one finds it as Conkebourne or indeed Coquebron. The family, settled and well established in Berry, carried for arms *Argent three cocks Gules*. Another family of the name showed these arms in a slightly different way, a *chevron between five cocks* and carried this as a quartering with another family. These arms are mentioned

by César de Grandpré as a family descending from the marriage of Adam Cockburn who was one of the Marshals of the Garde Écossaise. In Scotland, quarters appeared too for Cockburn as in the arms of Cockburn of Sutton Rock.

During the 16th century a very Scottish family became established in France, particularly in Picardy. This family descends from the family of Douglas. Mention is particularly made of the heart and the stars. The blue chief with the three silver stars is the earliest record of a Douglas coat in Scotland. The heart and crown were added a little latter to commemorate the links between the Douglases and the Bruces. Numerous members of the Douglas family, or as it became in France Duglas, settled and established firm connections with the new country. The name Duglas might not at first sight be thought to have any Scottish links at all, but the coat of arms could be nothing but Scottish. Not only is the crowned heart shown but also the blue chief with thereon three silver stars.

One more example is that of the Spens family. The Spenses have long served in foreign armies and the Swedish family of Spens is a well-known example of the links between the Spenses in Scotland and soldiering abroad. Patrick Spens went to France in 1450 as an archer in the Garde Écossaise. In 1466 he married a daughter of Pierre de Sault at Saint-Sever. Another of the family appears to have settled in the southwest of France near Bordeaux. The links with the homeland were retained by means of their coats of arms. The differences between the two French Spenses appeared only in the fourth quarter, where the southwestern branch of the family showed three gold anchors on a blue background. The first quarter in each case shows the familiar Scottish Spens coat of a red lion on a gold background, although in this case there is no bend as appears in the Scottish arms of Spens of Lathallan.

Moving further east to Russia, the links were relatively early with Scottish soldiers who were involved in Baltic battles in the early 15th century. But whether the Scots then roamed as far as the Grand Duchy of Muscovy remains unclear. At the very end of the 15th century, however, an ambassador was sent by King Christian I of Denmark to Tzar Ivan III, who was Petrus Davidis de Scotia Aberdonensis. This scholar, Peter Davidson, was a graduate of the Sorbonne. A few years later Scottish artillery experts were ordered to Moscow by King James IV of Scotland, nephew of the Danish King.

From the mid-16th century, however, the contacts with Muscovy increased and a foreign quarter was established in Moscow that included Scottish soldiers. Scottish mercenaries continued to serve in Russia throughout the 17th century with such notable Scottish names as Thomas Dalyell of the Binns; Colonel John Kinnimonth, who received a certificate of his birth and descent from the Scottish Privy Council in 1636; and the later Viscount Strathallan, William Drummond of Cromlix. Many more northeastern Scots journeyed and worked in Russia, including General Patrick Gordon from near Ellon in Aberdeenshire who left a diary with his account of life in Russia during his 38 years of service there.

In volumes of the Public Register of All Arms and Bearings in Scotland we find a number of recordings of arms for Scots serving the Tzar in a number of capacities. Many may have been there on a temporary civilian basis, such as engineers or doctors serving Catherine the Great or Peter the Great. There was John Grieve, physician in Muscovy and many others.

However, many of these people did not leave a family that became an armigerous Russian family. Work is being carried out now on what arms were granted or certified in Russia to ennobled Scots—and so many were not ennobled that there is no link between the arms recorded in Scotland for someone in the service of the Tzar and present-day Russian descendants. Luckily there are some, a few of which we can consider.

Heraldry developed in Russia in the 18th century, although early settlers may have used their familial arms from the 16th century. The earliest arms would appear to be those used by the Khomutovs who held lands near Moscow and held fiefdoms from the early 17th century. The ancestor of this family of Scottish origin was Thomas Hamilton, who arrived in Russia in 1542 with his son Peter and a daughter. In 1611 Grigorii Petrov Khomutov is listed among the city nobility of Moscow. His forenames indicate that he was Peter's son and thus grandson of Thomas. The distortion of the surname is not an entirely unbelievable change. The proof that he is of Hamilton descent is in his arms, which show a quarterly coat with in the first and fourth quarters an oak tree presumably taken from the Hamilton crest and in the second and third, two differing lions, but with over all on *an inescutcheon Purpure a heart within an orle Or between three roses Argent* and these roses look very like cinquefoils. We know that the Hamiltons of Raploch and others certainly showed a heart on their shield. Later Hamiltons who retained that form of the surname also used arms very similar to those of Hamilton of Raploch.

Perhaps one of the most notable Scoto-Russian families is that of the poet Lermontov, whose family descended from George Learmonth, who arrived in Russia via Polish service, as did so many others. In 1688 the grandsons of George produced a pedigree that showed a coat closely resembling Learmonth of Dairsie as it appears in the Great Armorial of Lord Lyon Sir David Lindsay of the Mount of 1542. The arms show *Or on a chevron Sable three mascles of the first.*

It is of particular interest to see that the simple arms of Bruce, shield of *Or, a saltire and chief Gules* is as recognisable in Russia as it is in Scotland. This chiefly coat of the name of Bruce appears as an inescutcheon on a quartered shield much as the arms of Hamilton were shown on a quartered shield. Inescutcheons were popular in Russia and show a diversion from Scottish practice. The crest is also very reminiscent of crests in various Bruce families although not the chiefly crest. My own line of Bruces has long shown an arm holding a broken sceptre. The supporters to the Russian arms of Count Bruce show a very Scottish link, being a lion and a unicorn, which supports the links between the old home and the new. This Scottish family of Bruce sent scions all over the globe and produced in Russia such notable people as Field Marshal James Bruce and his brother Robert, the First High Commandant of St. Petersburg. The links in the 18th century between the Scottish and Russian cousins were close, and Dimitry Fedesov, a present Russian scholar of note with a particular interest in Scoto-Russian connections, has studied this family in depth. He concludes that the arms granted in 1721, when James Daniel Bruce was created a Russian Count, were designed by the Grantee, the quarters behind the inescutcheon being in recognition of his valour and for his participation at the Congress of Oland as First Minister Plenipotentiary. Bruce was much concerned with heraldic and other matters in Russia and was closely involved in the founding of the Russian Heraldic Office.

It is of interest to note that the Chief of the name of Bruce, the Earl of Elgin, is a Knight of the Order of the Thistle in Scotland, and that Count Bruce was a Knight of the Russian Order of St. Andrew, and the links between the Bruces continued at that level as well.

The arms used by the family of Kar in Russia are indistinguishable from the principal arms of Kerr, even down to the motto, showing as they do, the chevron and stars and horse's head. The savage supporter does not appear common in Russian heraldry, whereas it is exceedingly common in Scottish heradry. Clearly, the Russian Kars, including Princess Katherine Golitsyn, looked to their family roots to establish their armorial identity.

However, the Russian family that perhaps springs very readily to mind is that of the Barclays de Tolly. The family settled in Riga and owes its fame to Prince Michael Barclay de Tolly of the early 19th century. The now recognizable paternal arms which appear as an inescutcheon, appear here with a shield parted per saltire that might allude to Scotland. The inescutcheon shows the unaltered Barclay coat with the motto LOYALTY AND PATIENCE translated into Russian. The Scottish Barclay coat shows a black field with thereon a *Gold chevron between three Silver crosses pattee* and this is the inescutcheon of the Russian coat. Thus the notable Russian family of Barclay de Tolly is still linked armorially very closely even in designation with the Chief of the Barclay family in Scotland, Barclay of Towie.

To return westwards, it is of interest that one of the writer's predecessors as Carrick Pursuivant of Arms to whom Scots owe much was David Reid of Robertland. He died far too young some 23 years ago, but in a paper he gave to the University of Glasgow on the background to the heraldry of Scottish emigrants to Sweden, he finished by stating that he hoped the paper might provide a stimulus to the study of one of the most important aspects of heraldry, that of international co-operation, and we seem to be fulfilling that wish. As early as the mid 13th century, a Henning Tait went on a military expedition to Sweden. The Tait arms in Sweden show a deer's head and stars similar to the Tait arms in Scotland.

Only France can rival Sweden for the number of Scots who left their homeland to serve a new country of the then established world. The Garde Écossaise was closely followed by the army of King Gustavus Adolphus as a "foreign legion," attracting the enterprising Scottish soldier of fortune.

Agnes Mure Mackenzie, in her essay *Scottish Literature to 1714*, writes: "The most famous example after the Garde Écossaise, is the Scots troops of Gustavus Adolphus. He had 34 Scots Colonels and 50 Lieutenant Colonels in his service with Scots commands and, like the King of France, had a Scots bodyguard. He was said to have made over 60 Scotsman governors of castles and towns in the conquered provinces of Germany. At the taking of Frankfurt in 1632 Lumsden's regiment alone captured 9 stands of colours from the enemy . . ." She continues "As late as 1857 the Marshal of the Kingdom of Sweden was a Hamilton." The link continues further for, in this present generation, a distinguished soldier Colonel Crafoord was Governor of Gripsholm Castle. The Scandinavian Crafoords descend from the Craufords of Fedderet and, like many others of Scottish descent, an early member of the family sought a birthbrief or certificate, in this case from the City of Aberdeen, as to the veracity of his Scottish birth and his connection with a Scottish landed family. Such certificates were not uncommon, particularly for those who settled in northern Europe and came from northeastern Scotland. They often showed the coats of arms of the various antecedents of the family. The Craufords arrived in Sweden in the early 17th century in a military context, a profession that has attracted members of the family for nearly four more centuries. The Crawfurds of Fedderet showed for arms *a Gules field with thereon an ermine fess between in chief a Gold mullet and in base a Gold garb* and these arms are the same as those borne by early members of the family in Sweden.

Another family found in Sweden since the military importation of Scots is that of Colquhoun, or now Gahn. Two brothers, Hugh and William, arrived in the mid-1560s. They are thought to have been the sons of Sir Alexander Colquhoun of Luss and certainly William used a saltire on his signet as did the Scottish family. At this period, the use of "bucket shop" heraldry or the Victorian misappropriation of arms was not the norm, and William's use of an armorial signet would lend credence to his armigerous status. His fate is unknown, but from his brother, Hugh, descends the Swedish line. Hugh was accused of impugning the honour of his brother officers—a crime so foul as to merit the loss of his head. But King John III did not desert his descendants, and in 1689, one was raised to the nobility and further in 1809,

General Pontus Gahn was raised to the nobility and took the name Gahn of Colquhoun.

A Swedish coat that is intriguing is that of Adelsköld. According to Otto Donner in 1884, Andrew Hanson, aged 14, escaped from Scotland when his parents were accused of high treason. In Sweden the descendants flourished and Johan Christian was ennobled in 1773, taking the name Adelsköld. The arrangement of pales on the Adelsköld shield presents a problem. It could indicate a somewhat unusual descent from Aragon, but more readily would indicate a descent from Keith especially in view of the Scottish connection. This raises the question, were the Hansons really Keiths assuming another name? The Keiths were well known in Sweden. Andreas Keith, Lord Dingwall, was a notable man. The illegitimate son of the Commendator of the Abbey of Deer and a nephew of the Earl Marischal of Scotland, he became Commandant of Vadstena Castle in 1574. His arms appear on his house at Baggensgaten and his links continued with Sweden even after his return to Scotland. After his death, some time in the late 1590s, his widow used a territorial designation derived from his Swedish estate. Might not other Keiths or dependants of that family with another name under a cloud in Scotland have still wished to allude back to their roots when adopting arms in Sweden?

There are two very distinctive Scandinavian coats of arms that illustrate how families retained their original identity when they physically had transcended frontiers. The name Bruce occurs again, the Swedish Bruces being descended from Bruce of Blackhall. The Swedish Bruces used a shield very closely linked with Scotland in that it shows a red saltire in chief against a gold field with a cross on the chief, this being the only element that might lead a Scottish Herald to have a question mark in his mind. On the other hand, the Swedish Murrays adapted the azure field and argent stars of Scottish Murrays to produce a most beautiful, but obviously continental European shield by incorporating a curved chevronel between the three stars [FIGURE 2].

There are so many families with Scottish/ Swedish links that more armorial research is required, but in a short paper it is only possible to dwell on the crossover that existed between the countries of northern Europe and the many Scots who served in Russia, Sweden and Finland. The name Leslie, for instance, springs to mind as a family providing soldiers throughout northern Europe. In Sweden half a dozen or more of the name are found serving in a military context. Alexander Leslie was sent to Russia by Gustavus Adolphus and the links between the Swedish and Russian families existed. The arms of these northern European Leslies were clearly derived directly from the Scottish parental family and are those of Leslie of Balquhain. Both shields show gold buckles on a blue fess [FIGURE 3].

It must not be thought that the armorial links were only with Scandinavia and Russia and France. Scots, as we know, travelled widely and far.

We have now covered a fairly wide area of Europe, but there are one or two interesting cases that we have not looked at. One of the most interesting families with a descent that has brought them into the most eminent families of Europe is that of Kirkpatrick of Conheath. These Kirkpatricks descend from the family of Kirkpatrick of Closeburn. It was the granddaughter of William Kirkpatrick of Conheath who became Eugenie Empress of the French and wife of Napoleon III. She was the daughter of Dona Marie Manuela, who was in turn the daughter of William Kirkpatrick of Conheath. William Kirkpatrick had one son and four daughters, of whom only three daughters survived. The first daughter married the Comte de Teba and his daughters became the Duchess of Berwick and Alba and the Empress Eugenie. The second daughter of William of Conheath married a kinsman of hers, Thomas James, son of another Kirkpatrick of Conheath and the third daughter married the Count of Cabarrus. An interesting story goes that when the Comte de Teba wished to marry Dona Maria Manuela Kirkpatrick it was necessary for William of Conheath to prove that he was of the right standing for his daughter to marry a Grandee of Spain. He said to his future son-in-law "You trace up to King Alphonso XI and thus if I can trace my descent to King Robert the Bruce, I suppose His Majesty will be satisfied." He obtained a certificate attesting this descent and laid this before the King who said "Let the noble Montijo marry the daughter of Fingal."

Not all Scottish-related coats in the New World came directly from Scotland. That most loved of ladies, H.M. Queen Elizabeth the Queen Mother, has an illustrious descent, but so does

Donna Adriana Lyon y Lynch and Don Arturo Lyon y Edwards in Chile. The Spanish-speaking Lyons descend from the same Earls of Strathmore as the Queen and *a blue tressured lion* appears on arms as far apart as Glamis in Perthshire and Santiago in Chile, proclaiming for all to see that it is the non-material characteristics and memories—and in this context, we include emblems—that families take when transcending frontiers.

Scotland

France

**FIGURE 1**: Blair

Scotland

Sweden

**FIGURE 2**: Murray

Scotland

Sweden

**FIGURE 3**: Leslie

# MEDICAL HERALDRY WITH FOUR RECENT EXAMPLES

Robert B. Salter

Although born during the Middle Ages in a rather brutal milieu, heraldry soon was employed to depict the compassion and caring of what was to become the medical profession. To this day, literally hundreds of associations and societies of physicians and surgeons, as well as faculties of medicine at universities and major hospitals, especially "teaching hospitals," have been granted their specific armorial bearings paying testimony to their uniqueness.

One of the fascinating things about heraldry as a hobby is that when one becomes familiar with the art and science of heraldry, including its many rules and regulations, one becomes capable of designing a coat of arms or armorial bearings for a given institution such as a professional association, a hospital or a university medical school.

Sir Anthony Wagner, a former Garter principal king of arms of England, has stated that "The worst heraldic proposals that I have known have come from committees where every member has had something different to suggest." In recent years, with Sir Anthony's quotation in mind, I have agreed to design armorial bearings for the following groups of physicians or surgeons:

- The International Federation of Surgical Colleges (IFSC)
- The Faculty of Medicine of Memorial University of Newfoundland
- The Canadian Orthopaedic Association
- The Hospital for Sick Children, Toronto

The symbolism and significance of these recently designed armorial achievements bear testimony to the fascination of medical heraldry.

## The International Federation of Surgical Colleges (IFSC)

This Federation, which includes virtually all of the major surgical colleges of the world, and which is affiliated with the World Health Organization, is concerned with the standard of undergraduate and postgraduate surgical education, as well as the quality of surgical care worldwide. While serving as president of the Federation, the author was requested to design its armorial bearings [FIGURE 1]. In the upper part of the shield is a map of the world indicating the true international composition of the Federation. Below are the two heraldic books representing teaching and learning. At the bottom, looking a little like the number 7, is a fleam, which is a very ancient type of lancet and a well-recognized heraldic symbol of surgery.

## The Faculty of Medicine of Memorial University of Newfoundland

As a former visiting professor at this relatively young medical school, the author was invited to design its armorial bearings [FIGURE 2]. At the top are the two heraldic books and the cross, which are part of the arms of the parent body, the Memorial University of Newfoundland. Since Memorial is a maritime medical school on the coast of the Atlantic Ocean, the sea has been depicted by the wavy white line. The shank of the anchor in the deep blue sea serves as the rod for the entwined snake of Aesculapius, the God of Medicine. The Latin motto, VITA CAMPUS MINISTERII, is taken from a statement by the late Sir Wilfred Grenfell, who had founded the Grenfell Medical Mission in 1892, namely "Life is a field of service."

## The Canadian Orthopaedic Association

As the president of the Canadian Orthopaedic Association (1981-1982), the author designed its armorial bearings as a personal gift to all members of the Association [FIGURE 3]. The coat of arms reflects the Association's tradition, philosophy, and goals, as well as the nature of orthopaedics.

## The crest

The crest, atop the shield, depicts the "orthopaedic tree" from Nicholas Andry's 18th-century book entitled *Orthopaedia, or the Art of Preventing and Correcting Deformities in Children*. This crooked tree, which, like a deformed child, can be helped to grow straight by the application of appropriate forces, has become the international symbol of orthopaedic surgery. For the Canadian Orthopaedic Association, the tree is a Canadian maple, the leaves of which have turned red as they do in the late autumn.

### The shield

Appearing in the middle section of the upper part of the shield is a red maple leaf with a superimposed gold fleur-de-lis from the Canadian Orthopaedic Association's original "seal," which had been designed by the late Dr. Alexander Gibson, a distinguished anatomist and orthopaedic surgeon. The maple leaf represents the Association's English-speaking members, while the fleur-de-lis represents the French-speaking members, and the common stock symbolizes the concept of national unity.

Since one of the goals of the Canadian Orthopaedic Association is *education*, the two open books in the upper part of the shield have been chosen as heraldic symbols of teaching and learning.

In the lower part of the shield, the femur represents the skeletal tissues with which orthopaedic surgeons work and, hence, symbolizes orthopaedic patient care.

The key is an ancient symbol of a closed mystery and a way by which to unlock it. Thus, the key has been chosen to represent research that the Association fosters. Because orthopaedic research involves skeletal tissues, a "skeleton key" has been depicted.

### The motto

The Latin motto, PIETATE, ARTE ET SCIENTIA CORRIGERE is a statement of orthopaedic philosophy.

*Pietate* means "with compasssion," which is so important in the art of patient care.

*Arte* is "skill," and refers to the combination of surgical dexterity and precision required in orthopaedic surgery.

*Scientia* is "knowledge," specifically scientific knowledge, which forms the basis for orthopaedic judgment.

*Corrigere* is a verb meaning to "correct, straighten, or set things right." For the sake of brevity, what we correct, namely musculoskeletal disorders and injuries, is unstated but implied.

Thus, the complete motto means: "With compassion, skill and knowledge we correct, straighten or set right (musculoskeletal disorders and injuries)."

These armorial bearings were matriculated by the Canadian Heraldic Authority in 1992.

### The Hospital for Sick Children, Toronto

In 1875, The Hospital for Sick Children was founded and, consequently, in 1975, the Hospital celebrated its Centennial. Up to that time, the Hospital had as its only emblem, a simple seal with the monogram "H.S.C." And so, as a personal centennial project, the author designed a coat of arms for the Hospital [FIGURE 4].

Five years earlier, as the Hospital's then surgeon-in-chief, the author had commissioned a well-known sculptor, Pauline Fediow, to produce for the Hospital's Rotunda, a symbolic statue of a mother supporting, rather than coddling, her young child, and helping to prepare the child for independence. This exquisite statue in bronze, which is entitled *Into Life*, is symbolic of those for whom we provide care—medical and nursing care for sick and injured children, and supportive care for their concerned parents.

Understandably, this statue is depicted as the crest atop the helmet. In the shield are depicted six heraldic devices.

The red cross of St. George of England on a white background is symbolic of the fact that the Hospital for Sick Children, Toronto, was named after a similar institution in London, England.

In a white square in the centre of the cross of St. George is the Canadian red maple leaf of the new Canadian flag. As the most appropriate national symbol of Canada, it is also symbolic of the fact that The Hospital for Sick Children is not only a municipal and provincial institution, but also a national, and even an international, institution.

The rod of Aesculapius with a serpent entwined is symbolic of the Hospital's medical staff. The glowing lamp of Florence Nightingale is symbolic of the Hospital's nursing staff.

Thus, the combined symbols for the medical and nursing staff symbolize the first responsibility of The Hospital for Sick Children, namely *patient care*.

The open book, a heraldic symbol used by many universities, is symbolic of the second responsibility of the Hospital, namely teaching at both the undergraduate and postgraduate level, as a *teaching* hospital for the University of Toronto.

The ancient heraldic key, a symbol of mystery or enigma and a method of solving it, symbolizes the Hospital's third responsibility, namely *research*. The wards of the key are intentionally drawn to form the letter "E," which may be considered a subtle indication of Excellence.

The motto begins with the word CARE in both its medical and its humanitarian sense, and is in keeping with the Hospital's Centennial slogan: "A century of care—a future of caring." The remainder of the motto is derived from an inspirational quotation by Louis Pasteur, the eminent French scientist and humanitarian, who wrote: "When I look upon a child, I am filled with admiration for that child, not so much for what it is today as for what it may become." Thus the motto is CARE FOR WHAT THE CHILD MAY BECOME.

Since the Hospital for Sick Children exists for the care of children and their concerned parents, and since we would like them to understand the humanitarianism of the motto, it is displayed in English rather than in Latin.

The coat of arms was approved and matriculated by the College of Arms of England in the Hospital's centennial year, and the Hospital was provided with the letters patent. It was necessary to apply to the English College for a grant of arms in 1975 because that was 13 years before the Canadian Heraldic Authority was established.

## Conclusion

From the descriptions of these four examples of medical heraldry, it can be appreciated that the art and science of this form of heraldry is alive and well and is enjoying a period of renewed interest and enthusiasm!

1

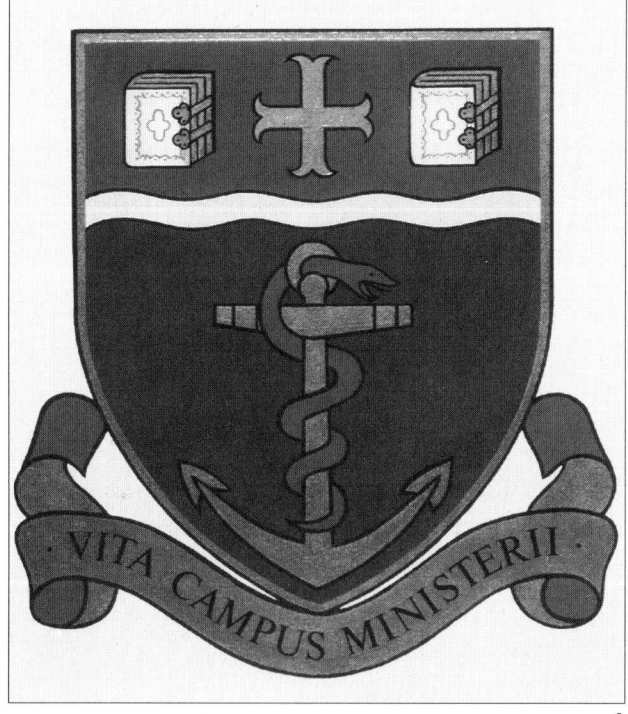

2

3

4

# SOME AMERICAN PERSPECTIVES ON HERALDRY AND VEXILLOLOGY

Whitney Smith

Since 1929 there has been a series that has always been known as the International Congresses of Genealogical and Heraldic Sciences. It is a characteristic of all sciences, both natural sciences and social sciences, to adhere to the fundamental standards of scholarship that set the scientific community apart from other areas of society. Every scientist is presumed to be objective, thorough, scholarly, and willing to alter his or her point of view—even in fundamental questions—should the facts under investigation require. In contrast, religion requires faith in the truth of certain beliefs; a political ideology likewise is founded on the commitment to advance a particular cause in a spirit of partisanship; and in the realm of esthetics, it is generally acknowledged that individuals may well have fundamental differences of opinion that cannot be adjudged scientifically as right or wrong.

Has heraldry adhered to the fundamental principles of science? It appears to this analyst that there are areas that have been consistently neglected by heraldic scholarship.[1] The subject dealt with is the development of heraldry in the United States, the specific circumstances that have led to its divergence from traditional European heraldic norms, the relationship between heraldry and flags in the United States, as well as the role that both the study of heraldry and vexillology have played in analyzing these characteristics.

Coats of arms and flags are parts of a wider realm of graphic symbolism that characterizes the social and political organization of human societies around the world. Other forms of graphic symbols include, but are not limited to, seals, logos, medals, decorations, uniforms, and regalia. The focus here is exclusively on the use of seals and arms by states and other organized political entities (i.e., civic heraldry) and on flags. Important as family and individual arms have been historically, in the United States it was state symbolism which always had primacy until it was outranked (but not displaced) by commercial symbols, such as trademarks and logos, in the late 19th century. Even today personal heraldry is a very small part of social symbolism in the United

States. Worthy as personal heraldry is of study, only a primary focus on state symbolism allows a realistic view to scholars seeking to elucidate general principles of importance for American heraldry.

It is conceded by most who have studied official symbols of the United States—the seals, coats of arms, and flags of the Federal government and the governments of the American states, territories, counties, and municipalities—that they do not generally conform to traditional heraldic norms of design and, furthermore, that they exhibit mediocre to execrable taste in their composition and execution. These symbols are, for example, characterized by naturalistic rather than stylized figures; they rely heavily on words, numbers, and other inscriptions; their colors are often impossible to describe in heraldic terms; the figures as represented are too frequently puerile renditions; and the compositions violate heraldic rules of distinctiveness, simplicity, and uniqueness. Without seeking to justify these symbols, let their history be analyzed and their logic perhaps become better understood.

The social context of every country determines the way in which its symbolism develops. Special circumstances in the United States—despite the common heritage it shares with Europe and, above all, with Great Britain—have been influential in defining the nature of American heraldry, just as American religion, literature, and other aspects of life differ from European models. Specifically, in explaining the unique nature of American heraldry, we must consider the social classes composing its citizenry, the circumstances of their emigration, the prevailing political systems before and after the American Revolution, the ideology informing American nationality, and the nature of trans-Atlantic heraldic influences.

Society in colonial America (1620-1775) was overwhelmingly composed of individuals descended from segments of the European population that had nothing to do with heraldry in their daily lives. While George Washington and a few other Americans may have had coats of arms, they were even more of a minority than their armigerous counterparts in Europe. Perhaps more importantly, their heraldic bearings did not engender the prestige and community support that the armigerous in Europe found in their societies in general and in government in particular. Moreover, the fact that many common people had emigrated to the United States because of persecution for their religious or political views, and that even the poorest of them had shown great initiative in uprooting themselves and their families from traditional patterns of life, meant that there existed in America a spirit of independence and, often, of iconoclasm generally lacking among comparable social classes in Europe. Thus public and private use of personal heraldry in the United States in the last quarter of the 18th century was very modest and there was relatively little social or political advantage to such use that might have encouraged heraldry's growth. Nevertheless, the decisive circumstances by which heraldry was "dethroned" came during the American Revolution, i.e., its war of independence.

Americans in the 1770s who utilized personal heraldry were, for the most part, among those Loyalists—about a third of the total population—who were opposed to separation from Britain. At the termination of the Revolution, a substantial number of Loyalists left the country for Canada, the Bahamas or Britain; those who remained tended to avoid flaunting prerogatives that were even less prestigious than they had been before the Revolution. The revulsion many Americans felt against the monarchical system was manifested in the tearing down of British coats of arms, statues, and similar monuments, which—if left untouched —might eventually have given a sense of dignity to a heraldry that most Americans saw as pretentious or foolish. Quite simply, in the private sector in the United States following independence, heraldry had a bad reputation. It was not so reviled as it was to be in France following the French Revolution perhaps, but only because it had never really permeated American society prior to the Revolution.

In the state sector, heraldry also suffered. Overwhelmingly, pre-Revolutionary seals and coats of arms had been created in England for use by officials whose allegiance and responsibility were to England and not to America. There were exceptions: the governments of Rhode Island, Connecticut, and Massachusetts-Bay were local ones and the symbols they adopted likewise were autochthonous. For the most part, however, the chartered companies, royal governors, and proprietors who exercised authority in the colonies of British North America relied on seals and arms that bore little or no relationship to the lives of ordinary people in the territories that those symbols represented. In many cases, the personal arms of royal governors were used on documents rather than the royal arms.

During and after the Revolution there was a total revulsion in the 13 new American states against the old symbols of public authority, resulting in the abandonment of every vestige of them. The arms of the Lords Baltimore used in Maryland were only resurrected more than a century later; moreover, Maryland is the only American state that has again taken up symbols from the era of English rule. Contrast this with the widespread use of old European symbols in other former colonies that are now independent states in the New World, Africa, the Pacific, or Asia —or with the resurrection of Ancien Régime symbols in modern France and Russia.

When Virginia, which has exhibited more aristocratic inclinations than most of the original states, looked to the 17th-century arms of the Virginia Company in the 1960s and 1980s as a possible source for new state symbols, the public attitude to this initiative was very negative. The Carolinas, Pennsylvania, and New Jersey all have pre-Revolutionary coats of arms that might be appropriate for use today and yet no suggestion that they be so used ever seems to have been made. Only rarely is there interest in traditional heraldry when consideration is being given to the creation of seals, arms, or flags for American counties, cities, or towns—even in the old Eastern seaboard states.

However unacceptable the old heraldry was to the men and women who from 1775 onward were creating new systems of government in a new country, the perceived necessity for public symbols led to the immediate adoption of alternatives. If a proclamation was embellished by engraved royal arms in the past, it must have a comparable graphic symbol under the new regime; if a wax seal previously authenticated documents, it must do so in the future. In theory, of course, *all* symbols of that kind could have been abolished: indeed, ceremonial forms such as ranks of nobility and military orders and decorations, which were part of a general European tradition in which Britain fully partook, were unceremoniously dumped by Americans. Titles of nobility have never since been recognized in the United States nor have orders of knighthood; even military decorations only very slowly began to find favor again a century after the Revolution. In theory, therefore, the seals and coats of arms which America had inherited from Britain could likewise have been abandoned. If the Puritan spirit of the Massachusetts-Bay Colony had prevailed, perhaps words alone, in written or oral form, would have substituted wherever an honorific or authenticator was called for.

In any event, the need for symbols was perceived by the fledgling republic and it was only the specific models that were rejected, not the usage. As with many other revolutionary governments, a conscious attempt was made to relate the visual content of seals and arms to the life of everyday citizens rather than to abstract historical notions or the traditional design elements of heraldry—mantling, pavilion, crown, crest, scepter, orb, lions, etc. Once that revolutionary mode of graphic expression was established, by definition it became the norm for all American heraldry. Both France and Russia underwent counter-revolutions and eventually their old symbols were partially restored. No such revulsion against revolutionary excesses ever arose in the United States and, consequently, there has never been a return to traditional European heraldic concepts of design or authority for American civic symbols. In any event, public heraldry of the late 18th century in Europe set few standards of excellence that Americans might appropriately have turned to in order to correct their own shortcomings. If anything, the closer American 18th century seals and arms were to traditional heraldry, the worse were the designs that resulted. It is rather American isolation from more recent heraldic standards in Europe that has kept the United States from attaining a better esthetic canon.

The same process can be seen in other parts of the world. In Latin America, which liberated itself from Spanish and Portuguese dominion in the early 19th century, modern civic heraldry is an outgrowth of the poorly designed Iberian models from the colonial era. Likewise in Africa, the Caribbean, and the Pacific there are many countries and territories whose contemporary civic heraldry is a reflection of mid-20th century British norms, for better or worse. In a few cases, of course, there have been positive modern external influences. For example, our late colleague Louis Mühlemann of Switzerland created designs for provincial arms in Gabon reflecting the striking simplicity of concept and rendition that characterizes Swiss heraldry, but this is very much the exception. Moreover, arms created by foreign experts inevitably raise the question of appropriateness, particularly when it is simply artistic taste rather than fundamental design principles that is being applied to a specific coat of arms.

Two other factors cannot be ignored in analyzing the origins and growth of the distinctive style of civic symbolism of America. Unlike 18th-century Europe, the young independent America was democratic and federal. While there certainly were restrictions on democracy—for example, unrepresentative state legislatures and property and gender qualifications for voting—nevertheless the average male in any of the 13 original states in the late 18th century was freer to participate in public decisions, including those affecting official symbolism, than his counterpart in almost any European country of that age. Access to the vote, constitutional and legal guarantees of civil liberties, widespread education, and economic self-reliance in the United States resulted in the strong exercise of what might have been only theoretical rights.

That fundamental American principle of popular involvement in the choice and even the designing of official symbols exists down to the present day. It expresses itself strongly in the feeling Americans have that authentic symbols can only be developed by, approved by, and utilized by those who are actually native to the area represented. Outsiders are generally not welcome in the process. Even heraldic and vexillographic experts—one is tempted to say *especially* experts —are looked upon with suspicion. Fundamentally, the unspoken American ethos denies the concept that there can be any expertise in matters of official symbolism. The design of a symbol, in the American view, is purely a matter of taste that is personal, local, and to be determined by vote. Democracy is seen not as the enemy of good heraldry but as its best guarantor.

Federalism is also a powerful force in American life, one that cannot easily be understood by those who live in countries where centralism has been the rule for centuries or where autonomous regions are looked on with suspicion. The life of public policy and administration in the

United States differs radically from what prevails in most of the world in the wide license given not only to states, but to state subdivisions—counties, cities, and towns—in many important matters. There is no national police force in the United States, for example, and in most states municipal police have a role that in many countries would be a function of the central government. Education at all levels, health care, tax policy, and public safety standards are among other areas where wide latitude exists for differences from one state or community to the next. Whatever the demerits of federalism may be in discouraging a uniform system of administration and law across the entire nation, its impact on popular attitudes creates a strong prejudice in favor of civil liberties and individual initiative.

This dramatically affects public symbolism. There is no central office in the United States responsible for designing, approving, or even registering coats of arms, seals, and flags; likewise none of the 50 states has such an office. A proposal to create such a "Bureau of Heraldry" has apparently never seriously been made, nor would such a proposal likely find any popular support. Some private initiatives have been undertaken, but almost exclusively on a profit-making basis. Their lack of success—in a country where everything is for sale and where every opportunity to exploit products, ideas, and people for profit has been attempted—is extraordinary. Nevertheless, in the 50 American states and six territories there are more than 3,000 counties and 100,000 cities and towns and the majority have seals for use in public business. Moreover, thousands of flags and hundreds of coats of arms are in existence—all developed almost entirely without any direct reference to other symbols, even those of neighboring communities.

Since heraldic knowledge is negligible, it is extraordinary that so many of the designs manage to manifest beauty and effectiveness. It is not surprising, however, that the greater number of these symbols are lacking in the fundamental respect for heraldic principles that even small communities in every European country exhibit. On the other hand, supervision by a government authority of symbol designs and their registration is never an absolute guarantee that only the best concepts and executions will be manifested in state arms, seals, and flags. Indeed, the proliferation of civic heraldry outside the United States in the decades since the end of World War II has taxed the ability of heraldists to find unique and imaginative designs. Moreover, certain canons of taste exist in each country such that even the best coats of arms and flags frequently exhibit a repetitiveness deriving from a strong family resemblance to each other. While diversity is no substitute for excellence of design, both simultaneously are not incompatible.

The great 19th century westward population dispersion in the United States left many relatively small communities physically isolated from established centers of government. This had even happened in the older states: two or three decades after the first European settlements in Massachusetts, for example, there were independent and self-sufficient cities and town existing hundreds of kilometres from the main population centers of the coast. Such communities had legislative bodies (town meetings) that made all the laws and ran local affairs in the same way that the states themselves did, albeit on a smaller scale. A seal was needed for documents such as property deeds. The choice of design naturally led community leaders to consider the milieu of the municipality since by their ethnic roots, their local economy, their religious convictions, and general mode of life they were often barely distinguishable from a thousand other communities along the eastern coast of North America. Local history was not a viable source of symbolism: when (ignoring the Indian population) the town itself was only five or 20 years old, there could be no "history" for use on its seal. The same issue arose increasingly as the population expanded westward. Creators of new communities had the common experience of being emigrants from Europe, yet that was a past which most new Americans had no interest in recalling or perpetuating. Their lives were oriented toward the circumstances they faced in their daily lives and the future.

Lacking famous battles, old castles, distinguished families, foreign invasions, and the many other sources for symbols so frequently found in Europe, these small communities—even the larger states into which they coalesced—took up images derived from their everyday existence as inspiration. The tree, the wheat sheaf, the mountain, the ox, the plow, the ship, the river, the rifle—these were their natural choices, over and over again. In addition, America was a highly literate society. Protestants were expected to read the Bible and at least a rudimentary education was nearly universal. It was natural, therefore, that words should appear in their seals—sometimes classical quotations, sometimes a biblical passage, but often only a statement of the most mundane kind such as the name of the community (or its eponym) and the date of its foundation.

Heraldic books and people familiar with heraldry were totally lacking. The only inspiration for graphic symbolism in the overwhelming majority of cases when new towns, counties, and states came into being, were the printed images of the seals used by the earliest states, many of which expressed the anti-heraldic attitudes of the Revolutionary War era. Americans instinctively felt that those symbols belonged to them: they were not the prerogative of a powerful noble class or of a distant impersonal government. Hence the seals of the states were frequently adapted artistically for use as letterheads, on newspapers, to decorate recruitment posters for local militia groups, even for presentation in commercial advertising. The point was quickly reached where their familiar pastoral scenes bore little or no resemblance to the coats of arms into which they had been (or might have been) converted.

Indeed it is a striking characteristic of American public symbolism that what modest knowledge of traditional heraldry had once existed in the United States was largely lost with the passage of years and the population expansion from East to West. While there are exceptions, basically by the end of the first 50 years of American independence all pretense had been abandoned of maintaining the fundamental artistic canons of European heraldic art. The shield had at best been reduced to a rococo border for a pictorial representation or to a beaded ring that fit in the circular compass of a seal. Supporters had become figures that dominated the emblem, when they were present at all. The crest was gone as were the torse, mantling, crown, badge, and order of knighthood. Quite simply, the designs were no longer coats of arms in appearance even though they filled that function on documents, monuments, flags, military uniforms, public buildings, and elsewhere.

It is likely that the official symbols of the American states in the 19th century were more widely used than the corresponding state and royal arms in Europe, even though they suffered in comparison with regard to purity of heraldic form. Moreover, 19th-century state heraldry in Europe was scarcely an appealing alternative for Americans as an artistic model. As a glance at any book or chart of "arms of the nations" from that era will show, the simplicity and purity of the earliest heraldry had long been abandoned. Even the smallest European states felt it necessary to overload their armorial achievements with baroque trappings and myriad quarterings. In contrast, the national coat of arms of the United States was an exemplar of simplicity, although it inspired few American examples.

An often overlooked but important source of artistic inspiration for the public symbols of the new country may be found in the "emblems" that flourished in 17th and 18th century Europe. These *imprese* showed allegorical scenes —often classical figures accompanied by mottoes or inscriptions intended to have a moral or inspirational value. Not only animals and human figures, but scenes from nature and neo-classical architecture abounded. Anyone familiar with the cavalry standards of the Thirty Years' War, the English Civil War, and other contemporary conflicts will recognize similar pictorial themes in the flags of the American Revolution. That tradition as an inspiration for military colors died off in Europe before the counterpart American trend was exhausted in the mid-19th century, but the influence of these images has never totally been extinguished in non-military American symbolism.

To represent an allegorical scene in naturalistic detail and to reinforce that by inscriptions became the standard form of public symbolism in the United States, displacing the early heraldic ideal of a single charge on a simple shield: the seal of Iowa is a perfect example of this trend. The simple elegance of the Massachusetts coat of arms of 1780 belies the significance of the new artistic approach, as reflected in the 1775-1780 seal of Massachusetts-Bay. Of the original 13 states, in only four—Massachusetts, Connecticut, New Jersey, and Rhode Island—did the symbols fully meet the traditional heraldic ideal. Of the remaining 36 states and six territories, with a total of 18 arms and 42 seals, only five seals (those of Texas, Louisiana, Mississippi, Washington, and the restored Maryland seal) and only five coats of arms (those of the District of Columbia, Texas, Mississippi, North Dakota, and Maryland) fully qualify as being in the heraldic tradition, although there are some others that approximate the traditional heraldic form—the arms of New York, Utah, Colorado, and Missouri.

American states are free to change their seals and arms at will, and over the years many have modified existing ones or adopted completely new ones, yet North Dakota is the only state that in doing so has turned to traditional heraldry. (Its coat of arms, incidentally, has very little recognition or use.) Nor can the absence of good design in the states and territories be attributed in most cases to their lack of population, educational achievement, economic resources, or interest in history. California, for example, has over 30 million people, 142 colleges and universities, and an annual production of goods and services valued at $850 billion. In contrast, California's level of public graphic symbolism may arguably be said to compare with what is found in El Salvador and Papua New Guinea.

The American design model used for seals and arms has carried over into American flags. While no statistical analysis has ever been undertaken, it seems likely that the largest category among all American flags is what might be called the "field-and-emblem" pattern, the latter including logos, seals, designs based on *imprese*, and some genuine coats of arms. Military colors from the Revolution to the present as used by the Federal armed forces, by state militia, local and irregular troops, and by the Confederate States of America have all relied heavily on this pattern in which the background is a single solid color bearing a fairly complex central emblem and, occasionally, a distinctive canton. During the Civil War of 1861-1865 especially, when the state militias of the North became the basis for the armies that defended the Union, this pattern was indelibly impressed on the American national consciousness as the proper one for all flags not based on the Stars and Stripes. The familiarity of those designs and the involvement of Civil War veterans in the adoption process for state and local flags strongly encouraged the transformation of that model from one employed only for the unique color of a military force to usage for any general purpose flags made in quantity. New flags were created after the same model by those whose limited knowledge of alternative flag designs prevented their questioning the appropriateness of the field-and-emblem pattern. Whether such flags might have followed traditional heraldic models if such had been available or if heraldry itself had been better known is a moot question.

The complexity of those seals and arms and the multiplicity of their colors made them expensive and difficult to manufacture, as well as almost impossible to distinguish when the flags of many states or cities were flying together. Nevertheless there was and is tremendous loyalty to these designs. Among the 24 states that have altered their flags in the 20th century, New Mexico is the only one to reject this vexillographic tradition and adopt a flag acceptable to traditional heraldry. Indeed, the other state flags that have been changed have all been replaced by worse designs. Moreover, emphasis on this type continues in contemporary America. Flag manufacturers routinely illustrate the field-and-emblem type of flag in their catalogs as a guide for organizations (schools, clubs, color guards, etc.) and for cities and counties that might want to create designs. Overwhelmingly, agencies of the Federal government and their "vexilliferous" officers have such flags. Company flags and advertising banners in the commercial world, whether or not professionally designed as part of a "corporate identity program," typically acquire a flag as an afterthought when a logo has been created. These logos, because they already contain several colors, are usually placed against a white background, although dark blue is sometimes used instead—as for government flags.

Despite the overwhelming popularity of this basic design, a vigorous alternative tradition dating back to the earliest days of European settlement in North America nevertheless exists. The original models were English naval flags—the Red Ensign, the Union Jack, and various signal flags—and, to a lesser extent, the colors carried by infantry. These non-heraldic flags tended to make use of two or three contrasting colors with distinctive design elements such as stripes, crosses, and simple badges. The earliest such flag created in America on English models dates from 1634, but the real flowering of these flags began just prior to the Revolutionary War, as Americans actively sought distinctive symbols for themselves. The British red, white, and blue continued to serve as the primary colors but green, yellow, and buff—even orange—were not unknown. Popular symbols included the eagle, crescent, pine tree, anchor, star, beaver, sheaf of rice, liberty cap, snake, sun, clouds, wreath, and sword. There were also inscriptions, but usually these were brief one-to-four-word phrases written large for visibility.

This new vexillographic style produced several flags still in use—the Stars and Stripes, the Pine Tree flag, the *Don't Tread on Me* flag, the Palmetto flag, and the Coast Guard flag. While there was an original or standard form for most of these, popular designs quickly became the subject of great variation. For example, the Stars and Stripes has existed in at least 200 versions used by the nation as a whole, by individual states, by military units, as a signal flag or personal rank flag—even by individuals determined to break their allegiance to the United States by overthrowing the government or forming a new nation. No other pattern has been so popular a model, but geometric figures—triangles, borders, circles, diagonal stripes, and even distinctive flag shapes—have also been put into use both officially and unofficially. The Confederate Battle flag, one of the most striking and widely used flags in the United States today, is not only an important example of the trend, but itself constitutes one of the basic design patterns frequently adapted to entirely new flags. These types—what might be called the "geometric flag," the "Stars and Stripes variant," and the "Battle flag variant"—have also not infrequently been combined with the field-and-emblem model. Thus the striking diagonally divided field of a civic flag may have a seal in the center even though from the standpoint of distinctiveness, cost effectiveness, and classic heraldic simplicity that seal is redundant.

While some heraldic writers have been ingenious in describing many modern flags according to the traditional language of the blazon, that alone does not determine whether a given design conforms to traditional canons of good heraldry. In fact, only a small percentage of the flags used in the United States, past and present, can legitimately be qualified as proper heraldry. The percentage of seals that could pass muster as heraldic is still less and even coats of arms in American state and civic heraldry often fail to meet or approximate heraldic standards. Yet overwhelmingly American civic heraldry is based primarily on seals, secondarily on flags, and only rarely on coats of arms. This fact raises a serious question—one that brings us back to the starting point of this analysis, namely the scientific nature of heraldic studies.

If the official and unofficial symbolism of a given country—and the United States is not unique in its symbols in this regard—incorporates very little that corresponds to the traditional laws of heraldry in terms of design, yet functionally performs in ways that are the same as or parallel to the usage of correct coats of arms as found in most European countries, what is the proper attitude for the scholarly investigator? Or, framed differently, does such non-heraldic symbolism deserve the equal attention of those who analyze heraldry? The question is particularly important in part because heraldry, until recently, has had a near monopoly in the realm of all studies relating to official symbols. The amount of research and publication about orders of knighthood, ceremonial regalia, military insignia, and seals has been modest in contrast to the volume of heraldic work produced. Research about flags was until recently also limited and practical guides (for those who needed to know the designs of the flags displayed at sea) constituted much of what was produced.

Heraldry has been the dominant theme in studies relating to official symbolism, yet heraldic scholars frequently have taken the position, overtly or covertly, that any symbols not conforming to traditional standards of heraldic correctness are to be dismissed as unworthy of serious attention. That attitude continues even today and broad areas of official symbolism—including most logos and non-armigerous seals and many flags—are generally ignored in heraldic publications. Moreover, the rejection of such symbols is not simply benign neglect: editorials, letters to the editor, lectures, private conversations, and other forms of communication make clear that there is an active hostility on the part of many heraldists to designs and usages that do not conform to the laws of heraldry.

This attitude is perhaps understandable in a country like Britain where the sovereign is traditionally "the font of all honor" and where control of symbols—who may claim what title, what corporation or individual may or may not display a certain flag, what graphic symbol encroaches on another by its similarity of design, etc.—are directly related to maintenance of the existing political and social system. Yet regardless of the self-interest that a government institution might have in preserving and promoting the heraldic status quo, the heraldic scholar presumably has an obligation to universality and objectivity in the pursuit of scientific knowledge. To ignore or denounce symbols that do not conform to good heraldic taste is inadequate and, ultimately, unacceptable as a way of dealing with symbols that clearly have widespread currency.

It is not simply the civil heraldry of the United States that has been treated in this fashion by American and non-American scholars and writers, but other symbols as well—for example, emblems of political parties and religions or the official arms of non-Western style used by many Third World countries and Communist countries. It is also remarkable that heraldic scholars have long looked at flags as being a subdivision of their own study, yet overwhelmingly books on heraldry either do not mention flags at all or present the subject in a few pages with an underlying assumption that flags are only manifestations of coats of arms in cloth form. It is surprising that so little attention has been given even to the study of *heraldic* flags by scholars of heraldry. For example, only 4.8% of the lectures delivered in the seven published proceedings of the International Congresses of Heraldic and Genealogical and Heraldic Sciences held between 1929 and 1968 relate to flags.

While there is no lack of examples of "bad heraldry" in the public symbolism of the United States, from the standpoint of the longevity of these symbols in American society, their number and the frequency of use, their permeation of popular and commercial culture, their official standing, and the concrete roles they play that parallel the "good heraldry" found in other countries, these symbols deserve serious and exhaustive examination as an important social phenomenon. For all their bad heraldry, they reflect that strong and ancient human impulse of choosing colors and emblems to represent individual and collective beliefs and activities.

If heraldry is truly to be a science, therefore, the challenge is for it to recognize the importance of such symbols, in the United States and elsewhere, that do not conform to traditional concepts of heraldry, and to apply objective, rigorous standards of scholarship in analyzing them. It is not necessary to promote or even to approve of the forms and practices and presumptions implicit in these non-heraldic symbol systems in attempting to analyze and document them, any more than a scholar of slavery or the Inquisition or the Holocaust need be an apologist for the subject areas he or she studies.

In this regard, it seems that certain differences exist between heraldry and vexillology. As conceived and developed since its formal beginnings 30 years ago, vexillology is dedicated to the scientific study of flags of all kinds, all eras, and all societies. Of course, many vexillologists hold strong points of view about the appropriateness of design and use of certain flags, yet the vexillologist *qua* vexillologist, in seeking to understand the roll of flags in human society, gives the same basic attention to an advertising pennant as to a royal standard. Those few who seek to promote a particular flag or flag usage under the guise of vexillology always do so improperly and without support from the world community of vexillologists.

Good and bad design for flags is recognized as properly being in the realm of vexillography, where questions of taste and preference rather than objectivity and rigorous analysis prevail. Whereas vexillology makes a clear distinction between the theses developed by scholars on the one hand and the subject matter of their study (namely, flags) on the other, in contrast, heraldry is often implicitly or explicity defined by the specific designs and practices that developed in Europe some 800 years ago as summarized by the traditional "laws of heraldry." Expressed somewhat differently, vexillologists, in principle, always stand apart from the flags they study, to derive scientific principles from knowledge of what is manifested in actual usage, rather than to evaluate such usage by applying a priori principles. The flag-waver holds a given flag sacred and does everything in his power to exalt that flag, but the vexillologist is not beholden to any flag nor to any immutable laws about what constitutes their proper use and design. In contrast, it would seem that heraldry has not completely separated itself from the agenda that was originally developed to preserve the exclusivity of arms granted, confirmed, or altered and the privileges of those responsible for those actions.

Seeking to preserve good heraldry as an art form is a noble goal, but its pursuit should never be at the expense of the advancement of heraldry as a science. To like or dislike American civic symbolism or some other form of "bad heraldry" should not be the goal for heraldry as a science, as it is for heraldry as an art. Like vexillology and other aspirant social sciences dealing with graphic forms in the social *milieux* of humankind, heraldry as a science must treat all symbols seriously by giving them rigorous, objective scrutiny.

## NOTES

1.   Analyzing why this may have been the case can only be hinted at in this presentation, which is primarily an essay, based on years of dealing with the points in question and without the rigorous documentation that a complete analysis requires. This lecture therefore must be considered only as a preliminary statement for a work in progress. Criticisms and comments will be welcomed by the author.

# LA CÉRAMIQUE ARMORIÉE D'IMPORTATION, REFLET DU NATIONALISME CANADIEN (1887-1921)

Auguste Vachon

L'emblème du Dominion du Canada avant l'acquisition d'armoiries officielles en 1921 rassemblait sur un écu les emblèmes des provinces et territoires canadiens. On y voyait des armoiries officielles, des armoiries conçues par des héraldistes amateurs et des motifs tirés de sceaux provinciaux. Autour de l'écu venaient s'agencer des éléments aussi de libre adoption : la couronne royale britannique, le castor et les feuilles d'érable. Si cette macédoine héraldique s'était constituée après 1867, date de la Confédération, elle comprenait des éléments dont l'histoire remonte à la Nouvelle-France, voire à la découverte même du pays.

## La recherche d'un emblème national

Au printemps de 1867, les délégués des quatre provinces canadiennes d'alors, se trouvant à Londres pour élaborer les conditions de leur union, furent appelés à proposer un emblème approprié pour la province qu'ils représentaient[1]. Ayant examiné les propositions soumises, le roi d'armes Jarretière accepta sans modifications les armoiries de la Nouvelle-Écosse et de la province de Québec. Il voulut cependant substituer au cheval blanc de Hanovre, proposé pour le Nouveau-Brunswick, un léopard d'or représentant mieux le duché de Brunswick[2]. Les délégués de la province d'Ontario, pour leur part, avaient demandé une branchette d'érable à trois feuilles et un chef au drapeau de l'Union (l'Union Jack), les trois croix du drapeau devant représenter le mélange presqu'égal d'Anglais, d'Écossais et d'Irlandais dans la province.

Vraisemblablement, du fait qu'il avait déjà accepté les feuilles d'érable pour le Québec et qu'il n'est pas d'usage de concéder intégralement un symbole national aussi important que l'Union Jack, Jarretière proposa pour l'Ontario : *de sinople à une gerbe de blé d'or, à un chef d'argent chargé d'une croix de gueules* (croix de saint George) [FIGURE 13][3]. Les délégués de l'Ontario firent, cependant, savoir au duc de Buckingham et Chandos, secrétaire d'État pour les colonies, qu'ils ne voulaient pas se départir de leurs feuilles

d'érable. Le duc demanda alors à Jarretière de respecter leurs vœux en éliminant la gerbe de blé en faveur de la branchette d'érable originale. Mais la croix de saint George, qui avait pu flotter sur le territoire ontarien au temps des premières explorations[4], était conservée[5].

Afin de comprendre les armoiries proposées pour le Québec, il faut remonter au 24 juillet 1534 alors que Jacques Cartier prenait possession du pays en hissant, sur la côte de Gaspé, une grande croix portant les armoiries du roi de France : *d'azur à trois fleurs de lis d'or*. Par la suite, on arborait les armoiries royales à presque chaque prise de possession d'un nouveau territoire. Elles figuraient aussi sur les principaux édifices, les places publiques et les forts. La bannière de France, une réplique des armoiries, ne fut, à ce qu'il semble, déployée au Canada que dans la première décennie du XVIIe siècle[6].

Les délégués du Québec, George-Étienne Cartier et Hector Langevin, avaient demandé l'inclusion de deux fleurs de lis dans les armoiries de leur province. On doit vraisemblablement cette initiative surtout à Cartier, le délégué le plus influent, qui revendiquait un lien de parenté avec Jacques Cartier. La volonté de George-Étienne de se rattacher à la lignée du découvreur allait aussi se refléter dans les armoiries que les hérauts d'armes d'Angleterre allaient lui concéder le 8 août 1868, juste avant son accession au titre de baronnet de l'Empire britannique. Ces armoiries, presqu'identiques à celles qu'on attribuait à l'époque à Jacques Cartier, ressemblaient étrangement aux armoiries de Saint-Malo, ville natale de l'explorateur. Le cimier qui se composait d'un écu *de gueules à une fleur de lis d'or* appendu à une ancre faisait aussi allusion au marin de Saint-Malo et aux origines françaises de George-Étienne. Il est presqu'assuré que c'est lui qui voulut placer dans les armoiries du Québec les fleurs de lis que son « ancêtre » avait arborées en prenant possession du Canada[7].

En 1763, la Nouvelle-France était cédée à l'Angleterre et le rôle de la fleur de lis comme marque du roi de France sur ce territoire prenait officiellement fin. Les troupes britanniques enlevèrent de la ville de Québec au moins deux grandes sculptures aux armoiries royales de France pour les apporter comme trophées en Angleterre. D'autres de ces sculptures semblent être restées sur place jusque vers la fin du siècle[8].

Comme les Canadiens français avaient, entretemps, délaissé les fleurs de lis pour le castor et la feuille d'érable[9], des délégués autres que Cartier et Langevin auraient vraisemblablement choisi ces deux emblèmes sans se soucier des lis. On peut même penser que le retour des lis au pays pour représenter les origines françaises des Québécois reflétait la seule volonté de Cartier. Quoiqu'il en soit, il ne s'agissait pas d'un choix de type populaire et le Québec acquérait ses lis en vertu d'un décret de la reine Victoria daté du 26 mai 1868[10]. Ainsi les fleurs de lis, qui jadis marquaient la souveraineté des rois de France sur de vastes territoires de l'Amérique du Nord qui incluaient le Québec, étaient redonnées officiellement aux Québécois par la reine d'Angleterre. Leur présence dans les armoiries du Québec revêtait, cependant, une grande importance car, à partir du début du XXe siècle, les Québécois s'attacheront de plus en plus à cette ancienne fleur royale[11]. Aujourd'hui, ils en ont fait leur emblème national par excellence, reléguant de plus en plus le castor et la feuille d'érable au rang d'emblèmes des Canadiens anglais.

La concession des lis au Québec se fit avec prudence car, en 1801, la Grande-Bretagne avait enlevé de ses propres armoiries les trois fleurs de lis signifiant sa prétention au trône de France. En rendant hommage aux origines françaises des Québécois, la Grande-Bretagne voulait aussi éviter que les lis concédés au Québec en 1868 soient interprétés comme une allusion à cette ancienne prétention. Cartier et Langevin semblaient être au courant de ce problème, car ils n'avaient demandé que deux fleurs de lis et non pas les trois lis de France. Les hérauts d'Angleterre y apportèrent la touche finale en inversant les couleurs de l'ancienne France de sorte que, en incluant deux fleurs de lis seulement, et d'azur sur or, on évitait de réanimer l'ancienne prétention, tout en signalant un changement de régime. Ainsi les lis figurant en chef, la place d'honneur, symbolisaient simplement les origines françaises des habitants de la province : c'est ce que souhaitaient les délégués[12].

Notons que plusieurs emblèmes des nations fondatrices se retrouvaient dans ces quatre armoiries : chardons d'Écosse, fleurs de lis de France et divers emblèmes de l'Angleterre. Seul l'Irlande manquait, les hérauts n'ayant pas retenu pour l'Ontario l'Union Jack avec ses trois croix.

Les délégués à Londres avaient aussi demandé que les armoiries des provinces unies soient celles des quatre provinces en écartelé. Le décret de concession contenait bien cet écu [FIGURE 4], mais précisait qu'il devait servir, non pas d'emblème au nouveau pays, mais de sceau commun aux quatre provinces confédérées sous le nom de « Dominion du Canada »[13]. Cet écartelé avait-il aussi le statut d'armoiries du pays? Si le décret ne concédait pas explicitement des armoiries au Canada, on peut prétendre qu'il le faisait implicitement, car les armoiries figurant sur le sceau d'un pays sont normalement celles du pays. Par contre, il est probable que, tout en s'efforçant de respecter les vœux des délégués, les hérauts n'avaient pas voulu que l'écartelé devienne des armoiries nationales. Ils se rendaient sûrement compte que les armoiries d'une confédération se devaient d'être plus que les armes de ses composantes rassemblées sur un écu.

Les lacunes de l'écartelé comme emblème national apparurent dès que Sa Majesté enjoigna aux frères Wyon de Londres de préparer le grand sceau du nouveau pays. Rien dans cet emblème ne représentait le Canada comme une entité en soi avec un gouvernement central ou comme une monarchie constitutionnelle dont les pouvoirs découlaient du souverain. C'est sans doute ce qui motiva les frères Wyon à opter pour un sceau de majesté où les armoiries des provinces figuraient, mais en temps qu'éléments secondaires répartis individuellement de chaque côté de la reine Victoria trônant avec sceptre et orbe [FIGURE 14][14].

L'écartelé ne disparut pas pour autant puisqu'on commença à l'utiliser comme emblème national. Rien d'étonnant à cela puisque tous les officiels, aussi bien au Canada qu'en Angleterre, semblaient croire à l'époque qu'il s'agissait d'armoiries en règle[15].

Lorsque de nouvelles provinces furent créées, on ajouta à l'écu du Canada, les motifs qui se trouvaient sur leur sceau. L'ignorance des Canadiens en matière d'armoiries n'était pas entièrement à blâmer pour cette curieuse initiative. Dès 1865, le Secrétaire d'État pour les colonies avait informé le gouverneur général que les navires de

Sa Majesté, ou à son service, devaient arborer le Blue Ensign avec le sceau ou l'insigne colonial sur le battant. Il demandait qu'on lui procure un dessin de ces marques et, en 1875, précisait que les provinces qui n'avaient pas d'armoiries devaient fournir à l'Amirauté britannique un dessin « en couleurs » de leur sceau [16].

S'inspirant de cette source officielle, les Canadiens placèrent armoiries et sceaux sur un même pied de sorte que l'écu du Canada de 1876 à 1902 environ, se composait des armoiries de l'Ontario, du Québec, de la Nouvelle-Écosse et du Nouveau-Brunswick et des sceaux du Manitoba, de la Colombie-Britannique et de l'Île-du-Prince-Édouard [FIGURE 1] [17]. Dès 1871, on somma l'écu de la couronne royale et on l'entoura de feuilles ou de branches d'érable [18]. Vers 1876, un castor, parfois sur un rondin, était posé sous l'écu [19]. Si ces ornements extérieurs et l'écu surchargé n'avaient rien d'officiel, les Canadiens avaient, comme les frères Wyon auparavant, senti instinctivement le besoin d'inclure des éléments signifiant que le Canada n'était pas uniquement la somme de ses provinces et territoires. La couronne marquait leur attachement à la monarchie ; le castor et la feuille d'érable, emblèmes du terroir, les représentaient comme nation.

En 1903, on assiste à un nouveau remaniement de l'écu. Un emblème conçu en 1895 par le chanoine anglican Arthur John Beanlands de Victoria pour un nouveau sceau de la Colombie-Britannique vient s'ajouter à l'écu [20]. S'y ajoutent aussi des emblèmes pour l'Île-du-Prince-Édouard, les territoires du Nord-Ouest et le Yukon créés de 1901 à 1903 par Edward Marion Chadwick, avocat et héraldiste à ses heures. Chadwick voulait un écu, dit « complet », c'est-à-dire, symétrique et représentant tout le pays. Avec les nouveautés de Beanlands et de Chadwick, le sceau du Manitoba et les quatre armoiries originales, l'écu contenait désormais neuf quartiers posés 3, 3 et 3 [FIGURE 2] [21]. De 1905 à 1906, le Manitoba, la Colombie-Britannique, la Saskatchewan et l'Île-du-Prince-Édouard s'étant dotés d'armoiries en règle, un nouveau remaniement de l'écu s'opéra, les emblèmes officielles remplaçant ceux d'adoption. Afin de conserver la symétrie des neuf, on fit disparaître de l'écu l'emblème des Territoires du Nord-Ouest de Chadwick pour y insérer celui de la Saskatchewan [FIGURE 3]. Lorsque l'Alberta se dota d'armoiries en 1907, l'emblème du Yukon connaissait le même sort [22].

Dès 1904, Joseph Pope, alors sous-secrétaire d'État, avait tenté de freiner cette « anarchie » en imprimant une illustration de l'écartelé original qu'il croyait être officiellement concédé [FIGURE 4] [23]. Il n'eut qu'un succès mitigé ; l'écu surchargé et ses ornements extérieurs de libre adoption retenaient toujours la faveur du public. Ils s'imposaient même à la vue de tous sur le battant d'une version du Red Ensign qu'on utilisait alors comme drapeau du Canada [24].

## Les emblèmes populaires dans la céramique

Si l'écu du Canada se montrait aussi changeant que la mode, les trois éléments ajoutés comme ornements extérieurs — couronne, castor et feuilles d'érable — donnaient à l'ensemble une certaine stabilité. Plusieurs des sources pour l'étude de ce phénomène — imprimés, médailles, sceaux et monuments — affichent le plus souvent un caractère formel. Par contre, les souvenirs comme les bibelots, les cartes postales et la céramique répondent à la dynamique d'un marché. La céramique armoriée, pour sa part, se particularise du fait qu'elle est produite exclusivement par des compagnies étrangères ayant pour seul souci de vendre leur produit aux Canadiens.

En 1881, un importateur canadien du nom d'Adam Darling commanda à la compagnie Havilands des États-Unis une réplique d'un service qu'elle avait fabriqué pour la Maison-Blanche, mais avec cette singularité que chacune des pièces était ornée des armoiries du Canada. Il s'agissait là, cependant, d'un service unique et non pas de production en série [25]. Le premier grand tirage connu aux armoiries du Canada a été l'œuvre d'un potier de Westbourne Grove à Londres nommé J. Abraham. L'année du jubilé d'or de la reine Victoria, en 1887, il réalisa une assiette très chargée rendant hommage à l'Empire britannique. On y trouve de tout : des déesses, des habitants de divers pays, des statistiques, des portraits, des armoiries, des scènes d'exploits et de guerre, une mappemonde et un cadran des fuseaux horaires. Les armoiries du Canada qu'on y voit comprennent les armoiries des quatre provinces et les sceaux du Manitoba, de la Colombie-Britannique et de l'Île-du-Prince-Édouard, l'écu étant surmonté du traditionnel castor rongeant sa branchette d'érable [FIGURE 5] [26]. Parmi les pièces produites en série pour la période 1887-1896, on ne connaît que cette assiette et deux autres aussi réalisées par Abraham. Ces dernières sont décorées des mêmes armoiries et du portrait d'un homme politique canadien, l'un étant sir John A. Macdonald, l'autre Edward Blake. Dans les trois cas, la forme de l'assiette et la représentation des armoiries sont identiques.

La production de pièces pour être vendues dans tout le Commonwealth continuera jusqu'à nos jours. On remarque, cependant, que plusieurs des pièces « impériales » destinées au marché canadien contenaient un message pro-canadien plus fort que celui se référant à l'Empire. Dans un service de table fabriqué à Karlsbad vers 1900, par exemple, on n'hésite pas à entourer la reine Victoria du castor, de branches d'érable et des armoiries des provinces [FIGURE 6]. Un autre service de table produit vers 1899 par William Lowe de Longton en Angleterre mêle des emblèmes canadiens à ceux de l'Empire. Au centre, un médaillon porte le slogan « CANADA OUR COUNTRY », et dessous, un listel arbore l'inscription « THE MAPLE LEAF FOR EVER ». En l'examinant à la loupe, on constate que le grand drapeau à dextre est le Red Ensign canadien portant sur le battant l'écartelé surmonté de la couronne royale. On constate également que le castor et sa branchette d'érable sont en chef de l'assiette alors que les armoiries de Grande-Bretagne, assez réduites, sont reléguées à la pointe [FIGURE 7].

Par la sincérité de leurs messages, ces pièces indiquent clairement que les Canadiens commençaient à développer une conscience nationale. Le chemin de fer Canadien-Pacifique, terminé en 1885 et liant le territoire d'un océan à l'autre, avait contribué à cette prise de conscience. La crainte d'annexion par les États-Unis disparaissait aussi avec l'avènement d'une période de prospérité et de progrès remarquables, par exemple l'industrialisation des villes et le peuplement de l'Ouest par l'immigration[27].

Si les souvenirs illustrant les aspects pittoresques du Canada trouvaient un marché à l'étranger dès le XVIIIe et davantage au XIXe siècle, ces souvenirs mirent plus de temps à trouver preneurs au pays. Les mémentos des premiers colonisateurs étaient ce qu'ils avaient amené de leur pays d'origine : bijoux, portraits, meubles, vaisselle, etc. Dans le sens inverse, les administrateurs, les troupes, les missionnaires et visiteurs de passage

en Nouvelle-France recueillaient des curiosités pour les apporter dans leur pays d'origine. Il en fut de même pour leurs homologues britanniques venus à partir de 1759[28].

Des estampes de sites pittoresques ont constitué la première forme de souvenirs commerciaux canadiens. Pendant longtemps, ces estampes étaient imprimées en Angleterre et vendues surtout à l'étranger. Une première série de vues d'Halifax imprimées au Canada en 1819 fut suivie de vues de Montréal dans les années 1830 et 1840[29]. Certes les Canadiens achetaient de ces estampes, mais une part du marché se retrouvait aussi chez les troupes britanniques jusqu'à leur départ en 1871.

Ces séries canadiennes, imprimées ici ou en Angleterre, servaient à illustrer des services de table produits en Angleterre et vendus tant aux États-Unis qu'au Canada. Pendant plusieurs décennies, les Canadiens manifestaient peu d'enthousiasme pour cette céramique illustrée de scènes de leur pays, ce qui indique que le marché pour des souvenirs de type canadiens demeurait faible au Canada[30].

À part Halifax et quelques autres endroits dans les Maritimes, le Canada considéré pittoresque à l'époque s'étendait de la ville de Québec aux chutes Niagara[31]. Les séries illustrant l'Ouest demeuraient plutôt épars, leur nombre étant comparable à celles liées à la recherche d'un passage maritime au nord du pays[32]. Ce n'est qu'avec la publication du *Picturesque Canada* de George Monro Grant en 1882 qu'est présenté au public canadien un recueil d'images représentatives de leur pays d'un océan à l'autre[33].

La céramique armoriée comporte des analogies avec le *Picturesque Canada* de Grant. Sur le plan emblématique, elle couvre le pays d'un océan à l'autre et exprime un patriotisme naissant. L'ouvrage de Grant illustre la beauté et la grandeur du pays alors que la céramique met en évidence les emblèmes qui l'identifient et qu'à l'époque on qualifiait de « souvenirs patriotiques »[34].

Les tableaux qui suivent contiennent les pièces ayant été inventoriées par l'auteur pendant près d'une décennie. Cet échantillon nous semble valable car y sont représentés tous les grands producteurs de céramique armoriée canadienne.

TABLEAU 1 : armoiries du Canada 1897-1903

| Pays de fabrication | Angleterre | Bohème | Allemagne | Totaux |
|---|---|---|---|---|
| Écu seul | | | | |
| + couronne | 7 | | | 7 |
| + feuilles d'érable | | | 1 | 1 |
| + couronne et feuilles d'érable | 2 | | | 2 |
| + feuilles d'érable et castor | 1 | | | 1 |
| + couronne, feuilles d'érable et castor | 4 | 10 | 4 | 18 |
| TOTAUX | 14 | 10 | 5 | 29 |

Le modèle presque unique pour la période de 1897 à 1903 est l'écu sommé de la couronne royale seulement. On n'a trouvé que trois pièces, produites à Karlsbad en Bohème et appartenant à un service de table, où le castor et des branches d'érable et de chêne viennent s'ajouter autour de l'écu [FIGURE 8]. Il est à noter aussi que, pour cette période, la production combinée de la Bohème et de l'Allemagne est plus importante que celle de l'Angleterre.

Après Goss, The Foley China (Wileman & Co., plus tard Shelley) fut, à partir de 1903 environ, la seconde compagnie à produire de la céramique armoriée sur une grande échelle en Angleterre. Elle fut cependant la toute première à exporter une importante production au Canada. Lors du jubilé de diamant de la reine Victoria en 1897, elle avait exporté des pièces ornées des armoiries royales de Grande-Bretagne et estampillées du nom de villes canadiennes[35]. Foley découvrit alors le marché canadien et commença à l'exploiter[36]. Cette céramique était souvent du genre « Dainty White » conçue en 1896 par Rowland James Morris, pour Foley. Il semble même, qu'à part les souvenirs du jubilé, les toutes premières pièces armoriées étaient destinées au marché canadien. Il s'agissait d'une porcelaine d'os très blanche et mince d'une qualité exceptionnelle ornée de cannelures, de coquilles et, sur les poignées, de motifs floraux en or[37]. Certaines de ces pièces étaient de type utilitaire, crémier, bol à sucre, bol à fruit, etc., parfois fabriquées pour des hôtels précis. Les rebords de pièces destinées au Canada, prenaient à l'occasion la forme des dentelures de la feuille d'érable : l'érablé avant la lettre du langage héraldique canadien [FIGURE 9].

Les armoiries du Canada représentées sur les premiers bibelots allemands étaient calquées sur une boucle de ceinture émaillée vendue par la compagnie Eaton à l'automne de 1899[38]. Les cloisonnés imprécis des figures émaillées se reflètent dans ces dessins d'un flou déconcertant illustrant une porcelaine dure, elle de bonne qualité [FIGURES 10 et 11]. L'étude des armoiries du Canada ornant les miniatures de Goss, semble indiquer que les exportations au Canada de cette compagnie ont débuté vers 1905.

TABLEAU 2 : armoiries du Canada 1904-1914

| Pays de fabrication | Angleterre | Bohème | Allemagne | Totaux |
|---|---|---|---|---|
| Écu seul | | | | |
| + couronne | 9 | 4 | 13 | 26 |
| + feuilles d'érable | | | | |
| + couronne et feuilles d'érable | 1 | | | 1 |
| + feuilles d'érable et castor | 1 | | | 1 |
| + couronne, feuilles d'érable et castor | | 3 | | 3 |
| **TOTAUX** | 11 | 7 | 13 | 31 |

Pour la période 1904-1914, l'écu entouré de la couronne, de feuilles d'érable et du castor prédomine nettement et ces pièces proviennent surtout des ateliers de Schmidt & Co. à Karlsbad (Karlovy Vary) en Bohème occidentale. Il se peut même que le modèle d'armoiries du Canada qu'on y trouve ait été élaboré par Schmidt [FIGU-RE 2] ou par une compagnie allemande car on ne l'a retrouvé que sur une seule pièce britannique plus tardive par Ridgways (v. 1912), et nulle part au Canada bien qu'un modèle s'en inspirant, et plus tardif lui aussi ait été publié en carte postale par Nerlich & Co. de Toronto vers 1907[39]. Les armoiries sur cette carte sont presque identiques à celles ornant des assiettes Wedgwood [FIGURE 3]. L'année 1914 marque la fin d'une période, car on ne retrouve que quelques pièces de céramique armoriées [FIGURE 19 par exemple] ayant été exportées au Canada pendant la Première Guerre mondiale et pour une bonne décennie après.

Le désir d'associer à leurs armes, soit la couronne royale, soit la couronne et des feuilles d'érable, se retrouvait au niveau des provinces et des villes.

TABLEAU 3 : armoiries des provinces 1900-1914

| Provinces | Écu seul | Écu + couronne | Écu + couronne + feuilles d'érable | Totaux |
|---|---|---|---|---|
| Ontario | 1 | 3 | 2 | 6 |
| Québec | 1 | | | 1 |
| Nouvelle-Écosse | | 1 | 1 | 2 |
| Nouveau-Brunswick | | 1 | 1 | 2 |
| Île-du-Prince-Édouard | | | | |
| Manitoba | 2 | | | 2 |
| Saskatchewan | | 1 | | 1 |
| Alberta | | 1 | | 1 |
| Colombie-Britannique | 3 | | | 3 |
| **TOTAUX** | 7 | 7 | 4 | 18 |

TABLEAU **4** : armoiries des villes 1900-1914

| Villes | Écu + couronne | Écu + couronne + feuilles d'érable | Totaux |
|---|---|---|---|
| St. John | 3 | | 3 |
| Québec | 3 | | 3 |
| Montréal | 1 | 1 | 2 |
| Orillia | 1 | | 1 |
| Perth | 1 | | 1 |
| Stratford | 1 | | 1 |
| Toronto | 2 | | 2 |
| **TOTAUX** | **12** | **1** | **13** |

Pour les provinces, on ne retrouve comme ornements extérieurs que la couronne et des feuilles d'érable [FIGURE 12]. Cependant, il existe un exemplaire des armes du Manitoba, sans couronne ou feuilles, mais sommées d'un casque avec lambrequins et ayant pour cimier un castor. Les armoiries des villes s'entouraient aussi de la couronne et de feuilles d'érable. On connaît également une demi-douzaine d'exemplaires aux armes de Toronto, sans couronne ou feuilles, mais sommées d'un castor sur une couronne murale.

L'étude de la céramique armoriée démontre que le trio couronne, castor et feuilles d'érable constituait les ornements extérieurs usuels de l'écu du Canada, particulièrement de 1904 jusqu'à la Première Guerre mondiale. La céramique révèle aussi que pendant cette même période les provinces et les villes adoptaient comme ornements extérieurs, tantôt la couronne seule, tantôt la couronne et les feuilles d'érable. Cependant, on constate que parmi les pièces municipales répertoriées, le trio couronne, feuilles d'érable et castor ne se retrouve pas. Une étude des médailles de l'époque semble confirmer la même tendance. Cette constatation surprend, car à l'époque, l'art héraldique populaire ne reculait pas devant les agencements les plus complexes et l'imitation plutôt que l'originalité était la règle. Les Canadiens croyaient-ils que ces trois éléments devaient demeurer l'apanage de l'emblème représentant à l'époque la nation ?

Le castor dont les origines remontent à la Nouvelle-France et la feuille d'érable d'adoption plus tardive avaient continué à s'imposer tout au long du XIX$^e$ siècle comme emblèmes nationaux, chez les francophones comme chez les anglophones. On les retrouvait sur des médailles, des pièces de monnaie, des jetons, des timbres, des reliures, des drapeaux et des armoiries.

Au Canada français, l'adoption comme emblèmes nationaux, aussi bien du castor que de la feuille d'érable, s'était généralisée dans la première moitié du XIX$^e$ siècle. Un important ensemble de table à caractère nationaliste produit vers 1856 par Edward Walley d'Angleterre montre un castor sur une branche d'érable feuillue. Sous le castor figure le slogan « NOS INSTITUTIONS ! NOTRE LANGUE ET NOS LOIS » d'abord paru en tête du journal le Canadien d'Étienne Parent du 7 mai 1832 et adopté en 1844 par la Société Saint-Jean Baptiste. Au-dessus apparaît « LABOR OMNIA VINCIT », devise du Département de l'instruction publique du Bas-Canada, le tout étant chapeauté par une guirlande de feuilles d'érable [FIGURE 15]. Le motif dans l'ensemble est calqué sur celui figurant comme en-tête à la première page du Canadien du 11 novembre 1836. Une note accompagnant la nouvelle vignette de ce journal précise que les emblèmes qui s'y trouvent n'ont pas besoin d'explications étant généralement reconnus comme ceux des Canadiens français[40]. On pense que ce service avait été commandé par la Société

Saint-Jean Baptiste ou par le Département de l'instruction publique pour servir dans les collèges[41]. Il s'agissait d'une quantité appréciable de vaisselle car il était offert en plusieurs modèles : les plus simples étant peut-être destinés aux collèges et les plus élaborés aux membres de la Société Saint-Jean Baptiste.

Deux assiettes commandées vers 1914 par le journal *La Patrie* pour commémorer le centenaire de la naissance de sir George-Étienne Cartier et fabriquées par Rowland & Marcellus Co. témoignent de l'attachement toujours vivant des Canadiens français à la feuille d'érable et au castor. L'une est illustrée du portrait de l'homme politique entouré de branches d'érable et ornée dans le bas des armoiries du Canada sommées d'un castor [FIGURE 16] ; l'autre est illustrée d'un dessin du monument qui sera dédié à sir George en 1919 et, sur le rebord, des armoiries des provinces séparées par des feuilles d'érable[42].

Au XIXe siècle et pendant une bonne partie du XXe, on retrouvait parmi les Canadiens français, l'idée qu'ils étaient héritiers de deux grandes traditions et cultures. Cette notion se traduisait par des phrases comme : « Être Canadiens-Français... c'est être Anglais par l'allégeance, Français par l'origine, catholique par la foi » (1894)[43] ; « Rameau détaché de la France, nous avions besoin de protection ; l'Angleterre étant devenue le véhicule des voies providentielles à notre égard, nous devons en conserver la mémoire » (1904)[44] ; « ...notre peuple participe à la fois au génie latin et au génie anglo-saxon à jamais réunis sur ce sol ...nous sommes à la fois fils de France et d'Angleterre » (1944)[45].

Cette dualité et le respect de l'allégeance britannique se retrouvent sur des assiettes produites par Wedgwood et par Buffalo Pottery (de Buffalo aux États-Unis) pour le tricentenaire de la ville de Québec. On y voit de part et d'autre les portraits de Wolfe et de Montcalm, les deux généraux en lice lors de la bataille des plaines d'Abraham. Dans le haut du rebord figurent les armoiries royales de Grande-Bretagne, dans le bas l'Union Jack et, entre ces deux emblèmes, les armoiries des provinces réunies par des guirlandes de feuilles d'érable [FIGURE 17]. Sur une petite tasse de fabrication anonyme figure le portrait traditionnel mais fictif de Champlain, fondateur de la ville, *accosté à dextre* de la bannière du roi de Grande-Bretagne *brisée* d'un écusson portant un castor et *à senestre* du tricolore de la France *brisé* d'une

fleur de lis. Entre les hampes croisées, on voit le monogramme d'Édouard VII et dessous, sur un listel, l'inscription « 1608-1908 » [FIGURE 18].

Les armoiries de Montréal [FIGURE 19] et celles de la ville de Québec, tirées de son sceau étaient les deux sommées de la couronne royale [voir TABLEAU 4] tout comme les armoiries de la province de Québec depuis 1883[46].

Au Canada anglais, la généralisation du castor et de la feuille d'érable avait plutôt eu lieu dans la deuxième moitié du XIXe siècle avec l'apparition du castor sur des timbres à partir de 1851, et des feuilles d'érable sur de nombreuses pièces de monnaie à partir de 1858. En 1863, le professeur sir William Dawson, s'adressant à des étudiants, sentait le besoin de leur dire que les deux emblèmes du Canada étaient le castor et la branche d'érable (*sic*). Le fait qu'il sente le besoin d'en informer les étudiants et qu'il parle de branche plutôt que de feuille d'érable semble indiquer que l'acceptation de ces deux éléments comme emblèmes du pays gagnait du terrain sans qu'il s'agisse d'un fait accompli[47]. La chanson d'Alexander Muir « The Maple Leaf Forever » lancée en 1871 contribua beaucoup à populariser la feuille d'érable chez les anglophones[48].

Sur la céramique destinée au Canada, les armoiries royales de Grande-Bretagne figurent très peu comme motif central et unique. On les retrouve sur deux assiettes réalisées par Wedgwood vers 1911, l'une pour Montréal, l'autre pour Niagara Falls [FIGURE 20], deux importants centres touristiques. Un crémier fabriqué par Foley pour l'hôtel Victoria vers 1902 porte aussi les armoiries royales et sur le listel l'inscription « LONG LIVE EDWARD VII ». Wedgwood a également produit de nombreux services à café ou à thé de formes très variées, quelques-uns en jaspe, mais surtout en noir (basalte) et en faïence blanche ornée de guirlande de chêne. Ce dernier modèle comprenait aussi des assiettes de 23,8 cm qui faisaient peut-être partie de services à thé ou à café ou de services de table entiers. Ces services étaient décorés des armoiries d'une ville, des armoiries de la province, des armoiries du Canada [FIGURE 3] et de celles de Grande-Bretagne, chacune des armoiries ornant une pièce différente[49]. Le peu de demande au sein d'un marché libre pour les armoiries de Grande-Bretagne seules indique que la majorité des Canadiens même anglophones, tout en demeurant attachés à leur souverain, symbolisé par la couronne, se considéraient avant tout Canadiens et ne semblaient pas attacher une grande importance au fait qu'ils étaient alors des sujets britanniques.

Il convient ici de se demander si cette céramique armoriée était vendue aux Canadiens ou à des touristes d'autres pays. De nombreuses visites chez des antiquaires aux États-Unis, des discussions avec d'autres collectionneurs ainsi que des enquêtes menées sur Internet indiquent que ce genre de pièces ne se retrouvent aujourd'hui à peu près pas ni aux États-Unis ni en Angleterre. Dans les ouvrages sur la céramique armoriée publiés en Angleterre, nous n'avons trouvé que la mention des pièces canadiennes produites par Goss. La production canadienne des autres compagnies semble être ignorée. Ces enquêtes et consultations nous portent à conclure que la céramique ornée d'armoiries canadiennes était probablement surtout achetée par les Canadiens.

Pour la période de 1897 à 1914, les plus importantes compagnies anglaises à créer de la céramique armoriée pour le Canada ont été Wileman et Shelley (The Foley China), Frank Beadmore & Co. (Sutherland Ware), Wedgwood, Adams, Wiltshaw et Robinson (Carlton China), Willow Art China, Taylor et Kent (Florentine China), Ridgways et Wood & Son(s) Ltd. En Bohème, la céramique armoriée provenait des fabriques de Schmidt & Co. (Gemma et Victoria) situées à Karlsbad, et d'une autre compagnie non-identifiée. Pour l'Allemagne, les pièces assez nombreuses ne portent parfois aucune marque ou la seule inscription « MADE IN GERMANY ». Vers 1899, Guérin-Pouyat-Élite de Limoges, France, fabriqua des chandeliers et peut-être des services de table pour le manoir Richelieu à Pointe-au-Pic, Québec [50].

Les pièces figurant dans les tableaux 1 à 4 et celles décrites individuellement plus haut font une centaine d'objet en tout. Si l'on estime, cependant, que ces pièces étaient reproduites en moyenne à 3 000 exemplaires chacune, ce qui est modeste, nous sommes confrontés à un corpus de bibelots et de vaisselle considérable. De plus, les pièces inventoriées ne constituent probablement pas plus d'un tiers de la production totale. On sait, par exemple, que Sutherland Ware, Wedgwood, et William Lowe, en Angleterre, Schmidt & Co., et au moins une autre compagnie, en Bohème, et au moins deux fabricants, en Allemagne, ont produit plusieurs services de table portant les armoiries du Canada et dont on ne retrouve aujourd'hui que quelques pièces. Bien qu'il ne soit

pas toujours évident s'il s'agit d'un service à thé ou à café ou d'un service complet, les pièces restantes témoignent d'une céramique abondante et diversifiée. Comme elle se vendait dans des magasins petits et grands, des boutiques, des kiosques touristiques, à des foires et expositions et vraisemblablement par des marchands ambulants, il est probable que presque tous les Canadiens connaissaient cette céramique et pouvaient s'en procurer. C'est avant tout sur la céramique que les Canadiens pouvaient voir de près les armoiries du Canada, de leur province et parfois de leur municipalité [51].

Fait amusant, on ne semblait pas, à l'époque, hésiter à trancher de la nourriture sur des marques nationales voire sur l'effigie du souverain ; certaines pièces portent même des marques de couteau. On remarque, par contre, que sur des assiettes utilitaires plus récentes, les armoiries ornent le rebord plutôt que le centre.

L'engouement des Canadiens pour la céramique armoriée dite patriotique, s'explique sans doute en partie par les raisons déjà évoquées : l'occupation du pays d'un océan à l'autre, la prospérité des années Laurier et Borden et le sentiment de pouvoir survivre comme pays vis-à-vis des États-Unis. Le jubilé de diamant de la reine Victoria en 1897 et le couronnement d'Édouard VII en 1901 avaient aussi permis à des compagnies de l'Angleterre, de la Bohème et de l'Allemagne de découvrir le marché canadien. Cependant, on ignore en général les raisons profondes qui font qu'un objet de consommation connaît pour un temps la faveur du public. On attribue le plus souvent leur succès aux caprices de la mode. Très populaire de 1900 jusqu'à 1914, l'exportation de céramique armoriée au Canada semble avoir presqu'entièrement cessée pendant la Première Guerre mondiale et les pièces d'entre les deux guerres étaient pour la plupart associées à l'Empire et la royauté et au jubilé de diamant de la Confédération en 1927. Après la Deuxième Guerre mondiale, cette céramique connut un regain de popularité.

Quoi qu'il en soit, la céramique d'avant la Première Guerre mondiale est particulièrement importante. À côté des écrits et des débats où se manifestaient, chez les uns, un patriotisme farouche, chez les autres, une solidarité prudente et, chez quelques-uns, une hostilité à l'endroit de l'Empire, la céramique nous donne un aperçu de ce que pensaient les gens ordinaires, ceux qui ne laissent pas de témoignages écrits. Il semble que, tout en respectant l'Empire, les anglophones comme les francophones aspiraient avant tout à être Canadiens. On a souvent dit que le nationalisme canadien était né avec la Première Guerre mondiale, mais la céramique vendue dans un marché concurrentiel au tournant du siècle jusqu'à 1914 indique que, tout en demeurant fidèles au souverain, les Canadiens plaçaient le Canada avant l'Empire plusieurs années avant la Guerre.

## Le Canada se dote d'armoiries en règle

Étant donné la popularité du castor, de la feuille d'érable et de la couronne royale, on se serait attendu à ce que les armoiries du Canada concédées en 1921 [FIGURE 21] mettent en vedette ces trois éléments. Pourquoi alors le comité chargé d'élaborer les armoiries du pays a-t-il opté pour une version canadienne des armoiries royales ? Ce n'est pas que ces membres ignoraient les préférences des Canadiens. Tous avaient vu sous une forme ou une autre les armoiries du Canada arborant ces trois éléments comme ornements extérieurs. Les nombreuses lettres adressées à Joseph Pope comme sous-secrétaire d'État de 1896 à 1909 n'avaient pas manqué de lui indiquer que les Canadiens considéraient le castor et la feuille d'érable comme leurs emblèmes nationaux. De plus, le comité avait, par la voie des journaux, sollicité des propositions du public et les dessins reçus, malgré l'hiatus de la Guerre, indiquaient que les Canadiens avaient conservé leur attachement au castor, à la feuille d'érable et à la couronne [52]. Pour comprendre le choix du comité, il faut examiner les dispositions personnelles de ceux qui le composaient.

Ce comité était formé de Thomas Mulvey (1863-1935), sous-secrétaire d'État, de sir Joseph Pope (1854-1926), sous-secrétaire d'État aux Affaires extérieures, d'Arthur George Doughty (1860-1936), archiviste du Dominion, et du major-général sir Willoughby G. Gwatkin (1859-1925) représentant le ministère de la Milice et de la Défense [53]. Mulvey et Pope étaient nés au Canada, Doughty et Gwatkin en Angleterre. Pope était le plus âgé et le plus expérimenté des quatre, ayant auparavant doté les quatre provinces de l'Ouest et Île-du-Prince-Édouard d'armoiries [54].

Mulvey comme sous-secrétaire d'État et président du comité avait la première responsabilité de mener ce projet à bon port. Il s'occupait d'établir des contacts avec l'Angleterre et de dresser les documents officiels. Il semble que le comité se réunissait souvent de façon informelle sans tenir de procès-verbal [55].

Doughty, comme archiviste fédéral et comme secrétaire, participait à la rédaction de documents et se chargeait des questions d'ordre historique.

Pope, la personnalité la plus forte du groupe, était un impérialiste convaincu. Il ne voulait pas de drapeau canadien distinct, étant heureux de vivre sous l'Union Jack. Pour lui les Canadiens étaient tout aussi britanniques que les citoyens de l'Angleterre et rien ne l'agaçait plus que les distinctions entre Canadiens d'une part et Britanniques de l'autre [56]. Contrairement aux autres membres du comité qui, tout en voulant maintenir des liens étroits avec le souverain, croyaient que des armoiries royales spécifiques signifieraient un statut spécial pour le Canada, Pope y voyait un moyen de mieux intégrer le Canada à l'Empire [57]. Il ne favorisait pas les emblèmes canadiens pouvant exprimer des sentiments trop nationalistes. L'adoption de leur sceau comme armoiries par les provinces et la confusion qui en avait résulté au niveau des armoiries du Canada lui avait causé beaucoup d'ennuis, lorsqu'il était sous-secrétaire d'État. Aussi se méfiait-il de toute manifestation non-officielle de l'héraldique. Il aimait que les choses se fassent correctement et efficacement [58].

Gwatkin, l'autre personnalité forte, avait probablement participé à la rédaction en 1918 d'un rapport présenté au gouvernement par sir Eugène Fiset, sous-ministre de la Milice et de la Défense, et qui prônait des armoiries simples pour le Canada : *d'argent à une feuille d'érable de gueules*, par exemple [59]. Un journaliste du nom de Charles Frederick Hamilton, travaillant pour le compte de la Gendarmerie royale du Canada, partageait le même enthousiasme pour la feuille d'érable unique [60]. Gwatkin s'était, cependant, épris de l'idée de neuf feuilles d'érable (une pour chacune des provinces canadiennes d'alors) dès qu'il fut appelé à siéger sur le comité. Mais n'étant pas à la première réunion, les autres membres avaient choisi le thème des nations fondatrices lequel se traduira dans les armoiries de 1921 par les armes d'Angleterre, d'Écosse, d'Irlande et de la France royale en écartelé [FIGURE 21] [61]. Après avoir fait connaître son penchant pour les neuf feuilles, Gwatkin sembla plutôt accepter la version des armoiries royales jusqu'à ce que sir Henry Farnham Burke, roi d'armes Jarretière, manifeste son opposition aux armoiries que le comité avait élaborées. Il tenta alors, une fois de plus, de faire valoir ses neuf feuilles [62].

En 1920, Mulvey délégua Gwatkin auprès du roi d'armes Jarretière [63]. Gwatkin découvrit alors que Jarretière était également favorable à des armoiries simples comprenant des symboles canadiens. Ensemble, ils conçurent des armes figurant une branche d'érable à neuf feuilles rouges surmontée de la couronne royale en champ d'argent ; un cimier comportant un castor d'or sur une couronne de feuilles d'érable du même posée sur un casque avec lambrequins de gueules et d'argent. Ils proposaient comme supports deux lions ou deux castors tenant, l'un la bannière de France, l'autre l'Union Jack que l'on retrouve d'ailleurs dans les armoiries qui seront concédées en 1921. Cette proposition incluait également la présente devise et les mêmes emblèmes floraux sous le listel. Les drapeaux et la gerbe florale représentaient ensemble les nations fondatrices [FIGURE 21] [64].

À notre avis, il eut été préférable de conserver comme supports les castors, de substituer une seule feuille d'érable aux neuf, de mettre la couronne au-dessus de l'écu pour indiquer qu'il s'agissait d'une monarchie constitutionnelle et d'enlever les drapeaux trop encombrants. On pourrait effectivement penser que cette conception, qui se serait rapprochée des propositions de Fiset, aurait mieux été accueillie par les Canadiens que les armoiries de types royales concédées ultérieurement.

Pope s'était préalablement entendu avec Mulvey pour que Gwatkin se rende en Angleterre demander informellement à Ambrose Lee, héraut d'York (non pas à Jarretière), si les armoiries proposées respectaient les règles et conventions de l'héraldique [65]. Dans le cas contraire, il devait apprendre quelles retouches il fallait y apporter pour les rendre conformes. L'intention était ensuite de demander formellement au roi d'enjoindre à Jarretière de concéder les armoiries [66]. Lorsque Pope apprit que Gwatkin s'était présenté directement à Jarretière, dont l'opposition à des armoiries royales était connue, il en fut très contrarié. Il ne tarda pas à convaincre le comité qu'il fallait tout mettre en œuvre pour avoir gain de cause [67].

Les inquiétudes de Jarretière étaient fondées, car l'acte d'Union de 1801 avait précisé le contenu des armoiries royales. L'ajout des fleurs de lis par le comité en changeait le contenu et pouvait être perçu comme symbolisant l'ancienne prétention de l'Angleterre au trône de France [68]. Lorsque Mulvey eut cependant obtenu de source officieuse l'assurance que le gouvernement français ne s'opposait pas aux lis et que les conseillers légaux de Jarretière l'eurent avisé qu'il pouvait contourner le problème légal par le biais d'une proclamation royale, il prépara ce document sans tarder [69].

Lors de sa visite en Angleterre Gwatkin n'avait pas bien compris l'opposition de Jarretière aux lis et celle-ci n'avait jamais été formellement communiquée au comité [70]. Ce n'est que lorsque Mulvey se rendit à son tour en Angleterre, en juin 1921, qu'il apprit de quoi il s'agissait [71]. Entre temps, les Canadiens, croyant que Jarretière était trop à cheval sur les principes, le traitaient de tous les noms [72]. Jarretière eut, en un sens, le dernier mot car la proclamation qu'il prépara évitait de préciser qu'il s'agissait d'armoiries royales [73].

Aujourd'hui le statut d'armoiries royales est acquis car depuis 1953, la reine porte le titre de reine du Canada et lorsqu'elle concéda le cimier des armoiries du Canada en augmentation aux armoiries du très honorable Vincent Massey en 1963, elle utilisa l'expression « notre cimier du Canada » [74].

En un sens, les armoiries choisies en 1921 étaient un peu rétrogrades ne faisant que peu de place aux emblèmes canadiens et se voulant un symbole de la continuité de l'Empire au moment même où les Dominions aspiraient à devenir des pays indépendants. De plus, au lieu de rechercher un symbole unique pour le Canada dans son ensemble, le comité avait repris des notions représentées dans l'écartelé de 1868 : les nations fondatrices et la branchette d'érable à trois feuilles. Il en résulta un emblème qui mettait l'accent sur les distinctions d'origine et la diversité aux dépens de l'idée d'unité nationale [75]. Par contre, la majorité des membres du comité avait aussi voulu exprimer un nouveau statut pour le Canada en le dotant, comme l'Écosse, de ses propres armoiries royales. Dans ce sens, les nouvelles armoiries canadiennes présageaient le jour où l'idée d'une Couronne canadienne ferait son chemin et où la reine porterait le titre de reine du Canada [76]. Mais la reine du Canada ne se serait-elle pas aussi bien accommodée de la feuille d'érable et du castor, qui seront plus tard reconnus comme emblèmes nationaux ? La feuille accédant à ce statut en vertu de la proclamation royale du drapeau national le 15 février 1965, le castor en vertu d'une loi sanctionnée par la reine le 24 mars 1975.

Doit-on aujourd'hui modifier les armoiries du Canada pour les rendre moins compliquées, pour leur donner un contenu plus canadien ? Nous pensons qu'il n'est pas opportun de le faire dans la conjoncture actuelle. La feuille d'érable figurant sur le drapeau canadien adopté en 1965 est maintenant présente partout au pays comme symbole unique de tous les Canadiens. En un sens, les deux emblèmes se complètent : les armoiries représentant le passé et le drapeau le statut actuel et vraisemblablement l'avenir du pays.

Par contre, si les Québécois acceptaient la feuille d'érable et le castor au XIX$^e$ siècle et encore au début du XX$^e$, ce n'est plus le cas aujourd'hui. Depuis l'adoption de la feuille d'érable comme marque nationale, les Québécois se sont attachés davantage à la fleur de lis comme emblème de leurs traditions et culture particulières. Si on modifiait les présentes armoiries, ils pourraient ne plus se sentir représentés au niveau de la Confédération. Beaucoup d'anglophones aussi auraient sans doute une réaction négative et protesteraient qu'on veut détruire tout vestige de la monarchie et de leurs racines européennes, et même, que l'on met tout en œuvre pour amadouer le Québec[77].

## Conclusion

En passant d'une colonie à un pays autonome, le Canada a modifié ses emblèmes à plusieurs reprises au cours de son évolution. L'avenir seul nous dira si les Canadiens voudront un jour, au gré de leur histoire, modifier encore les armoiries de leur pays ; laissons le temps agir.

## Illustrations[78]

1. Assiette aux armoiries de libre adoption du Canada composées de l'écartelé, de 1 à 4, des armes concédées à l'Ontario, au Québec, au Nouveau-Brunswick et à la Nouvelle-Écosse [voir FIGURE 4] et de, 5 à 7, des sceaux du Manitoba, de la Colombie-Britannique et de l'Île-du-Prince-Édouard, l'écu étant sommé de la couronne royale. Par Adams de Tunstall, Angleterre, faïence, v. 1902, 22,5 cm.

2. Porte-plat aux armoiries de libre adoption du Canada composées des armes et sceaux des provinces et territoires écartelés de 1 à 9 : Ontario, Québec, Nouvelle-Écosse et Nouveau-Brunswick (armes concédées), Co-

lombie-Britannique (sceau), Île-du-Prince-Édouard, Territoires du Nord-Ouest et Yukon (création d'Edward Marion Chadwick), Manitoba (sceau), ornements extérieurs : couronne royale, branches d'érable et castor. Par Schmidt & Co. de Karlsbad (Karlovy Vary) en Bohème Autriche, v. 1904, sous la marque VICTORIA, AUSTRIA, porcelaine dure, 17,6 cm.

3. Assiette aux armoiries de libre adoption du Canada composées des armes et sceaux des provinces et territoires écartelés de 1 à 9 : Ontario (armes concédées), Yukon (création d'Edward Marion Chadwick), Québec, Île-du-Prince-Édouard, Manitoba, Saskatchewan, Nouvelle-Écosse, Colombie-Britannique et Nouveau-Brunswick (armes concédées), ornements extérieurs : couronne royale, branches d'érable castor. Par Wedgwood, Etruria, Angleterre, faïence, 1908, 23,8 cm.

4. Estampe du sceau concédé au Canada par décret de la reine Victoria du 26 mai 1868. Cet écartelé ne fut jamais l'objet d'un sceau, mais on l'adopta comme armoiries nationales. Imprimée en 1904 par Mortimer and Co. (Ottawa) pour Joseph Pope, sous-secrétaire d'État. Photomécanique, 26,1 x 16,6 cm.

5. Assiette célébrant le jubilé d'or de la reine Victoria (1887) et la grandeur de l'Empire. On voit dans le haut, *à senestre*, les armoiries de libre adoption du Canada. Même écu que la figure 1 sommé d'un castor avec sa branchette d'érable. Par J. Abraham de Westbourne Grove, Londres, faïence, 24,5 cm.

6. Assiette à l'effigie de la reine Victoria entourée d'emblèmes canadiens. Par une compagnie de Karlsbad ayant pour marque les lettres NC superposées et surmontées d'une couronne à cinq pointes sommées chacune d'une perle, porcelaine dure, 18,5 cm.

7. Assiette ornée d'emblèmes de l'Empire et d'emblèmes et de slogans canadiens. Par William Lowe (W. L. L.), Longton, Angleterre, faïence, v. 1899, 24,1 cm.

8. Petite assiette aux armoiries de libre adoption du Canada. Même écu que la figure 1. Ornements extérieurs : couronne royale,

branche d'érable, branche de chêne et castor. Par une compagnie de Karlsbad ayant pour marque les lettres NC superposées et surmontées d'une couronne à cinq pointes sommées chacune d'une perle, porcelaine dure, 14,8 cm.

9. Bol à fruits aux anciennes armoiries de Toronto. Par Wileman & Co. (The Foley China), porcelaine d'os de style « Dainty White » dont les rebords prennent la forme des dentelures de la feuille d'érable, v. 1905, 21 x 24 x 5 cm.

10. Boucle de ceinture aux armoiries de libre adoption du Canada. Même écu que la figure 1 sommé de la couronne royale. Fabriquée pour la compagnie T. Eaton, argent sterling et émail, 1899, 6 x 6,2 cm.

11. Deux petits cochonnets *issants* d'une bourse ornée d'armoiries calquées sur celles de la boucle de ceinture [FIGURE 10]. Le sens de l'inscription « OTTAWA CONTRITUTION (*sic*) » sous l'écu nous échappe. Fabriqué en Allemagne, porcelaine dure, 6,5 x 9 x 4,5 cm.

12. Gobelet aux armes de la Nouvelle-Écosse concédées en 1868. Ornements extérieurs : couronne royale et branches d'érable. Fabriqué en Allemagne, porcelaine dure, v. 1905, 8.2 x 10 cm.

13. Sceau proposé pour le Canada, 1868, Archives nationales du Canada (ci-après ANC), nég. C 33849.

14. Grand sceau du Canada, reine Victoria, utilisé de 1869 à 1904, 12,4 cm, ANC, nég. C 6792.

15. Assiette ornée du castor sur une branche d'érable, accompagné, au-dessus, de la devise du Département de l'instruction publique du Bas-Canada et, au-dessous, de la devise de la Société Saint-Jean-Baptiste. Par Edward Walley, Staffordshire, Angleterre, v. 1856, grès, 24,5 cm.

16. Assiette portant l'effigie de sir George-Étienne Cartier entourée de branches d'érable et dans le bas les armoiries de libre adoption du Canada composées des armes des provinces écartelées de 1 à 9 : Ontario, Québec, Nouvelle-Écosse, Nouveau-Brunswick, Colombie-Britannique, Île-du-Prince-Édouard, Saskatchewan, Alberta, Manitoba. L'écu est sommé d'un castor. Toutes les armes sont concédées, mais très mal représentées. Fabriquée pour le journal *La Patrie* pour marquer le centenaire de la naissance de Cartier. Par Rowland & Marcellus Co., Staffordshire, Angleterre, v. 1914, faïence, 26,5 cm.

17. Assiette illustrée du monument érigé à l'endroit où Wolfe est mort à Québec, *accosté* des très peu ressemblantes effigies de Wolfe et de Montcalm. Ornée sur le rebord des armoiries des provinces et territoires canadiens, *en chef* des armoiries royales de Grande-Bretagne et *en pointe* de l'Union Jack. Fabriquée par Buffalo Pottery de Buffalo aux États-Unis, enregistrée W.A. Reynolds, *semi-vitreous*, 19 cm.

18. Petite tasse ornée du traditionnel et fictif portrait de Champlain, fondateur de la ville, accosté, *à dextre*, de la bannière du roi de Grande-Bretagne brisée d'un écusson portant un castor et, *à senestre*, du tricolore de France brisé d'une fleur de lis. Entre les hampes croisées figurent le monogramme d'Édouard VII et, dessous sur un listel, l'inscription « 1608-1908 ». Fabricant inconnu, faïence, 6 x 6,5 cm.

19. Assiette aux anciennes armoiries de Montréal conçues à l'origine par Jacques Viger, premier maire de Montréal de 1833 à 1836. Fabriquée par Wedgwood, Etruria, Angleterre, faïence, 1916, 25,7 cm.

20. Assiette aux armoiries royales de Grande-Bretagne. Fabriquée pour la ville de Niagara Falls par Wedgwood, Etruria, Angleterre, faïence, 1911, 25,2 cm.

21. Assiette aux armoiries du Canada concédées officiellement par proclamation royale du roi George V, datée du 21 novembre 1921, d'après un dessin d'Alexander Scott Carter. Par Adams de Tunstall, Angleterre pour le 175e anniversaire de la loge Albion des *Ancient Free and Accepted Masons* (A.F. & A.M.) de la ville de Québec, faïence, v. 1927, 21,1 x 21,3 cm.

## NOTES

1. Les provinces étaient : la province du Canada formée du Haut-Canada (Ontario) et du Bas-Canada (Québec), la Nouvelle-Écosse et le Nouveau-Brunswick.

2. Les armoiries du duché étaient : *de gueules à deux léopards d'or l'un sur l'autre.* En 1929, la Nouvelle-Écosse abandonnera les armoiries de 1868 pour se faire concéder des armoiries plus anciennes qu'elle possédait comme colonie. En 1939, le Québec adoptera par décret du lieutenant-gouverneur en conseil un chef *d'azur à trois fleurs de lis d'or* pour remplacer les deux fleurs de lis d'azur sur champ d'or concédées en 1868. La province du Nouveau-Brunswick créée en 1784 tire son nom du duché de Brunswick l'un des domaines héréditaires de la Couronne britannique à l'époque.

3. Archives nationales du Canada (ci-après ANC), « Memoranda (*sic*) Explanatory of the Proposed Armorial Bearings for the Provinces and Dominion of Canada ». Ce document et des dessins concernant les armoiries du Canada font partie de la collection d'art documentaire des Archives nationales du Canada. Ces documents se trouvent dans la boîte n° 5 intitulée « Coats of Arms ». Ils sont inventoriés dans le dossier 622-6 et portent le numéro d'acquisition 1949-1-2. Deux des dessins d'armoiries, la Nouvelle-Écosse et l'Ontario, sont reproduits dans CONRAD SWAN, *Canada Symbols of Sovereignty,* Toronto et Buffalo, University of Toronto Press, 1977, p. 123, 162.

4. Par exemple sur le fort Moose Factory fondé en 1672-1673 par la Compagnie de la baie d'Hudson. Soit la croix sur fond d'argent ou cette même croix au canton du Red Ensign arboré sur les forts de la Compagnie de la baie d'Hudson. Voir : AUGUSTE VACHON, « Le Red Ensign au Canada de Pierre Le Moyne d'Iberville à John George Diefenbaker » dans *L'Héraldique au Canada,* vol. 14, no. 1 (mars 1980), p. 2-10.

5. ANC, collections d'art documentaire, acquisition 1949-1-1, *loc. cit.,* sir Frederick Rogers à sir Charles G. Young, 29 avril 1868.

6. AUGUSTE VACHON, « L'emblème royal en Nouvelle-France » dans *l'Archiviste,* vol. 17, no. 1 (janv.-fév. 1990), p. 11-13.

7. AUGUSTE VACHON, « L'héraldique de Jacques Cartier » dans *L'Héraldique au Canada,* vol. 23, no. 3 (sept. 1984), p. 4-11. L'hypothèse que George-Étienne Cartier fut responsable de l'inclusion des fleurs de lis dans les armoiries du Québec est ici formulée pour la première fois.

8. L'une de ces sculptures amenée au collège naval de Portsmouth fut remise aux Archives nationales du Canada en 1917 et est aujourd'hui au Musée canadien de la guerre ; l'autre remise à la ville d'Hastings fut retournée à la ville de Québec en 1925. « Les trophées héraldiques de Québec » dans *L'Héraldique au Canada,* vol. 20, no. 3 (sept. 1986), p. 44. La consigne d'enlever les armoiries royales des églises et des cours de justice était adressée à lord Dorchester, gouverneur en chef du Bas-Canada, 16 septembre 1791 : ARTHUR G. DOUGHTY et DUNCAN A. MCARTHUR (éd.), *Documents Relating to the Constitutional History of Canada 1791-1818,* Ottawa, C.H. Parmelee, imprimeur de Sa Très Excellente Majesté pour les Archives publiques du Canada, 1914, p. 25.

9. F. A. BAILLARGÉ. *Le drapeau canadien-français.* Montréal, Granger, 1904, p. 19-21, 26-27 ; ALISTAIR B. FRASER, « Maple Leaf Chronology Revisited » dans *Flagscan,* sept.-oct.-nov. 1989, vol. 4, no. 3, p. 11-14.

10. Ce document est reproduit dans ALAN BEDDOE, *Beddoe's Canadian Heraldry revised by Col. Strome Galloway,* Belleville, Mika Pubishing Company, p. 68-70.

11. Voir à ce sujet LUC BOUVIER, « Du tricolore canadien au fleurdelisé québécois » dans *L'Héraldique au Canada/ Heraldry in Canada,* vol. 28, no. 1 à 4 (mars à déc. 1994), p. 30-40, 22-32, 25-32, 25-33 et vol. 29, no. 1 (mars 1995), p. 25-33.

12. Le « Memoranda », note 4, spécifiait deux fleurs de lis, mais ne précisait pas les émaux ni la disposition des pièces. La fasce étant *de gueules à un léopard d'or* pour représenter le nouveau régime britannique, les fleurs de lis d'azur devaient figurer sur l'or ou l'argent. Il est à noter que dans les présentes armoiries de l'Ontario, du Nouveau-Brunswick, de l'Île-du-Prince-Édouard, du Manitoba, de la Saskatchewan, de l'Alberta, de la Colombie-Britannique et du Yukon, les marques de l'Angleterre, léopard, croix de Saint-Georges et Union Jack sont placés en chef alors que dans le cas des armoiries du Québec, les fleurs de lis y figurent en chef au-dessus du léopard d'Angleterre, ce qui représente une importante marque de respect. En 1939, la province modifia le chef de ses armoiries pour reprendre les anciennes couleurs de France : *d'azur à trois fleurs de lis d'or.* Ce geste reflétait un souci d'exactitude historique et non pas la volonté d'effacer les marques du changement d'allégeance. Le lion britannique sur l'écu et la couronne royale britannique au-dessus étaient conservés. Malheureusement ce geste donnait à la province l'aspect d'une bonne ville de France. AUGUSTE VACHON, « La fleur de lis » dans *L'Héraldique au Canada,* vol. 20, no. 3 (sept. 1986), p. 42-44.

13. « ...that the said United Provinces of Canada being one Dominion under the name of Canada shall upon all occasions that may be required use a Common Seal to be called the Great Seal of Canada which said Seal shall be composed of the Arms of the said Four Provinces Quarterly... », BEDDOE, *loc. cit.,* p. 70.

14. « Seal of the Dominion of Canada » dans *The Volunteer Review,* vol. 3 (27 déc. 1867) ; « The Great Seal of Canada » dans *The Canadian Illustrated News* (11 déc. 1869), p. 93.

15. En expédiant le décret au Canada, le Secrétaire d'État pour les colonies le décrivait comme « Her Majesty's Warrant of Assignment of Armorial Bearings for the Dominion and Provinces of Canada ». Le document de l'Amirauté britannique autorisant le Red Ensign canadien en 1892 décrivait les armoiries sur le battant comme « les armoiries du Dominion ». COLIN CAMPBELL, « The Flag of Our Country » dans *The Canadian Almanac,* Toronto, Copp, Clark, 1894, p. 196 et 200. Dans sa correspondance avec le *colonial office,* le gouverneur général employait la même désignation. ANC, fonds sir Joseph Pope, RG 30, E 86, vol. 118, dossier 23, le baron Stanley of Preston au comte de Grandville, 30 juin 1870. Un dessin des quatre armoiries écartelées envoyé à Pope portait l'inscription « I hereby certify that the above are the arms of the Dominion of Canada as recorded in the College of Arms London. - College of Arms - 5 February 1903 - A.S. Scott-Gatty - York Herald - Acting Registrar ». *Idem.,* vol. 129, dossier 89.

16. ANC, Archives du bureau du gouverneur général, RG 7, G 21, vol. 163, dossier 290A, microfilm T-1160, le comte de Carnarvon au vicomte Monck, 11 août 1866 ; le comte de Grandville au gouverneur général du Canada, 14 sept. 1869 ; le comte de Carnarvon au gouverneur général du Canada, 23 août 1875.

17. Le premier sceau à être ajouté à l'écartelé fut celui du Manitoba peu de temps après l'entrée de la province dans la Confédération en 1870. Voir L'opinion publique, 2 (janv. 1873), p. 1. Le premier document connu par l'auteur où l'on voit les quatre armes et trois sceaux est la médaille de l'exposition du Dominion du Canada, 1876, par Ernest Paulin Tasset. Collection de médailles des ANC, no. 13224.

18. « The Provincial Arms and the Dominion Flags » dans Canadian Illustrated News (6 mai 1871), p. 274 et 281.

19. La médaille de 1876, voir note 17.

20. CONRAD SWAN, op. cit., Toronto et Buffalo, University of Toronto Press, 1977, p. 185.

21. ANC, MG 30, E 86, vol. 129, dossier 89, Chadwick à Pope, 25 avril 1904. Voir aussi CAMPBELL, op.cit., p. 203 ; CHARLES R. MAIER, « The Yukon Coat of Arms » dans L'Héraldique au Canada/Heraldry in Canada, vol. 16, no. 3 (sept. 1982) p. 8-13 ; ROBERT MERRILL BLACK, « Shagotyohgwisaks ; E.M. Chadwick and Canadian Heraldry » dans idem, vol. 24, no. 3 (sept. 1990), p. 2-17 ; RICHARD ROBERTS, « An Interesting Porcelain Plate: A Canadian Heraldic Puzzle » dans idem, vol. 13, no. 3 (sept. 1979), p. 8-10 et vol. 17, no. 3 (sept. 1983), p. 4-7.

22. Je n'ai retrouvé les neuf provinces que sur une pièce de céramique [FIGURE 16], mais on les retrouve ailleurs. Voir L'Héraldique au Canada/Heraldry in Canada, vol. 23, no. 4 (déc. 1989), p. 10.

23. ANC, MG 30, E 86, vol. 7, no. 40, Pope à J. Ogilvie, 31 mai 1897.

24. Les preuves de cet usage sont légion. Voir, par exemple, les broches et drapeaux en vente dans The Hudson's Bay Company Autumn and Winter Catalogue 1910-1911, no. 58, réimpression par Watson & Dwyer Publishing Ltd. Winnipeg, 1990, p. 85, 162 ; AUGUSTE VACHON, « Le Red Ensign... », loc. cit. Le Red Ensign canadien avec l'écartelé des quatre provinces originales sur le battant avait été autorisé en 1892 par l'Amirauté britannique pour identifier le Canada sur mer. Comme on augmentait cet écu de tous les symboles populaires, il devenait méconnaissable en mer. E. M. CHADWICK, « The Canadian Flag » dans The Canadian Almanac, Toronto, Copp, Clark, 1896, p. 227.

25. ELIZABETH COLLARD, Nineteenth-Century Pottery and Porcelain in Canada, Kingston et Montréal, McGill-Queen's University Press, 2ᵉ éd., 1984, p. 192-193.

26. Musée canadien des civilisations, document 20, fiche PARIS 98166/No inv. D-3148. La fiche cite un article de BEA HOWE « Souvenirs of Sovereignty » dans The Antique Dealer and Collector's Guide, mais aucune date de publication n'est précisée. Le castor préfère comme nourriture le tremble et le peuplier, mais l'érable aussi fait partie des branches qu'il entasse sous l'eau pour se nourrir en hiver.

27. Voir à ce sujet : ROBERT CRAIG BROWN et RAMSAY

COOK, Canada 1896-1921: A Nation Transformed, Toronto, McClelland and Stewart, 1974, xii-412 p.

28. Une peinture de Cornelius Krieghoff de 1846 montre la chambre d'un officier britannique remplie d'objets des plus disparates : tableaux par l'artiste, livres, animaux empaillés, artisanat amérindien, buste, poupée en costume de nonne et pièces de poterie, etc. Voir « Officer's Trophy Room » dans J. RUSSELL HARPER, Krieghoff, Toronto, University of Toronto Press, 1979, p. 22.

29. En 1819, J. E. Woolford publia à Halifax quatre vues de cette ville, la première série de ce genre à être imprimée au Canada. En 1830, paraît une deuxième série : six vues de Montréal par R. A. Sproule imprimées à Montréal par A. Bourne. Suivront ensuite deux autres séries de vues de Montréal imprimées au Canada : six vues par James Duncan 1843, quatre vues par John Murray, 1843 ou 1844. MARY ALODI, Printmaking in Canada: The Earliest Views and Portraits/Les débuts de l'estampe au Canada : vues et portraits, Toronto, Royal Ontario Museum, 1980, p. 34-43, 66-77, 174-179 et 193-199.

30. COLLARD, op. cit., p. 201-238.

31. Les images imprimées et les aquarelles par des officiers britanniques et leur épouse sont exécutées sur ce trajet. L'auteur a été conservateur de ce genre d'œuvre d'art pendant 22 ans aux Archives nationales du Canada. Voir aussi W. M. S. HUNTER JR., Hunter's Panoramic Guide from Niagara Falls to Quebec, Boston, John P. Jewett & Co., Cleveland Ohio, 1857, 66p., réimpression par Coles Publishing Co., Toronto, 1970.

32. On trouve un bon aperçu de ce phénomène dans MARY ALLODI, Canadian Watercolours and Drawings in the Royal Ontario Museum, Toronto, The Royal Ontario Museum, 1974 ; W. MARTHA E. COOKE, W. H. Coverdale Collection of Canadiana: Paintings, Water-colours and Drawings (Manoir Richelieu Collection), Ottawa, Public Archives of Canada, 1983, xix-297 p. et 500 ill. ; MICHAEL BELL, Painters in a New Land from Annapolis Royal to the Klondike, Toronto, McClelland and Stewart Limited, 224 p.; J. RUSSELL HARPER, Early Painters and Engravers in Canada, Toronto et Buffalo, University of Toronto Press, 1970, xv-376 p.

33. GEORGE M. GRANT, Picturesque Canada: the Country as it Was and Is. Illustrated under the supervision of L R. O'Brien, Toronto, J. Clarke, 1882, xv-880 p.

34. Les catalogues de la compagnie T. Eaton Limited, Toronto, 1899 à 1901.

35. AUDREY B. ZEDER, British Royal Commemoratives with Prices, Lombard, Illinois, Wallace-Homestead Book Company, 1986, p. 12.

36. Plusieurs pièces de la collection de l'auteur et de son épouse portent le numéro d'enregistrement 272101 qui date de 1896. Un petit gobelet de la collection orné des armoiries de la Nouvelle-Écosse est du même modèle qu'un autre portant les armoiries royales d'Angleterre et fabriqué pour le jubilé de diamant de la reine Victoria en 1897, voir ZEDER, op.cit., p. 18. Pour fins de datation, les numéros d'enregistrement ne sont que des indices, car un modèle peut demeurer en vogue de nombreuses années après son enregistrement. La pièce concluante pour notre datation est un petit vide-poches portant à l'avers les ar-

moiries de la Colombie-Britannique conçues par Beanlands en 1895 et sur le revers l'inscription « MANUFACTURED FOR J. A. SKINNER & CO., CROCKERY IMPORTERS, VANCOUVER ». Cette compagnie figure dans le guide de la ville de Vancouver de 1899, mais n'y figure plus en 1900 : *The Williams Official British Columbia Directory, 1899* et *Henderson's British Columbia Gazeteer and Directory and Mining Companies, with which is consolidated the Williams' British Columbia Directory for 1900-1901*.

37. ELISABETH CAMERON, *Encyclopedia of Pottery & Porcelain 1800-1960*, New York et Oxford, Facts On File Publications, 1986, p. 129, 232-233.

38. *The T. Eaton Company Catalogue for Fall & Winter 1899-1900*, no. 43, Toronto, T. Eaton Co. Limited, 1899, p. 20.

39. La carte contient les armoiries officielles concédées au Manitoba, à la Saskatchewan et à la Colombie-Britannique de 1905 à 1906 alors que le modèle de Bohème contient le sceau du Manitoba et les armes non-officielles de Beanlands et de Chadwick conçues antérieurement.

40. Notons que le slogan « NOS INSTITUTIONS ! NOTRE LANGUE ET NOS LOIS » ne signifie pas l'abandon du système parlementaire britannique ou du droit criminel anglais pour reprendre le mode de gouvernement plus autocratique du régime français. Il reflète, à l'époque, la lutte pour un gouvernement responsable où le gouverneur, représentant du souverain britannique, nommerait les membres de ses Conseils législatif et exécutif de concert avec l'Assemblée législative élue par le peuple. De cette façon, l'Assemblée exercerait un certain contrôle sur les nominations et les fonctions les plus importantes de l'État : éducatives, judiciaires, etc.

41. COLLARD, *op. cit.*, p. 223-224.

42. Cette assiette est exactement du même format que d'autres produites par Rowland & Marcellus Co. de Staffordshire, Angleterre. Il s'agit de la marque d'un importateur de céramique des États-Unis que l'on pense être British Anchor Pottery Co. Voir RALPH & TERRY KOVEL, *Kovels' New Dictionary of Marks*, New York, Crown Publishers Inc., p. 145 (j), 149 (p). Une assiette du même format fabriquée par Rowland et Marcellus pour G. W. Clarke and Co. de Montréal et illustrée de scènes de cette ville figure dans PETER UNITT, *Unitt's Canadian Price Guide to Antiques & Collectables*, Peterborough, Ontario, Clock House, 1979, vol. 8, p. 235.

43. « Le Canada : discours patriotique prononcé à Ottawa, à l'occasion de la fête de saint Jean-Baptiste, en 1894 » dans *Bibliothèque canadienne* (Collection Laval), Montréal, Librairie Beauchemin Limitée, 1925, p. 39.

44. BAILLARGÉ, *op. cit.*, p. 30.

45. EUGÈNE ACHARD, *L'Histoire du drapeau canadien*, Montréal, Librairie générale canadienne, 1944, p. 44.

46. ALAN BEDDOE, *op. cit.*, p. 72.

47. HORACE MARTIN, *Castorologia*, Montréal, Drysdale, 1892, p. 198.

48. *A Guide Book of Canadian Coins, Currency & Tokens*, Winnipeg, Canadian Numismatic Publishing Institute, 1958, 152 p. ; JOSEPH LEROUX, *Le médailler du*

*Canada/The Canadian Coin Cabinet*, Montréal, Beauchemin, 1888, 308 p .; BAILLARGÉ, *op. cit.*, p. 19-28 ; STROME GALLOWAY, « Why the Maple Leaf Is Our National Emblem » dans *Canadian Geographic* (août-sept. 1982) p. 30-32 ; « The Beaver Was Canada's First Emblem », *Heraldry in Canada*, vol. 20, no. 3 (sept. 1986), p.10-12 et 46 ; CONRAD SWAN, « The Beaver and the Maple Leaf in Heraldry » dans *The Coat of Arms*, vol. 10, no. 75 (juill. 1968), p. 97-109.

49. On retrouve quelques-unes de ces pièces dans PETER UNITT et ANNE WORRALL, *Unitt's Canadian Price Guide*, *loc. cit.*, vol. 9, 1981, p. 51 et *ibid.*, vol. 13, 1989-1990, section consacrée à Wedgwood ; « Wedgwood International Seminar-Meeting, Toronto, May 1994 » dans *The Upper Canadian*, vol. 14, no. 2 (mars-avril 1994), p. 20.

50. Ces pièces portaient les armoiries du cardinal Richelieu posées sur une ancre.

51. Chaque compagnie pouvait avoir une trentaine de représentants dans différentes villes à travers le Canada. Si chaque représentant vendait en moyenne 100 exemplaires d'une même pièce, l'estimation de 3 000 est atteint. Voir J. J. JARVIS (éd.), *The Goss Record*, Londres, Milestone Publication Limited, 1973, réimpression de la 9ᵉ éd. de 1921, p. 73. Nous savons aussi d'après les inscriptions qu'on y trouve que certains de ces objets armoriés étaient fabriqués pour des importateurs-distributeurs importants comme Cassidy's à Montréal et Goodwin & Co. ayant des entrepôts à Québec, à Montréal et à Toronto. D'autres étaient importés par des marchands de porcelaine et de souvenirs comme Nerlich & Co. à Toronto, D. H. Warwick et W. H. Hayward tous deux à Saint John et J. A. Skinner & Co. à Vancouver. D'autres portaient le nom d'endroits touristiques comme les Milles-Îles, Niagara Falls et la région de Muskoka en Ontario, Killarney au Manitoba et Banff en Alberta, etc.

52. Voir ANC, MG 30, E 86, vols. 6 à 31, 117 à 130 et ANC, MG 30, vol. 210, dossier 1156-1.

53. ANC, RG 6, vol. 210, dossier 1156-1, p. 291-292, procès-verbal de la réunion du comité du 3 avril 1919.

54. ANC, MG 30, E 86, vol. 27, no. 720, sir Joseph Pope à sir George E. Foster, 24 sept. 1917.

55. Le comité s'était réuni 14 fois du 3 avril 1919 au 8 décembre 1921, mais on ne trouve que quelques rapports ou procès-verbaux dans les dossiers. ANC, RG 6, A 1, vol. 210, dossier 1156-3, p. 165.

56. MAURICE POPE (éd.), *Public Servant: The Memoirs of Sir Joseph Pope*, Toronto, Oxford University Press, 1960, p. 283-284 ; SIR JOSEPH POPE, *The Flag of Canada*, Ottawa, 2ᵉ éd. 1912, 16 p. ; MG 30, E 86, vol. 129, dossier 89, Pope à Edward Marion Chadwick, 26 avril 1904.

57. ANC, RG 6, A 1, vol. 210, dossier 1156-3, p. 310, Pope à Thomas Mulvey, 4 nov. 1921.

58. ANC, MG 30, E 86, vol. 129, dossier 89, Pope au major Stanley Maude, 18 janv. 1904 ; JOHN ROSS MATHESON, *Canada's Flag: A Search for a Country*, Belleville, Ontario, Mika Publishing Company, 1986, p. 8-9 ; ANC, RG 6, A 1, vol. 210, dossier 2931-1916, p. 31-34, « Confidential Memorandum for Sir Robert Borden upon Mr. E. M. Chadwick's letter of the 18th December 1917, suggesting the adoption of a new coat-of-arms for Canada »,

31 déc. 1917.

59. ANC, RG 6, A 1, vol. 210, dossier 2931-1916, s. p., « Observations on the Armorial Bearings of Canada », le major-général sir Eugène Fiset à Mulvey, 4 fév. 1918.

60. *Idem*, dossier 1156-1, p. 225-231, George Herbert Todd au colonel Charles Frederick Hamilton, 22 avril 1919.

61. *Idem*, p. 271, le major-général sir Willoughby G. Gwatkin à Mulvey, 3 avril 1919 ; Maurice Pope, *op. cit.*, p. 282-283.

62. *Idem*, p. 49-48, Gwatkin à Mulvey, 10 et 11 avril 1920.

63. *Idem*, p.271, Gwatkin à Mulvey, 3 avril 1919.

64. *Idem*, dossier 1156-2, p. 255, Mulvey à Alfred Scott-Gatty, 21 juill. 1920 ; *idem*, p. 228, Gwatkin à Pope, 30 août 1920 ; *idem*, p. 227, Gwatkin à Pope, 1er sept. 1920.

65. Le comité avait d'abord travaillé avec Lee qui ne s'opposait pas à des armoiries de type royales pour le Canada. Mais Lee étant tombé malade, il n'avait pas pu terminer son travail. *Idem*, dossier 1156-1, p. 144-147, 60, 25-26, Ambrose Lee à Pope, 13 juin 1919 ; 16 janv. 1920 et 22 mars 1920.

66. *Idem*, dossier 1156-2, p. 257, Mulvey à Chadwick 23 juill. 1920 ; *idem*, p. 243, Pope à Mulvey, 28 juill. 1920.

67. *Idem*, p. 238, Pope à Mulvey, 24 août 1920.

68. *Idem*, dossier 1156-3, p. 350-351, sir Henry Farnham Burke à Mulvey, 13 sept. 1921.

69. *Idem*, p. 352-355, Louis Jarry à l'honorable Philippe Roy, 2 sept. 1921 ; *idem*, p. 339, Mulvey à Burke, 3 oct. 1921 ; SWAN, *Canada: Symbols...*, *loc. cit.*, p. 63.

70. ANC, RG 6, A 1, vol. 210, dossier 1156-2, p. 48, Mulvey à Chadwick, 15 août 1921.

71. *Idem*, p. 61-63, Mulvey à Roi, 11 juill. 1921.

72. *Idem*, p.45, Gwatkin à Mulvey, 16 août 1921 ; *idem*,

dossier 1156-3, p. 357, Gwatkin à Mulvey, 17 sept. 1921.

73. Le document précisait que le casque sur l'écu était un casque royal et que le tout était surmonté de la couronne impériale, mais cela ne voulait pas dire qu'il s'agissait d'armoiries royales car les armoiries du Royal Military College à Kingston sont surmontées d'une couronne impériale et les armoiries de la Nouvelle-Écosse comme celles de la Jamaïque sont sommées d'un casque royal. Voir la proclamation royale et la description des armoiries du Royal Military College dans BEDDOE, *op. cit.*, p. 64 et 102.

74. Voir le mandat accordant cette augmentation dans *ibid.*, p. 173.

75. Le Canada devenait un pays indépendant en vertu du rapport Balfour de 1926 et du Statut de Westminster de 1931. L'esprit populaire tend à attacher un symbolisme à tout ce qui est quantifiable allant jusqu'à tenir compte des 11 pointes de la feuille d'érable stylisée du drapeau du Canada. On y voit dans ces pointes les dix provinces et l'un des territoires, la queue de la feuille étant réservée au deuxième territoire. Pour la branchette à trois feuilles d'érable on pense que l'une représente les autochtones, les francophones et les anglophones ou encore l'est, le centre et l'ouest du pays. Si on peut trouver ce symbolisme populaire amusant, on doit admettre qu'il contribue à tenir un symbole vivant.

76. ANC, RG 6, A 1, dossier 1156-1, p.43-45, rapport du comité s.d.

77. La simple addition de la devise de l'Ordre du Canada sur un anneau autour des armoiries en 1995 avait provoqué ce genre de réaction. Voir DIANE FRANCIS, « Crest change a sellout to separatists », *Saskatoon Star-Phoenix*, 5 sept. 1996, p. A2 ; COLBY COSH, « A Coat to Fit Quebec », *Alberta Report*, 25 déc. 1995, p. 7. Au Canada anglais le Québec est parfois perçu comme une province revendicatrice qui veut tout changer.

78. L'ensemble des figures, à l'exception des figures 13 et 14, ont été photographiées par Jacqueline Vincent, DSI.

1

2

3

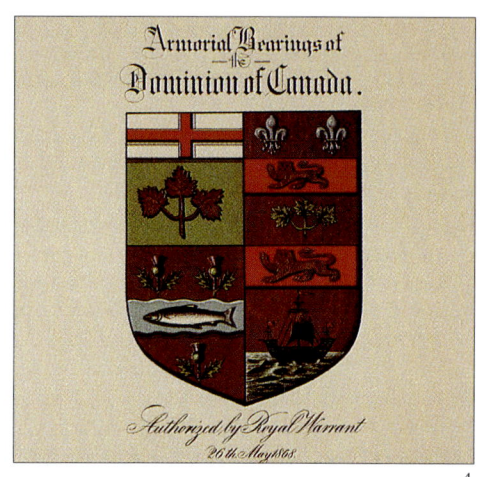

4

5

6

7

8

9

10

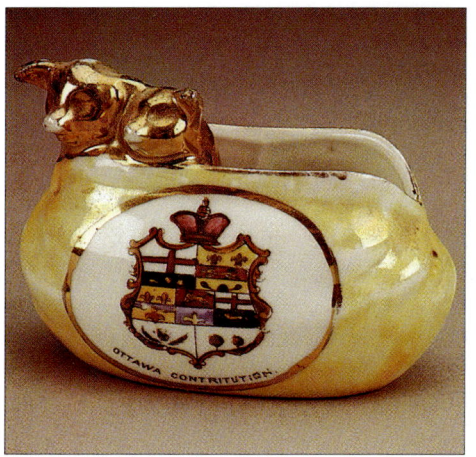

11

12

13

14

15

16

17

18

19

20

21

# A CENTURY OF CRESTS ON THE NORTHWEST COAST:
# A MULTIMEDIA PRESENTATION   Marjorie Halpin

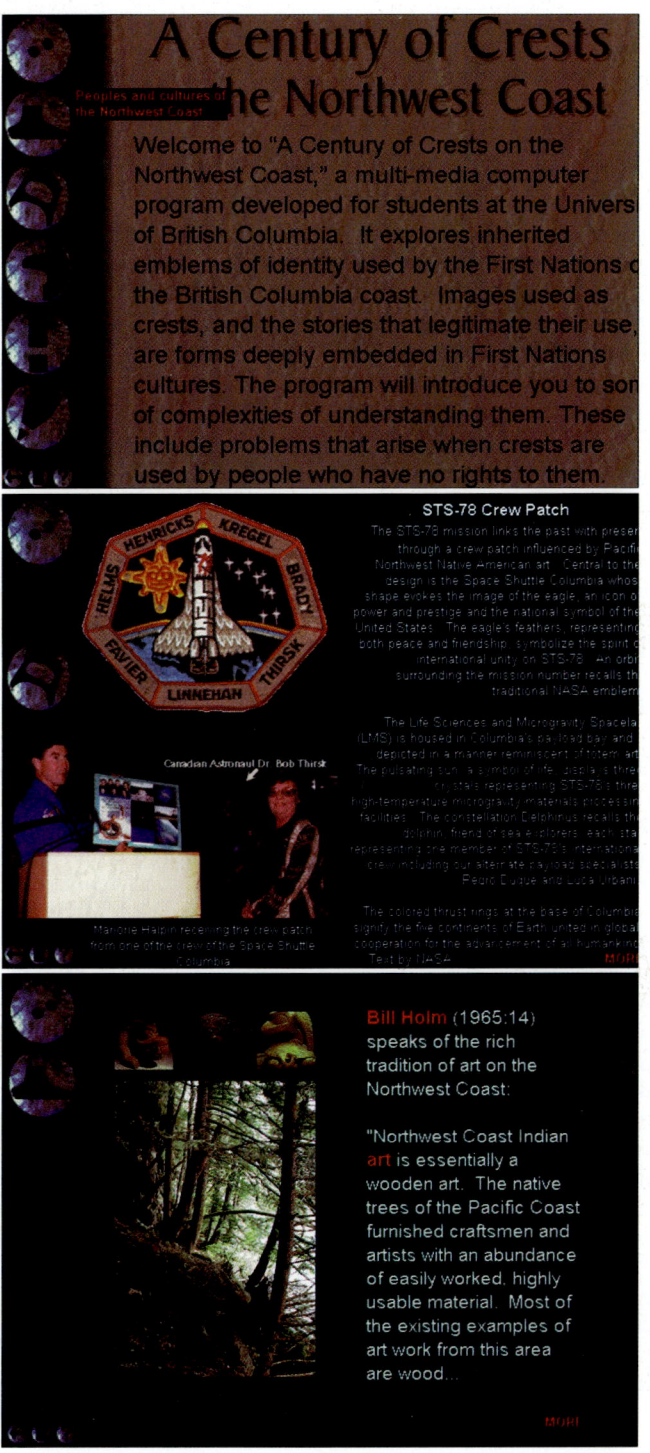

## A Century of Crests the Northwest Coast

Peoples and cultures of the Northwest Coast

Welcome to "A Century of Crests on the Northwest Coast," a multi-media computer program developed for students at the University of British Columbia. It explores inherited emblems of identity used by the First Nations of the British Columbia coast. Images used as crests, and the stories that legitimate their use, are forms deeply embedded in First Nations cultures. The program will introduce you to some of complexities of understanding them. These include problems that arise when crests are used by people who have no rights to them.

### STS-78 Crew Patch

The STS-78 mission links the past with present through a crew patch influenced by Pacific Northwest Native American art. Central to the design is the Space Shuttle Columbia whose shape evokes the image of the eagle, an icon of power and prestige and the national symbol of the United States. The eagle's feathers, representing both peace and friendship, symbolize the spirit of international unity on STS-78. An orbit surrounding the mission number recalls the traditional NASA emblem.

The Life Sciences and Microgravity Spacelab (LMS) is housed in Columbia's pay load bay and depicted in a manner reminiscent of totem art. The pulsating sun, a symbol of life, displays three crystals representing STS-78's three high-temperature microgravity materials processing facilities. The constellation Delphinus recalls the dolphin, friend of sea explorers, each star representing one member of STS-78's international crew including our alternate payload specialists Pedro Duque and Luca Urbani.

The colored thrust rings at the base of Columbia signify the five continents of Earth united in global cooperation for the advancement of all humankind. Text by NASA   MORE

Canadian Astronaut Dr. Bob Thirsk

Marjorie Halpin receiving the crew patch from one of the crew of the Space Shuttle Columbia

**Bill Holm** (1965:14) speaks of the rich tradition of art on the Northwest Coast:

"Northwest Coast Indian art is essentially a wooden art. The native trees of the Pacific Coast furnished craftsmen and artists with an abundance of easily worked, highly usable material. Most of the existing examples of art work from this area are wood...

MORE

# A CENTURY OF CRESTS ON THE NORTHWEST COAST:
# A MULTIMEDIA PRESENTATION

Marjorie Halpin

This "paper" was a multimedia presentation of a computer application[1] entitled "A Century of Crests on the Northwest Coast." The program included samplings of the large literature on Northwest Coast First Nations ("Indian") cultures, augmented by hundreds of photographic images and dozens of audio and video clips in which First Nations people speak for themselves.

Crests on the Northwest Coast are similar to European heraldry in that they are inherited emblems of identity. They are, however, much wider in scope than European crests. The following transcription of an audio clip from "A Century of Crests" is aboriginal historian Ron Hamilton's description of *topahti*, as crests are called by the Nuuchahnulth First Nation on Vancouver Island:

> *Topahti* is a limited right, and sometimes an exclusive right, to a ceremonial display, whether that is a vocal, visual, vocal and visual, or movement—so, songs and dances, names, crests, collections of crests on . . . the great painted screens and curtains used for different purposes, housefront paintings, canoe paintings, the names of canoes, the names of dogs, and so on.

Three months after presenting "A Century of Crests" at the Congress, I was privileged to tour five Canadian, French, and American astronauts from the STS-78 space mission through the Museum of Anthropology, where I work. After listening to me discuss the crests of the Northwest Coast, and learning that I had created a computer application based on them, the astronauts presented me with one of their "Crew Patches" for inclusion in "A Century of Crests." It is an octagonal embroidered badge showing an image of the space shuttle *Columbia* rendered in the Northwest Coast style, and was, in fact, based upon a design made for NASA by Bill Helin, a Coast Tsimshian artist. The text describing the Crew Patch is as follows:

> The STS-78 mission links past with present through a crew patch influenced by Pacific Northwest Native American art. Central to the design is the space Shuttle *Columbia* whose shape evokes the image of the eagle, an icon of power and prestige and the national symbol of the United States. The eagle's feathers, representing both peace and friendship, symbolize the spirit of international unity on STS-78. An orbit surrounding the mission number recalls the traditional NASA emblem.
>
> The Life Sciences and Microgravity Space Spacelab (LMS) is housed in *Columbia's* payload bay and is depicted in a manner reminiscent of totem art. The pulsing sun, a symbol of life, displays three crystals representing STS-78's three high-temperature microgravity materials processing facilities. The constellation Delphinius recalls the dolphin, friend of sea explorers, each star representing one member of STS-78's international crew including our alternate payload specialists: Pedro Duque and Luca Urbani.
>
> The colored thrust rings at the base of *Columbia* signify the five continents of Earth united in global cooperation for the advancement of all humankind.

This is perhaps the most contemporary and international expression of the crest idea that one could find. It is now included, along with a picture of the STS-78 Crew Patch, in the "A Century of Crests on the Northwest Coast" computer program.

## NOTES
1. The application was "authored" in Macromedia's Authorware software, version 3.0.

# THE ABORIGINAL IN HERALDRY WITH SOME EXAMPLES DRAWN FROM THE HERALDIC GARDEN AT BOXFORD HOUSE, SUFFOLK

Sir Conrad M. J. F. Swan

The video "*A Visit to the Heraldic Garden at Boxford House, Suffolk, with some Thoughts on Aboriginal Influences upon Heraldry,*" was created by Sir Conrad Swan, KCVO, formerly Garter King of Arms, for presentation at the Congress. For the first time at these meetings, viewers were able to pose questions via satellite to Sir Conrad who remained at his home in England.

Said to be unique in the world, the Heraldic Garden started in 1983 has made Sir Conrad's home, Boxford House, the site of many rare botanical specimens, some of which serve to illustrate this videotaped talk. A retired officer of the College of Arms in London, Sir Conrad, whose own ties of blood to Poland, the U.K. and Canada are well known, expresses his own wealth of affinities and depth of heraldic scholarship in exploring examples of armory in his personal collection drawn from a wide range of indigenous peoples,

fauna and flora of the Commonwealth and beyond. Some of these have been long adopted outside of their original environments dating back to the very beginnings of heraldry (Lion and Cedar), while other are importation of a more recent vintage. All serve to enrich the stock of armorial achievements produced from the heraldic imagination over seven centuries of the science's development. Examples were gleaned from the Boxford House library, with reference to the topiary "ordinaries" (pale, fess), arboreal rarities (palm, eucalyptus), aviary accessories (chough, pheasant), and floral charges (lotus, rose etc.) in the former Garter's garden and The Lady Hilda Memorial Arboretum.

The Heraldic Garden at Boxford can be toured at certain times of the year. Those interested should contact Sir Conrad directly at Boxford House, Suffolk, England, C010 5JT (Fax 1887-211-626).

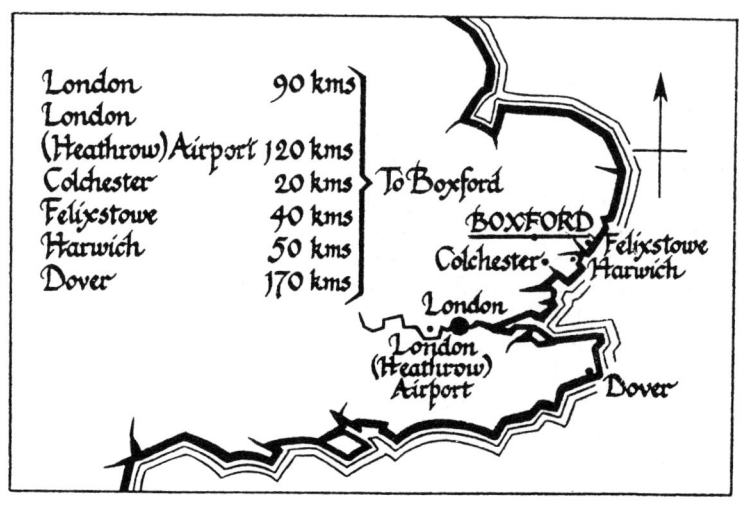

**FIGURE 1:** Boxford House, built 1819-20 on foundations of an older house. The East, along with the South façade are in the contemporary Georgian Gothic style; the West and North are Regency.

**FIGURE 2:** In the Herb Garden, one of "the Queen's Beasts'," in this instance the White Lion of March holding the Badge of York. This garden is planted with flora which occur in medical heraldry: the poppy, foxglove (both aboriginal) and so on, and not forgetting the Sweet Pea (from the Armorial Bearings of the British Association of Urological Surgeons!)

The paper used in this publication meets the minimum requirements
of American National Standard for Information Sciences –
Permanence of Paper for Printed Library Materials, ANSI Z39.48-1992.

PRINTED AND BOUND
IN BOUCHERVILLE, QUÉBEC, CANADA
BY MARC VEILLEUX IMPRIMEUR INC.
IN MARCH, 1998